HUMAN RESOURCES MANAGEMENT
Cases and Text

Second Edition

HUMAN RESOURCES MANAGEMENT
Cases and Text

Fred K. Foulkes

Professor of Management Policy and Director
Human Resources Policy Institute
School of Management
Boston University

E. Robert Livernash

Late of Harvard University

Prentice Hall, Englewood Cliffs, New Jersey 07632

LIBRARY OF CONGRESS
Library of Congress Cataloging-in-Publication Data

Foulkes, Fred K.
    Human resources management : text and cases / Fred K. Foulkes, E.
Robert Livernash. -- 2nd ed.
        p.   cm.
    Includes bibliographies.
    ISBN 0-13-445891-5
    1. Personnel management--United States. 2. Personnel management-
-United States--Case studies.   I. Livernash, E. Robert (Edward
Robert) II. Title.
HF5549.2.U5F67 1989
658.3'00973--dc19   88-23613
                                                        CIP

Editorial/production supervision and
  interior design: *Nancy Savio-Marcello*
Cover design: *George Cornell*
Manufacturing buyer: *Ed O'Dougherty*

 © 1989, 1982 by Prentice-Hall, Inc.
A Division of Simon & Schuster
Englewood Cliffs, New Jersey 07632

Printed in the United States of America

10 9 8 7 6 5 4 3 2 1

ISBN 0-13-445891-5

Prentice-Hall International (UK) Limited, *London*
Prentice-Hall of Australia Pty. Limited, *Sydney*
Prentice-Hall Canada Inc., *Toronto*
Prentice-Hall Hispanoamericana, S.A., *Mexico*
Prentice-Hall of India Private Limited, *New Delhi*
Prentice-Hall of Japan, Inc., *Tokyo*
Simon & Schuster Asia Pte. Ltd., *Singapore*
Editora Prentice-Hall do Brasil, Ltda., *Rio de Janeiro*

To

James J. Healy

and

M. Thomas Kennedy

CONTENTS

VI

Work Restructuring and Motivation   335

VII

The Role of Feedback Mechanisms, Communications Programs, and Training and Development   389

PREFACE

Although it includes introductory chapters and selected articles, the second edition of *Human Resources Management: Cases and Text* remains, first and foremost, a casebook. The approach of this book to the study of effective human resources management has as its primary learning process the analysis of cases. Our experience and conviction is that insights into personnel policies, procedures, and problems can be greatly enriched by case study. What is important, in our view, is not only more knowledge acquisition but improved knowledge utilization, better decision making, and more skill and ability to defend and implement plans of action. Immersing oneself totally in a case—that is, grappling seriously with the complex real-life problems faced by the managers and other actual actors in the situation, and being forced to make a decision designed to resolve or mitigate the problems in the case—while initially frustrating, prepares individuals in important ways to perform more effectively in an executive capacity. Cases are not neat logical problems to which answers may be found in the back of the book. Neither are they illustrations of some point made in the text. In fact, commonly no particular course of action will be supported broadly by a group of students nor a group of executives. The answers or decision that a given individual devises or supports will depend upon his or her interpretation of the facts in the case, his or her understanding of the institutional and environmental variables bearing upon the problems in the case, and upon the personal values and goals that the individual brings to the decision-making process. Group discussion of complex real-life situations thus typically exhibits considerable diversity as to the most appropriate course of action.

After the initial frustration, lasting insights are developed that condition the manner in which an individual will view similar problems in the future. In one sense nothing is deader than yesterday's case. A student will never again confront the facts of yesterday's case in yesterday's situation. But, out of guided immersion in a succession of cases, administrative skills are nurtured and developed, and a deeper understanding of personnel policies and practices created. Case study and discussion constitutes training in problem analysis, training in communication, training in decision making, and above all, a learning process that deepens understanding of administrative policies, processes, and problems. For instance, a student who studies a succession of different labor negotiations will become aware of crucial differences in the institutional and environment variables affecting each negotiation and will note how the process operated under the influence of different actors. Similarly, study of different company approaches to the administration of compensation will produce broadened and deepened understanding of that administrative function. Study of cases prepares students to undertake administrative assignments with considerable understanding of the problems facing them. This book, therefore, places primary emphasis on the analysis and discussion of a range of personnel and labor relations cases to build an understanding of administrative policies, processes, and problems.

As noted in the negotiation example, case situations are influenced substantially by "institutional and environmental variables." While no attempt will be made to catalog these variables, much of the subtlety of case analysis relates to them. Rather obvious economic variables are the growth or decline of the industry and company involved, the nature and degree of competition, and the profitability of the enterprise. Growth companies in expanding industries obviously have far more freedom to develop outstanding personnel policies than do organizations with severe financial, competitive, or regulatory constraints. The social environment, including community size and plant location, may be significant in particular situations. Clearly economic, social, and governmental variables play important roles in case analysis. These include such institutions as the National Labor Relations Board, the Equal Employment Opportunity Commission, the Occupational Safety and Health Administration, and such laws as the Equal Pay Act and others.

The term "institutional variables" is intended to include such factors as the history and character of the union-management relationship, the managerial culture including the values and goals of top management, and the ongoing policies and practices of the organization. These are subtle variables providing opportunities or constraints, as the case may be, for innovative human resources management. Students at times are unrealistic in suggesting a course of action that would have a minimal chance of adoption in the managerial climate of the case. A crucial element, therefore, is the identification and incorporation into the case analysis of important "institutional and environmental variables."

As a general guide to case discussion, each section is introduced by textual material analyzing the major policy options and other administrative dimensions of the topic under discussion. Each section also includes a limited number of selected references. Obviously the greater the familiarity of the student with the relevant personnel management literature, including the reader that accompanies this book, the greater will be the perspective he or she brings to the case analysis. The focus of the text material introducing each section will be on administrative processes and problems—that is, on policy options, on important administrative considerations, and on major problems.

This revised edition contains updated chapters that reflect changes that have taken place since the first edition was written, and 20 new cases. The new cases examine human resources problems in a variety of settings, from a unit of government in the Commonwealth of Massachusetts to a startup high-technology company located in Silicon Valley in California. The cases in this edition are from a broader array of organizations than those in the first edition.

We are indebted to many individuals and organizations for helping to make this book possible. In general, the authors of each case are listed at the beginning of each case. Many of the cases were developed for our students in personnel, human resources, and labor courses at Harvard and Boston University. They are reprinted with the permission of the President and Fellows of Harvard College and the Trustees of Boston University. In addition to being grateful to all the cooperating companies and their executives, we are also indebted to dozens of former students, research assistants, and faculty colleagues who helped produce these cases. We are especially pleased to acknowledge the assistance of Professors Norman Berg, William Bruns, Joel Cutcher-Gershenfeld, Paul Evans, William Fruhan, Jr., William Fulmer, James Healy, Jeffrey Hirsch, George Lodge, M. Thomas Kennedy, Thomas Kochan, David Kuechle, Earl Sasser, Leonard Schlesinger, Jeffrey Sonnenfeld; Mr. Robert Paul; and the work of former research assistants Hillery Ballantyne, Ellen Cain, Alison Been-Farquhar, Norman Fast, Donna Hale, Karen Hansen, Susan Johnson, Meredith Lazo, Lucy Lytle, Elizabeth Neustadt, Anna Walton, and Jane Wells. We are also appreciative of the advice and suggestions we have received from Professors Matthew Amano at Oregon State, Hrach Bedrusian at New York University, Joseph F. Byrnes at Bentley College, Anthony Campagna at Ohio State, Richard Dutton at the University of South Florida, Chris Hobart at Northeastern University, and James Klingler at Villanova University.

We are particularly appreciative of our association with Professors James J. Healy and M. Thomas Kennedy, to whom this book is dedicated. Their imaginative and creative case teaching and course development over several decades have been, and continue to be, both a landmark and an inspiration to students and faculty alike.

With respect to both the administrative and secretarial work that completion of this book required, we benefitted enormously from the fine work of Ellen Cain and Carmen Jacobson. We are also grateful to the staff of Prentice Hall, especially Alison Reeves and Nancy Savio-Marcello, for valuable assistance.

Fred K. Foulkes
Boston, Mass.

POSTSCRIPT

It saddens me to inform you that on February 2, 1987, Bob Livernash died. He was my teacher, colleague, and good friend for over 22 years. Right until his final days in the hospital he was working on the revisions to the last part of his chapter, "The Conduct of Labor Relations." Completing his portion of the revision, especially the chapter on collective bargaining, was a preoccupying concern of the final weeks of his life. He told me that if he was not able to complete it, I should make whatever changes I felt appropriate. Accordingly, with the assistance of Professors James J. Healy and Jeffrey Hirsch, I completed the revision of Chapter III.

F.K.F.

HUMAN
RESOURCES
MANAGEMENT
Cases and Text

1

INTRODUCTION:
THE MANAGEMENT
OF
HUMAN RESOURCES

The management of human resources continues to be elevated in relative importance among managerial functions in many union and nonunion companies, hospitals, universities, and governmental units. Personnel administration continues to become more sophisticated in content and refined in its administration, particularly in nonunion organizations. This increase in sophistication and refinement has been in part in response to new social legislation. And in part, improved personnel administration is a response to more militant employee attitudes that developed around 1965, attitudes that have waned during recent years.

In nonunion companies, the managerial objective of eliminating the need for a union continues to give personnel administration high priority. The union-nonunion struggle is nearly as active today as it was over fifty years ago, when the National Labor Relations Act was passed.

Some nonunion employers have become more aggressive in their anti-union stance with the decline in union membership and power. The struggle has changed primarily only in its sophistication and refinement of policy and practices.

The importance of human resources management has also been heightened by the conviction in many organizations of its strategic importance to the company's competitive success. Competitive superiority depends heavily on creative innovations. Such innovations may well be primarily dependent upon employee motivation and morale. How to elicit and sustain high levels of employee morale, perhaps particularly in large organizations, remains a highly complex topic. Desirable employee attitudes are by no means the automatic result of instituting certain personnel policies and practices. The one point that appears quite clear is that an autocratic style of management will not create the type of employee relations climate that is desired. For all of these reasons, effective and improved personnel management is receiving increasing attention from top management.

This section on the management of human resources relates to the nature and character of an organization's personnel function, both line and staff.[1] As an overview for this topic, an analytical framework for effective personnel management is presented. The following framework, while not comprehensive, should challenge the student to begin to formulate the critical elements in the effective management of human resources.

Effective personnel management may be conceptualized, and the personnel function explored, in terms of three primary interrelated and interactive dimensions of the topic:

- Some basic organizational requirements
- A comprehensive package of personnel policies
- An employee relations climate of confidence, trust, and openness

No doubt the payoff among these interactive elements is the achievement of a positive, cooperative, and productive employee relations climate that integrates organizational and employee needs.

Looking first, however, at basic organizational requirements, three crucial elements stand out: (a) top management commitment to effective personnel management; (b) a strong personnel depart-

ment; and (c) a well-integrated line-staff administration. Among these three organizational requirements, top management commitment to effective personnel management is an overriding consideration.

Real top management commitment to the personnel function necessitates active participation in personnel policy formulation and administration by the chief executive officer. Commitment also requires that human resource management be placed high among management's priorities. Members of top management indicate commitment by following and demonstrating established personnel policies in their own behavior. In addition, good human relations management must be required of all line and staff management and be built into the reward system.

Students, in thinking about the support given to the personnel function by top management, must recognize that historically personnel departments, with a few marked exceptions, have had low status, low regard, low pay, and low effectiveness. Realistically, top management believed that the survival and success functions for a business organization were marketing, finance, and production. Many business organizations, in fact, have been highly successful in financial terms while managing employees in a tough, autocratic, and rather inconsistent manner. Increasingly, however, top management is questioning the effectiveness of these styles of management. Managerial priorities and the nature of personnel administration are in the process of change, it is believed, in many organizations. However, differences remain; and a fundamental consideration in the effectiveness of personnel administration in any organization is the nature and the degree of sincere commitment by top management to the function.

A second basic organizational requirement for effective human resource management is the creation of a strong

---

[1] Various terms commonly found in the literature, such as "the management of human resources," "the personnel function," "personnel policy and administration," and "effective personnel management," are used in this text almost synonymously. The only differences are in emphasis. For example, the term "personnel function, both line and staff" is used to give emphasis to the management function as such, whereas the term "management of human resources" is used to convey the broad scope of the topic. No fundamental differences in meaning are intended.

personnel department, strong professionally and strong in influence. The department must be established at a high level within the organization to give it a voice in all relevant top management decisions, including the compensation and promotion of managerial personnel, the location of new plants, and so forth. This personnel input, to be truly effective, is required in the planning stage with respect to business decisions. This allows personnel to be more proactive and less reactive. Personnel strongly needs the opportunity to prevent rather than to put out fires. Viewed this way, personnel becomes a strategic partner of line management.

Also, a strong personnel department must have a meaningful audit or control role within the organization. In this control role, lower-level personnel administrators must have the right to elevate the point of decision to the chief executive officer if necessary. Giving personnel the right to elevate questionable line management decisions, and establishing the department at a high organizational level, demonstrate real organizational commitment to the function. Also, professional strength in personnel is increasingly demanded and demanding. Knowledge and skills are obviously required in high degree.

Today there are wide differences in status and professional strength among organizations in the personnel departments. Cases in the text reflect these differences. Also, organizations differ in the audit or control role given to the department. Historically, personnel began as a record-keeping and limited service function. Over the years the service function has become much more complex, and an audit or control role has developed in addition. Social legislation has expanded this control role, but as indicated below, control primarily is exercised indirectly through training and counselling. Only infrequently by elevating the point of decision does the personnel department override decisions of line management. The status, strength, and professional capacity of the personnel department is of interest in each case in the text.

A third basic organizational requirement is a balanced integration of line and staff responsibilities. Fundamentally personnel should remain a staff function. Line managers make the decisions affecting the employees they supervise. Personnel acts in an advisory manner. To be effective, however, personnel administrators must have strong influence. In organizations in which there is strong top management commitment to the function and a strong personnel department with the right to elevate the point of decision within the organization, the distinction between staff "advice" and line "decisions" may become blurred. While maintaining the distinction is fundamental, effective influence by personnel staff is greatly enhanced where line management's performance in the administration of personnel policies is built into the reward system through the organization's appraisal, compensation, and succession policies.

The most common problem in industrial and other organizations today is probably inadequate influence by the personnel department. If there is low top management commitment to the function, then personnel's staff advice will frequently not count when it is most needed. On the other hand, in some organizations where personnel has real power, staff may be tempted to take over and make what should be line decisions. Such action undercuts the line organization. Line management, to be effective, must have the right to be wrong in particular decisions. Personnel, however, should have the influence to remove a line manager with a low batting average in personnel performance who does not respond to training and counselling.

It is not easy for an organization to achieve balanced and integrated line responsibility with appropriate staff influence. Some degree of line-staff friction is perhaps inherent in their joint responsibilities. This friction can be minimized by well-developed personnel policies. The personnel policy formulation process should itself be utilized as a consensus mechanism. Line-staff consensus as to personnel policies is an essential integration mechanism. Balanced personnel policies, coupled with extensive training in their administration, will put line and staff on the same team.

The second dimension, noted earlier, of effective personnel management is a comprehensive package of personnel policies. This introduction is not the appropriate place to discuss in depth the range and content of personnel policies, which are developed in other chapters and in the cases. Economic policies include the wage and benefit aspects of compensation. Prominent among the compensation policies of leading nonunion companies is the extent to which they have employment security practices and good communications programs. Included in the total security package are diversified benefit plans, some of which go beyond standard protections from social risks.

A very important range of policies relates to promotion, layoff, and discipline and discharge. As noted, some nonunion companies have largely avoided the need for layoffs. Promotion policies have been greatly influenced by equal employment opportunity policies and affirmative action requirements. Many nonunion companies have extensive policies and procedures to assure the equitable treatment of individuals, such as various communication programs, complaint procedures and other "feedback" mechanisms, participa-

tion programs, career pathing with extensive training opportunities, policies to avoid "double standards," and the like. Many unionized companies are in the process of strengthening their personnel policies, and some have joint union-management "quality of worklife" committees and other cooperative programs.

The policies adopted by a given company are strongly influenced by its economic and institutional environment. A company with competitive and ability-to-pay constraints is forced to be conservative in its economic policies. Other personnel and labor relations policies are very much determined by the values and goals, and commitment to the personnel function, of top management. The policies adopted, in turn, have their impact on employee attitudes and the climate of employee relations in the organization. The remainder of the text deals with various issues in personnel policy and their administration. These issues will be developed further in the subsequent section introductions.

While the first two dimensions of effective personnel administration already discussed, some basic organizational requirements and a comprehensive package of personnel policies, may in some sense be regarded as fundamental, the third dimension in this interconnected and interactive system, the creation of an employee relations climate of confidence and trust and openness is, at least arguably, the bottom line and payoff consideration. Such climates are considered to be consistent with high productivity and the effective implementation of an organization's strategy.

If the organizational climate is an open one encouraging employees to express their dissatisfactions and concerns without fear of reprisal, then such concerns and dissatisfactions may be dealt with in a positive and constructive manner. A climate of openness, however, can only be created if employees have a high degree of confidence and trust in the fairness of managerial decisions and actions. Creating a climate of openness, confidence, and trust depends predominantly, it is believed, upon the values and goals of top management. It appears to require a sincere top management goal of treating employees fairly and an organizational objective of meeting and integrating both employee and organizational objectives and needs. There is, however, no mechanical method to capture the intangibles of creating and maintaining this type of positive employee relations climate. Nevertheless, the reality of important changes in the employee relations climate can readily be observed in association with changes in the supervisory leadership of a department, changes in the manager of a plant, and changes in the chief executive officer of an organization.

It is the view of the authors that the climate of an organization can be explained by the combination of the values and goals of top management, certain substantive policies, as well as the implementation and administration of those policies. Borrowing from Emerson, the corporation is the lengthened shadow of the man. If the chief executive officer of a company lacks integrity, cannot be trusted, and does not care about employees, there is little doubt that such attitudes will filter down and have an effect throughout the organization. If, on the other hand, the organization's top management is committed to good human relations and supports the personnel function and the various programs and policies concerned with the management of human resources, it is probable that the desired climate can be created and maintained. The substantive policies adopted by such companies may include the exercising of policy options with respect to certain environmental and institutional variables. For instance, locating a facility in one place may guarantee employee relations problems, whereas locating it someplace else would increase a company's chances of creating the desired positive employee relations climate.

The purpose of this introduction is to open a complex subject—important analytical considerations bearing upon the effective management of human resources—but not to resolve it. In fact, there is no standardized set of personnel policies that will automatically produce a favorable employee relations climate even though there are important similarities among the policies of leading companies. However, apart from policy as such, a most challenging fact with respect to the effectiveness of many personnel policies is the crucial importance of the manner of implementation. For example, a management by objective procedure in one organization may be an administrative headache with negative effects upon morale, while such a plan in another organization may be a positive influence resulting in a dynamic and creative managerial climate. As a second example, one system of measured daywork may be associated with ready acceptance by employees of technological change and with very favorable employee productivity, whereas an identical system in another organization may be associated with employee hostility and a relatively poor effort level. Clearly the intangibles of leadership and the manner of administration count very heavily in the results achieved from particular personnel policies. One might almost hazard the generalization that the more important the personnel policy, the more crucial is the manner of its development and implementation. Throughout this text, students are invited to deepen their insights into the variables that bear upon the effectiveness of the management of human resources.

A framework for analysis found to be particularly useful by one of the authors[2] can be illustrated by the diagram in Figure I–1. As the student will note, it is asserted that the combination of certain top management attitudes and values and certain substantive policies are capable of producing the desired results. To understand the employee relations climate and the management of human resources in any given company, it is suggested that the student would benefit by asking himself or herself questions such as the following:

1. What are the real attitudes, values, and philosophies of top management with respect to employees?
2. What environmental factors and company characteristics contribute in a positive or negative way to the employee relations climate? Where are company plants located? What size is the typical plant? How profitable is the company? Is the company growing at a satisfactory rate?
3. What amount of company resources are invested in employment and employment security? Are employees carefully hired for a career or is the company a hire and fire company?
4. Is promotion from within a reality? What, if any, training and career development programs exist to foster individual growth and development?
5. What is the status and role of the personnel department? Does the head of personnel report to the president? Are entry-level personnel jobs an avenue to general management? Do the views of the company's top personnel and industrial relations executives count?
6. Are the compensation and benefit programs adequate? Are they understood and perceived as fair and competitive?
7. Are there methods for employees to make

their views known? Are there methods for top management to keep its fingers "on the pulse"? Are there mechanisms for employee complaints?
8. How much attention is given to selection, development, and evaluation of managers? Do human relations skills, or lack thereof, count in selection and promotion decisions? What happens to the department head whose employees have an excessive number of grievances and complaints?

It is the authors' contention that if these questions are asked, the student's analysis will be strengthened and more realistic action possibilities will be considered.

Included in this section are two cases. The first, Sun Microsystems, Inc., raises important human resources management issues related to growth and organization. Sun, located in Mountain View, California, is an exciting startup company founded by four men in their twenties. The case focuses on both the business and human resources strategies of this young and very interesting company. The company will not continue to be successful unless it articulates and implements an effective human resources strategy, for the recruitment and retention of outstanding people is one of its principal competitive advantages.

In the second case, The First National Bank of California, the student is asked to be helpful to Michael Cooper, the new head of the personnel division. Cooper comes to his position from a line management career within the bank. The bank, part of the rapidly changing financial services industry, is being challenged by a more competitive environment. In addition to identifying a number of human resources problems, Cooper realizes there is much concern about the credibility and effectiveness of the personnel division itself. The case asks the student to help Cooper not only by diagnosing the situation at

[2] Fred K. Foulkes, *Personnel Policies in Large Nonunion Companies* (Englewood Cliffs, N.J.: Prentice-Hall, 1980).

FIGURE I-1

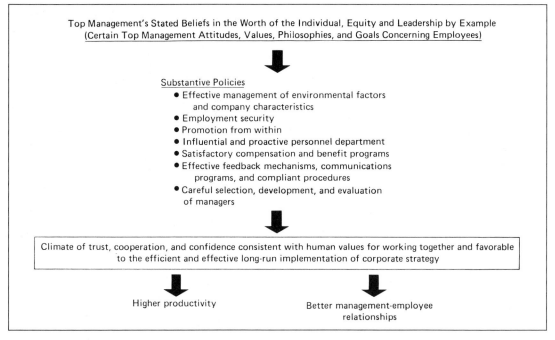

the bank but also by suggesting a viable course of action.

These introductory cases demonstrate clearly that the focus of this book is on strategic human resources management. We are concerned with the achievement of congruence between company strategy and human resources management. By building a partnership between line and staff, companies can establish and maintain a sustained competitive advantage by being strategic with respect to human resources management. All important human resources functions, from recruiting to employee benefits design, should be viewed from a strategic perspective.

Both cases in this section call for a balanced view of line and staff considerations. They also call for well-developed change programs from both company and human resources points of view. The how

of what is to be done is as important as the what. Developing comprehensive action plans and recommendations that can be implemented in the particular environments of each of the organizations, given the institutional variables, is crucial to the analysis of the cases. The strong hope of the authors is that students will develop and deepen their insights with respect to the requirements for effective human resources management, including the nature of the personnel function, as they study and discuss each case in this book.

BIBLIOGRAPHY: THE MANAGEMENT OF HUMAN RESOURCES

DERR, C. BROOKLYN. *Managing the New Careerists.* San Francisco: Jossey-Bass, 1986.

Eighties: An Employee Relations Forecast, The. New York: Organization Resources Counselors, Inc., February 1980.

FOMBRUN, CHARLES, N. TICHY, AND M. DEVANNA. *Strategic Human Resource Management.* New York: Wiley, 1984.

FOULKES, FRED K. *Personnel Policies in Large Nonunion Companies.* Englewood Cliffs, NJ: Prentice-Hall, 1980.

———. *Strategic Human Resources Management: A Guide for Effective Practice.* Englewood Cliffs, NJ: Prentice-Hall, 1986.

GLUECK, WILLIAM F. *Personnel: A Diagnostic Approach* (3rd ed.). Plano, TX: Business Publications, Inc., 1982.

HALL, DOUGLAS T., AND JAMES G. GOODALE. *Human Resources Management: Strategy, Design and Implementation.* Glenview, IL: Scott, Foresman, 1986.

HENEMEN, HERBERT G. III, DONALD P. SCHWAB, JOHN A. FOSSUM, AND LEE D. DYER. *Personnel/Human Resource Management* (3rd ed.). Homewood, IL: Irwin, 1986.

KOCHAN, THOMAS A., AND THOMAS A. BAROCCI. *Human Resource Management and Industrial Relations.* Boston: Little, Brown, 1985.

LING, CYRIL C. *The Management of Personnel Relations: History and Origins.* Homewood, IL: Irwin, 1965.

McFARLAND, DALTON E. *Cooperation and Conflict in Personnel Administration.* New York: American Foundations for Management Research, 1962.

McGREGOR, DOUGLAS. *The Human Side of Enterprise.* New York: McGraw-Hill, 1960.

———. *The Professional Manager.* New York: McGraw-Hill, 1960.

People, Progress and Employee Relations. Proceedings of the Fiftieth Anniversary Conference of Industrial Relations Counselors, Inc. June 9–11, 1976.

PETERS, THOMAS J., AND H. WATERMAN, JR. *In Search of Excellence: Lessons from America's Best-Run Companies.* New York: Harper & Row, 1982.

PIGORS, PAUL, AND CHARLES MYERS. *Personnel Administration: A Point of View and a Method* (9th ed.) New York: McGraw-Hill, 1981.

RAELIN, JOSEPH A. *The Clash of Cultures: Managers Managing Professionals.* Boston, Ma: Harvard Business School Press, 1986.

RITZER, GEORGE, AND HARRISON TRICE. *An Occupation in Conflict: A Study of the Personnel Manager.* Ithaca, NY: New York State School of Industrial Labor Relations, Cornell University, 1969.

SHEPPARD, C. STEWART, AND DONALD C. CARROLL (eds.). *Working in the Twenty-first Century.* New York: Wiley, 1980.

SPATES, THOMAS G. *Human Values Where People Work.* New York: Harper & Row, 1960.

WALKER, JAMES W. *Human Resource Planning.* New York: McGraw-Hill, 1980.

WALTON, RICHARD E., AND PAUL R. LAWRENCE (eds.). *HRM: Trends and Challenges.* Boston: Harvard Business School Press, 1985.

WOLF, WILLIAM B. (ed.). *Top Management of the Personnel Function.* Ithaca, NY: New York State School of Industrial and Labor Relations, Cornell University, 1980. (Frank W. Pierce Conference and Lecture Series No. 6, 1980, ILR Publications.)

Sun Microsystems, Inc.

INTRODUCTION

Scott McNealy, president and chairman of Sun Microsystems, ordered two more beers at the Dutch Goose Bar in Menlo Park, CA. It was June 3, 1986, four years and a few months since he and three other 27-year-olds had founded Sun, which was regarded as one of Silicon Valley's hottest startups. At 31, Scott was reflecting on his company's meteoric growth with an old college friend, John Bartlett.

Bartlett: Last time we got together, you were heading up operations at Onyx Systems. How'd you get involved with Sun?

McNealy: One of the other founders, Vinod Khosla, was a classmate of mine at Stanford Business School. He got the four of us together. The other two were Andy Bechtolsheim and Bill Joy, the engineers of the group. While working on his doctorate at Stanford, Bechtolsheim built what came to be Sun's primary product: a high-powered technical workstation for engineers and other sophisticated users. Because of its unique

This case was prepared by Ellen M. Cain, under the direction of Professor Fred K. Foulkes, as the basis for class discussion rather than to illustrate either an effective or ineffective handling of an administrative situation.
© Human Resources Policy Institute, School of Management, Boston University, 1988

design and low cost, a lot of companies were interested in it. Bechtolsheim turned them all down because he wanted to build a new company around his product. He teamed up with Khosla, and they recruited Joy and me. Joy, who was at Berkeley at the time, was our software guru. We raised $4.6 million in venture capital and started Sun, an acronym for Stanford University Network.

Bartlett: What's the status of the four of you today at Sun?

McNealy: Bechtolsheim's title is vice president of technology and Joy's is vice president of research and development. They're both in rather unique positions here, off on their own doing research. No one reports to them and they report to no one. Khosla left in 1985 to retire at the age of 30. He gets his kicks from starting companies. Once that was accomplished at Sun, he was ready to go. He's still a major stockholder, a director of the company, and a dabbler in venture capital.

Bartlett: I can imagine that in the first couple of years the excitement of working for a startup kept everyone going. But you're no longer the new kid on the block. Is it more difficult now to attract and retain the same kind of people that made Sun what it is?

McNealy: What Sun is—that's what I'd like to know. We know we're a different company today from what we were a year ago. We just need to figure out how. Last year, we recruited a vice president for human resources who's developed a system to define our "corporate culture."[1] Once I figure out who we are, I'll let you know how we intend to react to all the changes. There's no doubt in my mind that the human resource function is much more important at Sun today than it was a few years ago. We used to be able to recruit outstanding people for salaries much lower than what they were getting somewhere else. Our benefits package wasn't up to par. We didn't have time for things like formal training programs or performance appraisals. The excitement of the startup definitely kept the momentum going for the first few years. But things have changed a lot in the last few years. We've got over 2,000 employees and are hiring 150 new people a month. We're a public company. We are shipping at a rate greater than $300 million per year. We started in half of one building and now occupy more than eight buildings in Mountain View alone. In the past year, we've made our salary and benefits package competitive with the market. But we've got to spend a lot more time and money putting all the systems into place that will enable us to continue to attract and hold on to the best people.

The conversation went on, but this part of it stayed on McNealy's mind long after he dropped Bartlett off at his hotel. He knew that Sun could not maintain the entrepreneurial spirit that permeates a young startup. But he was convinced that something could be done so that the increase in bureaucracy did not change Sun as it had other high-tech startups. Employees at

[1] The project, first dubbed the "culture project," was later transformed into the "value study," discussed in detail in later section.

Sun overwhelmingly described Sun as a *fun* place to work. Despite his goal of reaching a billion dollars in sales, Mc-Nealy was intent on keeping Sun that way.

THE TECHNICAL WORKSTATION MARKET

In 1986, Sun's product line was primarily limited to workstations used by engineers, scientists, and other technical professionals. Sun's workstations were high-powered microcomputers that offered, on average, four times the processing speed and ten times the memory of a PC, as well as more sophisticated graphic capabilities. (Exhibit 1 shows a Sun workstation.) They were usually linked through a network that allowed, for instance, a team of engineers working on a new automobile to coordinate their designs. Because of the workstation's ability to increase productivity enormously, and a declining price, demand for Sun's systems was high.

The pioneer of the technical workstation market was not Sun but Apollo Computer, a company started in 1980 in Chelmsford, Massachusetts. By 1986, there were over two dozen producers, with Apollo and Sun controlling over 60% of the world market. According to Dataquest, a California market research firm, Apollo's market share fell from 50% to 39% in 1985. That same year, Sun's market share rose from 16% to 20%. Sun's installed base in June 1986 was approximately 17,000 machines, compared to Apollo's 20,000. The total number of systems in use was expected to increase from 40,000 in 1986 to nearly 2 million in 1990. Revenues over the same period were expected to grow from $1.1 billion to over $3 billion. A *Business Week* article of March 1986 described Sun's growth as "meteoric," listing Sun as one of the new "post-industrial" corporations because it relies on other companies for manufacturing and many crucial business functions. Considering that there are 6 million engineers in the world as well as other applications for the product, Sun and other producers of workstations had only reached a small portion of the potential market.

In May 1985, Digital Equipment Corporation entered the market with a stripped-down, low-cost machine that competed with Sun's low-end system. An even greater threat to Sun and Apollo was IBM, which introduced the RT PC in January 1986. The machine used a simplified design approach, known as Reduced Instruction Set Computer (RISC) architecture. Although the RT PC did not compete in performance with the Sun or Apollo products, IBM was expected to introduce a more sophisticated machine in late 1986 or early 1987. Because the typical workstation user was a knowledgable scientist or engineer rather than an analyst or manager, several industry observers believed that IBM would not enjoy its traditional advantage of sales in the technical workstation market based primarily on the IBM name.

SUN'S PRODUCT STRATEGY: "OPEN SYSTEMS FOR OPEN MINDS"

Sun's product strategy was focused in two closely linked areas: industry standard technologies and open systems architecture. Under these conditions, Sun was an assembler of existing high-performance systems rather than a manufacturer of components. Bechtolsheim's objective when designing the workstation was to combine low cost with high performance. To reduce production costs, he used standard components produced by other Silicon Valley manufacturers when possible. This strategy of purchasing "off-the-shelf" components from local suppliers differed greatly from that of Apollo and others that used components manufactured solely for their machines. This "art of making a Ferrari out of spare parts," as McNealy described it, enabled Sun to price its products approximately 20% to 40% lower than Apollo's.

Tied to a strategy of low-cost production was Sun's commitment to an open systems architecture. Sun's founders agreed that because of the diversity in computing, no vendor could supply equipment to serve every need of every user. As a result, Sun promoted standards that made it possible for the equipment of many vendors to work together. Because of Joy's and Bechtolsheim's involvement at Berkeley with the development of the Berkeley version of the UNIX operating system and early design of 32-bit microprocessor systems, Sun's initial product development team was able to achieve a high level of hardware and software integration. In addition to supporting the UNIX standard, Sun's systems were designed to support a number of other significant industry standards. In 1985, Sun began working with AT&T to develop jointly a next-generation operating system that would combine Sun's version of UNIX with AT&T's latest operating system, the System V.

Since its inception, Sun has introduced three generations of the Sun workstation—the Sun-1, the Sun-2, and the Sun-3 product families. Sun-2 was introduced in November 1983. Two years later, in November 1985, Sun began shipment of the Sun-3 product line. At this time, the Sun-1 product line was no longer available. Most Sun-1 systems were upgraded to Sun-2. According to a company executive: "Probably the most significant problem for us in product design is the speed at which we improve and replace our own technology. Since we plan to bring out a new product in approximately an 18-month timeframe, it becomes crucial to meet that deadline so that the product doesn't become obsolete before it has a chance to go to the marketplace properly."

In 1986, approximately 40% of the systems were sold to OEMs (original equipment manufacturers); the rest were sold to end users. Sun's largest OEMs included Computervision and Eastman Kodak; a list of its large end-user customers included such companies as EDS, General Electric, Hughes Aircraft and AT&T Bell Labs. Although most of its systems were used by engineers, there was a growing market in the financial services industry for high-powered workstations that allowed simultaneous display of information on a single screen.

OWNERSHIP AND FINANCING THE GROWTH

Ownership of Sun changed as the company sought additional financing for expansion. When Sun was started, the four founders had similar levels of ownership. By June 1986, none of the founders owned more than 8% of the company. Explained McNealy: "Here I am, a founder, with less than 5% of the company after only four years in business." Shortly after it began, Sun raised $4.6 million in venture capital from four firms in return for almost half the company.

Each of the founders strongly believed in ownership by employees. As a result, when hired every employee was given stock options, regardless of his or her position. For employees hired before the public offering, the price of the stock option was the company's book value. In early 1985 the book value of Sun's stock was approximately $2 per share.

A second round of private financing took place in the summer of 1984. The largest investor was Eastman Kodak, a customer of Sun, which purchased 7% of Sun for $20 million.

Faced with increased competition, Sun management agreed that the company needed to go public to acquire the funds necessary to finance new product development. The board had originally planned the initial public offering (IPO) for the summer of 1985, but held off because of slumps in both the computer and stock markets. The IPO was finally announced in March 1986, when Sun offered 4 million shares of stock at $16 per share.

After the IPO, venture capital firms owned approximately 27% of the stock. Eastman Kodak owned 5.7% of Sun's stock. The four founders became multimillionaires, with holdings valued between $15 and $26 million each. Over 50 other employees also became millionaires after the public offering. (See Exhibit 2 for a listing of post-IPO ownership of Sun.)

SALES AND PROFITABILITY

In the period of slow growth in high-tech that began in mid-1984, Sun remained one of the leaders in terms of sales growth and profitability. Sun turned its first profit just three months (August 1982) after it started shipping systems. In June 1983, the company ended its first full fiscal year of business with net income of $654,000 on revenues of $8.7 million. In 1984, revenues grew fourfold to $39 million and earnings climbed to $2.7 million. In 1985, revenues tripled to $115 million. They topped the $200 million mark in 1986, and the estimates for 1987 ranged from $350 to $450 million (see Exhibit 3 for financial data).

Several industry observers were wary of Sun's rapid growth. They were surprised that Sun's sales and profits continued to grow through 1984 and beyond as other high-tech companies faced difficult financial times. In Silicon Valley, the failure rate of startup companies in the first 12 to 15 months of operation was almost 80%. Bob Smith, chief financial officer at Sun, attributed the company's financial performance to the skill of the young management. According to Smith:

> Since joining Sun, I've been amazed at the perceptiveness of the management team in catching problems early on. The recession in the computer business is a perfect example. Instead of waiting until massive employee layoffs were necessary, we took smaller steps earlier. Hiring was done at a slower pace, production schedules were cut back, facility expansion was lessened, and fewer business trips were scheduled. Sun was one of a handful of computer companies that remained profitable throughout the computer slump. By eliminating perks like parties and picnics, which had gotten way out of hand in terms of cost in the Valley area, we were able to retain pay raises and other items with high value to the employee. We never had to lay off any employees.

DEVELOPMENT OF THE MANAGEMENT TEAM

Because of the company's continuous rapid growth, the organization at Sun was never the same for long. In the early days, the company was very informal: the founders were the only real managers within the company. For the first year, the majority of employees hired were engineers. During that time, the company's primary concern was getting the product out the door, so little time was spent worrying about adding layers of management. During the second and third years, when orders were coming in faster than the company could respond, concern about the organization of management in the company heightened. An early hire in operations commented:

> Things were happening so quickly around here that no one had time to devote to the kind of training we needed for middle management positions. As a result, a lot of young, inexperienced people were promoted before they were ready to handle the additional responsibility. This also led to a weak middle management and heavy top management later on.

As Sun grew, top management underwent a number of changes. Initially, Vinod Khosla served as president and chief operating officer. McNealy was vice president of operations, Bechtolsheim headed up the hardware group, and Joy managed software development. In 1983, Khosla became chairman and an outsider from Digital Equipment Corporation was brought in as president. He stayed only 10 months after facing difficulty blending in with the existing management team. McNealy then became president and chief operating officer. In McNealy's words:

> The decision that I would serve as president came almost by default. We decided on me because Joy and Bechtolsheim had no interest in running the show. They enjoy devoting their time to research—managing no one and being managed by no one. With Khosla leaving, I was given the job temporarily until we could find a "real" president. It never happened, and I was formally elected CEO six months later.

In 1984, McNealy realized that Sun needed not only the best engineers, but also the best management, and began to devote much more of his time to recruiting seasoned management from other high-tech companies. Bob Lux, recruited from Apollo in early 1986 as vice president of customer support, described McNealy's winning recruitment philosophy: "McNealy operates under the theory that if you always hire people better than yourself, you'll be successful."

McNealy spent a great deal of time pinpointing the one individual he wanted for each management position, and did not give up until he had recruited that person. Many of those eventually hired said that they hardly considered the opportunity at first. While they were impressed by Sun's rapid growth and quality products, they were wary of the young founders and the company's viability for the long term. Moreover, most of the high-level recruits were offered base salaries up to 50% lower than what they were currently making. Bob Smith, former chief operating officer and vice president of finance at Xerox Office Products Division, described his decision to take the chief financial officer position at Sun:

> I was involved in the startup of the Xerox Office Products Division. I always knew that I'd someday be ready to join another startup, and had a friend who was a venture capitalist who told me that when I was ready, he'd find me the right place. I received a Christmas card from him in 1984 saying, "I think the time is right—I've got the company for you." He was talking about Sun, and at that point, I wasn't interested. It was such a small company, run by such young guys that I doubted it needed what I could bring to a company. This friend of mine convinced me to consider it more seriously, so I did. I was extremely impressed by the foresight of the founders, and very attracted to the fast-paced environment. After talking to the senior staff, learning the product strategy, and reviewing the numbers, I was convinced that Sun would be a major part of an important industry. I gave up half my salary and all of my retirement fund, and have never worked so hard in my life.

An even more unlikely recruit was Crawford Beveridge, vice president of human resources, who came to Sun from Analog Devices in early 1985. Beveridge had worked at Analog for three and a half years, (before Analog he had been with both Hewlett-Packard and DEC in Europe)

and was very happy in his position when he received a phone call from McNealy in November 1984. Beveridge described his decision to go to Sun:

> I picked up the phone and heard, "Hello, this is Scott McNealy, president of Sun Microsystems. I hear you can walk on water." He then went on to tell me a little about Sun, and that he wanted me as the vice president of human resources. I was impressed with Sun's growth, and flattered by his interest, but I told him I wasn't ready to leave Analog. I did tell him that I could suggest some good candidates in the Valley. Since I was going out west for the Christmas holidays, I agreed to meet with him to discuss possible candidates. I met with him and some other members of the management team, and gave them some names to pursue. A month later, I got another call from McNealy. This time his words were, "Well, are you coming?" I was amused by his persistence, but thought I'd made it clear that I wasn't interested. He then replied that Bernie LaCroute, executive vice president, was on his way to Boston to make me an offer, and it would be rude if I didn't at least meet him for breakfast. The offer was what I had expected—considerably less money than I was making, but a great deal of stock. Although I thought my position was still firm, I began to think about the opportunities at Sun. At Analog, the founder had done an excellent job of articulating the company's values, and it was my responsibility to translate the philosophy into behavioral changes. At Sun, I could take a step backward, and work on defining the company's culture. I was intrigued by this, but it was actually a television program that made my decision to work at Sun final. It was a PBS special on *In Search of Excellence*, which included a short segment on Apple Computer. I was enthralled by the fast pace and excitement level at Apple. All of a sudden it occurred to me this was just what I had seen at Sun. Although I did underestimate the effort it takes to install sanity in a company growing so fast, I've never once regretted my decision.

Bob Lux, vice president of customer support and former vice president at Apollo, said that when he was first approached by Sun, he had three major concerns: McNealy's youth, the "instant millionaire syndrome," and Sun's ability to sustain its growth. While he admitted that he was attracted by the stock options, he emphasized the importance of McNealy's reputation within the company. According to Lux:

Scott is by far the most influential person inside Sun. The employees love his personable nature—that he gives you the high five rather than shaking your hand. For me, it's actually refreshing working for someone so young. He doesn't bring any baggage along since he's not tied to another corporate philosophy. He's got a lot of good ideas, but most important, he knows his limitations. He's told us more than once that he'd move over in a minute if his staff thought he wasn't the right person for the job. It's that kind of attitude that drew me to Sun.

By February 1986, there were thirteen vice presidents on McNealy's staff, aside from Joy and Bechtolsheim (Exhibit 4 lists the vice presidents and their backgrounds). With what he described as a strong management team intact, McNealy was able to spend more time with long-range planning, something he felt he never had time for before. In McNealy's words:

For the first couple of years, Sun was moving so quickly and was so short-staffed that no one had time to think about the future. It's actually quite amazing that we've gotten where we have today with so little planning. With the influx of some heavy new competitors, and technology changing so rapidly, sound strategic planning is critical. Although I rely on my staff to manage day-to-day activities, I also depend on them heavily for planning for the future. They're all experts in their fields, with a lot more experience than I have.

THE ENGINEERING DOMAIN

Despite the strong management team, it was widely reported that the engineers remained the dominant force within Sun. An administrative assistant who had been with Sun since the beginning stated, "The engineers run this place today, just as they did four years ago. It will always be that way. We're a technology-driven company and they're the ones who drive the technology."

The dominance of the engineers was reflected in the lifestyles they led at the company. While Fridays were designated as "jeans day" throughout the company, tee shirts, jeans and sneakers were the everyday garb for the engineers; a sport jacket might be worn when meeting with a client. Most of the engineers kept unusual hours, coming in at 10:00 A.M. and working well into the night. Many of the engineers had terminals at home to work from as well. Like people in other departments, most engineers worked at least part of the weekend, especially in the early years.

The engineering department had something of an "off-the-wall" reputation within the company. When asked to describe the department, one employee in the marketing department alluded to the engineers' enthusiasm on April 1:

The engineering department is becoming notorious for its April Fools' Day stunts. It started last year when a bunch of them came in the night before and moved the entire office of Eric Schmidt, vice president and general manager of the Software Products Division, into the middle of the brook in the courtyard outside. They just didn't move the stuff out there, however. You have to remember we're talking about engineers. They wired the whole thing up so his phone and computer worked. He actually spent the day out there! This year, they put a real 'software bug' in his office—a completely assembled Volkswagen Beetle.

SALES ORGANIZATION

Sun marketed and distributed its products to end users and OEMs through a direct sales force and independent distributors. At the end of 1985, Sun had 33 sales offices in the United States and nine abroad. The sales staff was composed of approximately 350 people. In addition to the direct sales organization, Sun used approximately 15 independent distributors to cover over 25 foreign countries. Sales to foreign customers accounted for about 18% of total sales in 1985.

Much of the attention of the sales organization was focused on Sun's 10 national accounts. Each of these accounts purchased at least $2.5 million, and combined made up 20–25% of Sun's revenue. A team of five senior sales people managed two national accounts each. Building a direct sales channel was difficult in this business, and required a very aggressive sales force. In June 1986, Sun's top salesperson, who had no previous sales experience, had brought in $6 million in sales, and the average sales per sales person was two and a half times the industry average. "We have an outstanding sales force," stated an officer of the company.

McNealy was strongly committed to the notion of "close to the customer." He and Joe Roebuck, the vice president for sales, were out in the field at least weekly to instill a reputation for service and support and determine the users' future needs. Although most employees welcomed the involvement of senior management in sales and customer support, some believed that there was a lack of effective middle management in the field.

MANUFACTURING

Because Sun bought all its parts from outside suppliers, the focus in manufacturing was on the assembly of parts. Five divisions reported into the vice president of operations. These included the operations group, new product growth, quality assurance, materials management, and production cost management. As Sun grew, management within the operations department found themselves extremely overworked. One manager commented: "The outlook in this department has to be very short term—like the next day. We don't have time for strategic planning. I know, for instance, that if I'm out sick some very important items won't get done. I guess that's what keeps us going over here. There's a great deal of personal pride and responsibility, knowing how important our work is to the success or failure of the business." Many of the complaints by the operations managers focused on the poor documentation and design from engineering. The operations department usually took the blame when a product was late in going out, even if the problem was traceable to engineering.

This frustration was also felt at the production level. In this group, there were three groups of workers: technicians, testers, and assemblers. In the summer of 1986, 30% of the production crew were temporary employees. Management had decided to increase the number of temporary hires to achieve greater flexibility in scheduling and reduced costs. The length of stay of a temporary employee averaged between three and six months. The public offering and subsequent rise in temporaries contributed to the decreasing morale of the department. One operations manager commented:

> Before the public offering, most of the production employees were permanent and received stock. Now with employees coming and going all the time, the morale seems to be a lot lower.

Compounding the morale problem was the overcrowding of facilities that resulted from growth in staff and materials. During the summer of 1986, half of the manufacturing department was moved to the East Bay, about 10 miles from the main location. Curt Woziniak, director of operations, explained the significance of the move:

> The planned expansion of facilities has had a major impact on the department. This place has been far too overcrowded, with no place for anyone to get their work done. In addition to alleviating this problem, the expansion is important because it gives the department its own place. Manufacturing has always taken a back seat to engineering; this investment is giving more credibility to our department.

EMPLOYEE RETENTION

The watershed for Sun came as the officers prepared for the company's first public sale of stock. McNealy and his team knew that once the company was public, recruitment of seasoned management and top engineers would be more difficult than before. In addition, Sun no longer had the same hold on some very valuable employees who would be millionaires after the IPO. McNealy and other officers were extremely concerned about the effect of the IPO on recruiting and maintaining valuable employees. In 1986, Sun's turnover rate averaged only 3 to 5%.

After the IPO, McNealy felt even stronger about retaining the spirit that made Sun a fun place to work. He believed the environment at Sun had played an important part in attracting some of the company's most valuable employees. A senior manager at Sun described the values of Sun's engineers:

> Engineers at Sun like the notion of a startup and the control they are given over their work. They like to see that their efforts have such a tremendous and immediate impact on the market. They don't like work environments such as IBM's, where a new product idea takes months before a decision to go with it is made. Probably what really motivates many of them is the opportunity to work with some of the world's top engineers.

What, then, would keep these people from joining a new startup, or starting a company themselves? One member of the human resource staff commented:

> I think that management is and should be concerned about losing some key software and hardware engineers. Those people are highly sought after, and once we're public, the risk of losing them is greater. I don't think this is the primary reason anyone would leave, however. I think the real threat is the growth of Sun. You don't find the same enthusiasm for reaching a billion in revenues with the engineers that you do with the officers. Obviously, the technical people want to see the company grow, since it means their efforts have been successful. On the other hand, they place a high value on autonomy and freedom in their work environment. The fact that Sun is growing at the rate of 150 employees per month is a real turnoff to some of the engineers, who came to Sun for the small-company, non-bureaucratic environment. Control has always been in the hands of the engineers here, and if that changes too much, I think we'll lose a lot of key people.

One attempt by McNealy to retain the "small company" atmosphere was the reorganization of Sun's operations into five divisions in early 1986. Another goal of the divisionalization was to create a wider career ladder for employees striving for management positions within the company.

The new divisions, each its own profit center, were Workstation, East Coast, Federal Systems, Customer Services, and

Software Products. The company's sales, administrative, customer services, and European operations continued to report to McNealy. Sun brought in Barry Folsom from Digital Equipment Corporation and Bob Lux from Apollo Computer to run two of the divisions, bringing the number of vice presidents to 15 (see Exhibit 5 for organization charts before and after divisionalization).

THE HUMAN RESOURCE FUNCTION

The focus of the human resource (HR) function has changed continuously as Sun has grown. In the early days, the officers did the hiring. There was no time for training, benefits design, and many other traditional HR functions. Recognizing the importance of this function, however, McNealy brought in Beveridge to organize and manage the HR department. While much of Beveridge's early efforts also focused on hiring, the department expanded to develop such functions as compensation and benefits, communications, and training and development. As of June 1986, the department consisted of 40 members.

Compensation and Benefits

McNealy knew that by the time Sun went public, salaries and benefits would have to be competitive. In the early years, the company had been able to offset its low salaries with stock incentives, and frequently new hires would accept a 30 to 50% salary cut in exchange for stock. But as Sun made the transition to a public company, with enormous needs for new people, it became critical to implement a more attractive compensation package, since the company could no longer offer stock below the market price.

The terms of the option were as follows: Nonexempt employees and grade 4 (the lowest grade) exempt employees received options to purchase between 100 and 200 shares; the exact number was based on the importance of the hire at a certain point in time, rather than the position or individual alone. Above grade 4, the number of options offered corresponded to the grade level (see Exhibit 6 for listing of options by grade). In addition to this plan, employees with the company for two years could purchase half the amounts listed in Exhibit 6 based on their performance. Approximately 85% to 90% of the employees eligible for this plan were offered stock.

Both plans were to be in place until January 1, 1987. After the IPO, however, instead of receiving options to purchase stock for $2 to $3 per share, options would be granted at the market price of the stock, which opened at $16. In January 1987 Sun management planned to put a new stock plan into place. Only new hires and employees of grade 7 or higher were eligible to receive stock options. Management expected this plan to be further constricted later in the spring of 1987 as the amount of stock reserved for this plan was depleted. These changes would include a reduction in the number of shares offered at each grade level, and a higher grade cutoff point.

In 1985, Sun implemented a bonus plan for its high-level executives. The plan was based on the performance of the organization, rather than on an individual or department, and was offered at the director level and higher.[2] Bonuses were determined annually as a percentage of salary, ranging from 15% to 40% based on the individual's position within the company. The percentage varied depending on the

[2] Positions that were eligible for bonuses included directors, vice presidents, vice president/officers, executive vice presidents, and president. In June 1986 this group totaled approximately 100 individuals.

yearly corporate results and varied from 80% to 140%. For example, if the company achieved 100% of its target profit, the president of the company would receive 40% of his salary as a bonus, while a director would receive 15%. Exhibit 7 provides a chart showing the various bonuses received at various positions and achieved corporate performance.

In 1986, Sun also made significant improvements in its benefits plan. The most notable improvements were in the area of medical coverage. Before the changes, Sun had offered employees a choice of three Health Maintenance Organizations (HMOs) or a self-insured plan. Employees paid no premium for the self-insured plan, but from $4 to $50 per month for the HMOs depending on the plan and the number of family members. The deductible for the self-insured plan was $100, and employees paid 20% of all medical expenses. Under the redesigned self-insured plan, called the Sun Plan, the company paid 100% (instead of 80%) for many common services. These services generally included types of preventive care, or alternative methods of health care delivery that offered cost savings while retaining the level of quality. Examples of these included outpatient preadmission testing, outpatient surgery, and birthing centers.

Another significant improvement in the Sun Plan was a reduction in the yearly maximum cost after the deductible from $5,000 to $2,000. This resulted in a maximum out-of-pocket cost to the employee dropping from $1,100 [$100 deductible + (20% × $5,000)] to $500[$100 + (20% × 2,000)].

Other changes to the benefits plan were implemented in the following areas: vision, dental, accidental death or dismemberment, business travel accident, employee disability and stock purchase (see Exhibit 8 for details of these changes).

As a result of the improvements in the Sun Plan, the percentage of employees enrolled in the plan rose from 73% to 83%.

Communications

With the tremendous growth came the inevitable expansion of Sun's facilities and a growing communications problem. When the company was started, the founders wondered if the building they had leased (45,000 square feet) was too large for them. In four years (1982–86), Sun expanded into eight buildings at the Mountain View facility (each within walking distance of the others), and moved part of manufacturing to a larger building about 10 miles from the main location. Many of the oldtimers attributed the changes in the environment at Sun to the physical separation of employees. According to one engineer:

> Things have really changed a lot around here with all this moving. I've moved three times, and this probably isn't even permanent. When there were just a hundred or so employees under one roof, everyone knew each other and there was a real sense of camaraderie. You realize how few people you know now when we have social gatherings like the Friday beer busts. We used to all hang out together no matter what department we worked for. Now there are a bunch of small cliques that only mix with each other.

Sun's primary tool in keeping the lines of communication open was the electronic mail system (known as e-mail), used daily by virtually every Sun employee: 85% of the employees had electronic mail terminals at their desks, and the remainder had access to one. The system enabled employees to send messages electronically to other employees, whether they were at the next desk or in a foreign office:

The e-mail system is a tremendous time saver. I used to spend hours playing telephone tag, or tracking people down around the office. With e-mail, I can send one message to the whole company in seconds if I want. It's also a great replacement for memos and letters, since you don't have to be as formal. It's amazing how much time can be saved when you're not concerned with how something is worded.

Although the e-mail system was a great productivity booster, its easy accessibility also created some problems. Because there were no controls on the messages sent, any employee could send an "all-home" message (a message to all the other terminals in the network), at a cost of between $500 and $600. Reflecting on the use and misuse of e-mail, one senior manager said:

E-mail is convenient. It saves us time, phone calls and meetings. But e-mail is not a perfect vehicle. It sacrifices a whole realm of communication devices that assist in the transition of ideas. Facial expressions, body language and intonation are lost when e-mail is used. If the message is very important, controversial, confidential, or one that can be easily misunderstood, I think we should think twice about sending it via e-mail. I have come to the view that e-mail is a good way to communicate but that it is not necessarily the best way to communicate every message.

The detachment and semi-anonymity of e-mail occasionally created an environment where bad manners seemed acceptable. Privacy, for instance, might be violated because it was so easy to access someone's mail or mail record. "Carbon copying" of messages too might be overdone or done for the wrong reasons. Finally, there had been occasional "flaming" messages from angry employees.

HIRING A COMMUNICATIONS EXPERT

Senior management at Sun was convinced that to avoid becoming "just another large company," communications within Sun, including e-mail, should be given considerably more attention. From his experience at Analog, Beveridge was convinced that at this stage of growth, a communications person was most effective within the human resources department, rather than the traditional marketing communications or public relations department. Beveridge recruited Jan Fry from Analog to develop a communications area within the human resources department.

Fry's mission upon joining Sun was twofold: to ensure that company information was readily available to employees and that the proper channels were in place so that employees could give feedback to the company. Fry's first priority was to develop a process to communicate to employees the details and implications of the new benefit package that was to be introduced in August 1986. In doing this, Fry organized focus groups to test the effectiveness of the communication process. She developed brochures, videotapes, and employee meetings to provide information on the new benefits package. The groups were asked to comment on the clarity of the brochures and other mediums of communication. In addition to improving the communication process, Fry was sure that the focus groups improved employee relations:

The focus groups turned out to be a real success and will undoubtedly be used for communications more in the future. Employees really enjoyed being a part of the decision-making process and were impressed that management had taken the time to organize a program that invited so much feedback from employees.

A second priority for Fry was developing guidelines for use of the e-mail system. In their effort to limit bureaucratization, many of the senior managers wanted to avoid placing physical constraints on the system. However, because of the high cost of sending messages to all desks and the potential misuse of this capability, guidelines on e-mail etiquette were needed. Exhibit 9 is a copy of the E-Mail Protocol distributed to employees in the spring of 1986.

Soon after Sun went public, management discovered another communications problem that became one of Fry's priorities. After the company went public, SEC rules restricted Sun from releasing any financial data to employees before the information was made available to the investment community. Before the public offering, financial information had been readily available to employees. Beginning in August 1986, Sun decided to hold quarterly meetings for the purpose of sharing financial information, future plans, and company goals with employees. Each VP was responsible for running his or her own meeting, but Fry would be involved in preparing the leaders for these meetings.

Another of Fry's responsibilities was to improve communications with potential Sun employees. As it became increasingly difficult to attract outstanding candidates, this role was given even greater attention. Specifically, Fry made sure that each piece of Sun literature and correspondence sent to a potential employee reflected Sun in a positive and accurate manner.

Fry was also heavily involved in the culture project that Beveridge designed to articulate the company's goals and values.

HIRING

In Sun's infancy, the investment in the human resources function was not signif-icant. Human resources was far below the level of growth of the corporation as a whole, especially in terms of its personnel needs. The HR function had also remained centralized when the company changed to a divisionalized structure. With an overwhelming number of open job requisitions (a fairly constant 200 openings for approximately four recruiters), it was natural that the ability of the HR organization to meet these needs or to be available to its clients was very low.

As a result of the shortage of recruiters, human resources was not involved in most hiring decisions. Overwhelmed managers often could not find enough time to conduct interviews and screen carefully, especially for "cultural fit." In many cases, managers turned to outside employment agencies, which had driven hiring costs up to $2 million a year.

In order to bring the hiring problem under control, several programs were instituted. The HR organization was decentralized and HR resources were dedicated to specific functional or divisional groups. Some of the money formerly spent on outside recruiters was used to hire in-house contracting employment people. These were individuals brought in to Sun from hiring agencies on a contract basis to offer full-time assistance in the hiring of new personnel. More rigid policies were introduced requiring higher levels of authority to use external agencies and limiting the fees the company was prepared to pay when agencies were used. An applicant tracking system was introduced to make managers better aware of the status of candidates in the hiring process. Over a twelve-month period, these changes resulted in Sun's ability to handle a constant backlog of nearly 400 requisitions. It also gave the company more control over the hiring process, slashing costs by two-thirds.

TRAINING AND DEVELOPMENT

A natural outcome of the company's growth was that many people were brought into supervisory and management positions above others who had been with the company for a longer period of time. Beveridge described the implications of this:

> Because individuals frequently associate their own growth with the growth of the company, they tend to believe that their careers are not being appropriately managed if they are not rapidly promoted at a place like Sun. In addition, growth means bringing in many experienced people from a variety of cultures. Without understanding "how things get done around here," they tend to bring their prior ideas with them, thus causing much confusion for employees who see vastly different approaches to the same issues by different managers. Finally, our rate of growth means that the time people need to spend on their own jobs leaves very little time for them to think about the development for their next jobs.

When the company reached about 1,000 people, a dedicated training and development organization was instituted. The basic charter was to understand the critical transitions that people need to go through when changing from individual contributor to supervisor, from supervisor to manager, and so on. The purpose was to ensure that employees were equipped with appropriate skills and the appropriate cultural understanding to be able to function effectively within the company. In addition, a series of peripheral programs dealt with such things as career management, negotiating skills, and effective presentations. According to Jan Becker, training and development manager:

> Due to the rapid growth of the company, the initial focus of training and development was the orientation program—a program dedicated to helping the large number of new employees quickly adjust and become effective in the Sun environment. This was particularly important as an opportunity to help operationalize the values articulated in the value study.

THE VALUE STUDY

In light of all the changes—the IPO, reorganization, building expansion, new competition—the culture at Sun had become much more difficult to define. Crawford Beveridge believed that in order to maintain the spirit that drove Sun in the early days, a formal assessment of the company's present culture was needed. In early 1986, using a model developed by Professor Stanley Davis of Boston University, Beveridge organized what came to be known as The Value Study. According to Beveridge, the purpose of the project was to define Sun's present culture and determine whether it was in line with the company's long-term goals.

Beveridge believed that much of Sun's success had resulted from the culture that had emerged in its early years. He had been told that the mood at Sun in its first year in business was one of high energy, free spirit, and risk-taking. There had been a tremendous feeling of worth throughout the company, since even the smallest task completed increased the chances of survival. An administrative assistant described the environment at Sun during its first year:

> We were all pretty big fish in quite a small pond back then. I can't say that there weren't some murky spots, but for the most part, the high-flying atmosphere really permeated the place. I don't think any of us have ever worked so hard, so many long hours, but no one cared. The "I really do make a difference" feeling was a thrill that

kept us all going. I don't know if I could be involved in another startup, but I wouldn't give up those early days at Sun for the world.

A technical support person had a similar view of Sun in the early days:

Things around here are quite different from the early days. Back then there was no time for bureaucracy, no time for planning, not even time for lunch! We were overworked and underpaid, but there were few complaints. We had a common goal—survival—and that's what really kept us all moving so quickly. It's sort of ironic that once survival was no longer an issue, the problems began to develop.

When asked to describe the culture at Sun, many employees focused on the approachability of senior management. A customer service representative compared the management at Sun with former employers:

The senior management here is very visible and approachable. I've worked for other high-tech companies where you rarely saw the top officers, let alone the president. Scott makes a real effort to get around and keep in touch with all departments here. When Sun had just a couple of hundred employees, he knew almost everyone's name. Now that we've expanded into so many different buildings, it's more segregated, since most of the officers are in the same building. Scott and some others are always at the Friday beer busts, so the effort is still there.

One of the company's telephone operators recalled an effort by the president to stay close to the employees. "On Halloween last year a bunch of employees came to work in costume. The word got around that I had a pretty good costume, and Scott came over, dressed up himself, to check my costume out. It's little things

like this that keep me here when I could be making more money somewhere else."

At an offsite meeting in May 1986, the executive staff (e-staff) came up with a group of general ideas that described the culture at Sun. With these ideas, Beveridge designed a questionnaire that included a number of statements about Sun's culture (Exhibit 10 is a copy of the questionnaire). The e-staff was asked to rate the importance of each statement to the business strategy of Sun and put in order of importance those statements that they believed to be important to the strategy. They were also asked to consider how compatible each statement was with Sun's present culture.

In addition to distributing the questionnaire to the e-staff, the human resources department organized representative groups of employees (Fry's focus groups) who were also asked to complete the questionnaire. According to Beveridge: "The results from the focus groups were remarkably similar to those from the offsite meeting."

At a second offsite meeting, the culture statement was again discussed, using an outside consultant as a facilitator for the meeting. Few problems were encountered as the group integrated the different responses and designed a third version of the value statement. Managers at Sun decided that the term "value" was more appropriate than "culture" since the statement described goals that the company strived for rather than what it was like to work at Sun. The new statement was sent out by electronic mail to all employees with an invitation for comments. A large number of employees responded, and a final value statement was produced (see Exhibit 11 for a copy of the value statement). Commenting on this development, one officer said: "Considering that it took companies such as HP and DEC many years to put their values in writing, our development of the value statement was very rapid. Some here, in fact, think it was too quick."

CONCLUSION

As McNealy headed home, he gave some more thought to Bartlett's questions. He felt that the value statement did a good job of describing Sun's objectives, but wondered if and how much the company's values would change as it continued to grow. In the area of compensation and benefits, Sun was certainly competitive and perhaps even above par for the market. But McNealy was concerned that even the most attractive salary and benefits package would not lure the same type of employee the company had drawn in its early days. McNealy wondered what other action might be taken to ensure that the company continued to hire the "entrepreneurial type" that had been so important to Sun's initial success.

SUN MICROSYSTEMS, INC. STUDY QUESTIONS:

1. Identify and evaluate Sun's business strategy.
2. Identify and evaluate Sun's human resources strategy.
3. What future human resources issues would you suggest Crawford Beveridge should be discussing with Scott McNealy? Why?

Exhibit 2 Ownership of Sun stock

Directors, Officers, and 5% Shareholders	Shares Beneficially Owned Prior to Offering		Shares to Be Sold	Shares Beneficially Owned after Offering	
	Number	Percent		Number	Percent
West Coast Venture Capital c/o Roger Mosher 525 University Avenue, #1410 Palo Alto, CA 94301	2,817,726	12.0%	588,182	2,229,544	8.4%
U.S. Venture Partners 2180 Sand Hill Road Menlo Park, CA 94025	2,224,254	9.5	—	2,224,254	8.4
Andreas Bechtolsheim 2550 Garcia Avenue Mountain View, CA 94043	1,571,093	6.7	33,333	1,537,760	5.8
Eastman Kodak Company 343 State Street Rochester, NY 14650	1,500,003	6.4	—	1,500,003	5.7
Kleiner Perkins Caufield & Byers III Four Embarcadero Center San Francisco, CA 94111	1,416,588	6.0	—	1,416,588	5.4
Technology Venture Investors-2 3000 Sand Hill Road Menlo Park, CA 94025	1,325,356	5.6	—	1,325,356	5.0
U.S. Ventures, S.A. 2180 Sand Hill Road Menlo Park, CA 94025	1,280,957	5.5	—	1,280,957	4.8
Vinod Khosla 31 Farm Road Los Altos, CA 94022	1,149,011	4.9	—	1,149,011	4.3
Scott McNealy 2550 Garcia Avenue Mountain View, CA 94043	1,147,263	4.9	33,333	1,113,930	4.2
William Joy	884,077	3.8	33,333	850,744	3.2
Vaughan Pratt	349,503	1.5	7,828	341,675	1.3
Bernard J. Lacroute	247,500	1.1	26,203	221,297	0.8
Douglas Broyles	—	—	—	—	—
L. John Doerr	—	—	—	—	—
David F. Marquardt	—	—	—	—	—
Robert B. Murray	—	—	—	—	—
Robert Sackman	—	—	—	—	—
22 other shareholders each owning less than 1.0% of the outstanding Common Stock prior to offering	2,295,611	9.8	277,788	2,017,823	7.6
All directors and officers as a group (17 persons)	6,377,430	27.2	200,000	6,177,430	23.4

SUN MICROSYSTEMS, INC.

Exhibit 3 Selected financial data (in thousands, except per share amounts)

	1986	1985	1984	1983	February 24, 1982 (inception) to June 30, 1982
			Years Ended June 30,		
Operating Data:					
Net revenues	$210,104	$115,249	$38,860	$8,657	$ 86
Costs and expenses:					
Cost of sales	101,965	61,697	21,309	4,486	56
Research and development	30,649	15,193	4,813	1,868	99
Selling, general and administrative	56,894	24,103	9,022	1,715	61
Total costs and expenses	189,508	100,993	35,144	8,069	216
Operating income (loss)	20,596	14,256	3,716	588	(130)
Interest income (expense), net	378	(14)	286	136	—
Income (loss) before income taxes	20,974	14,242	4,002	724	(130)
Provision for income taxes	9,025	5,709	1,344	70[(1)]	—
Net income (loss)	$ 11,949	$ 8,533	$ 2,658	$ 654	$ (130)
Net income (loss) per share	$ 0.46	$ 0.36	$ 0.13	$ 0.04[(1)]	$ (0.02)
Weighted average common and common equivalent shares outstanding	26,217	23,766	21,051	14,660	5,619

	1986	1985	1984	1983	1982
			June 30,		
Balance Sheet Data					
Working capital	$ 65,506	$37,475	$16,287	$3,357	$ (14)
Total assets	182,291	84,169	31,192	7,733	405
Short term borrowings	16,933	6,193	1,338	111	—
Long term obligations, less current maturities	4,062	6,514	3,421	749	—
Shareholders' equity	108,967	48,378	18,910	4,849	158

[1] Net of extraordinary item of $60 related to a reduction in income taxes from carryforward of prior period operating loss (less than $0.01 per share).

SUN MICROSYSTEMS, INC.

Exhibit 4 Sun Microsystems vice presidents

Name	Age	Position	Previous Employer
Bernard J. Lacroute	42	Executive Vice President	DEC
Darryl Barbe	46	Vice President and European General Manager	DEC
Carol A. Bartz	37	Vice President of Marketing, Workstation Division	DEC
James R. Bean	35	Vice President of Operations, Workstation Division	National Semiconductor
Andreas Bechtolsheim	30	Vice President of Technology and Director	Stanford Univ. Ph.D. candidate
Crawford Beveridge	40	Vice President of Human Resources	Analog Devices
Russel J. Bik	38	Vice President and General Manager, Government Systems Division	Intel Corp.
Harry James Folsom	38	Vice President and General Manager, East Coast Division	DEC
Robert Garrow	43	Vice President and General Manager, Workstation Division	Convergent Technologies
William N. Joy	31	Vice President of Research and Development	Univ. of CA, Berkeley
Robert R. Lux	41	Vice President of Customer Support	Apollo Computer, Inc.
Joseph P. Roebuck	50	Vice President of Sales	Osborne Computer Corp.
Wayne Rosing	39	Vice President of Engineering, Workstation Division	Apple Computer
Eric E. Schmidt	30	Vice President and General Manager, Software Products Division	Xerox Research Center
Robert G. Smith	50	Vice President of Finance, Chief Financial Officer	Xerox Corp.

SUN MICROSYSTEMS, INC.

Exhibit 5(a) Organization chart before divisionalization*

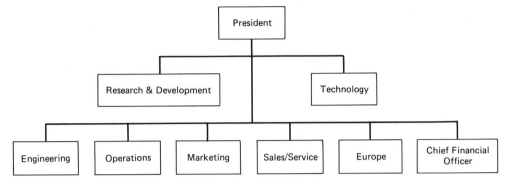

SUN MICROSYSTEMS, INC.

Exhibit 5(b) Organization chart after divisionalization*

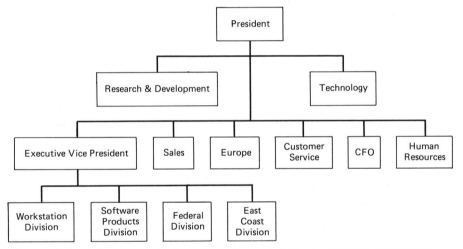

* These organization charts were compiled for the purposes of this case study. They are not generally used within Sun.

SUN MICROSYSTEMS, INC.

Exhibit 6 Stock options offered by grade level

Grade	No. of Shares	Job Categories
5	250 ⎤	
6	500 ⎬	Engineers, accountants, supervisors
7	750 ⎦	
8	1,000 ⎤	
9	1,500 ⎦	Entry-level managers, engineers
10	2,000 ⎤	
11	3,000 ⎬	Middle managers, engineers
12	7,000 ⎦	
13	12,000	Directors

SUN MICROSYSTEMS, INC.

Exhibit 7 Sun's executive bonus plan (as percentage of salary)*

Position	Percentage of Profit Target Achieved		
	80%	*100%*	*140%*
President	0%	40%	80%
Executive VP	0	35	70
Officer	0	30	60
Vice President	0	20	40
Director	0	15	30

* Numbers in exhibit refer to the percentage of salary an individual receives as a bonus at three different levels of corporate performance. A multiplier is used to determine percentages.

SUN MICROSYSTEMS, INC.

Exhibit 8 Additional changes to Sun's benefit plan

Vision—a new benefit added for employees of the Sun plan;

Dental—attached a separate $50 deductible for dental care; orthodontry coverage was added for children of employees; changed the coverage of preventive dental care (i.e., six-month check-up and cleaning) to 100% from 80%;

Accidental Death or Dismemberment—changed from two times annual salary to flat $50,000 for all employees and an option to purchase an additional $250,000 in coverage for employees and families;

Business Travel Accident—Employees are covered $200,000 if die in covered accident while on business travel;

Employee Disability—Disability coverage is required by the State of California. Sun adopted a self-insured plan that reduced the cost of the coverage to the employee;

Stock Purchase—1 to 10% of salary could be withheld twice a year for a six-month period. At the end of the six months, Sun uses the savings to purchase stock. The price of the stock is either 15% below the current market price, or the price at the beginning of the six-month period, whichever is lower.

21 February 1986

One of the best parts of Sun's culture is the open feeling of communication.
One of the greatest contributors to this "Open" feeling is our E-mail system.
E-mail allows us timely communication with our co-workers.

A Limited Tool

E-mail is convenient. It saves us time, phone calls and meetings. But
e-mail is not a perfect vehicle. It sacrifices a whole realm of communication devices which assist in the transfer of ideas. Facial expressions,
body language and intonation are lost when you use e-mail. If the message
is very important, controversial, confidential or one which could be easily
misunderstood, think twice about sending it via e-mail. E-mail is a good
way to communicate, but is NOT necessarily the BEST way for every message.

Praise in Public, Criticize in Private

E-mail is great for public "pats-on-the-back," public "thank you's," or
public questions of general interest. Public criticism of a co-worker,
department or organization is misuse of the medium.

Remember, e-mail is very public. You have little control over who will
see your message. Not all messages and questions are appropriate for
e-mail.

Privacy

Reading another's mail, without their specific invitation or permission,
is gross misconduct. The ease with which we may access someone's mail or
mail record is no excuse for this intrusion. This applies equally to printed
mail awaiting pick-up from the printer.

To CC: or not to CC:

CC is not CYA and should not be employed as a means of demonstrating to
the management above that you are doing your job.

The general rule of business is to carbon copy only those people with a
pressing business need to know what's going on.

Neither is CC an acronym for "See, see how clever I am!" If the purpose
of your eloquence is to keep others from speaking, you are not communicating.
If the chief purpose of your CC is to elevate a problem, please refer to
"Praise in public, criticize in private."

On the following pages you will find a summary of regrouping of the main statements that were made at the last offsite, about what we would like our culture to be.

To help prepare for the next one I need you to spend a few minutes answering the following questions.

1. For each of these statements please consider its importance to our business strategy for the next 2-3 years and rate it on a scale of low-medium-high.

2. For each statement consider how compatible you believe it to be with Sun's culture today.

3. If there are other critical-to-strategy statements that need to be made, please state them and for each one answer question 2.

4. When you finish please take those statements which you have rated as highly important (in terms of importance to strategy), and mark them in terms of your view of their importance to the company. Mark the most important #1, the next #2 and so on.

We will be testing out this questionnaire with some representative groups of employees and will use the data at our offsite to see if we can get closer to an articulation of our culture.

A) Statements About Our Culture

    1. We must never forget our competition.

Important to Strategy/Future	High	Medium	Low
Compatibility with Culture Today	High	Medium	Low

    2. We must never become complacent about losing a deal.

    3. Our customers view all parts of our organization as professional.

    4. Sun is a customer driven company.

    5. Dealing with Sun should be a good deal for both parties.

    6. Our customers agree that we have the best products in the marketplace.

B) Statements About Our Employees

    1. We treat our employees with dignity and trust.

    2. We try to understand the wants and needs of our people and to satisfy them through our organization and career opportunities.

    3. All employees have the right to be listened to.

4. We strive to promote and encourage the growth of our own people.

5. Sun hires the best people possible at every level of the company.

6. We value differences and diversity in our people and believe that divergent viewpoints add strength to the company.

C) Statements About Our Products

1. Sun products are known for extraordinary technical excellence.

2. Sun products make a contribution to the marketplace they serve.

3. Our goal is to maintain leadership by being first to market.

D) Statements About Our Style

1. Our atmosphere is frank and open.

2. Managers are expected to teach and mentor people rather than demand and berate them (teach don't scream).

3. Positive motivation is expected through a combination of positive feedback and candid, constructive, criticism.

4. While individual efforts are rewarded and recognized, teamwork is encouraged and rewarded.

5. We reward accomplishment versus effort, but we encourage people to take risks and tolerate their failures.

6. We insist on the highest standards for our people, products and processes.

7. We are willing to make, and will line up to, commitments to customers, vendors, employees and shareholders.

8. Our management style requires participation. While decision making is clearly the prerogative of line managements consensus is desirable.

9. We want to be the best people managers in the industry, not just in regard to our employees, but also in relation to our vendors and customers.

10. We would like a reputation of honesty with our employees, vendors, customers and shareholders.

11. We have an open door policy.

SUN VALUES

At Sun, we recognize that our long term success depends on both the results we achieve and the way we work to make those results happen. These five value statements describe what we believe to be the most important and fundamental principles of the way we do business at Sun. They were developed as a result of input from employees and managers and reflect ideals that we strive to meet. We realize that, in looking to the future, we will always have room for improvement. And while they are by no means all encompassing, we must constantly look for ways to put these fundamental values into practice.

I encourage you to read these carefully, and ask you to help us find ways to come closer to these ideals.

Scott McNealy, President

QUALITY AND EXCELLENCE IN ALL WE DO

Quality must set us apart.

We set and maintain high standards for our people, our products, and our processes. We set and maintain high standards of personal integrity and ethics in all our business ventures. We are known for quality and for honoring our commitments.

SATISFIED CUSTOMERS

We must make the customer our number one priority.

We maintain the highest level of commitment to our customers, listening and responding to their needs. We understand the customer perspective and provide quality products of excellent value that meet our customers' needs. We respect the competition while always striving for market leadership.

Profitable Company Growth and Development of Individuals

*We must acknowledge the essential link between company growth
and the development of individuals.*

We strive for profitable company growth through extraordinary technical excellence and effective long range planning. We remain at the leading edge of technology by developing products that meet our customers' present and future needs. We strive to have the best individuals in every job, at every level, and excellence throughout the company guides all promotion and hiring decisions. We maintain an environment that encourages personal growth and allows for internal career development and promotion. We encourage risk taking, and provide rewards based on accomplishment. We encourage the development of individuals by delegating responsibility and providing opportunities for growth and promotion.

A Positive Work Environment

*People must have an environment that is characterized by openness, challenge, equity
and respect for the individual in order to work most effectively.*

We look to every employee to share in the responsibility for developing and maintaining a positive work environment. We promote understanding of our company values, products, and the ways we do business. We are clear about expectations, and provide rewards and recognition on the basis of contribution. We treat people equitably and consistently.

Teamwork

We must have teamwork in order to maintain the integrity of the whole.

We encourage and reward teamwork in relationships among employees, customers, vendors, and shareholders. We approach all relationships as win-win partnerships with a willingness to make and honor commitments. Our management style reflects teamwork, characterized by participation, involvement and cooperation.

The First National Bank of California

As far as I'm concerned, Personnel is a collection of individuals who operate independently and who don't have their priorities straight. They're here to serve us, not to harass us.

Michael Cooper, a first vice president of The First National Bank of California, recalled this remark, which had been made by a senior vice president in the consumer services group. For the past three months Cooper had been on general staff assignment in the Personnel Division with the purpose of evaluating the division's services. He had initiated numerous discussions with division staff members and with line managers who made extensive use of Personnel's services. Now it was time to share his assessment with his boss, Roger Gray, executive vice president for staff services.

In Cooper's analysis, almost all of the division's seven departments had problems. To many line managers, inconsistency was the division's hallmark. As Cooper saw it, Personnel's effectiveness could be increased by using one of several options. The first would be to hire an ex-

ternal consultant to help the division's senior department heads formulate a strategy for the next three years. A second option was to establish an internal group to perform the same task. The final option he considered was to recommend an immediate program of specific changes designed to improve the division's performance and image within the bank.

ORGANIZATION OF THE BANK

With headquarters in San Francisco, The First National Bank of California (FNC) was among the largest commercial banks in California, and was ranked in the top 25 nationally. The oldest bank in San Francisco, FNC had grown from a regional concern to become a leader in the national and international banking arenas. It operated as an international bank holding company with current assets of $12 billion and deposits of $7.5 billion. FNC provided lending services to a diverse clientele, including customers in the high-tech, entertainment, and agricultural industries. A system of 28 branches in the Bay area, 42 branches throughout California, and 12 subsidiaries located throughout the nation made up the domestic operations. Internationally, bank branches, subsidiaries, and affiliates were located in 35 countries, with extensive representation in Japan,

This case was written by Jane Wells, Research Assistant, under the direction of Professor Fred K. Foulkes, as a basis for discussion rather than to illustrate either the effective or ineffective handling of an administrative situation.

the Philippines, Hong Kong, and Australia. The bank's presence in Africa had also increased substantially during the past ten years. Foreign operations accounted for nearly one-third of the bank's assets. Due to these activities, FNC was among the top 15 American banks abroad. Worldwide, FNC employed 8,800 people, 6,500 of whom were located in the United States. (See Exhibits 1 and 2 for an organization chart of the bank and staffing levels for U.S. operations, respectively.)

The bank's recent economic performance had disappointed the investment community and several members of the board. Return on assets and equity were below the average of comparable banks. The bank's stock, listed on the New York Stock Exchange, traded below book value and had not kept pace with market averages in the past several years.

With the objective of developing a broader customer base and expanding its market share, the bank was moving forward with plans to acquire additional in-state and Sunbelt banks. In addition, FNC planned to increase its customer business substantially through a greatly expanded system of automated teller machines and was introducing new services to affluent customers using electronic funds transfer technology, including home banking. Commenting on the bank's strategy, the bank's chairman said:

> If we are successful in becoming more profitable, we'll avoid becoming a takeover target ourselves. I'd like to see our stock sell at a premium to book as do the stocks of most of the better-managed regional banks.

THE BANKING ENVIRONMENT

The trend toward deregulation of financial markets was accelerating. Ceilings on permitted interest rates payable for de-posits had eroded. Regulatory permission to offer several new savings instruments had been granted. Competition for these funds, from nonbanking intermediaries, as well as from other commercial banks was fierce. In addition to banks, financial intermediaries now included retail organizations, insurance and credit card companies, and brokerage houses. Also, the prospects of national electronic banking networks heralded the beginning of a decade many analysts expected to be the most competitive ever for the banking industry. Satellite communications and the instantaneous exchange of funds and information by electronic means had laid the foundation for a fully integrated international and informational marketplace. Image technology too was expected to play a key role in the future.

In this changing environment FNC, with the help of a prominent management consulting firm, had developed a three-pronged strategy for the late 80s and early 90s. First, the bank planned to strengthen its regional base by providing better services and closer attention to medium-size corporations in California, with particular emphasis on high-tech companies in the Silicon Valley. This so-called middle market was viewed as very attractive. Second, having played a key role in organizing a regional automatic teller machine network, FNC was preparing to join with other interstate networks to build a national system. Finally, FNC planned to expand its international operations.

Critical elements of this strategy were FNC's ability to attract and keep top-quality staff at all levels of the organization. The bank competed not only with other banks in San Francisco, but also with New York and Chicago for talented staff. In addition, FNC was working to become more efficient and to create more effective management systems. To permit decisions to be made closer to the customer, the bank planned a major decentralization program.

HISTORY AND DEVELOPMENT OF THE PERSONNEL FUNCTION

Located at the bank's headquarters in San Francisco, the Personnel Division served headquarters, the branch offices, and the domestic affiliates. In 1987, there were 115 staff members employed in the division, which was organized into seven different departments: Employment, Training, Compensation, Staff Relations, Records and Benefits, Information Systems Administration, and the South San Francisco Data Processing Center (see Exhibit 3 for an organization chart for the Personnel Division).

Like the personnel function in many organizations, the size and scope of FNC's Personnel Division had increased as the bank grew. Initially it had been a "back shop" operation responsible for processing the information managers needed to hire or compensate their staffs. Over time, the division also served senior management by recommending compensation and bonus systems, developing recruitment strategies, establishing benefit plans, and keeping senior officers up to date on the bank's compliance with government regulations. One of the division's significant responsibilities was manpower planning; the head of the Division produced a plan for manpower growth and change at all staff levels each year.

Before 1984, the head of the Personnel Division reported directly to the chairman of the bank. However, in 1984 the position of executive vice president for staff services was created. Personnel, along with the Law Office and the Community Investment Office, reported to Executive Vice President Roger Gray under the new arrangement. Gray, a lawyer, had joined the bank in 1960 and had served in positions in Japan and Australia and as head of FNC's international leasing activities before being appointed senior vice president for the Asia Division in 1968.

This development seemed to have a profound effect on Oliver Franklin, who had been first vice president of the Personnel Division throughout the 1970s and early 1980s. Subordinates noticed a change in Franklin's behavior and performance following Gray's arrival. Some people speculated that Franklin felt he had been demoted. For whatever reasons, Franklin was seen as less effective and less motivated under the new arrangement. According to several oldtimers in the division, this perceived decline had adversely affected the morale and performance of staff throughout the division, and Franklin's credibility as a leader had waned. No one was surprised when he was asked to take early retirement in the summer of 1986.

The division's number two person, Sidney Martin, was assigned to be acting head. Soft-spoken in manner, Martin was a career professional in the human resources area. During the 20 years he had been with the division, he had been exposed to all aspects of its operation. His technical skill was superior and he enjoyed the respect of the staff in the division as well as managers throughout the bank.

Another year passed before any new developments occurred. In the fall of 1987, Roger Gray announced that First Vice President Michael Cooper would assume leadership of the Personnel Division, beginning his job on general staff assignment with the purpose of reviewing the division's activities. Under this arrangement, Martin served as a consultant to Cooper.

MICHAEL COOPER'S FIRST FEW MONTHS

Michael Cooper, age 34, had joined the bank as a young MBA in 1975. He had begun his career as a loan officer in the Commercial Banking Division and then moved to the International Banking Division as a credit analyst specializing in country risk evaluation. Here his facility for languages and his interest in foreign cultures were of benefit. Over time, he developed skills as a manager and a trouble-shooter. His two most recent assignments had involved revitalizing money-losing overseas branches in the Philippines and Hong Kong. These successful turnarounds had increased his interest in pursuing a management career. Thus, he saw the opportunity to review the personnel function as a chance to utilize his management skills in a visible position at corporate headquarters.

The personnel function appeared to have several problems. Among his colleagues in line management, it was regarded as a very conservative division that was out of step with the times and lacked relevance to the bank as a whole. There were plenty of horror stories about vice presidents who had referred promising candidates to Personnel only to hear that they had received "Dear John" letters from the department. Cooper looked forward to the challenge this new job offered.

According to many members of the division, Cooper's reputation preceded him in his new assignment. Stories about his previous successes in cleaning up failing departments had, in the opinion of several people, served to notify the division of its problem status. Since past turnarounds had involved changes in staff assignments and staffing levels, some speculated that Cooper was likely to disrupt the division's status quo. Some responded to these uncertainties with anxiety, others with anticipation and excitement; still others adopted a wait-and-see attitude.

Added to these sentiments was concern on Sidney Martin's behalf. In the division and outside of it, people were upset that Martin had been displaced by a younger person not experienced in personnel. Aware of these concerns, Cooper discussed them with Martin at the beginning of his assignment. From this fruitful talk, Martin recognized that Cooper's familiarity with bank operations could provide a valuable external perspective on the division's activities and could add credibility to the division's efforts. Cooper recognized the value of Martin's comprehensive knowledge of the division and of the importance of his support in order to evaluate the division accurately.

Cooper's first priority was to obtain information about the division's activities. In addition to reviewing division documents and progress reports, he planned to consult with department heads and with staff at all levels of the division. Concurrently, he wanted to talk with significant users of division services to obtain evaluations.

Within the division he found that very little information existed in the form of written reports. Although records and program descriptions were available, he noted the absence of goal or strategy statements or periodic progress reports. Individual discussions he had with the department heads and staff members were characterized by both the enthusiasm and the frustration many expressed. Many staff members had initiated meetings with him to present their ideas on how the division's performance could be improved. The division's poor reputation within the bank was a source of concern. Of equal concern was the feeling that it was hard to be effective within the division. People felt that they tended to be lone operators, with little sense of teamwork or support and that historically the division head's inaccessibility had set the tone for relations throughout the division.

Managers outside the division varied in their assessment of the individual departments. Many expressed negative opinions that lambasted all aspects of Personnel's operations. Others were more selective, and praised or criticized the efforts of specific individuals. As Michael Cooper reviewed the information he had obtained and the impressions he had acquired in meetings and conversations, his thoughts turned to specific activities and programs.

When the bank's chairman and CEO, just one year away from retirement, was asked about the Personnel Division and Michael Cooper's role, he said:

> The division is behind the times. I wish we could dump the entire department in the San Francisco Bay and start from scratch. But we can't. While the division has lots of nice people, they are not very creative or imaginative. They are not very business oriented either. I continue to be amazed by the way they lose résumés. Cooper has to shake them up, and he has my support, as well as the backing of the president and the vice chairman. I think he will do well in this assignment.

EMPLOYMENT

The largest of the departments in the Personnel Division, the Employment Department was organized into three areas: management staffing, clerical staffing, and job posting (see Exhibit 4 for an organization chart for the Employment Department). George Kendall was vice president of employment and, like many of the senior management in the division, had made his career in the personnel field. George had joined the bank in 1971 and been promoted to his current position in 1982.

In management staffing, there were three full-time and one part-time management recruiters. A major problem in the management staffing area was that over the years the Credit Department, which was not connected with Personnel, had taken over the administration of the main vehicle for attracting and training entry-level management staff—namely, the Loan Officer Development Program.

The Loan Officer Development Program (LODP) recruited and trained candidates for officer positions in the International Banking and Commercial Banking Division. Utilizing a combination of course work, project assignments, and internships, the program prepared participants for lending roles in all areas of the bank. Depending on prior background, a trainee's stay in the program ranged from 9 to 12 months. Over the past 5 years, the number of loan officer trainees hired each year had increased from 40 to the current level of 80. The Credit Department managed all aspects of the program, from college recruitment to final assignments. Michael Cooper talked with Chuck Hathaway, senior vice president of the Credit Department. Hathaway said:

> I don't have to tell you about the importance of this program to the bank. If we expect to get outstanding people to work here, this program and everything associated with it must be top-notch or better. We're competing with New York and Chicago to get bright MBAs and undergraduate finance majors to stay here or to come to San Francisco. We can't afford mistakes in this area; it's critical to the long-term success of the bank that we do an excellent job.
>
> Honestly, through the years we have made a conscious effort to take over the functions that we felt Personnel did not handle adequately. Now we run the whole show. We do everything from setting up recruiting schedules in colleges across the country, to selecting and training interviewers from among

the officers, to writing brochures and job descriptions. We even set salary levels and tell the Compensation Department how to administer them. It costs us a bundle, but it's worth every penny to have it go smoothly. We just couldn't get the level of service we needed from the Employment Department. There was a lot of turnover in the management staffing area. We'd deal with a different person every time. It got so that if a good person came along we'd hire him away from the management staffing to help us. They were happy to get out of there. Employment had no administrative control over the process. They were unable to pinpoint a candidate's status over time. They usually didn't even know how many people they had interviewed or offered jobs to. The worst case was when they sent a reject letter to our top candidate. Even though I talked to the lad personally and apologized for the mistake, we lost him. It was a complete disaster. The worst of it is that kind of thing happens all the time. It drives the chairman crazy every time he hears about it.

At the time of Michael Cooper's review of Personnel, Jim Chan had recently been hired to work on the problems of the management staffing area. Hired 6 months earlier and new to the management staffing area, Jim had already had complaints from several candidates and from a number of departments that résumés and applications had been lost. Four people had called to say that they had not received word about their status a month after being interviewed. Recruiters often did not have time to return calls to departments or to candidates, and paperwork to process a candidate or a new hire was frequently incomplete. Jim had been dismayed to find that frequently recruiters did not know the salaries of the jobs for which they were interviewing. Noting that there was great variation in how recruiters approached their jobs, Jim was not surprised to learn that no procedures manual existed for the recruitment pro-

cess. On the other hand, a recent conversation with Dan Scarlett, a vice president in Banking Operations, had been very positive. Scarlett had said:

Our division has been expanding quickly recently. We've averaged 12 management openings annually for the last three years. Currently, the management recruiter assigned to us has been doing a fine job. He has helped us find candidates, refers good résumés to us even when there is no specific opening, and chases down the paperwork if we find our own candidates.

Jim Chan felt his work was cut out for him.

Michael Cooper had also heard comments about the management staffing area. A senior vice president in the Trust Division had observed:

Maybe George Kendall has gotten his act together this time. He has finally hired someone to head management staffing who looks competent. It is a key, visible job. The last guy who had the position made a mess of it. Jim has the right credentials and he is sophisticated—knows how to work with officers. He's got some cleaning up to do though—some of those recruiters aren't very professional.

Seven employment representatives and a manager composed the clerical staffing area. For the past 5 years, the number of clerical openings had run at about 1,000 positions, or 15% annually. At any given time there were usually 25 openings; average time to fill a position was 6 weeks. Mary Bond, senior clerical staffing officer, had discussed the situation with Michael Cooper:

Clerical positions are harder to fill now. There is a severe supply problem. Competent clerical people are not as available as they once were. Fewer women are willing to become secretaries these days. Also we're competing with the high-tech firms in the area, which tend to offer higher salaries than banks and better opportunities for advancement. I'm disturbed by the fact that some of the departments in the bank are running their own ads, doing recruiting and screening for themselves. I've heard of one department that has hired a private employment agency. I'm surprised they're willing to pay the fees. George and I have discussed these problems several times. We are working hard on it and I think the job posting program is really starting to help.

The job posting program, the newest addition to the employment area, had been in operation for a year. It was instituted after a 2½ year study to reduce turnover and increase the number of internal promotions by ensuring that external candidates were not solicited until current employees had had a chance to apply for openings. The program applied not only to all clerical jobs, supervisory, and exempt positions, but also to management trainee positions.

Sandy Rubin, personnel officer for job posting, ran the program with help from a posting assistant and an administrative clerk. The program involved several activities: writing or revising job descriptions, reviewing salaries with the Compensation Department to ensure that positions carried a competitive wage rate, and monitoring job requirements to determine that they had not been set too high. Jobs were posted internally for one week. After one week, if no internal candidates had applied or if none of those applying was qualified, the position would be opened to external applicants. Timeliness was a critical aspect of the service. During the one-week period, all applicants were screened and interviews with supervisors were scheduled for those who qualified. Sandy acted as an intermediary between the departments and individuals wanting

to transfer. On occasion, she would work with a staff relations officer to handle someone seeking a transfer who was about to be terminated for poor performance. Supervisors and employees alike had responded positively to the program.

While discussing the activities of the Employment Department with Mike Cooper, George Kendall commented:

> A lot of the officers and vice presidents in this bank are very demanding people. They want immediate results although they have no concept of how competitive the market is. My philosophy is to wait until they've called a few times before getting back to them. That way I know they are serious and they know I am busy with more people than just them.

TRAINING

Unlike the rest of the Personnel Division, the training department was located on the eighth floor of the headquarters building. According to several people, in many ways this was symbolic of the department's relationship to the division. "Trainers see little of their colleagues in the other departments and think of themselves as a separate organization," observed one line manager. Headed by Assistant Vice President Alison Ray and staffed by 12 trainers, the department was responsible for serving the training and development needs of headquarters, the branches, and affiliates. Historically concerned with skills training, over the past seven years the department had designed a comprehensive array of programs directed at all levels of the staff. In-house courses and seminars included orientation programs, supervisory/management programs for officers and nonofficers, communications workshops, sales/marketing training for customer contact situations, language programs, including Berlitz, staff development workshops in time management and career development, and technical programs for typing and number skills. Out-of-bank opportunities included courses offered by the American Institute of Banking and the Tuition Assistance Program that provided bank employees with financial support while they pursued undergraduate or graduate degrees on a part-time basis.

In addition, organizational consulting and training-related consulting services were provided to departments upon request. Individual trainers had the freedom to design new programs or modify existing programs as user needs developed.

While analyzing the training department's strengths and weaknesses with Cooper, Alison Ray had commented:

> As you know, I was in the Banking Operations and Corporate Services Division before coming to Personnel a year ago. I'm still very conscious of how different it is here. Although training has always been a well-managed department with a good reputation, until I came little attention was given to how cost-effective programs were or whether they really had an impact on the bottom line or improved productivity. We have started to evaluate the effectiveness of our services and to establish goals for the future.
>
> I have to say, though, that I am very frustrated with the Personnel Division as a whole. There is a bureaucratic mentality here, a lot of buck-passing, and a great deal of resistance to new ideas. In my opinion, we are in desperate need of a management information system, and yet the other department heads cannot see beyond their own areas. One or two of them claim they don't have time to think about it. Unfortunately, they're probably right.

COMPENSATION

The Compensation Department was composed of three areas: organization planning, officer compensation, and non-officer compensation (see Exhibit 5). Organization planning was responsible for keeping track of changes in officer job titles, updating the organizational chart, and disseminating information about changes in the bank's organization. In addition, organization planning administered the system of external and internal signing authorities. (There were 19 types of signing authorities that related to over 3,000 different documents, including cashier's check authorizations, bank contracts, and vendor invoices.) While officer compensation handled salary decisions and bonus award programs for the bank's officers, non-officer compensation administered the salary program for the members of the non-officer staff.

Vice President Bill Tucker had been head of the Compensation Department for 12 years. Described as "outgoing" and "charming," he was a man with many friends at the bank; he seemed to thrive on the extensive interactions with managers in all divisions of the bank that his job required. In talking with Michael Cooper, he had described the department's weakness:

> Compensation is stretched too thin. We're understaffed now because we've recently begun a massive effort to review and update officer job descriptions. I have three people assigned full-time to that project. They all came out of the nonofficer compensation area, leaving it without adequate manpower. The officer's review is an important effort that we've needed for a long time. So it's got to get done, but in the meantime, we're really strapped.

For the past 10 years a consultant from Hay Associates had come in to update officer job descriptions on an annual basis, usually spending a day per week with the bank for about 6 weeks. During that time, he was able to analyze and describe about 20 positions. However, since the bank had approximately 1,500 officer positions in the United States, the department was chronically behind in maintaining the accuracy of officer job descriptions. The lack of timeliness in the officer area made decisions about appropriate compensation based on comparable positions within the bank and in other banks very difficult. The compensation system in use had been developed in 1955 and revised in 1970 and 1976, with no major changes since then.

The Officer Position Evaluation Committee (known as OPEC) was composed of four managers: vice presidents from Deposit Operations, Commercial Finance, Institutional Investments, and International Banking. It was chaired by Bill Tucker. It met once a month to assign salary levels to new positions and to consider revised job descriptions when a request for a position reclassification and compensation adjustment occurred. Often the butt of hostility, critics claimed that the committee was too easily influenced by the current officeholder's performance when deciding to reclassify a position, and that a manager's negotiating skill was the essential ingredient in arriving at compensation decisions for new positions. However, many people praised Bill Tucker. The vice president for Commercial Banking said:

> Bill is the only one in the department I can talk to. He has gone out of his way to be helpful to me. He's enabled me to reward some of my people at slightly higher rates at times when we might have lost them otherwise. He knows when to be flexible.

In a later conversation with Cooper, Tucker had made the following observation:

> I think the officer salary increase program could be restructured. As it stands now, managers receive salary increase allotments in September, during the annual planning process, which they are supposed to allocate during the following year. Because allotments are made a year in advance, managers often must make compensation decisions well in advance of when they give them out—that is, managers must predict in September how well their subordinates will perform during the coming year. Any changes in allocation decisions must receive approval from the president. All in all, the system lacks flexibility, and it is not effective in connecting reward to performance. Over the years people have learned how to manipulate it to get what they want, but this tends to undermine the whole process. I'd like to form a committee to develop a new system.

STAFF RELATIONS

Headed by Carolyn Hodges, one of the few women vice presidents at the bank, the Staff Relations Department consisted of four areas: staff relations, administration support, equal opportunity programs, and the staff health center (see Exhibit 6). Unemployment compensation, workers' compensation, retiree affairs, and recreational activities were handled by administration support. The EEO area monitored compliance with government regulations by collecting and submitting necessary documents. Located in another part of the building, the staff health center was a medical facility employees utilized on a walk-in basis. The largest area, staff relations, was directed by a manager, Fred Brown, and staffed by five officers who served all nonofficer staff throughout corporate headquarters, in the branches, and in the affiliates and subsidiaries. Their main role was to be the liaison between the Personnel Department and the bank's employees. In this capacity, they helped managers and supervisors interpret personnel policies and mediated employee disputes and grievances. Depending on the problem, they would act as advocates on behalf of a manager or an employee to resolve an attendance problem or counsel an employee about alternative career opportunities in another division, or assist a manager in obtaining adequate documentation to discharge a subordinate who was performing badly.

A vice president in the West Coast division had commented:

> Supervisory staff in my area often mention how responsive the staff relations people are. A problem comes up and they're on it immediately with a phone call or a visit. We had one case where a Japanese-American clerk felt she had been passed over for a promotion. There were personality problems between her and her supervisor and a history of misunderstandings. The staff relations officer really handled it well. Got her a good transfer to another department that ended up being a promotion. I credit him with keeping us out of court in that situation.

Fred Brown had initiated a meeting with Cooper to discuss his analysis of the staff relations function. Fred had gone on to reflect about the department's weaknesses from his perspective:

> I think we're strong in the service delivery area. It's our main business. We're good generalists and we have been successful at developing leverage with department heads to avoid potentially serious problems. There are two problems, both of which are systemic in nature. First, as generalists, the staff relations officers need to work with other departments in the Personnel Division. However, the quality of information we get is very uneven, depending on whom we contact. There's a lot of territoriality with the division and people let you know when they think you're on their turf. To solve problems effectively, the various components of the division need to communicate better with each other.

> Secondly, because we're in constant contact with employees, we are often made aware of how policies have become outmoded or of the need for new policies. I've proposed several policies to extend benefits to long term part-time employees and to revise the discipline procedures. The problem is these ideas get bogged down. You have to do a major community organizing effort within the division and outside to get support for changes. It took four years for the job posting policy to be accepted, even though all our competitors already had one. The atmosphere around here has been risk-averse for too long, and there needs to be more efficient mechanisms for change.

RECORDS AND BENEFITS

The Records and Benefits Department consisted of two sections: benefit and payroll administration, and benefits development. Largely a clerical effort, benefits and payroll administration provided operational support for the division's other functions. A primary responsibility was processing weekly, biweekly, monthly, and overseas payrolls, which included incorporating changes in salary or benefits. According to Barry Knight, the area's manager, it was operated as a production shop, with emphasis on meeting the payroll cycle schedule. It functioned as a self-contained unit within the division. The benefits development area was responsible for designing benefit programs and for evaluating and monitoring current benefit trends.

INFORMATION SYSTEMS ADMINISTRATION

A small and relatively new department, Information Systems Administration was a technical group concerned with ensuring reliable computer services within the division. Staff members provided systems development assistance to the division's departments (primarily records and benefits) and acted as a liaison between the Personnel Division and the bank's computer complex, The Information Systems and Services Division.

SOUTH SAN FRANCISCO DATA PROCESSING CENTER

The bank's data processing services center was located in a separate facility in a suburb, South San Francisco. A highly labor-intensive operation that handled stock transfers, check collection and processing, and automated corporate services, among other activities, the center employed 3,000 exempt and nonexempt staff. Due to its large size and remote location, the center had always had its own on-site personnel office, which reported on a solid line basis to the head of the Personnel Division at corporate headquarters.

A miniature version of headquarter's Personnel Division, the South San Francisco office had eight professional staff and offered assistance in five areas: staff relations, employment, medical claims and benefits information, training and development, and health care through the health center. The staff was organized as a team, and frequently collaborated when an employee's needs overlapped more than one area.

The center's team structure was the creation of Vice President Malcolm McNeil, who headed the South San Francisco personnel office. McNeil said:

> The center is in an isolated location in addition to being removed from the bank. We felt that the personnel department should really work hard to maintain a sense of community here. Consequently, we have striven to develop an integrated service, responsive to the needs of the center's employees.

An innovation fostered by the center's personnel department had been the establishment of volunteer committees composed of center employees. One of the committees had developed a lunchtime recreation program that featured movies and concerts. Another committee prepared a proposal that resulted in the conversion of vacant space in the basement to a fitness center. According to several employees, the existence of the committees and the opportunity to contribute to new projects were highly valued and had gone a long way to promote positive atmosphere there.

CONCLUSION

Michael Cooper reflected on what he had learned during his two months of meetings and conversations with members of the Personnel staff and with managers outside the division. He reminded himself that having asked about problems and weaknesses, he had heard mostly about the division's inadequacies. Nevertheless, some valid themes had emerged. Lack of coordination among the division's departments and dissatisfaction with the quality of some of the division's services stood out in his mind. In addition, entrenched negative attitudes about Personnel among many of the bank's officers and line managers appeared to have stymied past leaders of the division in making Personnel effective and relevant in meeting the bank's changing needs.

In thinking about how to proceed, he considered the three alternatives he planned to discuss with Roger Gray:

1. Bringing in an outside consultant to assist the division in developing its strengths and planning for the next three years
2. Analyzing the situation further by establishing an internal group to review the

division and recommend ways of improving its performance and image during the next three years

3. Initiating specific changes—such as adding staff to the compensation department, developing a public relations program to improve the division's image and to educate people about Personnel's services, and revamping the clerical staffing area.

Cooper pondered the challenges that faced the division. Although the ultimate goal of creating a Personnel office that could readily serve the recruitment, training, compensation, and development needs of the bank seemed clear to him, the question of how best to achieve this objective remained.

THE FIRST NATIONAL BANK OF CALIFORNIA STUDY QUESTIONS:

1. What is your assessment of the situation Michael Cooper faces at the end of the case?
2. In terms of priority, what do you see as the major problems?
3. What should Cooper's objectives be?
4. How will Cooper's performance be judged?
5. What are the realistic options open to Cooper?
6. What should Cooper do? Why?

THE FIRST NATIONAL BANK OF CALIFORNIA

Exhibit 1 FNC organization chart

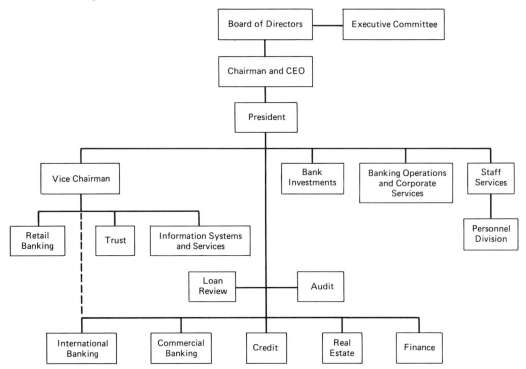

THE FIRST NATIONAL BANK OF CALIFORNIA

Exhibit 2 U.S. operations—staffing levels

Job Category	Number in Category
I. *Officers*	
Chairman	1
President	1
Vice Chairman	1
Executive Vice President	10
Senior Vice President	27
First Vice President	38
Vice President	300
Associate Vice President	300
Officer/Manager	825
Total	1,500
II. *Non-Officers*	
Supervisory and Technical Staff (Exempt)	375
Clerical (Nonexempt)	4,625
Total	5,000
III. *Total U.S. Operations*	6,500

THE FIRST NATIONAL BANK OF CALIFORNIA

Exhibit 3 Organization of the personnel division

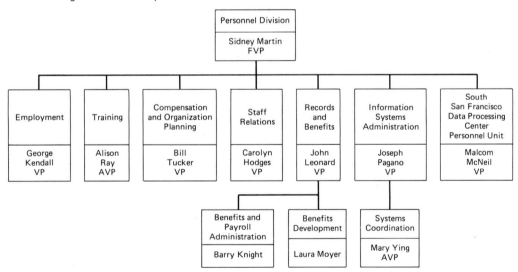

THE FIRST NATIONAL BANK OF CALIFORNIA
Exhibit 4 Employment department

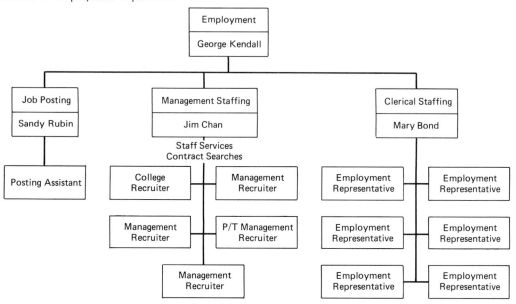

THE FIRST NATIONAL BANK OF CALIFORNIA
Exhibit 5 Compensation and organization planning department

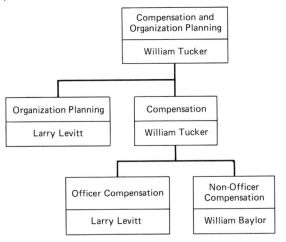

THE FIRST NATIONAL BANK OF CALIFORNIA

Exhibit 6 *Staff relations department*

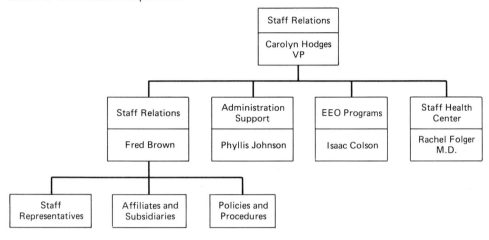

II

EMPLOYMENT AND PROMOTION POLICY AND ADMINISTRATION

Walter Wriston, retired chairman and chief executive officer of Citicorp, the parent of Citibank, has said, "I believe the only game in town is the personnel game . . . My theory is that if you have the right person in the right place, you don't have to do anything else. If you have the wrong person in the job, there's no management system known to man that can save you . . . The selection of the people that hold the key jobs is a principal function of the chief executive officer." And Akio Morita, chairman of Sony, has said: "In the long run, your business and its future are in the hands of the people you hire. To put it a bit more dramatically, the fate of your business is actually in the hands of the youngest recruit on the staff."[1]

Too often managers agonize and spend much time over firing decisions, whereas

a wiser investment of time would be in the hiring and promotion processes. People who become performance problems or people fired looked good when they were hired or promoted. Good hires and proper promotions can become the lifeblood of the organization. It is important, therefore, that sound employment and promotion decisions be made. Cost-effective employment and promotion processes are crucial. The readings and cases in this chapter, accordingly, are concerned with employment and promotion policy and administration, including the requirements of equal employment opportunity and affirmative action.

RECRUITMENT AND SELECTION

In hiring, one is trying to balance the needs of the organization, including its affirmative action commitments, with the

---

[1] *Made in Japan: Akio Morita and Sony* (New York: Dutton, 1986).

interests and career goals of the individual. The objective is to make good matches or fits. Wise selection decisions start not only by defining well the organization's people requirements and the specific jobs to be filled, but also by articulating thoughtfully the desired qualifications. While employing people who turn out to be unqualified is costly, hiring overqualified people also has its perils. Bored employees create their own special set of personnel problems. Finally, hiring plans also must take into account the organization's affirmative action goals with respect to minorities, women, and the disabled.

The student must recognize that there are frequent conflicts, especially in the short run, between the needs of the organization and the interests and career goals of the individual. The company may consider the training program for new recruits essential; the individual, wanting immediate challenge, may consider it unnecessary. The company may consider a developmental move to another job or country essential for career development, while the individual may view such a move as unattractive. There can also be conflicts between the company's desire to recruit the best people and the requirements of getting the job filled as soon as possible.

Before effective recruiting and selection decisions can be made, the employer must describe and analyze and then set wage or salary rates or ranges for the jobs that are to be filled. Selection criteria need to fit the job responsibilities and demands. For reasons of equal employment opportunity, the criteria must be reliable and valid. For a particular job, one has to determine the predictors of successful job performance. The use of criteria and predictors in a demonstration of the concept of validity is crucial to understanding the whole process of finding someone who will be appropriate for a job.

For example, at The Boston Consulting Group, a leading business strategy consulting firm, virtually all professionals have MBAs from top schools. The firm reports that it hires only those "highly motivated overachievers who are extremely bright." It interviews approximately 25 students each year for each one it hires. In 1979 80% of students receiving job offers accepted them, with the vast majority of those hired in the upper 10% of their MBA class. To help implement its rigorous selection process, before several in-depth interviews and reference checks the firm requires the interested student to provide college and graduate transcripts, SAT and GMAT scores and photocopies of graduate school admission applications in addition to the customary résumé. For a consulting company, the human resource is not simply an important resource—it is the *only* resource. It is therefore of strategic importance to invest heavily in the recruitment and development of extremely talented people. Ill-advised selections are costly from both the firm's and individual's point of view.

Delta Airlines also invests heavily in the employment process. All of Delta's hiring is done in Atlanta, Georgia, at corporate headquarters. A local manager may recommend candidates to the corporate group, but Atlanta does the hiring. The hiring process consists of interviews, reference checks and, for pilots, mechanics, flight attendants and certain staff jobs, such as programmers, a pyschological assessment. Delta, perceived as an extremely good place to work, has a huge number of applicants for its jobs. It may, for example, hire 500 flight attendants from among the 2,500 to 3,000 candidates interviewed. Delta has extremely low turnover and, under its promotion-from-within policy, hires people not so much for a particular job, but rather for a career. It might be added that once hired, employees are put through an extensive orientation and training seminar at the company's new learning center in Atlanta.

While past performance is the best predictor of future performance, if the past experience is relevant for the job or career being recruited for, what criteria should a consulting firm, for instance, use when evaluating MBAs from leading business schools? As one thinks about hiring a consultant, what are the valid measures? Moreover, suppose the measures utilized produce an adverse impact with respect to either women, or minorities, or both? If one is hiring a typist, a typing test can be an extremely relevant input into the hiring decision. But if one is hiring someone to be a consultant, what tests, if any, are appropriate? In airline work it is thought that stability of the individual is particularly important, for many airline employees at different times are involved in uncertain work, with safety of obvious importance.

Developing an effective bias-free selection system is no easy matter. Students must also understand that the development of in-depth screening procedures is simply an attempt to raise an organization's batting average with respect to the selection of people, as well as to attain an acceptable position toward the EEOC in the event of discrimination charges. Mistakes will always be made. But some companies do a better job than others, and those who do generally devote a good deal of time to the recruiting process.

Hiring procedures vary by job, company, and industry. More time and resources are invested in hiring a vice president from the outside than are devoted to hiring a sweeper. A sweeper can be watched during his probationary period, and, if his or her performance and/or attendance is not satisfactory, may be dismissed. Although vice presidents may also be discharged, mistakes at this level are

more costly. Delta, given its nonunion status and the importance it attaches to personnel, appears to invest more heavily in the employment process than its competitors do.

After the position descriptions, desired qualifications, and selection criteria have been established, the employment, orientation, training, performance appraisal and career development processes can be managed more productively. An outline of the College Placement Council's professional training and development modules for college recruiting and relations follows:

    I. College relations—definition and importance

   II. Establishing the on-campus recruiting program

  III. Select, train, and supervise the recruiters

  IV. Identify and attract candidates

   V. Interviewing skills

  VI. Equal Employment Opportunity/Affirmative Action requirements

 VII. Evaluate the candidate

VIII. In-house selection process

  IX. Follow-up—selling the candidate

   X. Evaluation of the recruiting program

To begin with, companies must do sound recruitment planning and then design and staff effective recruitment programs. If hiring is viewed as a purchasing activity, then one looks at the relative effectiveness of different talent pools or recruitment sources for different jobs. While executive search firms may be retained to fill middle and senior management positions where no insiders are considered qualified, campus recruiting programs can meet the needs for entry-level engineers, scientists, and management trainees. Newspaper advertisements, attractive brochures, job fairs, and open houses can all be useful recruiting aids. While hiring walk-ins and the friends and relatives of current employees are frequently used techniques, especially in smaller companies, these methods may not produce the best qualified candidates. They are also generally inconsistent with equal employment and affirmative action principles. This is because the friends and relatives of existing employees, if most existing employees are white, will most likely not be members of minority groups. Although it is usual practice to work through the college's placement office, an employer wanting minority students from a nonminority school may find it more effective to work through the minority student organizations on campus. This is because some minority students may not avail themselves of the services of the placement office.

Various selection tools can be used to narrow down the choices. Interviews, reference and school checking, psychological tests, résumés, the employment application itself, and perhaps assessment centers are ways to ascertain how good the person-organization fit might be. Some even claim that the services of graphologists (handwriting analysts) are useful in determining the character of prospective employees. Selecting the right people to conduct the initial and secondary interviews (as well as their orientation and training) is critical. Skill in judging people generally comes with experience. Recruiters must not turn off applicants. They must know their company and the nature of the jobs offered. Interviewers may tend to favor people who resemble themselves ("If you are like me you must be good") as well as those they view as physically attractive. Interviewer bias must be guarded against. Training the recruiter to be effective is a major problem because the turnover of college recruiters is very high—approximately one-third every year. Such turnover, obviously, is inconsistent with

the desire to build effective long-term relationships between a company and the campus.

To reduce turnover among college recruiters, recruiting must be made more attractive. Too often managers fail to receive any rewards for hiring outstanding people. While the performance of outstanding people is appreciated and recognized, the organization forgets those who recruited and hired those individuals. Some companies have made recruiting a more attractive activity for line managers by inviting a select few to be part of a top executive's recruiting team at a particular campus.

In addition to trying to reduce turnover, it is also important to decide well in advance who will make the final decision as well as communicate the results. Timely decisions are appreciated by applicants and can give companies a competitive advantage in hiring. Applicants who are kept dangling for too long become discouraged.

A company may use either specialized recruiters or line managers to conduct the initial interviews. What a company does will depend on many factors, including the size of the organization, the nature of the job, the importance the organization attaches to recruiting, and the costs involved. On the one hand, it would be inconceivable that a company would hire an executive vice president or a financial vice president without the president's and/or chairman's involvement. On the other hand, it would also be inconceivable for a company president, at least in a large company, to interview each potential new supervisor. Akio Morita of Sony, however, meets each year with the group of college graduates that join the company.

Ideally, a new employee's boss should always interview him or her as part of the selection process, but that is not always possible. In large, geographically dispersed companies where people are being hired for a career rather than a job, some line managers, to fill some jobs, may have to rely on the judgment of specialized recruiters. For example, it would not be practical for the Citibank trainee, hired in New York for a training program of several months, to be interviewed by a future boss in Saudi Arabia. While line managers can generally respond well to questions about the job, they may not be effective interviewers. Therefore, when line managers are used in recruiting programs, careful attention must be given to their selection, training, and performance. A most expensive part of recruiting is the period of time after a successful initial interview. If an applicant invited to the company is turned off by a middle manager, the student applicant in turn may turn off ten other students on campus.

The purpose of the interview is to learn about the candidate what cannot be known from an application or résumé. What, from a student and employer viewpoint, makes for effective interviews? How can the initial interviewing process be improved? If past performance is the best predictor of future performance, then a good interviewer must seek to ascertain how the person will act on the job. As for what employers are looking for and what makes a good MBA candidate, a group of surveyed companies ranked the attributes they look for in a potential employee as follows:[2]

1. Personality and leadership potential
2. Motivation and clear-cut goals
3. Maturity and previous business or military experience
4. Communications skills
5. Analytical ability

[2] Jacqueline A. Thompson, "Recruiting: The Best Year in a Decade," *MBA Magazine*, March 1974, p. 43.

6. Reputation of the business school attended
7. Grades

The selection criteria one company utilizes for college hires is as follows:

1. Personal Characteristics
   a. Drive, motivation
   b. Leadership
   c. Attitude
   d. Communication skills
   e. Appearance
   f. Decision-making skills
   g. Intelligence
   h. Maturity
2. Personal Goals—ambition
3. Educational background
4. Work experience
5. Extracurricular activities/accomplishments/interests

It is easy to agree with these attributes, but consider how one goes about assessing personality, motivation, and leadership and communication skills. What evidence is one looking for, and how can/should it be obtained? What questions should be asked? What can you tell from an interview? Behavior during an interview as well as past experience may be proxies for behavior on the job, but ways in addition to "gut feel" have to be devised to make such assessments. Selection criteria also need to be both job related and validated.

A good interviewer will not only let the interviewee do most of the talking, but will plan in advance what he or she wants to learn from the applicant and what questions might be appropriate to ask. For example, if leadership potential is important, what are the indicators of it? If, for instance, the résumé or application reveals that the applicant was an officer of his fraternity, one might ask about what he did. Similarly, if decision-making skills and/or analytical ability are important, one might pose actual job-related problems to see how the applicant's mind works.

Although there are a few general principles it is wise to follow, most employment problems must be solved on a case by case basis. Unless almost every condition is the same, what works for one company will not necessarily work for another. Consider, for example, the questions one large company asked itself, when, for competitive reasons, it decided it had to develop a more professional career-oriented sales force.

1. How should a professional sales force be developed?
   a. Should we use specialized recruiters?
   b. Should we use sales managers for recruiting?
   c. Should we use career weekends?
2. What should be the principal sources of new sales people?
   a. Colleges
   b. External outside hires
   c. Direct hires from competitors
   d. Internally developed people
   e. Personnel agencies and executive search firms
   f. Other
3. What specific selection criteria are appropriate for college graduates and what quality or attribute is demonstrated by the criteria? For example, grade point average—top half, indicates ability to comprehend technical problems.
   a. Grade point average
   b. Advanced degrees
   c. Degree field
   d. Technical-nontechnical background
   e. Types of schools
   f. Extracurricular activities
   g. Other
4. What value should we attach to previous experience? What kind of previous experience should we value?
5. What training is appropriate for new sales personnel?
   a. Should it vary with employee background?
   b. Should employees be assigned sales territories before completion of training?
6. Should employees with qualifications be hired for specific positions? Or, should employees be hired on a general basis and assigned positions on some other criteria?
7. What kind of assessment or prehiring screening should be used?
8. What programs should be established to track the success or lack thereof of the recruiting/hiring effort?
9. Given the selling task, should salespeople be paid on a straight salary or commission basis? If by commission, what should it be based on?
10. What kinds of career paths should we offer?
11. What kind of turnover should be expected?

Although these questions are interrelated, the right answers to them emerged only after a searching examination of the company's selling tasks, its competitive situation, its top management philosophy, the employment market, and the nature of the product markets in which the company expected to be a viable competitor.

One also needs to determine whether it is a buyer's or a seller's market. In the early 1980s, qualified engineers and technicians were in short supply. Over 1,000 companies recruited at Purdue University. At one time, the industry was hiring computer programmers as fast as universities could graduate them. By 1988, however, the industry had begun to turn away graduates with bachelor's degrees in computer science. Accordingly, there has been a decrease in undergraduate enrollment because there is no longer a great need for people with computer programming degrees. These jobs are now frequently filled by students from trade or technical schools. Liberal arts graduates, too, were becoming a glut on the market. Some companies, however, think that the strategic recruiting of liberal arts graduates followed by proper training, is a wise course of action for the long run. In a seller's market, the employer may have to resort to up-front bonuses, as well as special educational programs and advancement opportunities.

Illustrative of the booming Massachusett's economy in 1987, Brigham's Restaurants, a Boston-based chain of ice cream and sandwich shops, was advertising in all stores for management personnel. The ad said the following: "Brigham's Restaurants Are Seeking Management Personnel for Various Locations, Apply to Store Manager. *No Experience Necessary.* Equal Opportunity Employer M/F." (emphasis added) The advertisement reminds the student of employment that it is particularly important to pay close attention to the needs and opportunities of the employer, in relationship to its environment. An article in *The New York Times* in late 1987,[3] reporting on the bleak outlook for jobs for middle managers, noted a new and controversial trend affecting middle managers called "auditioning." Citing Adelco Oliver, who heads an outplacement firm: "It's a buyer's market. Companies want to make sure that they hire the right person." Hence, they offered temporary jobs for six months or so during which the jobholder must prove valuable. While au-

ditioning has been common in the theater and music world, and trial periods of three to six months after a week-long tryout in journalism have been used, such trial periods for middle managers of corporations is a new development with significant employee relations challenges.

Consider also the employment and employee relations problems of a retailing company whose management is concerned about a rising level of employee theft. How should a company select employees who will be honest? Prior to 1988, many employers, in states where it was legal, used a lie detector test on either or both new and current employees. In 1988, however, President Reagan signed The Employee Polygraph Protection Act that for the most part prohibits the use of the lie detector test by private employers for either job applicants or current employees. Exceptions will be made for drug companies and those providing security assistance.

In 1987, many employers were wrestling with the pros and cons of drug testing of employees and applicants. In response to increasing concern about drug and alcohol problems in the workplace, many companies developed substance abuse policies. While drug testing by urinalysis and alcohol testing by breath testers had become increasingly common for job applicants, such testing, except for cause, was relatively rare for existing employees. In general, tests for employees with no history of substance involvement is requested only when supervision or the company's medical department have reason to believe that job performance is being affected by substance use and when supervisors have reason to believe that the employee has recently used or possessed drugs or alcohol in the workplace. In June 1988, however, a lower court in California issued a preliminary injunction prohibiting a company from requiring job appli-

[3] Elizabeth M. Fowler, "Career: Job Prospects for '88 Seen as Mixed," *The New York Times,* December 29, 1987, p. D-17.

cants to submit to urine testing that can detect drug use. The judge held that the drug-testing policy violated the privacy provision of the California Constitution. The decision, according to *The New York Times*, is the first time a private employer has been barred from conducting pre-employment drug screening. The company immediately filed a request with the California State Court of Appeals, asking that the ruling be voided pending appeal.[4]

Beginning in 1987, moreover, all employers had to verify the citizenship status of all new employees, Americans and aliens, within 24 hours after they were hired. For proof, job applicants must show documents such as a passport, a driver's license, a social security card, or a birth certificate. These rules were issued by the Immigration and Naturalization Service under the Innmark immigration law passed by Congress and signed by President Reagan on November 6, 1986. Employers are required to insure that the papers "appear on their face to be genuine." The law prohibits the hiring of illegal aliens. The law also offered legal status or amnesty to illegal aliens who have lived in the United States continuously since before January 1, 1982. This is the first time Americans have had to present proof of citizenship when applying for a job.

Almost every personnel decision made today, especially in large organizations, also has an equal employment opportunity and affirmative action dimension. This is no more true than with respect to hiring and promotion decisions. Equal employment opportunity is the law of the land and a pervasive concept indeed. The law, judicial and/or administrative employment standards, as well as enforcement requirements, have had a profound effect on the behavior of employers. Hir-

ing criteria, for instance, must be both job related and validated and, at least for government contractors, take into account both "underutilization" and "availability" of members of the protected classes. Under the 1978 Uniform Guidelines on Employee Selection Procedures promulgated simultaneously by the Equal Employment Opportunity Commission, the Department of Labor, the Department of Justice, and the U.S. Civil Service Commission, the employer must also determine possible "adverse impact" of the implementation of the selection criteria.

Minorities (blacks, Hispanics, Pacific Islanders, and native Americans), women, religious and ethnic groups, the handicapped and veterans comprise the protected classes who are covered by the Department of Labor's Office of Federal Contract Compliance Program (OFCCP) regulations. Selection rates must be examined to ascertain if there is an adverse impact. If, for example, 100 whites and 25 blacks apply for a job in the course of a year and 40 whites and 5 blacks are selected, a comparison of the ratio of whites selected (40 of 100, or a rate of 40%), to the ratio of blacks slected (5 of 25, or a rate of 20%) reveals that there is an "adverse impact" against blacks, one of the "protected" groups. If there is adverse impact, then the employer must show the job-relatedness of the selection procedures having adverse impact. In addition, people over age 40 are protected by the Age Discrimination in Employment Act. Moreover, the 1988 Harkin-Humphrey amendment to the Federal Rehabilitation Act, passed as part of the Civil Rights Restoration Act, makes it illegal for employers to discriminate against people with AIDS and other contagious diseases or infections who are able to work and do not pose a direct threat to others, despite unfounded fears of contagion and misconceptions about AIDS. The amendment

---

[4] "Pre-Employment Drug Tests Blocked by California Court," *The New York Times*, June 11, 1988.

makes it clear not only that people with contagious diseases, like handicapped people, continue to be entitled to reasonable accommodation, such as modified work schedules when these are needed to enable them to work, but also that it is illegal to deny employment to individuals who are infected with HIV (the AIDS virus) or who have symptoms of AIDS. The legal pitfalls in the interviewing, hiring, promotion, and termination process, therefore, are considerable.

The Hart Enterprises case helps students deal with equal opportunity and affirmative action and real or perceived issues of discrimination. The Case of the Mismanaged Ms., too, raises many tough questions about subtle discrimination as a management problem. Like Hart, the case raises important issues that students need to identify and decide how to handle. Is the problem serious? Who is to blame? What, if anything, can management do to prevent subtle discrimination? Finally, what tactics can managers use to deal with such problems when they occur?

MBAs at Merrill Lynch is a comprehensive human resources management case. It asks the student not only to identify and evaluate Merrill Lynch's business strategy in a rapidly changing financial services industry but also to think systematically about the areas of recruitment, selection, placement, training, performance appraisal, compensation, and career development for MBAs.

Although the Hi-Tech Corporation case study is about "decruitment," or outplacement—the final aspects of an effective employment program—it, too, has an affirmative action dimension. The Hi-Tech case also allows students not only to think through the pros and cons of voluntary severance pay programs but also to balance human resources and financial considerations in such decisions. Workforce reduction, or resizing the corporation, is an inescapable reality of the employment picture in today's competitive global economy.

BIBLIOGRAPHY: EMPLOYMENT AND PROMOTION POLICY AND ADMINISTRATION

ARVEY, RICHARD K., AND ROBERT H. FALEY. *Fairness in Selecting Employees.* Reading, MA: Addison-Wesley, 1988.

BARDWICK, JUDITH M., *The Plateauing Trap: How to Avoid It in Your Career and Your Life.* New York: AMACOM, 1986.

BURTON, D., J. FILER, D. FRASER, AND R. MARSHALL. *The Jobs Challenge.* Cambridge, MA: Ballinger Books, 1985.

BYRNE, JOHN A. *The Headhunters.* New York: Macmillan, 1986.

CUMMINGS, LARRY L., AND DONALD P. SCHWAB. *Performance in Organizations: Determinants and Appraisal.* Glenview, IL: Scott-Foresman, 1973.

GOODALE, JAMES G. *The Fine Art of Interviewing.* Englewood Cliffs, NJ: Prentice-Hall, 1982.

HALL, DOUGLAS T. *Careers in Organizations.* Pacific Palisades, CA: Goodyear Publications, 1976.

————, ET AL. *Career Development in Organizations.* San Francisco: Jossey-Bass, 1986.

HENNING, MARGARET, AND ANNE JARDIM. *The Managerial Woman.* Garden City, NY: Anchor Press/Doubleday, 1977.

KOONTZ, HAROLD. *Appraising Managers as Managers.* New York: McGraw-Hill, 1971.

LLOYD, CYNTHIA B., AND OTHERS (eds.). *Women in the Labor Market.* New York: Columbia University Press, 1979.

LOPEZ, FELIX M., *Personnel Interviewing: Theory and Practice,* 2nd ed. New York: McGraw-Hill, 1975.

MCLANE, HELEN J. *Selecting, Developing and Retaining Women Executives.* New York: Van Nostrand Reinhold, 1980.

MAHLER, WALTER R. *How Effective Executives Interview.* Homewood, IL: Dow Jones-Irwin, 1976.

MEYER, JOHN L., AND M. W. DONAHO. *Get the Right Person for the Job: Managing Interviews and Selecting Employees.* Englewood Cliffs, NJ: Prentice-Hall, 1979.

MINER, MARY GREEN. *Separation Procedures and Severance Benefits.* Washington, DC: Bureau of National Affairs, 1978.

————, AND JOHN B. MINER. *Employee Selection within the Law.* Washington, DC: Bureau of National Affairs, 1978.

MOSES, JOSEPH L., AND WILLIAM C. BYHAM (eds.). *Applying the Assessment Center Method.* Elmsford, NY: Pergamon Press, 1977.

NORTHRUP, HERBERT R., AND JOHN A. LARSON. *The Impact of the AT&T-EEO Consent Decree.* Philadelphia: Industrial Research Unit, The Wharton School, University of Pennsylvania, 1979.

————, AND OTHERS. *The Objective Selection of Supervisors.* Philadelphia Industrial Research Unit. The Wharton School, University of Pennsylvania, 1978.

PATI, GOPAL C., J. I. ADKINS, JR., AND G. MORRISON. *Managing and Employing the Handicapped: The Untapped Potential.* Lake Forest, IL: Brace-Park Press, 1982.

ROGERS, JEAN L., AND WALTER L. FORTSON. *Fair Employment Interviewing.* Reading, MA: Addison-Wesley, 1976.

ROSEN, BENSON, AND THOMAS H. JERDEE. *Older Employees: New Rules for Valued Resources.* Homewood, IL: Dow Jones-Irwin, 1985.

SCHNEIDER, BENJAMIN. *Staffing Organizations.* Pacific Palisades, CA: Goodyear, 1976.

SCHNEIDER, STEPHEN A. *The Availability of Minorities and Women for Professional and Managerial Positions, 1970–1985.* Philadelphia: Industrial Research Unit, The Wharton School, University of Pennsylvania, 1977.

SWEET, DONALD H. *Decruitment: A Guide for Managers.* Reading, MA: Addison-Wesley, 1975.

————. *The Modern Employment Function.* Reading, MA: Addison-Wesley, 1973.

WANOUS, JOHN P. *Organizational Entry: Recruitment, Selection, and Socialization of Newcomers.* Reading, MA: Addison-Wesley, 1980.

YODER, DALE, AND HERBERT G. HENEMAN, JR. *Staffing Policies and Strategies.* Rockville, MD: Bureau of National Affairs, 1974.

Hart Enterprises

In January 1980 several personnel managers and a legal advisor at Hart Enterprises were preparing for a meeting to discuss the discrimination charges of an employee, Delores Mendoza. In the preceding 9 months, Ms. Mendoza had filed with the EEOC two complaints against the company. It had all started in April 1979 . . .

"Just because I'm a woman and I'm Hispanic . . . They're not going to get away with this," thought Delores Mendoza as she left the EEOC office in San Francisco in April 1979. Triumphant, yet still angry, Delores had just filed claims of sex and race discrimination against the company which had employed her for the past 12 years.

Delores was bewildered by the events of the preceding few months. She simply could not understand why certain people within the firm had suddenly seemed to turn against her. She thought she was well-respected by her fellow employees; just last year she had been selected by members of her division as their representative on the Annual Company Christmas Party Committee. Also, she was somewhat of a spokesperson for her Hispanic co-

workers and was treasurer of the East Bay Hispanic American Association.

Delores Mendoza had joined Hart Enterprises in January 1964 after completing 2 years at a local community college. Since that time she had gained the equivalent of a 4-year degree through night classes in business management and accounting.

Hart Enterprises, a major retail outlet in Oakland, California, had hired Ms. Mendoza as a low-level clerk/bookkeeper. She had been promoted 5 times during her 12 years with Hart.

In October 1976 Delores Mendoza had been promoted to assistant supervisor in the Accounts Receivable Division of the Treasurer's Department. Department Manager David Flood supervised 3 main divisions: Accounts Receivable, Accounts Payable, and General Ledger. Each Division comprised about 20 bookkeepers and clerks and was managed by a Division supervisor. In her new position, Ms. Mendoza had shared some responsibility with her supervisor, Bill Dorfmann.

In September 1978, William Dorfmann had retired. When such a vacancy occurred, the assistant supervisors in all of the divisions within the Department were considered for the promotion. In accordance with company policy, Flood, the Department manager, had considered Delores Mendoza along with the other De-

This case was prepared by Donna Hale, Research Assistant, under the direction of Professor Fred Foulkes. Reprinted by permission of the Harvard Business School.

partment employees in corresponding positions.

Because of a 3-month lag in selecting a replacement for Dorfmann, Delores Mendoza had been asked to assume many of his responsibilities. David Flood acted as interim supervisor (in addition to his duties as department manager), but Ms. Mendoza contributed many overtime hours in performing some of Dorfmann's duties.

In January 1979, Mr. Flood made a lateral transfer and Tom Adams, the supervisor of Accounts Payable, filled Dorfmann's vacancy. Ben Anderson, assistant supervisor of Accounts Payable was made supervisor of Accounts Payable.

Ms. Mendoza believed that she had been passed over for promotion because she was Hispanic and female. Accordingly, she filed a sex and race discrimination complaint against Hart with the EEOC on April 25, 1979. She wrote on the complaint:

> If I had not been a woman or Hispanic, I would have been promoted with *no* question. I was the most qualified for the job.

Management, when informed of the complaint with the EEOC, began a formal investigation through the Affirmative Action Division of the Hart Personnel Department. To keep abreast of developments in the area of Affirmative Action, senior management at Hart had established an Affirmative Action Division. Several people in the Division had been trained to investigate both informal and formal complaints of discrimination. In 1975 Hart had established an affirmative action plan. Since then the company had been an aggressive recruiter of women and minorities. "The problem today," stated one company official, "is not recruiting and hiring but rather upgrading and promotion."

The preliminary report of Jim McDonald, the Company's Affirmative Action Officer, contained several main findings:

Current Situation

One of the 3 current supervisors in the Treasurer's Department is Hispanic.

Past Promotion Record

In the past 5 years, in the Company as a whole, one third of those promoted to the position of the division supervisor have been female and one fifth have been Hispanic.

Record of Delores Mendoza

Personnel performance ratings of Delores Mendoza had been excellent throughout her history with the company.

Interview with Department Manager

David Flood (Department Manager) asserted that he did consider Ms. Mendoza for the promotion. He had consulted with the other 2 supervisors in the department. The Hispanic supervisor had stated that he did not feel that Ms. Mendoza was capable of assuming the responsibilities of being a supervisor. The supervisor went on to state that Ms. Mendoza frequently upset other employees in the department and that people were much happier when she was absent from work. Tom Adams, the supervisor who received the lateral transfer, confirmed the other supervisor's opinion of Ms. Mendoza. According to Adams, Delores Mendoza had personality conflicts with people in the entire department. By his estimation, Adams felt that about half of the department were so adamant in their negative feelings toward

Ms. Mendoza that they would probably resign if she became division supervisor. "She consistently irritates those people she has contact with; she makes people extremely unhappy," continued Adams. According to the supervisor, the promotion of Ms. Mendoza would be a serious impediment to the smooth operation of the department.

Position of Ms. Mendoza

She was the most well-qualified candidate for the job because she had been trained in her current position for over 2 years and had been properly trained to fill the vacancy.

She had been successfully performing many of Bill Dorfmann's duties since his retirement in September.

Her performance reports showed excellent past performance and no lack of productivity.

She had been with the Company for 12 years and had earned the equivalent of a college degree. During her period of employment, 2 white males had been promoted around her.

She believed that the lateral transfer of Adams was a deliberate attempt on the part of the department manager to deny her the promotion opportunity.

She knew that David Flood (Department Manager) was prejudiced against all women and Hispanic people. A friend of hers at work had once overheard a conversation between Flood and another manager in which the 2 men were complaining about "all those foolish women" and "incompetent minorities" who were trying to infiltrate the ranks of Company management.

Final Position of Department Manager

David Flood (Department Manager) took the position that Ms. Mendoza was the least qualified of those people who were considered for the position. Ms. Mendoza was not promoted because her abrasive personality had a detrimental effect on the work performance of others, and she had not demonstrated a capability to manage other people.

To substantiate his position on Ms. Mendoza's promotability, Mr. Flood cited several reasons:

1. Ms. Mendoza tended to degrade employees rather than trying to offer constructive criticism.
2. Ms. Mendoza was constantly criticizing the Company and upper management in front of the other employees.
3. Ms. Mendoza used her authority as assistant supervisor very unwisely.

Although Adams had been with the company for only 2½ years, he was the best candidate for the job.

Ms. Mendoza's August 1979 performance report showed that her conduct and attendance were borderline; her overall evaluation was "satisfactory." The report also indicated that in the first 9 months of the rating period, Ms. Mendoza was observed behaving inappropriately at work. Five examples were noted on her report:

1. Talked with other employees about personal matters for extended periods of time.
2. Used the company telephone for making lengthy personal calls of a non-emergency nature.
3. Left her work area for extended periods of time without notifying her supervisor.
4. Conducted her personal business, such as writing letters and balancing her checkbook, during business hours.
5. Read the morning paper, *The Oakland Tribune*, while she drank coffee at her desk.

The performance report also indicated that Ms. Mendoza lacked tact in her interactions with lower level employees. She was thoughtless in bringing errors to the attention of subordinates. Two employees had disclosed that Ms. Mendoza had visited their homes to ask for letters of personal recommendation from them. Both of the employees were concerned as to how their decisions not to comply with Ms. Mendoza's request would affect their job status. By means of her report Ms. Mendoza was advised that such intimidation must stop immediately.

The first five weaknesses mentioned above had been discussed with Ms. Mendoza on April 11, 1979. Also discussed was her lack of tact in discussing errors. The report indicated that some improvement in these areas had been noted between April and August.

When her performance report was discussed with Ms. Mendoza, she became very upset not only about its content but also about the fact that her performance rating had suddenly dropped from "excellent" to "satisfactory." The Department manager and Division supervisor explained that in the past all performance reports in the Department had been inflated. Now, however, performance reports would be used to help employees; no longer would everyone be rated "excellent." Thus, the August 1979 report was an accurate reflection of Ms. Mendoza's performance.

Under Hart's pay for performance plan, all increases were for merit; there were no cost of living increases for exempt personnel. In 1978, for example, excellent performers received a 9% increase; satisfactory performers received 7%. It was felt that some supervisors had overrated their people to help them keep up with the rapidly rising cost of living. Performance appraisals were supposed to be discussed with the employee each year; nonetheless,

some supervisors did not do it or did it in a very cursory manner.

An explanation was given to Ms. Mendoza about the changes in the use of the performance reports, but she was not satisfied. On September 15, 1979, she filed a second charge of discrimination. She claimed that her employer had taken reprisal action against her; she complained that she had been given a poor performance rating because she had filed an earlier complaint against the company.

In November, Jim McDonald, the Affirmative Action Officer at Hart who had investigated Ms. Mendoza's first complaint, completed an additional report dealing with the woman's second charge. McDonald quoted Ms. Mendoza's rebuttal of the charges in her performance report:

1. "Talking with other employees about personal matters for extended periods of time . . ."

   "My work involves discussions with other employees. Everyone at one time or another enters into personal conversations."

2. "Leaving her work area for extended periods of time without notifying her supervisor . . ."

   "This is an untrue statement."

3. "Conducting her personal business such as writing letters and balancing her checkbook during business hours . . ."

   "I have occasionally written letters and balanced my checkbook; however, other people in the department do likewise. There is no Company policy, nor have I ever been told that I could not engage in such activities."

4. "Reading the morning newspaper . . ."

   "Everyone does this. Besides, I generally do it on my own time before the office opens, during breaks or at lunch."

The Department manager and the Division supervisor reiterated what they had told Ms. Mendoza about the changes in the Department's performance reporting system. In fact, most of the reports coming from the Department were less favorable than they had been in the past. Two-thirds of the employees who had been evaluated in the current year had received ratings lower than those in the previous year (In this group were 25% of the male employees, 63% of the female employees, 32% of the white, 71% of the Black, 53% of the Hispanic, 21% of the Chinese). One-third of the employees rated had remained the same; no one had improved.

In January 1980, a meeting was to be held at Hart Enterprises to discuss the impending meeting with the local EEOC representatives over Delores Mendoza's complaints. Charles Hoffner, Vice-President for Personnel, had called to-gether Affirmative Action Officer Jim McDonald, Paula Gibbons, Manager of the Affirmative Action Division, and Peter McDermott, a company legal advisor. All of them were familiar with Ms. Mendoza's situation and had read Jim McDonald's reports. The purpose of the meeting was to define clearly the company's position with regard to Delores Mendoza's charges.

HART ENTERPRISES
STUDY QUESTIONS:

1. Has the company, in your judgment, discriminated against Delores Mendoza?
2. How is the EEOC likely to decide her case?
3. If you were a senior line manager at Hart, how would you want this case handled?

The Case of the Mismanaged Ms.

Sally Seymour

It started out as one of those rare quiet mornings when I could count on having the office to myself. The Mets had won the World Series the night before, and most of the people in the office had celebrated late into the night at a bar across the street. I'm a fan too, but they all like to go to one of those bars where the waitresses dress like slave girls and the few women customers have to run a mine field of leers when they go to the ladies' room labeled "Heifers." Instead, I watched the game at home with my husband and escaped a hangover.

So I was feeling pretty good, if a little smug, when Ruth Linsky, a sales manager here at Triton, stormed past my secretary and burst into my office. Before I could say good morning, she demanded to know what business it was of the company who she slept with and why. I didn't know what she was talking about, but I could tell it was serious. In fact, she was practically on the verge of tears, but I knew she wasn't the type to fly off the handle.

Ruth had been with the company for three years, and we all respected her as a sensible and intelligent woman. She had been top in her class at business school

and we recruited her hard when she graduated, but she didn't join us for a couple of years. She's since proved to be one of our best people in sales, and I didn't want to lose her. She fumed around the room for a while, not making much sense, until I talked her into sitting down.

"I've had it with this place and the way it treats women!" she shouted.

I allowed her to let off some more steam for a minute or two, and then I tried to calm her down. "Look, Ruth," I said, "I can see you're upset, but I need to know exactly what's going on before I can help you."

"I'm not just upset, Barbara," she said, "I'm damned mad. I came over to Triton because I thought I'd get more chances to advance here, and I just found out that I was passed over for director of the marketing division and Dick Simon got it instead. You know that I've had three outstanding years at the company, and my performance reviews have been excellent. Besides, I was led to believe that I had a pretty good shot at the job."

"What do you mean, 'led to believe'?"

"Steve heard through the grapevine that they were looking for a new marketing director, and he suggested I put in my name," she said. "He knows my work from when we worked together over at Forge Techtronics, and he said he'd write a letter in support. I wouldn't have even known they were looking for someone if Steve hadn't tipped me off."

Steve Baines is vice president of manufacturing. He's certainly a respected senior person in the company and he pulls some weight, but he doesn't have sole control of the marketing position. The hierarchy doesn't work that way, and I tried to get Ruth to see that, "Okay, so Steve wrote a letter for you, but he's only one of five or six VPs who have input in executive hiring decisions. Of course it helps to have his support, but lots of other factors need to be considered as well."

"Come off it, Barbara," Ruth snapped. "You know as well as I do there's only one thing that really matters around here and that's whether you're one of the boys. I've got a meeting this afternoon with my lawyer, and I'm going to file a sexual discrimination suit, a sexual harassment suit, and whatever other kind of suit she can come up with. I've had it with this old-boy crap. The only reason I'm here is that, as human resources director, you should know what's going on around here."

So the stakes were even higher than I had thought; not only did it look like we might lose Ruth, but we also might have a lawsuit on our hands. And to top it off, with the discrimination issue Ruth might be trying to get back at us for promoting Dick. I felt strongly about the importance of this legal remedy, but I also knew that using it frivolously would only undermine women's credibility in legitimate cases.

"Ruth," I said, "I don't doubt your perceptions, but you're going to need some awfully strong evidence to back them up."

"You want evidence? Here's your evidence. Number one: 20% of the employees in this company are women. Not one is on the board of directors, and not one holds an executive-level position. You and I are the only two in mid-level positions. Number two: there's no way for women to move into the mid-level positions because

they never know when they're available. When a vacancy comes up, the VPs—all men, of course—decide among themselves who should fill it. And then, over and over again I hear that some guy who hasn't worked half as hard as most of the women at his level has been given the plum. Number three: there are plenty of subtle and sometimes not-so-subtle messages around here that women are less than equal."

"Ruth, those are still pretty vague accusations," I interrupted. "You're going to have to come up with something more specific than feelings and suppositions."

"Don't worry, Barbara. Just keep listening and maybe you'll learn something about how this company you think so highly of operates. From the day Ed Coulter took over as vice president of marketing and became my boss, he's treated me differently from the male sales managers. Instead of saying good morning, he always has some comment about my looks—my dress is nice, or my hair looks pretty, or the color of my blouse brings out my eyes. I don't want to hear that stuff. Besides, he never comments on a guy's eyes. And then there's that calendar the sales reps have in their back office. Every time I go in there for a sales meeting, I feel like I've walked into a locker room."

So far, this all seemed pretty harmless to me, but I didn't want Ruth to feel I wasn't sympathetic. "To tell you the truth, Ruth, I'm not so sure all women here find compliments like that insulting, but maybe you can give me other examples of discriminatory treatment."

"You bet I can. It's not just in the office that these things happen. It's even worse in the field. Last month Ed and I and Bill, Tom, and Jack went out to Dryden Industries for a big project meeting. I'll admit I was a little nervous because there were some heavy hitters in the room, so I kept my mouth shut most of the morning. But I was a team member and I wanted to contribute.

"So when Ed stumbled at one point, I spoke up. Well, it was like I had committed a sacrilege in church. The Dryden guys just stared at me in surprise, and then they seemed actually angry. They ignored me completely. Later that afternoon, when I asked Ed why I had gotten that reaction, he chuckled a little and explained that since we hadn't been introduced by our specific titles, the Dryden guys had assumed I was a research assistant or a secretary. They thought I was being presumptuous. But when Ed explained who I was, they admitted that I had made an important point.

"But that wasn't all," she went on. "The next day, when we explained to them that I would be interviewing some of the factory foremen for a needs assessment, one of the executives requested that someone else do it because apparently there's a superstition about women on the factory floor bringing bad luck. Have you ever heard of anything so stupid? But that's not the worst of it. Ed actually went along with it. After I'd pulled his bacon out of the fire the day before. And when I nailed him for it, he had the gall to say 'Honey, whatever the client wants, the client gets.'

"Well, we got the contract, and that night we all went out to dinner and everything was hurray for our team. But then, when I figured we'd all go back to the hotel for a nightcap, Ed and the guys just kind of drifted off."

"Drifted off?" I asked.

"Yeah. To a bar. They wanted to watch some basketball game."

"And you weren't invited?"

"I wasn't invited and I wasn't disinvited," she said. "They acted like they didn't know what to say."

By this point Ruth had cooled down quite a bit, and although she still seemed angry, she was forthright in presenting her case. But now her manner changed. She became so agitated that she got up from her chair to stare out the window. After a few minutes, she sort of nodded her head, as if she had come to some private, difficult decision, and then crossed the room to sit down again. Looking at her lap and twisting a paper clip around in her hands, she spoke so softly that I had to lean forward to hear her.

"Barbara," she began, "what I'm going to tell you is, I hope, in confidence. It's not easy for me to talk about this because it's very personal and private, but I trust you and I want you to understand my position. So here goes. When Steve Baines and I were both at Forge, we had a brief affair. I was discreet about it; it never interfered with business, and we ended it shortly after we both came to work here. But we're still very close friends, and occasionally we have dinner or a drink together. But it's always as friends. I think Ed found out about it somehow. The day after I notified the head office that I wanted to be considered for the director position, Ed called me into his office and gave me a rambling lecture about how we have to behave like ladies and gentlemen these days because of lawsuits on sexual harassment.

"At the time, I assumed he was referring somehow to one of our junior sales reps who had gotten drunk at the Christmas party and made a fool of himself with a couple of secretaries; but later I began to think that the cryptic comment was meant for me. What's more, I think Ed used that rumor about my relationship with Steve to block my promotion. And that, Barbara, is pure, sexist, double-standard hypocrisy because I can name you at least five guys at various levels in this company who have had affairs with colleagues and clients, and Ed is at the top of the list."

I couldn't deny the truth of Ruth's last statement, but that wasn't the point, or not yet. First I had to find out which, if any, of her accusations were true. I told her I needed some time and asked if she could give me a week before calling in a lawyer. She said no way. Having taken the first step, she was anxious to take the next, especially since she didn't believe things would change at Triton anyway. We dickered back and forth, but all I could get from her was a promise to hold off for 24 hours. Not much of a concession, but it was better than nothing.

Needless to say, I had a lot to think about and not very much time to do it in. It was curious that this complaint should come shortly after our organization had taken steps to comply with affirmative action policies by issuing a companywide memo stating that we would continue to recruit, employ, train, and promote individuals without regard to race, color, religion, sex, age, national origin, physical or mental handicap, or status as a disabled veteran or veteran of the Vietnam era. And we did this to prevent any problems in the future, not because we'd had trouble in the past. In fact, in my five years as HRM director, I'd never had a sexual discrimination or harassment complaint.

But now I was beginning to wonder whether there had never been grounds for complaint or whether the women here felt it was useless or even dangerous to complain. If it was the latter, how had I contributed to allowing that feeling to exist? And this thought led me to an even more uncomfortable one: Had I been coopted into ignoring injustices in a system that, after all, did pretty well by me? Was I afraid to slap the hand that buttered my bread?

Questioning one's own motives may be enlightening, but it's also time consuming, and I had more pressing matters to deal with before I could indulge in what would likely be a painful self-analysis. I asked my secretary to find George Drake,

CEO of Triton, and get him on the phone. In the meantime, I wrote down as much as I could remember of what Ruth had just told me. When George finally called, I told him I knew his schedule was full but we had an emergency of sorts on our hands and I needed an hour of his time this morning. I also asked that Ed Coulter be called into the meeting. George told me I had the hour.

When I got to George's office, Ed and George were already waiting. They were undoubtedly curious about why I had called this meeting, but as I've seen people do in similar situations, they covered their anxiety with chitchat about ball games and hangovers. I was too impatient for these rituals, so I cut the conversation short and told them that we were going to have a serious lawsuit on our hands in a matter of days if we didn't act very quickly. That got their attention, so I proceeded to tell Ruth's story. When I began, George and Ed seemed more surprised than anything else, but as I built up Ruth's case their surprise turned to concern. When I finished, we all sat in silence for I don't know how long and then George asked Ed for comments.

"Well, George," Ed said, "I don't know what to say. Ruth certainly was a strong contender for the position, and her qualifications nearly equaled Dick's, but it finally came down to the fact that Dick had the seniority and a little more experience in the industrial sector. When you've got two almost equally qualified candidates, you've got to distinguish them somehow. The decision came down to the wire, which in this case was six months seniority and a few more visits to factory sites."

"Were those the only criteria that made a difference in the decision?" George wanted to know.

"Well, not exactly. You know as well

as I do that we base hiring decisions on a lot of things. On one hand, we look at what's on paper: years at the company, education, experience, recommendations. But we also rely on intuition, our feel for the situation. Sometimes, you don't know exactly why, but you just feel better about some people than others, and I've learned that those gut reactions are pretty reliable. The other VPs and I all felt good about Dick. There's something about him—he's got the feel of a winner. You know? He's confident—not arrogant—but solid and really sharp. Bruce had him out to the club a couple of times, and I played squash with him all last winter. We got to know him and we liked what we saw; he's a family man, kids in school here, could use the extra money, and is looking to stick around for a while. None of these things mean a lot by themselves, of course, but together they add up.

"Don't get me wrong. I like Ruth too. She's very ambitious and one of our best. On the other hand, I can't say that I or any of the VPs know her as well as we know Dick. Of course, that's not exactly Ruth's fault, but there it is."

I had to be careful with the question I wanted Ed to respond to next because Ruth had asked for my confidence about the affair. I worded it this way: "Ed, did any part of your decision take into account Ruth's relationship with anyone else at the company?"

The question visibly disturbed Ed. He walked across the room and bummed a cigarette from me—he had quit last week—before answering: "Okay, I didn't want to go into this, but since you brought it up.... There's a rumor—well it's stronger than a rumor—that Ruth is more than professionally involved with Steve Baines— I mean she's having an, ah, sexual affair with him. Now before you tell me that's none of my business, let me tell you about

some homework I did on this stuff. Of course it's real tricky. It turns out there are at least two court cases that found sexual discrimination where an employer involved in a sexual relationship with an employee promoted that person over more qualified candidates.

"So here's what that leaves us with: we've got Steve pushing his girlfriend for the job. You saw the letter he wrote. And we've got Dick with seniority. So if we go with Ruth, what's to keep Dick from charging Steve and the company on two counts of sexual discrimination: sexual favoritism because Ruth is Steve's honey and reverse discrimination because we pass over a better qualified man just to get a woman into an executive position. So we're damned if we do and damned if we don't. We've got lawsuits if we don't advance Dick, and, so you tell me, lawsuits if we don't advance Ruth!"

We let that sink in for a few seconds. Then George spoke up: "What evidence do you have, Ed, that Steve and Ruth are having an affair?" he asked.

"Look, I didn't hire some guy to follow them around with a camera, if that's what you mean," Ed said. "But come on, I wasn't born yesterday; you can't keep that kind of hanky-panky a secret forever. Look at the way she dresses; she obviously enjoys men looking at her, especially Steve. In fact, I saw them having drinks together at Dino's the other night and believe me, they didn't look like they were talking business. All that on top of the rumors, you put two and two together."

Well, that did it for me. I'd been trying to play the objective observer and let Ed and George do all the talking, but Ed's last comment, along with some budding guilt about my own blindness to certain things at Triton that Ruth had pointed out, drove me out in the open. "Come off it, Ed," I said. "That's not evidence, that's gossip."

Now Ed turned on me: "Look," he shouted, "I didn't want to talk about this, but now that you've brought it up, I'll tell you something else. Even if we didn't have to worry about this sexual discrimination business, I still wouldn't back Ruth for the director's job." He calmed down a bit. "No offense, Barbara, but I just don't think women work out as well as men in certain positions. Human resources is one thing. It's real soft, person-to-person stuff. But factories are still a man's world. And I'm not talking about what I want it to be like. I'm talking facts of life.

"You see what happens when we send a woman out on some jobs, especially in the factories. To be any good in marketing you have to know how to relate to your client; that means getting to know him, going out drinking with him, talking sports, hunting, whatever he's interested in. A lot of our clients feel uncomfortable around a woman in business. They know how to relate to their wives, mothers, and girlfriends, but when a woman comes to the office and wants to talk a deal on industrial drills—well, they don't know what to do.

"And then there's the plain fact that you can't depend on a woman the way you can on a guy. She'll get married and her husband will get transferred, or she'll have a baby and want time off and not be able to go on the road as much. I know, Barbara, you probably think I'm a pig, or whatever women's libbers call guys like me these days. But from where I'm sitting, it just made good business sense to choose Dick over Ruth."

"Ed, I don't believe it," I said. "The next thing you'll tell me is that women ought to stay at home, barefoot and pregnant." There was a long silence after that—my guess was that I had hit on exactly what Ed thought. At least he didn't deny it. Ed stared at the rug, and George frowned at his coffee cup. I tried to steer the conversation back to the subject at hand, but it dwindled into another silence. George took a few notes and then told Ed he could go back to work. I assumed I was excused too, but as I started to leave, George called me back.

"Barbara, I'm going to need your help thinking through this mess," he said. "Of course we've got to figure out how we can avoid a lawsuit before the day is out, but I also want to talk about what we can do to avoid more lawsuits in the future. While Ed was talking I took some notes, and I've got maybe four or five points I think we ought to hash out. I'm not saying we're going to come up with all the answers today, but it'll be a start. You ready?"

"Shoot."

"Okay, let's do the big one first," he began. "What should I have done or not done to avoid this situation? I mean, I was just patting myself on the back for being so proactive when I sent out that memo letting everyone know the company policy on discrimination. I wrote it not thinking we had any problem at Triton. But just in case we did, I figured that memo would take care of it."

"Well, it looks like it's not enough just to have a corporate policy if the people in the ranks aren't on board. Obviously it didn't have much of an effect on Ed."

"So what am I supposed to do? Fire Ed?"

Being asked for my honest opinion by my CEO was a new experience for me and I appreciated it, but I wasn't going to touch that last question with a ten-foot pole. Instead I went on to another aspect: "And even if you get your managers behind you, your policy won't work if the people it's supposed to help don't buy it. Ruth was the first woman to complain around here. Are the others afraid to speak up? Or do they feel like Ed about a woman's place, or have husbands who do?

Maybe they lack confidence even to try for better jobs, that is, if they knew about them."

"Okay," he said, "I'll admit that our system of having the VPs make recommendations, our 'old-boy network,' as Ruth called it, does seem to end up excluding women, even though the exclusion isn't intentional. And it's not obvious discrimination, like Ed's claim that Ruth is unqualified for a position because she is a woman. But wouldn't open job posting take away our right to manage as we see fit? Maybe we should concentrate instead on getting more women into the social network, make it an old boys' and old girls' club?"

"To tell you the truth, George, I don't want to play squash with you," I replied, "but maybe we're getting off the subject. The immediate question seems to be how we're going to get more women into executive positions here, or, more specifically, do we give Ruth the director of marketing position that we just gave Dick?"

"On that score, at least, it seems to me that Ed has a strong argument," George said. "Dick is more qualified. You can't get around that."

I had wanted to challenge Ed on this point when he brought it up earlier, but I wasn't quite sure of myself then. Now that George was asking me for advice and seemed to be taking what I had to say seriously, I began to think that I might have something valuable to offer. So I charged right in. "George, maybe we're cutting too fine a line with this qualifications business. I know a lot of people think affirmative action means promoting the unqualified over the qualified to achieve balance. I think that argument is hogwash at best and a wily diversion tactic at worst. To my mind, Ruth and Dick are equally qualified, or equal enough. And wouldn't it make good business sense to get a diverse set of perspectives—women's,

men's, blacks', whites'—in our executive group?"

"But isn't that reverse discrimination—not promoting Dick because he's a man? How would a judge respond to that? That's a question for a lawyer."

George leaned forward. "Let's talk about my last point, the one I think we've both been avoiding. What about this affair between Ruth and Steve? Boy, this is one reason why women in the work force are such trouble—no, just joking, Barbara, sorry about that. Look, I don't like lawsuits any more than anyone else, but I'd do anything to avoid this one. We'd be a laughing stock if it got out that Triton promoted unqualified people because they slept with the boss. I don't know how I'd explain that one to my wife."

"Look, George," I said, "in the first place, Dick's superior qualifications are debatable; in the second place, we have no proof that Ruth and Steve are involved in that way; and in the third place, what if they were once involved but no longer are? Does a past relationship condemn them for life? Isn't there a statute of limitations on that kind of thing, or are we going to make her put a scarlet letter on her briefcase? I thought these discrimination laws were supposed to protect women, but now it looks like a woman can be denied a promotion because someone thinks she's a floozy."

"Wait a second, Barbara. Don't make me look like such a prig," George said. "I realize that when men and women work together sexual issues are bound to crop up. I just don't know what I'm supposed to do about it, if anything. In some cases a woman may welcome a guy coming on to her, but what if it's her boss? And then there's that subtle stuff Ruth brought up—the calendar, dirty jokes, the male employees excluding women by going to bars to watch TV—and other women. And Ruth's treatment at that factory—how can we control our clients? I'm not sure these are things you can set policy on, but I am sure that I can't ignore them any longer."

And there we were. All the issues were on the table, and we had about 21 hours to make our decisions and act on them.

THE CASE OF THE MISMANAGED MS. STUDY QUESTIONS:

1. What is your analysis of the situation at Triton?

2. If you were Barbara, HRM director, what recommendations would you make to George Drake, CEO of Triton? Why?

MBAs at Merrill Lynch

As never before, the critical element in gaining a competitive edge on Wall Street in 1985 was the firm's ability to attract and retain the best and the brightest talent. Globalization, accelerating innovation, growing requirements for capital and advanced technology were leading to concentration of market share in the hands of a few major firms and increasing competition among them for both business and talent.

Jerome P. Kenney, president of Merrill Lynch Capital Markets (MLCM), was determined to ensure that his firm had the most effective recruiting strategies and communication programs to attract the best talent available from leading business schools.

While Merrill Lynch Capital Markets ranked first, second or third in almost all significant product categories and had been recruiting MBAs for many years, Mr. Kenney was concerned that his firm's image on campus lagged its competitive reality: apparently some students still thought of Merrill Lynch as primarily a retail securities house and not the equal of

This case was prepared by Research Assistant Anna Elise Walton, under the supervision of Professor George C. Lodge, as the basis for class discussion rather than to illustrate either effective or ineffective handling of an administrative situation. Reprinted by permission of the Harvard Business School.

Goldman Sachs, Salomon, or Morgan Stanley on the capital markets side of the business. He wondered what steps he and his organization could take to overcome this perception and ensure that top students recognized the opportunities available to them at Merrill Lynch, and, once recruited, that management policies encouraged long-term affiliation with the firm.

THE CAPITAL MARKETS INDUSTRY

Investment banking and securities brokerage have long played an important part in the American economy. Historically, the industry was extremely stable, and dominated by established firms who successfully limited entry of new competitors.

Traditionally, an investment bank's primary business was underwriting securities. The bank would originate (or design) a suitable issue of bonds or shares; manage the required regulatory procedures; guarantee that the money would be available to the issuer on a specific date; assemble a group of underwriters, each of which bought a piece of the issue in return for fees and commissions; and finally, distribute newly created securities to the underwriting group and to the investor market. The lead, or "book managing," investment bank earned a "spread," or the difference between the funds received by the issuer and the selling price of the securities issued. Investment bankers also provided their clients with financial advice such as suggesting acquisition candidates or a well-timed stock repurchase, charging a fee, usually geared to the total value of the transaction.

Corporations wanting to issue a new security faced a "buyers market." Said one now senior banker, "I remember being roundly chastised by my management for calling one of our accounts. The rule was never to call a client, but to 'oblige the client to call you.' " The investment bankers decided whether or not the company's financial needs merited a security offering. When the bank agreed to issue a new security, business proceeded according to the banker's timetable, taking weeks or months to complete.

In those days, each corporation conducted essentially all its business through one firm, on a "relationship" basis. The senior corporate officers had a personal relationship with the senior bankers, who became part of the "inner council" of the corporation. These bankers had substantially greater financial expertise than the corporation's own financial people. Once these relationships were established, it was quite unlikely that anything would induce the client to switch its business to another firm.

Wall Street also included wholesale trading and brokerage houses. These firms bought and sold blocks of securities for institutional investors—advising them which securities best met their portfolio needs and then executing the transaction for the client. Some major investment banks also provided these services, but mainly as an adjunct to their primary business. At that time, trading was considered less prestigious than investment banking.

In addition, firms such as Merrill Lynch,

Dean Witter and E. F. Hutton had extensive retail networks which sold securities primarily to individual investors and smaller institutions through their extensive office networks offering advice and charging a commission on transactions.

Finally, firms developed massive research departments to provide customers with information they could not afford to develop themselves. Excellent research departments supported the salesperson's expertise, helped traders evaluate securities and supported product innovation in all areas. A powerful research department helped to attract and retain clients.

Investment Banking

Separate and distinct skills developed within these traditional capital markets functions. The investment bankers needed to anticipate the client's financing needs and design the best way to meet them under given market conditions. Their success also depended on their ability to develop and cultivate relationships with senior corporate executives.

Some senior investment bankers were important public figures. Their opinions were sought on a variety of financial matters and they had influence with powerful industrial and government decision makers.

Traders

Traders bought and sold securities in the primary (new issues) and secondary market either for their clients, earning a commission, or for their firm's own account.

Before the development of computer-based information and analytical systems which now support traders at leading securities firms, traders needed to rely heavily on their own judgment, experience and "instinct" for the market. They speculated on security price movements and bought or sold accordingly. They had to make split-second decisions before market turns or market closings and stress was commonplace. The best traders were known for their soundness of judgment (calling the market right more often than wrong) and their tolerance for risk.

Sales

Institutional salespeople dealt with a variety of large investors such as portfolio managers, corporate investors, pension fund managers, thrifts and governments. The successful salesperson needed to understand market performance, yield, maturity and other characteristics of a given security and attempt to match its characteristics with client's needs—liquidity, flow, risk minimization, rate of return and so forth. Here, as in investment banking, interpersonal skills were critical. Institutional salespeople worked closely with pension fund managers, corporate treasurers and other investment officers on the telephone, and at lunches or dinners.

Retail salespeople acted as local securities brokers and financial advisers to individuals. Often, they were prominent figures in their local communities and critical to a firm's securities distribution system.

CHANGES IN THE INDUSTRY

Changes in the structure of the capital markets began in 1973, when international fixed currency exchange rates were eliminated. In 1975, the Securities Exchange Commission (SEC) abolished the fixed commission. The percentage that brokers charged for transactions could now be negotiated and set at any level, usually based on the size of the transaction and the investor's buying power. Further change came on May 1, 1982, when the SEC introduced "Rule 415," allowing shelf registrations whereby big companies could design and preregister a new issue without the assistance of an underwriter. The corporation could leave the issue "on the shelf" and, when market conditions appeared favorable, simply invite investment banks to compete for the underwriting.

Eventually, high profits and the loosening of regulatory restrictions in the securities business attracted commercial banks and others into the industry. Although the Glass-Steagall Act prevented commercial banks from underwriting, many commercial banks (for example, Citicorp, Morgan Guaranty, Bankers Trust, Chemical and Security Pacific) began testing the limits of the law. Some began to provide discount brokerage and other services and to compete directly with securities firms for such services as mergers and acquisitions. Insurance companies and large corporations bought securities firms: American Express bought Shearson Loeb Rhoades and then Lehman Brothers, Prudential bought Bache, Sears bought Dean Witter, Equitable bought Donaldson, Lufkin & Jenrette, John Hancock bought Tucker Anthony, thereby increasing the capital resources and potential competitiveness of the acquired firm.

Over the same period, customers became increasingly sophisticated. During the late 1970s, clients developed their own finance departments, staffed with professionals who had substantial financial expertise. As the finance function came to be seen as a source of profits, the chief financial officer rose to preeminence. Companies now realized that investment bankers needed them as much as they needed the bankers. They shopped around, looking for the firm which provided the best price, product delivery and service. Increasingly, clients distributed business among different firms based on the most attractive terms or a superior reputation in a given product area rather than overall reputation or traditional relationships. In response, investment banks began to market their services aggressively. Some large clients could receive as many as 15,000 solicitations a year for all financial products and services.

Securities firms were now expected to place their own capital at risk: clients wanted the investment bank not only to distribute a new security, but also to be prepared, if necessary, to buy and hold the securities in order to ensure successful completion of an offering. They not only wanted the firm to provide liquidity in the secondary market for their issues, but also to absorb risk, buying and selling securities on their own account, not just acting as agents. The net result of these changes was a vastly altered playing field in which capitalization, risk management expertise and distribution power played an increasingly important role.

In response to the need for greater liquidity in various sectors of the economy new securities variations sprang up almost overnight. Mortgage-backed securities, originally introduced by the Government National Mortgage Association (Ginnie Maes), were launched by Salomon in 1977 and grew to over $21 billion in 1985. This market was dominated by Salomon which still had about a 40% share in 1985.

To meet the financing need of companies with below investment grade ratings, Drexel Burnham Lambert introduced the high yield—often termed "junk bond"—security in 1983. Since that time, Drexel has held the lead position in high yield securities, and, in 1985, possessed 70% of the high yield market.

To secure low-cost financing for issuers and meet the desire of investors to protect their principal while taking risks with their interest and dividend income, Merrill Lynch pioneered a new product, Liquid Yield Option Notes (LYONS) in 1985. These notes combined a number of features currently available in separate products, such as straight debt, convertibles and zero coupon securities. This innovation brought in a number of new issuing and investing clients and resulted in substantial new business for MLCM.

While innovation became key to securing new financing business, new ideas were easily copied by competitors due to the absence of patent protection and little time lag between product design and product delivery. Once products were copied, price competition set in and margins declined for everyone. However, firms that failed to innovate or imitate ran the risk of losing a place in a potentially major market.

As competition intensified, firms sometimes accused each other of "suicide bids" for business at razor-thin spreads. For example, when Goldman Sachs bid to win back some business from Sears and Texaco that had gone to other firms, the firm had to sit on unsold bonds while prices fell, and, according to one source, accumulated losses in the millions of dollars. Goldman conceded that Texaco got its money at an interest rate far lower than Salomon had offered. Some Goldman employees expressed dismay, saying, "If we go after market share, that diminishes our return. Goldman makes less money, and people get paid less."[1]

As specific product reputation became a magnet for new business, Wall Street firms competed fiercely for top rankings in surveys published by independent sources on a regular basis. For example, on Friday, June 29, 1985, it appeared that First Boston would usurp Salomon's traditional

---

[1] Linda Sandburg, "Goldman Is Being Aggressive in Bidding for Firms' Bonds," *Wall Street Journal*, January 9, 1985, p. 4.

title as the volume leader in mortgage-backed debt in the half-year tables. Salomon quickly put together a $600 million deal which came to market Friday afternoon, leaving First Boston only a few hours to do something to maintain its newly won lead. First Boston then put together a similar transaction for $200 million, getting it to market at 5:05, after most Wall Street trading desks had closed. Managing directors at both firms admitted that these last minute deals were influenced by the desire for the volume leader title.[2]

As price competition eroded margins in traditional "plain vanilla" products, investment houses sought new ways to make money. They began earning significant income trading on their own account and increasingly pursued nonunderwriting business, e.g., the substantial fees that could be earned from mergers and acquisitions.

Major Wall Street firms made significant investment in "globalization" of their operations and packaging their services to meet market conditions as clients demanded more international service. Floating exchange rates and different interest rates in each international market offered the possibility of reducing financing costs through currency swaps (foreign exchange swaps grew from $2 billion in 1982 to $13 billion by 1984). For example, an unprofitable bond offering could become profitable if associated with a currency or interest rate swap.

The number and complexity of new products also affected trading. Debt or "fixed income" products became increasingly important and sold primarily on objective quantitative factors in contrast to the qualitative "story" aspects traditionally associated with equities. Markets were increasingly "linked" or interdependent. For example, mortgage-backed securities, commercial paper, corporate securities and money market instruments all traded at yield spreads related to those of U.S. Treasury securities reflecting the relative risk inherent in each type of security. International financing markets were related through different techniques such as exchange rate and interest rate swaps. The listed option, the right to buy or sell a stock at a set price some time in the future, also introduced new complexity to the equity markets.

Institutional investors changed too. More and more investment dollars were being channeled through institutions such as life insurance companies, pension funds, or mutual funds. These large institutions had access to market information, and constantly bought and sold securities to improve their returns. They put pressure on brokers' commissions and found they could pay less. As the size of deals grew, the number of "block trades" (large holdings of securities sold at one time) increased. Because those transactions were so substantial, the client paid a lower transaction price per share. Many large institutions switched their investment strategies from stock picking to programmed trading by making use of modeling techniques and derivative products such as options and futures.

Meanwhile, trading volume soared. In 1975, year-end trading volume of the New York Stock Exchange was 4.5 billion trades on 22.5 billion shares outstanding. In 1985, New York Stock Exchange trading volume was 23 billion trades on 49 billion shares outstanding,[3] but in 1985, ten years after the abolition of fixed commissions, commission rates for institutional investors, the most profitable

---

[2] Ann Moreau, "Salomon Brothers Makes First Boston Sweat for Victory," *Wall Street Journal*, July 2, 1985, p. 44.

[3] Carol Higgins, "May Day 10 Years After," *Investment Dealer's Digest*, April 30, 1985, p. 17.

customers, had fallen to less than a third of the 1975 level.[4]

THE NEW SKILLS

In this new world, ability became paramount. No longer could bankers "oblige the client" to call them but had to pursue the client aggressively, anticipating and preparing for the client's needs. They also had to solicit new business, often making "cold calls" and persevering in their attempts to explain and sell financing proposals to old and new clients alike.

Bankers needed to be creative. They had to imagine how an established product could be adapted to meet changing issuer and investor requirements. They needed teamwork to combine product features that met both issuer and investor needs, as MLCM did when a group of professionals from banking, trading and sales developed LYONs. They needed to be constantly alert to how market and environmental trends could create new product opportunities for their clients and for their firms.

They had to manage relationships, organizing effective teams of product specialists to structure and explain to the issuer how a highly technical financing approach would work. These specialists working in a coordinated fashion became key to serving customer needs.

Traders and salespeople also needed to be able to understand more complex concepts. Millions of dollars depended on the ability of a firm's traders. Salespeople needed extensive product expertise to explain new, highly complex financings to clients in understandable terms. With markets and products increasingly linked, traders and salespeople needed to know what was going on in several different

markets and what effect other markets had on their market of interest. Commented Dan Napoli, president of MLCM's Government Securities, Inc., "Traders now need to know what the Federal Reserve is doing, what the implications of current economic policies are, how the price in the U.S. government securities market will affect their market and so on." With more products selling on the basis of their relative value, traders also needed sophisticated mathematical skills and computer-based tools to evaluate trading opportunities and execute them quickly.

Cross-functional cooperation between investment bankers, traders and salespeople became increasingly critical. Product development teams formalized these links. Informal cooperation also made a difference. Described Jean Rousseau, who in 1985 was director of Municipal Markets at MLCM, "We were working with a North Carolina municipal power agency—an all-nuclear power agency—and one of our very best clients. They wanted to raise funds in 1983, but we learned through our underwriters and marketing people that nuclear power was anathema to the institutional investors. This was on the heels of a number of plant closedowns. As a result, we worked with our salespeople, the North Carolina agency people and our investment bankers. We had joint meetings with institutional buyers over six months. It had such a positive effect on institutional investor perception that when we brought the issue to market in 1984, North Carolina received the best terms since its first financing in 1978."

In addition to these skills, serious contenders needed capital technology and distribution to succeed. Size alone was an advantage. One foreign firm wishing to raise capital in the United States chose MLCM. Its treasurer commented, "We wanted to have the company's name widely known . . . Merrill Lynch seemed to

[4] International Banking Survey, *The Economist*, March 16, 1985, p. 27.

offer the widest investor base, and was, therefore, ideal for spreading our name in the U.S. market."[5] As deals got larger, the "lead" investment bank needed an ever-greater capital base to underwrite new issues and position large trades. Although lead managers sometimes team up with co-managers to buy deals, an investment bank could underwrite a whole issue itself to avoid sharing underwriting fees and sales commissions with partners, again requiring large capital commitment. In this situation, the firm usually had to use (or "risk") some of its own capital, holding some of the security to avoid flooding the market until the price stabilized. For the same reason, to be a serious player in the secondary market, a firm needed to employ substantial amounts of its own capital. Finally, because the spreads in transactions were narrowing, firms needed capital to buy and sell securities for their own account.

Technology represented a key competitive advantage. Firms had to execute large transactions at high speeds without error. Technology was also needed to support the management of risk. For example, computer programs have been essential in developing the swap markets since they can perform complex calculations linking the net exposure over the life of swap transactions to potential movements in interest rates and thus facilitate hedging. Computer programs became essential tools of the trader to identify, buy and sell opportunities and keep them informed of developments in linked markets as well as enabling appropriate hedging programs to be put in place.

When a firm successfully pulled together capital and talent, it could create a market. For example, MLCM developed the continuously offered medium-term

note market. Introduced in 1972, medium-term notes were issued primarily by automakers who distributed the notes themselves. In the 1980s, the SEC loosened regulations on continuously offered securities.

At the same time, fluctuating interest rates made long-term debt less attractive to investors and issuers alike. Seeing an opportunity, MLCM's Emanuel Falzon effectively extended maturities available in the money market area and put together a powerful sales effort and developed variations of the note: a mortgage-backed medium-term note for a California savings and loan; an equipment trust medium-term note for a railroad; a floating rate note for an automaker. To develop this market, MLCM had to use its capital, promising to buy back any note it sold, and making a commitment to the secondary market that extended to over $1 billion at the time. The effort paid off, and MLCM has a 60% share of a market with $30 billion notes outstanding, expected to grow to $100 billion by 1990.[6]

Despite deregulation and competition from new entrants, the market share of the top ten firms went from a pre-415 29.25% to 53.1% in 1984 for debt and from 17.1% to 33.52% in equities. Most of this gain accrued to the top five firms; Merrill's share in debt went from 5.3% to 6.9% and from 4.6% to 7.1% in equities.[7] Evidently, the largest firms had mustered the energy, creativity and resources to meet the formidable challenge presented by economic, regulatory and competitive change.

Market share and position now turned on the talent of individuals to assemble the competitive elements successfully.

---

[5] "Treasurers' Top Team," *Euromoney Corporate Finance*, March 1985, p. 20.

[6] Daniel Kadlec, "The New Medium-Term Notes and Merrill Lynch, The Dominator," *Investment Dealers' Digest*, November 4, 1985, pp. 17–20.

[7] "The Post-415 World: Top Ten Firms Rule the Street," *Corporate Financing Week*, vol. XI, no. 18, May 6, 1985.

Competition for proven professionals and top MBAs became intense. Those with the best and the brightest had the innovative ideas that made them first in the field. Their reputation in turn gave them first pick of new recruits.

PROFESSIONAL DEVELOPMENT AND CAREERS ON WALL STREET

On Wall Street, skills were largely learned by doing. Bankers, traders and salespeople had to prove their ability starting at the bottom. Rarely did an industry outsider move into a senior spot, and firms hiring seasoned external talent restricted themselves to competitors and possibly commercial banks. Therefore, a steady intake of newly minted talent was essential to maintaining a leadership position over time.

The assistance of senior associates, vice presidents and managing directors was critical to the new recruits' success. One banking vice president, reflecting on the importance of mentoring, commented, "A new recruit coming in here kind of drifts around without an anchor unless they have some one to show them the ropes. Coaching and informal praise can go a long way in developing people and preventing performance problems."

Junior investment banking associates felt it was important to see how their work fit into the picture or to link their names with specific clients. They saw this as a source of early credibility in the firm, and also as assurance of a clear career path; they could either increase their expertise in a specialty area of financing or take on more responsibility for relationships as they moved up the ladder. Associates were particularly satisfied in the regional offices or the small specialty groups where the senior bankers had to rely on only a few associates and needed to make them

part of the team. The process worked least well where a pool of associates was accessed by many senior bankers.

In investment banking, promotion had traditionally been based on length of service. Some of this remained: associates could expect to become vice presidents in approximately four years and managing directors in no less than eight to ten years. As a firm hired more MBAs, the pipeline of talent filled up and a broad base of junior associates at the bottom of the hierarchy competed for fewer senior spots unless the firm they had joined was growing rapidly. To ensure quality of their professional staff, firms used an "up and out" process, taking in the best talent at the entry level and promoting them to higher levels based on performance. Those who did not make it to the top of the investment bank were often able to move into senior financial positions in industry.

Traders and salespeople learned on the job as well. Said one outstanding trader, "I worked closely with the senior trader for two or three years, just watching what he did. There were many decisions he couldn't explain, but after a while, I found myself making the same decisions he would make. It's critical that the senior traders and salespeople put that effort in."

In sales and trading, promotions could be based on more quantitative measures of performance. Often, the trader or salesperson took on additional responsibilities such as leading a task force or working on a product development team. Depending on his performance on these tasks, this would also influence promotion. Since promotion often meant handling fewer accounts and earning less direct commissions, many traders and salespeople chose not to move into management where responsibilities were broader and compensation depended on more performance variables.

As far as assessing their own development, bankers, traders, and salespeople used a measure readily available—the size of their bonus. Said one, "You set check-points. If you haven't cleared certain management levels, or if you haven't received an excellent performer bonus, you had better start looking around."

Compensation

Wall Street's established investment houses had a tradition of high pay. And high pay was related to performance—a star trader could earn more than his manager, or even some managing directors. In addition to high pay, Wall Street's few remaining partnerships offered the potential for substantial capital accumulation; partners retired with millions in equity or sold out for millions. The nonpartnership firm offered some nontaxable compensation benefits, but few could match the long-run potential of a partnership. Said one compensation expert, "The partnerships can pay a little worse on the low end of the totem pole, because they have that partnership carrot. The only way other firms can compete with the partnerships is with cash payments."

Throughout the industry, investment bankers' pay was heavily influenced by seniority. Salaries were tied roughly to tenure. Bonuses started small relative to salary, but grew rapidly, eventually becoming double or triple the salary at senior levels. Traders and salespeople's bonuses and commissions, tied to bottom line performance, also grew to three or four times salary as the employee progressed.

When the firms needed to "buy" outside talent, they had to offer extravagant compensation packages. Usually firms tried to get "star" talent from the firm which had the strongest product position in the marketplace. Particularly in trading, stars could write their own tickets, sometimes getting compensation deals that guaranteed as much as $1 million. But a successful hire could be well worth the cost, earning millions for the firm.

Aided by compensation surveys and conversations among themselves, most firms' recruiters offered roughly similar salary and bonus packages to MBAs. There were often added amenities like funds for moving expense. In some cases, sign-on bonuses might be considered an advance on the year-end bonus. Some firms did not give bonuses or amenities unless the recruit specifically asked about them.

With this framework there was a fair amount of variation. A firm aggressively seeking new recruits in a given year might offer unusually high salaries in that year. Some smaller firms, or "boutiques," offered exceptionally high salaries to attract talent.

Many new recruits were not as concerned with starting salary as with long-run earnings potential. Future earnings were often unpredictable at hiring time, as one MBA pointed out, "A colleague of mine turned down an offer from Salomon to go to Drexel Burnham. We all thought she was crazy at the time, but she's earned more than any of us." Other MBAs pointed out that, though partnerships did offer the potential for capital accumulation, they might be sold or dissolved by the time a 1985 MBA graduate would be eligible for partnership. Said one MBA, "Whichever firm you choose, you're going to have a lot of fun and earn six figures, so it's more important to choose a place you're going to like working."

MERRILL LYNCH

Merrill Lynch, Pierce, Fenner & Smith traces its origin back to a partnership formed by two bond salesmen, Charlie Merrill and Eddie Lynch in 1914. Originally, the firm catered to the "average investor," those beyond the social and economic elite served by old-line investment houses. From its inception, Merrill Lynch & Co. functioned as a distributor of new securities for growing companies in emerging industries such as the chain store, oil, automotive and movie industries.

In 1940, Merrill Lynch & Co. merged with E. A. Pierce and Casset, one of the nation's largest wire houses (a brokerage firm with a large retail branch network connected by telegraph wires). Recognizing the coming explosion in the postwar economy, Charlie Merrill began building the "department store of finance," one that would "bring Wall Street to Main Street." In 1971, Merrill went public, gaining substantial capital resources, and in 1973 adopted a holding company structure, with Merrill Lynch, Pierce, Fenner & Smith as the registered brokerage subsidiary of the listed company, Merrill Lynch and Company, Inc.

Merrill Lynch has been involved in investment banking throughout its history, but began expanding these functions extensively in the mid-1970s. The first major expansion was into utility and municipal issues, based on local relationships Merrill Lynch had through its retail brokers. Since the bulk of their securities was sold to retail investors, these issuers needed a retail operation like Merrill's.

In 1978, the Capital Markets group was formed as a separate organizational unit consisting of trading and investment banking. In 1981, institutional sales accounts were separated from the retail distribution system and organized into MLCM's Institutional Sales division. International activities became part of Capital Markets in 1983. Integration of all Merrill's institutional business in Capital Markets was completed with the transfer of Commercial Real Estate in 1985.

MLCM also grew through acquisition. In 1978, Merrill acquired White Weld, an established and prestigious investment banking firm, along with many of its investment banking clients. In 1984, MLCM acquired A. G. Becker Paribas, which, added to Merrill's strong position in commercial paper and allowed MLCM to surpass the volume leader, Goldman Sachs. Becker personnel also filled some uncovered niches in investment banking and fixed income trading.

In 1984, Jerry Kenney was made president of Merrill Lynch Capital Markets. Kenney came from White Weld initially as assistant director of research and worked his way up to head of research, institutional sales and then, investment banking. By 1985, MLCM had structured itself into several business and management units headed by senior management that had grown up in the capital markets environment (see Exhibit 1).

Investment banking now had relationship managers whose responsibility was to put together teams which focused on clients' needs, and financing specialists who had responsibility for working with relationship managers to sell, structure and execute transactions. The Debt Transactions group was formed in response to Rule 415 to ensure smooth and rapid integration of the origination, structuring, pricing and placement functions for debt deals. Sales and trading were also more closely tied together through management processes and compensation systems. As the organization continued to evolve, MLCM's management believed a degree of structural fluidity should be maintained in order to ensure easy adaptation to external change and internal innovation. Over a ten-year period, Merrill Lynch Capital Markets, with more than 12,000 employees, had attained a significant position in the investment banking community, becoming the largest provider of funds in the global public markets. (In total Merrill Lynch employed some 44,000 people.)[8]

Work Life at MLCM

Professionals appreciated the quality of life at MLCM. Merrill Lynch and Company president, Dan Tully, said, "We hope Merrill's growth will be good for our employees and their families." Individuals were treated with respect and helped through difficulties they had with work or managers. Said Jean Rousseau, "MBAs are valuable and expensive resources. It's important to us that they work out."

There was considerable tolerance for diversity at MLCM. All types of individuals could fit in. Said one banker, "I know a senior banker, whose hair is a little long, who comes to work a bit disheveled. He doesn't fit the investment banker image, but this guy is incredibly good at his job. He can be successful here, but I don't think he would be at the more tradition bound firms."

Many were attracted by this aspect of MLCM. Said one associate banker, "I'm a relaxed person. I wear jeans on my day off. It's sad, but I've seen changes in a lot of my friends. They used to be regular guys and now I meet them socially and they're wearing horn rimmed glasses and suspenders. That's not for me." Women and minorities also benefited from the high tolerance for diversity. While women went to Wall Street in ever-greater numbers, few advanced into the partner or managing director ranks. Of the top firms, Merrill Lynch in 1985 had the greatest representation of women at the partner/managing director level and four of the seven female managing directors on the Street. Drexel Burnham Lambert, Goldman Sachs, Morgan Stanley, Salomon and Smith Barney had no women at this level.[9]

Others commented that people at Merrill were more considerate than was typical on Wall Street. One employee commented, "People who come here from some other firms think they died and went to heaven. We're nice to each other here. We help each other out." Related was the tendency towards humility. Even Kenney, the president, said, "I can give you no assurance that we will succeed (in becoming #1) other than the fact that our goals are clearly stated, there is a full concurrence on those goals, and there is determination.[10]

However, aspects of this culture had drawbacks. For example, one manager commented, "We always said that to get fired around here, you had to steal something or kill somebody. Mother Merrill takes care of you from the cradle to the grave." Junior associates criticized this approach as protecting "deadwood," managers and producers who didn't pull their weight.

Some junior associates found the hierarchy overwhelming. Said one trader, "I report to a desk manager, between him and the division manager are five managers. Those are expensive people and it's hard to know what they all do." One trader who had been with a smaller firm noted, "My previous firm was an investment bank, Merrill is a corporation. If I wanted to do a trade at my last job, I looked across the desk at my manager, explained the trade, and he told me if I

[8] MLCM's competitors are substantially smaller. Goldman Sachs and First Boston, for example, each employ between 3,000 and 4,100 people.

[9] Beth McGoldrick and Gregory Miller, "Wall Street Women: You've Come a Short Way, Baby," *Institutional Investor*, June 1985, pp. 88–89.

[10] Neil Osborn, "Merrill Lynch: A New Lunge at the World Capital Markets," *Euromoney*, December 1983, p. 62.

could do it. At Merrill, I have to get approval from higher up." Others complained of bureaucratic constraints and "red tape" particularly regarding headcount constraints (limits on the number of staff a manager could have).

Yet, experienced managers understood the reasons behind certain controls and knew that Merrill supported new ideas and initiative. Falzon, who developed the medium-term note market, said, "Senior management was very supportive of our efforts to develop the MTN product. We were able to add qualified people to originate, trade and market the product. In addition, we received increases in our inventory limits, which enabled Merrill Lynch to position the notes and provide consistent liquidity to our issuer and investor clients." Said Curtis McWilliams, an associate, "I had an idea for structuring a TIGR (zero coupon government bond) product in the U.K. It didn't work out because England didn't want to lose the associated tax base, but I got full support to pursue my idea and a lot of credit for trying." Another manager noted, "I run up against the cost-cutting drive of the firm. But I have a good reputation, and if I make a credible case for something, I usually can get it." Finally, one manager noted, "If there's one way to get something done, a Merrill Lynch manager will find 101 ways to do it. The organization doesn't stop us."

"The opportunities are fantastic," noted Scott Karr, a vice president after three years on MLCM's money market trading desk, "I'm supervising four people, some of whom are many years my senior." Though many traders had no MBA degree, those traders who did were a pool of talent from which to draw management talent. Added Karr, "I believe the future management of the company will come from trading."

MBA Recruiting

A great deal of effort went into recruiting MBAs. Competition for top talent was keen. Wall Street was hiring MBAs in ever-greater numbers; estimates suggested that over 500 MBAs joined Wall Street firms in 1985.

In the early years, MLCM's recruiting efforts were not coordinated between divisions. White Weld, acquired in 1978, had been recruiting from the major business schools for years into investment banking; it continued its effort independently so that the trading and sales divisions might not know when the investment banking division would be recruiting at a school. Hence, referrals from one division to another were then rare. Because Merrill's major commitment to Capital Markets was relatively recent, student clubs were unaware of its growing importance and overlooked MLCM when inviting representatives to their career days. MLCM's own prerecruiting events were less well attended than their competitors', and fewer students signed up for interviews.

By 1983, MLCM began to increase recuiting coordination among functions. Amy Margolis, an experienced executive recruiter, was hired to coordinate MBA recruiting full time and to manage recruiting for sales and trading.

In September each year, Margolis began scheduling prerecruiting events such as "dog and pony" shows for MBAs, introducing them to MLCM and describing career options. At the same time, Margolis would get together the recruiting teams for each campus made up of individuals from the line selected by each function area head which usually included a number of that school's alumni. In the early fall, Ms. Margolis updated MLCM staff on recruiting events and reviewed guidelines for the recruiting season.

By mid-October, MLCM's functional

groups (investment banking, trading, sales) had identified promising candidates from the résumé books published by the business schools, from students writing in to request interviews, by obtaining faculty recommendations, and from meeting interested candidates at prerecruiting events. These names were compiled into an assigned or "closed" interview schedule. As most firms, MLCM offered "open" interview time as well as closed or prearranged interviews.

At the same time, the individual functional group decided which summer associates who had worked for them to invite back. These people were grouped into three categories: those who were definitely wanted, those who should go through the interview process, and those who would definitely not receive offers. All summer associates were notified by December. Said Margolis, "We don't believe in the fill-or-kill approach that some Wall Street firms use—where you have a week to accept our offer or else lose your job."

Once the interview schedule was compiled, each recruiter interviewed approximately 13 candidates in the first round. Each recruiter had his own interviewing style and criteria. At the end of the day, the recruiters ranked their candidates on a number of dimensions (see Exhibit 2) and had to recommend candidates for second round interviews. In 1985 MLCM interviewed approximately 1,170 students from over eighteen schools through the first round.

About 655 of these 1,170 were invited back for second round interviews. These were conducted either in New York or in regional offices. During this phase, the candidates were likely to speak to a number of the firm's more senior managers. After this round, the school teams in each function decided which candidates to make offers to. In most cases, candidates received offers by the third round, though

some were called back for fourth and fifth round interviews. Said one recruit, "It's nice that MLCM makes offers fairly quickly. Some firms really drag it out with six or seven interview rounds—they want to be sure you're going to say yes if they make you an offer."

Once the offers had been made, MLCM had to attract the candidates to the firm. Since most of these MBAs had offers from several Wall Street firms, MLCM had to sell prime candidates on joining Merrill Lynch. In the corporate finance division, certain bankers were assigned to woo specific recruits. Key people were specifically assigned to answer questions or set up additional meetings. Most recruits were flown to New York for more meetings, dinners, and a general sales pitch typical of Wall Street recruiting.

MLCM felt it had a lot to offer its new recruits. It was an increasing power on Wall Street and the premier firm in several areas (municipal securities, commercial paper, competitive bid deals, etc.). Its large capitalization meant that future investment bankers, traders and salespeople would have the benefit of high underwriting and trading limits. The institutional, international and retail systems gave them excellent distribution capability. Bankers, traders and salespeople would all benefit from access to MLCM's research department, which was the most highly ranked on Wall Street.

MBAs joined Merrill because of the people they met in the interview process and the career opportunities they saw at the firm. One recruit pointed out, "I met a 28-year-old vice president and realized that the oldest person I had met was 35 years old. I saw a great deal of opportunity here, and looked forward to working with such a young group of people." Another MBA explained, "I was recruited by the head of all trading at MLCM. I knew I had a mentor here. In a few cases, a recruit decided against joining MLCM (as they might at other firms) because he met a manager he didn't get along with.

Training and Career Development

In the 1970s and early 1980s, MLCM recruits (investment bankers trading and salespeople) experienced separate introductions to the firm. Investment Banking had a three-month classroom training program, followed by two years of six-month job rotations. At the end of rotations, associates had to request assignment to a specific area, and also be "bid for" by that area. Usually the associate had built some relationships with management in the area of his choice, and receiving a desirable "bid" posed little problem. Said one recruiter, "About every three years we have an associate who doesn't find a permanent assignment. Usually, we consider that person a recruiting mistake."

During the same period, sales and trading recruits attended a different three-month training program, including orientation and product training, visits to regional sales offices and preparation for the Series 7 exam (or Registered Representatives exam, which licensed one to sell securities). Particularly in rapidly growing areas, some had little formal training and were put immediately to work. A money market trader described his initiation into MLCM, "I saw the Charlie Merrill movie and went right to the trading desk. It would've been nice to have a little more training—especially on the mechanics of MLCM, like where do I get forms from, who do I send them to, who handles the paychecks."

In 1985, the Sales and Trading training program merged with the Investment Banking training program. All 55 of the 1985 MBA recruits were in the same three-month program, which covered major project training as well as more general information of MLCM's strategy, competition and structure. Another intended benefit was that these new recruits would get to know their counterparts in other areas of the business and thereby develop their own network of relationships. That year, mandatory rotations in investment banking were discontinued.

While some MBAs wanted to go immediately into a particular area and chose firms that allowed that, many MBAs appreciated the flexibility of the training and rotation process. Said one manager, "If you sign up for mergers and acquisitions at another firm, and you don't like it when you get there, you're stuck. Here, you get to see how it works out—it protects you against some downside risk." One MBA with little industry experience described the training as "essential, the reason I came."

As at other firms, new recruits had adjustments to make when they started work. They often encountered a minimum 70-hour week. Junior associates had little control over their time, they had to sacrifice weekend plans to work on some senior banker's project or arrange last-minute travelling on client business. Traders and salespeople too worked long hours. Observed one, "There's a lot of work and reading we have to do after the markets close." The new recruits also had to do what they considered "grunt work," a stark contrast with the important issues they felt they had dealt with in business school. Finally, they often had to work in teams and those who had a legacy of individual stardom found this another necessary adjustment.

Professionals left the firm for a variety of reasons. Some were asked to leave for performance reasons. Most left because they had not made the progress they desired or felt they didn't "fit in." Some left for financial offers from a competing firm "too good to refuse."

Comparisons suggested that MLCM's turnover was equivalent to rates experienced at other firms, although fairly significant variations within MLCM suggested that some improvements could be made. Turnover in one group ran at about 17%, while other groups, such as Municipal Finance, had no turnover at all. The latter, perhaps by coincidence, were also where MLCM's market position was outperforming the competition.

Compensation

When originally established, MLCM management tied compensation closely to performance, and set up separate bonus pools for the different operations. Until 1984, there were over 30 separate pools set up for different groups, as specific as Eurobond Trading or High Yield Bonds. The bonus pool was based on a percentage of profits earned and funded with a base minimum amount. The area manager then distributed that bonus pool according to performance. These bonuses were reviewed and agreed upon by the senior management team.

Many praised this independent bonus pool system. Said Rick Fuscone, vice president of Money Markets, "These pools have really encouraged our entrepreneurial zeal. If our compensation had been tied to something more removed from our performance, our motivation would have been nowhere near as high. I'm certain that this independence contributed to our clear success in the short-term commercial paper market."

As the need for integration increased, the numerous separate pools became a liability and in 1985, MLCM reduced the number of pools to ten. Said one MLCM banker, "In some cases, we had been arguing about how to divide fees amongst ourselves rather than worrying about how to best serve the clients." Some managers questioned the change, since fewer pools reduced the individual area's control over bonus amount and payouts.

In the past, compensation created tension between salespersons and traders. Traders, compensated on the profitability of their transaction, felt that they were the true risk takers while the salespeople were compensated for "writing the ticket" whether or not the transaction made money. In 1985, MLCM changed the basis on which the salespeople were compensated. Whereas in the past, salespeople received a fixed credit or had commission and were paid three times a year, they now had "variable" credits and were paid twice a year. (Traders received bonuses once a year.) Subjective factors, such as traders' evaluations of the salesperson's performance, account penetration and product delivery expertise were included in determining the salesperson's bonus calculation. Although salespeople worried that the ever-shrinking payouts would someday cause their compensation to decline, experience argued that increasing volume would counterbalance or exceed the effect of lower commissions.

Over the decade since its creation as a separate and distinct business arm of Merrill Lynch, Capital Markets' recruiting results improved steadily.

In 1985, MLCM was receiving invitations to career days and "Distinguished Speaker" events. Senior management was increasingly involved with recruiting events. More MBAs than ever were attending MLCM's events and interviewing with MLCM. Furthermore, MLCM now had substantial numbers of analysts and summer associates attending business schools, who were able to "spread the word" about MLCM and increase the firm's profile on campus.

Yet, Jerry Kenney wanted to be sure that MLCM was doing as well as its five or six top competitors in attracting the best MBAs at each school. He knew the powerful images of Merrill's long-established competitors attracted many MBAs. Some of these firms had recruited MBAs for over 50 years; Goldman Sachs still offered the promise of partnership.

In comparison, MLCM lacked the history and the "image" of the top traditional firms: "When you think of Merrill," said one MBA, "you think of the branch on the corner and the local broker—not of an investment bank. Some people fail to distinguish MLCM from the retail side." Said another MBA, "When I told my friends and family I was joining Merrill Lynch, they said, 'Oh, you're going to be a stockbroker'." Some MBAs reported that competitors made a point of stressing Merrill's retail side as a way of detracting from MLCM's image as a capital markets firm. Press articles about changes and reorganizations led some to choose a more secure route with the smaller or older firms, while some MBAs saw change as an advantage. Said one recruit, "I was impressed by Merrill's active pursuit of self-improvement. The organizational changes were exciting to me—it meant opportunity to innovate and to move ahead quickly."

MBAs AT MERRILL LYNCH
STUDY QUESTIONS:

1. Identify and evaluate the business strategy of Merrill Lynch.
2. How is the industry changing and what implications do these changes have with respect to human resources?
3. What do you think Jerry Kenney is worried about?
4. Why is MLCM having recruiting problems?
5. What is your assessment of the recruiting, orientation, training, and career development policies and practices of MLCM? How could they be improved?
6. What advice, if any, do you have for Kenney?
7. What obstacles, if any, will Kenney encounter if he does what you recommend?

MBAs AT MERRILL LYNCH

Exhibit 1 Corporate offices and organization of major line units of Merrill Lynch Capital Markets, January 1, 1986

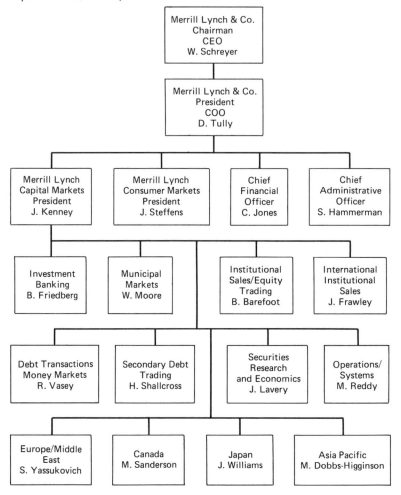

Merrill Lynch Capital Markets Interview Evaluation*

Applicant _____   Date of Interview _____

Interviewer _____   Interviewed For _____

I. Interpersonal Skills

	Rank			
A. Impact Impression (self-confidence, assertiveness and persistence, sales ability, enthusiasm)	Lower 1/3 Inadequate	Middle 1/3 Adequate	Top 1/3 Good	Top 5% Outstanding
B. Communication skills (Able to communicate—orally, listening ability, eye contact)	Lower 1/3 Inadequate	Middle 1/3 Adequate	Top 1/3 Good	Top 5% Outstanding
C. Teamwork (Flexibility)	Lower 1/3 Inadequate	Middle 1/3 Adequate	Top 1/3 Good	Top 5% Outstanding
D. Leadership	Lower 1/3 Inadequate	Middle 1/3 Adequate	Top 1/3 Good	Top 5% Outstanding

II. Competencies

	Rank			
A. Knowledge and skills (What does candidate know about Sales and Trading?)	Lower 1/3 Inadequate	Middle 1/3 Adequate	Top 1/3 Good	Top 5% Outstanding
B. Intellectual capabilities (Academic performance, analytical skills, math, economics, statistics and computer science background)	Lower 1/3 Inadequate	Middle 1/3 Adequate	Top 1/3 Good	Top 5% Outstanding
C. Success indicators (Risk taker, self starter, entrepreneurial initiative)	Lower 1/3 Inadequate	Middle 1/3 Adequate	Top 1/3 Good	Top 5% Outstanding

III. Motivation

	Rank			
A. Maturity	Lower 1/3 Inadequate	Middle 1/3 Adequate	Top 1/3 Good	Top 5% Outstanding
B. Strength (Achievement, drive, energy level, persistence and tenacity)	Lower 1/3 Inadequate	Middle 1/3 Adequate	Top 1/3 Good	Top 5% Outstanding

IV. Match to the Industry/Merrill Lynch.

Interest in this job .... Yes ☐ No ☐   Thoughtful career planning .... Yes ☐ No ☐   Realistic career goals .... Yes ☐ No ☐

V. Conclusion (Note: A highest rating—F lowest rating)

Hire   A   B   C   Not Hire   D   E   F

Comments and Follow-up Recommendations _____

_____

*Remember to conduct a lawful interview.

Professional Recruitment Copy

REMEMBER TO CONDUCT A LAWFUL INTERVIEW

CANDIDATE _____   INTERVIEWER _____

SCHOOL _____   DATE _____

	Excellent		Good		Poor
Intelligence	1	2	3	4	5
Knowledge of IBK	1	2	3	4	5
Value of Educational Experience	1	2	3	4	5
Value of Business Experience	1	2	3	4	5
Poise, maturity, appearance	1	2	3	4	5
Drive, ambition, initiative	1	2	3	4	5
Ability to work with others	1	2	3	4	5
Oral Persuasiveness	1	2	3	4	5
Preparation for Interview	1	2	3	4	5
Interest in Merrill Lynch	1	2	3	4	5

RATING SCALE FOR OVERALL EVALUATION 1 – 10

(1 – 5) denotes "No interest"   (6 – 7) denotes "Further Consideration"
(8 – 10) denotes "Possible Hire"

OVERALL EVALUATION _____

COMMENTS (IF ANY) _____

_____

*Merrill Lynch is committed to providing all employees and applicants for
employment equal opportunity without regard to race, religion, national
origin, age, sex or disability.

Hi-Tech Corporation

In October 1981 the senior management of Hi-Tech Corporation was engaged in budget planning for 1982. Adverse worldwide economic conditions had slowed the corporation's growth. Sales during the first nine months of 1981 were 2% below the comparable period in 1980 (see Exhibit 1). Profits had declined by 45%. Company management, seeing little prospect for near-term relief from troubled economic conditions worldwide, was actively engaged in an effort to reduce operating costs and overhead expenses. To achieve a better balance between the company's revenue expectation and the size of the work force, Hi-Tech determined to reduce its domestic U.S. work force by about 1,000. The company's work force worldwide was about 17,000, of which approximately 13,000 were U.S. employees, almost all in four locations in the state of Massachusetts. Hi-Tech was quite proud of the firm's record in dealing fairly with its employees. A work force reduction of the size indicated was thus a major concern for top management.

This case was developed cooperatively by Professor William E. Fruhan, a member of the Harvard Business School faculty, and Professor Fred K. Foulkes, director of the Human Resources Institute at Boston University School of Management. It was prepared as a basis for class discussion rather than to illustrate either effective or ineffective handling of an administrative situation.

BACKGROUND INFORMATION

Hi-Tech started as the creation of its founder in Cambridge, Massachusetts, in 1937. It was not until 1980, when he was 71, that the founder relinquished his title of chief executive officer to a longtime colleague. The founder remained as chairman and, with his family, was the largest single shareholder, controlling about 10% of the company's stock.

Hi-Tech designed, manufactured, and marketed worldwide a variety of products primarily in the photographic field. These included some specialized products for which Hi-Tech had developed and dominated the worldwide market. In 1981 Hi-Tech estimated its share of the relevant U.S. market at more than 65%.[1]

The company's top policy committee was an eight-man Management Executive Committee (MEC). Chaired by the president, it consisted of the company's three executive vice presidents and four senior vice presidents.

In 1944, the year before the invention of Hi-Tech's most distinctive products, the founder delivered a speech in which he promised to make the company "a new type of social unit." "All will regard themselves as labor in the sense of having as

[1] Prior to 1976, Hi-Tech had enjoyed a 28-year monopoly of the primary products in its field.

their common purpose learning new things and applying that knowledge for public welfare," he said. "The machinist will be proud of and informed about the company's scientific advances; the scientist will enjoy the reduction to practice of his basic perceptions."

The founder articulated early in the company's history the basic strategies of the company. In a document entitled "The Purpose of Our Company," he wrote:

> We have two basic aims here at Hi-Tech.
>
> One is to make products which are genuinely new and useful to the public, products of the highest quality and at reasonable cost. In this way we assure the financial success of the company, and each of us has the satisfaction of helping to make a creative contribution to society.
>
> The other is to give everyone working for Hi-Tech personal opportunity within the company for full exercise of his talents; to express his opinions, to share in the progress of the company as far as his capacities permit, to earn enough money so that the need for earning more will not always be the first thing on his mind—opportunity, in short, to make his work here a fully rewarding, important part of his life.
>
> These goals can make Hi-Tech a great company—great not merely in size, but great in the esteem of all the people for whom it makes new, good things, and great in its fulfillment of the individual ideals of its employees.

All personnel policies at Hi-Tech flowed from the second basic aim. A personnel policy committee consisted of top corporate officers, with a senior vice president as chairman and members of the personnel department serving as staff to the committee. Part of Hi-Tech's tradition, before the adoption of new personnel policies, was its "yellow draft" system whereby all levels of the organization reviewed proposed policy changes exten-

sively before adopting them formally. In the spring of 1981, a former line manager with 20 years of seniority with the company was appointed head of the personnel division.

Participation of hourly employees in the development and establishment of personnel policy was ensured through the involvement of members of the Employees' Committee, a group of representatives elected from all areas of the company. Although not a union in the traditional sense, the Employees' Committee was powerful and significant because top managers listened to it and had great respect for it.

EMPLOYMENT POLICIES

Historically, Hi-Tech had distinguished itself in both the innovativeness of its products and the quality of its employee relations. Hi-Tech was a leader in pay and benefits. It began its cash profit-sharing plan in 1959. To help make its "promotion from within" policy meaningful, Hi-Tech utilized an internal job-posting system that was recognized as a model for industry in terms of the career development opportunities it offered. Under this system all job openings were made known through bulletin board announcements and oral announcements by supervisors and managers. The posting had occupational, shift, compensation, and geographical dimensions. Interested applicants contacted designated personnel representatives regarding the opening or openings that interested them. Virtually all job openings were posted, and over 90% of the jobs posted were filled from within. The company's system recognized lateral moves as well as promotions. Approximately a quarter of the people who were selected for posted jobs filled them on a lateral basis. Lateral moves provided the opportunity for employees to broaden their experience within a discipline, and also to facilitate career changes. When asked what contributed to the high number of lateral bids, an administrator for the program reported that many employees were "chasing overtime opportunities" or "getting closer to home or to an opportunity to get a better shift or supervisor." While many supervisors objected to the practice of allowing bids for lateral moves, this administrator felt that in the long run "the company ends up with happier employees, with a greater degree of freedom.... They don't feel that they are being leaned on and they don't feel that they are being regimented."

Hi-Tech referred to its employees as "company members."

No Hi-Tech employee punched a time clock. Each specific manufacturing job at Hi-Tech, like other nonexempt positions in the firm, could be compensated at seven different merit pay levels.[2] Extensive training, education, and career counseling, and development opportunities were also offered employees. Hi-Tech was also recognized nationally for its leadership role with respect to the implementation of equal employment opportunity and affirmative action.

In addition to its job-posting and merit pay systems, Hi-Tech had formally adopted a policy which effectively promised employment until retirement for all employees with more than 10 years of exempt employment at the company. Hi-Tech's personnel policy manual contained this statement on the subject of reductions in personnel:

Furthermore, we want to assure all members (employees) who have 10 or more years of exempt seniority of an exempt job within the company although not necessarily at the same level of their present job.

For purposes of both promotion and layoffs, Hi-Tech's seniority system was companywide. For nonexempt employees, layoffs were affected in reverse order of seniority. The least senior employee in a given job title and basic unit in a specific location, when displaced, could displace the least senior member with the same job title and location in some other basic unit. When no such bumping possibility was available, the employee could either accept a voluntary layoff or bump the least senior member with the same job *title* at an alternate *location*. If the employee could not avoid being laid off through these steps, the same procedure could be followed based on job *level* as opposed to job *title* displacement.[3] If the employee could not avoid being laid off via this step, the same procedure could be followed based on *reductions* in job level.[4] The path to be followed is indicated in Figure A. When, as a result of this bumping process, the employee reached a point at which he or she had exhausted all bumping possibilities, the employee was laid off.

The employment protection provided to exempt employees with more than 10 years' service, combined with the multilocation, multititle, and multilevel bumping process for nonexempt employees, created unusual problems at Hi-Tech when significant reductions in force were

---

[2] Nonexempt employees were entitled to overtime pay when they worked more than 8 hours in a day or more than 40 hours in a week. Exempt employees were not normally entitled to overtime pay for hours worked beyond the normal work day.

[3] Bumping rights into new responsibilities were permitted only if the employee was deemed able to perform the normal work routine with limited supervision within a four-week period. Designated personnel administrators were responsible for making this decision.

[4] Any employee bumping into a job with a lower rate of pay was protected against a pay decrease for a period of two years.

Figure A The job bumping process at Hi-Tech

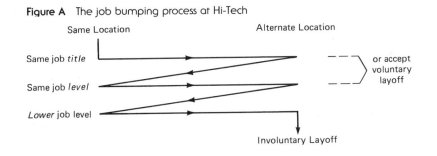

contemplated. The administration of this system, with respect to individual employees, generally took several months. As shown in Exhibit 2, if a layoff of 1,000 people was spread pro rata across the salaried and hourly work force, approximately 345 salaried employees and 655 hourly employees would have to be laid off. All of the 345 salaried employees laid off would have to come from the 1–9 year employment population of 1,532 individuals. This represented nearly 25% of the employees in this group.

Layoffs in the hourly work force would create equally difficult problems. If 80% of the 655 employees declared surplus could bump into other jobs in order to avoid layoff, 524 employees with less seniority would become surplus. If the 80% factor was applied to this group of 524 employees, they would, in turn, bump 419 less senior employees. At the end of this complex chain, 655 people would ultimately be laid off, and about 2,600 Hi-Tech employees would have changed jobs. Productivity losses as well as disruption in the personal lives of employees could be very significant. In addition, since Hi-Tech protected for two years the pay level of any employee bumped down into a lower job level, for that period Hi-Tech would probably save only the compensation level associated with the lowest paid 655 employees in the firm.

VOLUNTARY SEVERANCE PROGRAMS, 1973–1974 AND 1979–1980

In two prior periods of economic dislocation, Hi-Tech had experienced a need to reduce its work force significantly. In 1973–1974 Hi-Tech reduced its work force by 8.9% or 1,200 employees. About 1,000 of these reduced jobs were accomplished via layoffs. In 1974 about 150 salaried employees were laid off and an additional 150 returned to the nonexempt ranks. This was the only layoff that had ever occurred in the salaried ranks at Hi-Tech. This traumatic event was accompanied by a generous severance pay plan and extensive outplacement assistance. In 1979–1980, the work force was reduced by 16.4%, or 3,400 employees. Much of the 1979–1980 reduction was also accomplished via layoff. While many more employees were laid off in this period than in 1974, the 1979–1980 layoff was far less disruptive in terms of Hi-Tech's operations. Almost all of the 1979–1980 layoffs were concentrated in Hi-Tech's lowest pay categories, such as camera assemblers. Employees in these job categories often had little seniority and few alternatives for job bumping, so disruptions to Hi-Tech's operations were minimal.

In each of these prior periods, work force attrition had been accomplished through a combination of normal turnover, layoffs, and a special voluntary severance program aimed at inducing exempt employees to leave the work force. In 1973, employees aged 55 or over with 15 years of service had been offered an opportunity to leave Hi-Tech with full pay for the first 3 months and half pay for the next 33 months. In 1980, employees in the same category were offered the opportunity to leave Hi-Tech with full pay for the first 3 months, and half pay for the following 21 months. One hundred four and 191 employees, respectively, had voluntarily left Hi-Tech under the 1973 and 1980 programs. This amounted to 28% of those eligible, in both 1973 and 1980.

DESIGNING A NEW VOLUNTARY SEVERANCE PROGRAM

Since Hi-Tech had concluded a special severance program fairly recently, many of the exempt employees who might normally have responded favorably to such an offer had already left the company. For the plan to attract the desired number of volunteers in 1981–1982, the compensation terms of the program might have to be improved to appeal to some employees who had not been attracted to the 1980 program. The age and length of service requirements to qualify for the plan might also have to be relaxed to attract more participants. In addition, any program should be designed to provide equity across the exempt and nonexempt employee groups, reducing the costs and disruption caused by the job-bumping process described earlier.

Hi-Tech analyzed a number of variations for voluntary severance programs including:

- eliminating minimum age qualifications,
- reducing the minimum length of service qualifications to 10 years, and

- altering the number of months of pay which might be granted to employees volunteering to terminate employment under the plan.

The company was mindful of some of the legal ramifications of severance programs, such as their treatment under Social Security regulations and the Pension Reform Act of 1974. In particular, the company was concerned that it might be accused of discriminating against certain of its employees on the basis of age. Four hypothetical alternative plans covering most of the variations considered by Hi-Tech are presented in Exhibit 3. Alternative 1 in Exhibit 3 indicates that an employee *under age 45* with 10 years of service at Hi-Tech would receive 4 months of salary continuation payments for accepting voluntary termination.[5] Payment to employees *over age 45* with more than 10 years of service would increase linearly over the ranges indicated.[6]

Since severance compensation varied within the four hypothetical plans by age and length of service, Hi-Tech assumed that the percentage of employees accepting voluntary severance would also vary by age and length of service. The company's estimate of acceptance rates by age and length of service for Plan Alternative 4 is presented in Exhibit 4. These estimates were based on prior experience at Hi-Tech, as well as the experience of other large companies utilizing voluntary severance programs. The estimated average sever-

[5] Voluntary termination generally disqualified the employee from collecting unemployment compensation. In addition, an employee voluntarily terminating was not entitled to normal severance benefits associated with a layoff. Nonexempt employees (with three or more years of service) on permanent layoff at Hi-Tech received one week of pay for each full year of service. Exempt employees on permanent layoff received one month of pay for each two years of service.

[6] Payments to employees aged 62 to 70 were reduced somewhat to reflect Social Security payments. All payments stopped at age 70 (normal retirement age).

ance payment for employees occupying each category by age and length of service for Plan Alternative 4 is also presented in Exhibit 4.

Each of the four alternative voluntary severance plans presented in Exhibit 3 could be expected to produce different levels of success in terms of the number of employees who would leave Hi-Tech voluntarily. Any shortfall between voluntary terminations and Hi-Tech's work force reduction target of 1,000 would have to be made up by involuntary layoffs. Exhibit 5 presents an estimate of the number of Hi-Tech employees who might elect voluntary termination under each of the four alternative plans described in Exhibit 3. Lines 1, 3, 5, and 7 of Exhibit 5 indicate the "best guess" estimate of acceptances for the various alternative plans. Lines 2, 4, 6, and 8 present the estimate of acceptances for the "maximum cost" situation where:

- more than the anticipated number of employees accepted voluntary termination,
- the employees accepting the offer were skewed toward older employees whose severance costs tended to be higher, and
- the mix of employees terminating voluntarily tended to come more heavily from the hourly work force than from the salaried work force.

The left half of Exhibit 5 deals with employee headcounts. The right half of Exhibit 5 shows total estimated program costs, and both gross and net savings over the calendar years 1982 and 1983 that could be expected to result from implementation of each of the work force reduction plans.[7]

---

[7] The gross and net savings data of Exhibits 5 and 6 assume that any voluntary severance plan for reducing Hi-Tech's work force would be announced in November 1981 and would be effective as of February 15, 1982. The savings reported in columns 7 and 8 of Exhibit 5 thus cover the 22½ months spanning February 16, 1982, through December 31, 1983. For the layoff alternative (see Exhibit 7), it is assumed that layoffs would occur as of January 1, 1982.

Only summary calculations for total program costs and savings are presented in Exhibit 5. A more detailed breakout of the cost and savings calculation for severance plan Alternative 4 is presented in Exhibit 6. Similar data for the layoff alternative are presented in Exhibit 7.

The final decision would be made by the Management Executive Committee, listening to recommendations from the personnel department, personnel policy committee, and the employees' committee. Whatever the outcome, it would have to be announced to all members of the company by the president.

HI-TECH CORPORATION STUDY QUESTIONS:

1. Why has Hi-Tech been experiencing inadequate profitability? For how long has this condition continued?
2. What are the shareholder value implications of having 1,000 redundant employees at Hi-Tech?
3. What is your analysis of the principal human resources problem at Hi-Tech?
4. Will a reduction of 1,000 employees in Hi-Tech's workforce restore the company to an adequate level of profitability? How many redundant employees do you think Hi-Tech has?
5. Should Hi-Tech downsize, and if so, how?
6. What are the pros and cons of a voluntary severance program?
7. If you believe the voluntary severance program should be offered, which of the four alternative propositions presented in Exhibit 3 would you recommend? Why?
8. How would you implement the voluntary severance program?
9. What would your communications strategy be with regard to the program?
10. If you were to adopt a voluntary severance program, how would you evaluate the results?

HI-TECH CORPORATION

Exhibit 1 Selected financial data, 1968–1981 ($ in milions except per share data)

Hi-Tech Corp.	1968	1969	1970	1971	1972	1973	1974
Sales	$443.9	$522.2	$492.1	$525.5	$557.3	$685.5	$757.3
Cost of goods sold	202.4	257.4	240.3	243.4	259.1	358.3	485.2
Research and development expense	na	na	na	85.9[a]	130.4[a]	68.8[a]	76.8[a]
Advertising expense	109.1 }	127.4 }	140.5 }	29.6	33.7	37.5	49.4
Other selling, general, and admin. exp.	na }	na }	na }	65.8	73.5	145.6[b]	113.1
Other income less expenses[c]	8.8	15.9	15.5	15.8	12.7	14.8	12.3
Profit after taxes	62.2	71.2	66.0	61.0	42.5	51.8	28.4
Assets[d]	326.9	484.4	556.4	617.1	651.8	741.5	768.4
Cash and marketable securities	209.2	201.5	210.8	194.1	216.7	188.1	106.8
Net property, plant, and equipment	99.9	128.4	175.9	213.3	224.5	228.3	224.3
Borrowed money	—	—	—	—	—	—	9.3
Net worth	277	437.9	493.1	544.2	577.0	619.1	636.9
Shares outstanding (millions)	31.7	32.8	32.8	32.8	32.8	32.9	32.9
Market price/share	$117⅛	$125	$77	$89	$126⅛	$69⅞	$18⅝
Common stock β	na	na	na	na	na	na	na
Employees (end of period)	8,844	10,506	10,582	11,654	11,998	14,277	13,019
Total payroll and benefits	na	na	na	na	$160.2	$191.3	$223.2
Consumer price index (1967 = 100)	104.2	109.8	116.3	121.3	125.3	133.1	147.7
L. T. Treasury bond interest rate (%)	5.4	6.2	6.7	6.0	5.8	7.0	8.0

						9 Mos	
	1975	1976	1977	1978	1979	1980	1980	1981
---	---	---	---	---	---	---	---	---
Sales	$812.7	$950.0	$1,061.9	$1,376.6	$1,361.5	$1,450.8	$990.2	$974.3
Cost of goods sold	468.0	511.8	575.7	778.3	876.8	831.1	571.7	577.7
Research and development expense	64.2	77.6	88.9	86.5	109.6	114.0	na }	na }
Advertising expense	51.9	61.8	70.8	101.1	105.0	101.4	334.5 }	350.0 }
Other selling, general, and admin. exp.	120.9	155.4	177.6	230.6	234.8	268.5	na }	na }
Other income less expenses[c]	15.5	11.1	12.6	14.4	.5	8.4	3.2	15.0
Profit after taxes	62.6	79.7	92.3	118.4	36.2	85.4	53.1	29.4
Assets[d]	834.3	949.6	1,067.2	1,266.6	1,244.3	1,394.6	1,377.7	1,393.8
Cash and marketable securities	180.0	258.8	213.1	179.3	96.2	279.9	211.2	275.7
Net property, plant, and equipment	203.3	198.2	225.9	294.8	371.6	362.2	371.6	341.5
Borrowed money	12.0	30.7	50.0	92.7	100.1	196.6	199.3	223.0
Net worth	689.0	755.2	826.2	915.0	918.3	970.9	935.9	964.7
Shares outstanding (millions)	32.9	32.9	32.9	32.9	32.9	32.9	32.9	32.9
Market price/share	$31	$37⅞	$26⅛	$51¾	$28	$25	$28⅛	$23⅝
Common stock β	na	na	na	na	na	na	na	1.27
Employees (end of period)	13,387	14,506	16,394	20,884	18,416	17,454	na	na
Total payroll and benefits	$231.8	$289.6	$332.2	$421.4	$464.1	$497.3	na	na
Consumer price index (1967 = 100)	161.2	170.5	181.5	195.4	217.4	246.8	239.5	266.0
L. T. Treasury bond interest rate (%)	8.2	7.9	7.7	8.4	9.2	11.3	11.3	14.7

Eastman Kodak Company	1968	1969	1970	1971	1972	1973	1974
Sales	$2,644	$2,747	$2,785	$2,976	$3,478	$4,036	$4,584
Cost of goods sold	1,469	1,482	1,508	1,623	1,856	2,124	2,625
Research and development expense	na ⎤	na ⎤	na ⎤	na ⎤	215	248	274
Advertising expense	418 ⎬	465 ⎬	520 ⎬	565 ⎬	103	120	120
Other selling, general, and admin. exp.	na ⎦	na ⎦	na ⎦	na ⎦	329	396	458
Other income less expenses[c]	32	29	35	29	55	56	48
Profit after taxes	375	401	404	419	546	653	630
Assets	2,565	2,830	3,043	3,298	3,757	4,302	4,703
Cash and marketable securities	537	575	560	649	862	1,036	814
Net property, plant and equipment	1,084	1,226	1,385	1,510	1,559	1,714	2,051
Borrowed money	88	82	84	81	106	121	124
Net worth	1,836	2,035	2,226	2,430	2,775	3,118	3,427
Shares outstanding (millions)	161.2	161.2	161.2	161.2	161.3	161.3	161.3
Market price/share	$73¼	$82⅜	$75⅝	$97¼	$148⅜	$69⅞	$62⅞
Common stock β	na	na	na	na	na	na	na
Employees (end of period)	108,400	110,400	110,700	109,700	114,800	120,700	124,100
Total payroll and benefits	$999	$1,081	$1,157	$1,232	$1,403	$1,641	$1,857
Consumer price index (1967 = 100)	104.2	109.8	116.3	121.3	125.3	133.1	147.8
L. T. Treasury bond interest rate (%)	5.4	6.2	6.7	6.0	5.8	7.0	8.0

	1975	1976	1977	1978	1979	1980	9 mos 1980	9 mos 1981
Sales	$4,959	$5,438	$5,967	$7,013	$8,028	$9,734	$6,627	$7,265
Cost of goods sold	2,927	3,272	3,516	4,000	4,843	6,085	4,183	4,468
Research and development expense	313	335	351	389	459	520	na ⎤	na ⎤
Advertising expense	127	152	190	226	247	294	1,197 ⎬	1,334 ⎬
Other selling, general, and admin. exp.	505	552	622	752	830	939	na ⎦	na ⎦
Other income less expenses[c]	19	42	13	36	58	67	47	80
Profit after taxes	614	651	643	902	1,001	1,154	749	857
Assets	5,056	5,524	5,904	6,801	7,554	8,754	8,440	9,140
Cash and marketable securities	747	780	958	1,379	1,541	1,585	na	1,243
Net property, plant, and equipment	2,378	2,568	2,658	2,737	2,960	3,435	na	3,866
Borrowed money	126	173	151	188	199	219	na	na
Net worth	3,709	4,026	4,331	4,858	5,391	6,028	5,923	6,533
Shares outstanding (millions)	161.3	161.4	161.4	161.4	161.4	161.4	161.4	161.6
Market price/share	$106⅛	$86	$51⅓	$58⅝	$48⅛	$69¾	$65½	$65
Common stock β	na	na	na	na	na	na	na	.98
Employees (end of period)	124,000	127,000	123,700	124,800	126,300	129,500	na	na
Total payroll and benefits	$2,098	$2,309	$2,448	$2,776	$3,177	$3,643	na	na
Consumer price index (1967 = 100)	161.2	170.5	181.5	195.4	217.4	246.8	239.5	266.0
L. T. Treasury bond interest rate (%)	8.2	7.9	7.7	8.4	9.2	11.3	11.3	14.7

[a] Data for 1971–1974 are inflated due to development expenses for a major new photographic system.

[b] Includes introductory expenses of $54.6 million for the major new photographic system.

[c] Includes primarily royalty income and interest income less interest expense.

[d] Asset data for 1968–1969 are not fully comparable to later years because of a change in accounting for non–U.S. subsidiaries.

HI-TECH CORPORATION

Exhibit 2 Employee population categorized by age and length of employment (U.S.)

| | Age of Employee | | | |
Length of Service	Under 45	45–54	55 and Over	Total
Salaried Work Force				
1–9 years	na	na	na	1,532
10–14	773	282	79	1,134
15–19	569	315	99	983
20–24	161	287	86	534
25–29	3	99	56	158
30 and over	—	9	68	77
Total	na	na	na	4,418
Hourly Work Force				
1–9 years	na	na	na	5,121
10–14	972	421	365	1,758
15–19	602	332	220	1,154
20–24	90	164	166	420
25–29	1	44	40	85
30 and over	—	8	17	25
Total	na	na	na	8,563

HI-TECH CORPORATION

Exhibit 3 Total severance payments (measured in months of pay) under four alternative voluntary severance payment programs

| | Age of Employee | | | | | |
| | Alternative 1 | | | Alternative 2 | | |
Length of Service	Under 45	45–54	55 and Over	Under 45	45–54	55 and Over
10 years	4 mos	5 mos	6 mos	4 mos	6 mos	8 mos
20	8	10	12	8	12	16
30 or over	12	15	18	12	18	24
	Alternative 3			Alternative 4		
	Under 45	45–54	55 and Over	Under 45	45–54	55 and Over
10 years	5 mos	6.25 mos	7.5 mos	5 mos	7.5 mos	10 mos
20	10	12.5	15	10	15	20
30 or over	15	18.75	22.5	15	22.5	30

HI-TECH CORPORATION

Exhibit 4 Forecasted acceptance rates and severance payment costs per employee for voluntary severance plan alternative 4

	Age of Employee							
	Forecasted Acceptance Percentage				*Forecasted Average Severance Payment*			
Length of Service	*Under 45*	*45–54*	*55 and Over*	*Total*	*Under 45*	*45–54*	*55 and Over*	*Total*
Salaried Work Force								
10–14 years	12%	11%	13%		$20,200	$34,900	$46,400	
15–19	12	11	13		26,700	47,900	60,200	
20–24	12	13	16		33,200	57,800	74,600	
25–29	—	20	22		52,300	71,800	92,700	
30 and over	—	25	30		—	84,600	124,400	
Total				13%[a]				$44,700
Hourly Work Force								
10–14 years	14%	12%	18%		$10,900	$16,100	$20,000	
15–19	14	14	21		16,600	24,600	31,400	
20–24	14	14	21		21,800	31,600	40,100	
25–29	—	19	21		—	39,500	49,900	
30 and over	—	21	21		—	48,300	59,400	
Total				15%[b]				$21,200

[a] Equal to 374 employees as calculated from Exhibit 2.

[b] Equal to 519 employees as calculated from Exhibit 2.

HI-TECH CORPORATION

Exhibit 5 Forecast of head count reduction, total costs, and gross savings during 1982 and 1983 from four severance plan alternatives versus a layoff program

		(1) (2) Voluntary Severance		(3) (4) Headcount Reduction Layoff		(5)	(6)	(7) $ Millions	(8)
	Line	Hourly	Salaried	Hourly	Salaried	Total	Total Cost	Gross Savings 1982–1983	Net Savings 1982–1983
	Alternative 1								
1	Expected profile	395	264	260	81	1,000	$15.8	$52.4	$36.6
2	Heavier acceptance in hourly and older profile	450	251	205	94	1,000	19.8	57.2	37.4
	Alternative 2								
3	Expected profile	440	299	215	46	1,000	19.6	57.3	37.7
4	Heavier acceptance in hourly and older profile	541	296	114	49	1,000	26.2	58.9	32.7
	Alternative 3								
5	Expected profile	481	348	174	0	1,003	24.8	59.0	34.2
6	Heavier acceptance in hourly and older profile	569	313	86	32	1,000	30.7	59.5	28.8
	Alternative 4								
7	Expected profile	519	374	136	0	1,029	31.0	61.7	30.7
8	Heavier acceptance in hourly and older profile	657	363	0	0	1,020	43.4	62.5	19.1
9	All terminations via layoff			655	345	1,000	10.1	49.2	39.1

HI-TECH CORPORATION

Exhibit 6 Severance plan alternative 4: calculation of total costs, and 1982–1983 gross savings and net savings

Line		Amount Per Employee		Number of Employees		Total ($ millions)
	Total Costs					
1	Severance payments to hourly employees	$21,200[a]	×	519	=	$11.0
2	Severance payments to salaried employees	44,700[a]	×	374	=	16.7
3	Layoff payments to hourly employees	875	×	136	=	.1
4	Benefits[d]	[e]	×	1,029	=	2.5
5	Layoff process costs				=	.7
6	Total				=	$31.0[b]
	Gross Savings, 1982–1983 [c]					
7	Wage and benefit savings from hourly VSP employees	$46,700	×	519	=	$24.3
8	Salary and benefit savings from salaried VSP employees	87,600	×	374	=	32.8
9	Wages and benefit savings from hourly employees laid off	33,200	×	136	=	4.6
10	Total			1,029		$61.7[b]
11	*Net Savings, 1982–1983*					$30.7[b]

[a] Data drawn from Exhibit 4.

[b] As summarized in Exhibit 5, line 7.

[c] Equal to 22½ months of savings from February 16, 1982, through December 31, 1983.

[d] Assumes employees accepting VSP under age 55 could continue their medical insurance, dental insurance, and life insurance for 2 years by paying the normal fraction of the cost paid by active employees. Employees aged 55 or over could continue medical coverage on the same terms to age 65.

[e] Equal to $2,500 per VSP termination and $1,500 per employee laid off.

HI-TECH CORPORATION

Exhibit 7 Layoff alternative: calculation of total costs and 1982–1983 gross savings and net savings

Line		Amount Per Employee		Number of Employees		Total ($ millions)
	Total Costs					
1	Severance payments to hourly employees	$ 876[a]	×	655	=	$ .6
2	Severance payments to salaried employees	5,620[b]	×	345	=	1.9
3	Benefits	1,500	×	1,000	=	1.5
4	Layoff process costs					6.1
5	Total					$10.1[d]
	Gross Savings, 1982–1983					
6	Wage and benefit savings from hourly employees	$34,648[c]	×	655	=	$22.7
7	Salary and benefit savings from salaried employees	76,881[c]	×	345	=	26.5
8	Total					$49.2[d]
9	*Net Savings, 1982–1983*					$39.1[d]

[a] Equal to three weeks' termination pay.

[b] Equal to two months' termination pay.

[c] Equal to two years of pay including benefits.

[d] As summarized in Exhibit 5, line 9.

III

THE CONDUCT
OF
LABOR RELATIONS[1]

During the period from 1965 to 1987, there have been some quite fundamental changes in the industrial relations system in the United States. First, there has been an absolute decline of about 2 million union members. Somewhat less than half of this decline reflects changes in the pattern and structure of employment with the relative decline in blue collar jobs and the growth in white collar, service, and female employment. The changes also reflect the development and application of more sophisticated personnel policy and administration in nonunion companies, as well as seemingly more negative attitudes toward unions among employees.

Underlying these trends and develop-

ments have been: (1) intensified worldwide competition in many industries, (2) intensified domestic competition associated with the deregulation of certain industries, (3) concessionary collective bargaining with to date very limited restoration of concessions, (4) profit sharing established as a balancing element for concessions, (5) the considerable spread of quality of worklife programs in both union and nonunion organizations, (6) a development in National Labor Relations Board policy allowing "double breasted" corporate operation through competitive union and nonunion subsidiaries, (7) the development in nonunion companies of multiple communication programs, such as skip-level interviewing, "speak up" procedures, and various training programs and other mechanisms, (8) the elimination of "pattern bargaining" notably as linked to the automotive wage formula with its annual improvement factor and cost of liv-

[1] This chapter benefited from discussion with Professors Thomas H. Kochan and, more extensively, Robert B. McKersie; but it was written (including the above remarks) prior to the publication, with Harry L. Katz, of their outstanding book, *The Transformation of American Industrial Relations.* Extended discussion of this work is not necessary, since it will be required reading for those interested in the field.

ing escalator clause, (9) declining strike activity, and (10) increased development of "individual employee rights" through both statutes and judge-made law. These developments, trends, and conditions both reflect and allow new opportunities for management initiative and indicate fundamental change in our industrial relations system.

A BRIEF HISTORICAL OVERVIEW

Collective bargaining in the United States has been a continuously evolving institution shaped by the changing economic, social, political, and industrial relations trends and conditions. A system of union-management relations has been created with quite special characteristics compared to the systems prevailing in Western Europe and other areas.

Unions go back to the early industrialization of the country. A date frequently cited is 1796, when journeymen shoemakers founded a local union in Philadelphia. Locals of printers, shoemakers, caulkers, tailors, carpenters, and so forth sprang up, but these early unions were founded and refounded, since they did not survive recessions. The early unions consisted primarily of skilled craftsmen and were confined to eastern cities.

The National Typographical Union, the country's earliest permanent national union, was founded in 1850. Some fifteen crafts, such as the Machinists and Iron Molders, had organized on a national scale by 1860. The Civil War created a burst of organizing that brought the labor movement to some 2 percent of the total labor force. For a period of years after the Civil War, from 1878 to about 1900, unionism broke out of its narrow skilled-worker mold under the Noble and Holy Order of the Knights of Labor and reached a peak of some 700,000 in 1886,

after which the organization declined and disappeared.

In 1881 an enduring national organization began that in 1886 became the American Federation of Labor under the elected leadership of Samuel Gompers. Within this federation national unions (or international as they are now called primarily because of Canadian membership) were autonomous and bargained almost exclusively through local unions on a plant or small area basis. The AFL was established on the principle of exclusive jurisdiction and granted a charter to only one national union in a trade or industry to avoid the weakness of "dual" unionism. This principle in modified form is now reinforced by bargaining unit determinations under the National Labor Relations Act. Also, the young federation and its national unions followed a pragmatic philosophy of accepting the private property and profit system and bargaining for immediate wage-centered gains.

During the entire early period of the labor movement in this country, unionism was of very limited scope, played a modest national role, and developed characteristics, still retained in large measure, best suited for survival in a harsh climate. This harsh climate included: (1) widespread and militant employer opposition,[2] (2) a generally hostile legal environment, (3) widespread industrial job and other individual economic opportunities, (4) the pervasive spirit of individualism, (5) a lack of class consciousness, and (6) political, religious, and educational freedoms and opportunities achieved prior to and apart from a national labor movement.

---

[2] Employers had many potent weapons to use against unionism: discharge of union leaders and sympathizers, forcing individuals as a condition of employment to sign the individual "yellow-dog" employment contracts prohibiting union membership, espionage, blacklists and various other community punishments.

The Great Depression of the thirties brought drastic economic, social, and political changes. The modern labor movement in the United States was an outgrowth of these changes. The Norris-LaGuardia Act of 1932 was an early long-sought change that restricted greatly the power of federal courts to issue labor injunctions. Public policy underwent a fundamental change with the passage of the National Labor Relations Act in 1935 prohibiting employer unfair labor practices and basing legal recognition on a government conducted election. Also in 1935, through the initiative of John L. Lewis of the Mine Workers with Sidney Hillman of the Clothing Workers and David Dubinsky of the Ladies Garment Workers, the CIO (the Congress of Industrial Organizations) was created in a split with the AFL. "Dual" unionism became the order of the day (until the break was healed by merger in 1955), and the CIO launched major organizing drives to achieve industrial unions in the mass production industries.

The new spirit of unionization was more than a change created by law or organizational structure. The modern labor movement burst upon the country largely in the single decade 1935–1945 in which membership grew from 3 million to almost 15 million, 22 percent of the labor force. The heartland of industrial America, steel and automobiles, began to operate under collective bargaining. Workers flocked into unions, paid their dues and demanded "when do we strike." Unionism caught fire.

While union membership continued to grow during the decade 1945–1955, it grew much more slowly to a labor force peak of slightly over 25 percent, 17.5 million members. After a decline of a million members to 1961, slow growth was resumed as a trend essentially until the significant decline in the eighties.

THE EVOLUTION OF THE MODERN LABOR MOVEMENT

The modern labor movement in the years since 1932 may be said to have gone through various stages. First, an organizational stage, the period from 1932 or 1935 to 1945. Attitudes were hostile, strikes were commonplace. There were historic sitdowns in auto, rubber, and other industries. Violence was all too common. A second overlapping stage, a contract development stage, may be dated from 1940 to 1950. Initially labor agreements were simple documents. The first contract between U.S. Steel and the Steel Workers Organizing Committee took three typed pages. These agreements expanded in no small part through the happenstance of World War II with its War Labor Board, which wrote countless "no-strike," "arbitration," and other clauses into labor agreements. The end of this contract development stage has been set somewhat arbitrarily at 1950, the year in which the United Automobile Workers signed a 5-year historic contract with General Motors. This or any other union's willingness to hold its contract unchanged for 5 years would have been quite out of the question at an earlier date.

Attitudes were also changing and a third merging stage of growing accommodation may be dated from 1950 to 1965. Throughout this period the negotiation and particularly the administration of labor agreements became more orderly. More and more relationships could be described as ones of "accommodation" rather than "conflict" or "containment-aggression."

Growing accommodation has not, however, continued in a manifest destiny type of evolution. In part collective bargaining may have worked too well. At least in the larger relationships, such as steel and automobiles, bargaining grew remote from the rank and file, and a new rank and file militancy developed. Grievance rates increased, members refused to ratify contracts, pressures to remove no-strike clauses developed, and large numbers of local issues brought a new dimension to bargaining. Collective bargaining since the mid-sixties has entered a stage of greatly increased complexity both as to bargaining structure and as to issues, along with rank and file militancy.

The militancy since the mid-sixties has not been a return to the conflict of the thirties. Today in established relationships there is highly experienced and professional leadership on both sides of the table, but these leaders have been grappling with a series of difficult issues in an environment of membership unrest. Today's wave of new unionism, particularly among state and local government employees, is somewhat reminiscent of the thirties. In 1986, 33% of state and local employees were union members, a striking figure considering that the unionization of such employees has been legal in most states only since the mid-sixties. It was these new unions and associations, such as the American Federation of Teachers and the National Educational Association, that struck with great frequency. Collective bargaining encountered new problems in the seventies. As already pointed out, the eighties opened with a major membership decline and a loss of power and influence. The prospect that those trends will be reversed appears remote.

CHARACTERISTICS OF THE U.S. SYSTEM OF INDUSTRIAL RELATIONS

Students desiring to obtain a more complete perspective on the characteristics of the U.S. labor relations system, and its consequences are urged to read Bok and Dunlop.[3] The following constitutes an introductory comment on major characteristics.

Limited Scope

The U.S. labor movement has to date been a relatively limited one. In 1945 membership stood at 35.5% of the nonagricultural labor force, an all-time high. This percentage was 25.7 in 1974, or, if association membership counted, 29. By 1987 only 17% of all private nonagricultural wage and salaried workers were organized.

This limited scope serves to demonstrate that, while unions have become well-established institutions, nonunionism has remained strong. In the thirties unions won 85 to 90% of all National Labor Relations Board elections. In 1975, for the first time, the percentage won dropped below 50. The rate dropped to 46% in 1977 and to 42% in 1985.

Moreover, as recently as 1980, organized labor initiated 7,200 NLRB representative elections in which 478,000 workers were eligible to vote. Contrast this to 1986, when unions asked for only 3,300 elections involving just 208,000 employees. It is interesting to note that in Britain, too, there has been a decline in union membership. Since 1979, union membership in Britain has fallen by 3 million to approximately 9 million, with the unionized work force declining from 51 to 27%. In Great Britain, too, the unions are having difficulty recruiting members in the growing financial services and electronics industries.

In Japan, the influence of unions has also declined. While unions represented 55.7% of Japanese employees in 1949, in 1986 the penetration rate had fallen to

[3] Derek C. Bok and John T. Dunlop, *Labor and the American Community* (New York: Simon & Schuster, 1970).

28.2%. In a 1987 paper, Professor Kazutoshi Koshiro of Yokohama National University attributes the decline of organized labor in his country to five factors: (1) decreased employment in large companies where most union members are employed; (2) increased employment in the service sector, which has been less organized than the manufacturing sector; (3) increased female part-time employees, who usually are uninterested in joining unions; (4) changing value systems among younger workers that is part of a decreased zealousness toward the labor movement in the society as a whole; and (5) decreased employment in the public sector because of administrative reform and privatization.[4]

There are various contributing factors in the relative decline of unionism in the United States. A very important combination of circumstances has been the relative decline in blue collar employment coupled with the limited organizing success unions have had, apart from government employees, with white collar and professional employees. Also, many large predominantly unionized companies have kept their new plants nonunion. This point is partially associated with the continuing low degree of union organizing success in the Sunbelt states, since companies have located many of their new plants in these states. Many observers also believe that employers became more aggressive after President Reagan fired 11,500 federal air traffic controllers for their illegal strike in 1981, a move that put the controller's union out of business. Government, too, has taken over some of the functions previously done by unions. There has been in the past 25 years an expansion of individual employee rights through both federal and state antidiscrimination and safety and health statutes and judge-made law, including employment-at-will developments.

In recent years there has been legislative activity at the state level. In 1987, for example, Connecticut voted strict limits on employer's use of drug tests; Minnesota became the first state to require that companies provide up to 6 weeks of unpaid paternal as well as maternal leave; Montana passed a law protecting nonunion workers from dismissal except for good cause; Vermont said employers must provide a smoke-free workplace; and the U.S. Supreme Court upheld a Maine law forcing employers to pay severance and give advance notice to employees laid off by plant closings. While the term *employment law* used to refer to union organizing, collective bargaining, and proceedings under the NLRB, the field now includes litigation over unjust discharge, discrimination, pensions and benefits. There is now an ample supply of personal injury lawyers to handle wrongful discharge cases and civil rights attorneys to respond to discrimination cases.

An additional hindrance to unionization has been the continuing unorganized status of some large well-known and totally nonunion companies. Finally, unions have lost ground in some long-time traditional centers of union power, such as construction, trucking, coal mining, and newspaper publishing, where new nonunion sectors have emerged. The one dynamic area of union growth, government employees, has not been sufficient to offset the declines. The major question as to the future scope of collective bargaining, and possibly the political power of the union movement, is whether union organizing can achieve a breakthrough in the white collar and professional field. This appears doubtful.

---

[4] Kazutoshi Koshiro, "High-Tech: Societal Conditions of Introduction of New Technologies and Imports on the Society of Japan," pp. 32–33. Paper prepared for the Symposium on High Tech and Society in Japan and the Federal Republic of Germany, September 7–11, 1987, in West Berlin, organized by the Japanese-German Center, with scientific support of the Science Center Berlin.

Limited Political Objectives

Employers in the United States regard our unions as very active politically. To some extent, political activism is growing. But activity has been limited to "getting out the vote" and lobbying for various legislative programs. President Leonard Woodcock's speech to the special collective bargaining convention on March 18, 1976, for example, dealt at length with the United Automobile Workers' political, as well as collective bargaining, objectives.

But it is also true that labor is far from united politically, tends to have political objectives closely related to collective bargaining objectives, and participates politically for the most part only by campaigns to elect its friends and defeat its enemies and through lobbying activity.

Nonideological

As well as having limited political objectives, U.S. unions have accepted the basic private-property character of the U.S. economic system. At times labor has had to contend with left-wing factions and unions, but there has never been widespread rank and file support for revolutionary movements or reforms, and traditional unionists have won out in these struggles.

Business Unionism

The previous two points may be put positively by categorizing U.S. labor as "business unionism." Unionism in Western Europe is as much a political as a collective bargaining institution. Unions in the U.S. have sought almost exclusively to achieve their objectives directly through collective bargaining. This traditional position may change as government continues to expand the area of social legislation.

Indeed, some unions in large metropolitan areas have recently attempted to use nontraditional methods such as public boycotts and protests to achieve their goals. This strategy has been called the "corporate campaign" and involves union attempts to persuade the members of the public or even company directors or shareholders that the company is guilty of some poor practice.

Decentralized Plant-Focused Collective Bargaining

Collective bargaining is essentially a decentralized process in the United States. Most bargaining is at plant level or at the corporate (or combination) level. There is very little industrywide bargaining with employer associations (trucking, railroads, maritime, clothing, coal mining, and basic steel have been exceptions). To be sure, craft unions in construction and other industries bargain with employer associations, but the associations are confined to limited geographical areas. Multiple-level bargaining is growing, but negotiation units in the United States remain quite decentralized. There is nothing approaching the degree of industrywide coverage of Western Europe. And regardless of structure, the focus of bargaining is very much on plant level issues.

Comprehensive Labor Agreements

The meaning and strength of U.S. unionism is best demonstrated by the comprehensive labor agreements that have been achieved. In no other country have unions negotiated the comprehensive written specification of the real terms and conditions of employment as in the United States and Canada. Contracts in Europe are quite limited in scope and specify minimum rather than actual terms. Informal controls by custom and practice are strong in the United Kingdom and legislative controls are growing in Europe, but the United States alone has developed a system of very comprehensive labor agreements.

Exclusive Jurisdiction and Public Policy

Public policy toward unions and collective bargaining will not be discussed in this introduction, but the fundamental features will be noted here. The passage in 1935 of the Wagner Act (the National Labor Relations Act) marked a major change in public policy. The act encouraged organization and collective bargaining (a) by requiring an employer to bargain collectively with a union that had won a certification election in an appropriate bargaining unit and (b) by prohibiting specified employer unfair labor practices.

Exclusive representation in appropriate bargaining units prohibits multiple union representation, a significant difference compared to many European countries. The prohibition of unfair labor practices means that basically an employer can remain nonunion only through majority support of his employees in a secret ballot election. Creating a public policy under which an employer may remain nonunion by developing constructive employee relations policies and thereby maintaining majority employee support is as fundamental to the system as requiring union recognition when the majority so wishes.

These characteristics point out the major dimensions of the U.S. system of labor relations. While only briefly noted, significant contrasts with Western Europe are quite marked. Western Europe also has institutional arrangements, particularly Works or Worker Councils and a system of Labor Courts not found in the United States. Most notably, however, the highly cooperative systems of industrial relations in Europe have been undergoing modification under the impact of rising militancy. Increased militancy has been perhaps more characteristic of Europe than the United States and has found expression in various forms of worker participation.

VARIATIONS IN UNION-MANAGEMENT RELATIONSHIPS

Collective bargaining is a complex process. One reflection of this complexity is the wide variation in union-management relationships. This section will introduce and discuss eight related considerations that underlie these variations. These eight points may be used by students as a beginning framework for the analysis of labor relations cases. Each point has significance in its own right. Analysis using these factors also will greatly assist the student in avoiding stereotyped views of union-management relationships. Analysis of relationships over time will also bring out their evolutionary dimensions. The eight points are as follows: (1) the nature and character of the union challenge and the management response, (2) the type of union-management relationship, (3) the interplay of power, problem-solving, and attitude-structuring processes, (4) the personal characteristics of top union and management leaders, (5) the internal political forces within the union organization, (6) the problems and opportunities inherent in the economic, political, and social environment, (7) the special characteristics of the industrial relations system in the industry involved in the case, and (8) the character of the management policies revealed by the case. Other variables could be identified, but these eight can serve as a useful beginning analytical framework.

Nature and Character of the Union Challenge and the Management Response

In the examination of the nature and character of the union challenge and the management response, it should initially be recognized that unions introduce a second power center within an organization. Unions thus crete an institutional challenge-response mechanism within an organization. While this mechanism is fundamentally a two-way street, the direct, initial challenge is typically by the union. The union challenges management in two major ways: first, a negotiation challenge, and second, a day-to-day grievance challenge. The negotiation challenge is the more dramatic of the two. Negotiation captures the newspaper headlines, particularly if a strike is involved. The labor agreement arises from the negotiation challenge. Labor agreements today are typically very complex documents that may be regarded as "constitutions" setting forth the web of rules governing the relationship between the parties. The central focus of the industrial relations system in the United States is the negotiation and administration of labor agreements which, as noted, have evolved into highly comprehensive documents in many relationships.

While the negotiation challenge captures the headlines, the grievance challenge is of at least equal importance to the employee, the union, and to management. Almost all labor agreements contain a formal grievance procedure with several appeal steps, and some 90 percent of such procedures provide for arbitration as the final step. Agreements also typically have no-strike clauses that bar the union from taking direct action during the term of the contract. Arbitrators, not infrequently college professors or lawyers, render "final and binding" decisions with respect to grievances that have not otherwise been resolved by the parties. Labor agreements thus usually provide a judicial-type procedure for the resolution of grievance disputes.

The union on behalf of one or more employees may effectively "grieve"—that is, initiate formal challenge, using the contractual grievance machinery, to management decisions or actions involving wages, hours, or working conditions that are alleged to violate the labor agreement. Since many important provisions of a labor agreement are stated in very general terms, the union can allege that a wide variety of management decisions or actions violates some provision of the labor agreement.

The importance of the grievance challenge to management is witnessed by the fact that many managements have seriously fettered their contractual rights and created noncompetitive costs by the cumulative impact of concessions made in the grievance procedure. Management may also make unwise concessions in response to the negotiation challenge, particularly in the face of an actual or potential strike. Negotiation disputes are seldom arbitrated and are thus ultimately resolved by a power process—the economic presence of strikes, boycotts, or picketing, or their threat on the perceived ability of the company to operate during a strike.

The union challenge in both dimensions may be more or less militant and may reflect a greater or lesser degree of union power relative to the employer. The nature of the management response also varies in important respects. It varies fundamentally in the degree to which management accepts the legitimacy of the union. It varies also in the degree to which management's response is policy-oriented. It varies in the degree of initiative that management takes in both the labor relations and human resources functions. Of great significance is the degree to which management develops a policy response to the union challenge, and, with respect to the grievance challenge, makes this response operational at the supervisor level.

Type of Union-Management Relationship

The nature of the union challenge and the management response establishes the type of the union-management relationship. These relationships can vary widely. Two contrasting company-union relationships come immediately to mind. In one, the chief union negotiator, subsequently the international union president, and the company industrial relations director had established over the years a relationship in which neither seriously considered the possibility of a strike. No issue was too difficult to be worked out between them. Both sides took reasonable positions in what was essentially a problem-solving atmosphere. To be sure, the company was strong financially and competitively, but settlements were not one-sided. The quality of the relationship and the openness of communication were impressive.

A second relationship was laden with conflict. The author's first contact with these parties was in the beginning stages of a negotiation in which they were on the verge of a strike over the issue of where to meet to conduct negotiations, compromising by meeting in various locations. There was no question that there would be a strike; the only question was what the issues would be. This relationship continued over the years with a great deal of day-to-day conflict and regular contract renewal strikes. Conflict was ultimately

ended when the company took a firm position that the plant would be closed at the next union strike. The company had other plants and the position was credible for that and other reasons.

Variation in the character of union-management relationships has led to the development of typologies. The late Professor Benjamin M. Selekman created an early one in a 1949 *Harvard Business Review* article, "Varieties of Labor Relations."[5] Selekman created eight types but primarily used four in his teaching: (1) conflict, (2) containment-aggression, (3) accommodation, and (4) cooperation. The characteristics of the relationships are rather self-evident. The cooperative relationship as used today denotes a formal union-management cooperative arrangement such as a quality of work life program. Containment-aggression indicates a relationship in which management attempts to contain the union within a role unsatisfactory to it and from which the union aggressively attempts to escape. Relationships of accommodation may be more or less positive in character. There may be a high degree of informal cooperation in such a relationship. Classification of actual relationships is somewhat arbitrary, but the types are meaningful. While management at any given time is concerned primarily with near-term issues, a most important long-term objective commonly is to move the relationship toward the positive end on the continuum.

Just as individual union-management relationships vary and change over time, there has been an evolutionary development in the character of union-management relationships since the beginning of the modern labor movement in this country. As earlier discussed, the modern labor movement began with (1) an organizational stage from 1932 or

[5] Vol. XXVII, No. 2, March 1949, p. 125.

1935 to roughly 1945. This was a conflict-laden period that saw the establishment of collective bargaining in the so-called mass production industries. An overlapping contract development stage (2) may be dated from 1940 to 1950, the year in which the first long-term contracts were negotiated in the automobile industry. Fundamental provisions of comprehensive labor agreements, such as their layoff systems, were developed during this period. Once these fundamental provisions had been agreed upon, a stage of growing accommodation (3) developed, which may be dated from 1950 to 1965.

Finally, since 1965 a stage of greatly increased complexity and collective bargaining and increased rank and file militancy (4) has developed. Complexity has grown both as to issues and the structure of collective bargaining. Basic steel, for example, has, until very recently, negotiated on three levels—local plant, corporate, and industrywide. At the local level in steel, automobiles, and other industries, thousands of local issues are negotiated.

The increased complexity of issues is particularly notable in the benefit area. Increased rank and file militancy is evident in rising grievance rates, in masses of local issues, in refusals to ratify contracts, in racial tensions, and in a general unwillingness to accept authority, whether it be management or union.

It is believed that most observers of the collective bargaining scene would accept the generalization that complexity has increased rather dramatically in recent years. Also, the emphasis in collective bargaining has shifted in meaningful degree to the local level and to many aspects of working conditions. What is of most importance from a student point of view is to recognize the decidedly dynamic character of the union-management relationship.

Interplay of Power, Problem-Solving, and Attitude-Structuring Processes

The third of the eight points is the interplay of power, problem-solving, and attitude-structuring processes. There is no union-management relationship that does not involve some degree of power bargaining and some degree of problem-solving behavior, but the mixture in which these processes are involved varies greatly. In an over-simplified but fundamental sense whether problem-solving behavior or power bargaining predominates depends upon attitudes and hence upon the type of union-management relationship. If the union challenge is militant and the management response of poor quality, the relationship is likely to be on the negative side of the continuum and the power process will predominate. And problem-solving behavior is fundamentally a very different process from power bargaining.

In a problem-solving atmosphere neither party comes to the negotiation table with a strongly committed, unilaterally defined position. Rather, problems are presented, options explored, and an attempt made to develop a solution that meets the fundamental goals of both parties. In other words, a problem-solving atmosphere is likely to result in an integrative solution to problems. The power-bargaining process is logically very different. Positions are defined unilaterally, and parties take committed positions. While the power process varies, the outcome tends to depend upon the power balance and the ability of each party to bluff, maneuver, and compromise. The objective is to win, not to find integrative solutions. Of course, real-life situations are mixtures of power and problem-solving processes and the power process may have a decidedly constructive outcome. There is such a thing as the creative use of power. Dispute resolution is discussed in a subsequent part of this introduction.

Personal Characteristics of Top Union and Management Leaders

The fourth point is an examination of the personal characteristics of top union and management leaders. A major conclusion of one of the authors growing from some three years of labor relations field research could be simply stated by the generalization that people do count. It became evident from this research that the nature of union-management relationships at the departmental, enterprise, and corporate levels frequently underwent dramatic change with changes in union or management leadership. In other words, the basic policies of organizations and organizational units are closely associated with the values, goals, and attitudes of leaders. For example, one extremely militant union leader outlasted twelve plant managers, none of whom was able to develop a satisfactory plant. The plant, in fact, was finally closed. Many other examples could be cited indicating the importance of leadership characteristics as determinants of the type of union-management relationships. While leaders are in part products of their environment, to some extent leadership constitutes an independent variable warranting special analysis.

Internal Political Forces within the Union Organization

A fifth point for analysis is an examination of the internal political forces within the union. Unions are inherently political institutions and cannot be expected to behave in accordance with business logic. The job of the union leader is of necessity to get elected and to stay elected. It is also true that most unions in the United States tend not to be ideological, nor are members class conscious. Union leaders have emerged from the rank and file membership and reflect their pragmatic views. Recently, however, there have been some individuals specially trained in labor relations emerging in leadership positions in unions. Moreover, in the mid-1980s several successful labor consultants, performing work for labor union clients, began sophisticated efforts to organize employees at various companies and to influence corporate policies.

Management leaders can save themselves much emotional tension if they can learn to accept the reality of the political character of the union as an institution. At the same time, dealing with a politically divided and fragmented union is typically extremely difficult. While sometimes management can play one faction of a union against another to its advantage, most managements prefer to deal with a stable union organization. Unfortunately, many management leaders expect totally uncharacteristic behavior from union leaders. Students must examine the political forces within a given union in its particular circumstances, and never forget the fact that unions are, first and foremost, political organizations.

Problems and Opportunities

A sixth point consists of the problems and opportunities posed by the economic, political, and social environment evidenced in the case. A company faced by difficult economic and competitive problems will inevitably bring difficult issues to the bargaining table. A company in a strong competitive and financial position has much more latitude in its accommodation to the goals and objectives of the union. The social environment in a particular plant may also have a decisive impact upon employee attitudes. Widespread or quite dramatic technological change can have a substantial impact upon union-management relationships. Student analysis must encompass these broader forces in the environment to achieve an adequate perspective on the issues faced by the parties.

Special Characteristics of the Industrial Relations System

A seventh point for analysis, which cannot be adequately developed in a brief statement, is an examination of the special characteristics of the industrial relations system in the industry involved in the case. Many industries have very special systems of industrial relations. Transportation, or construction, or the performing arts have highly specialized industrial relations systems. These (and other) industries are dominated by groups of craft unions, and work rules and work jurisdictions play a major role in union-management relationships. While there is a certain similarity in the issues in union-management relationships within manufacturing industries, generalizations developed from these industries may be quite misleading when applied to other industries and occupations. There is no simple way in which these differences may be captured, but there are unique features of the industrial relations systems of particular industries.

Character of the Management Policies

An eighth and final point for analysis consists of the management policies revealed by the case. The student should search for the basic managerial policies revealed by the case, for the general and substantive policies involved in the issues of the case, and for various implementing policies. The focus of case discussion is quite typically the weaknesses in existing policies and the wisdom of particular changes.

On a broader level, students should be able to learn a great deal from the different degrees to which management has been able to establish "management by policy" in the case at hand. All managements proclaim management by policy, but there are obvious differences in the degree to which different managements have made their policies operational at the supervisor level. There is no such thing as a policy cookbook that provides all the answers. Policies frequently must be general in character and a great deal of training is required to achieve reasonable consistency in their application.

Managements also vary a great deal in the relative importance they attach to personnel and labor relations administration and the degree of initiative that they exhibit. It is believed that currently the management of human resources is achieving a higher status in many organizations. Apart from the relative importance attached to industrial relations, some organizations exhibit much more initiative in this area than do others.

Finally, good labor relations and efficiency tend to be associated. Appeasement rarely pays off in labor relations. Of course it is easy to make statements such as these, but extremely difficult to achieve and maintain a constructive union-management relationship. Analysis of cases, keeping in mind the eight points that have been presented, should provide at least a beginning understanding of the complexities involved.

DISPUTE RESOLUTION WITH EMPHASIS ON POWER BARGAINING

As previously noted, the focus of the industrial relations system in the United States is the negotiation and the administration of labor agreements. A related characteristic of the system is the comprehensive nature of the labor agreements that have been created. The central focus in the administration of labor agreements is the operation of the grievance procedure. The type of union-management relationship involved will be reflected in the grievance process. In turn, the type of union-management relationship will depend upon the nature and character of the union challenge and the management response.

A relationship of accommodation will be characterized by a high degree of problem-solving behavior in the administration of the grievance procedure. A high proportion of grievances will be resolved by the parties at the lower steps of the grievance machinery—that is, at the first and second steps (first-line supervisor as step one and a step two appeal). Only a small proportion of grievances will be appealed to the higher steps, with a very few precedent-type grievances going to arbitration. To resolve a high proportion of grievances at the lower steps requires well-developed policies. This resolution also requires that first-line supervisors have substantial responsibility in the administration of policies. Lower-level grievance decisions will only be accepted without appeal if there is a low probability of reversal or modification at higher steps in the procedure. To achieve this result, first-step grievance responses must be of high quality. Such responses must stand up if the grievance is carried to the higher steps, including arbitration. To develop and to maintain a relationship of accommodation requires a high degree of policy orientation in first-step grievance responses.

The grievance process, however, will exhibit considerable departmental variation. Operating conditions and technology create many more employee relations problems in some departments than in others. Union representatives in some departments are decidedly more militant than in other departments. First-line supervisors are much more effective in dealing with employee problems in some departments than in others. Higher management should not expect equality in grievance rates among departments and should subject departmental variations to thorough analysis. The outstanding characteristics of grievance administration in a relationship of accommodation will be a highly developed policy response to grievance challenges and a high degree of problem-solving behavior by both parties.

A relationship of conflict or containment-aggression will be characterized by a relatively high grievance rate, inconsistent grievance responses, and the employment by unions of various pressure tactics. The use of power by the union will be exhibited in actual and threatened strikes—that is, strikes during the term of the labor agreement in violation of the no-strike clause in the agreement, slowdowns, work-to-rule behavior, and various other practices by which employees can bring pressure on management. Pressure tactics are likely to be associated with inconsistent grievance responses by management in a chicken-and-egg fashion. Of course, the tone of the relationship will be one of hostility. Again there will be departmental variations in the manner in which the grievance procedure operates. A history of hostility in the relationship is difficult to modify. Conflict in the day-to-day relationship is difficult to modify. Conflict in the day-to-day relationship will typically be reflected in conflict in the negotiation process. The reverse is also true; negotiation conflict will tend to carry over to the grievance process.

Power bargaining in the negotiation process, however, should not necessarily be associated only with a conflict-laden relationship. Negotiation is inherently a power process in that there are no judicial-type standards to apply in the resolution of "interest" disputes, nor is there a judicial-type procedure for the resolution of these disputes. However, negotiation can embody a high degree of problem-solving behavior. Also, negotiation disputes are less difficult to resolve in some than in other situations. For example, pattern-setting disputes are likely to be more difficult to resolve than pattern-following situations. Power bargaining is a varied as well as a complex process.

There is no simple manner in which the outcome of power bargaining can be stated. The outcome depends upon:

- The power balance between the parties
- The collective bargaining and competitive environment in which the bargaining takes place
- The character of the relationship between the parties and the degree of problem-solving behavior exhibited
- The quality and character of the planned use of power, the manner in which negotiations are conducted, and the dynamics of the power process as it develops

The realities of the power balance may or may not be subject to some degree of planned change during the course of a given negotiation, but at least the character of the resolution process for particular issues is dependent upon the options presented and upon the character of the negotiation.

In discussing the variables enumerated in this section, balance of power is all-important in negotiations in which one party has dominant power. In such negotiations the dominant party essentially dictates terms of settlement, at least as to the cost level and major terms, though usually not as to all terms of settlement. When the late James Hoffa of the International Brotherhood of Teamsters Union negotiated the first Central States Agreement he called the employers together, presented a proposed contract, and is reported to have opened negotiations by stating: "The sooner you sign this, the less trouble we'll have." Multiplant companies negotiating on a local plant basis with different unions and with different termination dates have, at least in particular situations, dictated terms of settlement and exhibited dominant power.

Dominant power is neither a simple nor an absolute concept. Dominant union power may be based on the ability to impose prohibitively high costs of disagreement on the company, frequently a situation in which the company fears permanent loss of market in taking a strike. But dominant union power often appears to imply a low *competitive* cost of agreement. Competitive cost of agreement (not absolute cost) is again complex in that analysis of cost impact requires short and longer-term judgments as to market consequences, including loss of market to substitute products. Also, dominant power by one party does not mean that the collective bargaining and the competitive character of the environment, the character of the relationship, and other variables will not influence the outcome. It does imply that the weaker party usually feels compelled to accept the dominant party's determination as to the appropriateness of settlement terms. Of course, if the issue is sufficiently serious, the weaker party may accept very high costs of disagreement.

Outcome in relatively balanced power

relationships is simply not subject to clear specification. Outcome depends on relative power and on the remaining earlier enumerated variables. An important danger from a management point of view is making a short-term cost concession that turns out to have high-cost long-term consequences. An example of this situation is the initial concession by the railroads of a fireman on diesel locomotives when there were almost no diesels. Competitive and environmental changes are continuously modifying relative and absolute cost, and the labor relations significance, of particular issues. Serious issue strikes, also, rarely have their causes simply in the events of the recent past. The GM-UAW 1970 strike resulted from issues and tension that had been building up between the parties over some ten years. The 1959 basic steel strike can only be understood in the light of the 1955 and 1956 negotiations, the changed economic environment after 1955, and indeed, earlier collective bargaining experience. The 1949 UE-International Harvester strike, which broke that union at Harvester, was the product of the entire history of the relationship intertwined with Communist strategy during World War II. If it is believed that the planned and strategic use of power can be a crucial determinant of the outcome of strikes and of many power negotiations, an intriguing assumption, the planning horizon must extend well beyond a single negotiation and must be updated continuously in the light of competitive and environmental changes.

Comment on the third enumerated variable, the character of the relationship, will be limited to noting that the power process does not necessarily exclude good accommodation between the parties and a significant degree of problem-solving behavior. The Steelworkers' Union and the companies, for example, have made extensive use of joint study and have engaged in a great deal of problem-solving behavior at the bargaining table. These parties deserve high marks for the constructive resolution of a series of difficult issues that had to be swept under the rug in the White House imposed settlement in 1965.

In subsequent years (1968, 1972, and 1974) many of these issues were resolved constructively through problem solving. For example, the demand for the right to strike over grievances was resolved through joint study recommendations resulting in a much-improved grievance process and in expedited arbitration. Probably the most notable achievement of these parties was the Experimental Negotiation Agreement to arbitrate unresolved issues that was adopted by the parties to eliminate the stockpiling of steel prior to contract termination dates, followed by extensive layoffs if no strike took place. This agreement was the product of joint exploration over a series of years. A consent decree and the revision of the seniority system, achieved in 1974 to meet equal employment problems, had its roots in the joint study of seniority issues by the Human Relations Committee of 1960–1964.

The complexities involved in the negotiation of the above issues are far too great to introduce here, but viable and creative resolution of complex issues has frequently been achieved by these parties through the use of joint study. Collective bargaining in steel, however, has most certainly been imbedded in both a political and an economic power process.

The fourth enumerated point—the quality and character of the planned use of power, the manner in which negotiations are conducted, and the dynamics of the power process—introduce much potential variation in the relationship and in the negotiation process. In some situations the relationship and process are heavily conflict-laden and may constitute major confrontations. Such situations may result from temporary problems and circumstances or may be ongoing characteristics of the relationship. In addition to serious differences in expectations and a wide economic gap, such parties are likely to become locked in battles over principle. Strong commitment to a principle may preclude constructive resolution of an issue. Negotiation becomes a victory or defeat confrontation. This is not to say that parties should not be guided by principle, but rather that they should be extremely careful as to the manner and degree of commitment in negotiation. Not the least of the dangers of extreme commitment, apart from the loss of flexibility, is that thought processes may become frozen and realistic analysis of issues foregone.

Power bargaining, however, need not be cast in the above mold. Outcome may reflect extensive planning, and well-developed options and fall-back positions, and the clear preservation of flexibility. The outcome of power bargaining may be as creative and as constructive as that achieved through problem-solving behavior. For example, the 1955 UAW negotiation with the Ford Motor Company, in which the union sought to achieve the guaranteed annual wage, had all of the characteristics of a potential major confrontation. The union was totally committed to the objective but not, wisely, to the manner of its achievement. At the same time the union developed a detailed guaranteed employment plan with the assistance of outstanding academic experts. This plan was widely and emotionally denounced by industry groups stating that competitive realities made it impossible for management to guarantee employment. As the negotiation approached its deadline, the company placed on the bargaining table its very creative Supplemental Unemployment Benefit Plan, based upon a number of important principles (some of which have since been eroded)

including limited liability. The union, and particularly Walter Reuther, its president, proved in fact not to have been so committed to their own plan as to be unable to accept SUB. A major strike was averted and an interesting form of income security created.

The above negotiation was power-bargaining and not problem-solving behavior at the bargaining table, but each party internally did a great deal of problem solving. It is reported that substantial differences of opinion were overcome within management and very substantial research carried out over a considerable period of time. Developing the detailed plan, and the principles upon which it was based, was highly creative activity. In a different situation, the author has observed during a three-year period a small company dealing with several strong unions achieve its planned objectives, including a change in representation of one group. Changing representation involved the careful use of National Labor Relations Board procedures. The writer, when first made aware of this company's objectives, felt that it would be impossible to achieve them. They were achieved in the course of three annual negotiations without a strike but with the very careful use of internal power considerations.

Peaceful resolution of issues in power bargaining implies, at its best, their constructive resolution in terms of the mutual objectives of the parties and the realities of the competitive situation. Viable solutions are required if they are to be permanent. It is also believed that constructive resolution of issues moves the relationship toward the positive end of the continuum of types of relationships. The resolution of issues and the nature of the relationship state a chicken-and-egg problem. The long-term management strategy implied in this statement is one of constructive uses of force to resolve particular issues and by so doing to improve the relationship between the parties. Rules of behavior for the negotiator, particularly with experienced negotiators, appear far less important than strategic long-term planning in the light of the power elements. Competitive and power realities in some situations, however, can create issues that defy at least short-run mutual resolution. Major confrontation at times appears inevitable.

Dispute resolution is in a sense the essence of collective bargaining. The character of the resolution process is closely associated with the relationship between the parties as well as the issues. Analysis of each party's objectives, sources of power, and strategy is required.

THE GRIEVANCE PROCESS

Two primary dimensions of the grievance process are worth introducing and discussing. They are (1) the grievance rate, and (2) the settlement step. In 1950 the corporate grievance rate at General Motors was some 12 grievances per hundred employees per year, certainly not a high rate. In addition, the parties achieved a high proportion of low-step settlements and arbitrated very few grievances. Labor agreement administration in 1950 presented a very constructive picture. By 1970, the corporate grievance rate had increased some threefold and was particularly high in assembly plants.

Discussion of the grievance rate should introduce the wide range of variables that tend to result in a relatively high or a relatively low grievance rate. For example, suppose the rate is approximately 25 grievances per hundred employees per year. This is not an especially high rate. In plants in which grievances are written at the first step of the grievance procedure, the only basis on which roughly compara-

ble data may be obtained, it is not unusual to find plants with grievance rates in excess of 50 grievances per hundred employees per year. The rate of 25 grievances is also not a particularly low rate. A rate under 10 grievances per hundred employees per year would commonly be regarded as a low rate, but a rate may be low for "good" or for "bad" reasons.

The second dimension relates to the settlement step. If there is a very low rate of settlements at the lower steps of the grievance procedure, then all denied grievances are appealed to higher steps. This fact can be used to discuss a series of important and related questions: (1) Why is it desirable to have a high proportion of lower-step, particularly first-step, settlements? (2) How can a high proportion of lower-step settlements be achieved? And (3) How can complaints be resolved informally thus avoiding formal grievances? Some very fundamental considerations as to the grievance process can be discussed.

The most basic question to be considered is why it is desirable to achieve a high proportion of lower-step settlements. There are at least three reasons for seeking to achieve this result. In the first place, both the status and the effectiveness of the first-line supervisor is enhanced if settlements are achieved by that supervisor or on terms established by discussion at that level. A second reason is to get agreement where it really counts—that is, through a meeting of minds among those most directly concerned. A third reason is to resolve the grievance within its operating context. Many grievances change their character as they go higher in the appeal procedure. Such grievances subtly change from operating problems, such as how hard an individual employee should work, to technical and legal problems to be resolved by "experts." For at least these reasons, resolving grievances at the lowest possible step should be regarded as an important corporate policy. Additional relevant considerations were discussed on pages 120–121.

To achieve a high proportion of low-step settlements requires that management be more flexible in its first-step discussion than at higher levels. In other words, employees must learn through experience that appeals do not result in more liberal settlements. Following this policy also requires first-step answers of high quality to achieve support if the grievance is carried to arbitration. Finally, if supervisors have a good idea as to the probable first-step answer if a formal grievance is brought, they have a good opportunity to resolve the potential grievance as an informal complaint. The manner in which the grievance process operates is of particular importance in today's climate of industrial relations.

Two contrasting departmental grievance situations in one plant of a large integrated steel company will move forward the analysis of the grievance rate and settlement process in a particular union-management setting. One department, the blast furnace department, had a very low grievance rate though it is interesting to note as a historical fact that at one time the department had an exceedingly high rate. Many variables, some environmental and some behavioral, have a bearing upon the achievement of a low rate: (1) the character of the union leadership, (2) the character of the management leadership, (3) a highly automated technology that creates relatively few employee problems, (4) various considerations that contribute to low racial tensions, and (5) some other considerations.

The contrasting situation, the bricklayer department, had an extremely high grievance rate. The primary reason for the high rate was the high degree of racial tension that was associated with various factors. But the same set of considerations

that produced a low rate in the blast furnace department, namely, leadership considerations and technology, combine with racial tension to contribute to the high rate. A great deal of understanding of departmental variation in grievance rates, and also of the grievance process, can be achieved by an analysis of such situations.

THE BROADER IMPACT OF COLLECTIVE BARGAINING

This section can deal only in a very general manner with the controversial and complex issues which will be raised. The purpose is much more to raise issues than to deal adequately with them. Three broad areas of impact—industrial relations, social change, and economics—are discussed below.

1. *Impact upon Employee Relations.* The public policy of encouraging the organization of unions and the development of collective bargaining has had its most constructive result in forcing employers to develop and apply improved employee relations policies. Of all of the resulting policies, progressive discipline and protection of employees against arbitrary or discriminatory discharge may well be the most fundamental.

Employee relations policies fostered by collective bargaining include rationalized (frequently evaluated) job wage rate structures; layoff systems heavily keyed to seniority, transfer and promotion systems with considerable seniority emphasis; standards for manning and workload; technological change protections; work assignment and scheduling; payment systems and their administration; the subcontracting of work; provisions with respect to safety and health; and various employee benefit plans. Examination of any labor agreement illustrates the extent to which collective bargaining has led to the extensive development of employee relations policies.

Another dimension to public policy has been the encouragement to management to remain nonunion by practicing enlightened personnel policies. Certainly some of the best employee relations policies to be found in the country are in some of these leading nonunion companies.[6] While the spread of unionism has been limited by these company policies and practices, employees have not been the losers. In both union and nonunion plants, the right to organize and bargain collectively has brought substantial social advance through improved employee relations policies.

2. *Instruments of Social Change.* Unions in the United States are difficult to assess as instruments of social change. Undoubtedly the major contribution they have made has been their direct and indirect impact upon employee relations policies discussed above. They have not sought nationalization of industry or other far-reaching reform. They have been, however, probably the most broadly based group in the country supporting a wide range of social legislation. Social legislation has expanded dramatically within the past decade in significant part because of union pressures and lobbying activity.

3. *The Economic Consequences of Unionism.* The economic impact of unions has remained controversial. Some dimensions of the issues involved will be discussed briefly under the following headings: (a) impact upon relative wages, (b) impact upon productivity and the trend of real wages, (c) impact upon fringe benefits, and (d) impact upon money wages and inflation.

[6] See Fred K. Foulkes, *Personnel Policies in Large Nonunion Companies* (Englewood Cliffs, NJ: Prentice-Hall, 1980).

a. *Impact upon relative wages.* There is now considerable consensus that unions raise the relative wages of their members. The classic study of relative wages is that of H. Gregg Lewis, reported in his 1963 book, *Unionism and Relative Wages in the United States.* In a review of a series of studies he found that unions had raised the relative earnings of their members as of the late fifties by 10% to 15%. Subsequent to Lewis's work, Leonard W. Weiss, Frank P. Stafford, Adrian W.Throop, and Michael J. Boskin have made studies. While the results of these studies vary somewhat, they consistently report that unions raise the relative earnings of members by amounts modestly in excess of the conclusion of the Lewis study.

On an unsophisticated basis an analysis of earnings data by Paul L. Scheible (*MLR*, March 1975) over the period 1966 to 1972 in more than 5,000 establishments indicated that compensation (wages and benefits) of unionized nonoffice workers increased 61 percent compared to 51 percent in the nonunion establishments. There is considerable indication that union members have improved their relative position since Lewis reviewed the data for the late 1950s.

b. *Impact upon productivity and the long-term trend of real wages in the country.* It has been contended that unions reduce the country's productivity and thus reduce the growth of real wages. Proof of this contention is not convincing even though it is clear that in particular industries for particular periods of time unions have inhibited technological change or otherwise retarded productivity. But historical studies of resistance to technological change, a classic subject for study in labor economics, indicate repeatedly that such policies hold firm only over the short run. Most recently we have witnessed a collapse of union power in the printing trades and the widespread introduction of advanced technology. A different type of situation has been the long struggle with work rules and technological change in the railroad industry. In a

1975 volume published by the Industrial Relations Research Association titled *Collective Bargaining and Productivity*, various authors review many aspects of the productivity topic. In Chapter 2, "Bargaining and Productivity in the Private Sector," Joseph P. Goldberg gives capsule summaries of the difficult problems unions and employers have had with technological change in association with changing patterns of demand in the following industries: automobile, steel, construction, retail food, printing and publishing, meatpacking, railroad, and long-shoring. All these industries were forced in various degrees to deal with absolute and/or relative declines in employment.

c. *Impact on fringe benefits.* Most students believe that collective bargaining has considerably hastened and broadened the development of fringe benefits—paid holidays, vacations, pension coverage, supplemental unemployment benefits, health and medical benefits, and other benefit contributions.

The above types of employee protections constituted only an insignificant proportion of total compensation in 1929. By 1986, fringe benefits constituted over 39 percent of total compensation. Benefit contributions have grown considerably faster than pay for time worked. Payments for benefits in larger companies frequently amount to over 40 percent of wages.

When one combines the relative wage position of union employees with the substantial benefit packages in major union contracts, the members of at least the major unions have achieved an elite position as to their material benefits.

d. *Impact upon money wages and inflation.* There is considerable consensus among economists that collective bargaining has some degree of "cost push" influence upon money wage rates and thus contributes to inflationary forces. Perhaps most economists would now agree with the late Professor Sumner H. Slichter that the wage-fixing arrangements in the society have an inflationary bias. There can, however, be considerable difference of opinion as to the significance of wage push in a particular period of inflation. For example, when the United States in the late 1970s had double-digit inflation it was through food and fuel price increases and rising import prices with the decline in the value of the dollar. Wages played no initiating role in this particular period of inflation. More generally, money wages in the United States have historically followed the country's productivity trend combined with increases in the cost of living. The wage-price spiral was not created by unions, and no methodology will assess satisfactorily the degree to which collective bargaining has accentuated the spiral.

FUTURE PROSPECTS FOR LABOR UNIONS AND COLLECTIVE BARGAINING

While a new surge of growth for unions in the private sector is possible, growth appears unlikely with current employee attitudes and with prevailing human resources policies and their administration. More probable is a continuation of existing conditions and current trends. The more important of these conditions and trends appear to be the following:

1. *Loss of membership.* The absolute decline in union membership of roughly 2 million has resulted in a drop in the organized proportion of the nonagricultural labor force from somewhat over 30 to 17%. With today's attitudes and conditions, if the union-sponsored "corporate campaigns" are not successful, it is doubtful that labor has any other strategies that might reverse this decline.

2. *A significant decline in strike activity.* While there have been a few highly publicized defensive strikes, strikes involving, 1,000 or more members have

consistently declined year by year from 1980 to 1986.

3. *Growth in union-management coopera-tion.* A substantial number of new coop-erative programs, particularly in quality of work life, have been developed. It will require unusual union and management leadership to sustain this activity.

4. *Aggressive management activity to stay nonunion and to keep new plants unorga-nized.* If nonunion management be-comes too aggressive, it risks a resurgence of successful union organization.

How these various trends ultimately will work themselves out in the increas-ingly competitive world economy of the future is beyond our ability to forecast. We anticipate further union decline but hesitate to speculate as to its extent. The challenge unions will face may lead to new creative strategies, such as further use of labor union consulting firms or the strate-gic use of union pension funds. It is possi-ble that, with the decline in union membership, management will be overly aggressive and thus assist unions in stem-ming future losses. While our belief is that unions will remain a significant force in our industrial relations system, the pres-sures under which both management and labor will be operating in an increasingly competitive world economy will be sub-stantial.

It can be noted, however, that in addi-tion to becoming decisive leaders and in-novators in human resources management, nonunion companies have added to their strength through more strategic plant lo-cation and, frequently, smaller plant size. Union strength has also been weakened by the dissolution of centralized bargaining systems such as those in basic steel and trucking. The decline in power and influ-ence of the union sector can also be ex-pected to lead to somewhat lower wage increases and to enhanced competitive strength.

RELATION TO THE CASES

It is not possible in the limited number of labor relations cases included in the text to expose students to a meaningful range of substantive issues. The cases therefore concentrate on union organization and on the grievance and the negotiation proc-esses.

The first case in this section, First Cen-tral Bank of River City, relates to an or-ganizing drive in the bank. An interesting first question for consider-ation is why the bank has not been orga-nized in the past. Discussion of this question will bring out a range of con-siderations bearing upon the topic, in-cluding the attitude of white collar em-ployees toward unionization. A second question is the degree to which condi-tions within the bank and within the broader environment have changed to make organization more probable. As a phase of this discussion, various weak-nesses in the bank's personnel policies and in its personnel organization will be brought out. Discussion of these weak-nesses will lead into the question of whether the changes have been sufficient to lead to the organization of the bank. Analysis of this question may be orga-nized roughly to parallel the topics (and points in the analytical framework and thus elaborate upon and reinforce the content of the framework) introduced in the first section of this book.

The case has been written at the time just preceding the final days prior to the representation election. This fact natu-rally gives rise to the two questions as to what the bank should do, and what it will do, during this remaining 30 days. The probable outcome of the election can be discussed relative to the action pro-gram undertaken by the bank. Discussion may be broadened to include factors bearing upon the potential for unionization among white collar and professional employees.

The next four cases—Groton Chemical Company (A) and (B), The Case of Patrick Donovan, and *The Washington Post*—are concerned with the negotiation and/or the grievance process. The Groton Chemical Company (A) and (B) and The Case of Patrick Donovan, are concerned with the grievance process. These cases assist students in understanding the dynamics of the contract administration phase of collective bargaining. In Groton Chemical, two grievances are presented. Although the cases are about alleged contract violations, they have broader implications than the individual problems presented. Unless the parties—namely the management and the union—can resolve the grievances to their mutual satisfaction, they will have to be decided by an arbitrator. Students, in groups of four to six, are generally put into union and management teams and after individual and team discussions are given two to three hours to resolve the grievances or agree to disagree with respect to their resolution. Student participation in this exercise will result in an enhanced understanding of and respect for the dynamics and pressures of the grievance and arbitration process. The Case of Patrick Donovan lets students evaluate the handling of a difficult employee relations issue. They must not only assess what has taken place to date but also recommend what action, if any, should be taken.

A very interesting labor relations case included in this section, *The Washington Post*, portrays the development of a major confrontation. Analyzing the dynamic and shifting elements of power bearing upon the development of this confrontation is a very rewarding exercise. *The Washington Post* and the other cases can give the student considerable perspective on power bargaining.

BIBLIOGRAPHY: THE CONDUCT OF LABOR RELATIONS

Beal, Edwin F., and James P. Begin. *The Practice of Collective Bargaining* (6th ed.). Homewood, IL: Richard D. Irwin, 1982.

Bok, Derek C., and John T. Dunlop. *Labor and the American Community*. New York: Simon & Schuster, 1970.

Colosi, Thomas R., and Arthur Eliot Berkeley. *Collective Bargaining: How It Works and Why*. New York: AAA Publications, 1986.

Dunlop, John T. *Dispute Resolution*. Dover, MA: Auburn House, 1984.

———. *Industrial Relations Systems*. New York: Holt, Rinehart, and Winston, 1958.

Freeman, Richard B., and James L. Medoff. *What Do Unions Do?* New York: Basic Books, 1984.

Gould, William B. *Japan's Reshaping of American Labor Law*. Cambridge, MA: MIT Press, 1988.

Heckscher, Charles C. *The New Unionism*. New York: Basic Books, 1988.

Katz, Harry C. *Changing Labor Relations in the U.S. Automobile Industry*. Cambridge, MA: MIT Press, 1987.

Kochan, Thomas A., ed. *Challenges and Choices Facing American Labor*. Cambridge, MA: MIT Press, 1985.

———. *Worker Participation and American Unions*. Kalamazoo, MI: Upjohn Institute, 1985.

———, Harry C. Katz, and Robert B. McKersie. *The Transformation of American Industrial Relations*. New York: Basic Books, 1986.

Kolb, Deborah M. *The Mediators*. Cambridge, MA: MIT Press, 1983.

Levin, Edward, and Donald Grody. *Witnesses in Arbitration: Selection, Preparation, and Presentation*. Washington, DC: BNA Books, 1987.

Lewin, David, et al. *Public Sector Labor Relations*. Lexington, MA: Lexington Books, 1988.

Lipsky, David B., and Clifford B. Donn. *Collective Bargaining in American Industry: Contempo-*

rary Perspectives and Future Directions. Lexington MA: Lexington Books, 1987.

McKERSIE, ROBERT B., AND RICHARD E. WALTON. *A Behavioral Theory of Labor Negotiation.* New York: McGraw-Hill, 1965.

SCHOEN, STERLING H., AND RAYMOND L. HILGERT. *Cases in Collective Bargaining and Industrial Relations: A Decisional Approach* (4th ed.). Homewood, IL: Richard D. Irwin, 1982.

SIMKIN, WILLIAM E. *Mediation and the Dynamics of Collective Bargaining.* Washington, DC: Bureau of National Affairs, 1971.

WENDLING, WAYNE R. *The Plant-Closure Policy Dilemma: Labor, Law and Bargaining.* Kalamazoo, MI: Upjohn Institute, 1984.

First Central Bank of River City

On a Monday in 1986, Jack Kramer, President of the First Central Bank of River City, received a formal notice from the National Labor Relations Board (NLRB) that an election would be held at the bank's offices in 30 days to determine if the employees wished to be represented by the International Metalworkers Union (IMU). The NLRB's notice was the culmination of a long unionization campaign that management had dismissed at first, but which had gathered momentum to an extent that had bewildered the bank's top management.

Jack Kramer immediately arranged for a meeting to be held the following afternoon with the bank's labor attorney, Philip Smith, and a group of the bank's executives, including Steven Johnson, Vice President of Human Resources. Kramer stated that at the meeting the actions taken so far by the bank and the union would be reviewed. Kramer also wanted to discuss whether management should take any further action during the 30 days remaining before the election.

This case was prepared by M. Thomas Kennedy as the basis for class discussion rather than to illustrate either effective or ineffective handling of an administrative situation. It was modified by Jeffrey L. Hirsch, Esquire. Reprinted by permission of the Harvard Business School.

River City

River City, which was located in a north-central state, had a population of approximately 210,000, a number that had remained relatively constant during the past ten years. The economy of the community, until 1984, had been dependent upon one large automotive parts plant, which was owned by one of the big three of the auto industry. In 1984, a Japanese company opened an electronics plant 20 miles from River City where about 350 people were employed.

A "Union Town"

During the mid-thirties River City had had some turbulent labor strife when representatives from the national headquarters of the International Metalworkers Union (IMU) tried to organize the workers in the local automotive parts plant. In the late thirties the automobile company had signed a national agreement with the IMU that included the River City plant. Since 1956 the agreement had included a union shop clause, which required all workers at the plant to be members of the union. Employment at the auto plant peaked in the mid-sixties.

The IMU had been successful in organizing a number of machine shops and other types of small plants in the area.

Because of this and the fact that the IMU was also active in local politics, River City was in fact sometimes described as a "union town." Although the union had not made an attempt to organize the employees at the new Japanese plant, rumor was that the union had planted some organizers inside the company to test the water. While the electronics plant paid substantially less than the local union auto plant, it offered employment security, job rotation and substantial training opportunities. Three quarters of the employees at the Japanese plant were women, performing light assembly work.

Most of the employees of the bank had relatives or friends who worked at the auto plant and were members of the IMU. In fact, some of the bank's employees were closely related to the local IMU leaders. Four years ago the IMU had been successful in organizing the maintenance workers at one of the city's smaller banks. However, unionization at the bank had not spread to the tellers and the other white collar employees and none of the employees in the other banks of River City were organized. The IMU had recently failed in attempts to organize white collar employees at the auto plant.

Two groups of professional employees in the community were represented by a union—the school teachers and the college professors. Most of the grade school and high school teachers in River City had been members of the National Education Association (NEA) for many years, which until the sixties had been a purely professional society that opposed collective bargaining. In the seventies, however, the NEA, pressed by the success of a rival organization, the American Federation of Teachers (an affiliate of the AFL-CIO that had negotiated sizeable wage increases for teachers in some of the major cities) decided to support collective bargaining. The business community of River City was surprised and disturbed when some of the local teachers who were members of NEA began to organize for bargaining purposes under the protection of the State Public Employees Relations Act. They were even more surprised when in an election the teachers voted to have NEA serve as their bargaining agent. They also had trouble understanding the unionization of professors at the local community college several years later. It was generally agreed, however, that the teachers secured large economic gains as a result of unionization and bargaining. The first faculty contract at the local community college also included substantial pay increases.

FIRST CENTRAL PAY AND BENEFITS

First Central was the oldest commercial bank in the River City community. It had assets of approximately $800 million, which was twice the size of the next largest commercial bank in the area. Founded in 1892, First Central had remained a single bank until about ten years ago, when it had begun an expansion program by acquiring a number of smaller banks in nearby communities. As a result, it had 18 offices, including two that had been opened recently in newly developed suburban shopping areas.

Although First Central was the largest financial institution in the area, it was not the salary pacesetter in the community or even in the banking sector. First Central salaries were generally 15 to 25 percent below those for comparable jobs at the auto plant. In addition, two of the smaller banks had somewhat higher salary scales than the First did. However, the First seldom lost employees to other banks, although recently there had been some movement of younger employees to the auto plant and to work in data processing departments outside the bank.

Everyone at the bank, except the maintenance employees, was on salary. The bank had a formal job evaluation program in which there were ten classifications, each with a maximum and minimum rate. At the lowest job level, the maximum salary was 13% higher than the minimum; at the highest job level, the maximum salary was 30% above the minimum for that level. Within the ranges, increases were granted each year entirely on the basis of merit. All increases, whether as a result of a change of job or merit evaluation, became effective January 1 of each year. If an employee was promoted during the year, he or she received the new job title immediately, but his or her salary was not changed until the following January 1. Management believed that its somewhat low salary scale was more than made up for by its excellent working conditions, its job security, and its liberal profit-sharing plan.

"Over the years," said one officer, "First Central was looked at as a prestigious place to work." The offices were clean and pleasant and the atmosphere was congenial and unhurried. Most of the employees were proud to say that they worked at the First Central. The established work week was 38 hours during a five-day period, although most employees averaged only 35 hours. For work between 38 and 40 hours employees received additional compensation at straight-time rates. Beyond 40 hours per week, a rate of time and one-half was paid.

The bank was also viewed as a place where employees with only a basic high school education, especially men, could rise to important positions. Almost one half of the Bank's officers, including all but three of its top officers, had terminated their formal education with graduation from local high schools. After joining the First, many of them had attended American Institute of Banking (AIB) courses at night, which the bank encouraged and financed. A job at the First represented an avenue for dependable young men with a high school education to become important leaders in the community. In recent years, many women, some with MBAs, had joined the bank in both technical and managerial positions.

Jobs at the First were valued also because of their security. Employees were never laid off and discharge for poor work or offensive conduct was extremely rare. Once a person was hired he or she could usually count on a regular pay check until retirement. In the past, this job security had been very important in a community where the major industry was known for heavy overtime one year and heavy layoffs the next. However, over the years, the bank's advantage had disappeared as the Union in the fifties and early sixties negotiated supplementary unemployment benefits (SUB) and in 1967 topped off its drive for income security by negotiating a Guaranteed Annual Income (GAI) that replaced the SUB. (Under GAI, employees with seven years of service were guaranteed 95%, but for a lesser number of weeks.) Employees who were discharged at the auto plant could usually count on strong support from the union.

Management at First Central believed that their employee benefit package was excellent. They thought the profit-sharing plan was highly valued and appreciated, especially by older employees. Under the plan, all employees became eligible for profit-sharing after two years of employment. The percentage of salary participation was the same for everyone, including officers. The bank contributed an amount each year that was equal to $7\frac{1}{2}\%$ of its net operating income after customary reserves and dividends. The amount was then divided by the combined yearly salaries of the plan participants and that percentage was applied to each employee's base annual salary to determine his or her share. During the 50 years that the plan had been in effect it had never paid less than 10% of salaries and in recent years it had approached the 15% limit set on such plans by the Internal Revenue Service.

The payments from the profit-sharing plan were not immediately available to participants. They were held in a trust fund that earned interest until the employee either quit or retired. Employees who left the bank before retirement received less than the full amount depending upon the number of years they had been in the plan. At retirement the employee received 100% of the balance in his account. The money became 50% vested at the end of 5 years. Employees were allowed to withdraw any amount in their account that exceeded two and one-half times their annual salary. If an employee died, the entire amount in his or her account was paid to the estate.

First Central was the only bank in the River City area that had a profit-sharing plan. The IMU had tried to negotiate a profit-sharing plan with the auto company for many years, and had finally succeeded in 1984. Only a few of the other smaller industrial and commercial companies in the area offered profit-sharing.

In addition to the profit-sharing plan, the bank had a death benefit plan, a pension plan and a salary continuation plan. The death benefit plan was intended to supplement the amount that the employee's family or estate would receive at his or her death from the profit-sharing plan. It paid $10,000 to employees whose salary was $20,000 or less. It paid nothing for people with salaries over $20,000.

The bank's pension plan required an employee to have 10 years of service to be eligible for retirement benefits. Early retirement was possible at age 55, but because of state and federal law changes, there was no mandatory retirement. The plan also provided for payments at any age after 10 years of service in case of total and permanent disability.

Determining one's pension benefit under the plan was a complicated matter. It involved three separate calculations. Most of the employees had difficulty understanding it, although the bank had prepared and published a booklet that explained it.

Benefits under the pension plan were not as liberal as those provided under the union contract at the auto plant, especially for the lower-paid employees and for those who wished to retire early. However, they were as good or better than those paid by any of the other banks in the area. Management felt that when the pension plan and the profit-sharing plan were considered as a package, they compared well with the auto company benefits.

The bank's salary continuance program, which became effective 90 days after an employee's hiring date, provided one week of sick pay during the first year and six weeks per calendar year thereafter. The six weeks were not cumulative. The weekly pay check was decreased for any day of absence other than those covered by the salary continuance program.

The bank provided two weeks of paid vacation after one year of service, and three weeks after five years of service. This was identical with the vacation plans of the other banks in the area, but not as good as the vacation plan at the auto plant. First Central also paid for ten holidays, as did the other banks in the area; the auto plant provided thirteen.

The bank gave its employees free checking accounts, free traveller's checks, and reduced interest rates on mortgages, car loans and personal loans. On mortgage loans, for example, there were no points and the rate was reduced by ¼%, thus enabling an employee to save a considerable amount of interest over the life of the mortgage.

The bank also enrolled all of its employees who were interested in the American Institute of Banking (AIB). The AIB conducted night courses in River City in bank accounting and numerous other subjects. Approximately 15% of the employees took one or more courses each year without cost.

Conspicuous by its absence in the bank's benefit package was an employer-paid hospital and medical-care program. The management had discussed such a program with Blue Cross–Blue Shield and several insurance companies and on several occasions had presented proposals to the board. Each time, however, they had been turned down because of the vigorous opposition of Fred Jackson, who was in his late eighties and controlled the largest block of stock in the bank. Jackson felt very strongly that the good of the country would be served best if each person paid his or her own medical and hospital bills. Because of rising medical costs and his respected position as a long-time community leader, Jackson was able to bring enough pressure to bear on the President and the other members of the board to block any employer-paid hospital and medical plan.

The bank did set up a group plan with Blue Cross–Blue Shield that was paid for entirely by the employees. Rates ranged from $125 for individual coverage to $250 per month for family coverage. The Bank agreed to deduct the amounts from the paychecks if employees desired. The majority of the employees participated in the group coverage and many of those who did not were covered elsewhere because their spouses worked in other companies that provided family coverage. A handful of employees belong to an HMO in River City.

The First Central was the only bank in the area that did not have a hospital-medical plan that was at least partly financed by the employer. At the auto plant the union had negotiated a very liberal hospital-medical plan, the cost of which was borne entirely by the company. The great majority of the other industrial and retail companies in the area also had plans in which the employer paid all or part of the costs.

Human Resources

Steve Johnson had been appointed Vice President of Human Resources about ten months earlier. Prior to that time the human resources responsibilities had been handled by an officer of the Bank who had other major responsibilities. Johnson had no previous training or experience in human resources work or union organizing campaigns. Among the bank officers he was relatively young both in age (32) and service, having been hired only five years earlier. Before coming to the First he had worked with a big Chicago bank. At the First he had served as Vice President of Mortgages and manager of a branch before becoming head of human resources.

UNION ACTIVITY

The first indication of union activity at the bank occurred one Sunday morning. John Sampson, a guard at the main office discovered that membership cards had been distributed to the various teller stations on the first floor, the desks in the bookkeeping department on the second floor, at the switchboard and in the ladies lounge. Sampson reported the matter to the Director of Security, who, in turn, reported it to Steve Johnson. Johnson called Phil Smith, the bank's attorney, and upon his advice it was decided to collect and hold all the cards.

On Monday morning Jack Kramer, president of the bank, called Johnson to his office. Kramer, who was scheduled to retire in less than a year, had been president for fifteen years. He had spent his entire working career with the Bank. Starting out as a clerk, immediately after graduation from River City High School, he had worked his way up through the ranks to his present position. He had good reason to be proud of the progress that had been made at the bank during his presidency; from a single office it had expanded to the point where it now had 18 branch offices. Total assets and profits had increased far more rapidly than was the case for any other bank in the area.

Johnson showed the cards to Kramer and told him where they had been found. Kramer said that he and the other members of management with whom he had talked had no idea who might have been responsible for distributing them. Kramer did not appear to be disturbed. Johnson was surprised when Kramer said, "Steve, I don't think we should get too excited about this. After all, in a place like River City, I suppose it's inevitable that we will eventually have to deal with a union. Let's keep it all low key."

Management never was able to determine who was responsible for the distribution of the cards and the only action that was taken was to tighten security. Four months passed without any outward indication of further union activity and management came to feel that the incident could be dismissed as the act of a single disgruntled employee. Supervisors in the areas where the cards were found reported no evidence of any organizing activity. Then one Monday morning a number of employees reported to their supervisors that they had received a letter from the IMU addressed to their homes. Management soon learned that the letter had been sent to all of the employees. Evidently one of the employees had provided the union with a computer printout of employee names and addresses. The union letter is reproduced as Exhibit 1.

After reading the letter, Kramer scheduled a meeting of the top management people and Attorney Smith to discuss the matter. At the meeting Smith explained that the union would have to get 30% of the employees to sign membership cards before the NLRB would hold an election. He added that in his experience the IMU would not ask for an election unless it had at least 60% or 70% of the employees signed up. Those present at the meeting expressed surprise that the union felt it had enough interest among the employees to warrant sending out the letter. Management believed that only a very small number of the bank's employees were involved and that the union had no chance of getting 30% to sign cards. It was agreed that for the time being management would take no special action except to gather as much information as possible. Johnson was appointed by the president to serve as clearinghouse for any facts or rumors about unionization that might become known to any of them.

Approximately one month after the union's first letter it addressed a second letter to the employees. The second letter read, in part, as follows:

> Your response to our first letter was very encouraging. As a result an informative meeting will be held next Thursday evening at the River City Hotel at 8:00 P.M.
>
> We will tell you what we believe you can gain through collective bargaining and will answer any questions you may have.

The meeting was held as scheduled and management learned that between 100 and 125 of the bank's 350 employees had attended. The group who attended consisted largely of employees from the bookkeeping, personal loan, and main office tellers departments. Not all those who attended appeared to be in sympathy with unionization.

Although salaries, individual grievances and other matters were talked about at the meeting, the discussion centered around two major topics: (1) the pension and profit-sharing plans and (2) the lack of an employer-paid hospital-medical plan. Several of the older employees spoke favorably about the pension and profit-sharing plans and indicated that they were afraid that the bank might decrease the pension benefits and eliminate profit-sharing if it had to bargain with the union. The union representatives assured the employees that the union would never agree to changes in the pension and profit-sharing plans that would be to the detriment of the employees. Instead they said that the union would insist that the employees receive even better pensions and a larger share of the profits, too much of which, they declared, now went to the owners and to the management.

The issue that seemed to be of most concern to the majority of the employees at the meeting was the lack of an employer-paid hospitalization-medical plan. It was reported that the union leaders really played up this issue, saying that they found it hard to believe that in the 1980s a major bank like First Central could have so little interest in its employees' welfare as to refuse to cover them with hospital-medical insurance. They pointed out that even the smaller banks in the community provided their employees with such insurance. They showed the employees a copy of the employer-paid plan that they had negotiated for the employees at the auto plant. They also referred to a number of other contracts that the union had negotiated with other companies in the River City area that contained employer-paid hospital-medical plans. They said they knew of no contract that the IMU had negotiated in recent years in which they had not secured an employer-paid health plan. The employees were told that if they chose the IMU as their bargaining agent, the union would insist that the bank foot the entire bill for a good hospital-medical insurance plan. One of the union representatives stated that the value of this benefit alone would more than make up the cost of union dues, which were generally two hours of pay per month.

As reports of the union meeting reached Johnson, he became convinced that the bank was facing a serious unionization threat. He proposed to Kramer and to the other officers that the bank engage in an active "information and education" campaign to convince employees not to join the union. Attorney Smith also urged a very aggressive campaign, including a series of letters by President Kramer and a meeting of all the employees. It was decided that Johnson should work out a series of questions and answers with the attorney and that Johnson should read these to the employees in small groups (see Exhibit 2 for the list of questions and answers). Attorney Smith cautioned Johnson to be careful not to promise the employees anything as a result of not becoming unionized or to threaten them with anything if they did. "If you promise them anything or threaten them with anything the NLRB could find us guilty of an unfair labor practice and might even order us to bargain with them on the basis of their signed cards without ordering an election, assuming they have a majority of the employees signed up," Attorney Smith warned.

Group Meetings

Johnson discovered, after he had presented the questions and answers in the small group meetings, that the employees were interested primarily in discussing the bank's wage and benefit policies, which to his surprise most of them knew little about. (The bank had never developed an employee handbook or a pamphlet explaining the various benefit plans.) The newer employees seemed to be better informed than many of the older employees because during their recent employment interviews and orientation sessions the policies and plans had been explained. Johnson believed that the small group meetings were helpful, but came away from some of them convinced that there was a large employee group that really wanted the Union.

Johnson felt that he got a very cool reception in several particular departments. One of these was the data-processing center, which had been established in the bank's main office building six years earlier. In addition to the bank's work it did some outside work for customers. Although a few of the Bank's former employees had moved into jobs in the data center, the great majority of the thirty employees were new hires. Johnson had the impression that these employees looked upon themselves as a group separate and apart with very little loyalty to the bank. He said:

> Their loyalty is first to the equipment, then to the system, and only after that to the bank. They are a lot closer to the data processing people at the auto company and other companies and banks in the area than they are to employees in the other departments here at the First.

During the six years of its operation there had been a considerably higher turnover of employees in this division than in most other departments. Johnson felt that the bank served as a training school for employees in data processing who, once trained, moved to the auto company or in some cases even to out-of-town companies and banks, where they earned more money and better benefits.

Johnson addressed the data-processing employees in four groups. At each of these meetings the question of wage rates for similar jobs at the auto company was raised by the employees, who seemed to be very well informed. Johnson admitted that the bank's rates were not as high as those paid by the auto company, but said that in some cases this was due to the fact that there was a difference in the skill requirements of the jobs. Moreover, he said that if they took into account the whole pay package, including the profit-sharing plan, he believed the pay was as good or better at the bank. However, Johnson left the meetings feeling that the employees were unconvinced. He felt that all of the data processing employees were interested in the union and many of them were strongly interested.

Another area where Johnson felt hostility was in the consumer loans department in the main office. This division of the bank had been unusually successful compared with similar divisions in the other banks in the community, primarily because of the ability and drive of Frank Locklear, who had become vice president of consumer loans ten years earlier. Johnson was aware that although Locklear's performance in terms of profits to the bank was outstanding, he was abrasive and ineffective in dealing with employees. In the short time that Johnson had been vice president of human resources, several of the 35 employees from consumer loans had discussed with him actions by Locklear that they believed to be very unfair and autocratic. On one occasion an employee complained that she had been demoted from an interviewer to a loan teller without any explanation or warning. Locklear had simply attached a note to her time card that said, "As of today you will work as a Teller instead of an Interviewer." Turnover in this department was higher than anywhere else in the bank, including the data center. In the past year 35% of the employees had quit or transferred to jobs elsewhere in the bank. Johnson had discussed the problem with President Kramer and had recommended that some action be taken. Kramer had replied, "I know Frank has problems with people, but with his performance on loans I think we'll just have to live with his people problems." Johnson came away from the meetings with the consumer loan groups convinced that 100% of them favored the union.

When Johnson returned to his office from one of the question and answer meetings, Harold Newell, Vice President of Branch Operations, was waiting for him. Newell reported to him that a number of the branch office employees had informed him that the three assistant auditors were engaging in union organizing activities in the branch offices while ostensibly instructing employees on the use of a new computer. According to Newell's informants, the auditors spent only about 15 minutes explaining the new computer procedures and the remainder of the two-hour session talking about the advantages of having a union. At the end of the meetings they had passed out union membership cards. By the time Newell received the information, meetings had already been held by the auditors at about half of the branches. Newell cancelled the remaining meetings.

The news that the assistant auditors were engaging in union organizing activities came as a shock to the officers of the bank who had always considered them as part of the management team. It was agreed that Newell and the cashier should meet with the auditor and the three assistants. At the meeting the assistants admitted that they favored a union and had been trying to get other employees to join. Following the meeting Newell discussed the matter with Attorney Smith, who said it was his opinion that the assistant auditors were a part of management, and, therefore, that union activity by them was not protected under the National Labor Relations Act. Newell then recommended to Kramer that the three assistant auditors be discharged. However, Kramer thought that the discharge of the internal auditors would raise serious questions in the community regarding the financial integrity and soundness of the bank. As a result, no disciplinary action was taken. The meetings at the other branch offices were rescheduled at times when Newell could be in attendance and the assistant auditors limited their discussions to an explanation of the new computer system.

Two weeks after the union meeting at River City Hotel, Robert Markel, the International Representative of IMU, called on Johnson and informed him that 80% of all the bank's employees had signed up with the union. He offered to produce the signed cards for signature comparison. Johnson informed him that he would prefer not to see the cards, and had "an honest doubt" that the union really represented the majority of the employees. Markel then informed Johnson that the union would petition the NLRB to hold a representation election.

A week later, the union sent another letter to the employees, which is reproduced as Exhibit 3. Copies of the letter were given to management by several of the employees. A meeting of management representatives was then called, when it was decided that the president should reply. Kramer's letter, which was the first written communication from anyone in management to the employees on the union matter, is reproduced as Exhibit 4.

Two weeks after sending out its first letter to employees regarding the union-organizing drive, the bank filed with the Internal Revenue Service a request to institute a hospital-medical plan to be paid entirely by the bank. (Fred Jackson, the major stockholder and influential director of the bank who had opposed such plans had died eight months earlier.) Following the filing, announcements were sent to all department heads, supervisors, and branch managers informing them that the bank was instituting a free hospital-medical plan subject to approval by the necessary government agencies. No letter was sent directly to the employees on the hospital-medical plan at this time, but they were informed about it by their supervisors.

Two weeks after the bank announced its intention to assume the cost of a hospital-medical insurance plan the union filed a petition with the NLRB requesting a representation election. At the same time the union filed an unfair labor practices (ULP) charge against the Bank claiming that the promise to institute a hospital-medical plan paid by the employer was for the purpose of avoiding unionization. The charge, as filed by the union with the NLRB, read as follows:

> The above-named employer, by its officers, agents and representatives, has, by establishing a hospitalization plan for employees and their dependents and other acts and conduct, interfered with, restrained and coerced its employees in the exercise of the rights guaranteed in Section 7 of the Act.

As a result of this charge, the NLRB held in abeyance the union's requests for a representation election.

Four weeks later a hearing on the ULP charge was held before an officer of the NLRB. The bank produced witnesses and correspondence to show that work on the hospital-medical plan had been undertaken before the bank was aware that the union was attempting to organize its employees. Attorney Smith argued that if the bank had not proceeded to develop the plan and try to place it into effect according to its original schedule, then indeed the Bank would have been guilty of unfair labor practices. He requested that the hearing officer find that the union's charge was without merit.

One month later the Bank received a notice from the NLRB that the union had withdrawn the ULP charges. The president then addressed a letter to all employees informing them that the new hospital-medical plan would become effective in two months. (See Exhibit 5 for a copy of the president's letter.)

At about this time, three employees at the bank's main office were observed by a supervisor in a part of the bank other than where they worked, handing out union membership cards to other employees during working hours. The officers of the bank were surprised when they learned that one of the employees was Esther Jones, who had an excellent record of employment with the bank for the past 29 years. A review of her personnel record showed the following facts:

> Unmarried and supports her mother, hired 29 years ago as a clerk upon recommendation of Jack Kramer who attended same church; excellent attendance record; interested in advancement, took AIB courses at night and worked hard; advanced over time to better and better jobs; eight years ago placed in charge of general ledger bookkeeping that required her to bring together all the data from the main office and the branches and deliver it to the president by noon each day; two years ago bank computerized the general ledger and Esther was

moved to the savings department where she maintained controls over various matters; savings department job was important and bank maintained her prior salary; president still called upon her for data from time to time, but not every day; two months ago as a result of computerization of the savings department Esther was moved to the job of collection clerk with no decrease in salary; works with two other collection clerks who receive considerably less pay; still has desk at back of main floor but no reason for president to see or talk to her now.

Two of the vice presidents discussed the incident with Esther. She admitted that she had passed out the cards and urged employees to join the union. She agreed with the officers that it was not fair to the bank for her to do this during working time and assured them that she would not do it again. Attorney Smith recommended that Esther and the two other employees who were observed passing out the cards be discharged. However, President Kramer decided that it was better not to take any disciplinary action other than to deliver a warning. Esther continued to be interested in the union, but limited her activities to non-working time.

Two weeks after the withdrawal of the ULP charge the NLRB informed the Bank that it was proceeding with the union's request for a representation election. The bank refused to follow the informal procedure, but instead requested a formal hearing.

At the hearing, which was held a month later, the matter of which employees should be included in the bargaining unit, and, therefore, be eligible to vote, was discussed. Much to the surprise and pleasure of management the union did not ask to have the watchman and the other building and maintenance employees included in the unit. Management argued to exclude the secretaries of the president and the human resources vice president on the

grounds that they had access to confidential material; the union agreed.

The greatest difference of opinion developed regarding supervisory employees. The National Labor Relations Act provides that supervisors, as it defines them, should be excluded from the bargaining unit. (See Exhibit 6 for provisions of the National Labor Relations Act relating to supervisors and professionals.) Some of the employees whom the bank had given the title of supervisor did not meet the requirements as set forth in the Act. The bank argued that most of the branch managers and the purchasing agent should be included in the unit, but that the auditor and the assistant auditors should not be included. After discussing the content of the above jobs it was agreed that three of the branch managers, three of the assistant branch managers, the three assistant auditors, and the purchasing agent should be included and others excluded. However, the election was delayed because the bank challenged the validity of the union's signature cards and moved that the election petition be dismissed.

After the hearing the union sent another letter to the employees explaining the delay and assuring the employees regarding the profit-sharing plan. (See Exhibit 7 for a copy of this letter.) Two weeks later the hearing officer denied the bank's motion to dismiss and his decision was approved by the regional director of the NLRB. The bank then filed a petition for review with the NLRB that was denied two weeks later. The regional director of the NLRB then set a date for the election and sent formal notices to the bank and the union. The election was scheduled for a date almost exactly five months after the union had filed for an election. The election date was also a few days after the new hospital-medical plan would become effective.

On the Monday afternoon on which the

bank received the election notice, Steve Johnson discussed the matter briefly with President Kramer. They agreed it would be wise to have a meeting the next afternoon with Attorney Smith and the other senior executives of the Bank in order to plan management's strategy and tactics during the thirty days that remained before the election. Kramer informed Johnson that he would expect him to present a tentative plan of action that could form the basis for discussion and final decision.

THE FIRST CENTRAL BANK OF RIVER CITY STUDY QUESTIONS:

1. Why has the First Central Bank of River City not been organized to date?

2. Why are some of the employees now interested in collective bargaining? Have conditions so changed that the bank will probably be organized? Develop a list of all of the reasons why a felt need for a union arose among employees at the First Central Bank of River City. In what ways was the bank remiss in its "management of human resources?"

3. What is your assessment of the bank's response to the organizational campaign? What would you have done differently?

4. If you were an employee in the defined unit, how would you vote in this election, for or against the union?

5. If the bank wishes to remain nonunion, what actions should management take during the remaining thirty days prior to the election?

INTERNATIONAL METAL WORKERS UNION
Local 76

TO THE EMPLOYEES OF FIRST CENTRAL BANK OF RIVER CITY
(MAIN OFFICE AND BRANCH BANKS)

Greetings:

A considerable number of your co-workers have shown an extreme interest in the desire to unite for the good of all the First Central Bank employees in River City and area branches.

You have the right by law from the National Labor Relations Act to self organize to form, join or assist labor organizations for the purpose of collective bargaining. This is exactly what your co-workers are attempting to do.

In order to petition the National Labor Relations Board (N.L.R.B.) for an election, we must have a sufficient number of the enclosed cards signed! These signed cards are held in strict confidence and no one but a staff member of IMU or a field representative from the N.L.R.B. will see these cards.

No initiation fees or monthly dues are payable until an N.L.R.B. election is won. This is accomplished by each of you voting by secret ballot to accept IMU as your collective bargaining representative along with a committee of employees of your own choosing.

The professional employees of banking institutions are long overdue in exercising their right to self organize. You must realize that you are way behind professional employees pertaining to wages, vacations, pensions, paid hospitalization and accident and sickness insurance.

In just a few short years of self organizing, professional teachers of America have made substantial gains in all of the aforementioned benefits. You have that same privilege guaranteed by federal law. For your own benefit, take the first step as your fellow co-workers have and sign the enclosed card, which is held in strict confidence, and return it to IMU, Box 72, River City.

An extra card is enclosed for any of your fellow employees who wish to sign cards but did not receive a copy of this letter.

IMU ORGANIZING COMMITTEE

<u>Questions and Answers</u>

A number of questions have been asked about what would happen if a union were to get in. Here are the answers:

1. Question: Is there any real reason why you need a union to speak for you and to pay dues to a union?

   Answer: No. You are always free to speak to any officer of the bank about wages, working conditions, or other conditions of employment without paying dues to a union.

2. Question: If the union wins, would there automatically be a contract with the union?

   Answer: No. The bank doesn't have to sign any contract that is not in the best interests of the bank. There is no law to force the bank to agree to anything the union asks and there can be no contract until we agree.

3. Question: Under a union, would you automatically get the things that the unions promise?

   Answer: No. The bank doesn't have to grant any request which the union makes. Our bank would agree only to those things that it is willing and able to grant which are in the bank's opinion in its best interests.

4. Question: With a union, would the employees go out on a strike?

   Answer: We don't know; but if the bank cannot agree to grant the things that the union has been promising or that the union wants for its own interests, the only way the union can try to force the bank to do these things is to get the employees to go out on a strike. It is easy for the union to make all kinds of big promises to you, but these are not always easy to fulfill.

5. Question: If the union calls a strike, can I be replaced?

   Answer: Yes. If the union makes you strike to try to force the bank to agree to the union's demands, under the law an employer is free to continue to operate and to replace the strikers. In addition, if our customers do not wish to be bothered with a strike, they can decide to end their relationship with us. Without customers, where are we?

6. Question: Will I have to join the union if it gets in here?

    Answer: It is hard to tell what may happen if the union gets "in." Most unions try to force a company to sign a contract which requires all the employees to become union members or pay dues. Many strikes have been called to get just this kind of contract.

7. Question: If the union calls us out on strike, will we get paid while the strike is going on?

    Answer: NO. If you don't work, you won't get paid. An employer won't pay your wages and neither will the union.

8. Question: Why is it so often said that the employees lose by a strike even though they get a wage increase?

    Answer: An employee who earned $400 a week loses $2,000 pay during a strike of only 5 weeks. If at the end of the strike she got a 10% increase, how long do you think it would take to make up that kind of loss?

9. Question: If you did vote the union in and try it, and find that you don't like it, can you get rid of the union?

    Answer: Not easily. It is a lot harder to get a union out than it is getting one in. If you vote the union in, you will probably be stuck with it as long as you work here.

10. Question: Would the union get us higher wages, additional benefits, and more job security, or is it possible that we could lose something we now have?

    Answer: The union has probably told you that you have everything to gain and nothing to lose by voting it in. This is not true. The union can't guarantee you any new and additional benefits.

11. Question: Can a union do anything or punish an employee because he opposes it, speaks out against the union, or refuses to let them in him home?

    Answer: No. It is a violation of the Federal Law for a union to even attempt to discriminate against an individual in his job or pay, or to attempt in any way to punish an employee because he opposed the union. The right of the employee to oppose a union is guaranteed by Law. It is the employee's right and duty to make his own decision and make that decision known if he should so determine.

12. Question: IF I SIGNED A UNION CARD, CAN I VOTE AGAINST THE UNION
                IN AN ELECTION?

    Answer: YES, IF THERE IS AN ELECTION YOU CAN VOTE AGAINST THE
                UNION. IT DOESN'T MAKE ANY DIFFERENCE WHETHER YOU SIGNED
                A UNION CARD OR WENT TO THE UNION MEETINGS OR EVEN PAID
                THE UNION MONEY. WHAT YOU HAVE SIGNED OR HAVE TOLD
                ANYONE WOULD NOT COUNT IN ANY ELECTION. YOU WOULD HAVE
                AN OPPORTUNITY TO VOTE FREELY AND SECRETLY UNDER GOVERN-
                MENT SUPERVISION. IT IS ILLEGAL FOR A UNION TO THREATEN
                OR FORCE AN EMPLOYEE TO VOTE ITS WAY.

INTERNATIONAL METALWORKERS UNION
Local 76

For the benefit of the employees who were unable to attend our last meeting, I would like to point out the major question that arose during the meeting and that is of the current profit-sharing pension program.

There is absolutely <u>no</u> way that you can jeopardize this benefit or any other benefits that you presently enjoy by self organizing. Your pension program is currently available to all employees of the Bank including some twenty (20) or so officers who are not eligible by law to join with you in a collective bargaining agreement.

The monies in this program have been set aside for pension benefits and your employer has already received a tax exemption by meeting Internal Revenue Service requirements. The pension money which has been set aside cannot be used for anything else but pension benefits. Furthermore, the federal law forbids your employer from reducing any of your present benefits for the reason you chose to self organize.

Organization can improve on benefits in two ways. First, eliminate those not in the bargaining unit who take a lion's share from the fund, and second, negotiate higher benefits for those in the bargaining unit.

Unfortunately, a few employees at the First Central honestly believe they can gain more on their own. Take a good look at these individuals and see where this has led them. What have they gained? Even your employer is distrustful of them. However, he would use them to his advantage. What happens when they are no longer useful to him? In unity there is strength and in strength and unity there are rewards at the bargaining table with the employer.

TO: ALL EMPLOYEES — 6/7/86

I understand each of you received a letter signed by an international representative of the IMU, which states as follows:

> "Unfortunately, a few employees at the First Central Bank honestly believe they can gain more on their own. Take a good look at these individuals and see where this has led them. However, he would use them to his advantage. What happens when they are no longer useful to him? In unity there is strength and in strength and unity there are rewards at the bargaining table with the employer."

The statement that we are distrustful of any of our employees is absolutely and unqualifiedly false and untrue. If we were distrustful of an employee, he or she would not be working for us.

You have the right to deal with us directly without the intervention of a union on any matter, both with respect to either present benefits or the consideration of any new or additional benefits.

It has certainly not been necessary in the past to have a union intervening on your behalf and we would hope that our past record would indicate that a union is neither needed nor necessary in considering future benefits.

The letter states that we would use employees so long as they are advantageous to us and asks what happens when they are no longer useful to us. All of our employees are valued by us and are useful to us. We do not use any of you in the manner suggested in this letter.

In fact, these statements are outrageous and show to what lengths this union will go to get you to sign cards.

We wish to make it perfectly clear, however, that you have the right to join a union. You have just as much right not to join. No union can guarantee you economic benefits. If a union wins an election, the bank is not required to sign any contract that it feels is not in its best interest.

In their letter, the union refers to our profit sharing plan. Both our pension and profit sharing plans are purely voluntary on the part of the bank, and as you know, both are totally paid for by the bank. We hope to continue them, but there is nothing in the law to require us to do so if we feel economic considerations warrant a change. If you vote in favor of a union, all of these items are subject to negotiation.

I trust that each of you will give all these matters your serious consideration.

                                        Jack Kramer
                                        President

TO: ALL EMPLOYEES

We are writing this letter in order to report on the progress to date of our efforts to install a fully paid hospital and major medical plan of all of our employees.

You will recall that you were advised of the bank having to obtain clearance from the Internal Revenue Service prior to the introduction of such a plan.

After consultations with appropriate Internal Revenue Service officials, it has been determined that the earliest date when such installation would be permissible is January 1, of next year. This year's salary increases already granted and the increases in profit sharing and pension allocations prevented any earlier implementation of the new hospital and major medical plan.

We are pleased, therefore, to inform you that we will be instituting a fully paid hospital-major medical plan covering both you and your dependents and under which you as an employee make no contribution, approximately two months from the date of this letter.

Various proposals from insurance companies and Blue Cross-Blue Shield have been under study. As soon as complete details have been worked out, we will be sending them to you.

We are pleased that we are able to offer this protection to you because we recognize the pressures which unforeseen medical expenses can place upon family budgets.

Sincerely,

Jack Kramer,
President

Exhibit 6 Provisions of the National Labor Relations Act relating to supervisors and professionals

Section 2 (3)

The term "employee" shall include any employee, and shall not be limited to the employees of a particular employer, unless the Act explicitly states otherwise, and shall include any individual whose work has ceased as a consequence of, or in connection with, any current labor dispute or because of any unfair labor practice, and who has not obtained any other regular and substantially equivalent employment, but shall not include any individual employed as an agricultural laborer, or in the domestic service of any family or person at his home, or any individual employed by his parent or spouse, or any individual having the status of an independent contractor, or any individual employed as a supervisor, or any individual employed by an employer subject to the Railway Labor Act, as amended from time to time, or by any other person who is not an employer as herein defined.

Section 2 (11)

The term "supervisor" means any individual having authority, in the interest of the employer, to hire, transfer, suspend, lay off, recall, promote, discharge, assign, reward or discipline other employees, or responsibly to direct them, or to adjust their grievances, or effectively to recommend such action, if in connection with the foregoing the exercise of such authority is not of a merely routine or clerical nature, but requires the use of independent judgment.

Section 14 (a)

Nothing herein shall prohibit any individual employed as a supervisor from becoming or remaining a member of a labor organization, but no employer subject to this Act shall be compelled to deem individuals defined herein as supervisors as employees for the purpose of any law, either national or local, relating to collective bargaining.

Section 9 (b)

The Board shall decide in each case whether, in order to assure to employees the fullest freedom in exercising the rights guaranteed by this Act, the unit appropriate for the purposes of collective bargaining shall be the employer unit, craft unit, plant unit or subdivision thereof: *Provided,* That the Board shall not decide that any unit is appropriate for such purposes if such unit includes both professional employees and employees who are not professional employees unless a majority of such professional employees vote for inclusion in such unit.

INTERNATIONAL STEELWORKERS UNION
Local 76

TO: EMPLOYEES OF FIRST CENTRAL BANK OF RIVER CITY

This letter will explain the delay in our organizing campaign and is also intended to let you know that the IMU is still very much interested in you as a member of our Union and as an employee of the First Central Bank of River City.

I am sure the delay concerns you as much as it concerns me. I want you to know there is little the Union can do about the delay but I do want to explain the reason for it.

Recently a hearing was held before a Hearing Officer of the NLRB. Following the hearing, attorneys for the company and the Union were given twelve days to file post-hearing briefs. After the twelve days, the entire record is turned over to the Regional Director of the Labor Board. When he has completed his study he will then decide what jobs will be included in the bargaining unit, and will set the date for the election.

During the course of every union organizing campaign, many rumors, usually untrue, are circulated. These rumors are circulated in most instances by some supervisors or company propagandist who is taken in by the company's opposition to the Union.

Your company is no different. Our organizing committee has informed me that most of the present crop of rumors are so ridiculous that the men and women are laughing at them. However, there is one persistent rumor that the Committee has asked me to put to sleep once and for all!

These rumor mongers are saying that you will lose your profit sharing and pension benefits because you joined the IMU. Nothing could be further from the truth!

We challenge the company, its propaganda artists or anyone else to put in writing that you will lose benefits if the IMU wins.

Don't be taken in by these rumors that are intended to fool and confuse you.

Stick together and be a part of the victory parade of the Union.

Groton Chemical Company (A)

On August 22, 1987, the following grievance was presented to the supervisor in the maintenance department:

> I contend that the company is wrong in not awarding me the No. 2 mechanic-carpenter job. I further contend that I'm the senior bidder and have the qualifications for the job. I have worked as No. 2 mechanic-carpenter in construction for a number of years.
>
> /s/ *William W. Fite*

The mechanic classification at the Groton Chemical Company covered a variety of skills such as mechanic-electrician, mechanic-painter and mechanic-carpenter. Each mechanic skill classification was divided into three levels depending upon the amount of skill required. Thus, a carpenter might be rated as mechanic-carpenter No. 1, mechanic-carpenter No. 2 or mechanic-carpenter No. 3.

The mechanic-carpenter No. 1, which was the highest carpenter classification, required that a worker be able to read blueprints, lay out his or her own work, do his or her work with a minimum of supervision or, when necessary, direct the work of No. 2 and No. 3 carpenters.

The No. 2 carpenter worked under supervision, was given specific instruction, and only rarely was he or she required to work alone. The No. 2 carpenter was expected to exhibit some skill and ability in the use of carpenter tools.

The No. 3 position represented, for the most part, beginners in the craft. Workers in this classification had to exhibit only rough skill and ability in the use of carpenter tools, and they always worked under supervision with specific instructions. Most employees who did carpenter work started in this classification and were advanced as they exhibited greater skill. The relative skill difference between the No. 2 and No. 3 positions, however, was not as great as the difference between the No. 1 and the No. 2 positions.

The hourly rates paid the three positions were as follows:

Mechanic-carpenter No. 1—$14.67
Mechanic-carpenter No. 2—$14.38
Mechanic-carpenter No. 3—$14.12

The company, after determining the amount of work likely to be required in each grade of carpenter work, established the number of jobs needed in each classification. Thus the company increased or

This case, derived from another case titled Rocket Chemical Co. E, was prepared by Professor David Kuechle as the basis of class discussion rather than to illustrate either effective or ineffective handling of an administrative situation. Reprinted by permission of the Harvard Business School.

decreased the number of jobs in a classification according to the needs of the company. For example, if the need for work in the No. 1 classification jobs was decreased, the company eliminated some of the No. 1 positions. The displaced workers bid for other jobs, usually by bumping out No. 2 carpenters who in turn might bump No. 3 carpenters. When the need for No. 1 carpenters increased the No. 2 carpenters bid for the new jobs.

Early in August the company determined that there was sufficient demand for No. 2 class carpenter work to warrant three additional jobs in that classification. On August 8 the company posted Notice #307 (see Exhibit 1). Award Notice #307 was posted on August 19 (see Exhibit 2). Exhibit 3 contains the employment record of four employees who had bid for the jobs.

At the time of posting, Fite was working as a mechanic-painter No. 3 at $14.12 per hour. When Fite was first hired in 1954, he was hired as a mechanic-carpenter No. 2, and remained in that position until 1959 when he was forced to take a lower rated, lower-paying job as a result of a decrease in the work force. He returned to the No. 2 job in 1968, only to be removed from it two years later when management claimed that he did not exhibit the required qualifications. In 1974 he was again given a No. 2 carpenter-mechanic position, which he held until there was a reduction of the work force in 1985. At that time, Fite was given the No. 3 painter job which he was holding at the time the grievance arose (Appendix A presents contract clauses that might reflect on this issue).

NOTES FROM THE STEP TWO GRIEVANCE MEETINGS

The parties were represented as follows:

Company	Union
1. Hale, plant engineer	1. Turner, union steward
2. Fayerweather, assistant personnel manager	2. Slagle, union steward

Turner (u): This doesn't make sense to me at all. The company agrees that Fite has the seniority. But that's not all, Fite has been a No. 2 carpenter before. In fact the record shows that he's had about 18 years of it. In 1974 the company gave him the No. 2 classification, and he kept it until 1985 when the job was abolished. He must have done the job O.K. or the company would have taken him off.

Hale (m): Well our experience with Fite shows clearly that his abilities aren't equal to those of Scannel, Kingley or White. These three men have qualifications close to those required of a No. 1 carpenter, whereas Fite is barely above the No. 3 carpenter requirements.

Fayerweather (m): Awards made on the three No. 2 mechanic-carpenter jobs were in accordance with Article 5, paragraph G of the present contract which reads, "Promotions and transfers shall be made on the basis of relative ability, training, safety, knowledge, efficiency, and physical fitness provided that when the above qualifications are equal, plant-wide seniority shall be the determining factor. Qualifications acquired outside the plant must be authenticated." Fite does not possess as much *ability* as the three junior employees who were assigned to the job openings.

Slagle (u): Fite's past performance as a No. 2 mechanic-carpenter must have been satisfactory.

Fayerweather (m): I take exception to that statement. On more than one occasion Fite had been told that his work was unsatisfactory.

Turner (u): If that's true, why wasn't Fite removed from the job under Article 5, paragraph O of the contract?

Fite : The only time anybody talked to me about my work was when I bid on a No. 1 mechanic-carpenter job in 1980.

Hale (m): That's not right! Bailey talked to you, Fite, and so did Stern, your foreman. They both approached you about your performance.

Fite: Stern never talked to me!

Haler (m): Fite is just marginally qualified as a No. 2 carpenter. The company would have removed him under Article 5, paragraph O of the contract if his job hadn't been abolished before such action could be taken. Several people talked with Fite trying to get him to improve but he never did. In 1970 Fite was removed as a No. 2 mechanic-carpenter because he didn't possess the qualifications for the job. Ten years later Fite bid on a No. 1 job and at that time he was advised that the company was considering removing him from his No. 2 carpenter classification, because his work was not satisfactory. Fite went ahead

and entered a grievance because we didn't award him the No. 1 job. Here is a copy of the 1980 grievance (see Exhibit 4). Again in March 1985 in the presence of Edwards (union president) and Conner (steward), Fite was told that he was failing to show evidence of his ability to do No. 2 work and that if his work did not improve, the company would have to consider removing his name from the classification.

Fayerweather (m): Fite has been on the job a considerable length of time, and he has certainly had ample time to prove his ability to do the job; however, he has not done it and therefore it is evident that he does not possess the qualifications necessary to do the job.

Turner (u): It is hard to believe that some of the abilities and traits of the men working with Fite have not been adopted in Fite's performance. (There was general agreement from members of management that it was hard to understand but that Fite had failed to show improvement during the years.)

Hale (m): In Fite, all factors including quantity, quality, knowledge and cooperation are poor and in addition, Fite goldbricks. Other men in the carpenters' gang don't like to work with him, because he doesn't carry his share of the work.

Turner (u): Who are the men who don't want to work with him?

Hale (m): The company doesn't want to put an employee on the *spot, so I won't mention any names.*

Fox (u): I can't understand why Fite was permitted to hold a No. 2 carpenter's job after he was removed from that classification in 1970.

Fayerweather (m): Obviously an error was made in allowing Fite to return to the classification after being removed from it, but it would be equally wrong to permit him to return to this classification at this time, because he is not qualified to perform successfully the duties required by the job. Many times the union has requested that the company give consideration to advancing employees who were not part of the mechanics training program.

Most of the older workers are not graduates of the program and have acquired their skills on the job. We recognize that the training accorded to the graduates of the training program (such as the three selected to fill the three carpenter jobs) often makes them better qualified to fill openings and hence receive promotions. We have always reviewed the records of those individuals who have not been through the training program, and certain advancements have been made. The union could not expect the company to automatically put employees back on the job when they don't have potential for advancement and especially when they are not even qualified for the job which they bid.

Hale (m): I'd like to point out some specific instances to the union that I think reflected some of Fite's shortcomings. On September 11, 1985 Fite was supposed to be working on the roof of the Tower Concentrate Building, but he just stood on the scaffolding. He went for a smoke while the others worked and in general stood around most of the time instead of helping with the repairs on the roof. The next day, September 12, he was put to work repairing a roof on one of the River Experimental Labs. During that assignment Fite spent much of his time in the smoke shanty. On September 13, a Saturday—on overtime—he was found loafing in the carpenter and pipe shop. On September 19, he was assigned to help dismantle the Blasting Supplies Lab. He finished that job about 2:30 P.M. and admitted loafing in the lab for the balance of the day. Even as a painter, there have been numerous cases when he hasn't remained on his assigned job.

Fayerweather (m): These traits are certainly not desirable and definitely raise a question about the man's ability, interest and cooperative spirit.

. . . .

The union requested a short recess after which Turner stated:

The union feels Fite is qualified as a No. 2 carpenter, because he has worked in that classification for approximately 18 years; and, having been hired as a No. 2 carpenter originally, Fite certainly should have been awarded the job. The union wants a step three hearing.

On September 5, a step three grievance meeting was held. Present for the company were: Jason, Fayerweather, Hale, and Bernard, Maintenance Department supervisor. Present for the union were: Shaper, Turner, Davis, and Fox.

GROTON CHEMICAL COMPANY (A) STUDY QUESTIONS:

1. How should William Fite's grievance be resolved?
2. Students, in union and management teams, must, if they reach an agreement, put their resolution of the grievance in writing. If no agreement is reached, the union must decide whether to take the grievance to arbitration.

Notice # 307

The following jobs are open for bid, under the terms of the contract, effective August 8, 1987. All bids or withdrawals of bids must be deposited by 12:30 p.m., August 15, 1987.

Please Indicate Job Letter on Bid

Job Letter

Job Letter

Blasting Supplies Division

A. MATCH HEAD MACHINE ADJUSTER

Temporary vacancy
$14.12
Needed - 1
To replace: 26 G. Lutz

B. WIRE OPERATOR - Folding
               Machine Runner
Temporary vacancy
$14.00
Needed - 1
To replace: 329 J. Tolan

Dynamite Division - Powder

C. POWDER OPERATOR #1 - Gel. Cart

Temporary job
$14.35
Needed - 1

D. POWDER OPERATOR #2 - Gel. Cart

Temporary job
$14.25
Needed - 1

E. POWDER HELPER - Gel. Box Pack

Temporary jobs
$14.14
Needed - 2

F. POWDER HELPER - Powder Pool

Temporary jobs
$14.14
Needed - 2

Dynamite Division - Powder Cont.

G. POWDER HELPER - Hand Pack - #1 Hall

Temporary job
$14.14
Needed - 1
To replace: 42 H. Long

H. SHELL HOUSE HELPER
Temporary job
$14.10
Needed - 1

I. BOX PRINT HELPER

Temporary vacancy
$14.10
Needed - 1
To replace: 32 J. Steinert

Engineering Division

J. MECHANIC #2 - Carpenter

Temporary jobs
$14.38
Needed - 3

K. LABORER

Temporary jobs
$13.84
Needed - 2

PERSONNEL MANAGER

Award Notice # 307

Job Letter

Dynamite Division - Powder Cont.

I.   1 - BOX PRINT HELPER - T.V.

        154 L. Job   10-14-76
         42 H. Long   09-12-79
         82 A. Frable   10-03-79
        213 R. Stellfox   05-27-80
        224 F. Hinkle   07-31-81
        250 C. Christian   10-12-81

Awarded to: L. Job

Engineering Division

J.   3 - MECHANIC #2 - Carpenters - T.J.

        176 W. Fite   08-18-54
         99 C. Scannel   07-13-61
        771 F. Kingley   10-04-61
        343 F. Bain   09-21-64
         98 A. White   08-21-67
        275 N. Barton   06-11-83
        300 J. Vadner   05-22-80

Awarded to: C. Scannel
             F. Kingley
             A. White

K.   2 - LABORERS - T.J.

        140 J. Spudis   05-28-80
        135 F. Mlynek   05-28-80
        309 J. Domashevitz   06-13-83
        271 H. Berger   08-31-83
        231 D. Correll   08-31-83
        211 R. Clemson   08-31-83
        198 G. Tonkin   08-31-83

Awarded to: J. Spudis
             J. Domashevitz   _____
                                    ASSISTANT PERSONNEL MANAGER

157

Personnel Data

Employee #343 Frank Bain   Date Hired 09-21-64

Date	Classification	Specialty
	Cap helper	
04-30-63	E.B.C. Foreman	Soldering & sulfuring
07-14-69	E.B.C. Foreman	E.B.C.
06-05-72	E.B.C. Leadman	Trucker - caps
10-18-75	E.B.C. Operator	#2 Pack House
10-18-75	E.B.C. Leadman	#2 Pack House
10-12-80	Ordinance Operator #1	Primer line
02-25-82	Leadman #1	Labor gang
05-05-82	Truck helper	Powder - B.S. Transportation Dept.
07-16-82	Mechanic #3	Carpenter
04-13-83	Truck helper	Safety
04-04-84	Mechanic helper	Electrician
05-21-84	Truck helper	Safety
11-28-84	Mechanic #3	R.X.L.
09-25-85	Truck driver	Safety
04-01-86	Mechanic #3	D & D section
06-17-86	E.B.C. operator	Pack house operator
07-29-86	Mechanic #3	D & D section

Note: Bain claimed Mechanic #2 - Carpenter job on March 15, 1983. Claim
       was denied on qualifications.

Employee #771 Frank Kingley   Date Hired 10-04-61

Date	Classification	Specialty
	Powder helper	
	Acid helper	
	Acid operator	
09-19-77	Truck driver	Construction
10-12-79	Mechanic #3	Carpenter
09-12-84	Mechanic #2	Carpenter
10-03-85	Truck driver	Safety
08-18-87	Mechanic #2	Carpenter

Employee #99 Charles Scannel   Date Hired 07-13-61

Date	Classification	Specialty
	Shell helper	
	Shell operator #2	
	Shell helper	
12-15-76	Truck helper	Safety
10-12-79	Mechanic #3	Carpenter
09-11-84	Mechanic #2	Carpenter
10-01-85	Truck helper	Safety
08-18-87	Mechanic #2	Carpenter

Employee #98 Arthur White   Date Hired 08-21-67

Date	Classification	Specialty
	Shell draw helper	
01-09-76	Cap operator	
04-19-76	Acid helper	Finish house
08-29-77	Truck helper	Safety – B.S. Transportation Dept.
06-19-79	Truck driver	Safety – B.S. Transportation Dept.
11-01-79	Mechanic #3	Carpenter
06-16-80	Mechanic #2	Carpenter
10-03-85	Truck driver	Safety – Labor Dept.
10-16-85	Laborer	Janitor – Dyn. Division
08-18-87	Mechanic #2	Carpenter

1980 William Fite Grievance

The grievance submitted by Fite, dated June 18, 1980, read as follows:

> The company having posted three No. 1 carpenter jobs for bid only awarded two of these jobs and both of the awards were made to employees of lesser seniority than I have. I contend that I should have been awarded one of these jobs, both on my seniority and my qualifications. I am at present a No. 2 carpenter and have worked as a No. 2 carpenter for some time here at the plant. Therefore, with the experience I have on the job I feel that I should have been awarded one of these jobs.

Extracts from the June 1980 Grievance Meeting

Mr. Bailey, Fite's foreman, stated that the quality of Fite's work had not been satisfactory, that he had failed to carry out instructions, and that he had been observed to be argumentative when receiving instructions. Specific mention was made of a recent job in which he had failed to brace a water line properly while an excavation was being made underneath the line.

Fite asserted that in the latter instance he had complied with the general foreman's exact orders. Bailey, however, pointed out that had Fite displayed No. 1 carpenter's qualifications he would have recognized an obvious need to use a different method of bracing and would have brought the matter to the attention of the foreman. Bailey further stated that he had difficulty in keeping Fite at work. The union argued that Fite should be awarded a No. 1 job and that the incentive of the higher rate would encourage him to do a better job in the future.

The grievance went to the second step, and the union wanted a more explicit definition and description of Fite's failure to measure up to the requirements of a first-class carpenter.

Turner cited a recent job in the Blasting Supplies Works handled by Fite and a helper as evidence of Fite's ability. Bailey stated that that particular job demonstrated Fite's lack of ability. The work had been laid out by a leadman after which Fite and a helper spent over a week doing a simple job which should have been completed in about four days. Turner then characterized that statement as evidence that Fite was being watched and checked with more thoroughness than other carpenters.

It was felt by management that the case involved no question of relative qualifications but was only a challenge of their right and their ability to judge whether an employee did or did not possess qualifications. The company refused to change its position. The grievance was finally withdrawn by the union.

APPENDIX A
GROTON CHEMICAL COMPANY (A)

ARTICLE V

E. When job vacancies occur or a new job is created, the job will be posted.

Employees shall prepare bids or withdrawals in triplicate, depositing original in the company box, duplicate copy in the union box, and retaining the triplicate copy. All bids or withdrawals shall be available for inspection by the departmental steward at the latter's request.

Copies of all job notices and job award notices shall be furnished to the Local President and Chief Steward.

In considering bids for vacant jobs, the company will consider seniority and qualifications.

There shall be no interference by company or union with any employee in the exercise of his or her right to bid for or to claim a job.

The company shall either post job awards within five (5) full working days after the bidding period expires or post notices stating why awards are being delayed.

. . . .

G. Promotions and transfers shall be made on the basis of relative ability, training, safety, knowledge, efficiency, and physical fitness, provided that when the above qualifications are equal, plant-wide seniority shall be the determining factor. Qualifications acquired outside the plant must be authenticated.

In the application of the above factors governing the promotion and transfer of employees by bid and award, the company agrees that such factors will be determined and applied in a fair, unbiased, and nondiscriminatory manner. The above is a statement of policy and shall not change the intent of the preceding paragraph.

. . . .

H. In all cases of layoff or rehire, the seniority of employees involved shall be considered on a plant-wide basis and shall be the determining factor. However, if there is any job opening or job vacancy that cannot be filled by employees within the bargaining unit, or by qualified employees who have been laid off, the company may retain present employees with lesser seniority who are qualified to perform the work or then hire new employees. However, an open or vacant job will not be awarded to an employee if there is another employee with greater seniority on furlough, or laid off, who has qualifications to perform the work in the vacant or open job. Grievances with respect to the judgment of employees' qualifications for these purposes shall be subject to the full grievance procedure, including arbitration, except for those job classifications which are designated with an asterisk in Appendix A of the contract, in which case the plant manager shall be the sole judge and his decision shall not be subject to the grievance procedure beyond the first three steps. Senior employees who have been laid off or who are on furlough, will be notified by the company of job vacancies or job openings for which they have qualifications. Such employees will be given twenty-four (24) hours from the time of notification to advise the company of their intentions with respect to the open or vacant job.

. . . .

O. If an employee who has been awarded a job is unable to satisfactorily perform the work, the management may:

1. If he is on a temporary job, transfer him to his permanent job, or,
2. If he is on a permanent job, transfer him to the Labor Gang, Powder Helper Pool, Transportation Department or Utility Pool. Such transferee must make reasonable efforts to acquire a regular job by bid.

· · · ·

ARTICLE XX: TRAINING

Mechanics Training Program A Mechanics Training Program is hereby established with the following objectives:

1. To exercise due care in the selection of applicants for training in skilled trades.

2. To provide for suitable instruction and training which, upon completion, will result in first-class mechanics fully capable of meeting the demands of their occupations.
3. The parties agree to adopt a Training Procedure, copies of which will be given to the union officials and stewards. They also agree to establish a Training Committee with advisory functions as set forth in the Training Procedure. Membership of the Committee shall be as follows:

   two members representing the union,
   two members representing the management,
   one chairman (personnel manager)

4. The Training procedure may be amended at any time by mutual agreement of the company and the union. The union in this case shall mean the Grievance Committee.

· · · ·

Groton Chemical Company (B)

On August 9, the following grievance was presented in the Acid department of the Pennville plant:

> We, the Undersigned, take exception to the practice of the company insisting upon Acid Leadmen doing our work. This consists of transferring acid over Saturday and Sunday, weekends, when we are obliged to remain home.
>
> This constitutes our daily work, two shifts per day when Leadmen do not transfer acid. We therefore contend that any work of this nature which occurred over a weekend period rightly belongs to us as contracted overtime and cannot be performed by the Leadmen who again by contract are not allowed to replace any employee for a shift or part of a shift.
>
> On Saturday, August 6, the Acid Leadmen performed the following work:
>
> 1. Pumped mix from mix and weigh Scale Tank #3 to Tower and Cascade Storage Tank.
> 2. Pumped from Tank #5 to Scale Tank #1.
> 3. Pumped twice neutralizing Tank #3 to storage tank or truck. Each of these jobs takes approximately 1½ hours.

This case, derived from another case titled Rocket Chemical Co. (B), was prepared by Professor David Kuechle as a basis for class discussion rather than to illustrate either effective or ineffective handling of an administrative situation. Reprinted by permission of the Harvard Business School.

Signed Fred Scherer
Signed Anthony Vancura
Signed Joseph Cooper (Steward)

The manufacture of dynamite requires the use of certain acids, among which are nitric, sulphuric, and mixtures of these two. At the Pennville plant there was an operation where some of these acids were produced for use within the plant as well as for outside sales. The grievants and the leadmen referred to in the grievance were employed in this operation.

As part of the operation it was necessary to transfer the liquids from the storage tanks to the scale tanks where they were weighed and mixed, from the scale tanks to storage tanks, and also to and from tank trucks and tank cars. Some years ago these transfers were accomplished with compressed air and the operation became known as "acid blowing" and the operators as "acid blowers."

At the time of the grievance, acid transfers were accomplished by electric pumps. The employee performing the pumping set the lines and the valves so as to direct the flow of the liquid to the proper tank, started the flow of material, and then traced the line to see that the liquid was flowing as intended, without leakage. During the pumping the employee had no active duties but was responsible for the operation and had to be on hand in case of emergency.

When pumping to the scale tank the operator had to stop the process when the required quantities had been delivered.

Acid blowers were employed on the second and third shifts (8 A.M. to 4 P.M. and 4 P.M. to midnight) Monday through Friday. During that time most of the pumping was performed by them although some was done by the acid operators and the leadmen. It was sometimes necessary to pump acid, however, when the acid blowers were not at work, and the leadmen had performed the task at those times.[1] There were four acid leadmen who worked a schedule so as to cover the three shifts, seven days a week. One of them was always present at the plant during normal operations. Both the leadmen and the acid blowers[2] were hourly paid employees and in the bargaining unit.

THE FIRST STEP GRIEVANCE MEETING

On August 12, a first step grievance meeting was held to discuss the acid blowers' grievance. The parties were represented as follows:

Company	Union
1. Frank Kirsten, plant personnel director	1. George Davis, union president (worked in the acid area)
2. Ted Waltus, senior supervisor	2. Joseph Cooper, acid area steward
3. Leo Lowery, acid supervisor	3. Fred Scherer, acid blower
	4. Anthony Vancura, acid blower

[1] See Article II of the contract, which is reproduced in Appendix A.

[2] Acid Blowers had the same wage classification as acid operators ($14.19 per hour). Acid leadmen received $0.90 per hour more.

After Kirsten read the grievance Cooper asked Scherer to explain the men's complaint.

Scherer (u): Well, as the grievance says, last Saturday the leadman spent over four hours doing our work. This is the work us acid blowers do during the week. When there's work like this to be done on Saturday, we should be called out. We didn't mind the leadmen doing a little job once in a while, but this has grown and grown until it's beyond all reason. It isn't fair. Other groups get called out. Why shouldn't we? I can tell you one thing, the leadmen are plenty sore about all this extra work too. How are they supposed to get their regular work done?

Lowery (m): Fred, you fellows are wrong when you say we are loading up the leadmen with more and more pumping over the weekends. I have the figures for the past two years here, and you're welcome to look them over. Sure last Saturday was heavy, but there have been other Saturdays just as heavy in the past, and the figures don't show any general increase over the past two years.

Cooper (u): How much time do your figures show the leadmen spent on pumping last Saturday?

Lowery (m): The day leadman reported a total of three hours. This included pumping the tube twice which is not included in the grievance.

Cooper (u): Well whether it's been going on for two years or not, it's asking too damn much of these men to have the leadmen do them out of that much Saturday work. After all it's their work. I understand the leadmen also operated the neutralizer on Saturday. How can you expect the leadmen to do their regular work?

Fox (u): I'll tell you one thing, you'd never get away with this over in the maintenance gang.

Lowery (m): We've had no complaints from the leadmen. They're not overworked. After all the leadman is a higher paid classification, and under the contract we have the right to ask him to do this kind of work. It's no different than it's always been.

Davis (u): The men tell me that when Sam Sessions was acid supervisor he made an agreement with them that the leadmen would not pump over two hours on Saturday. If there was more than two hours pumping, the blowers would be called out.

Kirsten (m): Was that a written agreement, George? Do you have a copy of it?

Davis (u): Of course it wasn't written. It didn't have to be written. Sam was as good as his word and that's heck of a lot more than you can say about some people around here today. I can see we'll have to get everything down on paper from now on. I resent this whole business. Every time our men mention an understanding that was made in the past you as much as say we're a bunch of liars.

Kirsten (m): Now, George, I didn't say that at all—but this is the first time I heard of such an understanding and I wonder if it had been formalized. After all, in the last grievance, Ray asked me if I had a written record of the agreement made by the clean-up crew.

Scherer (u): You can't deny this is our work. We do it all week, but almost never are we called out on Saturday anymore. We're just interested in coming out here and doing our work. We're being done out of four hours at time and one-half almost every Saturday.

. . . .

A recess was then called during which each side reconsidered its position. Following the recess a further discussion was held but no agreement was reached.

THE SECOND STEP GRIEVANCE MEETING

At the second step grievance meeting, which was held on August 22, the parties were represented as follows:

Company	*Union*
1. Frank Kirsten, plant personnel director	1. George Davis, president of the union and grievance committee chairman
2. Leo Lowery, acid supervisor	2. Harry Tomason, chief steward
3. Ted Walters, senior supervisor	3. Ray Fox, maintenance mechanic and member of grievance committee
4. C. L. Hoover, superintendent dynamite division	4. Joseph Cooper, acid area steward
	5. Fred Scherer, acid blower

Kirsten read the grievance and stated that the company could not agree to it.

Cooper (u): The acid leadmen are doing more and more work which belongs to the men, not just pumping acid, as the grievance says, but on Saturday afternoons they act as storeroom helpers, and on the evening and night shifts they run the neutralizer.

Davis (m): The contract says you can't replace another employee for a part of a shift, but that's exactly what you're doing. You're replacing not just the blowers, but neutralizers and storeroom attenders. In the case of the neutralizers you're replacing a man for a whole shift. As I said in the other grievance—we give you fellows a little finger and you take a whole damn hand.

Lowery (m): George, the amount of work done by the leadmen has *not* increased. You can look at the records. It's true the blowers don't get as much overtime as they used to get. But that's not because the leadmen are working more. We used to have the tank trucks come in here on Saturday and Sunday, and the blowers were called in to load them. Recently we worked it out so we don't have to have the Saturday and Sunday shipments. Also, as you know, our production of acid is down so there just isn't as much pumping required.

The acid leadmen are not doing more work. It's true that they get things out of the storeroom when there's an emergency but that's nothing new. They've been doing that for years. Matter of fact they used to do it all day Saturday but now we have a storeroom attendant out here Saturday morning.

Fox (u): The storeroom work is completely outside the acid department. He has no business over there at all. The men tell me that one Saturday the acid leadman made 35 trips to the storeroom. That doesn't make sense. And what about the neutralizer? What's the leadman doing on that?

Walters (m): Well, we reached an agreement on that a couple of years ago—the leadman can operate the neutralizer when he has time. You remember when we settled that, Joe.

Cooper (u): Sure, we agreed he could do it in his free time, but it's like George says, you fellows are taking advantage of it. Some days now the leadman turns out a full shift's

operation. Heck, we never had that in mind.

Kirsten (m): George, you said we are violating the contract. We don't agree. As we read Appendix A, paragraph 2 on page 3, we have every right to use the leadmen this way. The last sentence which you refer to was not meant to cover this kind of situation.

It was adopted to cover a situation where a member of the work force was required to discontinue work during a shift, or who failed to report for scheduled work on a day. We agreed that leadmen would not do the work of an absent employee. That's not the case here at all.

Walters (m): Leo and I have looked over the production schedules and we can arrange things so that the tower and cascade concentrator won't have to be operated over the weekend. That will decrease the pumping by leadmen over the weekend, but, of course, it won't result in any more overtime for the blowers. We can fit it into their regular work schedule during the week.

Davis (u): Is there an overtime distribution plan in effect in the acid area?

Lowery (m): Yes, we have one. Joe and the boys drew it up, and I agreed to it after a couple of changes. We don't have any trouble with it as Joe will tell you, but we just haven't had any overtime for the blowers recently. That's no fault of the plan. It works O.K.

Davis (u): How can you say there's been no overtime for the blowers with all this Saturday pumping?

Cooper (u): As I recall it, our overtime plan said leadmen should not share. I'm trying to find it—yes—here it is, Item 7 says "Production leadmen will not share time in operational overtime duties."

Davis (u): Well there it is in black and white, Frank. You don't have to take our word for it this time. I think you'll have to agree that these overtime plans are part of the contract. It's spelled out here in paragraph 3 page 35 [see Appendix A, p. 8].

Kirsten (m): We agree, George, that the overtime plans are binding but we don't agree that the overtime plan has any bearing on this case.

Hoover (m): What you want in this grievance would increase our cost of making acid and we just can't afford it, especially with costs rising so fast these days. The margins are low here. The competition is tough. We've already lost some of our outside customers, and the company is even buying some of its own acid outside. That's why the blowers' overtime is down. If we have to bring the blowers out here on Saturday and Sunday every time there's a few hours of pumping there'll be less work, not more, for everybody.

. . . .

A recess was called during which each side discussed the grievance. When the meeting reconvened no agreement could be reached, and the union asked Mr. Kirsten to schedule a third step meeting.

The third step meeting was held on September 5. Present for the union were Martin Shaper, regional director, District #50 UMWA, Davis, Tomason, and Fox. Present for the company were Jim Jason, labor relations manager, Joseph Lowenberg, plant manager, Kirsten, and Hoover.

GROTON CHEMICAL COMPANY (B) STUDY QUESTIONS:

1. How should the grievance presented by Fred Scherer, Anthony Vancura, and Joseph Cooper of the Acid Department of the Pennville plant be resolved?

2. Students, in union and management teams, must, if they reach an agreement, put their resolution of the grievance in writing. If no agreement is reached, the union must decide whether to take the grievance to arbitration.

APPENDIX A
GROTON CHEMICAL
COMPANY (B)

Sections from the current agreement between the United Mine Workers of America and Groton Chemical Company (Pennville Plant).

ARTICLE II RECOGNITION

Leadman shall perform the duties of working gang-boss or leader. He shall exercise the authority to assign work and direct the performance thereof; to supervise the quality of workmanship and to maintain order, reporting any violation of rules. It shall be his responsibility to maintain standards of production, both quantity and quality, as established by the company, and to report to his foreman or supervisor any conditions which prevent the attainment of such standards of production. If such conditions result from the action of an employee, or employees, the leadman may consult with the departmental steward. A steward must be present whenever an employee is reported by the leadman for either violation of rules or for causing conditions detrimental to standards of production.

Supervisory duties as defined above shall be the primary function of a leadman. However, time not spent in the performance of supervisory duties may be spent in manual work, and there shall be no limit placed on the amount of time spent in such work. Leadmen will not be used to replace employees who are absent from work for a complete shift or who are required to discontinue their regular work for the balance of the shift, unless such leadmen are the only qualified employees available for that shift.

ARTICLE VII REPORTING PAY

a. Any employee not being notified at least two (2) hours before starting time of his regular shift not to report for work and reporting, shall be given four (4) hours work or shall be compensated for four (4) hours at his straight time rate unless the company's failure to notify him shall be for a cause beyond the company's control, in which case the employee shall be compensated for two (2) hours at his straight time rate. Employees so reporting will be provided with transportation if there are no means of transportation available.

b. Employees reporting for work as provided in paragraph (a) above or employees who are called out to work on a day that has not been scheduled for work will be compensated for either four (4) or two (2) hours in accordance with paragraph (a) above, on the following basis:

1. For reporting on Saturday or Sunday, compensation at the rate of time and one-half, subject to qualifying for such pay as provided in Article XI of this Agreement.

2. For reporting on the seventh consecutive day worked in his regularly scheduled workweek, compensation at the rate of double time, subject to qualifying for such pay as provided in Article IX of this Agreement.

3. For reporting on any other day, compensation at straight time unless the employee has worked forty (40) hours or more on the preceding days in that week in which case his reporting pay shall be at the rate of time and one-half.

ARTICLE IX HOURS OF WORK
(paragraph 3 on page 35)

Overtime work will be distributed equally as far as possible on a departmental basis. If requested by the Union, a cumulative record of overtime worked by every employee in a department will be posted and a copy will be sent to the Local Union President. The employees of a department may submit a plan for the distribution of overtime for all employees within such department within two (2) weeks of the effective date of the contract. However, the plan, if once approved by the company, may not be changed for the remainder of the contract term. In any department where no overtime plan is in effect, and no plan is submitted by any such department and approved by the company, the overtime will be distributed by the company in accordance with provisions of this Agreement.

ARTICLE XIII UNION (pp. 46–47)

a. The Union recognizes the responsibilities imposed upon it as the exclusive bargaining agent for the employees, and realizes that in order to provide maximum opportunities for continuing employment, good working conditions, and better than average wages, the company must be in a strong market position, which means it must produce at the lowest possible costs consistent with fair labor standards. The Union, through its bargaining position, assumes a joint responsibility in attainment of these goals.

b. The Union therefore agrees that it will cooperate with the company and support its efforts to assure a full day's work on the part of its members; that it actively will combat absenteeism and any other practices which restrict production. It further agrees that it will support the company in its efforts to eliminate waste in production; conserve materials and supplies; improve the quality of workmanship; prevent accidents and strengthen goodwill between the company, the employees, the customer, and the public.

The Case of Patrick Donovan
State of Connecticut Public Works Department and the Connecticut State Employees Association

Patrick Donovan, as of May, 1987, had 19 years, four months and six days of service with the Connecticut Department of Public Works. During these years he had earned a reputation as an excellent worker, and, at the age of 61, was paid the top rate for qualified craftsworkers: salary grade 11: $15.17 an hour, $27,685 a year. For the past eight years Donovan had been one of three plumbers assigned to the Department of Buildings and Grounds, the maintenance staff responsible for the upkeep of the state's principal buildings in Hartford. This position was regarded as one of trust, because Donovan frequently worked without direct supervision as he responded to emergencies at various locations in the capitol city. His supervisor, Chief of Buildings and Grounds Alan Crowley, had his office in the State Office Building on Capitol Avenue. Donovan was expected to carry out assignments relayed to him from this central office by telephone. On numerous occasions a single assignment might require several days to complete. His hours were from 8:00 A.M. to 3:30 P.M. with two brief rest periods and a half hour for lunch.

This case was adapted by Professor Fred K. Foulkes from a case written by Susan Johnson, Research Assistant, under the supervision of Professors David Kuechle and James J. Healy. It is not intended to demonstrate either correct or incorrect handling of an administrative situation.

On May 8, 1987, Domenic Casale, Superintendent for the State Capitol Building, received complaints at 9:45 A.M. from irate legislative aides that the toilets in the third floor men's room were still out of commission. Patrick Donovan had been assigned to this repair job the prior afternoon. Casale went to the third floor to speak to Donovan and, when he failed to find him there, searched the building for the missing plumber. Donovan was not to be found. Casale then called Crowley's office to ask whether Donovan had been called for an emergency assignment at another location. He was told that no such assignment had been made, nor had Donovan called in sick. Finally, at 10:30 A.M., Casale noticed that light was showing under the door of a storage room in a wing of the third floor. Normally this light was turned off and the door unlocked by the custodian just before the building was opened for the day at 7:45 A.M. To Casale's surprise, the door was locked. He went to get the head custodian who unlocked the door. Lying on the floor, his head cushioned by his work apron, Patrick Donovan was sound asleep.

Casale turned to the custodian and said, "You're a witness to this." The custodian replied, "It's not my job to be a witness." This conversation evidently roused Donovan, who sat up and, after looking around bewildered, said to Casale:

I'm sorry. I had one hell of a hangover, but I didn't want to miss work. I probably should have just called in to say I wouldn't be in today. I came in here to sleep it off. What time is it?

Casale told him that this was inexcusable, that he should go immediately to repair the toilets and that he would be told very soon what disciplinary measures would be taken. Donovan did as he was told, repaired the toilets, and left at his regular quitting time.

That night, at his home, he received a telegram from the Chief of Buildings and Grounds:

> Because of your conduct today, sleeping on the job and reporting for work in an unfit condition, and because of your prior record, you are terminated effective immediately.

These additional facts are pertinent: (1) The collective agreement between the State Employees Association and the Department of Public Works provided that the Department may discipline or discharge for "just and reasonable cause"; (2) The Department had issued rules, well-known to employees, that included statements that sleeping on the job or reporting to work under the influence of liquor may be causes for discharge; (3) There had been no prior problems of absenteeism with Donovan; (4) The following disciplinary notations appeared on his record:

a. September 18, 1986: Warned for refusal to report for duly posted Saturday work on September 16, 1986. (This was for overtime work, and 53 other employees were similarly warned; it was a concerted refusal to work overtime.) No grievance was filed.

b. February 10, 1983: Written warning for inattention to duties ("Deliberate idling in the washroom"). No grievance was filed.

c. January 10, 1968: Disciplined for fighting in department. Penalty (because he was found to be the aggressor): loss of seniority. (Donovan was actually hired on November 15, 1959. Because of this penalty, his seniority started over as of January, 1968.) No grievance was filed.

Thus, as of May 8, 1987, Donovan had worked for the Department of Public Works more than 28 years.

Immediately upon receipt of the telegram notifying him of his discharge, Donovan called his Association representative, George Bevelas, saying he wanted to file a grievance. He admitted that he had been in the wrong on that day, but that he felt the discharge penalty was unreasonably harsh, given (a) his long record of service; (b) his relatively unblemished record; and (c) the fact that he could have called in "sick" on May 8 and have received no penalty.

The Association staff representative filed a grievance the next day, Wednesday, May 9, 1987. Following Article XIV, section 6, step 1 of the grievance procedure established by the master contract, Crowley, Donovan's supervisor, gave a written answer and handed it to the staff representative on Thursday, May 10, 1987. It said simply, "Grievance denied." Reading this response, Bevelas told Crowley, "The Association certainly will appeal this. What you've done is unfair to Patrick. You and Casale are overreacting."

Under step 1.a, Bevelas submitted the grievance promptly to the Director of Public Works, who, within the prescribed seven days, affirmed Crowley's decision. Further appeal could be effected by written submission to step 2, the Personnel Officer for Building and Grounds at the central personnel office. In this case, Bevelas told the Association's top officers the result of the step 1.a filing; they told him to carry the appeal forward. Unfortunately, through inadvertence or negligence, neither Bevelas nor his superior, the Association's Director for the Maintenance Unit, John Perry, made any direct appeal to step 2 of the grievance procedure until June 7, 1987. The Association admitted that it had no explanation for the delay: "It was an oversight." However, Perry now said that he wanted to carry the grievance forward to step 2, and, if necessary, to step 3, the Office of Labor Relations and, beyond that, to arbitration.

Article XIV, section 6 of the contract provides that:

> Should any appeal from the decision on a grievance under step 1.a not be taken within 14 working days after such decision is given by the supervisor then the decision on such grievance shall be final and conclusive and not thereafter be reopened for discussion.

There was no known case where the Association had failed to appeal within the fourteen days or, having failed to make an appeal in a timely manner, had sought thereafter to have a grievance carried to a higher step. Nevertheless, on June 7, 1987, John Perry delivered a written grievance on Donovan's behalf to Thomas Gagnon, Personnel Officer for Buildings and Grounds, at the State Office Building. Mr. Gagnon refused to hear the case because the time limits called for in the grievance procedure had been exceeded.

After an apparently fruitless discussion with Gagnon, Perry requested an appointment with Paul Griswold, Director of the Office of Labor Relations. Perry said that if he didn't get a favorable response from Griswold, he would appeal the case to arbitration.

THE CASE OF PATRICK DONOVAN
STUDY QUESTIONS:

1. What is your assessment of management actions to date?
2. What advice do you have for Paul Griswold?

The Washington Post

On Wednesday afternoon, December 3, 1975, the strike of the pressmen's union against *The Washington Post* was 64 days old. To Katharine Graham, publisher of *The Post,* and Mark Meagher, the general manager, it was time to implement some decisions, the groundwork for which had been prepared over several weeks.

The Post management faced the pressmen's strike with the knowledge that their one rival, the *Washington Star,* would continue to publish. Based on precedent, if the pressmen's strike was a long one, *The Post* could anticipate serious short and long term losses. On December 3, *The Post* had beaten the odds for 6 weeks. Against expectations *The Post* had succeeded in publishing a paper which had held most of its market. *The Post*'s ability to print in the face of a craft strike, moreover, highlighted the issue which lay at the heart of the confrontation. A new technology was coming into the newspaper industry which opened to papers the possibility of operating with a substantially reduced workforce. Utilizing the new technology and a small group of non-craft employees, *The Post* had published.

This case is a condensed version, by Professor E. Robert Livernash, of one prepared by Professor William E. Fulmer. It is based in part on Robert H. Kaiser, "The Strike at *The Washington Post,*" *The Washington Post,* February 29, 1976.

However, if *The Post* had so far beaten the odds, Mrs. Graham and Mr. Meagher knew that only the heroic efforts of employees who did their regular jobs by day, then produced the paper by night, had made this possible. After 9 weeks, negotiations with the pressmen had shown no progress. As they evaluated their position on December 3, prominent among their thoughts was the knowledge that the endurance of the people in the building was dwindling, that after Christmas (at a good guess), the energy and morale which had sustained them would begin to flag.

THE NEWSPAPER INDUSTRY

The American newspaper industry in the 1970s was an industry under pressure. Labor costs, 30% to 50% of production costs, had risen steadily. Newsprint costs, another 25% of production costs, in 1975 were up over 40% from the beginning of 1973. Newspapers had difficulty in passing these increased costs to their customers.

Advertising revenue was particularly hard to increase. Advertising volume tended to drop significantly when linage rates increased. Often advertisers permanently transferred their business to radio or television. Though less sensitive than ad-linage rates, increases in circulation prices were limited by competition. Increases in newsstand prices also could make readers give up newspaper buying altogether.

The 1974–75 recession hurt both advertising and circulation revenues. In late 1975 expectations were that ad and circulation revenues would improve with a recovering economy. Whether increases in revenues could keep pace with increases in costs was uncertain and predictions were that for the immediate future, at least, the industry would continue in cost-price squeeze.

THE NEWSPAPER PRODUCTION PROCESS

Until the late 1960s the process technology used at large newspapers dated from the late 19th century (see Exhibit 1). This process technology was a true industrial art. Skilled craftsmen were required for most phases. Increasingly, from the mid-1960s onward, however, technological innovations became available with the potential to alter significantly the nature of the process.

The traditional method for preparing pages for printing was "hot-type" composition. In this process copy was sent to the composing room where printers set the copy into type using a variety of composing machines. For the most common of these, the linotype, the printer operated a keyboard that dropped brass molds and space bars into a line. Molten metal was poured into a line of molds creating a "slug"—hence "hot-type." Slugs were collected into columns of type and proofread. After proofing, columns of type with photo plates etched by photoengravers were put together by printers into page form. Page forms were sent to the stereotype department where an impression of the form was made on a soft pliable mat. The mat became the mold from which curved lead plates were made for use on the presses.

During the latter 1960s, the marriage of photographic with computer technology resulted in a new method of preparing pages—"cold-type" composition. In this process copy was inputted into a computer either by an optical scanner or by a keyboard on a terminal. In the most modern cold-type plants copy could be proofed, edited, and laid out in page form directly in the computer by means of video terminals. Computer produced photographic reproductions were pasted down on cardboard page grids. These grids were photographed by a photoengraving machine which produced a plastic or metal plate which stereotypes converted first into a mat and then into a lead plate.

Finished lead plates went to the pressroom where they were printed on web presses. The plates were bolted to cylinders which printed on both sides of continuous rolls of newsprint (the "web") which was fed through the intricate series of rollers and cylinders of the press. A modern web press had the capacity to print up to 80,000 papers/hour but seldom reached capacity because of breaks in the web. Rethreading the web resulted in at least a 10-minute shutdown. The maximum page capacity of a press at *The Post* was 112 pages. *The Post* routinely printed papers over 100 pages in length and used six or seven presses at once.

Once printed, the sheets of newsprint were combined, cut, and folded into finished papers and sent by conveyor to the mailroom. While technological changes comparable to those in the composing room had not yet taken place in the pressroom or mailroom, here too technological innovations were becoming available.

A major advantage of the new technologies was that they were much faster. The old procedures required skilled craftsmen in fair numbers. The new procedures called for less skill and training and in fewer numbers. To operate the hot-type plant it had on line in the early 1970s, *The Post* employed approximately 600 printers. To operate an equivalent facility, *The Post* would have needed a few skilled troubleshooters and approximately 350 semi-skilled workers who could have been trained for their jobs in a matter of one or two weeks. The savings in labor costs by conversion to cold-type would have paid for the facility within a year.

THE WASHINGTON POST

In 1975, *The Washington Post* was the seventh largest daily paper in the United States. When Katharine Graham's father, Eugene Meyer, bought the paper in 1933, it was the weakest of three Washington morning dailies. Meyer paid $835,000 at a bankruptcy auction. In 1946 Meyer's son-in-law, Philip Graham, became publisher.

The Post began its climb to a successful business in 1954 with the purchase of the *Times-Herald*. This acquisition gave *The Post* the largest circulation in Washington and inaugurated an era of prosperity. *The Post* grew rapidly. In 1960, it moved past the *Evening Star* to become the leading paper in Washington. Philip Graham was the moving force. His policy was one of controlled growth and careful management. His main interest was in editorial excellence. He used the growing revenues to hire more reporters and to establish the first foreign bureaus.

KATHARINE GRAHAM

When Katharine Graham became publisher upon the death of her husband in 1963, she commenced to "learn from the top." One of her first decisions was to expand efforts to build *The Post*'s reputation. Ben Bradlee was hired to run news operations. The editorial staff was increased by 20% and the number of foreign bureaus was doubled. Talented reporters were sought out and hired. A new plant was built. By September of 1975, *The Post*, now in competition only with the *Star*, commanded a 70% share of the ad linage and a 64% share of the paid circulation in its market area (Exhibit 2).

To improve the capital structure Mrs. Graham made the decision to take *The Post* public. Class A stock (full voting rights) remained with the Graham-Meyer family. Class B stock (limited voting rights) was opened to the public. In June 1971, *The Post* sold a first public issue of 1.3 million shares.

By unfortunate coincidence, 1971 heralded the end of increasing prosperity. From 1960 through 1969 pre-tax profit margins were 15% of revenues. In 1970 the gross margin dipped to 11%. From 1970 through 1974, though revenues increased by more than $45 million, the profit margin continued to decline. The margin fell to 8.5% in 1974 and looked to be lower yet for the months to October 1, 1975.

The profit decline did not threaten the Washington Post Company *Newsweek* magazine and radio and television holdings (Exhibit 3). Mrs. Graham felt, however, that each company activity must remain independent and maintain its own profitability.

To remain profitable, Mrs. Graham concluded that *The Post* needed better top management. Following the retirement of the then chief operating officer, John Sweeterman, Paul Ignatius, former Secretary of the Navy, was appointed president of the newspaper. In 1971 he was replaced by John Prescott, Jr., an executive of the Knight Newspaper chain. In 1974, Prescott was "promoted" to be president of the newspaper division and Mark Meagher, financial V.P., became the fourth general manager in 11 years (Exhibit 4).

If Mrs. Graham had difficulty in finding executives whom she felt could solve *The Post*'s problems, there was no difficulty in identifying the principal source of the problems, the production process. Beginning in the late 1960s, *The Post* came out later and later, often with a large number of typographical errors. Advertisers complained that their ads were badly set or printed. Circulation dealers, independent non-union entrepreneurs, complained that they had to wait for hours to pick up their papers. The newsroom complained of sloppy composing work and unreasonable restrictions on late-breaking news. New technology, however, offered the prospect of significant improvements if the labor situation at *The Post* could be surmounted.

LABOR AT *THE WASHINGTON POST*

Until the mid-1950s, the relationship between management and labor was open and cordial. *The Post*'s craftsmen were largely a homogeneous group drawn from the Washington area. After the acquisition of the *Times-Herald* in 1954 the relationship began to change. As *The Post* expanded, the wages paid its craft workers increased to satisfy union demands for a fair share of prosperity and to attract the new craft workers required at the growing paper (Exhibit 5). By 1967 only 75 of 590 printers were long-time *Post* employees. New employees had no particular loyalty to the paper and among them were a number of militants from papers in which unions had been broken.

Newspaper craft unions had a long history of imposing various regulations upon employers. During the years of prosperity, *The Post* management had viewed labor disputes as threats to growth to be avoided at all costs. In this environment the craft

unions (Exhibit 6) had steadily expanded their jurisdiction over work practices. For example, the printers' right to "reproduce" ads had been expanded to handle a reproduction "backlog" by allocating virtually unlimited overtime and/or by hiring new printers.

By the end of the 1960s printers would curse their supervisors and even throw lead slugs at them. Stereotypers had imposed a ban of silence on a new production manager believed to be anti-union. Pressmen had occasionally displayed their disapproval of certain executives by shutting down the presses when they came into the pressroom. In an attempt to maintain good relations union leaders were allowed to go directly to the general manager or the publisher, which served greatly to frustrate circumvented managers.

Negotiations with the printers in 1967 marked a turning point when the union conducted a slowdown during negotiations to pressure management. Rather than threaten operations, management settled. In 1969 and again in 1971 the Newspaper Guild rejected "final" contract offers. Both times management made "amended" final offers. Also in 1971 the printers staged a slowdown. This time they seriously disrupted operations for several weeks. By the early 1970s *The Post*'s craft unions had won great power for themselves and wage/benefit packages among the best in the industry.

The production craft unions (printers, stereotypers, photoengravers, pressmen, paper handlers, and mailers) had substantial power, based on the skills of their members, to control the production process. The production crafts also demonstrated how strong unions, through control of overtime and work-practice payments, could convert high wages into take-home pay which was higher still. As a general rule production operations at *The Post* took longer or required more workers than at most nonunion papers and even at many union shops. For instance, it took *Post* printers 32.5 man hours to set a page of type, over twice as long as the time required in an "average" union shop. In 1973, one out of every four hours worked in several of the production crafts was paid at an overtime rate (up to triple time) and $1 out of every $3 earned was paid out because of special work-practice provisions.

By the early 1970s, *The Post* was falling behind in adopting new technology, largely because of union resistance. Mrs. Graham became convinced that *The Post* had become "a goose laying golden eggs . . ." In November 1971, she appointed John Prescott general manager with a mandate to improve the labor situation. His first move was to develop the capacity to print a newspaper without craft union labor—Project X!

PROJECT X—A NEW APPROACH TO LABOR

Prescott's goal in starting Project X was to give Mrs. Graham a weapon with which to counter union ability to shut down *The Post*. Only if this were done, he believed, could management bargain successfully with the unions. To Prescott the new technology looked to be a means of challenging union strength. To achieve this end small groups of management-level employees were sent secretly to the Southern Production Program, Inc. (SPPI) of Oklahoma City for training. SPPI offered two classes of membership: full and associate. SPPI was blatantly anti-union. Full membership carried with it a mutual aid pledge among members to attempt to beat a union that struck. *The Post*'s goal was to improve its labor situation, not to turn anti-union. Consequently *The Post* became an associate member of SPPI with no

mutual-aid promise and no obligations. To train employees in cold-type composing, *The Post* established its own secret facility in Virginia.

Once Project X was well advanced, the unions were informed. This signal of a change in labor relations was reinforced in June 1973, by the appointment of Lawrence Wallace, formerly of the *Detroit Free Press*, as Labor Relations Director. Wallace had a reputation for fairness and for toughness. While Wallace recognized labor agreements as involving restrictions on management rights, he felt that management retained the right to test ambiguous points. Unions could respond to such tests with grievances. Wallace initiated a series of tests which were followed by grievances. Management looked upon this process as a means to improve the labor situation. The unions came to see it as an attempt to set them up as scapegoats.

In November 1973, the new approach resulted in a confrontation. The printers were negotiating a new contract and were staging a slowdown. Prescott had warned that such action could lead to discharges. On Friday, November 2, a foreman fined a printer for participation in a slowdown. In protest other printers stopped work. *The Post* missed two editions. Then, on Sunday, the decision was made to utilize Project X. By midnight Sunday, a special 40-page paper was ready to print. These preparations were watched by union engravers who had come to work expressly to keep other unions, who were not in the building, informed. As the presses were readied, 100 pressmen arrived. Their local President, James Dugan, told Prescott that rather than let amateurs work the presses, the pressmen would run them. The pressmen were allowed into the pressroom where they promptly seized the room. The presses would run, Dugan stated, only after management rehired the discharged printer. When Prescott protested that Dugan had given his word, Dugan replied. "I lied!" The pressmen ripped the web on the presses, committed other minor vandalism, and waited. Some hours later *The Post* agreed to reinstate the printer with only a reprimand. (Nothing was said about the damage.) The pressmen then ran the presses, taking care to efface the line of type stating that the edition had been prepared by non-union labor. James Dugan became the dominant union leader at *The Post*.

THE PRESSMEN

A pressman's job was dirty, noisy, and sometimes difficult. To produce a morning paper, the pressmen normally worked through the night. Saturday was described by some as "the hardest shift of the week." Yet, many pressmen enjoyed their work. According to a *Post* article;[1]

> The appeal of it is in the machinery, the magnificent presses. . . . Pressmen, compare their presses . . . to a beloved hot-rod car; they need careful handling to run properly. Keeping them running well can be an art, and a devoted pressman thrives on it.
> Pressmen perform numerous tasks, some routine, some very tricky. When they come on duty, the men all work together to bolt the lead plates which carry the imprints of the next day's paper onto the rollers of the presses. On a big paper like *The Post*, . . . this is a big job.
> When the press is running—creating a deafening roar and filling the air with a fine ink mist and tiny particles of newsprint—the crew has only a few tasks to perform. The sheets of newsprint must be kept straight and running correctly . . . the most substantial job is to repair broken "webs."

Dirty and difficult of necessity, *The Post* pressmen had long complained that their

[1] Robert H. Kaiser,"The Strike at *The Washington Post*," *The Washington Post*, February 29, 1976, p. 8.

work was made harder than it had to be by the poor design of the pressroom (which left too little space between the presses) and by inadequate safety precautions.

THE PRESSMEN'S UNION

The pressmen's union contained the most militant element in *The Post*'s craft unions. Management described them as a group maintaining a posture of complete alienation with management. Prior to 1973 the militants had not been a dominant force. The pressmen were, nevertheless, the worst exploiters of overtime and work practice provisions. After the 1973 confrontation, the militants gained ground.

The pressmen's quest for overtime took two forms. On one hand, they took advantage of manning provisions calling for as many as 19 men to run a press (non-union shops might be manned by 8 or 9) to work almost unlimited shifts. Also, management believed the pressmen were stringing out press runs to get end-of-shift overtime. Late press runs not dropped in time for the carrier to make deliveries and get to school meant that the papers didn't get delivered. Chronic late runs eroded circulation. In June, July, and August, 1975, 61 of 92 press runs were late. Of these, 27 finished after 5 A.M., ensuring late delivery of scores of thousands of newspapers.

The growing sense of confrontation with the pressmen at *The Post* reflected a national trend for that union. At a number of papers the union had been replaced with non-union labor. By 1974, *The Post* had among its pressmen a number of survivors from "broken" locals who believed there could be no meaningful accommodations with management.

Increasing militancy by the pressmen after 1973 may be contrasted with a rapid decline in militancy among the printers who in 1974 accepted the inevitability of cold-type composing. In exchange for life-time job guarantees and a generous "buy-out" provision. *The Post* obtained a free hand in introducing new technology. By 1975 all ads were being set in cold-type and this facility had the capacity to set all type for a full edition.

LABOR RELATIONS IN 1975

Mark Meagher, Vice President/Finance and Administration of The Washington Post Company, was appointed general manager shortly after the printers ratified their 1974 contract. The 1974 negotiations with Dugan were his first experience in labor relations. Little progress was made during 1974 and 1975 to lessen the atmosphere of confrontation with the pressmen.

The pressmen's contract and those of the other crafts except the Printers and the Guild expired on September 30, 1975. *The Post* had demanded major changes, particularly in manning and scheduling, that would greatly diminish union prerogatives. The union demanded a 4-day week, double time for all overtime, 5 weeks' vacation and retention of the status quo in every "non-economic" contract clause.

At each session Wallace stressed the following basic issues:

1. The union had to work more shifts at straight time.[2]
2. The company had to regain control of the pressroom, which meant exempting salaried supervisors from union discipline.

3. The union had to agree to "spell out" circumstances under which the "status quo" clause would be applied.[3]
4. All "past practices" had to be reduced to writing.

The pressmen refused to yield on any of the basic issues. As September 30 approached, Mrs. Graham learned that in the event of a strike *The Post* could expect no support from *The Star*. Historically the Washington newspapers had negotiated jointly with the crafts. This year, *The Star*, under new management and in shaky financial shape, announced that it intended to negotiate independently. Joseph Allbritton, the new owner, sought a one-year wage moratorium with the unions and feared that a strike would sink the paper. Mrs. Graham was not anxious to face a strike alone. "If we take a strike," Mrs. Graham told Meagher, "we can't win with other papers publishing." While she agreed that Wallace and Meagher should continue to push for significant concessions, she preferred a short-term time-buying settlement to a strike.

On September 30 new contracts had not been negotiated with any of the involved unions. Dugan terminated the pressmen's contract at midnight but stated a willingness to continue to work under the existing contract "as long as meaningful negotiations continue." He also proposed a one-week extension provided that a cost-of-living wage adjustment went into effect immediately and that all wage increases be retroactive. Wallace rejected the proposals but indicated a willingness to continue negotiations, and an October 1st negotiation date was set with the pressmen.

---

[2] The contract said that the union would make every effort to furnish straight-time coverage for 60% of employees on vacation, ill, etc. In the past, the union had made little effort to provide "straight-time" coverage.

[3] The "status quo" clause provided that when disputes over contract interpretation arose, the "status quo" would prevail pending settlement.

THE STRIKE

At 4:35 A.M. the night foreman in the pressroom noticed from his office that the presses had stopped running. On opening the door to the work area he was jumped by several men. One held a screwdriver to his throat. An unknown number of pressmen disabled all 72 units of the 9 presses. They sliced the cushions on the press cylinders, ripped out electrical wiring, removed key pieces, jammed the cylinders, cut air hoses and sabotaged other parts. The most serious damage was caused by fire. The extent of the damage was impossible to determine immediately. It was in fact three months before the most seriously damaged press was back in operation. The estimated bill for repairs was around $375,000.

Many of the 115 pressmen left when they saw what was happening. The severely beaten foreman managed to reach Mark Meagher's 7th floor office where he confirmed the report of "a riot going on in the pressroom." Meagher telephoned Mrs. Graham. Arriving at the office:

> The sight was unbelievable. When I got to 15th Street, I saw police cars, red lights flashing—I thought to myself, if I drive to the parking lot they'll wreck the car. I asked a policeman what to do. He said park it here, I'll keep an eye on it. I was so scared at this point. I just walked and went through (the picket line). They yelled but nothing happened. It was the most awful moment of my life.

One of Katharine Graham's first concerns was whether *The Post* could print that night. When told no, she telephoned Joe Allbritton of *The Star* to try to persuade him to lend *The Post* press time. He refused. A task-force under executive William Cooper canvassed small newspapers within 200 miles of Washington. Each paper was asked if they would print a small edition of *The Post*.

Many members of the Newspaper Guild, not knowing of the strike, showed up for work on October 1 and crossed the picket line. Top managers took them on tours of the pressroom which was still smokey and littered with debris. According to one executive: "They were unstrung." Meeting later that day, many expressed outrage and the group at *The Post* voted overwhelmingly to defy an order from the officers of their Baltimore-Washington local to honor the picket line.

Later that day, Jim Dugan told reporters that his men were "frustrated" by *The Post*'s anti-union policies. He offered no apologies. Several days later he told reporters that his men "just went crazy and panicked" in a moment of "temporary insanity." *The Post* seized the public relations initiative by issuing press releases and by having some top managers appear regularly on TV.

By the end of the second day *The Post* began to publish with the aid of six papers. Helicopters picked up paste-ups of a 24-page paper from the roof of *The Post* and flew them to the 6 plants. The heart of the makeshift production was cold-type technology.

All the unions except the Guild were honoring the pressmen's picket lines. The printers were bound by contract to honor mailer lines. The Guild met again and again voted by a narrow ten-vote margin to stay in. Without a working newsroom *The Post* could not have hoped to hold its readership and advertisers. With the Guild staying in there would be as much quality copy as the production process could handle.

On the night of October 6 non-union machinists repaired one press. *Post* employees trained in Oklahoma ran off 100,000 papers. After that night, printing capacity began to increase.

The company's most optimistic plans were to publish 40 pages a day with some supplementary sections printed elsewhere. This was enough to break even, given the $384,000 a week savings on craft work salaries. A larger paper was felt to be too difficult for the amateur crews.

These plans ignored the *esprit de corps* of the non-union employees. Many working in production lived at *The Post*, sleeping on cots in their offices. Whereas before October 1st, 1,220 craft workers were employed, after that date a work force of 210 to 375 produced *The Post*. Mrs. Graham spent almost every Saturday night gluing Sunday papers in brown wrappers for mail subscribers. In a few weeks working employees were competing with each other. A hand-lettered sign on one press proclaimed, "J. Press—printing its way into the hearts of thousands."

During this period, several executives expected Katharine Graham to give in to the pressmen. So also did the union leadership and initially *The Post* lost advertising to *The Star*. However, by mid-November *The Post* was running a 4-section paper. Dugan refused to believe that amateurs were running the presses.

Although *The Post* made two new proposals in negotiation, no progress was made. Several theories were discussed among top management regarding the pressmen's intransigence: (1) pressmen leadership was involved in the violence and could not negotiate until *The Post* offered amnesty: (2) Dugan did not know how to react in a situation in which he was no longer bargaining from a power position; (3) the pressmen misread the entire situation; and (4) Dugan's pride.

On November 5, at the request of various international officers, a secret meeting was held between *Post* officials and Dugan. The meeting was unproductive. A federal mediator's suggestion for arbitration was rejected by both sides.

By the beginning of December, *The Post* was fast approaching 95% of normal size and initial advertising defectors were returning. Mrs. Graham was being pressured by numerous publishers to "bust the pressmen's union." Mrs. Graham continued to respond that she hoped for a negotiated settlement.

Mrs. Graham and her executives were under no illusions that their production team could put out the paper indefinitely in spite of strong reluctance to giving in. At the beginning of the strike Larry Wallace had pegged the time limit at about Christmas. Mrs. Graham had come to agree and the effective date for some sort of turning point was set at the beginning of December.

DECEMBER 3, 1975

On the afternoon of December 3, Mrs. Graham and Mark Meagher reviewed the options as they saw them:

1. They could admit that the pressmen had outlasted them and "surrender" on the pressmen's terms. This would at least settle the strike before long-term damage was done to *The Post*.

2. They could attempt to buy time by rounding up enough trained help from outside to relieve the amateur crews. With the crews relieved, they could continue to wait and continue to try to start meaningful negotiation. This would signal the pressmen that *The Post* was prepared to continue the strike and would avoid irrevocable action. Hopefully pressure from other unions would induce the pressmen to negotiate seriously.

3. *The Post* could "go all the way." This option would involve a final offer to the pressmen which would grant substantial pay increases, and probably life-time employment, in return for surrender of union prerogatives. If this offer were refused, *The Post* would declare that a "legal impasse" had been reached in negotiation, bring in temporary replacements supplied by SPPI, and begin to hire permanent non-union replacements. This option held the promise of the greatest gain but also entailed the greatest risk.

This sort of irrevocable action could easily cause the Guild to strike, turn what had been a token national labor boycott into a serious union action adversely affecting circulation and advertising, harden all the striking unions behind the pressmen, or cause other reactions.

On the afternoon of December 3, one of these options would have to be chosen. Once the decision was made, the manner of its announcement would have to be decided.

THE WASHINGTON POST
STUDY QUESTIONS:

1. Analyze the management and union considerations that appear to be evolving toward a major confrontation.
2. What are the elements of power favoring management and the Pressman at the conclusion of the case?
3. What option should Mrs. Graham select? What are the advantages and risks of each option?

THE WASHINGTON POST
Exhibit 1 Newspaper production process, hot vs. cold type

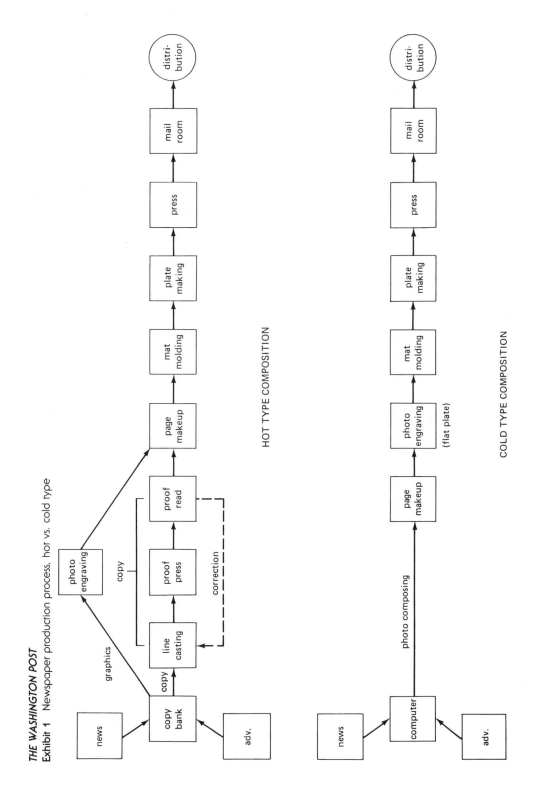

HOT TYPE COMPOSITION

COLD TYPE COMPOSITION

THE WASHINGTON POST

Exhibit 2 Circulation and advertising revenues, 1963–1974

| Year | Average Paid Circulation | | | Advertising | |
| | Daily | Sunday | Revenue | Linage | Revenue |
			(in 000's)	(in 000's)	(in 000's)
1963	423,401	513,751	$ 7,598	53,055	$ 33,431
1964	437,810	536,376	8,054	61,166	39,566
1965	446,342	556,252	9,064	68,443	44,811
1966	457,839	576,536	9,100	73,588	50,398
1967	469,972	599,596	9,297	70,470	52,061
1968	483,497	627,914	9,961	70,442	56,278
1969	489,123	641,121	11,859	71,933	62,183
1970	505,357	665,739	13,164	69,065	64,080
1971	511,540	677,663	14,353	72,197	69,533
1972	521,565	693,370	15,528	78,768	82,032
1973	534,373	706,005	16,391	84,728	92,955
1974	532,641	712,625	18,681	83,809	101,881

THE WASHINGTON POST
Exhibit 3 Revenue and income from operations by major divisions, 1963–1974 (in 000's)

Year	1963	1964	1965	1966	1967	1968	1969	1970	1971	1972	1973	1974
Net Operating Revenues												
Newspaper publishing & related operations	$41,139	$47,747	$54,011	$60,168	$63,404	$68,150	$75,859	$79,267	$85,892	$79,796	$111,997	$125,731
Magazine and book publishing & related operations	35,056	38,178	43,436	51,214	56,775	65,967	79,280	79,985	86,044	93,790	107,617	123,121
Broadcasting	9,319	10,118	10,603	11,445	11,316	12,480	13,994	18,779	20,813	24,258	27,335	38,727
Total	$85,514	$96,043	$108,050	$122,827	$131,495	$146,597	$169,133	$178,031	$192,749	$217,844	$246,949	$287,579
Income from Operations												
Newspaper publishing & related operations	$ 4,631	$ 6,470	$ 8,664	$ 9,604	$ 9,008	$ 10,295	$ 11,444	$ 8,883	$ 8,706	$ 10,222	$ 10,535	$ 10,746
Magazine and book publishing & related operations	1,525	689	2,764	3,581	2,140	4,266	6,515	2,584	2,738	5,660	9,161	10,202
Broadcasting	3,241	3,231	3,542	2,842	2,630	2,785	1,695	2,458	3,750	5,924	5,996	7,192
Total	$ 9,397	$10,390	$ 14,970	$ 16,027	$ 13,778	$ 17,346	$ 19,654	$ 13,925	$ 15,194	$ 21,806	$ 25,692	$ 28,140

THE WASHINGTON POST
Exhibit 4 Commercial departments organization chart, summer 1975

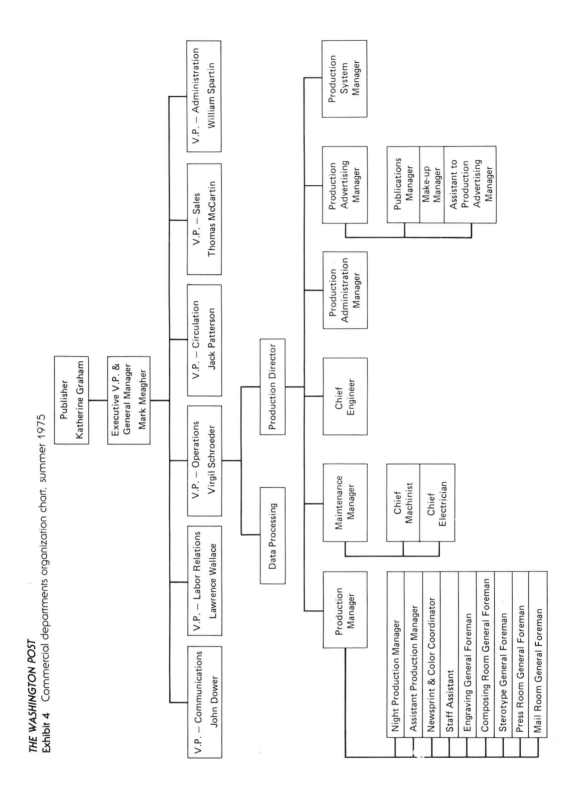

Exhibit 5 Weekly pay of production workers in various industries in the Washington metropolitan area, 1964 and 1974

	1964	1974	% Increase
	(Average Weekly Earnings)		
Manufacturing	$108.95	$199.16	82.8
Durable Goods	107.22	184.57	72.1
Food & Kindred Products	105.81	188.84	78.5
Printing & Publishing	117.87	240.46	104.0
Washington Post		*(Weighted Average Weekly Scale, Night Rate)*	
All Crafts	126.80	266.26	110.0
Pressmen	139.85	279.78	100.0
Sterotypers	137.00	280.65	104.9
Mailers	128.52	276.75	115.3
Photo-Engravers	155.50	301.00	93.6
Paper Handlers	95.32	218.36	129.1
Composing	148.42	290.27	95.6
Mailroom Helpers	83.68	217.07	159.4

Source: U.S. Department of Labor, Bureau of Labor Statistics, *Employment and Earnings, States and Areas, 1939–72*, Washington, 1974, and current additional data from various offices, Bureau of Labor Statistics, *Washington Post* data from the publisher.

Exhibit 6 Union and earnings, 1974

Unions	Number of Members	1974 Straight-Time Scale	1974 Average Earnings	1974 Highest Earnings
Mailers Union	245			
Mailers		$14,391.00	$19,054.83	$31,519.02
Newspaper and Graphic Communication Union	220			
Pressmen		14,588.95	22,568.00	34,649.00
Stereotypers		14,628.90	22,418.78	32,838.04
Printing Specialists and Paper Products Union	102			
Paperhandlers		11,354.85	17,932.73	26,824.23
General Workers		10,208.90	10,283.75	11,455.41
Graphic Arts International Union	37			
Photo-Engravers		15,847.00	18,564.31	27,787.45
International Association of Machinists	26			
Machinists		14,666.60	17,739.11	22,184.55
International Brotherhood of Electrical Workers	24			
Electricians		15,949.70	19,159.82	23,713.27
International Union of Operating Engineers	21			
Engineers		15,653.30	16,599.53	21,699.54
Carpenters and Painters		15,653.30	17,395.86	18,375.43
Typographical Union	540	NA	NA	NA
Printers				
Newspaper Guild	820	NA	NA	NA
Building Services Union	90	NA	NA	NA

NA = Not Available.

IV

THE
COMPENSATION SYSTEM:
SOME SELECTED
ISSUES

Compensation is the payment of wages and salaries, including incentive and bonus payments, and benefits to employees in exchange for work. The elements of compensation constitute an integrated system of payment and benefit policies and practices to achieve defined, and at times conflicting, organizational objectives. Much of the essence of the design of the compensation system is working out tradeoffs among more or less seriously conflicting objectives. In addition to the objectives to attract, to retain, and to motivate employees, compensation systems are designed to achieve certain more general objectives as well. They are:

1. The wage and salary system must be perceived by the great majority of employees as *equitable*. There are many dimensions to equity in compensation, some of which are highly subjective in character. The major aspects of equity relate to (1)

the relative pay to individuals working on the same job, (2) the relative rate of pay for more closely and for more distantly related jobs. The equity of pay among closely related jobs tends to be determined primarily by job content comparisons based on job evaluation factors. The relative pay for more distantly related jobs tends to be judged primarily by external market rate comparisons both directly and as incorporated in the selection and weighting of job evaluation factors. Both internal job content and external market rate standards are essential in making relative job rate comparisons as will be discussed subsequently. (3) In addition to the relative pay of individuals on the same job and to the relative pay among different jobs (a distinction that is less sharply made within the managerial hierarchy than at other occupational levels), an equity judgment is made as to the general level of wages and salaries in the commu-

189

nity or nationally for some jobs. This judgment is made by comparison to external rates by means of wage and salary surveys for selected "key" jobs.

2. Compensation systems must be *nondiscriminatory, open and defensible, and legal.* These aspects of compensation are evolving criteria. Equity considerations in compensation systems have frequently not been faced squarely within organizations. Payment to individuals has been regarded as confidential and kept secret. Increasingly systems must become more open. In part openness is being forced through equal employment opportunity challenges. Job descriptions, job requirements, performance standards, job evaluation systems, performance appraisal and merit pay plans, promotion policies and practices, and other elements of compensation must meet evolving equal employment opportunity standards. Union challenge historically and today has been and is important in shaping compensation systems. Unions tend to create more open and arguably more defensible systems. In the process unions tend to eliminate merit distinctions and to move toward seniority-based decisions. Equal employment opportunity requirements appear to be giving rise to similar policy changes. Compensation systems must meet other legal requirements including older requirements such as the Equal Pay Act. The Equal Pay Act mandates that companies pay men and women equally for work that requires equal skill, effort, and responsibility and which is performed under similar working conditions. Social legislation clearly is expanding the legal requirements of compensation systems, setting new equity standards, and forcing more open and more defensible administrative procedures.

3. Basic compensation objectives as stated are *to attract, to retain, and to moti-* *vate* employees. The motivational objective, however, is complex and somewhat controversial. There is no widely accepted theory of motivation. Theory does not provide a noncontroversial guide as to the extent to which an organization should use financial or nonfinancial incentive mechanisms. Legal, institutional, and employee group pressures would appear to be placing more and more constraints on the meaningful use of competitive financial reward systems. The relative weight which will be given to financial as contrasted with nonfinancial reward systems appears to depend heavily on the values and goals of a particular top management team.

4. The compensation system must be designed to meet the *competitive and ability to pay* necessities of the organization. Labor cost is of course a function of both the level of wages and salaries and of the level and quality of employee performance. The degree to which employees are in fact highly motivated and do achieve high performance standards appears frequently, if not typically, to be a more important competitive cost determinant than is the scope of variation in the relative general level of pay. Organizations in some industries are confronted by a situation in which their limited ability to pay seriously constrains their ability to meet community and national labor market rates.

In, for example, a capital-intensive industry, labor costs may account for only 8 to 10% of a company's cost of goods sold. For a hospital or a museum, however, payroll and payroll-related expenses might account for two-thirds to three-fourths of the budget.

5. One can also state that a compensation system should be *balanced* as to its relative emphasis on monetary compensation and benefits. Since 1940 benefit costs have grown dramatically as a percentage of pay or total compensation. There have been various reasons for this rapid growth; however, future emphasis and trends would appear to be subject to conflicting pressures. Perhaps the major issue is the degree to which benefit dollars as contrasted with wage and salary dollars contribute to employee motivation and to competitive realities. As discussed in the chapter on benefits, there is a broad social question as to the degree to which employees should be protected against social risks through public as contrasted with private systems. The United States possesses a double standard system of benefits in which individuals protected by both private and public benefits are far better off than those dependent entirely on public systems. European countries would not tolerate the double standards existing in the U.S. system.

It is obvious that the above five general objectives are not guides that can be easily applied in the design of particular systems. Conflicts and necessary tradeoffs between and among the criteria are obvious. How a given organization establishes its own specific compensation objectives in the design of its own system will depend upon the values and goals of top management and upon the institutional and environmental situation in which an organization is operating. These broad objectives, while difficult to apply, constitute fundamental considerations in working out both the policy and important administrative dimensions of a particular compensation system.

MAJOR ADMINISTRATIVE COMPONENTS IN WAGE AND SALARY SYSTEMS

The major administrative components in the determination of wages and salaries are decisions relating (1) to the general level of wages and salaries, (2) to the determination of wage rates or salaries for particular jobs or positions, and (3) to the determination of pay for the individual as distinct from the job. In establishing pay for the individual, (4) method of pay, including salary plans, incentive and bonus payments, must also be determined. While it is helpful to analyze these components separately, there are various relationships among them and each is complex.

The primary decision as to the general level of pay is where the organization will position itself within the range of market rates. Larger nonunion companies frequently articulate a policy of paying significantly above the average level of rates as identified through market surveys. Various objectives bear upon this primary decision.

In the first place, most managements no doubt desire to offer attractive wages and salaries to recruit and select more qualified employees, to reduce labor turnover, and to contribute to the motivation of employees. The extent to which a high-wage policy contributes to and sustains high morale can only be judged subjectively and will in fact be much influenced by the particular values and goals of top management. With nonunion companies, morale objectives will be closely linked to the desire to remain nonunion. In unionized companies, the general level of wages will be closely related to collective bargaining considerations. Unions obviously push companies toward higher general levels of pay.

A second objective, partially in conflict with the above employee relations considerations, is maintaining a strong competitive position in the product market. Some companies operate in highly competitive product markets—that is, highly competitive as to both wages and prices. Some highly competitive industries also have relatively low wage levels. Individual companies thus have, to varying degrees, an ability-to-pay constraint that makes difficult the implementation or a high-wage policy. However, competitive pressures bear upon unit labor cost and such costs are a function both of the level of pay and of productivity. Some companies achieve decidedly competitive labor costs in association with a high general wage level. While competitive realities place constraints on this happy outcome, designing and implementing policies to achieve these mutual objectives to the greatest possible degree should obviously have high managerial priority.

There are other dimensions to the general level question. For instance, wage structure and plant location decisions cannot usually be separated from general wage level decisions. Many multiplant companies follow a policy of decentralized wage determination. If a company establishes its general level of wages separately for each plant on the basis of local wage rate surveys, then plant location has a significant impact upon the company's general wage level. While unions frequently push for standardized wage rates throughout a company, they also often accept decentralized wage determination. Typically, plant location and decentralized wage determination have a significant impact on the determination of the general wage level.

Wage structure decisions are related in other ways to the general level of wages. In establishing wage rates by job evaluation, single or multiple job evaluation plans may be used. If a different job or salary evaluation plan is used for different groups of jobs, a more precise relationship to market rates will be established than will be the case with a single evaluation plan. If, for example, a separate job evaluation plan is used for clerical occupations, then in attaching wage rates separately to these jobs, a somewhat separate "general level" decision is being made for that group of jobs. Also, in the process of attaching wage rates to jobs, the "tilt" of the curve may be modified to pay, for example, relatively higher wages to higher-paying than to lower-paying jobs within the group.

The third administrative component in wage and salary systems, the determination of pay for the individual as distinct from the job, will be analyzed primarily in connection with the subsequent treatment of two issues: (1) merit pay and the effective use of performance appraisal and (2) the question of financial incentives. Some background considerations with respect to these issues will be presented later.

There are several points to be made in distinguishing different approaches to the compensation of individuals. In the first place, general increase adjustments are not typically used in nonunion organizations and frequently not for nonunion employees, particularly managerial employees, within union organizations. Most nonunion organizations do not make general wage and salary adjustments, but incorporate such adjustments into individual employee increases. Disguised general increases are thus given in the form of "merit" increases. The rationalization for not using general increase adjustments is to give greater scope for "merit" distinctions among individuals. However, as the merit principle increasingly yields, for reasons discussed subsequently, to more seniority-based systems, it may be that elements of a merit system could best be preserved by also using cost of living and productivity uniform adjustments. One can even question the heavy emphasis usually given to bonus payments in executive compensation.

In the second place, in compensating individuals an organization may use single rates or rate ranges. Job evaluation typically culminates in the classification of jobs into a larger or smaller number of labor grades or classes. With respect to each labor grade, a range of wage rates—that is, a minimum and a maximum rate—is usually established, but at times a single uniform rate is utilized. In fact, single rates are not uncommon in unionized organizations. Single rates eliminate all distinctions in pay among employees on the same job unless incentive compensation is also used in the system. Also, if union organizations utilize rate ranges, progression of individuals from the minimum to the maximum rate tends to be automatic, or nearly so, on the basis of time in grade. Progression systems may provide for more rapid advancement for individuals in lower labor grades, reflecting a shorter estimated learning time for the jobs in those grades. Advancement may also be speeded up to relieve inflationary pressures. However, apart from variations, even in many nonunion organizations so-called merit increases have become much more automatic and standardized.

There is a great deal of merit in distinguishing administratively between general wage increases, job rate changes, and individual employee compensation. If such a distinction is maintained, general increases to all employees tend to maintain their real wages and to pass on to them an improvement in standard of living reflecting at least the gains in the country's average improvement in output per man-hour. There is logical appeal in the regular use of general increases in wages and salaries as is the practice in unionized situations. Much less logical, however, is the replacement of merit-based compensation of individuals by nearly automatic increases. This question is central to the subsequent discussion of the financial incentive and performance appraisal issues.

JOB EVALUATION AND PAY FOR THE JOB

Job and salary evaluation is the cornerstone of compensation administration. Just how extensively evaluation is used is not known precisely, but formally or informally such methods appear to predominate in large-scale private employment. Some companies and industries use no formal method for the determination of job wage rates. Such companies and industries—as, for example, in construction—operate simply with a system of market wage rates. Other companies and industries utilize some form of wage classification but no formal evaluation. Also, where job and/or salary evaluation is used, different systems are commonly employed for blue collar, clerical, and for professional and executive job groups. Some of these differences will be discussed subsequently. In each instance, however, evaluation involves three processes: (1) job definition and description, (2) job rating, and (3) attaching wage rates to jobs.

Job Definition and Description

What constitutes a "job" is typically well accepted at any given time in any organization. Job titles and concepts are established by custom and practice, by technology, and by existing administrative procedures. Jobs are less fixed in content and have more elastic boundaries in administrative, professional, and executive employment than in plant and clerical employment, but typically job categories tend to be accepted and taken for granted. Exceptions to this statement are found where a job structure is being modified by changes in technology, operating practices, or through deliberate changes in organizational design. It is suggested, however, that more conscious attention should be paid in job design and to the concept of a "job" as embodied in a job description.

In the first place, the concept of a "job" is arbitrary and judgmental in important respects. Jobs can be defined in quite broad or in very narrow terms. When job evaluation was first being introduced, one of its contributions was to recognize job and payment distinctions within then existing broad categories such as clerk in the office and laborer in the plant. While equity then demanded narrower and more specialized job categories, such categories are flexible and should be determined in the light of hiring and entry-level requirements, transfer patterns associated with work fluctuations, and promotion patterns and sequences. At times, narrowly defined job categories have created needless administrative burdens.

For one company we know, the nonexempt pay plan includes three distinct features: (1) the concept of job families, (2) the structuring of jobs according to job families, and (3) distinct criteria for determining job values and classification levels. Within each job family, jobs are grouped into classification levels. Each level requires more complex skills and functions than the preceding; therefore, as an employee gains experience in one level, he or she is preparing for the next. Thus, because both career direction and the specific requirements to proceed in that direction are clearly visible to the employee, the system encourages the movement of individuals. The nineteen job families this company has are as follows: secretarial, data processing, graphics and audio visual, material control, general clerical, coating, chemical mixing and processing, machine manufacturing, evaluation technician, manual operations, optical processing, general services, metal trades, construction and maintenance trades, instrument technician, research and devel-

opment technician, drafting, medical, and general.

More important than the issue of more narrowly or broadly defined job categories is the issue of job design in and of itself. For many years industrial engineering principles have governed the design of jobs. The assumption has prevailed that the more specialized the job and the more finely divided the work tasks, the greater the employee efficiency. This assumption is more and more being called into question. At least in particular environmental and institutional circumstances, creating more challenging work through job enrichment or through various employee participation programs has resulted in both improved efficiency and in greater employee satisfaction. The managerial objective is a balanced search for an improved quality of working life and for improved employee productivity.

It is not clear just how these trends, which are only gradually developing in the United States, will affect traditional job evaluation procedures. It appears that employee participation and job enrichment programs and practices create rather continuous dynamic changes in work content. Possibly trends now exist toward more broadly defined jobs and also toward less standardized work content among individuals working in a given job category. While traditionally people are paid for what they do, perhaps in the future pay will be more closely related to potential, knowledge, and learning. The objective of a job enrichment program is to increase employee responsibility, traditionally a heavily weighted item in any job evaluation plan.

Another important influence modifying job design, job requirements, and job descriptions is equal employment requirements. Job descriptions vary considerably in length and in degree of detail incorporated in them, but all describe in as operational a manner as possible the general duties and responsibilities of the job. In writing descriptions, particular attention is paid to the "boundary" conditions of a given job to distinguish it, again in as operational a manner as possible, from closely related jobs. Poorly conceived jobs and poorly written job descriptions give rise to controversy in the classification of individuals.

In addition to a statement of general duties and responsibilities, job descriptions commonly list and state job requirements. Requirements are stated relative to the job factors (skill, responsibility, working conditions and physical effort— or as otherwise defined) used in the rating of jobs. With specific statements of job requirements in terms of job factors, the rating of jobs is almost mechanical once the requirements are stipulated in the description.

Job requirements have historically been stated in terms of minimum requirements to do the job. On the other hand, these minimum requirements might well have been designated as "desired" minimum qualifications or requirements rather than as "bare-bones" and "essential" minimum requirements. Former job descriptions and job requirements or qualifications may, for example, have excluded women employees in situations where such qualifications were not essential to job performance. Or, as a second example, the educational or physical requirements stated for a job may exclude a high proportion of minority and/or women employees, but not truly be necessary for satisfactory job performance. The thrust of EEO has been toward validated "job related" hiring and promotion criteria.

The determination of job content with its related job requirements has always been regarded as an important first step in the introduction of job evaluation plans. The historical approach to the determination of job content, however, has been an industrial engineering one. Today industrial engineering is a necessary but not sufficient analytical approach to job design and the determination of job content. Motivational, quality of work life, and equal employment considerations and requirements must also be given adequate attention.

A final point with respect to job descriptions is their status in collective bargaining contracts. Are job descriptions in essence negotiated agreements as to the content of the job? Or are they descriptions of the job as currently performed, with management having the right to modify job content subject only to the requirement that the revised job be redescribed and reevaluated as to appropriate rate of pay? There is no hard and fast answer to these questions. Among industries employing crafts workers where jurisdiction is a major union consideration, job descriptions have become agreements as to job content. In perhaps most manufacturing organizations, however, management has the contractual right to modify job content whenever it so desires, subject only to the job being reevaluated. If, however, management allows a job to become "deskilled" through technological change without reevaluating the job, vested interests are created which are difficult to correct. In union or nonunion circumstances, substantial employee relations problems are created if descriptions are not kept current.

The Rating of Jobs

An understanding of the process of job evaluation, particularly the rating of jobs, is an essential prelude to the discussion in this chapter of the issue of comparable worth. A paper by Professor Donald P. Schwab, University of Wisconsin, on "Job Evaluation and Pay Setting: Concepts and

Practices,"[1] contains a decidedly relevant contrast between job evaluation as practiced and job evaluation prescriptions. As Schwab notes, ". . . specifically, job evaluation is described as a procedure that makes judgments about jobs based on content or the demands made on job incumbents." (page 55) This, as noted earlier, suggests an internal as opposed to external or market orientation. Schwab subsequently points out that ". . . as practiced, job evaluation identifies and differentially weighs compensable factors to maximize the relationship between them and the wages on key jobs (which are assumed to reflect the market). Thus the actual criterion of job evaluation is not worth in a job content sense, but market wages. The model (compensable factors and weights) emerging from this process is then applied to non-key jobs for purposes of establishing a wage hierarchy." (page 63)

Not only is the model of compensable factors and weights, as stated by Schwab, developed to reflect the market rather than "worth" as such, but the actual ratings of particular jobs, it is believed, tends with dissimilar jobs rather unconsciously to reflect a market evaluation of skills. The process of rating skill elements, such as "job knowledge required" or "complexity" for distinctly different types of jobs (skills) is quite subjective. While a rather good consensus tends to emerge among members of a job evaluation rating committee in rating dissimilar jobs on the compensable factors, the belief is that this consensus tends to develop around labor market and existing wage and salary relationships. Among jobs within the same skill family, a more direct and independent assessment of relative skill based on job content tends to take place.

[1]Contained in *Comparable Worth: Issues and Alternatives*, E. Robert Livernash, ed. (Washington, D.C.: Equal Employment Advisory Council, 1980), pp. 51–77.

Job evaluation creates an improved wage structure, a more rational and a more defensible structure. The rating of jobs, however, is by no means a truly objective measurement process whether one is talking about quite dissimilar or similar jobs. Differences of opinion among members of a rating committee tend to bring out most clearly the subjective nature of the rating process.

The fact that the rating process by its nature cannot be highly objective tends to give emphasis to the value of using a committee. Committee analysis and discussion tends to overcome and override sharp differences in individual judgments. A committee operates by bringing together the different judgments of its individual members. In other words, individual members of a rating committee initially rate jobs independently of each other. When these independent ratings are displayed in a meeting, the ratings for some jobs will indicate a quite high initial consensus, and a group decision as to the rating of such jobs can readily be made. If sharp differences among individuals are revealed, these differences can be talked out and overcome or overridden. A committee decision process appears very logical in rating jobs. And research suggests, as pointed out by Schwab, that pooled estimates of five evaluators is acceptably reliable and clearly more reliable than individual rating.

Attaching Wage Rates to the Jobs

The process of attaching wage rates to the jobs is done by formal or informal correlation between points and market wage rates for key or so-called benchmark jobs. A market survey for key jobs indicates the general level of wage or salary rates for the group of jobs, but the survey requires decisions as to the jobs, the organizations, and the geographical area to be included. A line of best fit established by correlation or informal means between market rates and evaluated points enables a system of labor grades to be built upon the existing relationships, as explained in standard personnel or job evaluation texts.

While the line of best fit indicates the general level of prevailing rates and the broad contours of structural wage or salary relationships, various policy decisions are involved in establishing the wage structure for the organization. One company we know surveys the following: hiring rates, the manufacturing rate, and the top mechanical rate. They then look at the office, technical, manufacturing and mechanical job families and make pay judgments based on the benchmark jobs.

Important policy decisions involve the general level of rates, the number of labor grades and their point spread, and the wage or salary differentials between minimum and maximum rates within which individuals will be compensated. For example, nonunion companies desirous of remaining nonunion frequently have a policy of establishing a general level of rates in the upper quarter or third of the wage range revealed by the survey.

SELECTED ISSUES AND THE RELATED CASES

This section contains a brief discussion of two issues: (1) inflation, general increase adjustments, and merit pay; and (2) the question of financial incentives. The section also contains a more extended analysis of two additional issues: (3) merit-based pay and promotion and (4) the challenge of comparable worth.

The Lincoln Electric case allows the student to give thought to a variety of elements involved in the successful use by the company of several types of financial incentives. The student can and should examine the technical aspects of the various financial incentive plans. However, very important are certain institutional and environmental variables bearing upon the use of these incentives. Elements of managerial philosophy, which have remained quite steadfast over the years, are a particularly important topic for discussion. Lincoln is a company holding to, and implementing successfully, beliefs and practices that many other companies have abandoned or modified over the last couple of decades. What factors account for Lincoln's success?

The pay proposal in the Au Bon Pain case might be viewed as the service industry equivalent of the pay approaches described in the Lincoln Electric case. In the Au Bon Pain case, students must understand the factors associated with success in the restaurant business and evaluate a new pay plan for store managers.

The third case used with this compensation chapter is a case series—namely, Eli Lilly and Company (A) and (B). As developed in the analysis of merit-based pay and promotion, performance evaluation and career development systems are often more tolerated than accepted. Yet, if merit-based decisions for pay, promotion, and potential determination are to remain meaningful, the appraisal and career development systems on which they are based must achieve a high degree of employee and managerial support. The Eli Lilly cases provide the basis for discussion of a wide range of appraisal and career development issues, including the pros and cons of forming a group to evaluate an individual's performance and then recommend a development plan.

The Public Sector Data Processing Professionals case study gives students the opportunity to analyze a very serious and complex personnel management problem in the Commonwealth of Massachusetts. If data processing is to achieve its potential, then it is essential that the state be able to attract and retain competent professionals. Yet a number of factors, including the state's civil service system, are getting in the way of making adequate progress. Students, therefore, must identify with the goals of the manager, analyze the situation, and recommend a realistic course of action.

Inflation, General Increase Adjustments, and Merit Pay

The first edition of this text expressed major concern over the problem of inflation, pointing out that the underlying rate had advanced with each cycle of prosperity and recession during the postwar years. It stated: "To bring down this rate of inflation and to break the momentum of inflationary expectations will require fiscal and monetary restraint over an extended period of years. It is highly unlikely that political realities will support sufficient restraint to do more than mitigate modestly current levels of inflation."

In point of fact, inflation has been brought under control. An important element in its control has been the abandonment by the automobile industry of its wage formula, with the annual improvement factor and the cost-of-living escalator clauses. This formula was widely viewed as "an engine of inflation," in that correcting for past inflation created future inflation.

There has been and remains an important distinction between union and nonunion wage policy and administration. Very few nonunion companies follow the practice of giving "general" wage increases openly. As a consequence, "merit increases" incorporated an inflation adjustment, thus giving disguised general increases and blunting the avowed purpose of individual wage adjustments.

The competitive strength of the U.S. economy has undoubtedly been increased by the elimination of the automobile wage formula, with its widespread pattern-setting influence. Also, eliminating the wage formula and bringing inflation under control allows individual wage adjustments in nonunion firms to more closely follow their avowed purpose.

The Question of Financial Incentives

Many traditional wage incentive plans have not worked well under collective bargaining. The grievance challenge under militant unionism has frequently resulted in

(1) substantial inequities in earnings and effort. A mixture of tight and loose standards is both cause and effect in perpetuating a multitude of grievances over standards and a distorted wage structure; (2) a growing average incentive yield or bonus. The most dramatic figure found was a plan with a 60-point hour base, designed for an 80-point hour yield, which had, as of 1955, a 300-point hour average bonus. This figure, of course, indicates only payment results and not a high level of effort; (3) a declining average level of effort. Workers appear to take the gains of looser standards partly in increased earnings and partly in increased leisure. Informal quotas are met in seven or six, or, allegedly in one case, in four of the eight working hours; (4) a high proportion of "off-standard" payment and time. Incentive workers in one large multiplant company averaged 40% off-standard time for all plants. This may involve many factors, but an important element is abuse of various types of guarantees.[2]

[2]Sumner H. Slichter, James J. Healy, and E. Robert Livernash, *The Impact of Collective Bargaining on Management* (Washington, DC: The Brookings Institution, 1960), Chapter 16, "Wage Incentives," pp. 490–529, especially pp. 497–503.

The degree of incentive deterioration indicated above is an unstable situation and would lead to disaster or reform. Today many companies have replaced incentive systems particularly in their new plants by some form of measured day work or "fair day's work" system of payment, but the degree of incentive payment decline is not precisely known.[3] Data indicate that while incentive pay in 1958 in United States manufacturing industries (27% of production workers)[4] was more extensive than the percentage of production workers on piecework in 1890 (17.9% of production workers), some decline took place between 1945–46 and 1958. This latter decline was from 30% of production workers in 1945–1946 to 27% in 1958.[5] The strong suspicion is that there has been a further decline from the 27% in 1958 during the thirty years from 1958 to 1988.

Some incentive plans in less adversary union-management relationships have operated satisfactorily over the years, with production standards maintained in accordance with industrial engineering principles. Also, some poorly operating incentive systems have been revised so that a satisfactory level of effort has been achieved. Extensive fieldwork would be required to determine the operating characteristics of today's incentive plans and day work systems of payment, but the impression is that only a small proportion of incentive plans are operating in a manner that reflects a successful financial reward system.

The Lincoln Electric case is particularly interesting, as earlier noted, because of the various elements in the company's managerial philosophy. The continuing strong support for the use of financial incentives at Lincoln is in rather marked contrast to the experience of many companies.

Both long-term and short-term incentive compensation, however, is common for top management of many companies today. Many companies also regard commissions or incentive compensation as critical to the attraction, retention, and motivation of a sales force. Yet there are successful companies utilizing neither incentive compensation for management nor commissions for salespeople. To understand what is desirable with respect to incentive compensation, much has to be known about the nature of the jobs, the competitive environment, the climate of the company, and the goals and values of top management.

Merit-Based Pay and Promotion

While many managements profess to base "merit" increases and promotion decisions for production and maintenance employees upon merit, Fred K. Foulkes[6] found, even among a select group of large nonunion companies, a considerable degree of seniority orientation in these decisions. The impact of equal employment regulations has also, it is believed, strengthened the seniority emphasis in these decisions to avoid allegations and charges of discrimination. In fact, the extent of present emphasis on seniority raises a fundamental issue as to why there has been so much default in merit deci-

---

[3]See a chapter called "Work Effort On-the-Job Screening, and Alternative Methods of Remuneration" by John H. Pencavel, Stanford University, contained in *Research in Labor Economics*, Vol. 1, 1977, Ronald G. Ehrenberg, Cornell University, ed. (Greenwich CT: Jai Press), pp. 225ff.

[4]From U.S. Bureau of the Census, Census of Population 1890: Manufacturers, Part I, Table K. And Earl L. Lewis, *Monthly Labor Review* (May 1969) pp. 469–63.

[5]From Joseph M. Sherman, "Incentive Pay in American Industry, 1945–46," *Monthly Labor Review* (November 1947), pp. 535–38. And Earl L. Lewis, "Extent of Incentive Pay in Manufacturing," *Monthly Labor Review* (May 1969) pp. 460–63.

[6]Foulkes, Fred K., *Personnel Policies in Large Nonunion Companies* (Englewood Cliffs, NJ: Prentice-Hall, Inc., 1980), Chapter 9, pp. 168–89.

sion making and also how the merit principle might equitably be strengthened.

In 1977, the Conference Board published an excellent study on appraising managerial performance.[7] The authors of this study found that (1) formal appraisal plans were widely but not universally used for managerial employees—some 72% for middle and lower managerial employees and that (2) formal plans tended to be judged more effective by top management the more recently they had been introduced or revised. Plans more than three years old typically were judged not to be effective. It appears that formal plans undergo more or less continuous revision indicating considerable dissatisfaction with them. Another trend indicated by the study was (3) a shift toward a management-by-objectives type of plan. Some two-thirds of the plan used for middle and lower management were of this type. Finally, the general attitude toward formal appraisal was one of toleration and not true acceptance. Formal appraisal was regarded as a necessary evil.

There has long been a strong current of dissatisfaction in the literature on performance appraisal. A classic article in point was Douglas McGregor's "An Uneasy Look at Performance Appraisal" (*Harvard Business Review*, May–June, 1957). A second historically important article was by H. H. Meyer, E. Kay, and J. R. P. French, Jr., "Split Roles in Performance Appraisal" (*Harvard Business Review*, January–February, 1965). Finally, a most insightful article was Herbert H. Meyer's "The Pay-For-Performance Dilemma" (*Organizational Dynamics*, Winter 1975).

In his 1975 article, Meyer emphasized research indicating the impact of appraisal on self-esteem. He stated: "This re-

search would indicate that a merit pay salary plan is likely to have the effect of threatening the self-esteem of the great majority of employees" (page 42). The problem arises from the fact that employees all tend to regard themselves as being well above average. Meyer cites some extremely skewed distributions of self-ratings. Anything approaching a bell-shaped rating distribution forced by supervisors and management under a formal rating plan thus creates a most threatening situation for employees and is a substantial blow to their self-esteem. Meyer, as a consequence, questioned the competitive approach utilized by management in most appraisal systems.

We have long felt that there was a fundamental flaw in performance appraisal stemming from its multiple purposes and uses. The problem arises from attempting to use, simultaneously, the same mechanism and procedure both to judge employees and to motivate and develop them. Study of and experience with management-by-objectives, apart from its use in appraisal systems, has led us to a number of conclusions with respect to its effective use: (1) Such a program must have the active support and the active participation of top management. (2) A program must have a line management and not a personnel department orientation. It must be used as an important element in running the business. (3) The primary purpose of the program should be to motivate and develop employees, even though there will be an element of plan and control inherent in implementing management-by-objectives. (4) The objectives or targets established by employees should be limited in number. No attempt should be made for comprehensive coverage of all duties and objectives. Targets should be over and beyond normal duties. (5) Individual objectives can only be established appropriately within a framework of

[7]Robert I. Lazer and Walter S. Wikstrom, "Appraising Managerial Performance: Current Practices and Future Directions, 1977, The Conference Board, Inc., 845 Third Avenue, New York, NY 10022, pp. 1, 22.

top-down corporate goals and objectives. Individual and corporate goals require integration for an effective system. (6) Review by higher management of an individual's objectives should not be more extensive than the employee's immediate superior and one higher level of management.

As implied in the above enumeration of criteria, the effective implementation of management-by-objectives is difficult. Such implementation requires an organizational climate of support and a coaching relationship between superior and subordinate. The issue is whether, or how, an effective performance appraisal system program can be created within a management-by-objectives program. The fundamental flaw arises when the superior, in addition to coaching the subordinate, must also "play God," as stated by McGregor, and go on record in judging his behavior. Judging creates a threatening climate that tends to destroy the effectiveness of the coaching relationship.

It is possible to minimize this difficulty if the competitive element in appraisal is greatly reduced or eliminated and if coaching is carried out over a period of time. Initiative in establishing objectives can be given to the subordinate. The employee can be evaluated in terms of the objectives he himself establishes, with the coaching of his superior, and his degree of accomplishment against these objectives. Emphasis can be on self-appraisal within a coaching relationship. This process is very different from the traditional appraisal process, including its list of criticisms, handed out in a year-end interview. The belief also is that employees will accept nonthreatening appraisal within the framework suggested even though an element of insecurity inevitably remains. Finally, the name of the game is to motivate and develop employees and thus to create an employee relations environment that encourages them to improve their performance and to prepare them for promotion. Promotion decisions can be an element of planned career pathing.

Frankly, it is unclear as to how best to relate rewards to the suggested approach to performance evaluation. Possibly minimal differentiation in merit pay is the most appropriate approach. At least in growth organizations the primary reward can be associated with promotion. While rewards no doubt should be congruent with performance, they must, at the same time, be regarded as equitable within an increasingly open employee relationship and managerial climate. While there is obviously room for difference of opinion in the discussion of financial rewards, it has been demonstrated factually by a number of organizations that a highly motivational climate may be created with limited payment differentiation within the merit pay system. This entire subject is developed in the section on work restructuring, a process receiving increasing attention.

The fourth and final issue to be discussed is the concept of comparable worth.

The Challenge of Comparable Worth

The challenge of comparable worth is that it raises what might have been "the" wage payment issue of the eighties, namely, "What is the worth to society of a secretary's job compared to an automobile mechanic's job?" Why do secretaries, who are almost exclusively women, generally earn considerably less than auto mechanics, who are almost exclusively men? Moreover, how should one compare the worth of a secretary versus the worth of an automobile mechanic?

Notwithstanding the above questions, and the problems discussed below, there have been numerous implementations of comparable worth in the public sector. Other than the elimination of male-female differentials for comparable jobs, it is not known precisely how and to what degree job placement under these programs differs from job evaluation as typically practiced. While the private sector has reviewed and refined its payment policies and practices, the direct implementation of comparable worth appears to have been avoided.

The challenge of comparable worth arises from the dramatic worldwide increase in female participation rates in the labor force and from the fact that average earnings on jobs predominantly populated by women are well below average earnings on jobs predominantly populated by men. According to the U.S. Bureau of the Census, in 1985 the average earnings of women was only 62% of the average earnings of men. In 1978 it was 58%.

Supporters of comparable worth ascribe much of the earnings gap to discrimination. Comparable worth thus questions existing wage and salary relationships and the standards on which they are based—namely labor market rates and traditional job and salary evaluation systems. As stated in a *Wall Street Journal* article: "The real question, according to the doctrine, should be whether secretaries' work is as valuable to the organization as tool and die makers'. If it is, they should be paid the same, prevailing wages be damned."

The Equal Employment Advisory Council's 1980 study on comparable worth contains six substantive academic papers by George T. Milkovich, Donald P. Schwab, George H. Hildebrand, Herbert R. Northrup, Janice R. Bellace, and Harry V. Roberts.[8] The study also contains an overview paper by E. Robert Livermash and a revised paper on the legal framework of the equal pay controversy by Robert E. Williams and Douglas S. McDowell.

From these papers a strong case can be made against the concept of comparable worth. In the first place, the concept is highly ambiguous and has not been defined in operational terms. The concept is to date, as one author puts it, sheer rhetoric. In the second place, the concept is not likely to be defined in operational terms, since it rejects the only known operational wage structure standards—namely, labor market rates and traditional job evaluation procedures.

Supporters of comparable worth and some textbook authors appear to have a fundamental misconception as to the nature of job evaluation. Donald P. Schwab analyzes job evaluation in his paper in the study cited, and contrasts job evaluation as it is perceived and as it is practiced. Job evaluation tends to be perceived as a technique which measures in some fashion the intrinsic worth of jobs to the organization. In point of fact, job evaluation as practiced is so designed in its selection and weighting of compensable factors that it reflects wage and salary rate relationships prevailing in the market. Clearly the broad contour of wage and salary relationships as established by job evaluation follows prevailing rates. As Schwab says: "Thus the actual criterion of job evaluation is not worth, in a job content sense, but market wages" (p. 63).

Supporters of comparable worth tend to be ambivalent in their attitude toward job evaluation reflecting the contrast made by Schwab between perceptions of job evaluation and job evaluation as practiced. Those who have worked with job evaluation recognize that job content can only be used effectively to compare closely similar jobs. In comparing and in evaluating jobs with very different skill contents, evaluators fall back consciously and unconsciously on market relationships.

---

[8]"Comparable Worth: A Symposium on the Issues and Alternatives" (Washington D.C.: Equal Employment Advisory Council), November 21, 1980.

A third point in the case against comparable worth is that if an attempt were made to implement comparable worth in any comprehensive manner a hopeless administrative quagmire would be created, since the concept has not been operationally defined. George H. Hildebrand also makes clear that if by any chance comparable worth could surmount its administrative problems, it would have harsh unintended employment consequences for those it is intended to help.

The difficulties and problems of implementing comparable worth appear so formidable that it is doubtful that any such program will be carried forward. A limited program might, however, be attempted. Janice R. Bellace in her review of foreign experience in fourteen countries, in the study noted earlier, finds none that have attempted a comprehensive program of reform based on comparable worth. In fact many countries are at a stage in which they are eliminating male and female rates for the same job. In one or two countries, perhaps most notably in Germany, where something approaching comparable worth is being given consideration, reform is being directed primarily at job evaluation procedures. This type of limited approach might be taken in this country. The use of "physical effort required" might, for example, be questioned as a compensable factor. Also possible would be the requirement that a single job evaluation plan, rather than multiple plans, be utilized in a single establishment or organization. Such requirements, however, could be highly disturbing, since most wage and salary relationships have been professionally established.

A fundamental consideration in the case against comparable worth is that it is most doubtful that identifiable discrimination in rates of compensation exists in professional compensation systems. The shortfall in earnings is associated with the distribution of women within the wage and salary hierarchy rather than with rates of pay. It is true, however, that discrimination is very much a matter of individual value judgments, but what can be said is that professionally established rates of pay have not been arbitrarily determined. Such rates are set through the utilization of market rate and job evaluation standards.

In addition, Harry V. Roberts, of the University of Chicago, in his paper and in his more detailed study of employee compensation in the Harris Trust and Savings Bank[9] concluded that the adjusted data were more consistent with an assumption of nondiscrimination than with an assumption of discrimination. While there are many technical aspects to the Roberts' analysis, there are two major adjustments, one for "noncompeting groups" and a second for the "underadjustment bias." While the determination of noncompeting groups is somewhat arbitrary, in the legal case involving the Harris Bank these groups were established by agreement with the regulatory agency. Employees working on jobs within a single noncompeting group, simply defined, would be able to transfer from one to another job within the group with only a minimum degree of training. In the Roberts study he compares rates of pay only among employees within noncompeting groups. The second major adjustment is for differences among employees in age, experience, education, and length of service. After making these two adjustments, the shortfall in women's earnings is statistically explained and hence the adjusted data are more consistent with an assumption of nondiscrimination than with one of discrimination.

[9]Harry V. Roberts, Report 7946, *Harris Trust and Savings Bank: An Analysis of Employee Compensation,* Department of Economics and Graduate School of Business, University of Chicago, Chicago, Ill.

Roberts quite properly does not generalize beyond his data, but the probabilities appear high that most professional compensation systems would show similar results.

Most of the shortfall in earnings is removed by the adjustment of rates of pay for relative differences in age, experience, education and length of service. The viable method to remove the remainder of the shortfall is through increased upward mobility of women. With the skill shortages probable in the 1980s, economic forces will lead to increased upward mobility. It is undesirable, however, to depend solely on such economic forces. Positive programs to train and to promote women have and should continue to supplement economic forces. There is a social and economic need for such programs, and many organizations have already enormously increased the number of women within the managerial hierarchy. While there are the various logical objections to the concept of comparable worth previously discussed, the social and personal needs giving rise to the concept can be met in a much more viable manner by increased upward mobility of women through positive training and promotion programs.

The belief is that comparable worth is a less prominent issue today than when the first edition was published. This can probably be attributed in meaningful part to significant upward mobility of women within the wage and salary hierarchy. In 1987, however, bills on comparable worth were introduced in both the Senate and the House. The bill introduced in the Senate not only requires stricter enforcement of existing EEO laws to eliminate current wage-setting practices that discriminate, but also would require a study to be conducted of federal employee compensation and wage-setting practices. The House bills, too, are concerned with the federal pay system and wage-setting practices. One (H.R. 386) would change the compensation system for federal employees and test alternatives in setting wages. The other (H.R. 387) calls for a study of federal pay system and wage-setting practices to ascertain if they encourage sex discrimination.

BIBLIOGRAPHY:
THE COMPENSATION SYSTEM

BELCHER, DAVID W., AND THOMAS J. ATCHISON. *Compensation Administration, Second Edition.* Englewood Cliffs, NJ: Prentice-Hall, 1987.

BERG, J. GARY *Managing Compensation.* New York: American Management Association, 1976.

CRYSTAL, GRAEF S. *Executive Compensation: Money, Motivation and Imagination.* New York: AMACOM, 1978.

DAILEY, CHARLES, AND A. M. MADSEN. *How to Evaluate People in Business: The Track-Record Method of Making Correct Judgments.* New York: McGraw-Hill, 1979.

ELLIG, BRUCE R. *Executive Compensation: A Total Pay Perspective.* New York: McGraw-Hill, 1982.

FOX, HARLAND, AND CHARLES A. PECK. *Top Executive Compensation, 1986 Edition.* New York: The Conference Board, #875, 1985.

LAWLER, EDWARD W., III. *Pay and Organizational Effectiveness: A Psychological View.* New York: McGraw-Hill, 1971.

LIVERNASH, E. ROBERT (ed.). *Comparable Worth: Issues and Alternatives.* Washington: Equal Employment Advisory Council, 1980.

MCLAUGHLIN, DAVID J. *The Executive Money Map.* New York: McGraw-Hill, 1975.

MAHLER, WALTER R., AND WILLIAM F. WRIGHTNOUR. *Executive Continuity.* Homewood, IL: Dow Jones-Irwin, 1973.

PATTEN, THOMAS A., JR. *Manpower Planning and Development of Human Resources.* New York: Wiley, 1971.

———. *Employment Compensation and Incentive Plans.* New York: Free Press, 1977.

ROTHSCHILD, V. HENRY, AND ARTHUR D. SPORN. *Executive Compensation: Planning, Practice, Developments.* New York: Practising Law Institute, 1984.

SCHUSTER, JAY R. *High-Technology Management Compensation.* Lexington, MA: Lexington Books, 1983.

SHWINGER, PINHAS. *Wage Incentive Systems.* New York: Halstead Press, 1976.

STEELE, JAMES W. *Paying for Performance and Position: Dilemma in Salary Compression and Merit Pay.* New York: AMA Survey Report, 1982.

The Lincoln Electric Company

We're not a marketing company, we're not an R&D company, and we're not a service company. We're a manufacturing company, and I believe that we are the best manufacturing company in the world.

With these words, George E. Willis, President of The Lincoln Electric Company, described what he saw as his company's distinctive competence. For more than thirty years, Lincoln had been the world's largest manufacturer of arc welding products (see Exhibit 1). In 1974, Lincoln Electric was believed to have manufactured more than 40% of the arc welding equipment and supplies sold in the United States. In addition to its welding products, Lincoln produced a line of three-phase A.C. industrial electric motors, but these accounted for less than 10% of sales and profits.

Lincoln's 1974 domestic net income was $17½ million on sales of $236 million (see Exhibit 2). Perhaps more significant than a single year's result was Lincoln's record of steady growth over the preceding four decades, as shown by the graph on page 207.

During this period, after-tax return on

This case was prepared by Norman Fast, Research Assistant, under the direction of Professor Norman Berg. Reprinted by permission of the Harvard Business School.

equity had ranged between 10% and 15%. Lincoln's growth had been without benefit of acquisition and had been financed through internally generated funds. The company's historic dividend payout policy in the past had been to pay to the suppliers of capital a fair return each year for its use.

COMPANY HISTORY

Lincoln Electric was founded by John C. Lincoln in 1895 to manufacture electric motors and generators. James F. Lincoln, John's younger brother, joined the company in 1907. The brothers' skills and interests were complementary. John was a technical genius. During his lifetime he was awarded more than 50 patents for inventions as diverse as an apparatus for curing meat, an electric drill, a mine door activating mechanism and an electric arc lamp. James's skills were in management and administration. He began as a salesman but soon took over as general manager. The Lincoln Electric Company was undeniably built in his image.

In 1911, the company introduces its first arc welding machine. Both brothers were fascinated by welding, which was in its infancy at the time. They recognized it as an alternative use for the motor-generator sets they were already produc-

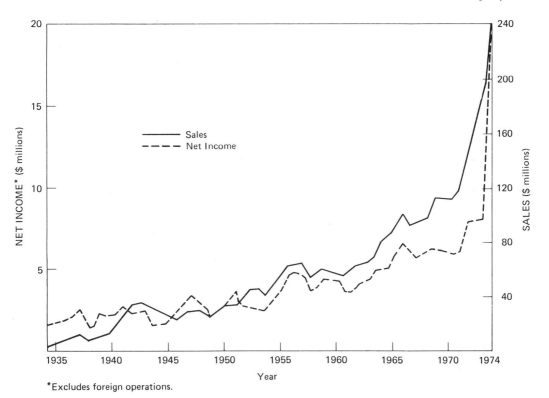

*Excludes foreign operations.

ing to recharge batteries for electric automobiles. It was becoming apparent from the success of Ford, Buick and others that the days of the electric auto might be numbered, and the brothers were anxious to find other markets for their skills and products.

John's mechanical talents gave the company a head start in welding machines which it never relinquished. He developed a portable welding machine (a significant improvement over existing stationary models) and incorporated a transformer to allow regulation of the current. As described by a biographer of John C. Lincoln:

This functional industrial development gave Lincoln Electric a lead in the field that it has always maintained, although the two giants—Westinghouse and General Electric —soon entered the market.[1]

By World War II, Lincoln Electric was the leading American manufacturer of arc welding equipment. Because of the importance of welding to the war effort, the company stopped producing electric motors and devoted its full capacity to welding products. Demand continued to outpace production, and the government asked the welding equipment manufacturers to add capacity. As described by Lincoln President George Willis:

Mr. Lincoln responded to the government's call by going to Washington and telling

[1]Raymond Moley, *The American Century of John C. Lincoln* (New York: Duell, Sloan & Pearce, 1962), p. 71

them that there was enough manufacturing capacity but it was being used inefficiently by everyone. He offered to share proprietary manufacturing methods and equipment designs with the rest of the industry. Washington took him up on it and that solved the problem. As a result of Mr. Lincoln's patriotic decision, our competitors had costs which were close to ours for a short period after the war, but we soon were outperforming them like before.

In 1955, Lincoln once again began manufacturing electric motors, and since then its position in the market had expanded steadily.

Through the years, Lincoln stock had been sold to employees and associates of Mr. Lincoln. In 1975, approximately 48% of employees were shareholders. About 80% of the oustanding stock was held by employees, the Lincoln family and their foundations.

In its eighty years to 1975, Lincoln had had only three board chairmen: John C. Lincoln, James F. Lincoln and William Irrgang, who became Chairman in 1972.

STRATEGY

Lincoln Electric's strategy was simple and unwavering. The company's strength was in manufacturing. Management believed that Lincoln could build quality products at a lower cost than their competitors. Their strategy was to concentrate on reducing costs and passing the savings through to the customer by continuously lowering prices. Management had adhered to this policy even when products were on allocation due to shortage of productive capacity. This had brought an expansion of both market share and primary demand for arc welding equipment and supplies over the past half century. It had also encouraged the exit of several major companies from the industry (including

General Electric) and had caused others to seek more specialized market niches.

Management believed its incentive system and the climate it fostered were responsible in large part for the continual increase in productivity upon which this strategy depended. Under the Lincoln incentive system, employees were handsomely rewarded for their productivity, high quality, cost reduction ideas, and individual contribution to the company. Year-end bonuses averaged close to 100% of regular compensation, and some workers on the factory floor had earned more than $45,000 in a single year.

Lincoln's strategy had remained virtually unchanged for decades. In a 1947 Harvard Business School case study on Lincoln Electric, James F. Lincoln described his company's strategy as follows:

> It is the job of The Lincoln Electric Company to give its customers more and more of a better product at a lower and lower price. This will also make it possible for the company to give to the worker and the stockholder a higher and higher return.

In 1975, Chairman William Irrgang's description was remarkably similar:

> The success of the Lincoln Electric Company has been built on two basic ideas. One is producing more and more of a progressively better product at a lower and lower price for a larger and larger group of customers. The other is that an employee's earnings and promotion are in direct proportion to his individual contribution toward the company's success.[2]

Management felt it had achieved an enviable record in following this strategy faithfully and saw no need to modify it in the future. Lincoln Electric's record of in-

[2]*Employee's Handbook*, The Lincoln Electric Company, 1974.

creasing productivity and declining costs and prices is shown in Exhibit 3.

COMPANY PHILOSOPHY

Lincoln Electric's corporate strategy was rooted in the management philosophy of James F. Lincoln. James F. Lincoln was a rugged individualist who believed that through competition and adequate incentives every person could develop to their fullest potential. In one of his numerous books and articles he wrote:

> Competition is the foundation of man's development. It has made the human race what it is. It is the spur that makes progress. Every nation that has eliminated it as the controlling force in its economy has disappeared, or will. We will do the same if we eliminate it by trying to give security, and for the same reason. Competition means that there will be losers as well as winners in the game. Competition will mean the disappearance of the lazy and incompetent, be they workers, industrialists or distributors. Competition promotes progress. Competition determines who will be the leader. It is the only known way that leadership and progress can be developed if history means anything. It is a hard taskmaster. It is completely necessary for anyone, be he worker, user, distributor or boss, if he is to grow.
>
> If some way could be found so that competition could be eliminated from life, the result would be disastrous. Any nation and any people disappear if life becomes too easy. There is no danger from a hard life as all history shows. Danger is from a life that is made soft by lack of competition.[3]

Lincoln's faith in the individual was almost unbounded. His personal experience with the success of Lincoln Electric reinforced his faith in what could be accomplished given the proper conditions. In 1951, he wrote:

> ... development in many directions is latent in every person. The difficulty has been that few recognize that fact. Fewer still will put themselves under the pressure or by chance are put under the pressure that will develop them greatly. Their latent abilities remain latent, hence useless. ...
>
> It is of course obvious that the development of man, on which the success of incentive management depends, is a progressive process. Any results, no matter how good, that come from the application of incentive management cannot be considered final. There will always be greater growth of man under continued proper incentive. ...
>
> Such increase of efficiency poses a very real problem to management. The profit that will result from such efficiency obviously will be enormous. The output per dollar of investment will be many times that of the usual shop which practices output limitation. The labor cost per piece will be relatively small and the overhead will be still less.
>
> The profits at competitive selling prices resulting from such efficiency will be far beyond any possible need for proper return and growth of an industry. ...
>
> How, then, should the enormous extra profit resulting from incentive management be split? The problems that are inherent in incentive dictate the answer. If the worker does not get a proper share, he does not desire to develop himself or his skill. Incentive, therefore, would not succeed. The worker must have a reward that he feels is commensurate with his contribution.
>
> If the customer does not have a part of the savings in lower prices, he will not buy the increased output. The size of the market is a decisive factor in costs of products. Therefore, the consumer must get a proper share of the saving.
>
> Management and ownership are usually considered as a unit. This is far from a fact, but in the problem here, they can be considered together. They must get a part of the

---

[3]James F. Lincoln, *Incentive Management* (Cleveland, Ohio: The Lincoln Electric Company, 1951), p. 33.

saving in larger salaries and perhaps larger dividends.

There is no hard and fast rule to cover this division, other than the following. The worker (which includes management), the customer, the owner and all those involved must be satisfied that they are properly recognized or they will not cooperate, and cooperation is essential to any and all successful applications of incentives.[4]

Additional comments by James F. Lincoln are presented in Exhibit 4.

COMPENSATION POLICIES

Compensation policies were the key element of James F. Lincoln's philosophy of "incentive management." Lincoln Electric's compensation system had three components:

- wages based solely on piecework output for most factory jobs
- a year-end bonus which could equal or exceed an individual's full year regular pay
- guaranteed employment for all workers

The first component of this compensation system was that almost all production workers at Lincoln were paid on a straight piecework plan. They had no base salary or hourly wage, but were paid a set "price" for each item they produced. William Irrgang explained:

Wherever practical, we use the piecework system. This system can be effective, and it can be destructive. The important part of the system is that it is completely fair to the worker. When we set a piecework price, that price cannot be changed just because, in management's opinion, the worker is making too much money. Whether he earns two times or three times his normal amount

makes no difference. Piecework prices can only be changed when management has made a change in the method of doing that particular job and under no other conditions. If this is not carried out 100 percent, piecework cannot work.

Today piecework is confined to production operations, although at one time we also used it for work done in our stenographic pool. Each typewriter was equipped with a counter that registered the number of times the typewriter keys were operated. This seemed to work all right for a time until it was noticed that one girl was earning much more than any of the others. This was looked into, and it was found that this young lady ate her lunch at her desk, using one hand for eating purposes and the other for punching the most convenient key on the typewriter as fast as she could; which simply goes to show that no matter how good a program you may have, it still needs careful supervision.[5]

A Time Study department established piecework prices which were guaranteed by the company, until there was a methods change or introduction of a new process. An employee could challenge the price if he felt it was unfair. The Time Study department would then retime the job and set a new rate. This could be higher or lower but was still open to challenge if the employee remained dissatisfied. Employees were expected to guarantee their own quality. They were not paid for defective work until it had been repaired on their own time.

All of the jobs in the company were rated according to skill, required effort, responsibility, etc., and a base wage rate for the job was assigned. Wage rates were comparable to those in similar jobs in the Cleveland area, and were adjusted annually based on Department of Labor statis-

---

[4]Ibid., pp. 7–11.

[5]William Irrgang, "The Lincoln Incentive Management Program," Lincoln Lecture Series, Arizona State University, 1972, p. 13.

tics and quarterly to reflect changes in the cost of living. This determined the salary or hourly wage. For piecework jobs the Time Study department set piece prices so that an employee could earn the base rate for a job if he produced at a standard rate.

The second element of the compensation system was a year-end bonus. Each year since 1934, Lincoln had paid a year-end bonus to its employees. As explained in the Employee Handbook: "The bonus, paid at the discretion of the company, is not a gift, but rather it is the sharing of the results of efficient operation on the basis of the contribution of each person to the success of the company for that year." In 1974, this totaled $25 million, an average of approximately $10,700 per employee, or 90% of pre-bonus wages.

The total amount to be paid out in bonuses each year was determined by the Board of Directors. The concentration on cost reduction kept costs low enough so that generally prices could be set (and not upset by competition) based on costs at the beginning of the year to produce a target return for stockholders and to give employees a bonus of approximately 100% of wages. The variance from the planned profits was usually added to (or subtracted from) the bonus pool to be distributed at year-end. Since 1945, the average bonus had varied from 78% to 129% of wages. In the past few years, it had been between 40% and 55% of pretax, prebonus profit, or as high as twice the net income after taxes.

An individual's share of the bonus was determined by a semiannual "merit rating" which measured individual performance compared to other members of the department or work group. Ratings for all employees had to average out to 100 on this relative scale. However, if an individual had made an unusual contribution, and deserved a rating above 110, there was a special corporate pool of bonus points

which could be awarded so as not to penalize co-workers. Ratings above 110 were thus reviewed by a corporate committee or vice presidents who evaluated the individual's contribution. Merit ratings varied widely from as low as 45 to as high as 160.

In determining an employee's merit rating, four factors were evaluated separately:

• Dependability
• Quality
• Output
• Ideas and cooperation

Foremen were responsible for the rating of all factory workers. They could request help from Assistant Foremen (dependability), the Production Control Department (output), the Inspection Department (quality), and Methods Department (ideas and cooperation). In the office, Supervisors rated their people on the same items. At least one executive reviewed all ratings. All employees were urged to discuss their ratings with their department heads if they were dissatisfied or unclear about them.

Lincoln complemented its rating and pay system with a Guaranteed Continuous Employment Plan. This plan provided security against layoffs and assured continuity of employment. The plan guaranteed employment for at least 75% of the standard 40-hour week to every full-time employee with the company two or more years. In fact, the company had not had any layoffs since 1951 when initial trials for the plan were put into effect. It was formally established in 1958.

This was seen by the company as an essential element in the incentive plan. Without it, it was believed that employees would be more likely to resist improved production and efficiency for fear of losing their jobs. In accepting the guaranteed continuous employment plan, employees agreed to perform any job that was assigned as conditions required, and to work overtime during periods of high activity.

The philosophy and procedures regarding the incentive plan were the same for management and workers, except that Mr. Irrgang and Mr. Willis did not share in the bonus.

EMPLOYEE VIEWS

To the casewriter, it appeared that employees generally liked working at Lincoln. The employee turnover rate was far below that of most other companies, and once a new employee made it through the first month or so, he rarely left for another company (see Exhibit 5). One employee explained:

> It's like trying out for a high school football team. If you make it through the first few practices, you're usually going to stay the whole season, especially after the games start.

One long-time employee who liked working at Lincoln was John "Tiny" Carrillo, an armature bander on the welding machine line, who had been with the company for twenty-four years. "Tiny" explained why:

> The thing I like here is that you're pretty much your own boss as long as you do your job. You're responsible for your own work and you even put your stencil on every machine you work on. That way if it breaks down in the field and they have to take it back, they know who's responsible.
>
> Before I came here, I worked at Cadillac as a welder. After two months there I had the top hourly rate. I wasn't allowed to tell anyone because there were guys who still had the starting rate after a year. But, I couldn't go any higher after two months.

I've done well. My rating is usually around 110, but I work hard, right through the smoke breaks. The only time I stop is a half hour for lunch. I make good money. I have two houses, one which I rent out, and four cars. They're all paid for. When I get my bills, I pay them the next day. That's the main thing. I don't owe anyone.

Sure, there are problems. There's sometimes a bind between the guys with low grades and the guys with high ones, like in school. And there are guys who sway everything their way so they'll get the points, but they [management] have good tabs on what's going on. . . .

A lot of new guys come in and leave right away. Most of them are just "mama's boys" and don't want to do the work. We had a new guy who was a produce manager at a supermarket. He worked a couple of weeks, then quit and went back to his old job.

At the end of the interview, the casewriter thanked "Tiny" for his time. He responded by pointing out that it had cost him $7.00 in lost time, but that he was glad to be of assistance.

Another piece worker, Jorge Espinoza, a fine wire operator in the Electrode Division, had been with the company for six years. He explained his feelings:

> I believe in being my own man. I want to use my drive for my own gain. It's worked. I built my family a house and have an acre of land, with a low mortgage. I have a car and an old truck I play around with. The money I get is because I earn it. I don't want anything given to me.
>
> The thing I don't like is having to depend on other people on the line and suppliers. We're getting bad steel occasionally. Our output is down as a result and my rating will suffer.
>
> There are men who have great drive here and can push for a job. They are not leaders and never will be, but they move up. That's a problem. . . .
>
> The first few times around, the ratings were painful for me. But now I stick near 100.

You really make what you want. We just had a methods change and our base rate went from 83 to 89 coils a day. This job is tougher now and more complex. But, it's all what you want. If you want 110 coils you can get it. You just take less breaks. Today, I gambled and won. I didn't change any dies and made over a hundred coils. If I had lost, and the die plugged up, it would have cost me at least half an hour. But, today I made it.

MANAGEMENT STYLE

Lincoln's incentive scheme was reinforced by top management's attitude toward the men on the factory floor. In 1951, James Lincoln wrote:

It becomes perfectly true to anyone who will think this thing through that there is no such thing in an industrial activity as Management and Men having different functions or being two different kinds of people. Why can't we think and why don't we think that all people are Management? Can you imagine any president of any factory or machine shop who can go down and manage a turret lathe as well as the machinist can? Can you imagine any manager of any organization who can go down and manage a broom—let us get down to that—who can manage a broom as well as a sweeper can? Can you imagine any secretary of any company who can go down and fire a furnace and manage that boiler as well as the man who does the job? Obviously, all are Management.[6]

Lincoln's President George Willis stressed the equality in the company:

We try to avoid barriers between management and workers. We're treated equally as much as possible. When I got to work this morning at 7:30, the parking lot was three-quarters full. I parked way out there like anyone else would. I don't have a special reserved spot. The same principle holds true in our cafeteria. There's no executive dining room. We eat with everyone else.[7]

Mr. Willis felt that open and frank communication between management and workers had been a critical factor in Lincoln's success, and he believed that the company's Advisory Board had played a very important role in achieving this.

An Advisory Board of elected employee representatives had been established by James F. Lincoln in 1914. It had met twice a month ever since then. The Advisory Board provided a forum of employees to bring issues of concern to top management's attention, to question company policies, and to make suggestions for their improvement. As described in the Employee's Handbook:

Board service is a privilege and responsibility of importance to the entire organization. In discussions or in reaching decisions Board members must be guided by the best interests of the Company. These also serve the best interests of its workers. They should seek at all times to improve the cooperative attitude of all workers and see that all realize they have an important part in our final results.

All Advisory Board meetings were chaired by either the chairman or president of Lincoln. Usually both were present. Issues brought up at board meetings were either resolved on the spot or assigned to an executive to be answered by the next meeting. After each meeting, Mr. Irrgang or Mr. Willis would send a memo to the

[6]James F. Lincoln, "What Makes Workers Work?" (Cleveland, Ohio: The Lincoln Electric Company, 1951), pp. 3–4.

[7]The cafeteria had large rectangular and round tables. In general, factory workers gravitated toward the rectangular tables. There were no strict rules, however, and management personnel often sat with factory workers. Toward the center was a square table that seated only four. This was reserved for Mr. Irrgang, Mr. Willis, and their guests when they were having a working lunch.

responsible executive for each unan- swered question, no matter how trivial, and he was expected to respond by the next meeting if possible.

Minutes of all board meetings were posted on bulletin boards in each depart- ment and members explained the board's actions to the other workers in their de- partment.

The questions raised in the minutes of a given meeting were usually answered in the next set of minutes. This procedure had not changed significantly since the first meeting in 1914, nor had the types of issues raised changed significantly since then (see Exhibit 6).

Workers felt that the Advisory Board provided a way of getting immediate at- tention for their problems. It was clear, however, that management still made the final decisions.[8] A former member of the Advisory Board commented:

> There are certain areas which are brought up in the meetings which Mr. Irrgang doesn't want to get into. He's adept at steer- ing the conversation away from these. It's definitely not a negotiating meeting. But, generally, you really get action or an answer on why action isn't being taken.

In addition to the Advisory Board, there was a twelve-member board of middle managers which met with Mr. Irrgang and Mr. Willis once a month. The topics of dis- cussion were broader than those of the Ad- visory Board. The primary function of these meetings was for top management to get better acquainted with these indi- viduals and to encourage cooperation be- tween departments.

Lincoln's two top executives, Mr. Irr-

gang and Mr. Willis, continued the prac- tice of James F. Lincoln in maintaining an open door to all employees. George Willis estimated that at least twice a week fac- tory employees took advantage of this op- portunity to talk with him.

Middle managers also felt that commu- nication with Mr. Willis and Mr. Irrgang was open and direct. Often it by-passed intermediate levels of the organization. Most saw this as an advantage but one commented:

> This company is run strictly by the two men at the top. Mr. Lincoln trained Mr. Irrgang in his image. It's very authoritarian and de- cisions flow top down. It never became a big company. There is very little delegated and top people are making too many small de- cisions. Mr. Irrgang and Mr. Willis work eighty hours a week, and no one I know in this company can say that his boss doesn't work harder than he does.

Mr. Willis saw management's concern for the worker as an essential ingredient in his company's formula for success. He knew at least five hundred employees per- sonally. In leading the casewriter through the plant, he greeted workers by name and paused several times to tell anecdotes about many of them.

At one point, an older man yelled to Mr. Willis good-naturedly, "Where's my raise?" Mr. Willis explained that this man had worked for 40 years in a job requiring him to lift up to 20 tons of material a day. His earnings had been quite high because of his rapid work pace, but Mr. Willis had been afraid that as he was advancing in age he could injure himself working in that job. After months of Mr. Willis' urg- ing, the man switched to an easier but lower paying job. He was disappointed in taking the earnings cut and even after sev- eral years let the president know when- ever he saw him.

---

[8]In some cases, management allowed issues to be decided by a vote of employees. A recent example was when employees voted down a proposal to give them dental benefits paid by the company, recognizing that it would come directly out of their bonus.

Mr. Willis pointed to another employee and explained that this man's wife had recently died and for several weeks he had been drinking heavily and reporting to work late. Mr. Willis had earlier spent about half an hour discussing the situation with him to console him and see if the company could help in any way. He explained:

I made a definite point of talking to him on the floor of the plant, near his work station. I wanted to make sure that the other employees who knew the situation could see me with him. Speaking to him had symbolic value. It is important for employees to know that the president is interested in their welfare.

Management's philosophy was also reflected in the company's physical facilities. A no-nonsense atmosphere was firmly established at the gate to the parking lot where the only mention of the company name was in a sign reading:

$1,000 REWARD for information leading to the arrest and conviction of persons stealing from the Lincoln Electric parking lot.

There was a single entrance to the offices and plant for workers, management, and visitors. As one entered, the company motto in large stainless steel letters extending thirty feet across the wall was unavoidable:

THE ACTUAL IS LIMITED
THE POSSIBLE IS IMMENSE

A flight of stairs led down to a tunnel system for pedestrian traffic which ran under the single-story plant. At the base of the stairs was a large bronze plaque on which were permanently inscribed the names of the eight employees who had served more than 50 years, and the more than 350 active employees with 25 or more years of service who were in the "Quarter Century Club."

The long tunnel under the plant which led to the offices was clean and well lit. The executive offices were located in a windowless, two story cement block office building which sat like a box in the center of the plant. At the base of the staircase leading up to the offices, a Lincoln automatic welding machine and portraits of J. C. Lincoln and J. F. Lincoln welcomed visitors. The handrail on the staircase was welded into place, as were the ashtrays in the tunnel.

In the center of the office building was a simple, undecorated reception room. A switchboard operator/receptionist greeted visitors between filing and phone calls. The reception room reflected the Spartan decor which was evident throughout the building. It was furnished with a metal coat rack, a wooden bookcase, and several plain wooden tables and chairs. All of the available reading material dealt with Lincoln Electric Company or welding.

One could leave the reception room through any of seven doors which would lead almost directly to the desired office or department. Most of the departments were large open rooms with closely spaced desks. One manager explained that "Mr. Lincoln didn't believe in walls. He felt they interrupted the flow of communications and paperwork." Most of the desks and files were plain, old and well worn, and there was a scarcity of modern office equipment. One reason for this was that the same criteria were applied for expenditures on equipment in the office as in the plant. The maintenance department had to certify that the equipment replaced could not be repaired. If acquired for cost reduction, the equipment had to have a one-year payback.[9]

The usually omnipresent Xerox machines were nowhere to be found. The ex-

[9]Mr. Willis explained that capital projects with paybacks of up to two years were sometimes funded when they involved a product for which demand was growing.

planation was that copying costs were tightly controlled and only certain individuals could use the Xerox copiers. Customer order forms, for example, which required eight copies, were run on a duplicating machine.

The private offices which existed were small, uncarpeted, and separated by green metal partitions. The president's office was slightly larger than the others, but still retained a Spartan appearance. There was only one carpeted office. Mr. Willis explained:

> That office was occupied by Mr. Lincoln until he died in 1965. For the next five years it was left vacant and now it is Mr. Irrgang's office and also the Board of Directors' and Advisory Board meeting room.

PERSONNEL

Lincoln Electric had a strict policy of filling all but entry level positions by promoting from within the company. Whenever an opening occurred, a notice was posted on the twenty-five bulletin boards in the plant and offices. Any interested employee could apply for an open position. Because of the company's sustained growth and policy of hiring outsiders for entry-level jobs only, employees had substantial opportunity for advancement.

An outsider generally could join the company in one of two ways: either taking a factory job working at an hourly or piece rate, or entering Lincoln's training programs in sales or engineering.[10] The company recruited their trainees at colleges and graduate schools, including Harvard Business School. Starting salary in 1975 for a trainee with a Bachelor's

---

[10]Lincoln's President and Chairman both advanced through the ranks in manufacturing. Mr. Irrgang began as a piece-worker in the armature winding department, and Mr. Willis began in plant engineering. (See Exhibit 7 for employment history of Lincoln's top management.)

Degree was $5.50 an hour plus a year-end bonus at an average of 40% of the normal rate. Wages for trainees with either a Master's degree or several years of relevant experience was 5% higher.

Although Lincoln's president, vice president of sales, and personnel director were all Harvard Business School graduates, the company had not hired many recent graduates. Clyde Loughridge, the Personnel Director, explained:

> We don't offer them fancy staff positions and we don't pretend to. Our starting pay is less than average, probably $17,000–$18,000 including bonus, and the work is harder than average. We start our trainees off by putting them in overalls and they spend up to seven weeks in the welding school. In a lot of ways it's like boot camp. Rather than leading them along by the hand, we like to let the self-starters show themselves.

The policy of promoting from within had rarely been violated, and then only in cases where a specialized skill was required. Mr. Loughridge commented:

> In most cases we've been able to stick to it, even where the required skills are entirely new to the company. Our employees have a lot of varied skills, and usually someone can fit the job. For example, when we recently got our first computer, we needed a programmer and systems analyst. We had twenty employees apply who had experience or training in computers. We chose two, and it really helps that they know the company and understand our business.

The company did not send its employees to outside management development programs and did not provide tuition grants for educational purposes.

Lincoln Electric had no formal organization chart and management did not feel that one was necessary. (Exhibit 8

shows a chart drawn for the purpose of this case.)

As explained by one executive:

> People retire and their jobs are parcelled out. We are very successful in overloading our overhead departments. We make sure this way that no unnecessary work is done and jobs which are not absolutely essential are eliminated. A disadvantage is that planning may suffer, as may outside development to keep up with your field.

Lincoln's organizational hierarchy was flat, with few levels between the bottom and the top. For example, Don Hastings, the Vice President of Sales, had 37 regional sales manager reporting to him. He commented.

> I have to work hard, there's no question about that. There are only four of us in the home office plus two secretaries. I could easily use three more people. I work every Saturday, at least half a day. Most of our regional men do too, and they like me to know it. You should see the switchboard light up when 37 regional managers call in at five minutes to twelve on Saturday.

The President and Chairman kept a tight rein over personnel matters. All changes in status of employees, even at the lowest levels, had to be approved by Mr. Willis. Mr. Irrgang also had to give his approval if they involved salaried employees. Raises or promotions had to be approved in advance. An employee could be fired by his supervisor on the spot for cause, but if it was on questionable grounds it had to be approved afterward by either Mr. Willis or Mr. Irrgang. Usually the supervisor was supported, but there had been cases where a firing decision was reversed.

MARKETING

Welding machines and electrodes were like "razors and razor blades." A Lincoln welding machine often had a useful life of thirty years or more, while electrodes (and fluxes) were consumed immediately in the welding process. The ratio of machine cost to annual consumables cost varies widely from perhaps 7:1 for a hand welder used in a small shop to 1:5 or more for an automatic welder used in a shipyard.

Although certain competitors might meet their costs and quality in selected products, management believed that no company could match Lincoln on their whole line. Another important competitive edge for Lincoln was its sales force. Al Patnik, Vice President of Sales Development, explained:

> Most competitors operate through distributors. We have our own top field sales force.[11] We start out with engineering graduates and put them through our seven-month training program. They learn how to weld, and we teach them everything we can about equipment, metallurgy, and design. Then they spend time on the rebuild line [where machines brought in from the field are rebuilt] and even spend time in the office seeing how orders are processed. Finally, before the trainees go out into the field, they have to go into our plant and find a better way of making something. Then they make a presentation to Mr. Irrgang, just as if he were one of our customers.
>
> Our approach to the customer is to go in and learn what he is doing and show him how to do it better. For many companies our people become their experts in welding. They go in and talk to a foreman. They might say, "Let me put on a headshield and show you what I'm talking about." That's how we sell them.

George Ward, a salesman in the San Francisco office, commented:

> The competition hires graduates with business degrees (without engineering back-

[11]The sales force was supplemented in some areas by distributors. Sales abroad were handled by wholly owned subsidiaries of Armco's International Division.

ground) and that's how they get hurt. This job is getting more technical every day. . . . A customer in California who is using our equipment to weld offshore oil rigs had a problem with one of our products. I couldn't get the solution for them over the phone, so I flew in to the plant Monday morning and showed it to our engineers. Mr. Willis said to me "Don't go back to California until this problem is solved. . . ." We use a "working together to solve your problem" approach. This, plus sticking to published prices, shows you're not interested in taking advantage of them.

I had a boss who used to say: "Once we're in, Lincoln never loses a customer except on delivery." It's basically true. The orders I lost last year were because we couldn't deliver fast enough. Lincoln gets hurt when there are shortages because of our guaranteed employment. We don't hire short-term factory workers when sales take off, and other companies beat us on delivery.

The sales force was paid a salary plus bonus. Mr. Ward believed that Lincoln's sales force was the best paid and hardest working in the industry:

We're aggressive, and want to work and get paid for it. The sales force prides itself on working more hours than anyone else. . . . My wife wonders sometimes if you can work for Lincoln and have a family too.

MANUFACTURING

Lincoln's plant was unusual in several respects. The casewriter was struck by how crowded with materials and equipment it was, and how few workers there were. It was obvious that employees worked very fast and efficiently with few breaks. Even during the ten-minute "smoke breaks" in the morning and afternoon employees often continued to work.

An innovative plant layout was partly responsible for the crowded appearance.

Raw materials entered one side of the plant and finished goods came out the other side. There was no central stockroom for materials or work-in-process. Instead, everything that entered the plant was transported directly to the work station where it would be used. At a work station, a single worker or group operated, in effect, as a "subcontractor." All required materials were piled around the station, allowing visual inventory control, and they were paid a piece "price" for their production. Wherever possible, the work flow followed a straight line through the plant from the side where raw materials entered to the side where finished goods exited. Because there was no union, the company had great flexibility with what could be performed at a work station. For example, foundry work and metal stamping could be carried out together by the same workers when necessary. Thus, work could flow almost directly along a line through the plant. Intermediate material handling was avoided to a great extent. The major exception was where a large or expensive piece of machinery was used by multiple production lines, and the work had to be brought to the machines.

Many of the operations in the plant were automated. Much of the manufacturing equipment was proprietary,[12] designed and built by Lincoln. In some cases, the company had modified machines built by others to run two or three times as fast as when originally delivered.

Close coordination between product design engineers and the Methods department from the time a product was originally conceptualized was seen as a key factor in reducing costs and rationalizing manufacturing. William Irrgang explained:

---

[12]Visitors were barred from the Electric Division unless they had a pass signed by Mr. Willis or Mr. Irrgang.

After we have [an] idea . . . we start thinking about manufacturing costs, before anything leaves the Design Engineering department. At that point, there is a complete "getting together" of manufacturing and design engineers—and plant engineers, too, if new equipment is involved.

Our tooling, for instance, is going to be looked at carefully while the design of a product is still in process. Obviously, we can increase or decrease the tooling very materially by certain considerations in the design of a product, and we can go on the basis of total costs at all times. In fact, as far as total cost is concerned, we even think about such matters as shipping, warehousing, etc. All of these factors are taken into consideration when we're still at the design stage. It's very essential that this be done: otherwise, you can lock yourself out from a lot of potential economies.[13]

In 1974, Lincoln's plant had reached full capacity, operating nearly around the clock. Land bordering its present location was unavailable and management was moving ahead with plans to build a second plant fifteen miles away on the same freeway as the present plant.

Over the years, Lincoln had slowly back integrated by "making" rather than "buying" a larger percentage of their components. For example, even though their unit volume of gasoline engines was only a fraction of their suppliers', Lincoln purchased engine blocks and components and assembled them rather than purchasing complete engines. Management was continually evaluating opportunities to back integrate and had not arbitrarily ruled out manufacturing any of their components or raw materials.

ADMINISTRATIVE PRODUCTIVITY

Lincoln's high productivity was not limited to manufacturing. Clyde Loughridge

[13]"Incentive Management in Action," *Assembly Engineering,* March 1967.

pointed to the Personnel Department as an example:

Normally, for 2,300 employees you would need a personnel department of about twenty, but we have only six, and that includes the nurse, and our responsibilities go beyond those of the typical personnel department.

Once a year, Mr. Loughridge had to outline his objectives for the upcoming year for Mr. Willis, but he did not operate on a budget.

I don't get a budget. There would be no point to it. I just spend as little as possible. I operate this just like my home. I don't spend on anything I don't need.

In the Traffic Department workers also seemed very busy. There, a staff of 12 controlled the shipment of two and a half million pounds of material a day. Their task was complex. Delivery was included in the price of their products. They thus could reduce the overall cost to the customer by mixing products in most loads and shipping the most efficient way possible to the company's 39 warehouses. Jim Biek, General Traffic Manager, explained how they accomplished this:

For every order, we decide whether it would be cheaper by rail or truck. Then we consolidate orders so that over 90% of what goes out of here is full carload or full truckload, as compared to perhaps 50% for most companies. We also mix products so that we come in at the top of the weight brackets. For example, if a rate is for 20,000 to 40,000 pounds, we will mix orders to bring the weight right up to that 40,000 limit. All this is computed manually. In fact, my old boss used to say, "We run traffic like a ma and pa grocery store."

As in the rest of Lincoln, the employees in the Traffic Development worked their way up from entry level positions. Jim Biek had come into his position of General Traffic Manager after nine years as a Purchasing Engineer. He had received an MBA degree from Northwestern, after a BS in Mechanical Engineering from Purdue, started in the engineering training program, and then spent five years in Product Development and Methods before going to Purchasing and finally to Traffic. Lack of experience in traffic was a disadvantage, but the policy of promoting from within also had its advantages. Mr. Biek explained:

> One of my first tasks was to go to Washington and fight to get welders reclassified as motors to qualify for a lower freight rate. With my engineering experience and knowledge of welders, I was in a better position to argue this than a straight traffic man . . .
>
> Just about everybody in here was new to traffic. One of my assistant traffic managers had worked on the loading platform here for ten years before he came into the department. He had to go to night school to learn about rates, but his experience is invaluable. He knows how to load trucks and rail cars backwards and forward. Who could do a better job of consolidating orders then he does? He can look at an order and think of it as rows of pallets.
>
> Someday we'll outgrow this way of operating, but right now I can't imagine a computer juggling loads like some of our employees do.

Lincoln's Order Department had recently begun computerizing its operations. It was the first time a computer was used anywhere in Lincoln except in Engineering and Research, and according to Russell Stauffer, head of the Order Department, "It was a three-year job for me to sell this to top management."

The computer was expected to replace twelve or thirteen employees who would gradually be moved into new jobs. There had been some resistance to the computer, according to Mr. Stauffer.

> It's like anything new. People get scared. Not all the people affected have been here for the two years required to be eligible for guaranteed employment. And even though the others are assured a job, they don't know what it will be and will have to take what's offered.

The computer was expected to produce savings of $100,000 a year, plus allow a greater degree of control. Mr. Stauffer explained:

> We're getting information out of this that we never knew before. The job here is very complex. We're sending out more than two million pounds of consumables a day. Each order might have thirty or forty items, and each item has a bracket price arrangement based on total order size. A clerk has to remember or determine quickly whether we are out of stock on any items and calculate whether the stock-out brings the order down into another bracket. This means they have to "remember" the prices and items out of stock. This way of operating was okay up to about $200 million in sales, but now we've outgrown the human capability to handle the problem.

Although he had no previous experience in computers, Mr. Stauffer had full responsibility for the conversion.

> I've been here for thirty-five years. The first day I started, I unloaded coal cars and painted fences. Then I went to the assembly line, first on small parts, then large ones. I've been running the Order Department for twelve years. Since I've been here, we've had studies on computers every year or two and it always came out that we couldn't save money. Finally, when it looked like we'd make the switch, I took some courses at IBM. Over the last

year and a half, they've totaled eight and a half weeks, which is supposed to equal a full semester of college.

To date, the conversion had gone well, but much slower than anticipated. Order pressure had been so high that many mistakes would have been catastrophic. Management pressure, therefore, had been to assure 100% quality operations rather than faster conversion.

LINCOLN'S FUTURE

The 1947 Harvard Business School case study of Lincoln Electric ended with a prediction by a union leader from the Cleveland area:

The real test of Lincoln will come when the going gets tough. The thing Lincoln holds out to the men is high earnings. They work like dogs at Lincoln, but it pays off. . . .

I think [Lincoln] puts too much store by monetary incentives—but then, there's no denying he has attracted people who respond to that type of incentive. But I think that very thing is a danger Lincoln faces. If the day comes when they can't offer those big bonuses, or his people decide there's more to life than killing yourself making money, I predict the Lincoln Electric Company is in for trouble.

Lincoln President George Willis joined the company the year that the above comment was made. Reflecting on his 28 years with the company, Mr. Willis observed:

The company hasn't changed very much since I've been here. It's still run pretty much like Mr. Lincoln ran it. But today's workers are different. They're more outspoken and interested in why things are being done, not just how. We have nothing to hide

and never did, so we can give them the answers to their questions.

Looking forward, Mr. Willis saw no need to alter Lincoln's strategy or its policies:

My job will continue to be to have everyone in the organization recognize that a common goal all of us can and must support is to give the customer the quality he needs, when he needs it, at the lowest cost. To do this, we have to have everyone's understanding of this goal and their effort to accomplish it. In one way or another, I have to motivate the organization to meet this goal. The basic forms of the motivation have evolved over the last forty years. However, keeping the system honed so that everyone understands it, agrees with it, and brings out disagreements so improvements can be made or thinking changed becomes my major responsibility.

If our employees did not believe that management was trustworthy, honest, and impartial, the system could not operate. We've worked out the mechanics. They are not secret. A good part of my responsibility is to make sure the mechanics are followed. This ties back to a trust and understanding between individuals at all levels of the organization.

I don't see any real limits to our size. Look at a world with a present population of just under four billion now and six and a quarter billion by the year 2000. Those people aren't going to tolerate a low standard of living. So there will be a lot of construction, cars, bridges, oil and all these things that have got to be to support a population that large.

My job will still be just the traditional things of assuring that we keep up with the technology and have sufficient profit to pay the suppliers of capital. Then, I have to make sure communication can be maintained adequately. That last task may be the biggest and most important part of my job in the years ahead as we grow larger and still more complex.

THE LINCOLN ELECTRIC COMPANY
STUDY QUESTIONS:

1. Wage incentive systems quite commonly function very poorly with worker established production quotas seriously restricting output. Why does the reward system at Lincoln Electric function so effectively?

2. How applicable is Lincoln's approach to other companies and situations? Why don't more companies operate like Lincoln?

3. What recommendations or cautions would you make to Mr. Willis?

THE LINCOLN ELECTRIC COMPANY
Exhibit 1

Arc welding is a group of joining processes that utilize an electric current produced by a transformer or motor generator (electric or engine powered) to fuse various metals. The temperature at the arc is approximately 10,000° Fahrenheit.

The welding circuit consists of a welding machine, ground clamp and electrode holder. The electrode carries electricity to the metal being welded and the heat from the arc causes the base metals to join together. The electrode may or may not act as a filler metal during the process; however, nearly 60% of all arc welding that is done in the United States utilizes a covered electrode that does act as a very high quality filler metal.

The Lincoln Electric Company manufactures a wide variety of covered electrodes, submerged arc welding wires and fluxes and a unique self-shielded, flux-cored electrode called Innershield. The company also manufactures welding machines, wire feeders and other supplies that are needed for arc welding.

Exhibit 2 Statement of financial condition on December 31, 1974 (foreign subsidiaries not included)

	1974		1974
Current Assets		*Current Liabilities*	
Cash and Certificates of Deposit	$ 5,691,120	Accounts Payable	$ 13,658,063
Government Securities	6,073,919	Accrued Wages	1,554,225
Notes and Accounts Receivable	29,995,694	Taxes, including Income Taxes	13,262,178
Deferred Taxes & Prepaid Expenses	2,266,409	Dividends Payable	3,373,524
	$ 73,478,303		$ 31,847,990
Other Assets		*Shareholders' Equity*	
Trustee—Notes & Interest Receivable	$ 1,906,871	Common Capital Stock, stated value	$ 281,127
Miscellaneous	384,572	Additional Paid-in Capital	3,374,570
	$ 2,291,443	Retained Earnings	66,615,762
			$ 70,271,459
Intercompany			
Investment in Foreign Subsidiaries	$ 4,695,610	*Total Liabilities & Shareholders'*	
Notes Receivable	-0-	*Equity*	$102,119,449
	$ 4,695,610		
Property, Plant and Equipment			
Land	$ 825,376		
Buildings*	9,555,562		
Machinery, Tools and Equipment*	11,273,155		
	$ 21,654,093		
Total Assets	$102,119,449		

	Year Ended December 31, 1974
Income	
Net sales	$232,771,475
Interest	1,048,561
Overhead and development charges to subsidiaries	1,452,877
Dividend income	843,533
Other income	515,034
	$236,631,480
Cost and Expenses:	
Cost of products sold	$154,752,735
Selling, administrative, and general expenses and freight out	20,791,301
Year-end incentive bonus	24,707,297
Pension expense	2,186,932
	$202,438,265
Income before income taxes	$ 34,193,215
Provision for Income Taxes:	
Federal	$ 14,800,000
State and local	1,866,000
	$ 16,666,000
Net Income	$ 17,527,215

*After depreciation.

THE LINCOLN ELECTRIC COMPANY

Exhibit 3 Lincoln Electric's record of pricing and productivity

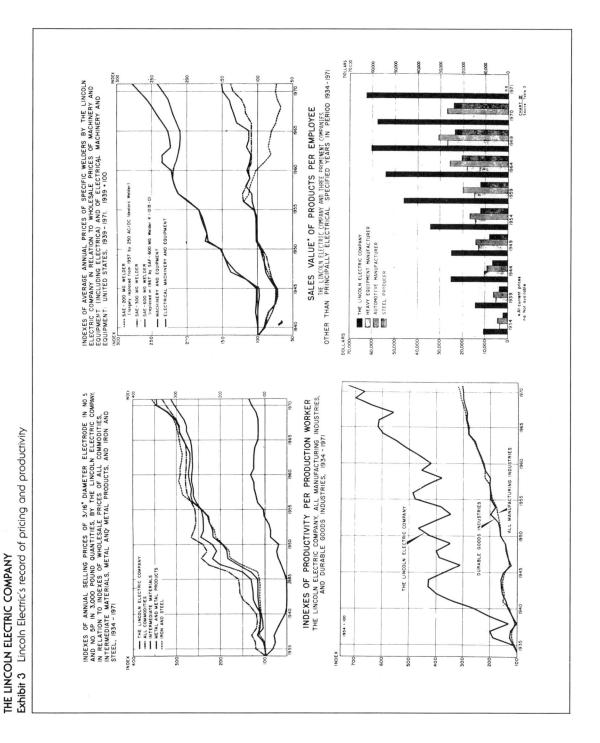

225

Exhibit 4   James F. Lincoln's observations on management

- Some think paying a man more money will produce cooperation. Not true. Many incentives are far more effective than money. Robert MacNamara gave up millions to become Secretary of Defense. Status is a much greater incentive.

- If those crying loudest about the inefficiencies of labor were put in the position of the wage earner, they would react as he does. The worker is not a man apart. He has the same needs, aspirations and reactions as the industrialist. A worker will not cooperate on any program that will penalize him. Does any manager?

- The industrial manager is very conscious of his company's need of uninterrupted income. He is completely oblivious, though, to the worker's same need. Management fails—i.e., profits fall off—and gets no punishment. The wage earner does not fail but is fired. Such injustice!

- Higher efficiency means fewer manhours to do a job. If the worker loses his job more quickly, he will oppose higher efficiency.

- There never will be enthusiasm for greater efficiency if the resulting profits are not properly distributed. If we continue to give it to the average stockholder, the worker will not cooperate.

- Most companies are run by hired managers, under the control of stockholders. As a result, the goal of the company has shifted from service to the customer, to making larger dividends for stockholders.

- The public will not yet believe that our standard of living could be doubled immediately if labor and management would cooperate.

- The manager is dealing with expert workers far more skillful. While you can boss these experts around in the usual lofty way, their eager cooperation will not be won.

- A wage earner is no more interested than a manager in making money for other people. The worker's job doesn't depend on pleasing stockholders, so he has no interest in dividends. Neither is he interested in increasing efficiency if he may lose his job because management has failed to get more orders.

- If a manager received the same treatment in matters of income, security, advancement, and dignity as the hourly worker, he would soon understand the real problem of management.

- The first question management should ask is: What is the company trying to do? In the minds of the average worker, the answer is: "The company is trying to make the largest possible profits by any method. Profits go to absentee stockholders and top management."

- There is all the difference imaginable between the grudging, distrustful, half-forced cooperation and the eager whole-hearted vigorous happy cooperation of men working together for a common purpose.

- Continuous employment of workers is essential to industrial efficiency. This is a management responsibility. Laying off workers during slack times is death to efficiency. The worker thrown out is a trained man. To replace him when business picks up will cost much more than the savings of wages during the layoff. Solution? The worker must have a guarantee that if he works properly his income will be continuous.

- Continuous employment is the first step to efficiency. But how? First, during slack periods, manufacture to build up inventory; costs will usually be less because of lower material costs, Second, develop new machines and methods of manufacturing; plans should be waiting on the shelf. Third, reduce prices by getting lower costs. When slack times come, workers are eager to help cut costs. Fourth, explore markets passed over when times are good. Fifth, hours of work can be reduced if the worker is agreeable. Sixth, develop new products. In sum, management should plan for slumps. They are useful.

- The incentives that are most potent when properly offered are:

  > Money in proportion to production.
  > Status as a reward for achievement.
  > Publicity of the worker's contributions and skill.

- The calling of the minister, the doctor, the lawyer, as well as the manager, contains incentive to excel. Excellence brings rewards, self-esteem, respect. Only the hourly worker has no reason to excel.

- Resistance to efficiency is not normal. It is present only when we are hired workers.

- Do unto others as you would have them do unto you. This is not just a Sunday school ideal, but a proper labor-management policy.

- An incentive plan should reward a man not only for the number of pieces turned out, but also for the accuracy of his work, his cooperation in improving methods of production, his attendance.

- The progress in industry so far stems from the developed potentialities of managers. Wage earners, who because of their greater numbers have far greater potential, are overlooked. Here is where the manager must look for his greatest progress.

- There should be an overall bonus based on the contribution each person makes to efficiency. If each person is properly rated and paid, there will not only be a fair reward to each worker but friendly and exciting competition.

- The present policy of operating industry for stockholders is unreasonable. The rewards now given to him are far too much. He gets income that should really go to the worker and the management. The usual absentee stockholder contributes nothing to efficiency. He buys a stock today and sells it tomorrow. He often doesn't even know what the company makes. Why should he be rewarded by large dividends?

- There are many forms and degrees of cooperation between the worker and the management. The worker's attitude can vary all the way from passivity to highly imaginative contributions to efficiency and progress.

Source: Civil Engineering—ASCE, January 1973.

Exhibit 5 Labor turnover rates and employee's years of service

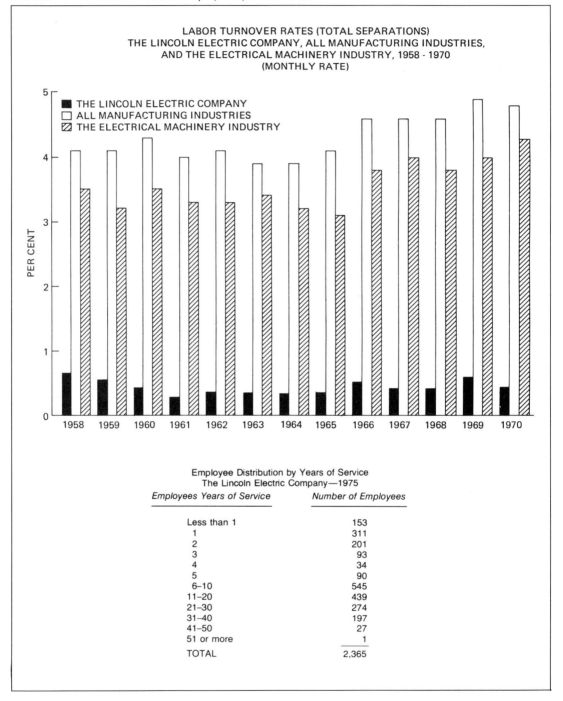

LABOR TURNOVER RATES (TOTAL SEPARATIONS)
THE LINCOLN ELECTRIC COMPANY, ALL MANUFACTURING INDUSTRIES,
AND THE ELECTRICAL MACHINERY INDUSTRY, 1958 - 1970
(MONTHLY RATE)

■ THE LINCOLN ELECTRIC COMPANY
□ ALL MANUFACTURING INDUSTRIES
▨ THE ELECTRICAL MACHINERY INDUSTRY

Employee Distribution by Years of Service
The Lincoln Electric Company—1975

Employees Years of Service	Number of Employees
Less than 1	153
1	311
2	201
3	93
4	34
5	90
6–10	545
11–20	439
21–30	274
31–40	197
41–50	27
51 or more	1
TOTAL	2,365

<u>Management Advisory Board Minutes - 1944</u>

September 26, 1944

———————

Absent: William Dillmuth

A discussion on piecework was again taken up. There was enough detail so it was thought best to appoint a committee to study it and bring a report into the meeting when that study is complete. That committee is composed of Messrs. Gilletly, Semko, Kneen and Steingass. Messrs. Erickson and White will be called in consultation, and the group will meet next Wednesday, October 4th.

The request was made that the members be permitted to bring guests to the meetings. The request was granted. Let's make sure we don't get too many at one time.

The point was made that materials are not being brought to the operation properly and promptly. There is no doubt of this difficulty. The matter was referred to Mr. Kneen for action. It is to be noted that conditions of deliveries from our suppliers have introduced a tremendous problem which has helped to increase this difficulty.

The request was made that over-time penalty be paid with the straight time. This will be done. There are some administrative difficulties which we will discuss at the next meeting but the over-time payment will start with the first pay in October.

Beginning October 1st employees' badges will be discontinued. Please turn them in to the watchmen.

It was requested that piecework prices be put on repair work in Dept. J. This matter was referred to Mr. Kneen for action.

A request was made that a plaque showing the names of those who died in action, separate from the present plaques, be put in the lobby. This was referred to Mr. Davis for action.

The question was asked as to what method for upgrading men is used. The ability of the individual is the sole reason for his progress. It was felt this is proper.

J. F. Lincoln
President

Management Advisory Board Minutes – 1974
(Excerpts)

September 23, 1974

Members absent: Tom Borkowski
                 Albert Sinn

Mr. Kupetz had asked about the Christmas and Thanksgiving schedules. These are being reviewed and we will have them available at the next meeting.

Mr. Howell had reported that the time clocks and the bells do not coincide. This is still being checked.

Mr. Sharpe had asked what the possibility would be to have a time clock installed in or near the Clean Room. This is being checked.

Mr. Joosten had raised the questions of the pliability of the wrapping material used in the Chemical Department for wrapping slugs. The material we use at the present time is the best we can obtain at this time...

Mr. Kostelac asked the question again whether the vacation arrangements could be changed, reducing the fifteen year period to some shorter period. It was pointed out that at the present time, where we have radically changing conditions every day, it is not the time to go into this. We will review this matter at some later date...

Mr. Martucci brought out the fact that there was considerable objection by the people involved to having to work on Saturday night to make up for holiday shutdowns. This was referred to Mr. Willis to be taken into consideration in schedule planning...

Mr. Joosten reported that in the Chemical Department on the Saturday midnight shift they have a setup where individuals do not have sufficient work so that it is an uneconomical situation. This has been referred to Mr. Willis to be reviewed.

Mr. Joosten asked whether there would be some way to get chest x-rays for people who work in dusty areas. Mr. Loughridge was asked to check a schedule of where chest x-rays are available at various times...

Mr. Robinson asked what the procedure is for merit raises. The procedure is that the foreman recommends the individual for a merit raise if by his performance he has shown that he merits the increase...

                                        Chairman

William Irrgang:MW
September 25, 1974

Exhibit 7 Employment history of top executives

Mr. William Irrgang—Board Chairman

1929—Hired, Repair Dept.
1930—Final Inspection
1934—Inspection, Wire Dept.
1946—Director of Factory Engineering
1951—Executive Vice President for Manufacturing and Engineering
1954—President & General Manager
1972—Chairman of the Board of Directors

Mr. George E. Willis—President

1947—Hired, Factory Engineering
1951—Superintendent—Electrode Division
1959—Vice President
1969—Executive Vice President of Manufacturing & Associated Functions
1972—President

Mr. William Miskoe—Vice President—International

1932—Hired, Chicago Sales Office
1941—President of Australian Plant
1969—To Cleveland as Vice President—International

Mr. Edwin M. Miller—Vice President & Assistant to the President

1923—Hired, Factory Worker
1925—Assistant Foreman
1929—Production Dept.
1940—Assistant Dept. Head—Production Dept.
1952—Superintendent—Machine Division
1959—Vice President
1973—Vice President & Assistant to the President

Mr. D. Neal Manross—Vice President— Machine and Motor Divisions

1941—Hired, Factory Worker
1942—Welding Inspector
1952—General Foreman, Extruding Dept. and Asst. Plant Superintendent
1953—Foreman—Special Products Dept., Machine Div.
1956—Superintendent—Special Products Division
1959—Superintendent—Motor Manufacturing
1966—Vice President—Motor Division
1973—Vice President in Charge of Motor & Machine Divisions

Mr. Albert S. Patnik—Vice President of Sales Development

1940—Hired, Sales Student
1940—New London, Conn. as Welder
1941—Los Angeles Office as Jr. Salesman
1942—Seattle Office as Salesman
1945—To Military Service
1945—Re-instated to Seattle
1951—Cleveland Sales Office as Rural Dealer Mgr.
1964—Asst. to the Vice President of Sales
1972—Vice President

Mr. Donald F. Hastings—Vice President and General Sales Manager

1953—Hired, Sales Trainee
1954—Emeryville, Calif. as Welding Engineer
1959—District Manager—Moline Office
1970—To Cleveland as General Sales Manager
1972—Vice President & General Sales Manager

THE LINCOLN ELECTRIC COMPANY
Exhibit 8   Organization chart

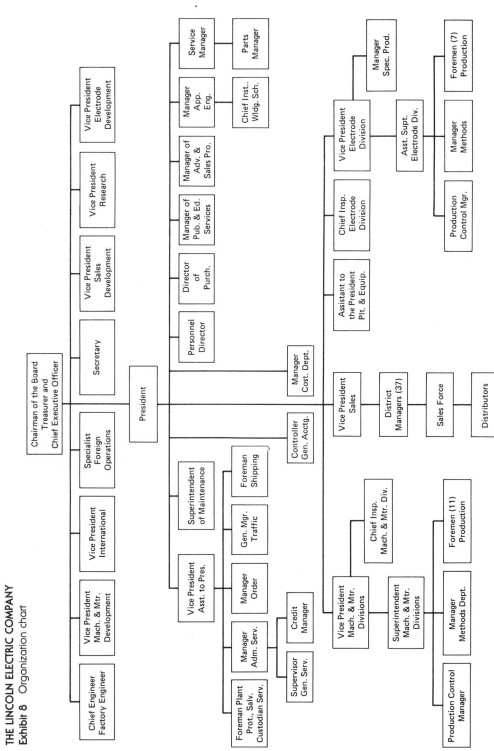

Exhibit 9   After reading the completed case study, Mr. Richard S. Sabo, Manager of Publicity & Educational Services, sent the following letter to the case writer.

July 31, 1975

To: Mr. Norman Fast

Dear Mr. Fast:

      I believe that you have summarized the Incentive Management System of The Lincoln Electric Company very well; however, readers may feel that the success of the Company is due only to the psychological principles included in your presentation.

      Please consider adding the efforts of our executives who devote a great deal of time to the following items that are so important to the consistent profit and long range growth of the Company.

    I.   Management has limited research, development and manufacturing to a standard product line designed to meet the major needs of the welding industry.

    II. New products must be reviewed by manufacturing and all production costs verified before being approved by management.

   III. Purchasing is challenged to not only procure materials at the lowest cost, but also to work closely with engineering and manufacturing to assure that the latest innovations are implemented.

   IV. Manufacturing supervision and all personnel are held accountable for reduction of scrap, energy conservation, and maintenance of product quality.

    V. Production control, material handling and methods engineering are closely supervised by top management.

   VI. Material and finished goods inventory control, accurate cost accounting and attention to sales costs, credit and other financial areas have constantly reduced overhead and led to excellent profitability.

  VII. Management has made cost reduction a way of life at Lincoln and definite programs are established in many areas, including traffic and shipping, where tremendous savings can result.

 VIII. Management has established a sales department that is technically trained to reduce customer welding cost. This sales technique and other real customer services have eliminated non-essential frills and resulted in long term benefits to all concerned.

   IX. Management has encouraged education, technical publishing and long range programs that have resulted in industry growth, thereby assuring market potential for The Lincoln Electric Company.

        Richard S. Sabo

BJS

Au Bon Pain

The Partner/Manager Program

Au Bon Pain has tried every progressive human-resource strategy or policy available—we've had them all. Quite honestly, I don't believe that any incremental strategies work long term in the multi-site service business, particularly in a labor market—like Boston—that is characterized by low unemployment levels. I'm convinced that developing *new* solutions for human-resource management at the unit level is the basis of competitive advantage. Instituting our *Partner/Manager Program* throughout the company now could give us an important edge. This is our chance to blow the company out, or to blow ourselves up.

This is how Len Schlesinger, executive vice president and treasurer of the Au Bon Pain (ABP) Company, described the situation he and company president Ron Shaich faced in January 1987. Six months earlier, in July 1986, two of the 24 company-owned stores had embarked on an experiment which could lead to a revolutionary change in the company's store-manager compensation system. *The Partner/Manager Program Experiment*, as it was called, ran for six "periods" of four weeks each (i.e., the

This case was presented by Lucy N. Lytle under the direction of W. Earl Sasser as the basis for class discussion rather than to illustrate either effective or ineffective handling of an administrative situation. Reprinted by permission of the Harvard Business School.

first period of the experiment, Period 8, ran from July 13 through August 9). The experiment concluded on December 20, 1986. Now, Schlesinger and Shaich had to decide whether to roll out the programs in all of the company's stores, to run it on a trial basis involving only some of the stores, to withdraw it to make needed improvements, or to abandon it.

HISTORY

Au Bon Pain, a chain of upscale French bakeries/sandwich cafes, opened its first store in Boston's Faneuil Hall in 1977. It was originally developed as a marketing vehicle for Pavallier, a French manufacturer of ovens and other bakery equipment. In 1978, Louis Kane, an experienced venture capitalist, bought the store and the rights to the concept. Two years later, Kane teamed up with Ron Shaich, a Harvard MBA who had worked as the director of operations for the Original Cookie Company, a national chain of over 80 retail cookie stores, and who had just opened The Cookie Jar, a cookie store in a high-traffic location in downtown Boston. The two agreed to merge their businesses, enabling Kane to utilize his extensive real estate skills while Shaich handled the operational end of the business.

ABP quickly became known both for the

high quality of its croissants and baguettes and for its prime locations. Although the company was based in Boston, Massachusetts, during the next six years the chain rapidly expanded to include stores in New York, New Jersey, Maine, and Pennsylvania, among others. By 1986, there were 24 company-owned units in the ABP chain. (For a complete list of ABP store locations and sizes, see Exhibit 1.)

Originally, each of the ABP units operated as a self-contained production bakery in the back with a retail store and seating area in the front. A bakery chef was assigned to each store to handle the demanding process of rolling out croissants and baking breads in the classic French style. In addition to the croissants and breads available, sandwiches, coffee, and beverages were also sold. Some "test stores" offered soups, salads, omelettes, cookies, and sorbets as well. Generally, 65% of a unit's business was take-out.

In 1980, Shaich and Kane decided to centralize production, and fifteen of the company's eighteen bakers were fired. The remaining three were transferred to the Prudential Center store, where the dough was prepared, frozen, and then shipped to the other units. This eliminated the need for a highly trained chef in each unit, improved inventory control, increased product consistency, and reduced the size of the production area in each unit. Three years later, production was moved to ABP headquarters in South Boston. Frozen dough, which had a shelf life of eight weeks, continued to be shipped to all the units on a weekly, or semi-weekly, basis.

Len Schlesinger, formerly an associate professor in Organizational Behavior at the Harvard Business School, joined the company as its executive vice president and treasurer in early 1985. He was charged with the task of systematizing efforts to increase sales and improve quality throughout ABP by increasing employee ownership—both financial and psychological—in the organization.

ABP's major competitors included Vie de France, PepsiCo's La Petite Boulangerie, and Sara Lee's Michelle's Baguette and French Bakery. By 1986, however, all three were suffering from a combination of low profitability and decreased sales.

THE CYCLE OF FAILURE

According to Schlesinger and Shaich, in 1985 ABP's retail operations confronted for the first time a set of human resource problems endemic to the fast food industry. Labeled by Shaich as "the cycle of failure," these problems interrelated in a systematic way to induce a pattern of poor performance at the store level. The problems included a continuing crew labor shortage, a chronic shortage of associate managers, an inability to attract and select high-quality management candidates, an inadequately trained management staff, and what Schlesinger referred to as the tendency of many district managers to play "super GM" (general manager)—meaning that they obsessively focused on following up day-to-day activities (a GM's responsibility) at the expense of a clear definition of the district manager's role.

Shaich noted:

> Our lack of attention to these issues had created problems at the crew level that remained unsolved. These, in turn, magnified managerial problems, and vice-versa. It created a vicious cycle—the cycle of failure—and led to a significant degradation of the customer experience. Len and I concluded that if Au Bon Pain was to achieve its objectives of delivering a high-quality customer experience which resulted in sales and profitability, we had to break out of this cycle once and for all.

Schlesinger added:

It was clear, especially in the Boston market, that the labor crisis had engendered a serious decline in the quality of the crew candidates we attracted and ultimately hired. In the past, we had focused on simply staffing our stores rather than on attracting desirable candidates. All of our energies were devoted to the short-term operational needs of the business in this area.

At the same time, training for the crew was practically nonexistent and, where it did exist, poorly executed. Development, too, tended to follow a Darwinian "survival of the fittest" approach. The problem was compounded by the fact that we were committed to a promote-from-within policy which precluded the opportunity to acquire skilled talent from outside.

Beyond that, considerable work remained to be done to develop our reward system into a long-term compensation system which more directly tied the managers into the success of their stores.

EXISTING COMPENSATION SYSTEM IN 1986

Our existing compensation system, which we devised in 1985, goes a long way toward addressing the problems contributing to the cycle of failure. It's a creative attempt to deal with a lot of difficult issues.

Shaich made this observation as he outlined the two basic components of ABP's existing compensation system: base pay and a volume adjustment.

Base Pay

A manager's base pay was determined by his or her level in the organization: general manager, senior associate manager, first associate manager, or second associate manager (which included manager trainees). In July 1985, the base pay levels were as follows:

Level	Weekly Pay	Annual Pay
General Manager	$375.00	$19,500
Senior Associate Manager	350.00	18,200
First Associate Manager	341.54	17,760
Second Associate Manager	336.54	17,500

Volume Adjustment

In addition to base pay, a volume adjustment was calculated each week for first associate, senior associate, and general managers. (Second associate managers were not eligible for a volume adjustment). As ABP had a wide range of store volumes with varying managerial responsibilities and workloads, three categories of stores were established:

Store Volume	Weekly Sales
Low	$ 4,000–10,000
Medium	$10,000–20,000
High	over $20,000

The formulae for determing the salaries for general, senior associate, and first associate managers (i.e., base pay plus volume adjustment) are presented in Exhibit 2.

THE DEVELOPMENT OF THE PARTNER/MANAGER PROGRAM

In the spring of 1986, Schlesinger and Shaich developed a draft of a new compensation/incentive system for the managers of ABP's stores: *The Partner/Manager Program.* Shaich explained:

Len and I had identified the problems inherent in the cycle of failure. The next step was to figure out how to pay people more. Since 1985, under our existing compensation system, we had tried to develop a pay system which allowed the managers to make more money than they had before while still tying them to the success of their stores and the company.

In brief, The Partner/Manager Program would reclassify general managers as "partner/managers" and provide them with a base salary of $500 per week. Each partner/manager could choose an associate manager, who would be paid $400 per week. The partner/manager would be entitled to a 35% share of the unit's incremental profits under the new system; the associate manager would receive 15%; and ABP would receive the remaining 50%. A store-lease payment would be deducted monthly from the store controllable profits to cover unit level fixed expenses, corporate overhead, and reasonable profit expectations. The amount of the store-lease payment would be guaranteed for 13 periods (i.e., one year), with the following exceptions which would require an adjustment. The addition of fixed assets would trigger an increase in the store-lease payment of 25% of the total fixed asset cost divided across 13 periods. Secondly, additional sales which triggered a percentage rent clause in the real estate lease would increase the store-lease payment by the percentage specified in the real estate lease. Incremental profits would be equal to a unit's net controllable profits minus its store-lease payment. These profits would be distributed to the managers at the close of each "period" (i.e., every four weeks), with $7,500 held in reserve for the partner/manager and $2,500 held in reserve for the associate manager by ABP until the end of their contract, which could last one, two, or three years.[1]

The managers would be required to work a minimum of fifty hours per week,

and the partner/manager and/or the associate manager would have to be on duty in the store during 90% of its operating hours. The quality of each store would be monitored through mystery shopping reports, white glove inspections, and 100% customer satisfaction "moment of truth" indicators. A violation of any of the listed rules could result in the dismissal of either or both of the managers if the problem was not corrected within a specified amount of time. (See Appendix A for a working draft of The Partner/Manager Program.)

PHILOSOPHY BEHIND THE PARTNER/MANAGER PROGRAM

Product of Research

The Partner/Manager Program was the result of research and careful thought, according to Schlesinger:

> It's not something that we developed overnight. We looked into the compensation systems of a number of fast-food chains, including Sambo's, Chick-Fil-A, Golden Corral, and Kentucky Fried Chicken. The Partner/Manager Program is a customized imitation of the processes we studied. In some ways, it is revolutionary—but it is not without precedent in this industry.
>
> Under this system, we would manage our partner/managers with loose controls and less overhead, hold them tightly accountable to outputs (i.e., customer satisfaction as determined by mystery shopping) rather than inputs, and require them to invest themselves in their stores. Hopefully, through their efforts, the good managers would earn considerably more than they do now.

Shaich added:

> We want to hire people who really care . . . the kind of person you'd want on your side

---

[1]During The Partner/Manager Program Experiment, which is described in detail later in this case, Schlesinger and Shaich opted to distribute the managers' share of the incremental profits in a lump sum at the end of the six-month trial period.

when you go into a street fight. A person who does a good job for the people beneath him, not to impress somebody higher up. This is an organization that has rewarded *trying* for years. Now it's time to reward *results*.

One of the aims of this program would be to employ fewer managers, who would work harder, and make more money than their predecessors. We want people willing to pay the price to earn big bucks.

Personally, I believe that people earning less than $30,000 per year should be managed through individually-based incentive/compensation plans.[2] People higher up in an organization, with a longer time horizon and broader responsibilities, should have a low salary and stock options, like at People Express. The problem at People was that while stock ownership is meaningful, it's money that gets results.[3]

The Role of the District Manager

Not only would The Partner/Manager Program change ABP's compensation system, it would alter the ways in which the individual units were supervised. Schlesinger explained:

> Under this program, the district managers would function as coaches, rather than as policemen—and they would supervise eight to ten stores rather than the traditional three or four. The district managers would serve as consultants by generating ideas for sales building and cost reduction, and as support people by helping out during busy seasons and assisting with the training of new associate managers. They would earn perhaps 5% of the incremental profits generated by each of the units they supervise. Of course, we haven't worked out all the details yet.

One of the factors necessitating the change in the district managers' role was

what Shaich termed the "Stockholm effect." He referred to the psychological phenomenon which occurs when, over time, hostage victims develop sympathetic feelings toward their captors. He noted:

> In the past, the district managers, like the general managers, became excuse-givers. Instead of holding the general managers accountable to Au Bon Pain's standards—as customers do—the district managers began to sympathize with the managers' excuses. They became agents of the status quo rather than agents of change.
>
> Now it's clear that the partner/managers would be primarily responsible for handling any problems that arise. I expect that 90% of the problems we used to deal with at headquarters, the managers would now figure out on their own.

Increasing Stability

One of the goals of The Partner/Manager Program would be to increase stability at the unit level by reducing turnover, and by encouraging managers to commit themselves to working at a specific unit for at least one year. Shaich discussed this idea:

> The program would require each manager to have a real financial commitment to his or her store in the form of his or her share of the incremental profits—some of which would be held back by Au Bon Pain until the end of the contract. We expect that after working in the same unit for at least a year, a manager would have the chance to become very familiar with the store's cycle—what its sales volume is like, when its peak periods are, and so on. In the long run, this knowledge would increase the quality of each store's operations.
>
> At the same time, the managers would get to know their customers and crew on a personal basis. Significantly, consulting psychologists have found that the most

[2]For an example of such a company, see Harvard Business School case #9-376-028 on The Lincoln Electric Company.

[3]For further information, see Harvard Business School case #9-483-103 on People Express (A).

important single variable that keeps a customer coming back to a store is whether or not someone in the store knows that customer's name. There are employees at Golden Corral, for example, who know the names of 2,700 customers. This "retention quotient" has major implications for a company like Au Bon Pain as our research indicates that some of our customers—the ones we refer to as the "Au Bon Pain Club"—visit our stores up to 108 times a year.

Quality Control

Although The Partner/Manager Program would reduce the degree of corporate supervision of the individual stores, a number of quality control measures were written into the system, including a provision requiring that the units would be mystery shopped at least once a week. Mystery shopping involved having a "professional shopper" hired from outside ABP evaluate the store from a customer's perspective based on criteria such as service speed, the quality of food, store cleanliness, and the friendliness of store employees. In addition, "white glove" inspections, using a 140 item checklist covering all phases of store operations, would be conducted by an Au Bon Pain auditor every period. The inspection lasted eight hours, and the days when they would occur would not be announced in advance. Finally, the managers would also be expected to comply with 12 "moment of truth" indicators (based on criteria generated in customer focus groups) which were aimed at achieving 100% customer satisfaction.

Decreased Recruiting Budget

Schlesinger expected a dramatic decrease in ABP's recruiting budget as a result of the publicity surrounding the news that it would be changing its compensation system. He predicted:

If we go public with this program, the resulting newspaper and trade journal articles would help us to attract and stockpile a new group of managerial candidates. We could cut our annual recruiting budget from $230,000 to $60,000 by substituting press for want ads.

Burning Out

One issue raised by both Shaich and Schlesinger concerned the managers who might burn out during the program. They agreed that being a partner/manager or an associate manager under the new program would be a potentially stressful experience—sufficiently stressful that it could cause some managers to drop out before their contract ended. Schlesinger, however, was philosophic about it:

Burning out managers would be one concern. But the way I see it, we're all adults entering into a business contract. We understand the benefits and the risks.

Physical Limitations

There were at least three physical factors that limited productivity and sales: (1) the proofing capacity of each unit (i.e., the capacity of the machines in which the dough was placed to rise for approximately two hours), (2) the freezer capacity of each unit, and (3) the limitations of Au Bon Pain's product line.

Schlesinger predicted:

If Au Bon Pain adopts The Partner/Manager Program, people will claim that we have come up with a new way to con people—but that wouldn't be true. The program would establish a clear, tangible link between the results the managers achieved and the money they would make.

We wouldn't hold up goals that aren't attainable, because we would need to create a base of heroes. Under The Partner/Manager

Program most people would make about
$40,000 a year. The heroes would make be-
tween $60,000 and $100,000, and they would
set an example for which everyone would
strive.

THE PARTNER/MANAGER PROGRAM EXPERIMENT

Eager to discover if the program would be
successful in a real-life situation, Schlesinger and Shaich invited the general and
associate managers of two stores to participate in a six-month-long trial run of
The Partner/Manager Program. Gary Aronson, the general manager of ABP's Burlington Mall store (15 miles west of
Boston), and Frank Ciampa, his associate
manager, agreed to give it a try. So did
Brian McEvoy, the general manager of the
CityPlace store in Hartford, Connecticut
(100 miles south of Boston), and his associate manager, Stephen Dunn.

The managers did not feel that they
were coerced into participating in the experiment. "We were able to choose whether
or not we wanted to participate," McEvoy
said. Before the experiment began, both
Aronson and McEvoy met with Schlesinger and Shaich to discuss a rough draft of
the program. "We gave them our input,
and they incorporated our suggestions
into a revised version," Aronson explained. Later, all four managers met with
Schlesinger and Shaich to review the
changes and discuss any questions about
the program.

Aronson explained why he agreed to
participate in the experiment:

> Frank and I decided that our #1 priority
> was to show that a program like this could
> work. We wanted to convince people that
> this was something revolutionary, and that
> it would not only turn around this company,
> but that it has the potential to change the
> whole industry. The way I see it, this pro-

gram is going to turn us all into a bunch of
professionals.

McEvoy was motivated both by the "financial incentives of the program," and
by his perception that it was an alternative to following the traditional route—
which would have involved moving to
Boston and trying to get promoted to the
position of district manager. He noted,
"First of all, my wife and I didn't really
want to relocate because it would have
upset her career. At the same time, even if
we did move, there wouldn't have been
any guarantees that I would have been
able to move up in the company."

Managers' Backgrounds

> What initially attracted me to Au Bon Pain
> was that they allowed their managers more
> mobility and more access to upper-level
> management than most fast-food chains.
> They also let their managers have an input
> into the decision process.
> I believe that the only way you can grow as
> a manager is to work in a less-structured
> environment. At Au Bon Pain, you can't run
> on buzzers and bells like you can at McDon-
> ald's or Burger King; you have to be able to
> think.

This is how Stephen Dunn, associate
manager of the CityPlace store in Hartford, recalled his first impression of ABP.
Dunn graduated from the University of
Massachusetts in 1981 with a business degree in hotel/restaurant/travel administration, and he had experience working in
full-service, fast-food, catering, and ban-
quet situations. In 1985, he was recruited
by a headhunter retained by ABP and accepted a position as the associate manager
of the CityPlace store.

Ironically, Brian McEvoy, Dunn's partner and the general manager of the City-
Place store, never intended to work for

ABP. After graduating from the University of Massachusetts in 1980 with a degree in history, followed by two years of teaching experience and a brief stint in the Navy; he viewed his original meeting with Shaich as a "practice interview." Later, impressed with the company, he took an entry-level job as an associate manager. At the start of The Partner/Manager Program Experiment, he had been with the company for three years.

Gary Aronson, the general manager of the Burlington Mall store, worked for Kentucky Fried Chicken for eight years before joining ABP in 1983 as an associate manager. He explained, "I switched jobs because I saw a lot of opportunity for me at a place like this. I didn't feel that the management team I was training with was that experienced, and I knew I'd find a way to shine real quickly."

Aronson's associate manager, Frank Ciampa, graduated from Bentley College in 1984 with a B.S. in marketing management and an associate degree in accounting. He joined ABP in 1985 as a manager trainee—in the hope that he could use it as a stepping stone to a job in the corporate side of the business. He admitted:

If you'd asked me a year ago what I wanted to be after working here for several months, it sure wasn't to be a partner/manager. But since I've been working with Gary under The Partner/Manager Program, my whole mentality has changed. Now, I'm in no hurry to work in the office—I enjoy being a manager.

Managers' Activities during the Experiment

"Len tells people that I run the place like a family deli, and I suppose that could be true," Aronson admitted. Both his wife and Ciampa's mother worked in the store, and Ciampa's father, a manufacturing equipment mechanic, helped out with maintenance.

Originally, Aronson employed two associate managers. When the experiment began, however, he took the opportunity to have one of the two transferred to another unit. He explained that, according to the program, he didn't need three managers to run the store. "It means that Frank and I have to work longer hours," he conceded, "but it's worth it." The Burlington Mall store was open from 9:00 A.M. until 10:00 P.M. Monday through Saturday, and 11:00 A.M. through 6:00 P.M. on Sunday.

During the experiment, Aronson took on a number of wholesale accounts, noting:

The store doesn't open until 9:00 A.M., but Frank and I get here by 4:30 or 5:00 most mornings to prepare our wholesale products. We've even begun to do a little catering. If we can keep the four or five accounts we've got right now, I bet we could make about $40,000 worth of sales next year just on the wholesale line.

Aronson and Ciampa also took advantage of the increased managerial responsibility called for in the program and initiated some money-saving repairs. Ciampa recalled:

During the first week of the experiment, we decided to knock out a platform built against one wall in order to make room for eight more seats in the cafe area. Of course, making this change wasn't high on the list of priorities for the company's construction department, so Au Bon Pain estimated it would cost $10,000. We found a guy who'd do it for only $3,000, and we did it right away.

Similarly, when it was time to repaint the store, headquarters estimated it would cost $1,200 to paint one wall. We had the whole store painted ourselves for about $800.

At the same time, Aronson began calculating food cost on a monthly, rather than daily, basis. "It drives the people at headquarters crazy," he grinned, "but I'm running the best food cost of any of the stores. As long as I'm alert, and trust the people I'm working with, I've never had a problem with stealing or cheating." He added that the turnover rate in his store was close to 0%.

The CityPlace store was open from 6:30 A.M. until 6:00 P.M. Monday through Friday. it was closed on the weekends. McEvoy admitted, "I don't want to work eighty hours a week the way Gary does now. I'm starting to like having my weekends off." He alternated shifts between himself, Dunn, and Barbara Jones, his shift supervisor.

Dunn observed:

Au Bon Pain provides us with a labor grid to guide us in making decisions about how many people to schedule to work at different times during the day. We generally employ more people than the grid specifies. For example, they say that in the morning we should be able to run the store with four people. We always try to schedule six in an attempt to decrease the amount of time it takes to fill a customer's order.

McEvoy added:

In order to schedule extra crew members to work during peak hours, we had to pay them more because they were only working a two-hour-long shift. However, having the extra workers allowed us to improve our service and decrease the time customers had to wait for their order, so it paid off in increased sales.

Approximately three months into the experiment, McEvoy and Dunn began a telephone express service. Under the new system, office workers called in orders of $25.00 or more, which they picked up a little while later. "It's a lot quicker than having to stand in line and wait while the order is filled, and it helps us to serve all our customers more efficiently," McEvoy explained. The telephone express service was currently available only to the office workers in the CityPlace building, but he was considering expanding it to other areas.

Managers' Evaluation of The Partner/Manager Program

All four managers agreed that one of the program's benefits was less corporate supervision of the units. This change was most apparent in the new role assumed by the district managers. Schlesinger acted as the district manager for both stores, and Ciampa noted that he had visited the Burlington Mall store no more than three or four times in as many months, although he kept in touch over the phone.

McEvoy predicted, "The district managers will become less like policemen, and more like advisors and coaches. Instead of being told *'You* must do this,' managers will hear comments like 'How can *we* build sales?' and 'How can *we* improve the store?' "

Aronson added:

Some managers love to have the district manager come around so that he or she can admire how clean the floor is. Frank and I don't need that. We know exactly what to do. Having someone else around actually brought down the quality of our work because we were busy explaining everything.

Aronson and Ciampa believed that the program had the potential to reduce the tendency of many managers in the fast-food industry to move from one job to another, starting at the ground level each time and slowly working their way up. Aronson explained:

In most professions, if you're good at what you do, when you change jobs you start out making more money than you did before. The fast-food industry's mentality is different. For example, when I left International Food Services, I was the highest-paid manager there and I was working in the highest-volume store. But when I decided to join Au Bon Pain, I had to start at the ground floor again and work my way up. It's the same story everywhere. I had to take a $135/week cut in pay in addition to going through the emotional upheaval of moving from one job to another. The prevailing attitude seemed to be "Well, maybe you're a whiz with fried chicken, but you don't know anything about croissants."

Now, Ron and Len have realized that they can't operate the way the Wendys and the Burger Kings deal with people. To be successful in the future, this company will have to bring in established people who've shown that they can do the job. A manager with five or six years' experience in the fast-food industry has to be worth a lot more than someone just out of school. If we start paying people what they're worth, I believe we can pick up some prime-time players and make this a really interesting company.

Aronson felt that, in the past, some of the instability generated by managers moving from store to store was the result of decisions made at the company headquarters. He asserted:

Once a manager had a store running smoothly, BINGO! They suddenly wanted to transfer you to a problem store. The better a manager you were, the more problems you had to take care of. After a while you began to ask, "What am I? A clean-up crew?"

Dunn believed that holding back part of the managers' share of the incremental profits until the end of their contract would reduce the desire to store-hop. He said "Now, I'm a lot less company-oriented, and a lot more store-oriented. I'm less willing to leave the unit where I'm working and move to another store."

McEvoy pointed out, however, that "the way for an ambitious person to make even more money would be to move to a higher-volume store. Personally, I'm not interested in relocating right now, but the temptation is always there."

Despite the decrease in corporate supervision of the units under the program, the managers still perceived a continuing corporate overemphasis on details and paperwork. Aronson exclaimed:

There's too much emphasis on the detail end, not enough on the meat-and-potatoes end. The majority of my customers want good food, quality service, and they want it fast. But every time we've been mystery shopped during the experiment, we've received the same basic criticism. Although our overall score is quite high, the mystery shopper generally objects that the floor hasn't been swept. Frankly, during lunchtime this place is a zoo. If we tried to sweep then, we'd get complaints from the customers about the dust flying in their food.

McEvoy generally agreed with Aronson's point, but admitted that he was more concerned that he was getting close to reaching maximum output on much of his equipment.

Dunn brought up another issue:

Under this new program, an associate manager's greatest fear will be that everything that he or she can make or lose hinges on the partner/manager they're working with. The partner/manager calls the shots, that's the bottom line, even though you've got your money tied into this thing too.

The length of a manager's workweek was also discussed. Aronson reported that he and Ciampa were working an average of eighty hours per week—twenty-five more hours per week than they had been working before.

Aronson recalled:

I knew that during the experiment I wouldn't have much time left over for anything else, and that was a real consideration. I finally told my family to put up with it for six months, and in the end I would make it worth their while. In the first sixteen weeks, we had two days off. I've worked some days from 4:30 in the morning until 11:00 at night.

McEvoy and Dunn worked fifty to fifty-five hours a week. McEvoy explained, "The amount of hours we're working hasn't really changed that much." Dunn added, "We work as long as it takes to get the job done. Whenever we've worked extra hours, it has been because we were understaffed, not because we decided to work long hours because of the experiment."

Dunn concluded:

To be blunt, parts of the program are good, and parts are bad. Burnout, particularly in this industry, is high. If someone is going to be locked into this thing, and they're going to have the added pressure of knowing that their money—a large part of their share of the bonus—is tied up in whether or not they can last out their contract, well, in my opinion, that kind of stress could actually cause a person *not* to perform as well as they could. I'm not trying to be negative, but they've got to be careful who they choose to be managers and how they monitor them.

There are also the shift supervisors to deal with. A lot of them act like managers in every degree but in the paperwork, including sales building. In fact, when we began this experiment, Brian decided to pay our shift supervisor 2% of our half of the incremental profits. When other shift supervisors hear about the phenomenal amounts of money being made by the managers, how will that affect their motivation?

Finally, even if this program dramatically improves the quality of our applicants for managerial positions, what are we going to do about the turnover rate for lower-level employees? It's close to 400% a year in this store. High turnover is an industry norm. How does that effect the quality of the customer experience?

Results

During the experiment, sales in the Burlington Mall and CityPlace stores increased dramatically. The operating statements for both units during Periods 1–7 and during the experiment (Periods 8–13) are shown in Exhibit 3. Exhibit 4 summarizes the stores' performances against the company's plan and compares it to their performance in 1985. While both McEvoy's and Aronson's base salaries remained at $500 per week, their actual earnings on an annualized basis were closer to $50,000 and $70,000, respectively.[4] A memo outlining the final distribution of profits is presented in Exhibit 5.

THE DECISION

Shaich considered the experiment a resounding success, and suggested that:

The problems don't lie in the concept, which I'm convinced is basically sound. The challenges will be in its execution. There are a lot of implementation issues we still have to deal with—that's one of the costs of being in the vanguard on an issue like this—but I think the potential gain is worth the risks.

The key to success will be for us to get out of the way once this thing starts. We've developed the concept, and now we have to stand back and let the managers operate it. In time, I believe we'll witness startling re-

[4]Art Veves, Burger King's regional director of Human Resources in Boston, reported in a telephone conversation that the average Burger King manager earned between $24,000 and $30,000 annually, plus a bonus of approximately $2,500. The salary expectations for a McDonald's manager were roughly equivalent to these figures.

sults. In my opinion, at least 25% more sales can be made. Len puts the figure closer to 50%, and Louis Kane thinks it's even higher. I'd love to flip the switch tomorrow and set the program in motion.

Schlesinger added, "In time, this plan will be broadly applicable to any multi-unit service concept on the face of the earth."

Aronson was more guarded, asserting:

With the right people, this program can work. But to suddenly turn it over to all the stores—personally, I think that would be a big mistake. There are some people who would try and squeeze it dry. In the short term they could show fantastic results, food and labor costs down, etc., but in the long term you wind up with underportioning and dirty stores.

McEvoy agreed:

I don't think they should roll out this program to every store right away, especially if they're hiring a lot of new managers. It takes a while for a person to settle in. The strict deadlines for solving problems set out in the Partner/Manager document would put too much pressure on new managers who aren't used to handling everything by themselves. Holding them accountable could blow them right out of the water.

Ciampa added:

Even under the best of circumstances, the company will be lucky if 50% of the people working for them now make it under the new program. People are used to getting a lot of supervision. It used to be that the louder you cried, the more attention you got.

Dunn added a final caution:

During the experiment, we've had phenomenal sales growth. But, and I've said this to

Len and Ron, 85% of that growth would have occurred in any case because of the type of individuals Brian and I are. It just happened that the experiment began when we were starting to get things together. Specifically, at that point, Brian and I had been working together for nine months. We were comfortable with each other and we knew our customers. It was the middle of the summer and we were fully staffed because a lot of high school kids wanted summer jobs. Our equipment was functioning correctly for the first time in a long time, and we had just converted from an inefficient cafeteria-style system to one in which the person working the cash register automatically keyed in the sandwich order to the kitchen.

When asked if they planned to sign up for the long-term deal, Aronson, Ciampa, and McEvoy indicated they would if certain conditions were met (i.e., Aronson would only sign up for a one-year deal). Dunn replied, "No comment."

After a meeting in early January, during which he reviewed both his own and Shaich's comments and the reactions of the managers involved in the experiment, Schlesinger concluded:

From an MBA viewpoint, it's an interesting situation. We've got two hand-picked managers and six months of data on which to base a decision whether or not to shake up this whole company. Are we foolish if we grab at this opportunity?

AU BON PAIN STUDY QUESTIONS:

1. Identify and evaluate the Au Bon Pain business strategy. How does one make money in this business? What difference does the performance of an individual restaurant manager make?

2. If the company is to achieve its business objectives, what are the human resources imperatives?

3. What is your evaluation of the Partner/ Manager Program (PMP)? Will PMP give ABP a competitive edge?

4. What is your evaluation of the experiment? Should the PMP be rolled out to all the restaurants? Why hasn't the Au Bon Pain type of plan become more widespread in multi-site service businesses?

AU BON PAIN: THE PARTNER/MANAGER PROGRAM

Exhibit 1 Company-owned stores

Location	City	State	Year Opened	Square Footage	Number of Managers
Faneuil Hall Marketplace	Boston	MA	1977	1,400	4
Burlington Mall	Burlington	MA	1978	1,400	2
Logan Airport	Boston	MA	1981	800	4
Cherry Hill Mall	Cherry Hill	NJ	1984	1,000	2
Harvard Square	Cambridge	MA	1983	2,500	4
Park Plaza	Boston	MA	1984	1,000	4
Arsenal Mall	Watertown	MA	1984	2,300	3
CityPlace	Hartford	CT	1984	2,400	2
2 Penn Center	Philadelphia	PA	1985	2,700	2
Riverside Square	Hackensack	NJ	1984	1,800	3
Crossgates Mall	Albany	NY	1984	1,400	1
Cape Cod Mall	Hyannis	MA	1985	1,000	3
Crystal Mall	Waterford	CT	1984	600	2
Rockefeller Center	New York	NY	1985	2,500	5
Prudential Center	Boston	MA	1985	3,000	4
Filene's	Boston	MA	1984	800	3
Filene's (Franklin St.)	Boston	MA	1985	150	4
Filene's (Basement)	Boston	MA	1984	600	
Copley Place	Boston	MA	1984	2,500	4
Copley Place (Stuart St.)	Boston	MA	1985	1,000	2
Maine Mall	South Portland	ME	1983	500	1
Cookie Jar	Boston	MA	1980	700	2
Newington	Newington	NH	1984	800	2
Kendall Square	Cambridge	MA	1986	2,600	3
Dewey Square	Boston	MA	1986	2,400	2

Exhibit 2 Weekly manager salaries for given weekly sales volumes

Volume/ Week	General Manager (Base = $375)		Senior Associate Manager (Base = $350)		First Associate Manager (Base = $341.54)	
	Volume Adjustment	*Weekly Total*	*Volume Adjustment*	*Weekly Total*	*Volume Adjustment*	*Weekly Total*
$1–4,000	0	$375.00	0	$350.00	0	$341.54
5,000	13.12	388.12	5.25	355.25	2.53	344.07
10,000	78.75	453.75	31.50	381.50	15.21	356.75
15,000	118.13	493.13	47.25	397.25	22.81	364.35
20,000	157.50	532.50	63.00	413.00	30.42	371.96
25,000	174.38	549.38	69.75	419.75	33.67	375.21
30,000	191.25	566.25	76.50	426.50	36.93	378.47
35,000	208.13	583.13	83.25	433.25	40.19	381.73
40,000	225.00	600.00	90.00	440.00	43.46	385.00
45,000	241.88	616.88	96.75	446.75	46.71	388.25
50,000	258.75	633.75	103.50	453.50	49.97	391.51

To compute the weekly salary at the general manager level, the following formulae were used:
  Low volume store: Base pay + .013125 (Volume − $4,000)
  Medium volume store: Base pay + $78.75 + .00785 (Volume − $10,000)
  High volume store: Base pay + $157.50 + .003375 (Volume − $20,000)

For senior associate managers, the formulae were:
  Low volume store: Base pay + .00525 (Volume − $4,000)
  Medium volume store: Base pay + $31.50 + .00315 (Volume − $10,000)
  High volume store: Base pay + $63.00 + .0135 (Volume − $20,000)

For first associate managers, the formulae were:
  Low volume store: Base pay + .002535 (Volume − $4,000)
  Medium volume store: Base pay + 15.21 + .001521 (Volume − $10,000)
  High volume store: Base pay + 30.42 + .000652 (Volume − $20,000)

Exhibit 3(a) Store operating statement, Burlington Mall (pre-experiment)

Percentage of Net Sales[a]	Periods						
	1	2	3	4	5	6	7
Regular Sales	100.0	98.5	98.9	100.0	100.0	100.0	100.0
Wholesale	0.0	0.0	0.0	0.0	0.0	0.0	0.0
Promotions	0.0	1.5	1.1	0.0	0.0	0.0	0.0
Net Sales	100.0	100.0	100.0	100.0	100.0	100.0	100.0
Discounts	0.4	0.4	0.6	0.7	1.0	0.9	0.5
Net Net Sales	99.6	99.6	99.4	99.3	99.0	99.1	99.5
Management	9.1	9.8	11.7	11.4	7.8	9.0	8.9
Shift Supervisor	0.0	0.0	0.0	0.0	0.0	1.2	1.1
Crew	15.1	14.3	14.9	13.8	14.1	13.2	13.9
Benefits	2.6	3.0	2.9	4.1	3.1	1.6	3.1
Total Labor	26.8	27.0	29.4	29.3	25.0	24.9	27.0
Food Cost	29.4	30.1	31.1	30.0	30.5	30.2	32.0
Paper Cost	1.8	1.2	1.4	1.2	2.0	1.4	1.8
Controllables	1.5	1.4	1.1	2.0	2.1	1.8	2.3
Utilities	1.9	2.8	2.3	2.3	1.8	2.1	2.2
Controllable Profit	38.3	37.0	34.1	34.4	37.6	38.7	34.2
Fixed Expenses	3.4	3.6	3.5	3.4	3.0	3.1	3.3
Occupancy	9.3	9.5	9.6	9.5	12.3	10.3	10.4
Store Profit	25.6	23.9	21.0	21.5	22.3	25.2	20.5

[a] These numbers have been disguised.

Exhibit 3(b)   Store operating statement, Burlington Mall (experiment)

Percentage of Net Sales[a]	Periods					
	8	9	10	11	12	13
Regular Sales	97.0	97.1	96.0	95.2	93.9	95.8
Wholesale	3.0	2.9	4.0	4.3	6.1	4.2
Promotions	0.0	0.0	0.0	0.0	0.0	0.0
Net Sales	100.0	100.0	100.0	100.0	100.0	100.0
Discounts	0.4	0.3	0.2	0.2	0.2	0.2
Net Net Sales	99.6	99.7	99.8	99.8	99.8	99.8
Food Cost	28.7	29.1	29.7	29.4	29.4	28.6
Paper Cost	1.7	1.5	2.0	1.6	1.9	1.7
Management	6.4	5.6	5.7	5.4	4.9	3.7
Shift Supervisor	1.8	0.8	0.1	1.3	2.4	2.3
Crew	13.0	12.9	12.9	12.5	11.9	11.3
Benefits	2.0	1.7	1.7	1.6	1.6	1.0
Total Labor	23.2	20.9	20.5	20.8	20.8	18.3
Controllables	1.3	0.8	1.1	0.9	1.1	1.5
Utilities	3.4	2.7	2.8	2.2	1.3	0.4
Controllable Profit	41.2	44.8	43.9	44.9	45.3	49.3
Fixed Expenses	3.0	2.9	2.8	2.8	2.4	2.0
Occupancy	11.8	9.2	9.5	9.5	11.2	9.2
Store Profit	26.4	32.7	30.3	32.5	31.7	38.2

[a] These numbers have been disguised.

250

Exhibit 3(c) Store operating statement, CityPlace (pre-experiment)

Percentage of Net Sales[a]	Periods						
	1	2	3	4	5	6	7
Regular Sales	100.0	96.5	97.8	100.0	100.0	100.0	100.0
Wholesale	0.0	0.0	0.0	0.0	0.0	0.0	0.0
Promotions	0.0	3.5	2.2	0.0	0.0	0.0	0.0
Net Sales	100.0	100.0	100.0	100.0	100.0	100.0	100.0
Discounts	0.3	0.3	0.4	0.4	0.3	0.3	0.4
Net Net Sales	93.1	99.7	99.6	99.6	99.7	99.7	99.6
Food Cost	28.0	29.1	29.9	31.2	27.5	29.1	30.9
Paper Cost	2.4	2.7	2.8	2.8	3.1	3.2	3.2
Management	7.0	6.8	7.3	6.5	7.1	7.1	6.8
Shift Supervisor	1.8	2.0	1.9	2.1	2.3	2.0	1.5
Crew	12.2	13.1	13.6	13.2	12.4	13.2	14.6
Benefits	2.3	2.9	2.1	2.9	2.3	2.3	2.8
Total Labor	23.2	24.8	24.9	24.7	24.1	24.6	25.7
Controllables	1.3	1.5	1.9	3.8	2.0	4.7	1.8
Utilities	1.6	1.5	2.1	1.6	1.8	1.7	1.7
Controllable Profit	36.6	40.0	38.1	35.5	41.2	36.3	36.3
Fixed Expenses	8.5	8.9	9.9	8.3	8.8	9.1	7.8
Occupancy	12.4	12.9	12.4	12.2	12.1	12.1	11.7
Store Profit	15.7	18.3	15.7	14.9	20.3	15.1	16.8

[a] These numbers have been disguised.

Exhibit 3(d)   Store operating statement, CityPlace (experiment)

Percentage of Net Sales[a]			Periods			
	8	9	10	11	12	13
Regular Sales	100.0	100.0	100.0	100.0	98.6	98.1
Wholesale	0.0	0.0	0.0	0.0	1.4	1.9
Promotions	0.0	0.0	0.0	0.0	0.0	0.0
Net Sales	100.0	100.0	100.0	100.0	100.0	100.0
Discounts	0.3	0.3	0.3	0.4	0.5	0.3
Net Net Sales	99.7	99.7	99.7	99.6	99.5	99.7
Food Cost	27.6	29.6	29.6	29.9	31.0	30.6
Paper Cost	2.8	3.1	2.9	2.9	3.0	3.1
Management	6.0	5.8	6.2	5.0	5.7	5.7
Shift Supervisor	1.9	2.0	2.0	1.7	1.9	1.8
Crew	14.6	14.6	13.4	15.0	13.9	14.3
Benefits	2.2	3.0	2.1	3.0	2.1	2.0
Total Labor	24.7	25.4	23.7	24.8	23.6	23.8
Controllables	2.6	2.3	1.6	2.1	1.7	1.6
Utilities	1.2	1.7	9.6	0.6	9.7	3.8
Controllable Profit	40.9	37.6	32.3	39.3	30.5	36.9
Fixed Expenses	6.9	7.6	11.3	7.2	5.9	7.4
Occupancy	9.6	10.3	9.7	9.2	13.0	8.9
Store Profit	24.3	19.7	11.3	22.9	11.6	20.6

[a] These numbers have been disguised.

Exhibit 4 Performance against plan and prior year (current dollars)

		Periods 1–7	Periods 8–13
Sales vs. Plan	Burlington	− 11,695	+ 56,719
	CityPlace	+ 12,903	+ 69,311
	Total	+ 1,208	126,030
		Periods 1–7	**Periods 8–13**
Sales vs. Last Year	Burlington	− 1,600	+ 70,478
	CityPlace	+ 33,512	+ 93,558
	Total	31,912	164,036
		Periods 1–7	**Periods 8–13**
Controllable Profits vs. Plan	Burlington	− 3,844	+ 53,562
	CityPlace	+ 4,613	+ 18,580
	Total	+ 769	+ 72,142
		Periods 1–7	**Periods 8–13**
Controllable Profits vs. Last Year	Burlington	− 2	+ 57,449
	CityPlace	+ 2,706	+ 29,741
	Total	+ 2,704	+ 87,190

Exhibit 5 Partner/manager profit distributions

```
                    M E M O R A N D U M

TO:    Gary Aronson, Frank Ciampa, Steve Dunn, Brian McEvoy

FROM:  Len Schlesinger

DATE:  January 15, 1987

RE:    Partner/Manager Profit Distributions
cc:    Ron Shaich
       Louis Kane
```

	BURLINGTON	CITYPLACE
Store Lease Payment	127,526.25	103,619.50
Fixed Asset Additions	110.62	45.49
Percentage Rent	3,556.48	0.00
TOTAL DUE ABP	131,193.35	103,664.99
CREDITS		
Period 8	23,225.00	23,680.65
Period 9	28,740.00	20,218.65
Period 10	27,705.00	23,444.46
Period 11	29,445.00	23,809.65
Period 12	33,172.00	24,071.65
Period 13	45,122.00	23,024.65
TOTAL CREDITS	187,409.00	138,249.71
LESS TOTAL DUE ABP	131,193.35	103,644.99
PROFIT POOL	56,215.65	34,584.72
ABP Share	28,107.82	17,292.36
P/M Share	19,675.48	12,104.65
Assoc. P/M Share	8,432.35	5,187.71

P/M Weekly Wage

	BURLINGTON	CITYPLACE
Salary	500.00	500.00
Share	819.81	504.36
TOTAL	1,319.81	1,004.36
ANNUALIZED	68,630.12	52,226.72

Assoc. P/M Weekly Wage

	BURLINGTON	CITYPLACE
Salary	400.00	400.00
Share	351.35	216.15
TOTAL	751.35	616.15
ANNUALIZED	39,070.20	32,039.80

APPENDIX A
AU BON PAIN: THE PARTNER/MANAGER PROGRAM

AN INTRODUCTION TO THE PARTNER/MANAGER PROGRAM

I. Company Objectives

As Au Bon Pain moves ahead into the future, it is critical that we develop a compensation/incentive system for our bakery/cafe managers which is second to none in our industry segment. The foundation of ABP's success is talented people who achieve results and, in turn, share in the financial rewards of their efforts. *The Partner/Manager Program* provides the opportunity for a select group of managers to be in business *for* themselves, but not *by* themselves. The company provides support in the form of monitoring of quality standards which will be vigorously enforced, and in the refinement and expansion of our retail concept and system.

Our ability to attract talented and enthusiastic people who thrive in our environment is nothing less than the prime ingredient necessary to achieve all that we have set out for.

Au Bon Pain fundamentally believes that the sales and profitability of the individual bakery/cafe units are strongly influenced by the quality of their retail operations. Furthermore, we believe that the quality of retail operations is directly affected by the presence of:

- A management team that truly cares about the quality of the customer experience.
- A management team with experience and commitment to working at a specific unit for an extended period of time.

Drafted: Spring 1986 by Len Schlesinger and Ron Shaich. Abridged by Research Assistant Lucy N. Lytle, under the supervision of Professor W. Earl Sasser, January 1987.

- A management team with a commitment to the Au Bon Pain operating system, but with the flexibility for some degree of local decision-making/adaptation to build sales in its market.
- A crew with a strong relationship and commitment to delivering for the management team, and thus to the customer.
- An explicit focus on the management of outputs (service, sales, food cost, controllable costs, labor cost) vs. inputs.
- A store-manager/company "you win-we win" approach.

However, the dynamics of the fast-food labor market and the internal structure of Au Bon Pain itself have made it very difficult to achieve these traits, due to:

- A managerial labor pool which forces us to take more "chances" in hiring entry-level talent, plus significant turnover at the associate manager level.
- A centralized system-wide orientation toward the operations and marketing functions in our bakery/cafes which currently stifles our ability to exercise initiative at the store level.
- Excessive crew turnover and sloppy hiring which severely degrade the quality of the customer experience and exacerbate the day-to-day problems of the management team.

To address these problems and to move down the road toward reaching an idealized version of our retail operations, we are proposing a radically reconceptualized framework for the management of human resources in Au Bon Pain bakery/cafe units. It is titled *The Partner/Manager Program.*

II. Objectives of The Partner/Manager Program

- To develop a management compensation system which dramatically enhances our ability to *attract* and *retain* the finest managers in the industry.

- To shift our organizational focus from promotion to district manager as the desired career path to achieving partner/manager status (a terminal general manager's position).
- To dramatically increase the tenure of a store management team with consequent feelings of "local ownership."
- To lessen our top-down management approach to retail operations by:

    1. Increasing local unit responsibilities for decision-making and execution, simultaneously with a reward system that increases management commitment to unit results.
    2. Encouraging partner/managers to "push" the corporate office to respond to local needs.

- To dramatically reduce district manager supervision of retail stores and to shift the district manager's role from a policeman/checker to a business/sales consultant.
- To provide a human-resource mechanism which frees ABP to grow at an accelerated rate without great pain ("hyperphased growth").
- To maximize store level profits, ABP return on investment, and management salaries, simultaneously.
- To provide the opportunity for our partner/managers to build financial "nest eggs."
- To provide job security for those people who perform for ABP and themselves.

III. Management of The Partner/Manager Experiment

The experiment will run for six periods, from July 13 until December 20, 1986. Len Schlesinger will assume direct responsibility as the district manager for the two stores selected to participate.

Experimentation at the Burlington Mall store will test our abilities to revive a ma-

ture shopping mall location and to tap into area offices as a growth vehicle in the face of increased competition. The City-Place experiment will provide us with considerable data on how to best leverage an office building location to its fullest potential.

IV. The Economics of The Partner/Manager Program

A. Each store's general manager will be reclassified as a partner/manager at a base salary of $500 per week. They will be authorized to hire/retain one associate manager at a base salary of $400 per week. Any additional management support can be added at the discretion of the partner/manager. However, all managers must take their bonus from a fixed profit pool (i.e., their 50% share of the store's incremental profits).

B. Au Bon Pain will determine a "store-lease" payment required to support a unit's fixed expenses, corporate overhead, and reasonable profit expectations. During the experiment, this payment will be $127,526 for the Burlington Mall unit, and $103,619 for the CityPlace unit.

C. The store-lease payment will be guaranteed for the period of the experiment, with the following exceptions which will require adjustments:

    1. The addition of fixed assets will trigger an increase in the store-lease payment of: .25 × total fixed asset cost.
    EXAMPLE: A new counter is added to Hartford at a cost of $10,000. On an annual basis, this would increase the store-lease payment by $2,500.
    2. Additional sales which trigger a percentage rent clause in the real estate lease will increase the store-lease payment by the percentage specified in the real estate lease.
    EXAMPLE: The rent for the Burlington unit assumes that the store will

achieve the 1986 plan. All sales over this plan will increase the store-lease payment to Au Bon Pain by 8% of the incremental sales dollars.

D. Profits will be distributed to the partner/manager and associate manager as follows: actual store controllable profits minus store-lease payment equals incremental profits or losses.

incremental profits × .50 = ABP share

incremental profits × .35 = partner/manager share

incremental profits × .15 = associate manager share

E. The partner/manager and associate manager's share of the incremental profits will be distributed at the close of each period, with $7,500 held in reserve for the partner/manager and $2,500 held in reserve for the associate manager by Au Bon Pain until the end of their contract.

F. For the *Partner/Manager Program Experiment,* profit distributions will occur after the final review of the experiment is completed (approximately February 1, 1987).

V. Supervising and Managing The Partner/Manager Experiment

A. The two stores will be heavily mystery shopped (at least once a week), and the mystery shopping reports will serve as critical indicators of store-level quality standards.

B. The two stores will be subjected to three "white glove" inspections. These will be conducted by an independent ABP auditor not connected with the experiment. They will cover all phases of store operations from top to bottom, and will be a major input to the overall evaluation of the experiment.

C. The two stores will be expected to comply with the 100% customer satisfaction "moments of truth" indicators, and will be evaluated against them.

D. The partner/manager, associate manager, or a certified ABP shift supervisor must be on duty in the store during all store hours. The partner/manager and associate manager must work in the store a minimum of fifty hours a week, and the partner/manager and/or the associate manager must be on duty in the story during 90% of its operating hours.

E. Au Bon Pain reserves the right to discharge, remove, or replace the partner/manager or associate manager at any time. All store managers, crew, and shift supervisors will remain employees of Au Bon Pain.

VI. "The Rules"

Violation of the following conditions will engender a default and/or termination of the partner/manager and/or associate manager:

A. Partner/manager shall use the Au Bon Pain bakery/cafe premises solely for the operation of the business; keep the business open and in normal operation for such minimum hours and days as ABP may from time to time prescribe; and refrain from using or suffering the use of the premises for any other purpose or activity at any time.

B. Partner/manager shall maintain the bakery/cafe in the highest degree of sanitation, repair, and condition, and in connection therewith shall make such additions, alterations, repairs and replacements thereto as ABP may require of partner/manager, including without limitation, periodic repainting, repairs to impaired equipment, furniture and fixtures, and replacement of obsolete signs.

C. Partner/manager further understands and acknowledges that in order to insure that all products produced and sold by bakery/cafe meet ABP's high standards of taste, texture, appearance, and freshness, and in order to protect ABP's goodwill and proprietary marks, partner/manager agrees that all products shall be prepared only by properly trained personnel strictly in accordance with the Retail Baker's Training Program.

D. Partner/manager shall meet and maintain the highest health standards and ratings applicable to the operation of the bakery/cafe.

E. Partner/manager shall operate the bakery/cafe in conformity with such uniform methods, standards, and specifications as ABP may from time to time prescribe to insure that the highest degree of quality and service is uniformly maintained.

F. Unless transferred at the request of Au Bon Pain, the partner/manager and/or associate manager will not be eligible for the profit-sharing disbursements unless they complete the full time-period of the experiment. If transferred, the affected manager will receive a pro-rated share based on the percentage of total controllable profit contributed while he or she was employed in the store.

Partner/manager agrees:

1. To maintain in sufficient supply, and use at all times, only such products, materials, ingredients, supplies, and paper goods as conform with ABP's standards and specifications, and partner/manager shall not deviate therefrom by using nonconforming items.

2. To employ such number of employees as may be needed to meet the standards of service and quality as may be prescribed by ABP.

3. To comply with all applicable federal, state, and local laws, rules, and regulations with respect to ABP employees.

4. Partner/manager shall permit ABP or its agents or representatives to enter upon the premises at any time for the purposes of conducting inspections; shall cooperate fully with ABP's agents or representatives in such inspections by rendering such assistance as they may reasonably request; and, upon notice from ABP or its agents or representatives, shall take such steps as may be necessary to correct immediately any deficiencies detected during such inspections.

Partner/manager agrees that failure to comply with the requirements of this paragraph will cause ABP irreparable injury and will subject partner/manager to termination and the loss of any incremental profit funds held in reserve.

In addition, the partner/manager shall be deemed to be in default and ABP may, at its option, terminate this agreement without affording partner/manager any opportunity to cure the default, upon the occurrence of any of the following events:

A. If a threat or danger to public health or safety results from the operation of the bakery/cafe which is not cured by the partner/manager within one week of notice.

B. If partner/manager is convicted of a felony or any other crime or offense that is reasonably likely, in the sole opinion of ABP, to adversely affect the ABP system or goodwill associated therewith.

C. If partner/manager fails to comply with the covenants in A–E above hereof, provided however that for any failure which is curable, partner/manager shall have thirty (30) days to cure after notice from ABP.

D. If partner/manager, after curing any default, engages in the same activity, giving rise to the prior default, whether or not cured after notice.

E. If partner/manager repeatedly is in default of or fails to comply substantially with any of the requirements imposed by this agreement, whether or not cured after notice.

Eli Lilly and Company (A)

One of the most important problems I faced when I was named to this job was the lack of a well designed succession plan to insure continual financial management of the company. For a variety of reasons, there was a missing generation of financial managers. So, while the company was growing, financial management was relatively inexperienced and not well rounded.

The Management Appraisal and Profile System has been particularly helpful to me. It has helped me sort through my financial directors and look again at our talent here when I arrived. It's also specified for me some of the performance dimensions which separate an effective financial manager from one who is simply a good financial analyst or accountant.

The issue is that the process which is implicit in the Appraisal and Profile System requires an enormous amount of time and effort. Even though only managers above salary class M are subject to the process, and not all of the hundred or so of those managers who report to me have been profiled, the time the process has consumed is far from trivial. I would really like to have the profile process applied to all 325 people who report directly to me, but I don't be-

lieve that it would be easy to show that the benefits would make the cost of doing so worthwhile.

The other question with which we have to grapple is the appropriate frequency of appraisal and profiling in activities like financial management and accounting. The written guidelines provided by the Personnel Resources Planning Group say that each member of management should have the opportunity for appraisal and profiling at least once a year, but we're falling well short of that. I wonder how the process will work if we repeat it on a two or three year cycle, as it now looks like we will.

Jim Cornelius, vice president of finance and chief financial officer of Eli Lilly and Company, was speaking about the management appraisal system used at the company since 1983. Replacing less formal and unsystematic appraisal and personnel development systems, the new system achieved great specificity in appraisal, development, and possible behavioral changes for all managers. It also increased the time required for personnel appraisal and highlighted a number of problems in measuring the performance of professional financial managers.

ELI LILLY AND COMPANY

Founded in Indianapolis, Indiana, in 1876 by Colonel Eli Lilly, a pharmaceutical

This case was prepared by Associate for Case Development Karen E. Hansen, under the supervision of Professor William J. Bruns, Jr., as the basis for class discussion rather than to illustrate either effective or ineffective handling of an administrative situation. Reprinted by permission of the Harvard Business School.

chemist, Eli Lilly and Company was one of the oldest producers of prescription medicines in the United States. From the very beginning, Colonel Lilly chose to manufacture "ethical" drugs with a basis of effectiveness in science which would be dispensed only on orders from a physician.

The company grew steadily through the years and achieved sales of $3.3 billion in 1985. The company has nearly tripled in size during the last decade. By early 1986, Eli Lilly characterized itself as "a research based corporation that develops, manufactures, and markets human medicines as well as electronic medical instruments, agricultural products, and cosmetics." Selected financial data for recent years are summarized in Exhibit 1, and selected highlights from the company history are summarized in Exhibit 2.

As a result of its personnel policies, which were frequently cited favorably by people within and from outside the company, Lilly was regarded by almost all employees as an outstanding employer that provided continuity of employment. In 1985, Lilly was comprised of more than 28,000 employees located throughout the world. More than 10% of those employees were directly engaged in research and development activities. Although worldwide corporate headquarters remained in Indianapolis, Lilly had manufacturing operations in North America, Europe, Asia, Latin America, and Africa, and its products were marketed in more than 130 countries.

Emphasizing recognition of the importance of personnel resources, a company publication summarized:

We know that the outstanding performance of our corporation is the direct result of the commitment of the people who make up the company—the wise use of their skills, their dedication to excellence, and their continued personal growth. Every effort is made to create both an atmosphere and an attitude at the company that are conducive to personal development, for we know that the leadership team can be, in and of itself, a distinct competitive advantage.

Lilly traditionally has operated under a promotion-from-within policy. This policy—coupled with company growth—has meant advancement at all levels and has made possible the selection of highly competent persons for positions of responsibility and leadership throughout the organization. Personnel policies are designed and carried out so that individuals can move through their initial assignment area into other areas as rapidly as their abilities, drive, and performance merit.

THE DEVELOPMENT OF THE MANAGEMENT APPRAISAL AND PROFILE SYSTEM

The task of making judgments about managers' performance had become more complicated and had evolved significantly as the company grew in size, scope, and international commitment. The processes employed were based on the personnel philosophies of careful selection, commitment, and continuous employment with the company. Although appraisals had always been done for the purpose of setting salary levels, they were often somewhat informal.

By the mid-1970s, it became important to establish mechanisms which would encourage consistent management performance appraisals across international boundaries and functional areas in the company. Recognition of this need led the personnel resources staff to think about improving the process by more explicitly identifying performance dimensions and making appraisal processes more uniform. International operations managers were the first to see the advantage of using uniform dimensions from country to country.

The Appraisal and Profile System evolved to its current form by late 1983, when it was introduced at corporate headquarters in Indianapolis.

Prior to the development of the Management Appraisal and Profile System (MAPS) at Eli Lilly and Company, there were few appraisals, and reviews were held only for purposes of setting salary and awarding stock options. But there was little to help people plan their careers on a year-to-year basis, or to help supervisors plot individual development, decide on the relative importance of technical versus managerial skills, or evaluate individual contributions and leadership skills. As a result, managers and supervisory employees often did not know which aspects of their performance to stress.

The primary objectives of the personnel resources staff in discussing and developing a MAPS were to reduce confusion and inconsistency about managerial roles, performance and compensation actions; to increase feedback to managers regarding areas for improvement and their personal development; and to avoid costly selection and management development mistakes. Explicit attention was given to the publication and discussion of these objectives, and to their consistent use across organizational boundaries and levels. As the personnel resources staff worked on the new system, they concentrated on appropriate performance dimensions, a process for appraising managers against those dimensions, and an explicit development plan that would be tailored to each manager's needs. The system had to help develop leadership qualities and problem-solving abilities through guidance from superiors. The personnel resources staff paid particular attention to resolving the dilemma of appraising people who performed well technically, but who had not yet developed the necessary leadership qualities to achieve their projected potential in the company.

Exhibit 3 summarizes some of the thinking and evolution of the dimensions of management performance. The management profile dimensions in the "Current" column were adopted in late 1983 as part of the MAPS and have been used since. The selection of 13 to 15 performance dimensions was never regarded as final; rather, it reflected the need to develop a system which could evolve if necessary.

The personnel resources group in Indianapolis, which managed worldwide personnel policy, decided to proceed with the MAPS and to adopt the same system for all managers, regardless of location or function. Developing a system which would be used for all managers dictated the broad dimensions specified in the Appraisal and Profile System.

THE MANAGEMENT APPRAISAL AND PROFILE SYSTEM

While many elements of the MAPS are detailed below, an overview of its parts will assist the reader in understanding the process:

- *Dimensions of management performance* were specified in the system (these are the dimensions shown in the "Current" column of Exhibit 3).
- An *appraisal group* was selected to include two levels of immediate supervision, a personnel manager/director, and other individuals who had worked closely with the individual being appraised.
- A *Management Appraisal and Profile meeting* was held during which the profile panel rated the manager on each dimension on a four-point scale.
- An *overall management effectiveness rating* was determined.

- A *development and follow-up plan* was prepared.
- A *feedback discussion* was held with the manager during which development objectives, which were mutually agreed upon, and employee comments were recorded.

The MAPS process was initiated by personnel staff, a member of which acted as scribe for each profile panel. The scribe identified the need for a profile, helped select the panel members by referring to supervisors and the individual, and invited participation one or two months before the meeting. The makeup of a panel could vary, but in most cases was likely to include the immediate supervisor and one level above, the prior supervisor, intracompany clients from outside the manager's area of activity, and one representative from personnel. The objective was to choose a panel of people who could give the most relevant feedback to the employee.

Prior to the first meeting of the panel, members were contacted and told to come prepared. They were encouraged to write on a previously distributed worksheet their views of the dimensions which would be evaluated and summarized by the panel. The objective of this step was to get relevant input from a variety of people. When a profile had been previously prepared on an individual, its observations might be provided to panel members. Most panel members would have served on other panels and would therefore be familiar with the performance dimensions; information was distributed to provide definitions of dimensions and possible ratings.

When the panel met, it had to reach a consensus. Meetings generally lasted about 1½ hours, but not more than 3 hours. The scribe prepared notes and created summaries of statements which were reviewed by all panel members and the supervisor, who then reviewed these with the employee. The employee had an opportunity to agree or disagree with the results of the process and the development plan, and then signed the plan, which became part of the personnel record. Personnel was then charged with responsibility for following up on this development plan which was the output of the process.

The forms which the profile panel completed are shown in Exhibit 4. Summary descriptions of the management performance dimensions were included in the profile form. Each dimension was rated by the panel according to the rating key shown at the bottom of each of the first two pages. Instructions to the panel amplified the ratings as follows:

In considering each dimension, the following scale should be used. It is expected that most individuals will exhibit a range of skill levels dependent upon their particular abilities and background. Thus, raters should use as much of the scale as appropriate. Only a highly exceptional person would be rated as Good or Top in every dimension.

Top signifies competence significantly beyond job requirements relating to a particular dimension. Exceptional achievement is demonstrated in key areas of responsibility. Performance is generally excellent in quality and quantity.

Good signifies competence that meets and sometimes exceeds job requirements relating to a particular dimension. Performance is above average in quality and quantity.

Satisfactory competence indicates that all job requirements are met with regard to that dimension. Major responsibilities are carried out in an acceptable manner. Continued development effort will ensure meeting future requirements.

Needs Improvement describes an individual's lack of skill or knowledge to meet significant requirements in a particular dimension. Development action steps should be designed to enable the individual to attain the necessary skills or knowledge.

In evaluating performance against appraisal dimensions, a STAR—an acronym standing for Situation, Task, Action, and Result—system was used. The panel, recalling its contact with the individual, described STARs, which provided the basis for evaluating the degree to which the individual had achieved a high or low performance against a particular appraisal dimension. In almost all profiles, in spite of the 13 or more performance dimensions and multiple STARs, one theme would develop as the panel proceeded with its work. The theme tended to concur with the strengths and the weaknesses with which an individual was associated. Coaching was then planned and developed around the result of the appraisal discussion.

Having rated the manager on each dimension, the panel prepared a summary of overall management effectiveness based on a five-point scale described as follows:

There are five zones to define overall management effectiveness. There is no set formula that establishes the placement of an individual in a given zone. Most people will have a variety of ratings on the skill dimensions and varying performance levels. Overall Management Effectiveness is determined on an individual basis, giving consideration to performance, skills, and potential. Obviously, an individual's placement in a zone will change over time. The following are guidelines that should be used to determine the Overall Management Effectiveness zone:

ACHIEVER—Performance consistently exceeds job requirements. Has potential for a higher level of responsibility.

OR

Performance consistently exceeds job requirements. Potential for higher level of responsibility is questionable.

CONTRIBUTOR—Performance consistent-

ly meets job requirements and occasionally exceeds them. Potential for a higher level of responsibility is questionable.

LEARNER—Performance exceeded job requirements in previous position. Potential for a higher level of responsibility is being assessed.

MAINTAINER—Performance meets job requirements. Potential for a higher level of responsibility is limited.

MARGINAL PERFORMER—Performance does not meet job requirements. Improvement in performance must be shown or demotion or termination is probable.

The overall management effectiveness rating was intended to provide a summary measure of both a manager's potential and performance. Exhibit 5 is a graphic representation of the five possible effectiveness zones.

The final stage of the panel's work was the creation of a development plan which summarized key areas for improvement, action to be taken, proposed timing, and follow-up.

When the panel had completed its work, a summary was prepared to be reviewed with the employee. A copy of this summary, as well as the Management Appraisal and Profile form, were distributed to the employee's supervisor, the personnel director, and the person responsible for personnel resource planning. The personnel director was responsible for reviewing the development plan, following up on the plan to see that it was being implemented, and for recording the development of actions taken.

MANAGEMENT VIEWS ON THE APPRAISAL AND PROFILE SYSTEM

Jim Cornelius spoke about his feeling that the profile system was exceptionally important:

One of my major tasks has been reestablishing the depth of talent of the financial organization on a worldwide basis so it can function more efficiently with or without my direct supervision. I've been trying to centralize many of the treasury functions, particularly those that relate to international operations. At the same time, I've been trying to improve the "back-office accounting/ administrative" functions and consolidate them here in Indianapolis.

To do this, I have to sort through the senior financial management group to be sure that I have the right people in the right places. The Management Appraisal and Profiling System has been particularly helpful to me. Also, it has probably helped us in a dozen instances where current performance didn't match up with job requirements.

I suppose I would have had to work on talent and succession issues anyway, but the appraisals and profiles helped a great deal. In particular, they helped us in dealing with those who were no longer performing adequately. They also helped to identify people who might be ready for and appropriate for early promotions. And finally, they helped me decide when we had to go outside the company for experienced talent in areas like auditing and strategic planning. Although our focus here at Lilly is on internal personnel development, we occasionally go outside to hire. In the long run, the Appraisal and Profile process will help us maintain a better long-term focus on future talent.

One of the things I like about the system is that it provides a "crisper" process and an ongoing "code" for communication with my management. They will now be reviewed periodically and systematically through the remainder of their careers. To me, the main purpose in this process is behavioral change. It provides a way of focusing people's attention on areas where they need to change if they are to develop and achieve their full potential. The purpose is to encourage everybody to work at 100% of their abilities. Quite often, before we had this system, there was an assumption that some people simply didn't have the necessary talents; I think the system has also shown us that talent can be developed. If we work together more productively over time through the profile and appraisal system, we will have accomplished a major breakthrough in the personnel management process within the financial organization.

As chief financial officer, I would normally receive copies of the profiles of all management people in my division. From these, we have identified five to ten possible successors to myself and prepared a list of people who are tracking toward the other key positions of controller, treasurer, strategic planner, etc. The profile process is enormously helpful in this because it summarizes past assignments and accomplishments. At the same time, it shows where people need to grow and what they have to do to broaden their management skills. It reveals the people who communicate well and it creates an environment that signals when learning or new experiences are necessary.

The profiling system quite frequently encourages people to stretch beyond the point they have previously achieved. We hired a specialist from the outside who was profiled as a clear achiever in that role. However, when we transferred him, he was only rated a learner. As a result of this rating through the profiling process, we signaled him that he should ask for more help on occasion and that he needed to develop his communication abilities further. The profiling forced feedback to him and as a result of this he now has five or six areas to improve in order to regain the Achiever status. The system got his attention and I'm fairly confident that he can make the change.

Mike Hunt, vice president and treasurer reporting directly to Cornelius, also spoke about the Appraisal and Profile System:

The most obvious result of our implementing the profiling system is that developmental programs are now very specific. This specificity includes not only job assignments, but people's behavior and how it might be modified to be more effective.

In the financial group, our use of the profile

has had substantial effect. In the old days, people were evaluated to a very large extent on their technical/accounting competence. Involvement in the business was not rewarded. But as we have grown to a large highly diversified corporation, a proactive financial organization is also very important. Profiling has helped us manage the change. It allows us to focus on leadership and the ability to effectively work in our environment. The system has some real teeth in it, too. It is tied directly to the administration of salary, performance awards, and stock options. Because so much information is explicitly summarized, we can better differentiate people in terms of current performance, potential, and compensation. The information from the profiling system helps us identify candidates for promotion and determine what we need to do to prepare them for added responsibility.

I serve on many of the panels for people in my area as well as other areas. Each panel member comes prepared with specific examples of behavior along each dimension of performance. The most important part of the process is to provide formal communication to people about what is expected and how they are performing against our expectations. Only when this happens can people improve their performance.

Dick Warne, vice president and controller reporting to Cornelius, compared the profiling system to other management appraisal systems that had been used at Lilly:

There is simply no question that the present appraisal and profiling system is much better than anything we used before. Prior systems lacked specificity and were not reviewed with the manager being appraised. They tended to be sporadic, narrowly based, and subjective.

However, we still have some sorting out to do for the system to achieve its maximum benefit. While the dimensions provide insight into specific activities relevant to management, it makes the process complex and time consuming, and sometimes the dimensions don't reflect the nature of staff work since it tends to have a higher advisory and quantitative, as opposed to supervisory and directive, content.

The rating *grid* for performance and potential is another area for gaining greater understanding. Since we are dealing with management succession, it would seem that potential is as important, or more important, than performance, but the process and dimensions appear to emphasize the latter; and, as we go further down in the organization, I'm concerned that the system tends to value performance more than potential.

Another issue with the rating grid is the use of the specific words: Achiever, Learner, Contributor, Maintainer, Marginal Performer. These words evoke emotional reactions from appraisees when they are given feedback on the appraisal system—everyone wants to be an achiever. People who are told they are maintainers feel they are being perceived negatively when, actually, they are doing a good job. The labels can become a hindrance in the appraisal process. I don't know, maybe a numerical rating system would serve us better. The Pharmaceutical Division uses numbers in its appraisal of salesmen; maybe we should also, to avoid "word" labels with their emotional content.

A final point of concern on the ratings is one common to many grading systems, and that is the tendency to appraise everyone as a medium performer—in this system a contributor. I wonder if we aren't tending to rank maintainers as low contributors. More importantly, I'm concerned that we may be rating high potential people as high contributors who might, with encouragement and coaching, be achievers. We don't have enough achievers to replace present senior management. We need, therefore, to identify deeper into the organization, or face the reality of outside hiring, which then has to be reconciled with our promotion-from-within philosophy.

But don't get me wrong. There's no question that the present system is working. It's much better than what we've done previously and is providing excellent input into our management succession planning.

Finally, Fred Ruebeck, controller of the Pharmaceutical Division, talked about specific profiles and his opinion of the Appraisal and Profile System:

> One case I remember was a person who was labeled a maintainer. The profiling system gave him a clear opportunity to see where he stood and to think about changing his performance. The individual had been with the company for most of his career and was a credit manager in my division. He was thoroughly professional and he performed the credit managing function very well. However, the maintainer category reflected his limited desire and potential to perform in other financial jobs.
>
> The system does not reward people who do just one thing well. Therefore, when an individual is not adding value to the job and is labeled a maintainer, he may conclude, as this individual did, "the company is changing and it's tougher on people than it used to be." But when I compare that manager (who retired) to his replacement, I see that the present manager has broader capability and is willing to learn at the same time.
>
> A second case that I recall was a person about 35 years of age. He had unrealistically favorable perceptions of himself and, after profiling, it took him a year to accept the results. He did many things well and was a good supervisor. He probably could have come around, since a large part of his problem, I think, stemmed directly from his self-concept. He couldn't accept the need for upward communication and lacked flexibility.
>
> When he was told that an evaluation panel would be selected, he suggested two persons to be on it and asked that two others not be selected. He had no objection to the process, and he respected the system. But when the profile led to a less favorable evaluation than he felt was justified, he said, "This has ruined my career. I want to be a director by age 40; I'll leave." He left Lilly to join a smaller competitor.
>
> A third case which I think illustrates that the system is working involves a very young manager. He has moved up quickly and his brash style has caused problems with some people. He's had a great deal of sponsorship from top management. When I provided feedback from the profiling process which labeled him as a contributor, he didn't like the message. Nevertheless, he is dealing the feedback, and I think he is likely to grow from it. By giving hard appraisals and basing compensation on those appraisals, the profile is an effective multidimensional motivation process.
>
> Because the Management Appraisal and Profile System uses common dimensions for all managers, I think it tends to encourage line behavior in the staff functions. To succeed in a staff function, a person has to be able to make presentations, to convince others, both higher and lower, about ideas and things that need to be done. The dimensions used in the profile reward breadth of management, talent, experience, and performance.

Jim Cornelius summed up his questions about the Management Appraisal and Profile System:

> I'm trying to build a first-class financial managers' organization here at Eli Lilly. There's been about a 100% growth in my function's headcount since 1982 while the rest of the company has been consolidating in terms of size. My real questions concern how I can best use the profiling process. Should I apply it to more people, even though this will take more time? Or should I just focus on top managers and my "fast trackers" by initiating profiles on them more frequently? I'm still grappling with the system's costs and benefits to me as chief financial officer. What do you think?

ELI LILLY AND COMPANY (A)

Exhibit 1 Selected financial data ($ millions, except per-share data)

	1985	1984	1983	1982	1981
Operations					
Net sales	$3,270.6	$3,109.2	$3,033.7	$2,962.7	$2,773.2
Operating costs and expenses	2,506.2	2,364.9	2,308.8	2,291.8	2,156.6
Other income (deductions)—net	32.2	26.4	29.9	13.3	29.4
Income taxes	279.0	280.5	297.4	272.4	271.5
Net income	517.6	490.2	457.4	411.8	374.5
Dividends declared	230.4	220.8	209.6	197.3	186.2
Dividends paid	224.9	216.8	205.6	197.5	180.4
Earnings retained[1]	287.2	269.4	247.8	214.5	188.3
Earnings per common share[2]	3.69	3.36	3.06	2.71	2.47
Dividends declared per common share[2]	1.65	1.525	1.4125	1.30	1.225
Dividends paid per common share[2]	1.60	1.4875	1.375	1.30	1.1875
Average common shares outstanding (thousands)[2]	140,281	145,710	149,248	151,868	151,884
Financial Position					
Current assets	$1,940.2	$1,827.5	$1,830.1	$1,680.5	$1,665.4
Current liabilities	1,045.8	1,067.2	988.3	873.6	817.8
Working capital	894.4	760.3	841.8	806.9	847.6
Other assets	639.5	536.0	371.1	339.0	230.7
Property and equipment	1,374.0	1,280.4	1,212.6	1,135.6	1,006.2
Total assets	3,953.7	3,643.9	3,413.8	3,155.1	2,902.3
Long-term debt	238.6	116.6	90.7	49.4	53.8
Deferred income taxes	281.6	238.9	213.8	176.6	142.4
Shareholders' equity	2,387.7	2,221.2	2,121.0	2,055.5	1,888.3
Financial Ratios					
Net income as a percent of sales	15.8 %	15.8 %	15.1 %	13.9 %	13.5 %
Turnover of average total assets	.86	.88	.92	.98	1.01
Return on average total assets	13.6 %	13.9 %	13.9 %	13.6 %	13.6 %
Return on average shareholders' equity	22.5	22.6	21.9	20.9	20.7
Effective tax rate	35.0	36.4	39.4	39.8	42.0
R&D as a percent of sales	11.3	11.0	9.7	9.0	8.5
Net sales per employee (thousands)	$116.8	$108.3	$103.9	$101.1	$97.0
Net income per employee (thousands)	18.5	17.1	15.7	14.1	13.1
Current ratio	1.9	1.7	1.9	1.9	2.0
Long-term debt as a percentage of total capitalization	10.0%	5.0%	4.1%	2.3%	2.8 %
Statistical Data					
Research and development expenses	$369.8	$341.3	$293.6	$267.4	$234.8
Capital expenditures	207.1	205.3	199.9	236.6	253.7
Depreciation and amortization	136.2	120.7	98.3	83.1	69.2
Number of employees	28,000	28,700	29,200	29,300	28,600
Number of shareholders	26,900	29,000	28,200	28,800	30,100

[1] Includes capitalized stock dividend.
[2] Adjusted for a two-for-one stock split, effected in the form of a stock dividend in December 1985.

Exhibit 2   Selected historical highlights

1876	Colonel Eli Lilly founds company in Indianapolis, Indiana.
1916	J. K. Lilly, Jr., submits landmark company document, "Report on the Subject of Employment," which forms the foundation of the Lilly personnel philosophy.
1923	Lilly makes first commercial insulin available. First foreign sales division formed.
1948	Lilly biochemists find way to greatly increase yields of penicillin G.
1955	Lilly's knowledge of tissue-culture techniques plays a leading role in developing and mass-producting Salk poliomyelitis vaccine.
1957	Darvon®, a widely accepted painkiller discovered by Lilly research, made available to the medical profession.
1963	Treflan®, a weed control agent discovered by Lilly, is introduced to the American agricultural market and is widely accepted.
1964	The first agent to be developed from the cephalosporin family of antibiotics is marketed under the name Keflin®. LIlly introduces six more cephalosporins by 1979.
1971	Lilly purchases Elizabeth Arden, Inc.
1977–1980	Lilly diversifies into the medical instrument systems market with the acquisition of IVAC Corporation, Cardiac Pacemakers, Inc., and Physio-Control Corporation.
1980	Elizabeth Arden markets Millenium®, a dramatic new skin-care treatment line that actually improves the quality of the skin cells.
	Biosynthetic human insulin produced by Lilly becomes the first product of recombinant DNA technology to be tested in humans.
1983	Humulin®, human insulin, is the first pharmaceutical product made from recombinant DNA technology to be marketed in the world.
1984	Lilly purchases Advanced Cardiovascular Systems, Inc.

Exhibit 3 Dimensions of management performance

Evolution of Management Profile Dimensions

1978	1979–1983	Current

I. Task Performance
   Performance Record
   Management Process
   Organization
   Understanding of the Market
     Sit.
   Understanding of the
     Marketing Proc.
   Understanding of Business
     Fund.
   Understanding of Economic,
     Political & Cultural
     Factors
	I. Problem Solving
	   Problem Conceptualization &
	     Analysis
	   Quantitative Skills
	   Ideal / Alternative Generation
	   Alternative Comparison /
	     Decision Making
	   Planning
	   Implementation / Follow-Up
	   Resource Utilization
		Management Process
		Problem Solving
		Leadership
		Communication Skills
		Interpersonal Skills
		Effort
		Developing People
		Job Content Knowl-
		  edge
		Resource Utilization
		Creativity/Innovation
		Presence
		Commitment
		Constructive
		  Confrontation
		(2—Free Choice)

II. Interpersonal Performance
   Communication
   Relationships
   Sensitivity
   Training / Coaching /
     Development of Others
	II. Communication
	   Downward
	   Lateral
	   Upward
	   Written
	   Formal Presentations
	   Language Ability	

III. Intellectual Characteristics
   Mental Capacity
   Logic
   Analytical Capacity
   Conceptualization
   Decision Capability
	III. Leadership
	   Initiative
	   Drive / Energy / Enthusiasm
	   Motivating Others
	   Priority Setting / Time Utilization
	   Team Building
	   Unit Improvement
	   Support for Company	

IV. Operational Characteristics
   Initiative
   Drive
   Innovation
   Breadth
   Language Adaptability
	IV. Interpersonal Competence
	   Collaboration
	   Openness to Influence
	   Credibility
	   Constructive Confrontation
	   Coaching/Developing
	   Breadth
	   Flexibility	

	V. Technical Job Related Skills and Knowledge	

	VI. Business Competence
	   Local Market
	   Marketing
	   Finance
	   Personnel
	   Production	

	VII. Self-Improvement/ Self-Development	

Exhibit 4   Forms completed by the profile panel

MANAGEMENT APPRAISAL AND PROFILE

Name (Last)	(First)	(MI)	Job Title:

Department Number/Location:	Social Security Number/Identification Number:	Date of Last Appraisal:	Current Date:
		MO DAY YR	MO DAY YR

Appraisal Group:

_____ Yrs. _____ Mo.
Supervised Employee

Supervisor	Participant
Scribe	Participant
Personnel	Participant

Management Process - Analyzes situations, decides on a course of action, plans, implements, and follows up on results.

Rating _____

Problem Solving - Identifies problems, evaluates relevant facts, generates ideas/alternatives, and reaches sound conclusions.

Rating _____

Leadership - Influences others to reach decisions, plan a course of action, and work towards common goals and objectives.

Rating _____

Communication Skills - Understands what is meant by others and clearly expresses one's own message.
(Note: Consider how communications are handled upward, laterally, and downward—orally and in writing.)

Rating _____

RATING KEY: N I = N e e d s   I m p r o v e m e n t;   S = S a t i s f a c t o r y;   G = G o o d;   T = T o p

Page 1

09 DM 9168 PRINTED IN USA SEPT 83

270

Interpersonal Skills - Interacts and collaborates with a variety of people, especially in difficult and sensitive situations.

Rating _____

Effort - Initiates action(s), meets tight deadlines, and maintains a positive outlook despite obstacles.

Rating _____

Developing People - Selects, appraises, trains, and coaches employees; sets standards of performance and develops employees to assume greater responsibility.

Rating _____

Job Content Knowledge - Demonstrates knowledge of requirements, methods, techniques, and business fundamentals involved in doing the job, and applies this to increase productivity.

Rating _____

Resource Utilization - Identifies, locates, and mobilizes internal and external resources necessary for the completion of job objectives.

Rating _____

Creativity/Innovation - Generates worthwhile new ideas or techniques; builds on the ideas of others, and helps others apply their ideas.

Rating _____

Presence - Instills confidence and does not add to the stress on others when under pressure.

Rating _____

RATING KEY: NI = Needs Improvement; S = Satisfactory; G = Good; T = Top

Commitment - Understands and accepts corporate goals and values; makes sacrifices, when necessary, to accomplish them.

Rating _____

Constructive Confrontation - Expresses ideas that differ with supervision, peers, and/or subordinates without being offensive and shares negative information when necessary.

Rating _____

OTHER DIMENSION -

Rating _____

OTHER DIMENSION

Rating _____

RATING KEY: N I = N e e d s I m p r o v e m e n t; S = S a t i s f a c t o r y; G = G o o d; T = T o p

Summary of Management Effectiveness—
(Describe the individual's major job accomplishments and summarize his/her skill level in the above dimensions.)

OVERALL MANAGEMENT EFFECTIVENESS - According to the Managerial Grid definitions, which zone best describes the appraised individual?	Marginal Performer	Maintainer	Learner	Contributor	Achiever

DEVELOPMENT PLAN

I.

Development Objectives	Action Steps to Accomplish Development Objectives	Timing

II. Follow-up on the Development Plan

Date	Personnel Director Responsible for Follow-up	Action Taken

ELI LILLY AND COMPANY

Exhibit 5   The five possible effective zones

MANAGEMENT PLANNING GRID

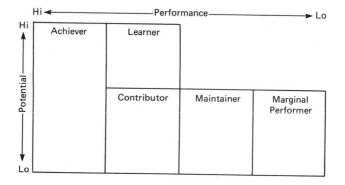

Eli Lilly and Company (B)

The Appraisal and Profile Panel reviewing David Campbell's performance as controller for manufacturing had completed their late morning discussion. Campbell's supervisor, Eric Neilsen, executive director of manufacturing, had suggested breaking for lunch before they assigned an Overall Management Effectiveness rating and created an employee development plan. Other panel members, from manufacturing, product development, systems, and control, agreed that a break would help them digest all of the views they had heard.

Campbell had worked for Eli Lilly for over 20 years, and had been in his present function for about 10 years. Each panel member was chosen because of his or her familiarity with a different area of Campbell's work. For the most part, they had agreed with each other's assessments of Campbell's job performance, interpersonal characteristics, and leadership abilities. Martin Rand, director of personnel, acting as scribe, had summarized the panel's comments about Campbell in each of the categories on the Management Appraisal and Profile form (Exhibit 1); as the panel gathered their information and opinions together, he quickly read the summaries to focus everyone's thinking.

After lunch, the six panel members reconvened in the conference room. Now, standing before them, Neilsen reminded them that they had to agree on the rating (Needs Improvement, Satisfactory, Good, Top) for each category on the Profile form, as well as the Overall Management Effectiveness rating (Achiever, Contributor, Learner, Maintainer, Marginal Performer). Neilsen was concerned with how best to serve the needs of Campbell, the manufacturing group, and the financial organization within Eli Lilly. As he prepared to open the discussion of performance ratings and development plans, he wondered what he should recommend.

ELI LILLY AND COMPANY (A) AND (B) STUDY QUESTIONS:

1. Identify and evaluate both the business and human resources strategies of the Eli Lilly Company.

2. What are the strengths and weaknesses of the Management Appraisal and Profile System (MAPS) developed and used by Eli Lilly and Company?

3. How would you answer the questions raised by Jim Cornelius at the end of the Eli Lilly and Company (A) Case?

This case was prepared by Associate for Case Development Karen E. Hansen, under the supervision of Professor William J. Bruns, Jr., as the basis for class discussion rather than to illustrate either effective or ineffective handling of an administrative situation. Some of the information in this case has been disguised or deleted. Reprinted by permission of the Harvard Business School.

4. What Overall Management Effectiveness rating would you assign to Campbell? Why?

5. What would you recommend be written for Campbell's development plan? Why?

6. Using the information in Exhibit 1 of the Eli Lilly and Company (B) case:

   a. Prepare a summary of management effectiveness for David Campbell.

   b. Rate Campbell's overall management effectiveness.

   c. Prepare a development plan for Campbell.

7. What are your personal reactions to the MAPS System? Would you like to work in an organization that uses this or a similar process for evaluation?

ELI LILLY AND COMPANY (B)

Exhibit 1 Management appraisal and profile

Name (Last)	(First)	(MI)	Job Title:
CAMPBELL	DAVID	.	Controller-Manufacturing

Department Number/Location:	Social Security Number/Identification Number:	Date of Last Appraisal:	Current Date:
			2 23 85
		MO DAY YR	MO DAY YR

Appraisal Group:

Executive Dir.-Manufacturing	___ Yrs. ___ Mo.	V.P. Manufacturing (Product Development)	
Supervisor	Supervised Employee	Participant	
Director of Personnel		V.P. Systems	
Scribe		Participant	
		V.P. Manufacturing	
Personnel		Participant	
		V.P. Controller	

Management Process - Analyzes situations, decides on a course of action, plans, implements, and follows up on results.

David has been a good participant in the manufacturing management process, especially on the development side. He has shown that he is very effective in taking direction and in implementation. His focus, however, is narrow (accounting versus the broader management/ business issues). He should strive to push out, to challenge and improve on a broad front. He needs to initiate actions in order to improve his management process.

Rating ___S___

Problem Solving - Identifies problems, evaluates relevant facts, generates ideas/alternatives, and reaches sound conclusions.

David has approached problem-solving more often than not from a rather narrow financial (accounting) perspective. While his strength has not been in problem identification, he has been most effective in implementing agreed-upon solutions. David should concentrate on approaching broader business issues (for example, the opportunity that the idle plant provided for "pushing out").

Rating ___G___

Leadership - Influences others to reach decisions, plan a course of action, and work towards common goals and objectives.

David has shown that he is a strong influence on others, choosing to accommodate versus challenge. An example of this can be seen in the manner in which he is handling the subordinate personnel issue--an issue that has not as yet been clearly defined, but which clearly needs to be dealt with. He needs to be a more active participant in many of the meetings he attends (staff/F.P.P., etc.). David is very good in one-on-one situations, and has demonstrated that he is very responsive to the issues of his user areas.

Rating ___S___

Communication Skills - Understands what is meant by others and clearly expresses one's own message.
(Note: Consider how communications are handled upward, laterally, and downward—orally and in writing.)

David is a good listener. He has demonstrated this through follow-up to issues brought forth in the various meetings he attends. He is very good in one-on-one situations, but his reserved style limits his impact (low-key approach with a presentation style that, while factual and concise, is lacking in enthusiasm).

Rating ___S___

R A T I N G   K E Y: N I = N e e d s   I m p r o v e m e n t; **S** = S a t i s f a c t o r y; **G** = G o o d; **T** = T o p

Page 1

09 DM 9168 PRINTED IN USA SEPT 83

277

Interpersonal Skills - Interacts and collaborates with a variety of people, especially in difficult and sensitive situations.

David needs to be a more active participant in group settings, but he is very effective in one-on-one situations geared to implementation. He possesses a very warm, but quiet passive approach. He comes across to all people as definitely interested in their issues, and as most sincere.

Rating ___S___

Effort - Initiates action(s), meets tight deadlines, and maintains a positive outlook despite obstacles.

Meets deadlines in most cases. He possesses a positive attitude. David cannot be faulted in his effort; rather, he could help himself by channeling his involvement into broader business issues and initiating issues (as described elsewhere in this write-up). David clearly puts a lot of effort into all that is asked of him.

Rating ___T___

Developing People - Selects, appraises, trains, and coaches employees; sets standards of performance and develops employees to assume greater responsibility.

David has been involved with a couple of the younger people where he has worked through people issues (the MBA in Finance and the BS in Accounting). He is not known for setting tough standards, but rather uses a lenient style in motivation. Executive Director needed to encourage David to push an employee, to give her guidance as a young professional. Once done, it was very effective. David uses a "father" type leadership style.

Rating ___G___

Job Content Knowledge - Demonstrates knowledge of requirements, methods, techniques, and business fundamentals involved in doing the job, and applies this to increase productivity.

David possesses an outstanding knowledge in the controller function within manufacturing. He knows the history and the accounting to a point where he can effectively respond to all inquiries. He could improve in the area of Job Content Knowledge by expanding beyond the accounting issue to focus also on the broader business issues facing the component (idle plant/Capital Appropriations/M.R.P.).

Rating ___G___

Resource Utilization - Identifies, locates, and mobilizes internal and external resources necessary for the completion of job objectives.

Working within the production/development areas, David does a very effective job of utilizing the resources available. Again, there is the continuation of the theme of broadening his involvement beyond the accounting function. He needs to develop a broader involvement with pharmaceuticals and the planning group, C.M.C.S., etc. Some of the problems in B.H.I. might have been better dealt with had David acted in a more proactive manner.

Rating ___S/G___

Creativity/Innovation - Generates worthwhile new ideas or techniques; builds on the ideas of others, and helps others apply their ideas.

David does not merchandise creativity, but is very responsive to the issues raised by his user areas. He has had a tendency to be somewhat inflexible on occasion.

Rating ___S___

Presence - Instills confidence and does not add to the stress on others when under pressure.

David is seen as maybe too tactful. While this style does not necessarily create stress, it can reduce his influence when coupled with his tendency to be somewhat passive.

Rating ___S___

RATING KEY: NI = Needs Improvement; S = Satisfactory; G = Good; T = Top

Page 2

278

Commitment - Understands and accepts corporate goals and values; makes sacrifices, when necessary, to accomplish them.

David will give of himself in any way possible to accomplish objectives. He accepts and fairly represents our corporate goals and values.

Rating ___T___

Constructive Confrontation - Expresses ideas that differ with supervision, peers, and/or subordinates without being offensive and shares negative information when necessary.

David needs to develop a stronger stand with subordinates [specific situation deleted]. David seems to seek out agreement rather than to confront issues immediately or directly.

Rating ___S___

OTHER DIMENSION -

Rating _____

OTHER DIMENSION -

Rating _____

R A T I N G   K E Y: N I = N e e d s   I m p r o v e m e n t: S = S a t i s f a c t o r y; G = G o o d; T = T o p

Summary of Management Effectiveness—
(Describe the individual's major job accomplishments and summarize his/her skill level in the above dimensions.)

OVERALL MANAGEMENT EFFECTIVENESS - According to the Managerial Grid definitions, which zone best describes the appraised individual?	Marginal Performer	Maintainer	Learner	Contributor	Achiever

DEVELOPMENT PLAN

I.

Development Objectives	Action Steps to Accomplish Development Objectives	Timing

II. Follow-up on the Development Plan

Date	Personnel Director Responsible for Follow-up	Action Taken

MANAGEMENT APPRAISAL AND PROFILE DISCUSSION

Summary of Management Effectiveness:

Development Objectives:

Overall Management Effectiveness: _____

Comments: _____
_____
_____

I acknowledge this appraisal was reviewed with me on _____
Date

_____
Employee Signature

_____
Supervisor

_____
Personnel

_____
Next Level Supervision

281

Public Sector Data Processing Professionals

The Commonwealth spends tens of millions of dollars per year on computer hardware, software and consultants, yet does not pay competitive salaries to the state employees who build, operate and maintain these systems. In the face of the many private sector employment opportunities in Massachusetts for data processing professionals, our efforts to recruit and retain the technical staff necessary to utilize our computer resources effectively are severely constrained by salary inequities.

As today's information processing environment becomes more widespread and complex, our ability to attract employees with the necessary technical expertise to utilize computer resources both efficiently and effectively is an increasingly serious problem. If the Commonwealth is not prepared to pay the salaries necessary to ensure that we have high quality data processing professionals, then we should phase out of the business of operating computers.[1]

Michael S. Dukakis
Governor, Commonwealth of Massachusetts

[1] From a message by the Governor to the Massachusetts Legislature, May 18, 1983.

This case was written by Elizabeth A. Neustadt, Ph.D. candidate, under the direction of Professor Fred K. Foulkes, as the basis for discussion rather than to illustrate either effective or ineffective handling of an administrative situation.

For David Bernstein, newly appointed director of the Office of Management Information Systems and assistant secretary for systems in the Executive Office for Administration and Finance, the governor's statement came as no surprise. Perhaps more than anyone else, Bernstein was in a position to know the complexity and severity of the problem to which the governor referred. Bernstein also understood that it was his job to find a solution. The challenges he faced were formidable, and the stakes were very high.

DATA PROCESSING IN THE COMMONWEALTH

During his first term as governor (1975–1979), Michael Dukakis launched a number of initiatives intended to improve management practices in state government. One major focus was data processing. Computer technology already was employed in many government operations, and as the technology evolved and new applications became available, use of data processing could only be expected to increase. Therefore, as the authors of the Dukakis administration's 1976 "Management Plan for Massachusetts" pointed out, there was a growing need for centralized management of data processing operations, and for statewide DP planning to ensure coordinated procurement and use of data processing resources.

Although there is no way to identify data processing expenditures with complete accuracy, it is estimated that approximately $28 million in direct expenses and $60 million for EDP-related functions are required on an annual basis.

At present, there is no evidence of statewide planning, coordination, or effective resource utilization in the data processing area. Standardized approaches to applications development, hardware facilities, data communications, and remote or local entry and output requirements are totally lacking.

What planning has taken place is fragmented and limited in scope. There is little agreement within the Executive Branch as to what the responsibilities of the Bureau of Data Processing and Telecommunications should be or what resources it needs to pursue its objectives effectively. There is no agency at present that has sufficient expertise regarding EDP equipment and related services. The absence of a central mechanism for collecting expenditure information makes it impossible to obtain valid figures. State agencies contract for new equipment independently, resulting in specifications and systems that do not meet identified needs. There is also a substantial lack of standardization in regard to EDP job classification while management-level salaries are simply not competitive with industry.

Most of the administration's efforts were interrupted when, in the fall of 1978, Governor Dukakis lost the primary. However, in 1979 a new executive branch agency, the Office of Management Information Systems (OMIS), was established in the Fiscal Affairs Division within the Executive Office for Administration and Finance. (An organization chart depicting OMIS's placement within the executive branch appears in Exhibit 1.)[2] According to a report subsequently prepared by the state auditor, OMIS was formed "for the purpose of performing EDP policy-making and planning functions, and to manage and operate the data center which was created from the consolidation of the Administration and Finance Computer Services Center and the Department of Public Welfare Office of Management Services."[3]

The Bureau of Systems Operations (BSO)

OMIS was organized into two major divisions, the Bureau of Systems Operations (BSO) and the Bureau of System Policy and Planning (BSPP). BSO operated a large data center that served more than fifty state offices, and BSPP was charged with overseeing statewide data processing planning and procurements.

BSO was an amalgamation of two former data centers, one connected with the Executive Office for Administration and Finance (EOA&F) and the other with the Department of Public Welfare. Former DPW managers were appointed to head several of the seven units of the new BSO; the new administration unit was staffed almost entirely by former DPW employees; and the new Bureau's director, Ben Seigal, had previously managed Public Welfare's Medical Claims Control Center (MCCC).

Space was allocated for most of the BSO units and for the smaller BSPP on several floors of the John W. McCormack State Office Building, at One Ashburton

[2] For a more detailed account of the Commonwealth's data processing policy before and during this transition period, see *Registry of Motor Vehicles: MIS*, a teaching case of the Boston University Public Management Program.

[3] "Report on the Examination of the Accounts of the Bureau of Systems Operations within the Executive Office for Administration and Finance, July 1, 1978 to June 30, 1980," No. 81-7-S-884.

Place in Boston, across from the State House. (Due to its size and essentially autonomous key-punching and record-keeping function, the medical claims control center retained its separate Westboro location.) The McCormack Building was a logical site for OMIS, since the Administration and Finance computer services center had been housed there, along with a number of other EOA&F agencies. For some state employees, there was the additional benefit of moving from Public Welfare offices at 600 Washington Street, a site in the middle of Boston's "combat zone," to this modern, relatively attractive, and well-located office building.

For many employees, however, the consolidation was not regarded favorably. According to one: "The merger was viewed as Welfare taking over A&F. The A&F people resented having Welfare's procedures, approaches and managers imposed on them. And there were some firings."

The resentment was not all one-sided. In addition to the strain over whose systems would have priority, and the "Welfare side's" tendency to feel proprietary about the new data center and to look upon people on the "A&F side" as users, there were more deeply rooted tensions between the two groups. Another state worker explained:

> There have always been differences between A&F and the DPW, anyway. In many instances, A&F both makes the rules and regulates. So, rightly or wrongly, the impression has formed that A&F people are better paid. That it's easier for them to get resources. And to make exceptions. It's their red tape, so one naturally assumes it's easier for them to cut through it. That makes for resentments.

The Bureau of Systems Policy and Planning (BSPP)

Although statewide in its focus, BSPP was a relatively small entity within OMIS,

employing, during fiscal year 1983, less than one-tenth of the agency's total staff of 382. (This agency total included 67 individuals who worked under "03" contracts[4] as full-time consultants performing technical, data processing functions.) In keeping with the bureau's developmental role, as well as its small size, the first director of BSPP had organized his professional staff as analysts reporting directly to him, and involved himself personally in all of the line agencies' procurements. He had hired a number of bright, young staff who made up for their lack of "real world" experience with their enthusiasm about this opportunity to use new technology to improve state government. He had also employed several individuals with education backgrounds to establish a DP training center for the Commonwealth.

Mike Sullivan first learned about BSPP's DP training in the spring of 1981 while he was working as training coordinator for the Division of Employment Security (DES), an agency that had its own data center. This was a Univac shop with a total department of 160 people, including a fairly large data entry staff, computer operators, and 60 or more technical professionals. At DES morale was low, turnover was high, and there was no DP training. Sullivan was interested in what BSPP might have to offer.

As it turned out, the courses provided by BSPP were primarily "soft," not "technical." They were courses like "Intro to DP," "Systems Analysis," "Systems Design," and "Project Management." They ran anywhere from a half day to three to five days. Sullivan observed:

> We have to qualify the term "user." Users of DP services in the general sense have a need for general concepts; users of, say, BSO ser-

---

[4] "03" refers to the subsidiary, within a given appropriation account, that can be used to pay for services and expenses rendered by nonemployees.

vices require more nitty gritty information about the particular hardware and software utilized by that IBM shop. But the really important missing piece was training for internal, technical staff: high level, sophisticated training—and it wasn't provided. BSPP did have videos, but not ones that were relevant for DES DP equipment. In any case, I have prejudices about video as a method for training adults. People tend not to interact. It becomes like watching TV.

USE OF TECHNICAL CONSULTANTS

Most positions in state service were subject to civil service law. (The only exemptions were management positions and gubernatorial appointments to positions outside the state's classification and pay plan.) In addition, with the enactment of Chapter 150E of the Massachusetts General Laws, in 1973, state employees gained the right to organize and to bargain collectively over terms and conditions of employment.

When computer technology was introduced during the 1960s, outside experts were often employed. Proponents of automation—often high-level managers and policy makers in the state government—solicited and hired these consultants. Other state workers, either skeptical about or threatened by the prospect of automation in their realm, criticized what they viewed as extravagant, wasteful expenditure of taxpayers' dollars on such contracts. Judith Kingsley, an OMIS manager with over twenty years of state experience, recalled the early days of data processing in Massachusetts:

> In a way, I knew as well as anyone that there was a need . . . I was working as a junior clerk and typist in a city job when the state decided to take over managing the welfare system, in 1968. Basically, there were two systems,

both manual, one for issuing checks to clients and the other for Medicaid vendor payments. The cities' welfare offices were running 9 to 12 months behind on payments. There were inaccuracies. Duplications. Clients on multiple roles in different cities. Tremendous potential for client or vendor abuse. Then in 1966 new federal laws put additional pressure on local government to perform. The cities weren't up to it, so the state took over welfare operations. But the state wasn't any better prepared than the cities.

> Overnight, we all became state employees. But DPW's personnel/payroll system was manual; there no way to convert that fast from 200 to 5,000 employees. So the first Friday after the Commonwealth took over management of the welfare system, none of the new state employees were paid.

Kingsley's personal experience was evidence of the need for systems improvements. Nevertheless, her stance toward automation was characteristic of many state employees at that time.

> I had that "It will never work" attitude. I remember watching Booz Allen and Hamilton trying to automate Medicaid processing. They were the first big time consultants I'd ever seen. Sure enough, they fell on their faces.

Outside consultants brought technical knowledge but were dependent on insiders to define the business problem. To be effective, consultants would locate state employees who knew the regulations and understood a particular system's requirements from the user's perspective. In return for this information, consultants provided state employees with the opportunity to learn technical skills on the job.

Public Sector DP Personnel

Over time, state workers who participated in these exchanges began to develop a "data processing" identity. They saw themselves not simply as users of automated systems, but as experts on those systems. The creation of OMIS strengthened this self-perception; the new agency's name and purpose served as clear evidence, to those employed there, that they were data processing professionals.

Obtaining external recognition for this transformation was, however, another matter. An OMIS employee described the experience:

> You've gained these skills; you've paid your dues; and you're not even recognized in terms of your civil service title. . . . Some kid right out of school comes in and picks your brains, does some packaging, and presents "his" solution to management. He gets all the credit. And all the big bucks. What do you get? Your annual step increase.

At first, the civil service system had neither functional titles nor a suitable salary structure for data processing. The Department of Personnel Administration (DPA), an EOA&F agency, had been responsible for the creation of new civil service titles, associated job descriptions, and civil service examinations. Titles were classified into grades of positions, and salaries were set for these grades through the collective bargaining process. Mark Greeley, personnel manager at OMIS under David Bernstein, commented on the job descriptions associated with these titles:

> We have some civil service titles that are technical. But the job descriptions for these titles were written years ago, before computer technology took hold in state government. The job descriptions make no mention of language or systems requirements; they were probably written during the era of Univac systems and punch cards to describe the maintenance of whatever systems were then in place.

Once written, civil service job descriptions could be changed only if DPA initiated a reclassification study. Such a reclassification had most recently occurred in 1975. Before that, existing positions had not been studied since 1956.

State employees could appeal to be given a position with a different title, at a higher salary. Greeley described the process:

> Reallocation is initiated as a request by the union on behalf of the employee. It is a cumbersome, tedious process that entails a series of DPA hearings. For reallocation to take effect, it must be approved by the legislature; traditionally, this has been done by tying the reallocation to the annual budget request. The whole process can take as long as a year and a half.

In Greeley's view, state employees who took this route clearly did so for other than monetary reasons.

THE LEGISLATIVE PERSPECTIVE

OMIS had been established by an act of the legislature to ensure the cost-effective introduction of computer technology into state government. Through its House and Senate Ways and Means Committees, however, the legislature continued its broader oversight function, reviewing the executive branch's budget request each year, examining agencies' priorities and assessing the soundness of their performance in fiscal planning and management. This resulted in a certain amount of overlap between Ways and Means activities and the DP procurement review function with which BSPP was charged. A House Ways and Means budget analyst observed:

> Much of what we do is fiscally oriented: Does the agency have enough money to do what it wants to do? Were funds appropriated for this expenditure, in particular, or

will the agency be taking money from some other appropriation? It isn't BSPP's role to check on this, but unless someone does, there is always the possibility that an agency's DP plan will be approved and implemented, and then when it comes time to pay the bill, no money will have been set aside for it.

From the time that OMIS was created, data processing was "in," so there was a sense that every DP procurement request should go through. We had no evidence that anything was being turned down. It wasn't just procurements for other agencies, either; there was a lot of fast growth going on within OMIS.

Take the personnel/payroll management information system (PMIS). It seemed that year after year they'd request another appropriation in the millions for that system, and nothing was going up. It became a joke. They just never stopped designing the thing. Over time that was bound to cause doubts about the technical skills and management capability of the whole operation.

They never seemed to plan computer capacity, either. They were always running across the street [to the State House] to scream that we had an urgent need for a new mainframe, right now!

NEW MANAGEMENT AT OMIS

Legislators and state civil servants involved in data processing were not the only ones who experienced frustration. Consultants and managers from the private sector were equally taken aback by how long it took to get anything done in state government. BSO's implementation of the PMIS, the Commonwealth's first statewide automated system, was a good example. Roberta Hardy, whose introduction to Massachusetts state government was as a consultant hired to assist with PMIS, recalled:

I came in the spring of 1982. The system was literally years behind schedule. I reported to

Joe Constantine, who reported to John Kalevik, who reported to Ben Seigal, who reported to Tom Cavanaugh.[5] (I didn't know these people, but a consultant always knows the reporting structure.) I was trying to effect change from eight million layers down, to implement the system at the pilot agency, the Department of Public Health. There was no plan, no strategy, no anything.

Six months after Hardy arrived, the incumbent governor of Massachusetts, Edward King, lost the primary to Michael Dukakis. In November, Dukakis was duly reelected as governor. Inevitably, this led to changes in high-level administrative appointments. David Bernstein, most recently employed in a management consulting firm, was appointed to a senior management position and given the dual titles of director of OMIS and assistant secretary for systems, EOA&F. Bernstein recruited James Corum, who had been the assistant commissioner of administration at the Department of Public Health (DPH), to assume the position of director of BSPP.

Hardy had worked with Corum on PMIS implementation at DPH. She explained:

I decided that I had to take charge, or leave. Jim had just taken the BSPP job. I wouldn't have pressed him if I hadn't really thought it was important. He talked to Bernstein, and I got the job as director of PMIS.

There was no management questionnaire for my position; I had to write my own. I hired eighty million "03" consultants; we went from eight to over forty of them. We needed talent, there was none, and I couldn't attract people any other way. Within the state system we couldn't pay competitively;

---

[5] Cavanaugh was the second Director of OMIS appointed during the King Administration. Both he and his predecessor, John Harrington, were paid as "03" consultants; therefore, according to civil service regulations and collective bargaining agreements, neither was permitted to supervise state employees. Many OMIS employees viewed Ben Seigal as the agency's senior manager.

there was a stigma about working for the state; and the hiring process for civil service positions—because nothing was based on merit and you had to weed out all those other people—would have taken forever.

I didn't know, or want to know, how the personnel process worked. I just had one objective: implement PMIS. That's why I moved the PMIS unit to 110 Tremont Street, too—so that we could pretend we were in the private sector.

STRATEGIC PLAN

In his new job, one of David Bernstein's first projects was to formulate a strategic plan for problems and possible solutions at OMIS. He identified the poor quality of data processing personnel as a key problem. In his view, there were two solutions to this. First, technical training was essential. As he put it:

In the computer industry, because new technology keeps being developed, you need ongoing training to stay effective. At OMIS we also needed it in order to *get* effective.

The other major constraint Bernstein identified was civil service—the lists, the salaries, and the inflexibility of the pay structure. (A comparison of public and private sector salaries for data processing professionals appears in Exhibit 2.)

He decided there was only one way to solve that.

PUBLIC SECTOR DATA PROCESSING PROFESSIONALS STUDY QUESTIONS:

1. What is your analysis of the situation Bernstein faces at the end of the case?
2. What advice do you have for him?

PUBLIC SECTOR DATA PROCESSING PROFESSIONALS

Exhibit 1 Executive offices and departments organizational chart

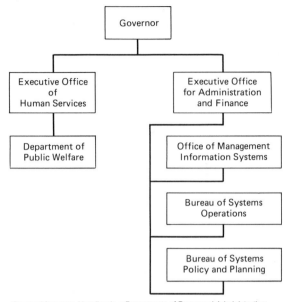

Source: Managers Handbook, a Department of Personnel Administration publication, FY85.

PUBLIC SECTOR DATA PROCESSING PROFESSIONALS

Exhibit 2 FY 1983 DPA salary survey—data processing professionals (salaries in 000s)

| Civil Service Titles | Mass. Unit 6 | | Datamation Survey | | | | | | John Hancock | | |
| | JC | Salary Range | Size | | Industry | | Geography | | Entry | Average | Top |
			All	Large	All	Govt.	All	Boston			
EDP Staff Supervisor	23	23.0–31.6									
EDP Systems Coordinator	23	23.0–31.6									
Data Processing Coordinator	23	23.0–31.6									
Data Proc. Project Leader	NC										
EDP Consultant	NC										
Systems Programmer I	NC		28.9	29.9	28.9	28.7	28.9	28.8	(1)25.2	32.0	40.7
Systems Programmer II	NC										
Systems Programmer III	NC		34.3	35.0	34.3	34.1	34.3	32.4	(2)31.7	42.2	52.8
System Program IV	NC										
Data Comm. Network Spec.	22	21.9–28.9	284	29.4	28.4	27.7	28.4	29.9			
EDP Software Specialist	22	21.9–28.9									
EDP Systems Analyst IV	22	21.9–28.9	34.9	36.1	34.9	33.7	34.9	31.0			
EDP Programmer V	22	21.9–28.9	30.9	32.7	30.9	31.8	30.9	29.7			
EDP Systems Analyst III	20	19.9–26.2	31.8	33.8	31.8	30.3	31.8	*42.8			
EDP Programmer IV	20	19.9–26.2	28.2	30.2	28.2	28.8	28.2	30.1			
Programmer Staff Supervisor	21	20.8–27.5									
*Asst. Mgr. Computer Oper.	19	19.2–25.0	23.5	24.8	23.5	25.5	23.5	—			
EDP Systems Analyst II	18	18.0–23.7	29.4	30.8	29.4	31.2	29.4	—			
EDP Programmer III	18	18.0–23.7	22.6	21.2	22.6	24.0	22.6	21.9			
EDP Systems Analyst I	16	16.1–21.3	—	—	—	—	—	—			
EDP Programmer I	14	14.5–18.9	17.8	19.7	17.8	17.8	17.8	19.9			
	Annual Salary as of 7/1/83		*Annual Salary as of 5/1/83*						*Current*		

(1) Technical Programmer (10 Positions)
(2) Manager Software Services (3 Positions)
(3) Director

* Shift Supervisor
NC = No Position in Boston
Source: Agency records.

V

BENEFIT POLICIES
AND ADMINISTRATION

OVERVIEW

Employee benefit plans can be divided into three categories. First, there are those that replace income. As social security and pensions replace income at the time of retirement, salary continuation and short- and long-term disability plans replace income lost through sickness or disability. Similarly, unemployment compensation and supplemental unemployment benefits (SUB), if the company has such an income security plan, replace income in the event of a layoff. Second, there are the benefits that provide increased security to employees by paying for extra or extraordinary expenses the employee may unexpectedly incur. Such benefit plans as health and dental care fall into this category. Though the employee does not wish to benefit from such plans, he or she is glad they are available during times of emergency and need. For many employees, were it not for company-provided major medical plans, the costs of certain illnesses would result in the complete wipeout of a family's lifetime savings. Finally, there are the benefits that can be viewed as employee opportunities. These can range from tuition reimbursement plans to vacations and holidays. These benefits relate to the quality of the employee's life apart from work.

At one time the term fringe benefits was appropriate. At that time virtually all compensation was in the form of pay for time worked. But considering what has happened over the years with respect to benefits, the term "fringe" has become a misnomer. According to the most recent Chamber of Commerce survey, the costs of benefits averaged 39.3% of payroll in 1986. In 1975 benefits averaged 35.4% of payroll. Annual benefit costs in 1986 amounted to $10,283 per employee, up from $5,560 seven years earlier. As noted from Table V–1, these figures include those benefits that are required by law. Total benefit payments as a percentage of wages and salaries have advanced from less than 1% in 1929. Industry payments vary widely. Department stores averaged 30.7%; chemicals and allied prod-

ucts paid 43.0%. Traditionally those companies in the P-industries—pharmaceutical, petroleum, and photography—have offered their employees outstanding benefit packages. For some large companies, the figure for 1986 is in excess of 45%.

Many employees today seem to view

TABLE V–1 Employee Benefits, by Type of Benefit, 1986

Type of Benefit	Total, All Companies	Total, All Manu-facturing	Total, All Nonmanu-facturing
Total employee benefits as percent of payroll	39.3%	42.0%	36.8%
1. Legally required payments (employer's share only)	8.9	8.7	9.1
a. Old-Age, Survivors, Disability, and Health Insurance (employer FICA taxes) and Railroad Retirement Tax	6.1	6.6	5.6
b. Unemployment Compensation	1.0	1.3	0.7
c. Workers' Compensation (including estimated cost of self-insured)	1.1	0.8	1.3
d. State sickness benefits insurance	0.8	0.0	1.5
2. Retirement and Savings Plan Payments (employer's share only)	6.7	7.2	6.3
a. Defined benefit pension plan contributions	3.3	4.1	2.5
b. Defined contribution plan payments	1.5	2.0	1.0
c. Money purchase plans	0.1	0.1	0.0
d. Pension plan premiums (net) under insurance and annuity contracts (insured and trusteed)	1.3	0.3	2.2
e. Cost of plan administration	0.1	0.1	0.1
f. Other	0.5	0.6	0.3
3. Life Insurance and Death Benefits (employer's share only)	0.5	0.5	0.5
4. Medical and Medically-Related Benefit Payments (employer's share only)	8.3	10.2	6.7
a. Hospital, surgical, medical, and major medical insurance pemiums (net)	6.1	6.9	5.4
b. Retiree (payments for retired employees) hospital, surgical, medical, and major medical insurance premiums (net)	0.6	1.0	0.2
c. Short-term disability, sickness or accident insurance (company plan or insured plan)	0.5	0.9	0.2
d. Long-term disability or wage continuation (insured, self-administered, or trust)	0.2	0.2	0.2
e. Dental insurance premiums	0.6	0.8	0.3
f. Other (vision care, physical and mental fitness, benefits for former employees)	0.3	0.3	0.3
5. Paid Rest Periods, Coffee Breaks, Lunch Periods, Wash-Up Time, Travel Time, Clothes-Change Time, Get Ready Time, etc.	3.4	3.3	3.4
6. Payments for Time Not Worked	10.2	10.2	10.1
a. Payments for or in lieu of vacations	5.2	5.2	5.2
b. Payments for or in lieu of holidays	3.1	3.5	2.8
c. Sick leave pay	1.4	0.9	1.8
d. Parental leave (maternity and paternity leave payments)	0.2	0.1	0.2
e. Other	0.3	0.5	0.2
7. Miscellaneous Benefit Payments	1.3	1.9	0.8
a. Discounts on goods and services purchased from company by employees	0.2	0.2	0.3
b. Employee meals furnished by company	0.1	0.1	0.1
c. Employee education expenditures	0.2	0.2	0.1
d. Child Care	0.6	1.1	0.2
e. Other	0.2	0.3	0.1
Total employee benefits as cents per payroll hour	496.2¢	570.7¢	436.2¢
Total employee benefits as dollars per year per employee	10,283	12,035	8,917

Source: 1986 Chamber of Commerce Study.

benefits not as special privileges but rather as employee rights. Employees, moreover, seem to prefer them to additional cash compensation. In a 1985 study based on paper-and-pencil surveys and focus group interviews with over 12,000 employees, Hewitt Associates, a leading employee benefits consulting firm, had three significant findings. First, a significant proportion of employees consider benefits equally as important or more important than pay. Over half of the surveyed employees considered benefits "equal in importance" to pay, and nearly one-third rated benefits "more important" than pay. Second, employee attitudes toward benefits vary little by income. And, finally, while employees realize that benefits cost something, they have little idea how large that expenditure is to their employer.[1]

Effective employee benefits administration is also extremely important. In a 1986 survey conducted with over 30,000 employees, Hewitt found that positive employee perceptions of an employer's benefit program seemed to track fairly closely with favorable attitudes toward claims administration. For example, the survey revealed that among employees with positive reactions to medical claims handling, only 4% gave the overall program a "negative" rating—versus 21% of employees with unfavorable perceptions of medical claims processing. Hewitt also found that "knowing where or how to get benefit information" also seemed to have much to do with employee attitudes toward a benefits program. Where access was rated "easy," only 4% of employees expressed a low opinion of the overall program versus 24% of those rating access "difficult."[2]

Benefit costs are escalating not only because of the costs of new programs and improvements, but also simply because of the spiraling costs of maintaining existing plans. Because so many benefits are directly related to salaries, benefit costs, too, increase. Company-provided insurance related to salary level increases as pay rises. Insurance premiums for health care have soared. Health insurance costs, over which the employer has little control, are the fastest increasing benefit cost. Among major companies, the yearly cost of the average family health insurance plan in 1987 was over $2,000.

Management at Honeywell, Inc., projected that in 1986 the company would spend $186 million on direct health care costs. This figure does not include indirect costs, which result from such factors as absenteeism, loss of efficiency due to the breakup of a work group, costs of training a new employee, damage or downtime of equipment, and environmental risks. At many companies the health insurance carrier has become a very large outside supplier. The increased premium costs have resulted primarily from higher prices and greater utilization of health and medical care plans. In 1984, more than $2.3 billion, or 40% of General Motors' total cost of benefits, was spent on health care. Costs in 1984, which include GM retirees and their spouses, reflected a 14% average annual increase from the $629 million GM spent on health care in 1973.

While committed to cost containment efforts, an official of the General Motors Corporation said, ". . . no significant moderation of these increases at any time in the foreseeable future appears visible, and we have no indisputable practical solution for the problem."

As the cost of benefits has escalated, so has the attention paid to both the methods of planning, designing, administering, and communicating benefit programs. Benefit

---

[1] "Hewitt Associates on Employee Benefits" (Lincolnshire, IL), November–December 1985.

[2] "Hewitt Associates on Employee Benefits" (Lincolnshire, IL), March 1986.

objectives that take into account both the needs of the company and of the employees have to be articulated so that benefit plans will be well designed, coordinated, and cost effective. Effective communications programs with employees, with insurers outside the company, and with various government agencies become increasingly important, as does keeping abreast and complying with federal and state legislation such as the federal Employee Retirement Income and Security Act of 1974 (ERISA), the consolidated Omnibus Budget Reconciliation Act of 1985 (COBRA), and the Tax Reform Act of 1986. COBRA, for example, requires the employer to make available participation in the group health insurance plan to widows, divorcees, and dependents of deceased or Medicare-eligible employees for up to 3 years and to discharged or laid-off employees for up to 18 months. The continued health care coverage provided to terminated employees and qualified beneficiaries must be identical to those benefits offered to employees who have not been laid off or terminated. COBRA, however, permits the employer to charge those who elect to continue coverage 102% of the premiums the company pays for each employee. The extra 2% is intended to defray the additional administrative costs of the program.

The Tax Reform Act of 1986 substantially affected employee benefit programs. For example, it introduced new requirements for insured programs, changed the normal retirement age of 65 to the floating age found in the Social Security Act, provided for earlier vesting of defined benefit pension plans, required employer contributions to the pension plan for employees who continue working after "normal" retirement age, cut the maximum employees could contribute to a 401(K) plan from $30,000 to $7,000 on an indexed basis, and spelled out a uniform definition of "highly compensated employee" for employee benefit and retirement plans.

As Table V–1 indicates, there are many different types of benefits. There are the legally required, such as social security, unemployment insurance, and worker's compensation. These public fringe benefits are mandated by government. In 1988, for example, social security amounted to 7.51% of all wages and salaries up to a base of $45,000 for both the individual and the corporation. There are, in addition, and unlike the custom in other countries, those benefits that are either privately negotiated in collective bargaining or offered voluntarily by the employer. These include pensions, profit-sharing, tuition reimbursement, paid vacations and holidays, group medical and life insurance plans, and savings and thrift plans. Private benefits of this type of more recent vintage include dental, optical, prepaid legal insurance plans, floating holidays, day care, coverage for second opinion surgery, adoption assistance, and eldercare.

Both child care concerns and responsibility for the care of an elderly dependent can cause stress and absenteeism, and affect job performance. Recent studies have shown that at least 20% of middle-aged employees are actively involved in the continuing care of an older person. A survey by the New York Business Group on Health stated that when employees care for the elderly, the costs to employers range from excessive use of telephones to chronic absenteeism. In recent years many companies have supported employee child care needs. Sometimes this support has been through a redesigned employee benefit program; at other times it has been through a child care facility on company premises or the establishment of an information and referral center for child care facilities in the community. Corporations have also been involved in supporting community resource centers, in creating on-site centers in industrial parks, and in the development of public-private partnerships to respond to specific child care situations. With respect to eldercare, some companies have offered referral services, flexible hours, hot lines, seminars and other educational programs, and financial aid.

Another relatively new benefit is child care vouchers, a plan that lets companies assist working parents in meeting their child care expenses at a modest cost and with minimal liability. Under such plans, which work through payroll deductions, the employee, after determining his or her child care costs for the year, asks the company to deduct a set amount of pretax dollars from each paycheck. The money is then converted to a voucher, which the employee receives. The voucher is used to pay the child care provider and is redeemed by a third party, frequently the Voucher Corporation. The employee receives significant tax savings, and working parents are free to choose their child care provider. The company, through this program, can enhance its image, improve recruiting and retention, and save money because of reduced FICA payments on employees' reduced gross salaries.

In 1988 Congress was considering a number of important benefit issues, including IRA-type health care savings accounts, coverage for catastrophic illness, "risk pools" for the uninsured, and mandatory family/medical leave.

WHY BENEFIT PROGRAMS?

Five major reasons explain both the widespread prevalence of generous benefit programs as well as their growth. First, perhaps growing out of paternalism, many employers felt an obligation to take care of those who worked for them. It was thought that employees should simply have, for example, adequate medical and pension plans. These companies also viewed the expenditures as good business. A worker freed from worrying about how a spouse's medical expenses are to be paid is a more productive worker because he or she, the thinking goes, has greater peace of mind.

Second, in the late 1930s and 1940s after key industries were unionized and pensions and insurance were held to be bargainable issues under the National Labor Relations Act, there was intense union interest, responding to perceived member desires, in benefits and benefit improvements. Also, during World War II, wages were frozen and companies offered benefits as a way to recruit workers. Once major unions negotiated specific benefit plans, this created pressure for other unionized as well as nonunion companies to match or exceed such programs. Unions also viewed increased time-off benefits such as longer vacations and more holidays as ways to increase employment by spreading the available work during periods of high unemployment. Major unions have been particularly interested in various employment and income security programs.

Third, in the United States the tax laws encourage the growth and development of substantial private benefit programs. In most cases the benefit purchased is not taxable to the individual, but its cost is fully deductible for tax purposes to the corporation. The kinds of benefits for which deductions are permitted under the Internal Revenue Code are group life, health and retirement, supplementary unemployment benefit programs and group legal plans. Company contributions to employee benefits such as pension and deferred profit-sharing plans, health insurance and other comparable coverages are exempted from employee taxation by existing law. For example, a company deducts its pension costs but the value of that benefit is not taxable to the individual until he or she actually retires and begins receiving retirement income. Also, when the employee buys life insurance, it is purchased with after-tax dollars. Company-provided life insurance, on the other hand, is bought with pretax dollars.

Savings and thrift plans, which generally permit employees to contribute as much as 6% of annual salaries to a managed fund, are particulary attractive. First, the regular employee contribution is generally matched by a company contribution. While the most common match is 50%, some companies match 75% or even dollar for dollar. Second, the fund is professionally managed. Finally, if the employee is able to leave his or her nest egg alone, the contributions earn interest and dividends on a tax-deferred basis. The net effect of this is that long-service employees, at the time of retirement, can have a nest egg or pool of cash of as much or more than twice their final salary. Consider also the attractiveness of a group legal service plan. Under such plans, employer contributions as well as plan benefits are also excluded from the worker's taxable income.

There are also other types of employee benefits that have been exempted from taxation by Internal Revenue Service regulations. Examples of such benefits are the price discounts enjoyed by department store employees, reduced air fares for airline employees, free or subsidized meals in company cafeterias and supper money for employees who work overtime.

Fourth, benefits purchased through the company can be bought more cheaply than those purchased individually. In addition to the convenience and tax aspects, group insurance rates are simply lower than the rates for individuals. There are economies of scale with respect to group buying. Many employees are pleased to be able to participate through payroll deductions in company-sponsored benefits in which the cost is passed over to the participating employees. This is because the cost through the group is generally considerably less than an employee would have to pay on his or her own. Some examples of these "no or low cost" to the company benefits are as follows: family and dependent life insurance, group automobile insurance, homeowners and tenants insurance, extra disability income, and additional life insurance.

Fifth, companies may have to improve or add benefit programs simply to remain reasonably competitive in the labor markets in which they compete for employees. For instance, a company without a dental plan in a geographic area where most employers have such plans may, unless its other benefit programs are unusually generous, find it difficult to continue to resist either employee or union pressures for such plans. This is a particularly difficult issue for the large national employer that, by design, offers the same benefit package to all employees regardless of where in the United States they work. While a prepaid legal plan in West Coast plants may be necessary for competitive reasons, the national adoption of such a plan may be both too expensive for the employer and unnecessary for competitive purposes. The fact that benefit costs have been rising more rapidly than wage costs would suggest that there is a change in values and preferences among employees. It would appear that employees value more highly benefit improvements as well as new benefits, as opposed to greater pay increases.

Companies may design and offer benefit plans that give them a competitive advantage in the attraction and retention of employees. Some companies have also been unusually effective in recruiting outstanding engineering undergraduates by giving them an opportunity to earn a master's degree by taking courses on company premises offered by professors from cooperating universities. Offering child care facilities, flexible working hours, wellness programs, physical fitness centers, or the four-day-week are also other ways some companies have been able to recruit and retain employees.

OBJECTIVES

It is important for companies to develop philosophies and objectives with respect to benefits. Such goals function as both a framework and a standard by which potential benefit changes can be evaluated. Some large companies wishing to remain nonunion attempt to maintain leadership positions with respect to benefits. Some of these companies, moreover, operate on the egalitarian principle of equal treatment. Whether the employee is the janitor or a vice president, he will receive the same benefit plan. One such company is Hewlett-Packard. Hewlett-Packard's corporate people objective is as follows:

Objective: To help HP [Hewlett-Packard] people share in the company's success, which they make possible; to provide job security based on their performance; to recognize their individual achievements; and to help people gain a sense of personal satisfaction and accomplishment from their work.

Under this umbrella objective, one better understands the company's benefit plans. Commenting on the company's approach, William Hewlett, co-founder of the company, writes in an employee publication:

There are a number of corollaries to this policy. One is that employees should be in a position to benefit directly from the success of the organization. This led to the early introduction of a profit-sharing plan, and

eventually to the employee stock purchase plan. A second corollary was that if an employee was worried about pressing problems at home, he could not be expected to concentrate fully on the job. This, and the fact that in the early days Dave [Packard] and I were very closely associated with people throughout the company and thus had a chance to see firsthand the devastating effect of domestic tragedy, led, amongst other things, to the very early introduction of medical insurance for catastrophic illness.

Other companies provide more attractive benefit packages and many "perks" (perquisites) for executives, a practice which the founders of the former group of companies would not tolerate. Rather than approaching benefits in a piecemeal and uncoordinated fashion, management should establish benefit objectives that relate to business goals. What, for example, is the retirement income plan to accomplish? Unless realistic goals are established, it is impossible to evaluate benefit changes intelligently.

POLICY AND ADMINISTRATIVE ISSUES

Design and Communication

Designing benefit plans that respond to employee needs is not easy when there is much diversity within the workforce. In addition to the basic tradeoff between pay and benefits, younger workers may be interested in longer vacations and more holidays, while older employees will favor higher pension benefits. Designing benefit plans for "the average employee," especially with so many dual-income couples in the workforce, is becoming increasingly complex. Attitude surveys and other forms of employee input are frequently used to determine employee preferences. It may be that to employees the perceived value of a lower-cost benefit is higher than the perceived value of a higher-cost benefit. If so, such employee preference analysis is invaluable to the company desiring to minimize benefit costs while maximizing employee satisfaction. At one company we know it was discovered through such analysis that employees preferred two additional holidays over an additional week of vacation. Another company substituted a dental plan in exchange for the cancellation of its annual Christmas party. The increased diversity of the workforce is also forcing many companies to consider offering a range of benefit plans more in line with new circumstances and new lifestyles. The so-called cafeteria approach to benefits, as described in the Modernizing Benefits: American Banking Corporation case, may be one such approach.

Since most employees generally do not understand or appreciate either their benefits or the costs (unless the employee encounters a serious problem), company benefit communication programs are becoming increasingly common. Delta Airlines presents an annual slide show to its employees which, among other purposes, depicts Delta's benefits relative to its competitors. United Technologies developed a humorous slide film, featuring its principal benefit plans, which stars Jonathan Winters, the TV comedian. Companies also frequently send an annual benefit statement to employees at home which educates and informs the worker and his or her spouse. A spouse, for example, might learn that the company gives $50,000 of free life insurance. Other companies have developed other means of communicating benefits. Included in such methods are meetings, publications, cartoons, and contests requiring employees to use their benefit handbooks. Table V–2 contains material from an annual report that the chairman of Kodak sends to each employee. The first part is a summary of Ko-

dak benefits; the second is the estimated cost of the company's benefits.

An interesting question is the manner in which a new benefit or a benefit improvement should be announced. If the change comes about through collective bargaining, should the company permit the union to take credit for it or should the company try to claim credit for it? A joint announcement, of course, allows both parties to take credit for the improvement. In one large nonunion company, a top management debate once took place over the announcement of a new benefit. The president thought he should announce it in a personalized letter addressed to all employees. Some others felt that employees should learn of the new benefit through their supervisor, using this as an opportunity to develop the supervisor-employee relationship.

Cost Control

Cost control associated with employee benefits, as has been indicated, receives top management priority today. Talented benefits managers and consultants are recommending a variety of ways to contain costs. Increased pressure is being put on investment managers to perform with respect to the management of pension or profit-sharing funds. Those who do not receive satisfactory investment results may lose the account. Self-insurance is being tried in some areas, as are administrative service contracts. For large companies, the establishment of special tax-exempt trusts for funding employee benefits, such as health, accident, and disability insurance, can also result in substantial reductions in costs compared to conventional insurance plans. With health costs soaring, company managers are taking keen interest in the inefficiencies of the nation's health care delivery system. Some companies are training executives who are also hospital board members to ask the hard questions at trustee meetings. Why, for instance, can't more tests be done on an outpatient basis?

Company initiatives in this area include preadmission authorization and concurrent review programs to make sure that hospitalization is appropriate for individual, nonemergency users; utilization review to check the appropriateness and quality of medical services provided to employees; mandatory second surgical opinions for certain nonemergency elective procedures; case management for certain high-cost cases, generally for patients in need of chronic care or those with catastrophic conditions; and the encouragement of alternative delivery systems, including outpatient treatment and surgery for many common procedures, Preferred Provider Organizations (PPOs), and Health Maintenance Organizations (HMOs). The objective of managed care programs is to prevent unnecessary hospital admissions, promote alternative care, and coordinate the resources required for high-cost illnesses.

To control costs and improve health and employee relations, many companies have implemented on-site wellness and physical fitness programs. These programs include: dietary counseling, regular exercise and aerobic training, lectures on controlling stress and early breast cancer detection, diagnostic testing, free or reduced tuition for smoking cessation programs, and low-calorie menus in the company cafeteria. Many companies have entered into joint arrangements with health clubs or installed exercise equipment on company premises for the benefit of their employees.

In 1987, according to Interstudy, a Minneapolis research firm, 653 HMO had 32 million Americans enrolled. The 1973 HMO Act required companies employing twenty-five or more to offer some kind of HMO as an alternative to conventional health insurance if a "qualified" HMO is available and if either the employees or the HMO requests it. Of the 600 HMOs in the United States in 1988, 480 were federally qualified. Competition from the growth of HMOs, themselves concerned with lowering costs through preventive medicine and the elimination of needless tests, has forced Blue Cross-Blue Shield and other conventional health insurers to be more cost conscious. HMOs, essentially a system of prepaid medical care, attempt to provide all services—including regular checkups, eye exams, and laboratory tests. The comprehensive medical services, including hospitalization, are offered for a fixed, prepaid, periodic fee. There are no claim forms, no coinsurance, and no deductibles. By emphasizing preventive medicine, HMOs are supposed to reduce medical costs. Top management interest and action as well as location and perceived quality has a great impact on whether many company employees enroll in an HMO.

In the Twin Cities area, 78% of Honeywell employees belonged to an HMO in 1986, compared to 31% in 1978. In 1988, however, the growth of HMOs appeared to be slowing. Many, perhaps as many as half, were losing money, and some analysts were predicting a wave of failures and consolidations. While states had encouraged HMO growth, several in 1988 were developing regulations to make sure that members of failed HMOs were not stuck for these bills.

Employer experience with HMOs has not been all positive. Some have found the expected savings illusory. An unanticipated consequence for many companies was the adverse selection phenomenon. Typically, younger, single and other healthy employees signed up for the HMO option. This meant that older and less healthy employees remained covered by

Table V–2 1988 Personal Benefits Statement

Prepared especially for . . .
JOHN A DOE SR
343 STATE STREET
ROCHESTER, NY 14650

Kodak is pleased to provide you with this summary of your 1988 benefits, based on information in company records. Please refer to your *You and Kodak* book for a more detailed explanation. If you have any questions about this statement, please call Benefits Information at KO ext. 41000, 724-1000 or 800-221-6543.	Employment date (continuous or adjusted)	07-06-53
	Birthdate	05-05-27
	Benefits marital status on record	Married
	Insurance Annual Salary Rate (IASR)	$ 51,000
	Spouse's birthdate	02-05-31

Life Insurance . . .

These are your coverages as of January 1, 1988, under the Family Protection Program. In addition, eligible dependents will receive these monthly survivor income benefits.	Basic Life Insurance (.5 × IASR)	$ 25,500
	Optional Life insurance (3.5 × IASR)	178,500
	Dependents Life Insurance—spouse	20,000
	—each child	4,000
	Occupational Accidental Death Insurance (2 × IASR)	102,000
	Monthly Basic Survivor Income Benefit	552
	Monthly Optional Survivor Income Benefit	368

Health and Dental Care . . .

You have these health and dental care coverages as of May 1, 1988.	Kmed (National)	Family
	Dental Assistance Plan	

Short Term Disability (STD) . . .

If you are sick or injured, you may continue receiving your regular pay.	You are eligible for pay continuation of up to	52 weeks

Long Term Disability (LTD) . . .

If your Short Term Disability runs out, you may qualify for monthly Long Term Disability payments until you reach retirement age or no longer qualify for LTD.	Maximum estimated monthly disability payment.	$ 1,700
	Your health, dental and life insurance coverages will be continued on a contributory and/or company-paid basis.	

Retirement . . .

These are estimated amounts of your retirement income benefit. Your monthly benefit at age 65 includes service projected to age 65.	Accrued monthly benefit through 1987 payable January 1, 1988	$ 1,815
	Your monthly benefit at age 65 (including a $48 reduction for survivor income benefits you elected)	1,893
	Social Security benefits are in addition to these amounts.	

Kodak Tax Credit Stock Ownership Plan . . .

Although contributions can no longer, by law, be made to KTRASOP, employee accounts will continue to be maintained.	Your account value on February 1, 1988 was	$ 2,915
	Dividend paid December 1987	108

Savings and Investment Plan (SIP) . . .
These are the fund values of your account in the Savings and Investment Plan as of April 1, 1988.

Total value of your account			$ 81,210.34
Total contributions to your account			56,506.51
Fund	**Number of Units**	**Unit Value**	**Fund Value**
A	3,572.4142	$ 7.6844	27,451.86
D	7,991.0932	6.7273	53,758.48

Other Benefits . . .

Wage Dividend paid March 11, 1988	$5,239
1988 Vacation days (carryover not included)	30
1988 Paid holidays	10

Cost of Your Benefits. . .
This is the company's 1987 cost, as well as any contributions you made, to provide these benefits.

Total company cost	$16,040
Including Social Security taxes of	3,289
You paid Social Security taxes of	3,289
You paid insurance premiums of	628

Your Beneficiaries . . .
These are your beneficiary designations as of May 1, 1988. (*A spouse is, by law, automatically the only beneficiary of the SIP and KTRASOP plans unless the spouse agrees by waiver to another designation.*)

Plan	Beneficiary	Beneficiary Class	Special Instructions
Basic Life Insurance	Susie Doe	Primary	
Kodak Tax Credit Stock Ownership Plan	Mary Doe	Primary	
Savings and Investment Plan	Sarah Doe	Primary	
All Plans Not Otherwise Designated	Jane Doe	Primary	

Used with permission of Eastman Kodak company, 1988.

the conventional insurance plan. Because premiums went up in response to the higher costs associated with those who remained in the traditional insurance plan, the HMOs raised their rates. To counter this development, employers in 1988 are beginning to think about the idea of negotiating rates with HMOs that will reflect the actual costs associated with their employees.

Employers are also managing costs by installing and raising deductibles and by sharing costs with employees. These measures not only contain costs, but create more employee awareness of benefits and their costs. Rather than raising the deductible from $100 to $250 per family, some companies are relating the deductibles to a percentage of an employee's pay. A deductible of 2% of pay means, for example, that the $20,000 per year employee has a deductible of $400, while the $40,000 per year employee has a deductible of $800. In 1988, General Motors required its 114,000 salaried employees in the United States to pay part of their health care benefits. These GM employees are not only required to pay deductibles and fees for health care, but lost coverage for hearing and vision care.

A benefit package that is contributory rather than noncontributory is a big change for many companies and their employees. In noncontributory programs, the company pays 100% of the costs. If the employee must contribute toward a health care and pension plan, he or she, some think, better appreciates what the company is providing. Employee contributions also reduce the company's cost. Union leaders generally find such arguments unpersuasive. They favor noncontributary benefit programs. It has been shown that higher deductibles and cost sharing result in less use of the medical system. It must be recognized that a company, especially in the area of health, neither wants to ban a benefit's use nor encourage overuse. While it is desirable for an employee to see a doctor if it is *necessary*, it is undesirable if it is *unnecessary*. A free benefit may be abused, and this is another argument for deductibles and copayments.

An area of increased concern in 1988 is the rapid rise in mental health costs. Analysis of claims data for mental-health-related hospital admissions generally show that children of employees are the primary source of the problem, with substance abuse a major issue. While hard to control, many companies are beginning to employ case management to reduce these costs.

The Honeywell case describes well the problems and is a model for other corporations wrestling with questions of cost and effectiveness in the health area. The case raises many challenging issues and permits the student to deal with both the policy and administrative matters.

GOVERNMENT REGULATIONS

Compliance with various federal and state legislation requires an increasingly larger share of company resources. Administered by both the Labor and Treasury departments, the federal Employee Retirement Income and Security Act of 1974 (ERISA) established, among other objectives, new standards with respect to eligibility, coverage and vesting, funding, reporting and disclosure, and fiduciary responsibilities. Pension plans had to be amended to comply with this law. Greater employee communications programs as well as reports to the government were required. ERISA,

as amended, and the Internal Revenue Code also provide rules for cost and deferred compensation plans (section 401(K) plans), rules for individual retirement accounts (IRAs), benefit and contribution limits under section 415, and nondiscrimination rules for welfare benefit plans. Under ERISA, in April 1979 the Department of Labor issued regulations containing the exact wording to be used in summary annual reports distributed to plan participants and beneficiaries. 1980 ERISA regulations required that participants be told total benefit amount, amount vested, and vesting date. COBRA and the Tax Reform Act of 1986, as mentioned above, required many more changes than either ERISA or any other single piece of earlier legislation. The 1986 amendments to the Age Discrimination in Employment Act (ADEA) became effective in 1987. They extend the protection of ADEA to workers in the private sector and to most state and local government employees beyond the age of 70. The amendments eliminate mandatory retirement for workers over age 70. The company cannot discriminate against any individual over age 40 in terms of pay, benefits, or continued employment. In addition to both federal and state laws and their interpretation by various government agencies (the IRS, the EEOC, the Department of Labor), benefit managers also need to follow federal and state court decisions. For example, in 1983 the Supreme Court ruled that pension plans were discriminatory if they paid women smaller monthly retirement benefits than they paid men, even though they might have relied on actuarial tables that predict women are more likely to outlive men.

The international side of benefits for the multinational company poses additional challenges. Many voluntary benefits in the United States are legally required elsewhere in the world. In Sweden, Great Britain, Japan, and many other countries, most benefits are provided through the government. Various governments may also have strict requirements with respect to profit-sharing, termination pay, and the indexing of retirement income with the cost of living. Profit-sharing and required training are government requirements in France; in Belgium high severance pay and indexing are the law of the land.

Because of the increased complexity of employee benefits as well as the significant costs involved, talented employee-benefit managers as well as employee-benefit consultants have been much in demand. Benefit managers at large companies command high salaries. In addition, in both small and large companies, increased use is being made of the expertise of benefit consultants.

The benefit picture today, moreover, forces one to question our nation's social policy. Private benefits represent a world of the haves and have-nots. If Joe Worker is an employee of General Motors or IBM, then he has an outstanding package of benefits. If, however, he works for the XYZ machine tool company, he may have little more than the legally required benefits. Only half of the private sector workforce have pension plans. While the GM or IBM worker retires with a handsome pension, the XYZ employee receives a retirement income provided exclusively from social security, personal savings, and, since ERISA, possibly an Individual Retirement Account. Any serious student must question the national policies that allow such discrepancies to exist.

It is significant to note that the COBRA legislation may represent a significant departure from past employee benefits legislation. According to Judith R. Mazo, director of research for the Martin E. Segal Company, a national actuarial consulting firm: "The law (COBRA) has important symbolic significance. It is the first broad-based federal law mandating employee benefits. We may be heading toward a period of greater federal design and regulation of corporate health plans."[3] There have also been proposals for a universal advance-funded minimum pension program and for tax-deductible health accounts along the lines of the Individual Retirement Account.

CASES

The cases in this section give students the opportunity to think analytically about the objectives, design, and funding of various benefit plans. The cases also emphasize both the administrative and communicative aspects of benefit programs. The Honeywell case focuses on the policy and administrative issues associated with the area of health care management. Honeywell has been a leader in this area, and students can learn much from its experience.

The Modernizing Benefits: American Banking Corporation case asks students to decide whether a limited form of flexible benefits, or the so-called cafeteria approach to compensation, makes sense in this setting. Responding to both a new competitive strategy and a more diverse workforce, a cafeteria plan might not only allow employees to participate in a basic decision-making process by permitting them to elect certain benefits from a package of company-provided options but also enable the bank to better control costs. Such plans have gained more acceptance not only because they respond to the diversity in the workforce but also because they can be a means to slow down the rate of increase in benefit costs.

[3] Deborah Rankin, "Hanging On to Your Health Insurance," *The New York Times*, May 11, 1986.

In a 1987 study ("Flexible Benefits and Employee Choice") by David E. Bloom and Jane T. Traham of Harvard University's Department of Economics, published by the Work in America Institute, it was found that while the number of companies offering employees "beneflex," "cafeteria compensation," and other variations of flexible compensation was still relatively limited, they predicted it would grow substantially in the future not only because of economic and demographic factors, but also because of the generally positive experience of most companies that have pioneered the trend. Calling the growing proportion of the workforce that is female (from 29% in 1950 to 44% in 1984) "the single most important change that has ever taken place in the American labor market," they see flexible benefits as an appropriate response to today's heterogeneous workforce.

In a recent study by Hewitt Associates of flexible compensation by size of employer, they found that flexible compensation programs have been implemented by companies in all size categories, but that most of the recent growth has been fueled by medium-size organizations, those with 1,000 to 2,000 employees. Among the largest companies in the United States, 29% of the Fortune 100 Industrials and 16% of the Fortune 500 Service companies had implemented programs by January 1, 1987, including 34% of the 100 largest commercial banks, 22% of the 50 largest life insurers, 16% of the 50 largest utilities, and 12% of the 50 largest retailers.[4] In addition to helping students think more strategically with respect to benefit objectives, the American Banking Corporation case provides better understanding of the administration and employee relation issues associated with benefit plans.

BIBLIOGRAPHY: BENEFIT POLICIES AND ADMINISTRATION

CHADWICK, WILLIAM J. *Regulation of Employee Benefits: ERISA and the Other Federal Laws.* Brookfield, WI: International Foundation of Employee Benefit Plans, 1978.

Chamber of Commerce of the United States. *Employee Benefits 1986.* Washington, DC, 1987.

FOULKES, FRED K. (ed.). *Employee Benefits Handbook.* New York: Warren, Gorham, and Lamont, 1982.

FROST, CARL, JOHN H. WAKELY, AND ROBERT A. RUH. *The Scanlon Plan for Organization Development: Identity, Participation, and Equity.* East Lansing, MI: Michigan State University Press, 1974.

HICKS, LAURENCE J. *Health Care Cost Management: Solutions for Employers.* Chicago: Illinois State Chamber of Commerce, Center for Business Management, 1986.

LESIEUR, FREDERICK G. (ed.). *The Scanlon Plan: A Frontier in Labor-Management Cooperation.* Cambridge, MA: The MIT Press, 1958.

LINCOLN, JAMES F. *A New Approach to Industrial Economics.* New York: The Devin-Adair Company, 1961.

McCAFFERTY, ROBERT M. *Employee Benefit Programs: A Total Compensation Perspective.* Boston: PWS-Kent, 1988.

———. *Managing the Employee Benefits Program* (rev.). New York: AMACOM, 1983.

MASI, DALE. *Designing Employee Assistance Programs.* New York: AMACOM, 1984.

METZGER, BERTRAM L. *Profit Sharing in 38 Large Companies.* Evanston, IL: Profit Sharing Research Foundation, 1975.

REJDA, GEORGE E. *Social Insurance and Economic Security.* Englewood Cliffs, NJ: Prentice-Hall, 1976.

Retirement Income Policy: Considerations for Effective Decision Making—An EBRI Issue Report. Washington, DC: Employee Benefit Research Institute, 1980.

---

[4]"Hewitt Associates on Flexible Compensation" (Lincolnshire, IL), July–August 1987.

Rosenbloom, Jerry S., and Victor Hallman. *Employee Benefit Planning.* Englewood Cliffs, NJ: Prentice-Hall, 1981.

Rosenbloom, Jerry S. (ed.). *The Handbook of Employee Benefits: Design, Funding, and Administration.* Homewood, IL: Dow Jones-Irwin, 1984.

Tilove, Robert. *Public Employee Pension Funds.* New York: Columbia University Press, 1976

Whyte, William F. *Money and Motivation: An Analysis of Incentives in Industry.* New York: Harper & Row, 1955.

Honeywell, Inc.

INTRODUCTION

Late one afternoon in May 1986, John Burns, vice president of health and environmental resources at Honeywell, studied the three objectives stated in the department's newly created five-year plan: (1) improve health, (2) manage costs, and (3) reduce risks. The five-year plan embodied the department's new "integrated" approach to health care, an approach that Burns believed would result in better care for Honeywell employees at lower cost, and might even change the nature of health care delivery across the nation.

The changes in Honeywell's health care department had started three years earlier in 1983, when senior management at the company formed a committee of inside executives and outside health care experts to discuss recent developments in health care and recommend a plan of action for the company. Rising costs were one of the committee's major concerns, and as a result, a health care cost containment team had been formed. Based on recommendations from this team, a new department, recently renamed Health and

This case was prepared by Ellen M. Cain, Research Assistant, under the direction of Professor Fred K. Foulkes, as the basis for discussion rather than to illustrate either effective or ineffective handling of an administrative situation.

Environmental Resources (HER), was also organized. John Burns, an internist and member of the health care cost containment team, was named head of the department. Burns was successful in attracting a number of outstanding individuals, all of whom believed a more aggressive approach to health care by users could result in better care at a lower cost. After two years of hard work and dedication, the department's philosophy had begun to take effect. As he studied the new five-year plan, Burns thought it was appropriate to review the work of the past few years and rethink the department's mission and objectives. "For 1987 and beyond," said Burns, "implementation of our strategies will be the issue."

COMPANY BACKGROUND

1985 marked Honeywell's 100th anniversary. The company had diversified over the years and in 1985 was a leading supplier of information and control systems for manufacturing and building automation. The company's major businesses were aerospace and defense, building control products and systems, and information systems. Honeywell's strategy, as stated in its 1985 annual report, was to maintain the lead or strong number two position in these market segments. In

1985, revenues totalled $6.6 billion, up 9% from 1984. During the same year net profit rose 18% to $282 million. The company employed over 94,000 people, with almost one-third of the employees working overseas. In the United States, the work force was spread across 60 locations. (See Exhibit 1 for financial information.)

Honeywell employed nearly 18,000 people in Minneapolis and its suburbs, an estimated 12,000 of whom were employed in production or factory-related operations that constituted Minneapolis Operations. Local 1145 of the International Brotherhood of Teamsters represented the nearly 6,500 factory employees who worked in assembly, manufacturing and skilled trades. Local 1145 was a centralized bargaining agent, with centralized, or "citywide," seniority rights that covered over 20 facilities. The company and Local 1145 negotiated one contract covering wages, benefits and working conditions that applied to all divisions within Minneapolis operations.

Honeywell operated under a decentralized structure. While the overall business strategy was the responsibility of senior management, managers of the individual units were given much autonomy. In most instances, the corporate office acted as a consultant to the locations and a facilitator of communication throughout the company.

ORGANIZATION

There were four members of the HER Department who reported directly to Burns: Ben Aune, director of health resources; Laird Miller, director of health systems; Tom Montag, director of environmental health and safety; and Lee Wenzel, manager of employee assistance programs. Each manager had a staff of up to three people, as shown in the department's or-

ganizational chart in Exhibit 2. In addition, the department employed 10 student interns. As head of the department, Burns worked under Fosten Boyle, vice president of human resources. Boyle reported directly to Edson Spencer, chairman and chief executive officer of Honeywell.

At the local level, each Honeywell division employed a director of human resources. These directors were not directly responsible to the corporate office, but they did use the corporate HER Department for assistance in the design and implementation of new programs and policies. They generally reported, however, on a solid line basis to their unit's general manager.

THE TWIN CITY CULTURE

Much of Honeywell's approach to health care was shaped by its location in the twin cities of Minneapolis and St. Paul. The Twin Cities house a number of Fortune 500 corporate headquarters in addition to Honeywell, including Control Data, General Mills, Pillsbury and 3M. The progressiveness of the Twin Cities has been especially apparent in local industries' health care activities. According to a report in the *New England Journal of Medicine:*

> Minneapolis-St. Paul is the home of open and progressive government, a conservative but constructive business community, and medical care providers who have demonstrated a greater willingness to innovate than their professional brethren in most other regions of the country.[1]

The nature of the community prompted the development of a number of non-profit

[1] "Health Policy Report: The Twin Cities Medical Marketplace," John K. Iglehart, *The New England Journal of Medicine,* August 2, 1984, p. 344.

agencies that focused on health care issues. Located in one building across from the University of Minnesota were the Minnesota Coalition on Health, the Minnesota Medical Association, the Center for Policy Studies, and a number of other health-related organizations. In 1985, the primary focus of several of these organizations shifted from cost to quality concerns, and from provider to purchaser behavior. The term "purchaser" is used to refer to individuals, corporations and other entities that buy health services; the term "provider" is used to describe hospitals, HMOs, physicians, and other individuals or groups that supply the health services. Dale Shaller, executive vice president of the Center for Policy Studies, commented on the changes:

> Historically, the focus in health care has been on supply side issues—hospitals, physicians, HMOs, etc. Soaring health care costs prompted an effort to control the providers. We've now found that this problem has been self-correcting due to the oversupply of physicians and hospital beds. As a result, we're trying to shape the demand side—the purchasers of health services. The major purchasers are business and government, but we also need to influence individuals since they are often making the ultimate choices. The goal now is to increase purchasing power in order to control costs *and* to improve quality.

Because many of the managers in Honeywell's HER department came from the provider sector, there was a high level of understanding that increasing competition among providers had shifted power from the provider to the purchaser. (See Exhibit 3 for background information on HER department members.) The director of health systems, Laird Miller, was most directly affected by this trend. Before he began negotiating with providers, he worked with members of the Midwest

Business Group on Health (MBGH), a Chicago-based health care coalition interested in this new development in the relationship between provider and purchaser. Miller recognized that Honeywell's plan would, in essence, put the theoretical "buy right" strategy, developed by Walter McClure of the Center for Policy Studies, into practice. McClure explained the buy right approach and its implications:

> If purchasers choose to buy right—make providers compete for their patients on quality and efficiency—then the mediocre plans and barracudas among the new provider organizations will find themselves rapidly losing patients. Provider organizations committed to quality and efficiency gradually should dominate the system. But if purchasers buy wrong—that is, steer, or even worse, lock their patients into providers with merely the lowest cost—then the barracudas will shave quality in every subtle way that will gain a cost advantage. Since patients usually cannot tell when they have had less than the best outcome, quality shaving will be difficult for them to detect. Thus, both patients and quality providers will suffer while mediocrity and commercial barracudas flourish, and purchasers will be paying far more than they are getting back.[2]

IMPETUS FOR CHANGE

Members of the HER department realized that the best way to attract support for their ideas was to focus on dollars and cents. Miller took on the task of compiling the figures. The information he presented to senior management was compelling. Miller projected that in 1986 Honeywell would spend $930 million on direct and indirect health-related areas. Foss Boyle, vice president of human resources, and

[2] "Buying Right: The Consequences of Glut," Walter McClure, *Business and Health,* September 1985, p. 46.

Lou Navin, chief financial officer, were surprised by this figure since Boyle had estimated it to be approximately $200 million, and even this had concerned him. Miller explained the discrepancy in numbers as follows:

> It is true that Honeywell's *direct* health care costs are estimated to be $186 million for the year, but that is only one-quarter of the total picture. We've estimated *indirect* costs to be four times this figure, which brings us close to $1 billion. Indirect costs result from a number of factors, including absenteeism, loss of efficiency due to the breakup of a work group, costs of training a new employee, damage or downtime of tools or equipment, etc. Industry has accepted that indirect health costs are two to three times direct costs, but this doesn't take into account other factors such as environmental risks. Including these and using a conservative estimate, the multiplication factor increases to four.

(See Exhibit 4 for a breakdown of costs.)

Miller also drew attention to the cost problems caused by the proliferation of health maintenance organizations (HMOs). An HMO differs from a private physician's office or hospital in that members pay a monthly flat fee and a small fixed fee per visit rather than being billed individually for services (typically referred to as fee-for-service). This prepayment system offers an incentive to the HMO to control costs since a profit or loss is incurred if costs are below or above revenues. In the belief that HMOs would reduce health care costs by controlling unnecessary physician visits and hospital stays, Honeywell had made an aggressive attempt to move employees out of the fee-for-service system and into HMOs. In those geographic areas where HMOs were common, enrollment of Honeywell employees had grown substantially. In the Twin Cities area, 78% of Honeywell employees belonged to an HMO in 1986 compared to 62% in 1980 and 31% in 1978. In 1986, there were six HMOs operating in the Twin Cities area. While Honeywell offered five of these HMOs, 50% of employees were enrolled in one of the HMOs.

Before 1985, Honeywell provided 100% medical benefit coverage through HMOs and Blue Cross-Blue Shield for salaried employees. In 1985, Honeywell added a copayment to all plans in which salaried employees would pay 20% of charges for overnight hospital stays to a maximum of $200. The copayment was increased in 1986 to $300. For unionized employees, Honeywell provided 100% medical benefit coverage through HMOs and 80/20 coverage (company pays 80% and employee pays 20%) after a $50 deductible for Blue Cross-Blue Shield. The intent of offering 100% HMO coverage (aside from the deductible) was to provide an incentive for the employee to choose the HMO plans.

The effects of the shift to HMOs, however, had not been what Honeywell had expected. Instead of reducing health care expenditures, the increase in HMO enrollment had actually driven health care costs upward. Miller explained what had happened in the Twin Cities:

> The reason for the cost increase is now clear. Initially, HMOs may attract younger, healthier employees who have not had prior reason to choose a regular physician and are primarily interested in eliminating copayments and deductibles. Because the population of the traditional fee-for-service plans is now older and less healthy, the premium for the plan increases. HMOs can then "price snuggle," i.e. follow the price increases of the fee-for-service providers at a slightly lower rate. The end result is higher costs for Honeywell as a whole.

Miller estimated that the shift to HMOs had cost the company $5 million more than if employees had remained in the fee-for-service plan.

Management at Honeywell was convinced that changes needed to be made. Not only were health care expenditures rising, but there had been no obvious improvement in the services delivered or the health of the employees. Therefore, in early 1986 the company decided to adopt formally the integrated approach that had been developed throughout 1984 and 1985. The remainder of the case describes the "managed care" approach of each group within the department. It is organized according to the four primary groups under Dr. Burns: Health Systems, Health Resources, Environmental Health and Safety, and Mental Health and Chemical Dependency.

HEALTH SYSTEMS

Miller's strategy to reduce costs focused on contracting with a variety of health care providers. Management at Honeywell recognized that the same purchasing patterns Honeywell used to buy components and other supplies used in the manufacturing process could be applied to health care. Miller also planned to negotiate with providers to obtain the services Honeywell employees needed at the cheapest rate. Miller's initial efforts in the area of managed care were primarily focused in two areas: the comprehensive health system (CHS) and HMO contract negotiation.

The Comprehensive Health System (CHS)

Miller's belief that managed care could be accomplished with providers other than HMOs resulted in the development of the CHS. Under the CHS, one "vendor" chosen for the best proposal would tie together the services of many providers in

accordance with the needs of a given Honeywell location. A vendor might be a large hospital or insurance carrier with the capability of bringing together the services of a variety of health service providers. In mid-1985, Miller and others began the development of a generic CHS program, to be followed by tailoring for specific locations.

Participation in the program and development of the specifications would be up to the "location representative"—most likely the human resource director or employee benefits manager at a Honeywell location. It was unlikely that a new employee would be hired to manage the program; rather, the incumbent benefits manager would be asked to take on the additional responsibility. After determining the specific requirements of the location and using the model developed by Miller, the project manager would develop a request for proposal (RFP) to be distributed to vendors in the area, who would, in turn, submit their bids. The vendor who could bring together the highest quality combination of services at the lowest cost would be granted the contract. Initially, the program arranged by the vendor would be offered to employees as an alternative option to the company's traditional plans. However, after a given period of time, the thought was to attach a financial disincentive to the other plans to attract employees to the CHS plan.

In order to select the best alternative, Honeywell needed to evaluate the quality of care to be delivered through the various vendors. With no objective form of measurement, end users of health care had traditionally relied on word-of-mouth to determine a provider's reputation. Some corporations and other large-scale purchasers, however, were beginning to use standards of measurement such as preadmission rates, peer reviews and employee satisfaction surveys. Only recently, a comprehensive system had been introduced that objectively measured the outcome of health care delivery.

One such system that had attracted much interest from both health care purchasers and providers was the Medical Illness Severity Grouping System (ME-DISGRPS) developed by MediQual, a health research organization located in Westborough, MA. Instead of focusing on utilization review and the appropriateness of treatment, the MEDISGRPS system measured quality of care as an *outcome* rather than a *process*. Utilization review is the process of assessing what services at what cost are provided by a hospital or other provider. Under the system, each patient was reviewed upon admission to the hospital using common clinical tests to determine the severity of the illness in relation to the potential for organ failure. The patient was then given a severity score (on a 0–4 point scale). After treatment or discharge the patient was reviewed again and given another severity score. While Honeywell planned to use traditional forms of quality assessment, each provider would be required to provide MEDISGRPS or comparable information to bid on the proposal.

Although Honeywell had not intended to implement the CHS program until 1987, David Parker, manager of employee benefits at the Large Computer Products Division (LCPD) in Phoenix, was very enthusiastic about the program and began work on an implementation plan in early 1986. Parker explained his reasons for an early start:

Our location in Phoenix offers a number of factors conducive to the CHS program. These include: a physician glut, 45–50% excess hospital bed capacity, rapid HMO growth (1 to over 15 in just two years) and the lack of dominance by the Blues. Most significantly, we have current medical claims costs in the LCPD over $9 million, and this is growing at a 17–20% annual rate. In addition, with over 5,000 employees we are one of the largest local employers. This puts us in a strong position to negotiate with providers.

Before the proposed changes, employees chose between an HMO or Blue Cross-Blue Shield. Honeywell paid 100% of basic coverage, including labs, X rays and inpatient charges, and 80% after a deductible of $100 on major medical items such as office visits, injections, prescriptions and medical supplies. Under the proposed new plan, by formulating specifications for the selected provider, Honeywell planned to reduce costs by eliminating unnecessary services that were included in the traditional plan. Working closely with members of the corporate staff, Parker developed an RFP to distribute to local vendors interested in establishing a long-term provider agreement with Honeywell. The RFP was completed in April of 1986 and was to be distributed to potential vendors in late April or early May.

In June, Honeywell expected to receive bids from 10 to 12 vendors in Phoenix. It would then choose one vendor with whom a multiyear contract would be established. The summer months would be spent on communication of the new program to the employees in order that the program could be launched in January of 1987. Parker was optimistic about the new plan. He predicted a 15–20% savings in health care expenditures in its first full year of implementation.

HMO Purchasing

In an attempt to extend the "buy right" approach to all methods of health service purchasing, Honeywell began in 1985 to develop a strategy similar to the CHS to be used with HMOs. Candace Dow, who worked as a contract consultant at Honeywell under Miller, was designated as the person to organize the process and subsequently work with the location representatives to customize the HMO contracts.

The HMO contracting process entailed four phases. The first step was to increase the location representatives' understanding of the HMO industry. Dow compiled information on the industry and produced a one-page summary of current trends (see Exhibit 5 for a listing of these trends).

The second step was to develop a model evaluation form that could be used by location representatives to measure HMO effectiveness in a number of areas including quality assurance, health services delivery, finance, and management. This evaluation process was aimed at determining, on a general level, the areas in which an HMO ranked highly and those in which it may have been weak.

The third phase was the development of an RFP to be distributed among HMOs that might want to submit bids. When the HMOs responded, the location representatives would use evaluation criteria to determine which bid most closely met location needs. The intent was to offer a limited number of HMOs. Honeywell wanted the HMO's rates to be based on their experience with Honeywell employees rather than the average rates for the community.

Once an HMO was selected, a service agreement (phase four) would be drawn up based on the RFP and location needs. In addition to information regarding the services to be provided, technical issues such as employer-specific utilization rates would be included in an agreement.

The first and second phases were to be performed solely at the corporate level by Dow to assist location representatives. The final two phases were to be completed by both Dow and location representatives, with Dow developing "models" that could then be customized by the location representatives.

According to Dow, progress in the area of HMO purchasing had been slower than expected because of the priority given to other programs such as the CHS and organ transplants (see Case Management section). During the summer of 1986, however, Dow planned to complete the educational material and model evaluations and RFPs to be distributed to the locations in the fall. By mid-1987, Dow expected to reach the final stage at a few pilot locations.

HEALTH RESOURCES

While Miller worked on promoting Honeywell's new approach to health care to other corporations and health care providers around the country, Ben Aune, director of health resources, was responsible for communicating the message internally to Honeywell's management and employees. Aune spent the majority of his time on health communications and health promotion program development throughout the company.

Health Promotion

Late in 1985 Aune submitted an unusual budget request. He wanted 1% of the $186 million medical allocation to be spent on a management program to improve or promote health at Honeywell. He estimated that a $1.8 million investment in programs in preventive rather than curative health care would produce a three to one return on investment. According to Aune:

> Honeywell spends, on average, $2,238 per employee on medical benefits each year. I'm asking for just $22 per employee to invest in health promotion, medical management,

and communications. If you include the dependents that can benefit from these programs, the cost per person is even lower. It's time to move from a "fix when broke" to a "prevent breakage" orientation here. (See Exhibit 6 for a description of this strategy). From a business strategy standpoint, health promotion will do more than simply reduce health care costs for the company. A healthy environment at Honeywell is likely to result in greater job satisfaction, reduced absenteeism, increased productivity, and lower employee turnover.

Aune's five-year plan called for an annual increase in the percentage of funds allocated to health promotion until 1990, at which time 3% of the medical benefits package would go to health promotion. Aune intended to pass on $20 per employee to each location in the first year (1986) so that the programs could be tailored to the specific health needs of particular sites. In order to receive the funds, each location program manager was required to submit a proposal detailing program goals, evaluation plans and anticipated return on investment. Upon approval by Aune, the location would receive the funds. If no proposal was submitted, the funds would remain in the medical allocation or be applied to general operating expenses. A small percentage would be retained by the corporate office to promote improved communication of health promotion ideas and implementation strategies on a companywide basis.

In line with the department's common philosophy to improve health, reduce risks, and manage costs, Aune's initial plan was to assess the health status and risk factors of Honeywell employees. Aune wanted to determine an aggregate profile of the health status of Honeywell employees, as well as individual data so that risk factors could be measured by location. To obtain this information, Aune contracted with General Health, Inc., a health risk management organization based in Washington, D.C., to offer the health plan personal risk profile to Honeywell employees. The personal risk profile was a computer-prepared individual health status report based on a questionnaire completed by the employee. It provided information about an individual's major risk factors which might contribute to heart attacks, strokes, and lung cancer. The profile revealed a current "health age" and an attainable health age if all the factors affecting risk were at their recommended levels. The profile also offered behavioral suggestions that could reduce health risks and increase survival rates. (Exhibit 7 is a summary of a sample personal risk profile.) Of the company's 64,000 U.S. employees, more than 10,000 at all locations had voluntarily completed the personal risk profile through 1986. The method of communicating the program varied slightly among locations; in general, company newsletters, memos and videos were used to inform employees about the availability of the risk profile. To promote participation, Honeywell offered the appraisal on a voluntary basis at no cost to the employee.

In addition to influencing employees' behavioral patterns, the personal risk profile was a mechanism for determining the health care needs of an employee group at large. The department intended to use the risk profile data to determine the specific health care needs for individual locations when organizing a CHS program. Miller believed that tailoring health plans to the needs of particular locations was very important. According to Miller:

Purchasers of health care traditionally have focused too much on benefit design without knowing what the needs of the employee population actually were. Attracting the best heart surgeon in town is not worth much if the employee population has a very low risk of developing a heart problem. The same group may have a high number of smokers but no smoking cessation program or access to a good lung specialist.

Although each location was responsible for organizing its own health promotion program, Aune produced a variety of literature to communicate the wellness campaign throughout the company. The "Your Health" fact sheet was one of the most widely distributed pieces of literature. These were a series of one-page fact sheets that addressed issues such as stress management, breast self-examination and physician selection. By mid-1986, over 30 fact sheets had been produced.

Aune worked closely with certain location program managers to implement a standard health promotion program in 1985 for all field employees (15,000 sales and service employees) and Information Systems employees. He developed a program manager's guide that gave step-by-step instructions on how to implement the core phases of the program, as well as suggestions on specific health promotion activities. Because the field employees were located across the country, Honeywell contracted with the YMCA, a national organization, to offer programs to both field and Information Systems employees. Aune estimated that 6,000 employees in these two groups completed the Personal Risk Profile and 10% to 15% of these individuals enrolled in the YMCA courses. The courses included stress management, nutrition and weight management, smoking cessation and physical fitness, among others. Honeywell paid for 50% of the tuition for the courses. If there was sufficient enrollment in the class, the YMCA would teach the class at the Honeywell location.

In addition to the core health promotion program, the Program Manager's Guide outlined a number of specific programs for health promotion: walking for fitness, cardiopulmonary resuscitation (CPR), Smokeout Day and blood pressure screening.

Aune was optimistic not only about the concept, but also that such a small budget request would be granted. But there were a number of issues that needed to be addressed for the health promotion program to be awarded an increasing amount of funds in the future. One was a method of measuring the program's success. It was logical that improving the health of employees should lower health costs, but how direct a correlation was possible? Moreover, the lag time between behavioral changes, improved health and thus reduced costs was likely to be five years or more. Another concern of Aune's was getting the locations committed to health promotion. At those locations with no health professionals on staff, how were the programs to be implemented? An even more challenging question was constantly posed to Aune by health promotion pessimists: Can a corporation actually influence employees to change such embedded habits as eating poorly, drinking excessively, failing to exercise, or smoking? Aune knew he had a tough job in front of him, but was committed to his task. He strongly believed that corporate health care should go beyond traditional cost containment activities, and saw health promotion as a key component to Honeywell's integrated approach.

Case Management

Aune was also responsible for the nursing program Denise Konicek managed before Mary Foley joined Honeywell in March 1986. Under Konicek, Honeywell's nurses had been encouraged to take more responsibility for "case management." Konicek explained the case management concept:

Case management is any of a number of approaches to planning, coordinating and providing health care, while managing health care expenditures at the same time. More specifically, case management involves ensuring a correct diagnosis, arranging for services and treatment that have a known value in restoring or preserving health, avoiding duplication of services and planning for transitional services and psychosocial support that enables the individual to return to normal activities as soon as possible.

In 1986 case management was accomplished through a limited number of programs, some much more complex and costly than others. The sophistication of the case management process varied considerably among locations, depending on the experience level of the health professional staff, and the interest of the location general manager. A simple form of case management done at some locations was prescreening and follow-up of patients before and after a hospital stay. This was completed at Honeywell regardless of the type of insurer (HMO, Blue Cross-Blue Shield) chosen by the employee.

At select locations, a more extensive form of case management was completed through an individual known as a health service advisor. This role was developed and filled by either a Honeywell nurse or a contracted health professional. The primary role of the health service advisor was to act as a liaison between employees and the health care system. The advisor worked with employees and their families to:

1. Help them find the best medical care for the best price
2. Assess their current lifestyle and advise them of available options for changing if they wish
3. Answer questions about particular medical procedures as they enter the health care system

4. Help them decide whether a second physician's opinion is necessary before hospitalization or treatment of a medical problem
5. Examine alternatives to hospitalization, such as home care, intermediate care facilities and outpatient surgery

In the fall of 1984 four pilot locations at which the staff nurse would take on the additional role of health service advisor were selected. These locations were Minneapolis, MN; Tampa, FL; Joliet, IL; and Colorado Springs, CO. Nurses and management at the four locations prepared for the startup by conducting employee information sessions, preparing promotional literature, developing linkages with insurers and benefits administrators, working with Honeywell-contracted physicians to ensure backup for case review and provider contracts, and establishing familiarity with community health resources.

Although the corporate office had not developed a system to record and track the data, a few of the locations compiled data and provided the results to the corporate office. In a group of approximately 100 cases tracked, an average of two hospital days were avoided. Lost work days were reduced in more than 30 of these 100 situations. In addition, at least 15 individuals chose alternatives to proposed surgery.

In an effort to measure employee satisfaction with the program, Honeywell contracted with a Minneapolis research firm to conduct a survey, the results of which were not yet available in mid-1986. On an informal basis, however, high employee satisfaction was observed. In Konicek's words, "Employees say it is a pleasant surprise to find a professional ally who will help refer them to a competent, second-opinion provider, is able to arrange for home health care when it's needed, and will translate medical terminology into plain English."

Transplant Cases

A more specialized managed-care program was implemented to handle heart, heart-lung, liver and pancreas transplant cases. In this area, Konicek worked closely with Miller to arrange the optimal situation for the transplant patient. In order to receive cost-efficient, high-quality care, each transplant case was handled individually. In addition to contracting with the provider of health care, Honeywell brought in an outside case management organization, Intracorp, to assist the individual and family with many of the non-medical needs.

Honeywell began the transplant program in 1983, but not all locations chose to provide coverage. At those locations that did offer transplant coverage, single coverage was provided at no charge to the employee and every employee with family coverage was required to pay an additional monthly premium (usually between $1.00 and $2.00). As of mid-1986, Honeywell had covered approximately 6 transplant cases. The cost of Honeywell varied greatly depending on the type of organ transplant. According to the May 1985 issue of *American Medical News*, the cost of organ transplants is as follows: $57,000 to $110,000 for heart, $135,000 to $238,000 for liver, and $30,000 to $40,000 for pancreas.

A recent case example that remained unresolved as of May 1986 illustrates the problems that arise in a transplant case. The wife of a Honeywell employee in Houston needed a liver transplant. Because few transplants of this kind had been done in Houston, Miller contracted with a provider in Pittsburgh who specialized in liver transplants. The patient was flown to Pittsburgh for an evaluation. It was determined that the case was not severe enough to be done at the present time, but that the patient needed to stay in the Pittsburgh area to undergo additional tests and preoperative treatment. This posed considerable problems for the couple. The couple did not want to be separated, but there was no Honeywell division in Pittsburgh to which the husband could transfer. There were a number of alternatives, but Miller wanted to find the one that best suited the employee's needs while remaining affordable.

ENVIRONMENTAL HEALTH AND SAFETY

Tom Montag, director of environmental health and safety (EHS) was the only member of the HER department who was with Honeywell before 1981. Montag was influential in the decision to bring in Burns and strongly supported Burns's efforts to refocus Honeywell's approach to health management. According to Miller, "Burns would have had a very difficult time reshaping the mission and direction of this department without the strong support of Montag from the outset."

As the HER department began to take shape, the existing environmental health and safety group broadened its approach in line with the new notion of integrated health management. Like Aune with his health promotion campaign, the EHS group began to take a proactive rather than reactive approach to reduce the risk of environmental health and safety hazards. At the corporate level, the group worked closely with other members of the HER department, as well as with members of the corporate legal staff. The majority of their time, however, was spent "consulting" with the environment and safety/health managers at the location level.

Honeywell's focus on proactive risk management was triggered by a number of external factors. First, the regulatory climate in 1985 was becoming more stringent. The Occupational Safety and Health Administration (OSHA) and the Environmental Protection Agency (EPA) were enforcing stricter rules to ensure that industry was in compliance with government regulations. Another stimulus for intervention were industry disasters such as Union Carbide's Bhopal incident and the Johns-Manville asbestos problem. Moreover, the prospect of individual responsibility caused managers to be more conscientious. Corporate EHS worked with divisions to reevaluate their emergency preparedness, and assess the risk of chemical emergencies. In addition, several Honeywell divisions had worked with local firefighters to identify ways in which information can be shared so they can respond faster to emergencies. For example, the division in Minneapolis has provided chemical hazard training for the local fire department.

In order to recommend effective programs for the locations, objective performance measures such as accident and illness rates were needed so that the areas of greatest risk could be addressed. Bill Heim, manager of occupational health and safety, was responsible for organizing and collecting this data, which was submitted every six months to the corporate office by the locations. Members of the corporate staff were careful not to take a punitive approach to poor results in order to avoid dishonesty in the data reporting. According to Heim:

> If we start finger-pointing, supervisors will play the game too and begin to fudge the statistics. No one wins in that game. Instead of taking a punitive approach, we've tried to provide positive reinforcement for complete and accurate data. That way we can work together with the location managers to tackle the problems.

The corporate EHS staff developed a number of programs for the locations in safety and environmental management. One of these was the environmental assessment protection program, implemented in 1984 and carried out annually since. The program provided a verification mechanism to check facilities' compliance with eight major federal environmental and safety laws. In Tom Montag's words, "the liabilities associated with non-compliance are so great now that this type of program is essential."

Another program aimed at reducing environmental risk was the raw material exchange list, initiated in 1985. This list consisted of chemicals and other materials that Honeywell plants had in storage and no longer needed. The list was compiled on a computerized database and distributed to all locations, so that plant managers could exchange excess raw materials. Utilizing this approach, less raw material needed to be discarded. The Minnesota Waste Management Board encouraged Honeywell to submit the program idea for the 1986 Minnesota Governor's Award for Outstanding Achievement in Hazardous Waste Management.

In 1986 Honeywell organized the household hazardous waste collection program for employees in the Minneapolis area. Employees were asked to bring cleaning products, paint, pesticides, and any other hazardous household substances to collection sites to be transported to a commercial hazardous waste storage facility. Most of the waste was then sent to hazardous waste incinerators. Participating employees contributed over 5,000 pounds of materials. The program not only reduced the risk of hazardous waste products, but also increased the awareness of environmental risks among employees and their families.

MENTAL HEALTH AND CHEMICAL DEPENDENCY

Although Honeywell attempted to apply a "managed care" approach in the area of mental health and chemical dependency, the nature of these health problems made it difficult to manage the cases as effectively as, for instance, an organ transplant case. Lee Wenzel, manager of employee assistance programs/human services, explained that unlike medical health, the distinction between sick and well is difficult to determine in the area of mental health. As a result, it was difficult for Honeywell to identify situations where the care provided had been excessive or inadequate due to a financial incentive on the part of the provider. According to Wenzel:

> Under the traditional fee-for-service payment system, there is an incentive to provide more care than is necessary. This is especially threatening in the area of human services where it is often difficult to determine at the outset the cost and length of need for services such as psychiatric counseling, drug abuse, etc. In other areas, HMOs have reversed the incentives to "over-provide," but then we face the dilemma of undercare.

Honeywell's traditional approach had been to insure mental health without restricting the services or tracking a patient's progress. According to Wenzel, "coverage of these services at an uncontrolled rate has resulted in insurance costs averaging $300 per employee per year, which is clearly excessive."

In January 1987 Honeywell planned to implement a managed mental health program for its 11,000 field sales and service employees. Honeywell had contracted with Human Affairs International (HAI), a case management service organization in Salt Lake City, to manage the program. Although the details of the contract were not settled in mid-1986, the plan was to give HAI a budget to be apportioned to the employees and families through their case managers.

Wenzel described the new program as a "mental health HMO" with four important differences:

1. Honeywell would determine the appropriate budget to be spent.
2. Honeywell would retain the risk; i.e. if the budget was not depleted the remainder would be returned to Honeywell.
3. Additional services including marriage counseling, domestic abuse, and career direction, would be part of the program.
4. Employees would have a greater variety of choices available.

Wenzel believed that the new program would reach a much larger group of employees in need of mental health services. Under a traditional fee-for-service plan, expensive inpatient care has been excessive. Under the new program, case managers would recommend (and fund) a much higher percentage of outpatient care, thus serving a greater number of people. Wenzel believed that improved communications at the workplace and new services such as an 800 hotline would increase the program's visibility.

CONCLUSION

As Burns reviewed the progress of each group within the department, he thought again of the three objectives stated in the five-year plan: improve health, manage costs, and reduce risks. He believed that some large steps had been taken to accomplish these goals, but realized that there were a number of challenges still to be resolved.

HONEYWELL, INC. STUDY QUESTIONS:

1. What is your analysis of Honeywell's integrated approach to health care delivery?
2. What advice, if any, do you have for John Burns?

HONEYWELL, INC.

Exhibit 1 Summary of financial statements (*dollars and shares in millions except per share amounts*)

	1985	1984	1983	1982	1981
Results of Operations					
Sales	$5,754.0	$5,185.1	$4,779.1	$4,490.6	$4,382.2
Computer rental and service revenue	870.6	888.5	888.3	896.5	879.1
	6,624.6	6,073.6	5,667.4	5,387.1	5,261.3
Cost of sales	3,914.3	3,494.8	3,241.0	2,971.3	2,851.5
Cost of computer rental and service revenue	451.8	485.0	483.3	488.0	505.2
Research and development	451.4	422.0	414.1	386.4	362.8
Selling, general and administrative	1,352.8	1,216.9	1,149.4	1,189.3	1,133.9
Interest	60.3	24.0	22.1	51.9	51.2
	6,230.6	5,642.7	5,309.9	5,086.9	4,904.6
Gain on sale of interests in Cii-HB and GEISCO				90.8	
Income from continuing operations before income taxes	394.0	430.9	357.5	391.0	356.7
Income taxes[1]	118.6	96.1	106.8	119.5	102.5
Income from continuing operations	275.4	334.8	250.7	271.5	254.2
Income (loss) from discontinued operations net of income tax benefits		(25.2)	(19.5)	1.4	5.1
Recovery (loss) on disposal of discontinued operations net of income tax benefits	6.2	(70.6)			
Net income	$ 281.6	$ 239.0	$ 231.2	$ 272.9	$ 259.3
Earnings (Loss) per Common Share					
Continuing operations[1]	$ 6.02	$ 7.14	$ 5.46	$ 6.05	$ 5.57
Discontinued operations		(.54)	(.43)	.03	.12
Recovery (loss) on disposal of discontinued operations	.14	(1.50			
Net income	$ 6.16	$ 5.10	$ 5.03	$ 6.08	$ 5.69
Cash Dividends per Common Share	$ 1.95	$ 1.90	$ 1.80	$ 1.75	$ 1.60
Financial Position					
Working capital—Current assets	$2,671.0	$2,561.6	$2,497.8	$2,387.5	$2,121.9
Current liabilities	1,548.7	1,387.4	1,338.0	1,251.0	1,182.7
	$1,122.3	$1,174.2	$1,159.8	$1,136.5	$ 939.2
Capitalization—Short-term debt	$ 179.3	$ 92.8	$ 139.0	$ 115.9	$ 115.0
Long-term debt	641.6	665.6	695.5	676.3	605.8

continued

	1985	1984	1983	1982	1981
Total debt	820.9	758.4	834.5	792.2	720.8
Stockholders' equity	2,566.9	2,380.9	2,313.7	2,143.4	2,098.0
	$3,387.8	$3,139.3	$3,148.2	$2,935.6	$2,818.8
Revenue					
Aerospace and Defense	$1,899.2	$1,608.0	$1,540.1	$1,258.3	$1,103.5
Control Products	1,015.7	1,024.5	890.4	822.0	854.7
Control Systems	1,757.8	1,615.8	1,570.8	1,622.1	1,529.4
Information Systems	1,951.9	1,825.3	1,666.1	1,684.7	1,773.7
	$6,624.6	$6,073.6	$5,667.4	$5,387.1	$5,261.3
Operating Profit					
Aerospace and Defense	$124.6	$116.2	$109.0	$87.4	$77.2
Control Products	114.4	141.1	83.0	79.3	82.1
Control Systems	140.2	135.9	134.9	187.2	175.0
Information Systems	200.1	179.7	130.8	79.8	158.3
Operating profit	579.3	572.9	457.7	433.7	492.6
Gain on sale of interests in Cii-HB and GEISCO				90.8	
Unallocated items[2]	(185.3)	(142.0)	(100.2)	(133.5)	(135.9)
Income before income taxes	$394.0	$430.9	$357.5	$391.0	$356.7
Assets					
Aerospace and Defense	$885.4	$800.5	$701.8	$674.4	$478.1
Control Products	757.1	671.3	661.5	584.6	584.3
Control Systems	1,135.8	1,074.1	972.9	930.7	899.7
Information Systems	1,405.9	1,310.4	1,322.6	1,369.1	1,371.4
Corporate	849.5	841.9	885.3	769.8	893.8
Discontinued operations		61.6	119.6	126.8	86.7
	$5,033.7	$4,759.8	$4,663.7	$4,455.4	$4,314.0
Additional Information					
Average number of common shares outstanding	45.7	46.9	45.9	44.9	45.6
Return on average stockholders' equity	11.8%	10.1%	10.5%	13.2%	13.2%
Stockholders' equity per common share	$ 56.08	$ 50.97	$ 49.37	$ 47.15	$ 45.27
Percent of debt to total capitalization	24%	25%	27%	27%	26%
Research and development—Honeywell-funded	$451.4	$422.0	$414.1	$386.4	$362.8
Customer-funded	429.4	390.5	348.5	353.9	328.2
Capital expenditures—Equipment for lease to others	129.0	165.8	148.9	245.2	308.3
Other property, plant and equipment	405.7	321.4	350.4	351.4	331.3
Depreciation—Equipment for lease to others	92.3	99.0	120.2	128.1	154.5
Other property, plant and equipment	251.6	215.1	210.7	171.6	145.5
Employees at year end	94,022	94,274	93,514	94,062	96,923

[1] 1984 includes $40.0 ($0.85 per share) from gain related to tax law changes affecting domestic international sales corporation (DISC).

[2] Unallocated items include interest expense and general corporate income and expense.

HONEYWELL, INC.
Exhibit 2 Organizational chart

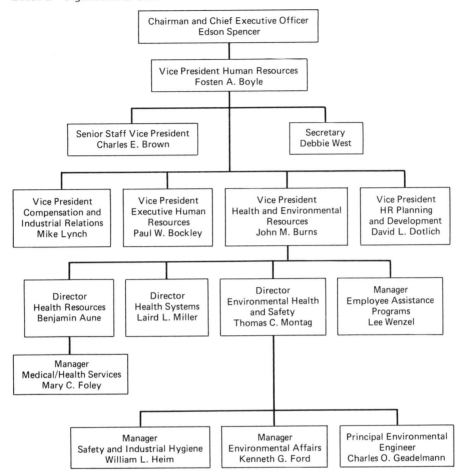

HONEYWELL, INC.

Exhibit 3   Previous work experience of health & environmental resources department members

Name	Organization	Position
Benjamin Aune	Health Central	Executive Director, Center for Health Promotion
John Burns	Central Internal Medicine Associates, P.A.	Internal Medicine Physician
Mary Foley	Control Data Corporation	Manager, Staywell Program
Kenneth Ford	Gould Metals Division	Division Environmental Manager
Charles Geadelmann	Phillips Petroleum	Environmental Engineer
William Heim	3M	Corporate Industrial Hygienist
Laird Miller	University of Minnesota	Director of Operations, Boynton Health Service
Thomas Montag	Idaho Nuclear Corporation	Health and Safety Engineer
Lee Wenzel	Process Dynamics	Employee Assistance Provider

HONEYWELL, INC.

Exhibit 4   Estimated total health & environmental management costs

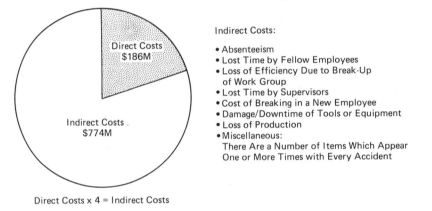

Indirect Costs:

• Absenteeism
• Lost Time by Fellow Employees
• Loss of Efficiency Due to Break-Up
  of Work Group
• Lost Time by Supervisors
• Cost of Breaking in a New Employee
• Damage/Downtime of Tools or Equipment
• Loss of Production
• Miscellaneous:
  There Are a Number of Items Which Appear
  One or More Times with Every Accident

Direct Costs x 4 = Indirect Costs

Exhibit 5 The changing health industry: impact on HMOs serving Honeywell employees

---

A. **Practice Patterns Change as Health Services Corporations of the 1990s Evolve**

1. Growth in alternative delivery systems as way to integrate health services financing and delivery.
2. Surplus of institutional and professional providers.
3. Proliferation of HMOs as free-standing, hospital-sponsored, hospital management company-sponsored or insurance company-sponsored plans.
4. HMOs will provide services through IPAs (individual practice associations) or contract physicians, rather than through the traditional group or staff models, thus increasing delivery sites and consumer acceptance.
5. Insurance carrier or hospital-affiliated HMOs may also offer PPOs.
6. Integrated buyers' and providers' interests.
7. Decreased utilization due to shift from higher cost, higher intensity to lower cost, less invasive treatment.
8. Increasing numbers of elderly will put cost pressures on public financing mechanisms.
9. Shrinking number, yet growing size of providers.

B. **Greater Employer Involvement in Health Management**

1. Increased interaction between employer and provider.
2. New ways to purchase and deliver services.
3. Desire to limit health services expenditures while maintaining or improving quality.
4. Increasing use of discounts and selective contracting.
5. Economic incentives for employees and their dependents to use cost-effective, appropriate health services and to practice healthy life-styles.

C. **Increased Employee Involvement in Health Management**

1. Major life-style changes.
2. Increased interest in health information and wellness.
3. Increased sensitivity to cost and quality.
4. Increased employee cost sharing.
5. Increased consumer acceptance of HMOs, particularly of hospital-sponsored HMOs, as HMOs become more numerous.

D. **HMOs**

1. Operational HMOs will have more members.
2. The number of HMOs will increase as more HMOs become operational.
3. HMOs will increase their range of services by creating networks of physicians.
4. Individual HMOs will consolidate into larger national networks.

HONEYWELL, INC.

Exhibit 6 Health care promotion strategy

FUTURE DIRECTION. . .
HONEYWELL'S HEALTH CARE STRATEGY

	Individual	Honeywell

Health Care (Prevent Breakage)	• Employee financial involvement
	• Healthy life style
	• Health management
	  —Self
	  —Dependents
	• Incentives for wellness
		• Climate of health
		• Educational awareness
		• Screening program
		• Health promotion strategy
		• Health-oriented incentives

Medical Care (Fix When Broke)	• React to symptoms
	• Treat sickness
	  —In-patient
	  —Outpatient
		• Encourages sickness by paying open-ended dollars for treatment

HONEYWELL, INC.

Exhibit 7 Personal risk profile summary

YOUR HEALTH RISKS

Below is a summary of the five leading health problems that you have a chance of dying from in the next 10 years. The first column indicates your risk today, the second column shows the average risk for other men your age, and the third column displays your attainable risk, i.e., your risk if all your health behaviors were at ideal levels.

	Risk Today	Average Risk	Attainable Risk
Heart attack	2.9%	1.9%	0.2%
Lung cancer	1.2	0.4	0.1
Motor vehicle accident	0.9	0.2	0.2
Cirrhosis	0.5	0.4	0.1
Stroke	0.3	0.2	0.1

YOUR LIFE EXPECTANCY

Your life expectancy is currently 69.5 years. If you change all of your health behaviors to the levels shown below, you may increase your life expectancy by up to 12.7 years.

Years You Can Add to Your Life By:

Not smoking	6.0 years
Controlling your type A behavior	2.5
Reducing your cholesterol to 180 mg/dl	1.9
Lowering your systolic blood pressure to 110	1.1
Drinking less alcohol	0.8
Getting 4,000 kcals of exercise per week	0.3
Always wearing your safety belt	0.1

SPECIAL MESSAGES

You may want to ask your physician about scheduling periodic check-ups, since your risk of lung cancer is considerably above average.

Modernizing Benefits: American Banking Corporation

INTRODUCTION

In mid-1986, Ed Warner reached the conclusion that American Banking Corporation's employee benefits program was out of date. Warner had been promoted to the position of senior vice president of human resources only two months earlier. He had come to ABC from a position as head of human resources at Motor State Bank, the largest of ABC's acquisitions in a series of recent mergers. Warner reported to Dan Knox, ABC's chairman and chief executive officer.

When he assumed his new job, Warner began taking a hard look at the bank's benefits plan, and he soon realized that the past few years of rapid growth had not only expanded ABC's work force but had increased dramatically the proportion of young, female employees in the bank. Yet as he examined ABC's benefit package, particularly its generous pension plan, he became convinced that the cost was greater than its value to the bank's current employee population. Not only were the existing benefits inordinately expensive to the bank, but the provisions did not meet

This case was prepared by Robert Paul, vice chairman of the Martin E. Segal Company, as the basis for classroom discussion rather than to illustrate either the effective or ineffective handling of an administrative situation.

© Human Resources Policy Institute, School of Management, Boston University, 1988

the needs of its people. He believed that ABC should examine the possibility of replacing its current plan with a flexible benefits program. With the Tax Reform Act of 1986 a certainty, Warner thought the timing for such a review could not be better.

Warner shared his thoughts with Jane Corbett, vice president of employee benefits, and William Ely, a vice president in the human resource division. Although Corbett and Ely both agreed with Warner in general, they recommended seeking outside help in making such a radical change in ABC's benefit plan. Accordingly, several consulting firms were interviewed. All advised against cutting back the pension plan, on principle that a competitive, defined-benefit pension plan was the cornerstone of a sound benefits program.

Then Ed Warner spoke on the phone with a good friend who was chief human resources officer at a large Chicago bank. In the process of going through a similar reappraisal of its benefits program, the Chicago bank had hired the national consulting firm Benefit Consultants, Inc., which had recommended a reduction in the bank's pension plan. The human resources team at ABC decided to interview Benefit Consultants. Although Knox looked to Warner and his team to make recommendations, all final decisions on employee benefit plans were made by the bank's management compensation committee (a group commonly referred to as the "Big Five"), consisting of the bank's chairman, the president and three executive vice presidents.

HISTORY OF AMERICAN BANKING CORPORATION

ABC had been formed 25 years earlier when two small neighboring banks in Indianapolis had merged. In its early years, ABC became known in Indiana for its lending to small businesses, cash management and similar services, and aggressive recruiting of young officers.

ABC's management had recognized in the early eighties that intensifying competition in the banking industry would result in substantial consolidation of financial institutions, and, therefore had pursued an energetic strategy of expansion through internal growth and interstate banking regulations to move into Michigan, and since then had increased the number of its branch offices to nearly 400 in two states. In the past five years, net income had risen by 135%, and assets had risen by 131%, making ABC one of the most profitable regional banks in the nation. In 1986, ABC was the leading bank in Indiana, with a market share of over 20% of deposits. In Michigan, it was the fourth largest bank. ABC's financial data for 1982 through 1986 (in millions) appear below.

Year	Net Income	Assets	Deposits
1982	$ 78	$ 9,099	$ 6,343
1983	88	12,826	8,943
1984	106	14,240	9,973
1985	133	17,354	12,698
1986*	164	19,754	13,950

* 1986 numbers are internal year-end estimates.

ABC had developed a reputation for its assertive stance toward takeover targets.

Once acquired, management at ABC paid special attention to assimilating quickly the operations of its purchases with those of the central bank. CEO Dan Knox was proud of the fact that "during many years of growth through mergers, ABC has operated as a single, consolidated bank." When ABC first moved beyond the borders of its home state into Michigan, it took what had previously been 25 separate banks and created one statewide bank with common systems and products.

In addition to growing through mergers, ABC was concentrating on expanding its business with existing customers, attracting new customers, and increasing market share within Indiana and Michigan. Deregulation had allowed ABC to develop new financial products and services, which the bank marketed under an aggressive program of "relationship management," or the cross-selling of the widest possible range of products to each customer. ABC focused on middle market companies—those with annual sales of from $5 to $250 million—and had recently been named in an independent survey the leading midwestern banker for middle market companies in terms of number of customer relationships, aggressiveness in soliciting business, and overall market coverage.

By the end of 1986, ABC will have completed Part I of its interstate expansion program, and planned to implement Part II during 1987 under new reciprocal interstate banking laws. Under Part II, ABC would expand its operations into Illinois and Ohio through several major acquisitions. The past few years of mergers and the purchases announced or planned for 1986 would bring the total number of employees at ABC to just over 10,000, a growth of over 5,000 since 1980. Three quarters of these were women; nearly half were under 30 years of age. Eighty-three percent of the employees at ABC earned less than $20,000. The majority of employees at ABC had worked at the bank fewer than five years. (See Exhibits 1 and 2 for employee statistics.)

CURRENT BENEFITS

In addition to direct compensation (salary, sick leave, vacation, holidays, bonuses, and overtime), ABC employees received an array of benefits. These included protective compensation (hospital, surgical, and major medical); replacement compensation (life insurance, business travel and voluntary accident insurance, short-term disability, and the pension plan); and capital compensation (stock/thrift plan). As the human resources team at ABC prepared to meet with Benefit Consultants, they reviewed the provisions of each benefit and the problems associated with each.

ABC's Pension Plan

Designed 15 years earlier by a former ABC chairman (now a member of the Board of Directors), ABC's defined-benefit pension plan rewarded long-term service with a generous post-retirement income. According to the pension plan's provisions, employees received 2% of their final average salary (the average of the last five years of employment) for each year of employment up to 30 years (or 60% of final average salary for 30 years of service) plus one percent of final average salary for each year of service over 30, minus one and two-thirds percent of their Social Security for each year of service (or 50% of Social Security for 30 years or more of service). Employees became fully vested after ten years at ABC. (The vesting period would be changed by the Tax Reform Act of 1986.)

Theoretically, employees with 40 years of service could expect a total retirement income (including Social Security) of over 90% of their final average salary. In actual practice, however, few employees at ABC had a career with the bank of 40 or even 30 years. More typically, an ABC employee might receive a pension that together with Social Security produced over 75% of his or her final salary after 25 years of service (after taxes). At higher salary levels, the current plan paid more than 75% of final salary after 30 years of service. (The replacement rate was lower for higher-paid employees because of the pattern of Social Security benefits.) In addition, ABC's contributions to the stock/thrift plan permitted employees to raise their retirement income another 1% to 26%, depending on length of service, amount of yearly contribution, and investment results of the funds offered. It was Warner's goal to reduce these benefits to a total retirement income of roughly 75% of final salary after 30 years of service.

Health and Life Insurance

A copy of ABC's current medical plan may be found as Exhibit 3. Under the plan, employees assumed little responsibility for their initial health-care expenditures. (See Exhibit 4 for the maximum cost to single and married employees at six different salary levels for medical expenses. Exhibit 5 shows the cost of medical expenses for high, medium and low charges for single and married employees at all salary levels.) Deductibles were low and the plan covered 100% of the first 70 days of hospital care and 85% of surgical costs. The so-called first dollar hospitalization benefits were expensive. Their costs, moreover, had been rising rapidly. Health care costs at ABC had increased nearly 60% during the past three years.

On the other hand, the existing health

plan set ceilings on its coverage. That meant that catastrophic illness could be financially devastating, particularly for lower-paid employees. Warner felt a more effective plan would make employees responsible for a large portion of initial medical expenses yet provide increased protection against catastrophic illness.

Another problem with the existing medical plan was that dental care was not available to all employees. In this respect the health plan was not uniform throughout the bank, since the recently-acquired Motor State Bank had a dental plan. Warner knew that ABC employees wanted a dental plan.

The existing life insurance at ABC provided survivors with an amount equal to two times salary up to a maximum of $200,000.

Stock/Thrift Plan

The major drawback of ABC's stock/thrift plan was that it required employees' contributions to be made in after-tax dollars. The bank then matched these contributions in the form of company stock. Ed Warner felt that a 401(k) plan, which allowed employees to make their contributions in before-tax dollars, would be popular with ABC employees. He recognized, however, that the Tax Reform Act of 1986 would make 401(k) plans less attractive than they were previously.

CONSULTANTS' INITIAL PRESENTATION

A few days later, John Mill, of Benefits Consultants, visited the bank and outlined his company's proposal for ABC. Mill proposed beginning work by developing what he called a "benefits strategy." He suggested that the kind of scanning that the bank's strategic planners routinely performed—of the demography and attitudes of the workforce and the bank's specific economic and business environments—was information that human resources needed in order to develop benefit and compensation plans that were consistent with the bank's strategy and the needs of its employees.

After analyzing the demographic and business environments in which the bank operated, Mill proposed to review the bank's five-year strategic plan to determine the future thrust of the business and what ABC's personnel needs were likely to be. Then the consultants would construct a demographic and compensation profile of the bank's current employees.

With both preliminary investigations in mind, Benefit Consultants would then compare the benefits yielded under the existing benefit program with the compensation available under new or redesigned programs. Mill estimated that the entire study would take 12 months to complete, and would cost the bank approximately $200,000.

After John Mill left, Warner and his colleagues argued about whether it might not be better to proceed directly to a flexible benefits program. Several of the human resources executives at the meeting felt that the preliminary parts of the study were side roads that would not only require a substantial expenditure of time and money but would also unnecessarily delay implementation of a flexible benefits program. Others believed that Benefit Consultants' approach was not only more likely to produce a long-term solution acceptable to the Big Five and the board, but it would also provide a framework in which to implement future changes. With some reluctance on the part of one or two executives, the management decided, after six weeks of discussion and debate, to engage Benefit Consultants.

MODERNIZING BENEFITS: AMERICAN BANKING CORPORATION STUDY QUESTIONS:

1. Describe your best estimate of the environments in which ABC will be operating. What changes would you expect in those environments in the next year; the next five years?

2. What is the bank's business strategy? How might an employee benefits strategy support it?

3. What goals would you establish for replacement income in the event of retirement, disability or death? Would those goals be measured in before-tax or after-tax dollars? Would they be the same for single and married employees?

4. What changes would you make in ABC's health benefits?

MODERNIZING BENEFITS: AMERICAN BANKING CORPORATION

Exhibit 1   Age and length of service of employees

Attained Age	Years of Service									Total
	5	5–9	10–14	15–19	20–24	25–29	30–34	35–39	40+	
<20	39	0	0	0	0	0	0	0	0	39
20–24	1,730	67	0	0	0	0	0	0	0	1,798
25–29	1,669	610	56	0	0	0	0	0	0	2,335
30–34	829	571	302	0	0	0	0	0	0	1,702
35–39	510	308	364	84	6	0	0	0	0	1,271
40–44	336	179	274	78	17	0	0	0	0	885
45–49	146	162	168	101	67	34	6	0	0	683
50–54	146	123	118	78	56	50	34	6	0	610
55–59	67	62	39	56	50	50	39	28	6	398
60–64	39	39	73	34	28	22	6	22	11	274
65–69	6	6	17	0	6	0	0	0	0	34
70+	0	11	0	0	0	6	6	0	0	22
Total number of employees	5,516	2,139	1,411	431	230	162	90	56	17	10,052

Count		Total Salary		Average Attained Age		Average Entry Age	
Men	Women	Men	Women	Men	Women	Men	Women
2,509	7,543	$60,995,200	$86,273,600	36.7	34.7	28.9	28

MODERNIZING BENEFITS: AMERICAN BANKING CORPORATION

Exhibit 2   ABC salary levels

	Number of Employees			Percent of Total	Cumulative Percent
Salary	Men	Women	Total		
<$10,000	224	2,542	2,766	27.5%	27.5%
$ 10,000<20,000	902	4,710	5,611	55.8	83.3
20,000<30,000	795	263	1,058	10.5	93.9
30,000<40,000	330	22	353	3.5	97.4
40,000<50,000	140	6	146	1.4	98.8
50,000<60,000	56	0	56	0.6	99.4
60,000<70,000	22	0	22	0.2	99.6
70,000<80,000	0	0	0	0.0	99.6
80,000<90,000	6	0	6	0.1	99.7
90,000<100,000	17	0	17	0.2	99.8
$100,000+	17	0	17	0.2	100.0
Total	2,509	7,543	10,052	100.0%	

MODERNIZING BENEFITS: AMERICAN BANKING CORPORATION

Exhibit 3   Summary of medical plan provisions

Hospital

Pays semiprivate room rate for 70 days
$1,000 in hospital services per confinement

Surgical

Pays 85% of reasonable and customary to a maximum of $5,000 per procedure

In-hospital doctor visits

$10 per day for 70 days

Outpatient diagnostic X-rays and laboratory tests

$100 per year

Major medical

Deductible: $100 per person with a maximum of $300 per year for a family
Coinsurance: 80%
Stop-loss limit: $1,000 per year
Maximum: $250,000

MODERNIZING BENEFITS: AMERICAN BANKING
CORPORATION

Exhibit 4 Medical expenses: maximum cost to employees (in dollars and as a percentage of salary)

Salary	Current Plan	
	Single	Married*
$ 10,000	$1,000 (10.0%)	$3,000 (30.0%)
15,000	1,000 (6.7%)	3,000 (20.0%)
20,000	1,000 (5.0%)	3,000 (15.0%)
25,000	1,000 (4.0%)	3,000 (12.0%)
50,000	1,000 (2.0%)	3,000 (6.0%)
100,000	1,000 (1.0%)	3,000 (3.0%)

* Assumes married employee with two dependents.

MODERNIZING BENEFITS:

Exhibit 5 Medical expenses for high, medium, and low charges for single and married employees at all salary levels

Level of Charges			Current Plan Payments	
Single Employees				
High:	Hospital	$2,650	100% Hospital	$2,650
	Surgical	1,730	85% Surgical	1,470
	Other	990	80% Other after $100 deductible	712
		$5,370	Total plan payment	$4,832
			Employee payment	$ 538
Medium:	Hospital	$ 0	100% Hospital	$ 0
	Surgical	370	85% Surgical	314
	Other	220	80% Other after $100 deductible	96
		$ 590		
			Total plan payment	$ 410
			Employee payment	$ 180
Low:	Hospital	$ 0	100% Hospital	$ 0
	Surgical	0	85% Surgical	0
	Other	220	80% Other after $100 deductible	96
		$ 220	Total plan payment	$ 96
			Employee payment	$ 124
Married Employees				
High:	Hospital	$4,240	100% Hospital	$4,240
	Surgical	2,670	85% Surgical	2,270
	Other	1,725	80% Other after $300 deductible	$1,140
		$8,635	Total plan payment	$7,150
			Employee payment	985
Medium:	Hospital	$ 0	100% Hospital	$ 0
	Surgical	900	85% Surgical	765
	Other	500	80% Other after $300 deductible	$ 160
		$1,400	Total plan payment	865
			Employee payment	435
Low:	Hospital	$ 0	100% Hospital	$ 0
	Surgical	0	85% Surgical	0
	Other	500	80% Other after $300 deductible	$ 160
		$ 500	Total plan payment	$ 160
			Employee payment	$ 340

VI

WORK RESTRUCTURING
AND MOTIVATION

This chapter, and its associated readings, give the student an opportunity to think through the conditions and requirements for effective participatory programs. Work restructuring has been a growing and an evolving phenomenon. An analysis by Richard E. Walton, in his insightful article on work innovations in the United States, is included in this section of the text.[1] Activity in the field during the late 1960s and early 1970s was primarily a response to so-called worker alienation. This response created a meaningful period of "job enrichment," which built upon an earlier concept of job enlargement. Further stimulus for the job enrichment response was the work of Douglas McGregor[2] with his "theory X and theory Y" and Frederick Herzberg's two-factor, "hygiene and motivator" theory of motivation. These developments will be reviewed in an attempt to highlight the essence of the trends.

According to Herzberg, the factors that created job dissatisfaction (job context) were different from those creating job satisfaction (job content). Removing sources of dissatisfaction led only to "no dissatisfaction." Job satisfaction resulted from improving job content by creating more challenging work—namely, job enrichment. A now nearly classic article by Frederick Herzberg, "One More Time: How Do You Motivate Employees?" (*Harvard Business Review*, January–February, 1968), outlines Herzberg's theory and discusses a successful application of job enrichment to a group of stockholder correspondents. The specific manner in which jobs were enriched is discussed.

Various approaches to job enrichment

---

[1] Richard E. Walton, "Work Innovations in the United States," *Harvard Business Review*, July–August, 1979, pp. 88–98.

[2] Particularly *The Human Side of Enterprise* (New York: McGraw-Hill, 1960).

were developed during this period, as pointed out by Fred K. Foulkes at that time (*Creating More Meaningful Work*, American Management Association, 1969). Shorter or longer lists of enrichment factors or principles were used; one such list follows:

1. Remove some controls without removing accountability
2. Increase accountability of individuals for their own work
3. Give individuals a whole natural unit of work
4. Give added authority to do or decide—job freedom
5. Make reports directly available to the worker himself rather than to supervisor—direct feedback
6. Introduce new and more difficult tasks
7. Assign specific or specialized tasks—aid employees to become experts

While Foulkes found that the essence of the enrichment process was much the same regardless of the list of principles applied, there was one fundamental difference in approach—the use or absence of employee participation in the process. Herzberg, in his article, was decidedly negative toward employee participation. But an evolutionary development in work restructuring has been toward approaches utilizing employee participation. This was true, for example, with respect to the work done within the American Telephone and Telegraph Company.[3] Foulkes's work also made it clear that elements in job *context* did count in terms of the relative degree of success of different enrichment programs. Relatively poor applications of job enrichment tended to be associated with a nonsupportive organizational climate or with authoritarian managerial styles or other such barriers.

Foulkes concluded that a major barrier to successful job design programs was supervisory attitudes and behavior. Job enrichment, in the final analysis, generally involved supervisory risk-taking. In many companies, where managers tend to be rewarded for short-run bottom-line results, managers and supervisors feel uncomfortable in taking job enrichment risks, for the benefits are generally in the long term.

While job enrichment as such no longer occupies center stage, and some well known company enrichment programs have lost their original dynamic character, the fundamentals of job enrichment are to be found in nearly all work restructuring programs and activities. However, as Walton emphasizes, "Attention shifted during 1972–1975 to a relatively few visible experiment-solutions to worker disaffection, such as the highly participative work system in General Food's plant at Topeka, Kansas; Volvo's pioneering modifications of the car assembly line; and the industrial democracy project at the Bolivar, Tennessee, plant of Harmon Industries, sponsored jointly by the management and the UAW."[4]

These projects had strong elements of "industrial democracy" in their approach to work restructuring and also were, to a degree, "autonomous work group" experiments. However, prior to discussing these plans and approaches, recognition should be given to the fact that since the early days of the modern labor movement, there have always been a small number of active union-management cooperation plans. The Scanlon Plan is perhaps the best known of these cooperative approaches. While Scanlon Plans vary somewhat, participation is typically achieved through a two-level committee system

---

[3] See "World of Work Report," *Work in American Institute, Inc.*, Vol. 4, No. 7, July, 1979.

[4] Richard E. Walton, "1977 Perspectives on Work Restructuring," *Sociotechnical Systems: A Sourcebook*, ed. W. A. Pasmoore and J. Sherwood (La Jolla, CA: University Associates, 1978).

that receives and considers employee suggestions to improve efficiency and cut costs. The savings achieved are paid in whole or in part to employees through a uniform percentage plantwide bonus. This type of bonus arrangement is sometimes called a "plantwide incentive plan." While particular Scanlon Plan applications have come and gone, many have lasted for a long time and have contributed substantially to the productivity and morale of the companies involved.

A single in-depth study of one Scanlon Plan and a review of twenty-two studies (forty-four firms) is contained in *A Plant-Wide Productivity Plan in Action: Three Years of Experience with the Scanlon Plan, May 1975.*[5] While study of the successful operation of the individual plan (DeSota, Inc., Chemical Coatings Division) is very worthy of attention, the review of twenty-two studies gives a good overview of experiences with the Scanlon Plan. The implementation of the plan in these forty-four firms was judged a success in thirty cases and a failure in fourteen. Those judged failures typically operated only for short periods of time. The successes frequently lasted for substantial periods of years. The successes were judged to involve "very good" union-management cooperation and produced roughly a 10 percent or higher bonus. A modest rather than a spectacular bonus characterized the more successful plans. Perhaps the most characteristic feature of successful plans was a steady and significant flow of valid cost-saving suggestions.

While various reasons are stated for plan failures, no reasons are given for the termination of successful plans. One of the authors, who is familiar with a number of successful Scanlon Plan operations, would hazard that termination of successful

plans has usually resulted from changes in management or union leadership which, in turn, is frequently associated with changes in the ownership of the companies.

Successful Scanlon Plans have been dependent upon unusual union and management leadership. Unusual union leadership is required to suggest or support cooperation with management. Even in a union-management relationship of good accommodation, a union leader is rarely willing to suggest a plan of cooperation to improve the efficiency of the company. In much the same fashion, it requires a most unusual management to desire the cooperation of the union in improving efficiency.

A meaningful book that goes well beyond an analysis of the Scanlon Plan as such is *The Scanlon Plan for Organization Development: Identity, Participation, and Equity.*[6] The book opens by noting that the Scanlon Plan is "a philosophy, a theory of organization, and a set of management principles." Following two orientation chapters, analytical chapters are devoted to the following essential conditions for successful implementation: (1) "The First Condition: Identification of the Organization and of the Employees;" (2) "The Second Condition: Opportunity to Participate and Become Responsible," and (3) "The Third Condition: Realization of Equity." The book concludes with discussions of earlier and more recent research on the Scanlon Plan.[7]

[5] The National Commission on Productivity and Work Quality, Washington, DC 20036.

[6] Carl F. Frost, John H. Wakeley, and Robert A. Ruh, Michigan State University Press, 1974.

[7] Several articles stemming from this same research also should be noted: (1) "What Employees Think of the Scanlon Plan," Robert K. Goodman, J. H. Wakeley, and R. H. Ruh, *Personnel*, September–October, 1972; (2) "An Approach to Increased Productivity: The Scanlon Plan," Timothy L. Ross and Gardner M. Jones, *Financial Executive*, February 1972; and (3) "Why America Can't Afford to Overlook the Human Side of Productivity," Joseph V. Barks and Keith W. Bennett, *Iron Age*, October 1, 1979, p. 28.

The research underlying this analytical treatment of the Scanlon Plan and "participative decision making" was done in companies that were or had been members of the Scanlon Plan Associates, a nonprofit group of companies constituting a center of Scanlon Plan activity developed at Michigan State University under the leadership of Dr. Carl Frost. Activity in this group went beyond traditional Scanlon Plan implementation, in that nonunion companies participated and a "value-added" ratio was utilized in some companies.

Historically Scanlon Plan bonus arrangements were built upon a base standard ratio of payroll to "sales value of production"—that is, sales plus (or minus) inventory increases (or decreases). (Scanlon himself urged an all-inclusive president-to-sweeper payroll participation.) With this simple ratio, if conditions undergo fundamental change, such as drastic alteration in product mix or major technological alterations, the ratio is to be revised.[8] In contrast to the Scanlon ratio, the Rucker Plan was based on production worker payroll to the "value-added" sales value of production—that is, raw materials were excluded. This ratio rarely required modification. In fact, Alan Rucker devised his entire approach from the constancy of this ratio in manufacturing census data over the many years such data had existed. Some members of the Scanlon Plan Associates use a value-added ratio which, no doubt, lends stability to the implementation of the plan. In point of fact, Scanlon Plan ratios historically rarely require alteration.

The essence of the Frost, Wakeley, and Ruh book is to be found in its three conditions for successful implementation. Each of these conditions warrants comment. Identification of the past achievements of the organization, of its problems, and of its competitive potential is a necessary first step, and must be an ongoing process, to establish and to maintain participation. Realistic identification through group discussion of the competitive strengths and weaknesses of the organization is the basis upon which both organizational and individual goals and objectives can and should be set. Identifying the unique elements in the organization's survival and growth potential is the fundamental characteristic of this particular process. The second condition, the opportunity to participate and become responsible, is achieved through the two-level suggestion system, and it is this continuing suggestion activity which integrates individual and corporate goals. Finally, equity is built into the system through the gain-sharing bonus arrangement. Financial savings resulting from improvements in efficiency are shared with all employees participating in the plan by means of an equal percentage payment to all employees. The reader is urged to study the Frost, Wakeley, and Ruh book to develop an improved understanding of the motivational dimensions of successful Scanlon Plan implementation. The conditions for successful implementation obviously are applicable to most consultative participation plans regardless of the technical characteristics of the plan.

Most participation plans appear to be of the consultative type; that is, some form of mechanism in which management officials accept or reject suggestions for productivity improvements made by employees. By 1980 an approach similar to the Scanlon Plan, "Quality Circles" had taken off and been implemented by some

[8] For those interested in Scanlon Plan implementation, see Brian E. Moore and Timothy L. Ross, *The Scanlon Way to Improved Productivity: A Practical Guide* (New York: Wiley, 1978). See also as an earlier reference, *The Scanlon Plan—A Frontier in Labor-Management Cooperation*, Frederick G. Lesieur, ed. (New York: The Technology Press of M.I.T. and Wiley, 1958).

sixty-five companies.[9] By 1985 some 1500 enrichment programs were reported to be in existence.

Quality circles, practiced extensively in Japan, is a process in which small groups of employees meet regularly, after training, to discover, and solve through group discussion, production problems in their areas. An interesting analysis of the quality circle approach and one application is by Robert H. Guest, "Quality of Work Life—Learning from Tarrytown."[10]

The Tarrytown QWL (quality of work life) program brought drastic positive change at this General Motors assembly plant. Union-management relations had been extremely antagonistic, with continuous conflict over massive numbers of grievances. Employee morale was low, with high labor turnover, excessive absenteeism, and poor workmanship. Efficiency was low and costs were high. By 1979 the relationship with the United Automobile Workers was highly positive, an open, problem-solving, participatory employee relations climate had been created, and the plant was an efficient one.

The factors initiating and sustaining this change at Tarrytown were unique and complex. The reasons for change included:

1. Top corporate and union support for a participatory approach as embodied in the 1973 labor agreement language which created the GM-UAW National Committee to Improve the Quality of Work Life. At the national level the leadership of Irving Bluestone, vice president, United Automobile Workers, has been particularly important, as has been the corporate staff support of Delmar L. Landen, director, Organizational Research and Development, General Motors Corporation.

2. The initiatives of a plant manager who felt that "there must be a better way" coupled with the felt need for change by both parties.

3. The patient support of the local union committee and the leadership of a persistent local-level union-management QWL group that did not give up when confronted with a variety of business and technological obstacles.

4. An initial nonadversarial training endeavor to which both parties contributed and which was an essential starting point.

5. The momentum of accomplishment and the intrinsic individual rewards in enhanced dignity and respect from active participation in solving difficult problems.

GM and the UAW have made substantial progress in their relationship through a rapidly expanding number of QWL programs. By 1985 some degree of activity was reported to exist in every plant. The GM-Toyota venture, New United Motor Manufacturing, Inc. (NUMMI), in Fremont, California, is reported to reflect a new degree of cooperation with the UAW and new status for the work force. Featuring teams, worker participation, and much flexibility through a multiple job concept, the plant is reported to be 20 to 40% more efficient than most GM plants. Through its success at NUMMI and at other GM plants, GM has been spreading the teamwork concept to all its plants. In the aggregate, these programs represent both a major change from the past in the management of people and a noteworthy accomplishment by the parties.

Participation going beyond consultation may be described as decision making by "autonomous work groups." In this type of participation management gives decision-making power to the employee group. One of the best known examples of this approach, now much modified, was

[9] *Wall Street Journal*, February 21, 1980, page 48. The characteristics of quality circles are described in this article.

[10] *Harvard Business Review*, July–August, 1979, pp. 76–78.

the Topeka plant of the Pet Foods Division of General Foods. The characteristics of the system can best be captured in a fairly long quotation from *Work in America.*[11]

> *Autonomous work groups*—Self-management work teams were formed and given collective responsibility for larger segments of the production process. The teams are composed of from eight to 12 members—large enough to cover a full set of tasks, and small enough to allow effective face-to-face meetings for decision-making and coordination. The teams decide who will do what tasks, and most members learn to do each other's jobs, both for the sake of variety and to be able to cover for a sick or absent co-worker.
>
> *Integrated support functions*—Activities typically performed by maintenance, quality control, custodial, industrial engineering, and personnel units were built into the operating team's responsibilities. The teams accepted both first and final responsibility for performing quality tests and ensuring that they maintained quality standards.
>
> *Challenging job assignments*—An attempt was made to design every set of tasks in a way that would include functions requiring higher human abilities and responsibilities. The basic technology employed in the plant had been designed to eliminate dull or routine jobs insofar as possible. Still, some nonchallenging but basic tasks remained. The team member responsible for these operations is given other tasks that are mentally more demanding. The housekeeping activities were included in every assignment—despite the fact that they contributed nothing to enriching the work—in order to avoid having members of the plant community who did nothing but cleaning.
>
> *Job mobility and rewards for learning*—The aim was to make all sets of tasks equally challenging although each set would comprise unique skill demands. Consistent with

this aim was a single job classification for all operators, with pay increases geared to mastering an increasing proportion of jobs, first within the team and then in the total plant. Thus, team members were rewarded for learning more and more aspects of the total manufacturing system. Because there were no limits to how many team members could qualify for higher pay brackets, employees were encouraged to teach each other.

> *Facilitative leadership*—In lieu of supervisors whose responsibilities are to plan, direct, and control the work of subordinates, a team leader position was created with the responsibility to facilitate team development and decision making. It is envisioned that in time the team leader position might not be required.
>
> *Managerial decision information for operators*—The design of the new plant called for providing operators with economic information and managerial decision rules. This enables production decisions ordinarily made at the second level of supervision to be made at the operator level.
>
> *Self-government for the plant community*—Management refrained from specifying in advance any plant rules; rather, it was committed to let the rules evolve from collective experience.
>
> *Congruent physical and social context*—Differential status symbols that characterize traditional work organizations were minimized in the new plant—for example, by a parking lot open to all regardless of position, single office-plant entrance, and common decor throughout office, cafeteria, and locker room. The technology and architecture were designed to facilitate rather than discourage the congregating of team members during working hours. The assumption was that these ad hoc meetings often would be enjoyable human exchanges as well as opportunities to coordinate work and to learn about each other's jobs.

Using standard principles, industrial engineers had indicated that 110 workers would be needed to man the plant. But when the team concept (rather than individual assignments) was applied, and when support

---

[11] Reprinted from "Report of a Special Task Force to the Secretary of Health, Education, and Welfare," *Work in America*, Ch. 4, pp. 96–98. By permission of The MIT Press, Cambridge, Mass. © 1973 The MIT Press, Cambridge, Mass.

activities were integrated into team responsibilities, the result was a manning level of less than 70 workers. While this 40% smaller work force is impressive, it is not the major economic benefit, because labor costs per unit are not a large percentage of the cost of goods sold in this particular business. The major economic benefit has come from such factors as improved yields, minimized waste, and avoidance of shutdowns. Significantly, these are productivity items that are related to technology but are especially sensitive to the work attitudes of operators.

The above system no longer exists in its original form,[12] but the original plan illustrates the extent to which employee decision making may be extended. While autonomous work groups can be established with less extensive power than in the Topeka case, this is not the major point at issue. The major point, discussed subsequently, is that group decision making impinges upon managerial authority far more than consultative groups. Autonomous work groups may make extensive improvements in efficiency, as was the case at Topeka, but they are not directly under management control. Some groups have worked out poorly so far as the achievement of managerial goals is concerned. Consultation or suggestion type plans do not carry this degree of managerial risk.

Employee participation plans are not widespread nor are plans of union-management cooperation. An important reason for their restricted use is management fear of constraints upon its right to manage. This is an important topic for student consideration, but students should also recognize that management may achieve objectives through employee participation that would be next to impossible with more traditional relationships.

[12] "Stonewalling Plant Democracy," *Business Week*, March 28, 1977, p. 78.

A most interesting example of work restructuring, combining consultation and group decision making is Volvo. Volvo adopted work restructuring as a response to high employee turnover, high absenteeism, poor quality of workmanship, and other employee and productivity problems. The Volvo response too has been an evolving one. Perhaps the most discussed Volvo plant has been Kalmar. Quoting from an article by Volvo president Pehr Gyllenhammar:

The design for Kalmar incorporated pleasant, quiet surroundings, arranged for group working, with each group having its own individual rest and meeting areas. The work itself is organized so that each group is responsible for a particular, identifiable portion of the car—electrical systems, interiors, doors, and so on. Individual cars are built up on self-propelling "carriers" that run around the factory following a movable conductive tape on the floor. Computers normally direct the carriers, but manual controls can override the taped route. If someone notices a scratch in the paint on a car, he or she can immediately turn the carrier back to the painting station. Under computer control again, the car will return later to the production process wherever it left off.

Each work group has its own buffer areas for incoming and outgoing carriers so it can pace itself as it wishes and organize the work inside its own area so that its members work individually or in subgroups to suit themselves. Most of the employees have chosen to learn more than one small job; the individual increase in skills also gives the team itself added flexibility.

To gain a sense of identification with its work, a group must also take responsibility for its work. The myriad inspection stations with "watchdog" overtones that characterize most factories have been abandoned at Kalmar. Instead, each team does its own inspection. After a car passes about three work-group stations, it passes through a special inspection station where people with special training test each car. A computer-based system takes quality information reports from these stations and, if there are any persistent or recurring problems, flashes the results to the proper group station, telling them also how they solved similar problems the last time. The computer also informs the teams when their work has been particularly problem-free.

When we started at Kalmar, we made the assumption that the productivity could equal that of any comparable traditional plant. Today we have not one but five new plants, organized in a nontraditional way, all scaled for 600 employees or less. These new plants cost a little bit more to build than traditional factories of similar size, but they are already showing good productivity. We believe productivity will continue to increase because the people who work in them have better jobs. One of the most important measures of our success came in autumn 1976 when we received the results of a union survey of all Kalmar employees. Almost all of them were in favor of the new working patterns; one result of the survey has been to increase our focus on working groups at other plants.[13]

One can only hope to catch some of the dynamics of development at Volvo in these brief statements. *The Volvo Report*, by Rolf Lindholm and Jan-Peder Norstedt (The Swedish Employer's Confederation, Stockholm, 1975), provides a more comprehensive survey and analysis of work restructuring at Volvo. Some selected considerations deserve particular emphasis. In the first place, the enormous improvement in working conditions, with greatly reduced noise levels (an average of about 65 db at Kalmar) is enough in itself to have enhanced markedly the attractiveness of the work environment. Second, while the assembly line as such has been

abolished, and employees have an important element of freedom, assembly still requires considerable control. Volvo is not a "free-wheeling" job enrichment environment. In the third place, important elements in the system are negotiated with the union, such as compensation, the effort level, and the speed of the line. In an important sense, Volvo is an example of union-management cooperation in which the union has a strong voice.

In the fourth place, certain characteristics of work restructuring stand out: (1) Participation methods in use are constantly being adapted to new circumstances. (2) Jobs in which the worker is rigidly tied to a fixed speed and a fixed set of movements are being radically modified. (3) Job rotation and work in teams are being applied increasingly widely. (4) Mechanization of heavy and tiring work has been accomplished at more and more plants. (5) The purely physical work environment is undergoing constant improvement. (6) New types of jobs and work methods are continuously being developed.

Finally, the constructive nature of the managerial response to a set of problems obviously owes a great deal to the active involvement of Pehr G. Gyllenhammar and the young managers associated with him. Volvo, on the one hand, has been accused of being softheaded and oblivious to the importance of profitability, and, on the other hand, of being obsessed with profitability and of using changes in the organization of work to manipulate employees. Perhaps the balance between these twin objectives is crucial to understanding the Volvo experience and successful implementation of other employee participation programs.

Work restructuring appears without much doubt to be increasingly utilized. Walton expresses the view that it is in the rapidly expanding stage of a typical

[13] Reprinted by permission of the *Harvard Business Review*. Excerpt from "How Volvo Adapts Work to People" by Pehr G. Gyllenhammar (July–August 1977). Copyright © 1977 by the President and Fellows of Harvard College; all rights reserved.

S-shaped growth curve. Also it appears that quite regularly new approaches appear on the industrial scene.

A second new approach, pioneered some years ago by Edward J. Feeney at Emery Air Freight Corporation,[14] which has gained a meaningful number of adherents in recent years, is behavior modification or positive reinforcement. *Business Week* reported that some 100 major companies, including Frito-Lay, 3M, Adressograph-Multigraph, B.F. Goodrich, Warner-Lambert, and others, used this approach and obtained substantial increases in productivity. Another approach is "deep sensing";[15] again, favorable results are reported by a number of major companies. The focus in this approach is monthly "sensing" meetings held by executives. Employees are encouraged to express their gripes in no-holds-barred meetings. Similar approaches are given consideration in the chapter of this book on feedback mechanisms.

As one looks back over the years, there is and has been a fad element in the various approaches that have gained and lost popularity. While there has been much similarity among approaches, there have also been important differences. Most important, perhaps, has been the general trend toward increased emphasis, in one or another form, on employee participation. Various approaches have been implemented successfully under favorable circumstances. On the other hand, no approach is always successful. As with so many aspects of personnel management, the manner of implementation is crucial.

An important element in successful implementation is balance in goals. One goal of work restructuring has been to increase employee productivity and another goal

has been to improve the quality of work life. Increasingly both goals have been recognized as necessary. In a union-management environment and also under nonunion conditions, it is believed, major emphasis on worker productivity exclusively will very likely doom a program to failure. Unions and employees will not cooperate unless they are convinced that management has a sincere interest in improving the quality of work life. Unions want no part of a disguised speedup. In a nonunion program, management integrity will be tested by its sincerity in improving working conditions. Perhaps most advocates of participate work restructuring would place primary emphasis, as found by Frost, Wakeley and Ruh, on creating a favorable employee relations climate. On the other hand, an essential element in the employee climate is acceptance by employees and union officials of the legitimacy of striving for improvement in the competitive position of the company while preserving equity for employees. A healthy plan, whether it is a Volvo or a Scanlon Plan, requires balance in its objectives.

Another favorable evolutionary development is that work restructuring is being implemented within a longer-term perspective. What is of basic significance in this regard is that managements increasingly have come to the point of view that changes in the manner in which people are managed are not only desirable but inevitable. If management shifts away from an authoritarian approach, then work restructuring will no longer be a program, but a way of life. Again, as noted by Walton, the managerial beliefs under which work restructuring now takes place are increasingly eclectic. There is less argument today as to whether extrinsic rewards (pay and advancement) or intrinsic rewards (work satisfaction) are more important. Increasingly, balanced goals are seen as essential.

[14] See *Business Week*, January 23, 1978, p. 56.
[15] See "Deep Sensing: A Pipeline to Employee Morale," *Business Week*, January 29, 1977, p. 124.

Related to the development of balanced objectives has been, perhaps, somewhat more meaningful motivational theory, including consistency theory, equity theory, and particularly expectancy theory. Wendell L. French provides an excellent survey of this entire topic.[16] The fact, however, is that there is no comprehensive theory of motivation, and each of the various theories has its controversial elements.

While only a small number of unionized companies have taken the initiative to attempt to develop formal plans for union-management cooperation, the number of such plans is growing. Employee involvement and joint labor-management action have been part of the negotiations between the Communications Workers of America (CWA) and American Telephone and Telegraph (AT&T) during the eighties. In 1980 the CWA and AT&T, as part of a national agreement, established a joint labor-management committee to respond to matters of mutual concern. The 1983 agreement, the last before divestiture broke up the Bell system, not only reaffirmed the parties' commitment to quality of working life, but also extended joint action to other areas, including a Common Interest Forum of top-level labor and management representatives. One purpose of the forum was to monitor the QWL process.

The 1986 contract contained additional breakthroughs. In addition to a jointly administered training and retraining program, the agreement took the parties a step further toward self-managed work teams. The contract commits the company and the union to joint selection, design, implementation, and evaluation of experimental work design projects. The reason for such projects, as written in the contract, is "to explore how a more participa-

tive style of operation and management can contribute to enhancing effectiveness, productivity, and the delegation of responsibility and authority to levels closest to the actual work process." These agreements are designed to increase the role of participation and multilevel cooperation in dealing effectively with the problems raised by technology, divestiture, employee insecurity, and the new attention being given to customer service and marketing.

In nonunion companies as well, more managements have become interested in employee participation programs. In the United States, one of the leading companies with respect to participative management, teams, and bonuses based on team performance has been Motorola. The company's Participative Management Program (PMP) consists of three basic elements—participation in the form of teams, goal setting with realistic measurements and communication of results, and rewards and appropriate recognition. Motorola's manufacturing teams, for example, are small and cross-functional, and the time period for feedback of operating results is one month. When asked to describe the essence of PMP, James Burge, corporate vice president, described it as follows:

> PMP is a centralized structure with much flexibility for local adaptation to the characteristics of each business unit. It is a management system, not a plug-in program, and is management encouragement and support of teamwork, idea sharing and mutual trust. Furthermore, it is increased communication, more decision-making at the most appropriate level, more employee responsibility, and a financial sharing of the benefits of improved productivity between the employees and the company.

Burge felt that financial sharing was important because it put the stamp of cred-

---

[16] *The Personnel Management Process*, 4th ed. (Boston: Houghton Mifflin, 1978), Ch. 6.

ibility on PMP: "That's when our employees realized that the company was serious and that this wasn't just another buzzword program that would run its course and disappear in due time."

In these situations relatively negative managerial attitudes are related to a fear of erosion of management authority. While there is an element of risk for management in participatory programs, there is certainly no necessary loss, and there may well be a gain, in the ability of management to achieve its objectives. This is most obviously the case with union or nonunion consultative programs.

There is no reason to believe, for instance, that a Scanlon Plan or quality circles will threaten management authority. Under such systems management gains respect by making honest decisions on suggestions. Accepting poor suggestions is not in the interest of the union, the management, nor the employees. Able management gains in status under such a system. It is true, however, that weak first-level supervisors do not survive; the challenge of employee suggestions highlights their managerial weaknesses. The period of introduction of a participatory plan is a rough one for first-line supervision. But, as such a plan continues, good management wins respect and technological and other changes can be made more readily than in a traditional union-management relationship. A good case can be made that management authority is strengthened, not weakened, under a successful participatory program.

Managerial behavior should be similar in its administration in a nonunion employee participation plan. The greatest danger in both union and nonunion situations is that supervisors will not respond wholeheartedly to good employee suggestions because of fear that their own competence is being called into question. If employees are put down when they come forward with suggestions, the flow of suggestions will cease. Competent supervisors are not likely to feel threatened by employee suggestions. Much depends upon the attitude of higher management officials and the climate of employee relations. The conditions for success with any participation plan are essentially as analyzed by Frost, Wakeley, and Ruh.

Autonomous work groups and group decision making by employees involve a higher degree of managerial risk taking than do suggestion plans, though it appears that the conditions for success are fundamentally similar. Group decision making by definition fetters management authority. A group may come up with a particular decision very different from the one that would have been made within a managerial hierarchy. However, again granting a positive employee relations climate with integration of individual and organizational goals, group decisions may well be superior, on balance, to hierarchical decisions. In no properly functioning system has management abdicated.

The president of Volvo, Pehr G. Gyllenhammar, gives a very interesting negative answer to any adverse impact of changes at Volvo upon management authority. In his article, "How Volvo Adapts Work to People," in the July–August 1977 issue of *Harvard Business Review*, Gyllenhammar states:

(1) "I don't believe the new values and new laws call for 'permissiveness'. Instead, I think managers have to be stronger and more disciplined. It is the weak people in management who have difficulties dealing with employee representatives. . . ." (2) "In this atmosphere of employee participation and rapid change, management is an exacting task. If you don't manage tautly, you can drift into inefficiency that endangers the entire venture." (3) "Participation demands more work, not less, from everybody. Idle people become bored and sloppy, so it is an

important part of the manager's job to be taking the temperature all the time, injecting some of his or her own alertness whenever he or she senses signs of apathy or boredom. As other companies have learned—and so have we—the manager who is reluctant or just gives lip service to the idea of participation can hold back employee-based changes that are actually in the best interest of both the corporation and its employees." (pages 112–113; see footnote 13)

Arnold S. Tannenbaum, University of Michigan, expresses a similar view:[17]

Participation is often thought to imply taking power from managers and giving it to subordinates, but in fact managers need not exercise less control where there is participation. A reduction in managerial power *may* occur but it need not, and there is evidence to suggest that participation may be a means through which managers actually increase their own control along with that of workers. Thus, contrary to stereotypes that assume participation to be a vaguely permissive or laissez-faire system, the participative organization may be one in which the *total amount of control* is higher than in the nonparticipative organization. There is no escaping the need for some system of control in organizations, participative organizations included, and the success of participative approaches hinges not on reducing control, but on achieving a system of control that is more effective than that of other systems.

While continued growth in the number of companies adopting formal employee participation programs is to be expected, study of the conditions for successful implementation of such systems has decided significance for all companies desirous of

improving the management of human resources. More and more normal managerial procedures involve informal employee participation programs. Communication meetings at all levels require constructive response to employee suggestions, and meetings should be so conducted as to elicit the views of those participating. Forums for management training and development will bring forth challenges to existing policies and practices. Formal and informal grievance procedures in union and nonunion organizations require constructive response to a wide variety of problems. The bottom line in the management of human resources is the creation of an open and positive climate of employee relations. Such a climate inherently requires participatory methods of management.

There is today considerable and valuable literature on work restructuring. Students can achieve a good beginning in the understanding of this topic by: (1) analysis and discussion of Xerox and the ACTWU case study; (2) study of the Walton article on work innovations in the United States; and (3) the perceptive analysis by Frost, Wakeley, and Ruh in their book on the Scanlon Plan.

Xerox and the ACTWU is a fascinating and comprehensive case study that begins in 1980. It is centered in Xerox's home manufacturing complex in Webster, a suburb of Rochester, New York, during a time in which Xerox's competitive position in the market was threatened. Eight critical episodes are highlighted in the case, beginning with a joint union-management decision to establish a program on employee involvement and ending with the 1986 negotiations that strengthened the participative efforts not only with the continuation of the no-layoff policy, but also with the exploration of new forms of rewards and recognition. Study of the sequence of events reveals the ex-

[17] *Organizational Behavior: Research and Issues*, eds. George Strauss, Raymond E. Miles, Charles C. Snow, and Arnold S. Tannenbaum (Madison, WI: Industrial Relations Research Association, 1974, p. 78).

tent to which the parties' capacity to pursue common interests depended on their ability to resolve deep conflicts.

BIBLIOGRAPHY: WORK RESTRUCTURING AND MOTIVATION

ADIZES, ICHAK. *Industrial Democracy: Yugoslav Style.* New York: Free Press, 1971.

BERNSTEIN, PAUL. *Workplace Democratization: Its Internal Dynamics.* New Brunswick, NJ: Transaction Books, 1980.

BLACKER, F. H. M. *Job Redesign and Management Control: Studies in British Leyland and Volvo.* New York: Praeger, 1978.

BLAUNDER, ROBERT. *Alienation and Freedom: The Factory Worker and His Industry.* Chicago: University of Chicago Press, 1964.

DAVIS, LOUIS E., AND ALBERT B. CHERNS. *The Quality of Working Life: Two Volumes.* New York: The Free Press, 1975.

EMERY, FRED, AND EINAR THORSRUD. *Democracy at Work: The Report of the Norwegian Industrial Democracy Program.* Leiden, the Netherlands: Martinus Nijhoff Social Sciences Division, 1976.

FOULKES, FRED K. *Creating More Meaningful Work.* New York: American Management Association, 1969.

GREENBERG, PAUL D., AND EDWARD M. GLASER. *Some Issues in Joint Union-Management Quality of Worklife Improvement Efforts.* Kalamazoo, MI: The W. E. Upjohn Institute for Employment Research, 1980.

GYLLENHAMMAR, PEHR G. *People at Work.* Reading, MA: Addison-Wesley, 1977.

HACKMAN, J. RICHARD, AND GREG R. OLDHAM. *Work Redesign.* Reading, MA: Addison-Wesley, 1980.

HERRICK, N. Q. (ed.). *Improving Government: Experiments with Quality of Working Life Systems.* New York: Praeger, 1983.

LOFTUS, JOSEPH A., AND BEATRICE WALFISH (eds.). *Breakthroughs in Union-Management Cooperation.* Scarsdale, NY: Work in American Institute, Inc., 1977.

LUND, ROBERT, AND JOHN A. HANSEN. *Keeping America at Work: Strategies for Employing the New Technologies.* New York: Wiley, 1986.

O'TOOLE, JAMES. *Work and the Quality of Life: Resource Papers for Work in America.* Cambridge, MA: MIT Press, 1974.

ROSOW, JEROME M. (ed.). *Teamwork: Joint Labor Management Programs in America.* New York: Pergamon Press, 1986.

TERKEL, STUDS. *American Dreams.* New York: Pantheon Books. 1980.

———. *Working.* New York: Pantheon Books, 1974.

VROOM, VICTOR H. *Work and Motivation.* New York: Wiley, 1964.

———, AND ARTHUR G. JAGO. *The New Leadership: Managing Participation in Organizations.* Englewood Cliffs, NJ: Prentice Hall, 1988.

WALTERS, ROY W., & ASSOCIATES, INC. *Job Enrichment for Results: Strategies for Successful Implementation.* Reading, MA: Addison-Wesley, 1975.

WALTON, RICHARD E., AND LEONARD A. SCHLESINGER. *The Structure and Meaning of Work.* New York: Wiley, 1980.

Xerox and the ACTWU:
Tracing a Transformation in Industrial Relations

INTRODUCTION

From 1976 to 1982, Xerox's share of worldwide copier revenues dropped from eighty-two percent to forty-one percent.[1] The company was facing unprecedented competition from corporations such as Canon, Ricoh, Kodak, IBM, 3M, Minolta, Océ, Savin, Konishiroku, Mita, Toshiba, Panasonic, Royal , and Pitney Bowes. This was a marketplace filled with firms renowned for their capabilities in sales, service, manufacturing, and product development. Meeting this challenge and regaining significant market share, which Xerox has done, has required dramatic change throughout a Corporation that employs over 100,000 people.

Xerox's competitive resurgence has earned it a reputation as a leading case of "beating the Japanese at their own game."[2] Public attention has particularly focused on the transformation of product development, sales, and service—involving, in each case, a return to the principles and dynamism that characterized Xerox's early years. Though less in the spotlight, similar changes in manufacturing are notable, in part, since they preceded and influenced changes elsewhere in the corporation. Moreover, since this portion of the Xerox Corporation is unionized, the experience in manufacturing speaks directly to the concerns of many other unions and managers facing similar economic and social pressures. For both reasons, it is the developments in manufacturing that will be the focus here.[3]

[1] Xerox includes the parent Xerox Corporation (The Haloid Company was founded in 1906, became Haloid Xerox, Inc. in 1958, and the Xerox Corporation in 1961.); Rank Xerox Limited (A fifty-fifty partnership with the Rank Organization Limited in the United Kingdom that was created in 1956; in 1969 Xerox bought an additional share, giving it majority ownership); and Fuji Xerox Company, Limited (A fifty-fifty partnership created in 1962 between Rank Xerox and Fuji Photo Film of Japan).

Prepared by Joel Cutcher-Gershenfeld, Industrial Relations Section, Massachusetts Institute of Technology, September 1987. © Joel Cutcher-Gershenfeld, 1987.

This research was conducted under the auspices of the Industrial Relations Section at the Sloan School of Management at the Massachusetts Institute of Technology. Support for the research was provided by the U.S. Department of Labor, Bureau of Labor-Management Relations and Cooperative Programs (Contract No. J 9-P-4-0021). Except where otherwise noted, the case is based on over one hundred interviews conducted during the last three years, archival analysis, and other sources of information at Xerox and ACTWU. The support and assistance of the employees, union officials, and managers at Xerox and ACTWU is deeply appreciated. This case was further enriched by input from the full research team associated with the DOL study—especially Thomas Kochan, who introduced me to the parties at Xerox and ACTWU and has contributed to the development of the research at every stage.

[2] Gary Jacobson and John Hillkirk, *Xerox: American Samurai*, New York: Macmillan Publishing Company, 1986.

[3] The larger set of corporate changes, while certainly of interest, is well beyond the scope of this case. Developments in other parts of Xerox will be noted only to the extent that they directly influence or derive from changing patterns of labor-management relations in manufacturing. Issues of diffusion within manufacturing, will, however, receive direct attention at a number of points in the case.

So many collaborative efforts in unionized settings have begun narrowly focused around employee involvement, only to be overwhelmed by contentious issues such as layoffs, disinvestment, and the lack of a sharing of the gains. A handful of unionized cases have so embraced the importance of cooperation that they have gone to an extreme characteristic of some non-union cooperative efforts, in which there is little room for internal dissent. This case illustrates the dynamics of a third alternative, which is an expansion and institutionalization of the collaborative effort in conjunction with a continued recognition of the legitimacy of conflict and the importance of the institutions of collective bargaining. The case is notable since it traces what might now be considered a transformed employment relationship in an established, unionized worksite—without the construction of a new facility or the recruitment of a new (presumably non-union) workforce.

Background

The bulk of U.S. manufacturing for Xerox is based in Webster, New York, which is near Rochester. This was the city in which Joseph C. Wilson, Sr. transformed the tiny Haloid Corporation into Xerox with the sale of the world's first plain paper copier in 1959. Wilson imprinted on the organization strong community and employee-oriented values.[4] He recognized, without resistance, the dominant union in Rochester—the Amalgamated Clothing

[4] By all accounts, Wilson strove to manage Xerox and live his life consistent with the following statement, which was found on a frayed blue index card in his wallet after he passed away: "To be a whole man, to attain serenity through the creation of a family life of uncommon richness; through leadership of a business which brings happiness to its workers, serves well its customers and brings prosperity to its owners; by aiding a society threatened by fratricidal division to gain unity." (Jacobson and Hillkirk, *op. cit.*).

and Textile Workers Union (ACTWU)—as the designated representative of Xerox employees. Today there are just under 4,000 bargaining unit members, though unionized employment has been as high as 7,000 and overall Rochester area employment has been over twice that.

The Webster site includes facilities for the final assembly of mid-size and high-volume photo copiers, the fabrication and assembly of various copier components, the production of related products (such as toner, a black talc-like substance used in copying), and product distribution. There are some research and development operations in Webster, which are linked to activities in a major Xerox engineering center about twenty miles from Webster.

As one of the largest and highest-wage employers in the Rochester area, Xerox has a relatively stable, high-seniority work force. Within the union leadership, there has also been a high degree of stability over the years. Within the top ranks of manufacturing management, however, there has been a high degree of job movement. As we will see, the consequences of this movement are more acutely felt during a time when the patterns of labor-management relations are in transition.

Relations between the company and union were relatively peaceful during the 1960s and the 1970s, although there was one major strike and occasional unofficial job actions. During this period, the relationship was typical of many unionized U.S. employment relationships in the centrality accorded to the negotiation and administration of bargaining agreements.

The Point of Departure

This case study begins in 1980, a time when these traditional forms of dispute resolution—collective bargaining and the grievance procedure—were well developed between Xerox and ACTWU. The parties' capacity to identify and pursue common concerns, however, was limited to informal arrangements on the shop floor and regular, but informal, briefings by top management with union leaders. The case traces the development of this capacity to pursue common concerns, without the abandonment of traditional collective bargaining responsibilities.

It has not been, in any sense, a smooth or natural evolution. Rather, the period from 1980 to the present has been punctuated by a series of double-edged crises that carried the potential either to undercut or to reinforce the new patterns of labor-management relations. These are referred to in the case as "choice points" or "pivotal events" and they represent more than an analytical device. Not only are the interests of labor and management more vivid at these points, but their very existence suggests a change process that is long-term, characterized by extensive formal and informal negotiations, and marked by a succession of discrete shifts in labor-management relations.

The choice points are presented in the case in roughly chronological order. However, some sections follow the consequences of choices up to the present (in order to clarify their implications) before returning back in time to the beginning of the next section. Today, as we will see, there is a clear pattern suggesting that these parties are on a path toward a transformed industrial relations system. But it will also become clear that there are pivotal events still to come for the parties. While it is hard to predict the outcomes of these future events, we can be quite confident in expecting that pivotal events will continue to occur—thus ensuring that one feature of a transformed labor-management relationship involves continued difficult choices about the direction of

the relationship. [See Exhibit 1 for a time-line of events.]

THE FIRST STEP: EMPLOYEE INVOLVEMENT

When Local 14A of ACTWU and Xerox entered into collective bargaining negotiations in 1980 the company had already begun to experience shrinking market share, but had not shifted its business strategy in response. Though similar in most respects to previous negotiations, the parties did agree to experiment with what was then termed a quality of work life (QWL) effort. The focus was on creating shop floor problem-solving groups comparable to quality circles. Oversight would be handled jointly through union-management plant advisory committees (PACs) in each of the four main manufacturing plants in the Webster complex, along with a network of department-level steering committees. Union and company officials each designated "trainer/coordinators" who received extensive training in facilitating the work of the problem-solving groups (PSGs). Membership on a PSG was voluntary and accompanied by about forty hours of training in problem-solving, statistical methods, and group dynamics.

The QWL proposal was made by management and, initially, drew skepticism from the union. They agreed to proceed only after assurances that oversight would indeed be joint, that management saw QWL as something more than a short-lived program, and that QWL would be kept separate from the management structure, the union structure, and the collective bargaining relationship. Thus, the different levels of joint committees and PSGs were intended to function as a separate (but parallel) structure. As well, the language of collective bargaining was employed to explicitly designate issues that were "permissible" for discussion in PSGs and issues that were "off limits." These distinctions were as follows:[5]

Off-Limits Areas
Salaries; union grievances; union contract; benefits; company policy; working hours; rates; breaks; classification; overtime; personalities; payroll; discipline; problems shop chairmen are working on; production standards

Permissible Areas
Product quality; work environment safety; savings in material and inventory costs; improvements in process, methods or systems; improvements in facilities, tools or equipment; reduction in paperwork; elimination of waste of materials and supplies; quality; scrap; rework; locations of equipment/materials

A further guarantee was provided by management in the form of a letter stating that no employees would lose their jobs due to productivity gains generated by QWL teams.

The reception to this initiative from first-line supervisors and from union stewards was mixed. Some were openly hostile, some were highly receptive, and most were skeptical that it would have anything more than the short-term, limited impact of previous employee-oriented programs. However, few questioned what was seen as the importance of keeping QWL distinct from collective bargaining and from the internal operations of the company and the union.

Within the first year and a half, over ninety problem-solving groups were established in the four main plants. After two years, about twenty-five percent of the 4,000 employees in the bargaining unit

had volunteered for QWL training and participated in a problem-solving group. By two and a half years, the collaborative efforts had spread throughout the four manufacturing plants and into other facilities in the Webster complex, accounting for a total of over 150 problem-solving groups.

The range of problems successfully solved by these groups included: improving the quality of manufactured parts, developing training for new technology, eliminating chemical fumes, reducing paperwork, machine upgrading, reducing downtime, eliminating oil spills, organizing tool storage, improving communications across departments, developing orientation for new employees, and redesigning floor layout to be more efficient. About twenty percent of the successful proposal included estimates of cost savings, which totaled close to a half a million dollars.[6] The initial QWL structure is depicted on the next page.[7]

Early Barriers to QWL

Despite the successful problem-solving experiences, there were clear limitations on the QWL effort. Some of the barriers derived from the traditional structure of collective bargaining and labor-management relations. For example, as a result of the extensive bumping and bidding rights guaranteed by the contract, there was high turnover in many of the groups. These job moves occurred almost every two months. Layoffs of over 5,000 Rochester area employees during 1981 and 1982—approximately 1,200 of whom

[5] These lists are from Peter Lazes and Tony Costanzo, *Xerox Cuts Costs Without Layoffs Through Union-Management Collaboration* (Washington, D.C.: U.S. Department of Labor, 1984).

[6] Data tracing actual cost savings on all the suggestions after implementation is not available. Overall performance data is discussed at the end of the case, which indicates at least a correlation between improved performance and the changes in labor-management relations.

[7] Chart from Lazes and Costanza, *op. cit.*

Initial labor-management monitoring and support structure for problem-solving teams

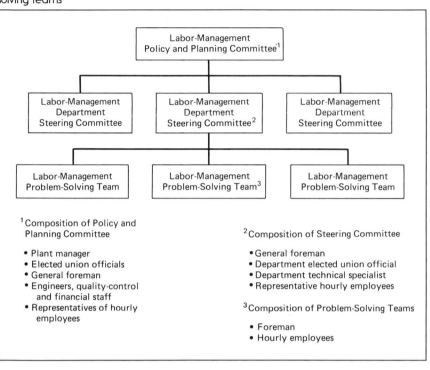

were union members—brought additional turnover on the teams. Moreover, while the layoffs were an accepted part of a traditional collective bargaining relationship, they directly undercut attempts to emphasize the commonality of interests between labor and management.

Some of the barriers derived from the QWL process itself. For example, there was dissatisfaction with the time required to solve major problems and, more frequently, dissatisfaction with the time required to implement the solutions. During the three years, the average time required just to generate a solution to a problem was between three and four months. A handful of problems took a year or more before they were proposed for implementation.[8] These perceived delays reflected, in part, workers tackling problems not amenable to quick solutions, but they also reflected the need to develop procedures (and overcome internal politics) associated with workers being given access to people and information not previously available to them.

The constraints on the QWL effort—seniority job movement, layoffs, and delays—involved issues that were either at the core of the collective bargaining contract or that directly involved issues

[8] In fact, this experience is quite consistent with the time period required for problem-solving in other locations studied in the course of the larger U.S. Department of Labor Study of which this case is a part. This issue, however, is that the workers' expectations were apparently for a much speedier process.

traditionally considered managerial rights. Addressing these barriers was well beyond the scope of QWL, which was intended to serve as an adjunct to bargaining. The barriers were choice points in which the choice was made in favor of the status quo. Yet, in the second year of the QWL efforts, a crisis led to direct union and management consideration of all these core issues.

EXTENDING THE PRINCIPLE OF JOINT DECISION-MAKING

Early in 1981 the union learned that management was in the process of vending out certain work in the Sheet Metal area of the Components Manufacturing plant. Originally, it had been both parties' intention to keep QWL separate from the adversarial side of the labor-management relationship. However, the potential loss of jobs was so divisive an issue that the union informed management that it could not continue to cooperate on the joint QWL effort, on the one hand, and yet see work vended out without joint consideration, on the other hand. Thus, the union's threat to pull out of the QWL effort was a pivotal event.

If QWL was to persist as a joint effort, the union in effect was demanding that the principles of joint decision-making would have to extend to other aspects of the employment relationship. In response, management agreed to halt the subcontracting in the Sheet Metal area. Further, there was an understanding that future decisions on subcontracting would not take place on a unilateral basis.[9] That this first challenge to the cooperative efforts emerged in the components portion of the manufacturing organization should come

[9] Legally, of course, the union could only insist on its right to bargain over the effects of such a decision, not over the decision itself.

as no surprise, since this is the portion of the business most subject to external market pressures and hence most likely to encounter conflicts of interest.

The Wire Harness Study Team

The first test of the new understanding around subcontracting also arose in the components plant in October, 1981. At that time the company announced the possibility of a $3.2 million savings from subcontracting the assembly of wire harnesses used in Xerox machines. This raised the specter of an entire department—around 180 people—being laid off. Not only would this have been devastating for the individuals involved, but the handling of this issue would now have clear consequences for the joint QWL efforts. Tony Costanza, now an International Vice-President and Director of ACTWU, was Chief Shop Steward at the time. He recalls that this was an issue clearly outside the purview of QWL, yet it so deeply affected the quality of so many people's work lives that any unilateral decision would have been inconsistent with the principle of joint decision-making around QWL issues.

A series of top-level union-management meetings led to management's suspending outsourcing plans for the wire harness area pending the establishment of a joint Study Team to be composed of six workers from the affected area, an engineer, and a manager. In essence, the parties saw themselves as applying the QWL problem-solving model to a new set of issues. Many in management privately protested the establishment of a Study Team, feeling that all reasonable possibilities for saving the work had been investigated. Nevertheless, six months was allowed for a team to fulfill the following mission:

> Find ways to be competitive, improve quality, cost and delivery performance of the

business to levels which will assure a positive competitive position and ultimately, to secure jobs.

Over one-hundred and eighty hourly employees volunteered for the team—practically all the employees in the affected area of the plant. The union shop chairmen and top union officers made the selection. Management picked the engineer and manager who were to serve on the team and both sides conferred to assure that the final work group would be compatible.

The Study Team's task would not be easy. Xerox had recently established a competitive benchmarking program so as to evaluate its operations and products against the competition along the following dimensions: customer satisfaction, product reliability, design effectiveness, service cost, installation quality, and manufacturing cost.[10] Over $3 million in savings had to be achieved while meeting all of the benchmarks that had been set.

At the outset, the team was trained in group problem-solving skills, communications techniques, and Xerox's accounting and financial methods. They were given office space, telephones, and a promise of complete access to anyone in the corporation. A plant labor-management Steering Committee, with its own executive committee, was established to meet regularly with the team in the expectation that some of the team's work would need approval beyond the authority of the plant and divisional union and management officials.

Initially, it was not only the scope of their task that frustrated the team. The

rest of the management organization was not prepared to deal with such a group. Financial information was not always available when it was needed. Policy decisions had to be made about access to confidential information, such as supervisors' salaries. At times, projects or progress were undermined by operations managers or general supervisors who "took independent action to implement the changes before the team had presented its ideas to appropriate managers or union officials."[11] Pete Lazes, an external consultant to the QWL initiatives, assisted the Study Team in surfacing these issues, channelling support from top labor and management leaders, and in sorting out the internal frictions that initially emerged between hourly and salaried team members. The Study Team also succeeded in building the trust of other hourly workers through a request for suggestions (over 200 suggestions were generated) and via weekly "walk-around" visits within all parts of the department.

At the conclusion of six months of study, the team proposed changes ranging from physically redesigning the department, to expanding employee responsibilities, to upgrading equipment, to changing the calculation of certain overhead expenses. The biggest concentration of anticipated savings (over 38%) involved changes in the organizational structure and procedures, such as limiting job movement, redesigning work procedures and consolidating jobs. In all, the estimated value of the savings significantly exceeded the team's target of $3.2 million.

Some of the proposals, however, were directly contrary to provisions in the collective bargaining agreement. For example, the reduction of job movement directly contravened the seniority bumping and bidding rights specified in the contract.

---

[10] This competitive benchmarking represented one of the most significant early responses of Xerox to increasing world competition. For some operations, parts and products Xerox has concluded that its own work represents the world benchmark; in other cases, the benchmark is held by one of Xerox's competitors; and, sometimes, the benchmark is in an unrelated industry; for example, after studying automated warehouse procedures in a variety of firms, Xerox identified the L.L. Bean mail-order company as the benchmark in this area.

[11] Lazes and Costanza, op. cit.

(At the time, these contractual provisions might account for as many as two or three job changes a year for a low seniority worker.) As well, the team recommended a reduction in ten minutes in the personal fatigue and delay allowance. Changes in the organization of work required changes in contractual work rules regarding lines of demarkation. Further, proposed reductions in the amount of supervision and in the calculation of overhead went directly to issues usually considered in the province of management rights. After considerable discussion, the parties agreed to implement the suggestions that involved no contractual changes, keep the outsourcing decision on hold, and grapple with the balance of the issues in the upcoming 1983 negotiations.

Future Instances of Subcontracting

Placing the Study Team issues on the bargaining table was a pivotal decision. It suggests that broadening the concept of joint decision-making could not occur without having implications for other aspects of the relationship—especially collective bargaining. During the 1983 negotiations (which will be discussed in more detail in the next section of the case), the parties agreed to implement the remaining recommendations (concurrent with a three-year guarantee of no layoffs for those ACTWU employees in Webster on the March 1983 payroll). Moreover, the parties agreed to institutionalize the Study Team concept by stating that subcontracting decisions would have to be subject to the establishment of such a team.

In the years since 1983, four additional Study Teams have completed similar analyses. In addition to the Wire Harness Study Team, these teams have been in the following areas: turnings, castings, extrusions, and sheet metal. In four out of the five efforts the recommendations have led to the continued in-house operation of these activities (rather than the anticipated subcontracting). The results have been enthusiastically received by labor and management at all levels. One senior executive stated:

> The task forces are the ultimate. With circles it's hard to have religion every day, but here there is a crisis driving the effort. These groups have made changes that would have been impossible for me to achieve on my own as a manager. They've come up with ways for 120 people to do the work of 200 and we've provided other work for the remaining 80.

The experience with the Study Teams reveals that, in order for this collaboration to effectively contribute to the goals of the employees and the employer, it was preceded, first, by a conflict that could not be resolved without some degree of hard bargaining. In essence, the union had to establish its legitimacy in this domain—which involved some contention—and then it was possible for collaboration to occur. The union, which initially sought to keep participative activities entirely distinct from collective bargaining, now highly values this expansion of the principle of joint decision-making and the consequent ability to better represent its members regarding these critical issues.

The targeted, crisis-driven nature of the Study Team concept—while clearly a key to its successes—is also a source of some new problems in the organization. For example, one top union official voiced the following concern:

> We've never found a way to bring study team members back to the floor effectively. Some say "thank God" when it's all done because the pressure is off, but others would like to continue to use the skills they've developed. They are called on in-

formally, but we should be able to do something more.

A related but much deeper issue also arises from the short-term nature of the Study Teams. This was vividly illustrated recently when it was announced that the Wire Harness area, the site of the first Study Team, was again non-competitive. The result was the establishment of a second Study Team. In reflecting on this development, one hourly member of both the original team and the new team pointed out that "a continuously moving target requires far more monitoring than we have been doing." Further, the appointment of the new team quickly highlighted the fact that some of the original Study Team recommendations had not been implemented. There was thus a practical question as to whether the new team could claim potential cost savings from unimplemented earlier suggestions (it was decided that it could) and a more fundamental question about the location of accountability for the implementation of Study Team recommendations.

The outcome of this newest Study Team's research is not yet clear. The experience suggests, however, the importance of linking this sort of targeted assessment and linking broad scanning on competitive trends back into daily operations. Before tracing some of the links that are indeed occurring in business operations, it will be helpful to return to 1983 and review the parties' negotiation of a critical collective bargaining agreement.

PIVOTAL NEGOTIATIONS

The institutionalization of the Study Team concept in the 1983 contract between Xerox and ACTWU was but one example of a larger, two-way linkage between the participatory efforts and the system of rules and regulations established via collective bargaining. Another equally important example of a participative issue that has bumped up into the collective bargaining forum was the company's agreement in 1983 to a moratorium on layoffs of ACTWU members in Webster for the full three-year term of the contract. This provision was, in part, a *quid pro quo* for other changes in the contract that are discussed below. However, it had clear implications for the participative effort. It addressed a concern not just of the employees associated with the Wire Harness Study Team or QWL groups, but of all employees at a time when workers were exploring improvements in organizational operations. No one wanted to be associated with suggestions that might cost them or co-workers their jobs and this agreement served to minimize potentially divisive internal debate over such issues.

Once the decision was made in collective bargaining, however, its administration was different in many ways from the administration of other parts of the agreement. It has required a continuous and sophisticated level of human resource planning. As will be discussed below, this includes an equal role for the union on a Horizon Team established to do strategic planning around these same human resource issues.

Not all of the consequences of the 1983 negotiations served to reinforce and extend the collaborative activities. Three portions of the agreement had the opposite effect. The contract had no wage increase in the first year, it included changes regarding co-pay provisions for health benefits, and contained a highly restrictive no-fault absenteeism program. The health benefits changes and the one-year wage freeze were seen as concessionary and hence resented. The absenteeism control program was addressed at what was seen as overly high absentee rates. Beyond a set of contractually guaranteed reasons for not being at work (vacations, jury duty, holidays, et cetera), employees were only permitted a limited number of instances during which they were absent from work—regardless of the reason. While absenteeism subsequently dropped, an unintended consequence was that it put employees with good records at substantially greater risk than they otherwise would have been in the event of illness or other events beyond their control. As such, it was seen as contrary to the union and management emphasis on participation.

Following the agreement, there was not only an increase in grievances (reflecting dissatisfaction with portions of the settlement), but there was a decline in volunteers for the QWL problem-solving groups and a disbanding of some existing groups. Thus, the 1983 negotiations illustrate the double-edged capacity for collective bargaining to both reinforce *and* undercut collaborative activities. The potentially negative impact of collective bargaining on collaborative activities was even more acutely felt in the case of a small local of the International Union of Operating Engineers (IUOE), which represents some engineers at the Webster location.

The contract for the IUOE was similar to the ACTWU contract, with two critical exceptions. It did not include the no-layoff guarantee and it did not include the subcontracting language, both of which had emerged out of the collaborative experiences between ACTWU and Xerox. Without these reinforcing features, the negative features of this agreement became particularly salient to the IUOE. In protest, the union filed an unfair labor practice charge claiming improper company actions regarding the co-pay change in health benefits. At the same time, it felt that it could not continue to endorse its members' participation in QWL activities and so withdrew from any formal role in this process.

Ultimately, the unfair labor practice charge was dismissed, but this reveals how polarizing a lack of reinforcement via collective bargaining can be.

The event also provides some insight into the limitations of using withdrawal from QWL as leverage on other issues. Unlike ACTWU's experience in the case of the Sheet Metal area, the IUOE action split the union. Apparently, for the IUOE members who were involved in QWL groups, this form of participation was more important than their dissatisfaction with the health benefit changes. Employees not involved in the QWL process felt otherwise. This experience suggests that the threat of withdrawal from collaborative activities can only be used by a union in a limited number of cases where the issue is either of overarching importance to most members or where the issue clearly involves an inconsistency with the norms and values associated with the collaboration.

During the term of the agreement the parties made informal modifications in the operation of the absenteeism control program and, as we will see later, formally addressed what were seen as the harshest aspects of the program in their 1986 negotiations. The informal changes alone, however, did not stem the decline in volunteers for QWL or the disbanding of additional groups. As such, this plateau and decline in participative activity represents that next major episode in the unfolding of this labor-management relationship.

RESPONSES TO A PLATEAU IN QWL ACTIVITY

Beginning in 1982, the number of new volunteers for QWL training and for membership in a problem-solving group began to decline. This was partly a reflection of dissatisfaction with the delays associated with the QWL process. As well, however, the decline in volunteers can be traced to the disruption and resentment associated with a series of layoffs in that year. While it would be expected that the no-layoff guarantees for ACTWU employees in Webster would have addressed this issue, the impact of the agreement was, in fact, mixed.

Interviews with employees who were involved in the QWL effort at that time suggest that these employees saw the no-layoff guarantee and the language on Study Teams and subcontracting as direct reinforcements of their QWL activities. They viewed the contract as a step in the right direction. However, there was no rush of new employees to become involved in the participative activities. Apparently, some of these employees stayed out of the process in protest over the changes in the health benefits and the new absenteeism control program. As one union official noted, "participation in QWL was one of the few things people had control over, so they used to protest their feelings on other issues." As well, there was still skepticism or disagreement with the idea of QWL.

Since the top leadership of the company and the union had, by this time, come to value the participative efforts, discussions began over how best to address the decline. It was felt that part of the problem was a lack of understanding of the nature of QWL, so a decision was reached to make QWL training mandatory for all employees. In fact, the impact of this decision was exactly the reverse of what was expected. Rather than building a shared understanding of (and, it was hoped, a shared commitment to) QWL, the shift to mandatory training polarized the workforce. Some individuals did come to value the participative activities as a result of the training, but many more were only at the sessions physically—they were not there in spirit. Indeed, some of these individuals were highly disruptive of these sessions.

This polarization was deeply felt in the QWL groups. During interviews with two such groups at this time, the group members were asked to identify what they had experienced as the principal forces that were barriers to their effective functioning. The perception of these groups was remarkably similar even though the groups were of different composition (one was composed of almost all white males and the other highly heterogeneous); they had different work responsibilities (one involved skilled trades employees and the other involved employees that engaged in assembly and materials handling work); and they had been in existence for different periods of time (one for less than a year and the other for almost four years). Among the many barriers independently identified by the groups, the five voted as most important by each group are listed below—indicating a common concern with issues related to a polarization in the workforce.

Skilled Trades Group

Politics (with engineering, other workers on the floor & management)

Misunderstandings of QWL by those not on the team (including the perception that it's cutting jobs) and the resulting peer pressure

Communications (people outside the group not delving into ideas sufficiently)

Insufficient support from people with specific, needed abilities

Not enough time (for problem-solving)

Production and Materials Handing Group

Not enough cooperation from white-collar workers—passing the buck

Recent union contract stops people from getting involved

Not enough cooperation from other hourlies

Employee distrust and indifference (about QWL)

Lack of dynamic leadership in the team

Further discussions with these and other employees highlighted the very real danger of a growing split in the workforce. Of critical importance was the extent to which this split reflected disagreement over QWL per se, or dissatisfaction over other issues being expressed in the context of QWL. In order to examine these and related issues, the company and the union worked with a consultant to design an employee questionnaire.[12]

An Attitude Survey

The attitude survey was administered in March of 1984 in the Components Manufacturing Operations, which employs about 1,000 hourly and salaried workers in Webster. The survey confirmed that employee attitudes about QWL were sharply divided. Employees involved in the process saw it as helping them, improving productivity, strengthening the union, contributing to improved labor-management relations, and functioning effectively as a process. Employees who had no interest in joining teams (regardless of whether or not they were previously on teams) had negative views along these and other dimensions. A small number of employees who were not members of QWL groups, but indicated an interest in joining these groups basically shared the views of current groups members.[13] The general results are illustrated in Table 1.

The gap in attitudes was reflected in many other dimensions of the survey, all of which served to corroborate the parties'

sense that there was a relatively large number of employees who were not involved in the QWL process, had no interest in being involved, and had negative views of the process. Indeed, this is reinforced by the fact that both employees with no interest in QWL and employees involved in QWL have negative perceptions of co-workers' support for QWL. However, embedded within the survey, there were a set of responses that went on to point the way for a fundamental change in the nature of QWL.

Specifically, there was overwhelming concurrence by the employees with statements concerning whether or not they wanted more say in their work (82.9% said they did), more information (86.0% said they did), and whether they liked the idea of employee involvement (89.8% said they did). This is consistent with the findings of recent national surveys on these issues.[14] Essentially, the employees were saying they valued participative principles, but that they did not all value QWL as the vehicle of this participation.

The Business Area Work Group Structure

In response to the survey, the parties developed a new structure for participation in this components plant. They identified over thirty functional groupings of workers, each of which was designated as a Business Area Work Group (BAWG). It was decided that supervisors would be appointed as BAWG leaders and that biweekly meetings for the purpose of sharing information would be mandatory for all workers. The membership of the BAWG included the engineers, supervisors, and

[12] The attitude survey was constructed and administered by Larry Pace, Manager for Organizational Effectiveness in Reprographics Manufacturing at Xerox, and Ron Mitchell, an internal consultant to Xerox's manufacturing operations.

[13] The similarity of views suggests, but does not demonstrate, that some attitudes about QWL may be independent of actual experience with QWL—an issue with far-reaching implications.

[14] See, for example, Alper, S. William, Bruce N. Pfau, and David Sirota, "The 1985 National Survey of Employee Attitudes: Executive Report." New York: *Business Week & Sirota and Alper Associates*, 1985.

TABLE 1   1984 perceptions of quality of work life by CMO employees, based on QWL experience and interest in future involvement

Attitude Measures	Not Involved and Not Interested in Joining (n = 497)	Not Involved, But Interested in Joining (n = 103)	Involved as a member of a QWL/EI group (n = 175)
QWL is on the right path (5 item scale, alpha = .77)	3.0* (1.0)	4.0 (0.9)	4.0 (0.9)
QWL has contributed positively to:			
My morale, say, and work (3 item scale, alpha = .85)	2.5* (1.2)	3.6 (1.0)	3.8 (1.3)
Attachment to my job and the firm (3 item scale, alpha = .81)	2.5* (1.2)	3.7 (1.0)	3.6 (1.3)
Firm productivity and efficiency (3 item scale, alpha = .84)	2.9* (1.3)	4.1 (0.9)	3.9 (1.2)
In general to the union (single item)	3.2* (1.6)	4.0 (1.2)	4.1 (1.5)
Labor-management relations (4 item scale, alpha = .85)	2.7* (1.2)	3.7 (1.0)	3.7 (1.1)
Management supports QWL (3 item scale, alpha = .64)	3.7 (0.9)	3.8 (0.9)	3.9 (0.7)
The union supports QWL (2 item scale, alpha = .67)	3.6 (1.3)	3.9 (1.2)	4.0 (1.4)
Co-workers support QWL (3 item scale, alpha = .70)	2.3* (1.1)	3.2* (1.0)	2.7 (1.1)

Note: All mean responses are in relation to a six point scale where 1 = disagree strongly; 3 = disagree somewhat; 4 = agree somewhat; and 6 = agree strongly (2 and 5 were unlabeled). Standard Deviations are in parentheses. Where the attitude measures are constructed from multiple items on the questionnaire, the reliability alpha of the combined scale is included.

* Indicates that the difference between the mean response of these "not involved and not interested employees" is significantly different from the response of *both* of the other two group at the 0.1 level based on a three-way scheffe test. In all but one instance, there is no significant difference between the interested employees and the involved employees. That one item is the last one regarding co-worker support and that is marked with an asterisk as well.

union officials associated with a given area. Beyond this relatively modest baseline level of participation, BAWG members would have the option to continue any QWL problem-solving groups, to form *ad hoc* groups to address specific problems, to serve as "individual contributors," and/or to establish themselves as an autonomous work group.

The BAWG concept can be thought of as a contingent approach to participation. It is a structure that reflects the fact that participation means different things to different people. It has the advantages of being more tightly linked into the management structure and allowing for multiple forms of participation. It also carries the potential of moderating the tensions around "in-groups" and "out-groups."

The first BAWGs went into operation in the spring of 1985. With their creation, the term QWL has become less common. Employee involvement (EI) is now the generic term. Although the BAWG structure allows for multiple forms of employee involvement, it is important to note that it was not designed to replace the grievance procedure or to otherwise serve as a formal vehicle for dispute resolution. Although, as we will see below, the administration of the grievance procedure has become more informal, its existence is clearly a necessary complement to the BAWG activities.

A reflection of the merits of the BAWG concept is the diffusion of similarly flexible structures to at least two other plants in the Webster complex. In fact, in one plant—the New Build Organization (NBO)—the development of a parallel concept called "work families" was preceded by an intermediate shift away from QWL. In this plant, which is where new copiers are assembled, the number of problem-solving groups meeting on a weekly basis declined in 1984 from twenty-four to eight. While initially viewed with alarm by the QWL facilitators, it quickly became clear that "sunrise meetings" involving over half of the workers in the plant had been substituted in their place. During these meetings supervisors reviewed with work groups recent data on performance, quality, and materials. Given this experience it is clear that NBO's version of the Business Area Work Group concept was an extension of participative principles, not a reversal.

As to the operation of the BAWGs, the individuals most closely associated with this organizational change point out that the designation of supervisors as group leaders had a mixed impact. Where the supervisor was supportive of participative efforts, the additional BAWG role was seen as complementary. Those supervisors that were less supportive, however, resented this new responsibility. As well, some supervisors and employees saw the imposition of a leader as inconsistent with the idea of participation. For these reasons and because many groups had hourly members who were strong informal leaders, it was recently decided that the BAWGs could elect their own leader. About half have switched from having a supervisor to having an hourly employee in this facilitating role.

While a separate analysis is being conducted to more precisely assess the impact of the shift to the BAWG structure, three patterns or implications seem clear. First, without the change in structure, it is likely that the QWL effort would not have progressed substantially beyond its pla-

teau. Indeed, a distributive issue might have undercut those efforts. Second, the contributions of the BAWGs to economic performance, employee concerns, and the union's institutional security seem largely positive, but modest and highly variable across work areas, perhaps reflecting what is still an incomplete institutionalization of participative principles into organizational operations. Third, this incomplete integration may suggest that the BAWG structure will reach its own plateau. Interestingly, within this structure, we see the elements of a deeper integration between participation and work operations, along with a concurrent increase in patterns of autonomy. This is the focus of the next section.

TRANSFORMATION IN THE ORGANIZATION OF WORK

With neither advance planning nor fanfare, a handful of work groups at Xerox have been functioning for over five years as semi-autonomous work groups—long before the advent of the Business Area Work Group concept. This form of work organization, in which work groups operate without direct supervision, typically emerged in selected areas where workers were used to operating independently and either a supervisor retired or was overextended.

The first such group was established in the Components Manufacturing Organization in 1982 under a proviso from the plant manager that (1) all work would be completed on time and (2) that there would be no defects. Twelve people were in the initial group, which split a year later into two groups due to product changes. Over the last six years these two groups have fulfilled their initial commitment to the plant manager. In this, an area that reportedly had a reputation for poor quality, these groups have managed for over four years to complete their complex sub-assembly routines without a single defect reported from the field.

While there have been a number of studies of such semi-autonomous work groups in new manufacturing facilities, little has been written about the emergence of such groups in established facilities. As such, it will be instructive to review the way these groups allocate work, handle membership, conduct training, and interact both with the union and management.

Autonomous Work Group Operations

In describing the functioning of one of the groups, a member observed:

It used to be that you were assigned to a job and that was it. Now we get together as a group and decide which jobs should be run, and how they should be run. Also, we do our own inspection and our own material handling. The people at quality assurance and material handling are not crazy about this, but there hasn't been enough hollering for us to stop. We report directly to the plant manager and do our own attendance and lateness sheets. We order our own material. Production control gives us orders thirty days in advance.

An engineer works directly with each group, sometimes providing information across shifts. One such engineer expressed enthusiasm for the arrangement, stating, "these people break their backs for you. This is beautiful; this is perfect; I've never worked anywhere like this."

Apparently, however, there is some variability in group relations with engineers, including some instances of sharp disagreement. In this sense, the increased worker autonomy can be thought of as elevating the importance of relations between engineers and workers. It thus poses a pivotal choice in which the outcome is either much deeper collaboration between workers and engineers *or* more contentious relations.

Although group members still tend to specialize in certain jobs, they note that they always make sure that at least two people know how to do each job to fill in for one another. This holds true for paperwork as well. According to group members, once people join, their attendance improves along with the quality of their work. One member explained:

It's because the company gives us responsibility. When you're in the main subassembly area you figure that if you build it wrong they'll be inspecting it. In our area your number is on your ticket. There is no blaming anyone else but you. It used to be that you would get up in the morning and only think about having to go to a bench, but now you want to see your buddies. I look forward to days off as much as anyone, it's just that I also look forward to being in.

The groups often deal with vendors and sales representatives on their own. Most of the training of new members is on the job. At most, three hours may be spent initially to show a new member how the system works and the rest is learned over time.

In discussing relations with the union, group members indicated that they had first approached the union representatives at the same time that they initially approached the plant manager. It was particularly these union officials that urged that the groups be established on a voluntary basis. Still, there is some ambiguity in the situation since some of what the groups are doing does not precisely fit within the contract. For example, the employees in this area are technically working out of classification with respect to certain quality inspection and materials handling activities. As a result, as one group member noted, "the floor union representatives are behind us. They back us behind the scenes, but they can't do it publicly."

Given their initial quasi-official status, it was critical for the groups to remain voluntary. That created tension, however, with the seniority-based system for job bumping and bidding. Job moves happen on approximately a quarterly basis and as many as four of the six members of a group have been bumped in a single move. This turnover makes the record of continuous, high quality performance all the more striking, though it does not make the job moves any more popular with the group members. Commenting on the impact of these job moves, one group member stated: "When you have a group, you all work together and socialize together. The promotions and transfers break that up. It's two steps forward and one back. This is the fourth full turnover in two years."

Within the past year, there have even been involuntary bumps into the autonomous work groups, with the consequent disruption of additional training and a greater degree of initial specialization. Former autonomous work group members who have been bumped into other areas have contributed to a diffusion of the general concept of semi-autonomous operations. Still, the overall experience raises an important institutional question. This is the direct tension between the seniority job rights of individuals and the continuity needs of groups.

In comparing this experience to that in facilities designed from the outset to be team oriented, what is most striking is that the daily work operations are quite similar. However, two distinctions are notable. First, the tensions with the existing system of rules are more salient here

(though these issues do emerge over time to some extent in the team facilities). Second, the system is both more informal and more permeable. That is, there is greater informality in training and orientation (which may reflect generally high seniority and skill levels in the workforce); and there is greater movement in and out of the teams (which is, of course, a product of the system of rules). Given the high levels of economic performance of these groups under these circumstances (informal training and extensive job movement), there is evidence to suggest that this mode of work organization is really quite robust.

Diffusion of Autonomous Work Practices

While the initial autonomous work groups emerged under unique circumstances, there are indications that they are at the forefront of a larger transformation in work organization at Xerox. A recent visit to the Webster Complex revealed that a number of new autonomous work groups had emerged of their own accord in various plants. Further, the idea of operating in this mode had been given explicit legitimacy under the BAWG structure and similar support in other Webster facilities.

An important test of the autonomous work group portion of the BAWG concept in the Components Manufacturing Operations occurred recently when Xerox offered an early retirement program for managers and other non-bargaining unit personnel. In about a half dozen cases, work groups whose supervisors took the early retirements have petitioned to operate on their own. Gradually, managers are evolving a set of questions to put to these groups to assess their readiness to operate in this mode and preliminary indications are that groups will be established in most of these cases.

Further, across the facilities in the

Webster Complex, there are emerging increasing levels of complementary informal activities. Both managers and union officials indicated a wide range of work groups, while formally under the responsibility of a supervisor, that have begun to operate more autonomously in one or more of the following activities: handling their own scheduling/assignments; monitoring their own inventory; meeting on their own with suppliers; maintaining their own records on quality; maintaining their own records on absenteeism; taking an active role in work redesign, especially around the introduction of new technology; and engaging in safety planning. Thus, in a quiet way, the very organization of work is undergoing a dramatic change.

Implications of Increased Work Group Autonomy

The developments represent a clear choice point for the parties. It is clearly a natural opportunity to extend the participative structure, but as these flexible (and hence more varied) forms of work organization become more common, fundamental questions are raised. For many supervisors these developments can be seen as direct threats to their employment security (despite assurances to the contrary) and as a threat to their authority. For union representatives—even those who are most supportive of these collaborative activities—there are concerns about maintaining equity in an environment of growing variation in work practices.

In part, the response of union leaders has been to develop informal criteria for when to allow variation and when not to. Basically it is a two part test of (1) whether or not the new practice is likely to affect employees in other work areas and (2) the extent to which management is or is not

taking advantage of the situation. One union official commented that:

> The hardest part of all this is that we sometimes agree to do things that are different than the contract. Then you get variation. But we have to be competitive. This sort of policy is possible only so long as the company continues to see us as partners. In turn, we have to trust the company. When they say the house is burning inside we have to trust them even if we can't see it. What George Meany and John L. Lewis did thirty or forty years ago is not acceptable now.

These union leaders report that their job now involves more up-front research, rather than reactive contract enforcement.

Based on the increased prevalence of autonomous activities, the union brought a demand to the bargaining table in 1986 to institutionalize some of the activities. It proposed that a special classification be created for informal group leaders so that they get an additional pay premium and dispensation to use fifteen percent of their work time for administrative activities. As one shop chairman noted:

> Our intention was to see if management was going to really support these new activities or if they were just taking advantage of the members. The risk, of course, was that if they rejected the demand we would have to tell the members to stop these informal activities.

In fact, despite the cost implications, this was an issue of some interest to higher management. As a result, an agreement was soon reached to create such a classification. Here we see shop floor experiences giving rise to an issue that, although potentially contentious, was addressed in a way that actually reinforced the participative activities.

There is a similar double-edged potential arising out of autonomous work group relations with engineers. It is not yet clear what will be required to more systematically assure that the cooperative potential between engineers and work groups is realized. Also persisting as an unresolved area of tension is the balance between the importance of individual seniority rights and the importance of work group stability. Both the seniority and the engineering matters remain as potentially pivotal issues for the future.

LINKAGE AT A STRATEGIC LEVEL

For years, two ACTWU leaders (at the international level) had maintained an informal arrangement with Xerox Chairmen and Chief Executive Officers by which they would be updated on corporate strategic plans at least once a year. Corporate industrial relations staff also had direct and easy access to channel key issues for top-level consideration. Still, collective bargaining remained the central focus of the relationship.

During the early 1980s, top-level corporate restructuring suggested that a wide range of new human resource activities were viewed as at least as important as the traditional industrial relations functions. While these internal corporate issues were being sorted out, a fundamental question arose at the plant level in manufacturing concerning the role of the union in strategic management decision making. This was, of course, the decision to handle subcontracting issues on a collaborative basis through the use of the Study Team concept. Following the decision have come a succession of further degrees of union involvement in strategic decisions at the plant level.

Horizon Teams

In late 1983 the degree of union involvement in strategic human resource planning expanded considerably. In the manufacturing complex an important response to heightened competition involved the creation of about a half-dozen Horizon Teams to explore the future of the reprographic business over the next decade. Although there was some union involvement on a number of the teams, it was particularly on the team responsible for scanning the future on human resources management issues that local ACTWU officials played a central role. This new level of strategic activity was important, as well, because the 1983 contract included a no-layoff guarantee for ACTWU members in Webster. In the ensuing years, through this team and through separate planning sessions, the union has become a permanent partner in these critical forecasting activities.

Toner Plant Design and Construction

The centrality of the union in strategic planning was revealed in 1985, when it became clear that there was a need for the construction of a new plant for the manufacturing of toner, a black talc-like substance used in creating images in photocopiers. While the company's initial investigations suggested that a Southern U.S. location would be economically preferable (especially due to lower energy costs), the prior experience with the union on subcontracting issues and the ongoing joint discussions on human resource planning facilitated a union-management agreement to explore cost-effective ways to construct the new facility in Webster. A planning team was established with a majority of hourly members from the existing Toner Plant. With substantial changes in work organization, the use of new computer inventory and control equipment, reductions in the level of supervision, and other changes, it was demonstrated that the facility could be both cost effective and achieve superior quality levels. Ground was broken in the same year and the new facility is now in operation.

Interviews with workers and managers that served on the plant planning team revealed an experience comparable in some ways to the Study Teams. That is, there were initially difficulties interfacing with organizational procedures. For example, reimbursement systems were not established to handle independent travel by hourly workers, yet this was a key part of the work of a number of team members. It was these sorts of administrative difficulties and the amount of learning required for the task that were identified by team members as the greatest barriers to their functioning effectively. While these barriers are not to be taken lightly, it is significant that the group did not encounter the same degree of overt resistance experienced by the first Study Team.

Product Development

In the Fall of 1982 Xerox announced its new "10 series of Marathon copiers," which included the mid-size 1075 machine that has since led the way in recapturing market share for the corporation. There is pride throughout the corporation in this set of third-generation machines. ACTWU even requested that a union label be put on each machine, which has occurred. For the corporation, however, there was no room for complacency. In the development of the newest machines there have been yet further advances in the way ACTWU and Xerox have been working together.

For past products, hourly workers would only see the new machines during trial production runs late in their development. Now, however, a team of hourly workers have been assigned full-time to work with the engineers in the early stages of product development for the newest Xe-

rox copier—especially around manufacturability issues. Special flexibility has been allowed for in terms of their classifications. Similar parallel product development occurred across different elements of the engineering process that had formerly proceeded linearly. The net result of this experience, according to a senior engineer associated with the project, is that almost a year has been cut off the time that would have otherwise been required for the development of the new product. Interviews with some of the workers associated with this project confirm that countless potential production problems have been found and solved at far earlier stages than would normally be the case.

Supplier Relations

The latest development at the strategic level concerns supplier relations. This represents a natural next step for the company, but a mixed set of issues from the union's perspective. In recent years Xerox has reduced the number of parts vendors with whom it deals from 5,000 to 400. It has sought just-in-time delivery arrangements and quality standards that approach zero defects. Indeed, in 1985 it earned *Purchasing* magazine's Medal of Excellence after reducing its parts inventory levels by $240 million and automating its parts warehouses.[15] These developments are highly visible in Xerox's Components Manufacturing Operations, where hundreds of square feet formerly allocated to storage is now being reclaimed for production.[16]

---

[15] Jacobson and Hillkirk, *op. cit.*

[16] Specifically, the area is now being use for the development of a world class injection-mold plastics capability. The technology for injection molded panels and parts continues to advance and replace metal, prompting Xerox to hire a leading engineering expert in this area and to make the extensive investment in capital and training associated with developing this capacity.

While the amount of inventory and storage work has been reduced, and the number of quality control inspectors has declined, management has been aggressive in bringing new production work into CMO. This is, at least partly, a result of the no-layoff guarantee. A strategic decision by the corporation to centralize even more of its manufacturing operations in the Rochester area has also assured a steady flow of work for the employees in Local 14A. However, it is with respect to the changes in relations with external suppliers that there are emerging some troubling issues from the union's point of view. Lately, for example, Xerox has begun to explore sharing the skills of its engineers, organizational effectiveness specialists (the new title for individuals who were formerly QWL facilitators) and internal consultants with its suppliers. For the union this raises fears that its own members will be helping to reduce the pool of work that might be brought into the Webster complex. It is too soon to tell how this issue will be resolved, but it illustrates the continuing, iterative nature of this transformation process. For each triumph in collaboration there emerges yet another potentially contentious issue that is double-edged. If the issue is addressed to the satisfaction of all the stakeholders, it does not hold back cooperation and may reinforce such efforts. If it is not addressed it threatens all prior collaborative achievements.

One event has not occurred at the strategic level. This is a choice by the ACTWU leadership to decline management offers of formal membership on the management operations committee for manufacturing. Despite the union's many other forms of involvement, the decision reflects a concern that this formal role could too tightly link the union to managerial decisions that it might have to turn around and oppose. While local union leaders feel

it is appropriate to be involved in the discussion of key strategic issues at the earliest possible times, they want to do so in a way that preserves their independence.[17]

TRANSFORMATION OF THE MANAGEMENT ORGANIZATION

Based in part on the successful experiences in the manufacturing organization (and in part on lessons from other organizations), the current Chairman and Chief Executive Officer of Xerox, David Kearns, embarked in 1984 on an effort to transform the way the entire management structure operates. Termed "Leadership Through Quality" (LTQ), the initiative began with a meeting of Kearns with the senior executives who report directly to him. Treating each other as "customers" for their respective output, they sought to define standards for quality performance and to establish regular meetings or other mechanisms for meeting these customer requirements. In turn, these senior executives met with their direct reports to engage in the same exchange of requirements and plans for meeting these requirements. Preceding each of these sessions, the individuals were given training in communications skills, decision-making skills and various LTQ principles. Following the same format as these top-level sessions, this interactive process has continued, as one individual put it: "cascading down the organization." In a sense, this process puts in place a process of continuous two-way negotiations that has the potential to allow for high degrees of adaptability throughout the management structure.

When the training of senior managers

---

[17] This issue—a central concern of union leaders as they enter new collaborative relations—is developed more fully in a companion research study conducted by M.I.T. for the U.S. Department of Labor. This study is entitled: "The Changing Role of Union Leaders."

in the manufacturing portion of Xerox began, however, a source of tension emerged. It was clear that senior union officials were among the main "customers" for the senior manufacturing managers, but the LTQ plan did not contemplate union participation. Indeed, there were some in the union who feared that management was seeking to create a strategic alternative to QWL that did not depend on joint governance. A specific concern of the union was its wanting to preserve its say in the sort of training that would be received by its members. Further, the LTQ team of trainers were using techniques and materials similar in many ways to those used by the union and management QWL facilitators, raising an issue as to who would provide this training. The first critical development to emerge out of this tension was the establishment of a Core Committee with top union leaders, top managers, LTQ trainers, and QWL coordinators. The main task confronting this committee was this bundle of integration issues.

It was decided that LTQ would occur in manufacturing, but in a modified form. The first session included not only top managers, but also top union leaders (a significant event), and the QWL coordinators. These QWL coordinators along with the LTQ trainers jointly delivered the subsequent sessions as they "cascaded" down the manufacturing side of the organization. As well, the content of the LTQ process was modified to fit a unionized setting. Today, every single manager and union official in manufacturing has been through the three days of LTQ training and almost every union member has been through the same sessions subsequently with their respective managers.

One of the key limitations of the QWL process, which has persisted in part into the BAWG structure, concerns the responsiveness of the management organization to these participative efforts. One potential advantage of LTQ, however, is that it more explicitly develops a common managerial language for how to think about the role of managers. This may at least temper some of the negative consequences of managerial rotation and turnover.

While it is not possible here to assess fully the impact of LTQ, it is clearly a step in the direction of building a necessary, complementary adaptive capacity among managers. Preliminary evidence of a positive impact is suggested by a look at the quality performance in the New Build Organization. During the period of the early QWL efforts (from 1982 to 1984), reject rates declined by about half. During the next two years (during the implementation of LTQ) the rate of improvement increased by a factor of seven. While many factors contributed to the improvement, the organizational changes are clearly concurrent and probably major contributors. Like so many other developments in this relationship, the experience with LTQ also illustrates how even an ostensibly collaborative change brings potentially contentious issues that must be addressed if it is to proceed.

CONTINUITY IN THE 1986 NEGOTIATIONS

While the 1983 negotiations marked a significant integration of the collaborative efforts with the traditional rule-oriented aspects of the relationship, the key question in the minds of union members, union leaders, and union managers was whether the 1986 negotiations would continue along that path. Five potentially contentious questions threatened to disrupt such continuity. First, the original QWL program had been established with a mission statement that included broad language concerning a sharing of the benefits of co-operative efforts. Increasingly, there was pressure from the shop floor to make a sharing of the gains explicit and more sub-stantive than the existing corporate-wide profit sharing program (which was quite distant in its relation with the perfor-mance of work areas), the suggestions pro-grams, and the contest-gift programs. Second, there was a real concern as to whether the no-layoff guarantee would continue. Third, the company was feeling pressure to move compensation in a direc-tion that would promote the firm's com-petitive position. Fourth, the issue of a new classification for leaders of groups taking on more autonomous responsibili-ties was on the table. Finally, the union could not leave the negotiations without some formal change in the absenteeism control program.

In fact, the parties succeeded in tack-ling all of these issues. They agreed to extend the no-layoff policy another three years, which is now seen by many work-ers as a key foundation to the coopera-tive efforts. A pilot study of new forms of rewards and recognition was also begun as a result of the agreement and the ab-senteeism control program was modified to be less restrictive regarding events be-yond an employee's control. As was noted earlier, a settlement was also reached on the new classification for group leaders. Finally, a wage package was assembled that included a lump sum payment of $2,000 in the first year and a lump sum 6% payment in the following year. It was felt that this would be seen as an attractive increase by the employ-ees, but that keeping the increase out of the base would enhance Xerox's ability to bid on new business. Apparently the parties read the union membership cor-rectly. The agreement was approved by over a three-to-one margin, one of the strongest ratification votes ever.

Not only did the substance of the agreement further attend to the joint needs of the parties, but the process of the bargaining was itself distinctive. At a number of times during the negotiations, joint study groups were established to explore various issues. At the main table, there were two brainstorming sessions. This occurred, for example, around the design of a modified absenteeism control program. This shift in the tone at the ta-ble reflects a transformation that is grad-ually occurring more generally in the handling of conflict between labor and management.

It is also at the shop floor that supervi-sors, labor relations professionals and union representatives (in at least some ar-eas) report increasing degrees of problem-solving around contentious issues. This is true in the tolerance for variation in work practices, but can also be seen in the records of one labor relations professional who made an explicit attempt over the last year to solve conflicts prior to their being logged as grievances. Over three times as many disputes were resolved be-fore being logged in, resulting in more grievances being settled at earlier stages and in an overall decline in the number of grievances.

Just as the nature of participation grad-ually evolved to be integrated with the union and management organizations, it is clear that the traditional activities of collective bargaining and contract en-forcement have evolved to more closely complement the collaborative efforts. The 1983 language on Study Teams and job security, as well as the 1986 language on group leaders, suggests that collective bargaining can be a powerful institution-alizing force. Further, while conflicts are increasingly being resolved through com-paratively subtle exercises of power and more explicit problem-solving, the griev-ance procedure and the contract still provide a valuable anchor to the dispute resolution.

CONCLUSIONS

Today, Xerox continues to dominate the copier industry.[18] Moreover, with product, manufacturing, and sales innovations it has managed to regain market share (from 20% to over 35%) in the critical market for mid-volume copiers. With the aid of Fuji Xerox it has managed to maintain a presence in the low-volume portion of the market. And, it has held onto a full seventy-five percent of the market share for high-volume copiers. Many elements of the organization have been critical in this turn-around. In this case, we have examined the complex dynamics associated with this change in the manufacturing portion of the business.

Social and Performance Outcomes

Assessing the relationship between the changing patterns of labor-management relations and various "outcome" measures is highly complex. While a separate analysis is currently underway around these issues, it is possible to report some overall trends along performance and social dimensions. The steady improvements along many of these dimensions do not demonstrate causality; however, they are at least suggestive that the impact is in a positive direction.

Quality improvements in the New Build Operations were mentioned earlier, in the discussion of the impact of the Leadership Through Quality effort. Additional information on quality and

other factors is available on the Components Manufacturing Operations. For example, during the period from 1981 to 1985 there was a steady improvement in quality (based on lots accepted and line fallout) from 89.3 percent to 99.1 percent. There was a parallel improvement in "on time" shipment of parts from 87.0 percent in 1981 to 100 percent in 1985. During the same period of time, the months of supply of finished goods on hand has been reduced by more than one hundred percent. In other words, the organization is more lean in the way it operates, yet is better at meeting the needs of its internal and external customers.

In terms of social outcomes, the period from 1981 saw a decline in the ratio of salaried to direct labor by eighteen percent and a decline in the ratio of indirect to direct labor of about twenty-three percent. Both of these measures are reflective of the increased levels of shop floor autonomy. Grievances declined slightly from 4.6 per 100 union employees in 1981 to 3.02 per 100 union employees in 1985, though the number of grievances did fluctuate during this period (with a high of 6.2 in 1982—during the layoffs and preceding the 1983 negotiations). In recent local union elections nearly all of the union stewards in the Webster complex have been returned to office and the most recent collective bargaining contract received one of its strongest ratification votes ever. Attendance, as was noted earlier, has improved from 92.0 percent in 1981 to 97.3 percent in 1985.

The combined set of social and performance indicators suggest that, in general, the interests of the employees, the union, and the firm are indeed all being met. As we saw in the case, this is not to say that there have not been important conflicts within and across these collectivities; nor is it to say that there will

[18] Ranked by copier revenues, Xerox (at $8.9 billion in 1985) is still many times the size of its closest rivals, which are Canon (at $2.2 billion), Ricoh (at $1.9 billion), Kodak (at $0.9 billion), and IBM (at $0.7 billion).

not continue to be conflicts in the future. Rather, it suggests that it is possible to have such conflicts and still achieve joint gains.

In Summary

Like so many organizations and unions, Xerox and the ACTWU sought to foster employee involvement as a distinct concept—separate from the internal operations of the company and the union and independent of collective bargaining. Over time, a series of potentially contentious issues have emerged, ranging from layoffs to outsourcing decisions to unpopular contractual changes to a corporate-wide management change effort. In these and other cases, the issues proved double-edged. Where they were incompletely addressed, they served to undermine collaborative activities. Where the conflicts were resolved, however, they did not impede and often reinforced the collaboration.

Concurrently, the nature of the participatory effort has evolved considerably—reflecting a diversity of preferences about participation that became salient as it became more directly integrated into the management organization, the union organization, and informal shop floor relations. The result has been a more flexible set of institutional arrangements. As well, there are evolving a set of norms and rules to ensure that equity and institutional security are not sacrificed in the name of increased flexibility. This is evident in the norms for when to allow variation in work practices and in the norms regarding the legitimacy of union input into top-level resource allocation decisions.

Finally, what is most striking about this case is that it reveals just how difficult and yet how important it is for the parties in an employment relationship to develop an adaptive learning capacity. That is, the parties have frequently been able to recognize pivotal events as just that—opportunities for reflection and choice. It is out of such reflection, for example, that a core employee interest (such as a concern about job security) is distinguished from a particular manifestation of that concern (such as highly specialized work rules) and an alternative institutional response becomes possible (such as the no-layoff guarantee). The key to the success of Xerox and ACTWU is not any one innovation. It is not QWL, Study Teams, BAWGs, autonomous work groups, Horizon Teams, new forms of product development or plant design, Leadership Through Quality, or any of the other developments documented in this case. Rather, it has been the ability to learn when (and how) to develop these new institutional arrangements that is the key.

The early history of concern for employees at Xerox and the tradition in ACTWU of attention to the competitive situation of employers have both facilitated the initiative discussed in this case. It helped, too, that this local was sufficiently independent of other ACTWU locals that it could innovate without producing tension across the international union. The very existence of a union, in this case, also proved critical in sustaining and diffusing many of the innovations—particularly when there was managerial turnover.

In all, the experience of Xerox and ACTWU suggests that the institutionalization of innovation in employment relations depends, first, on recognizing that employment relations contain a mixture of common and conflicting interests. The importance of identifying and pursuing common concerns is revealed as intimately intertwined with the importance of identifying and resolving conflicts. Further, the case suggests that attending to this interrelationship does not happen all at once. Rather, it is a continuous process punctuated by a succession of pivotal events that demand reflection, and, occasionally, the re-design of institutional arrangements. It is no wonder that it is difficult, but it is important to know that it is possible.

XEROX AND THE ACTWU
STUDY QUESTIONS:

1. What is your analysis of the "transformation" in the relationship between the Xerox Corporation and the ACTWU?
2. What lessons, if any, are there for other companies and unions?

Exhibit 1 Timeline

1980	QWL language in collective bargaining agreement
	Four joint Plant Advisory Committees and departmental steering committees established to create and support employee problem-solving groups
1981	Over 90 problem-solving groups established
	Outsourcing of 180 jobs on hold pending analysis of joint Study-Action Team
	Participative efforts begin in three remaining facilities in manufacturing complex
1982	Study Team identifies over $3.2 million potential savings, jobs not subcontracted.
	Over 150 problem-solving groups exist in seven facilities
	Massive layoffs of unionized and exempt personnel
	First semi-autonomous work groups established on their own initiative
1983	Contract includes no-layoff clause and mandated use of Study Teams in potential outsourcing cases, along with a first-year wage freeze, co-pay medical changes, and a restrictive absenteeism control program
	Horizon Teams include the union to assess the future of the reprographic business
	QWL training made mandatory, polarizes the workforce
	Study Teams established in two additional areas, with work kept in-house in each case
1984	Operating engineers union withdraws from QWL in protest over medical benefit change issues
	QWL groups decline in New Build Operations, informal pre-shift meetings emerge in their place
	Study Teams established in three areas, with work kept in-house in two cases
	Employee attitude survey in Components Manufacturing Operations prompts re-examination of QWL
1985	Launch of Business Area Work Group concept at CMO
	New Toner plant built in Webster based on joint analysis and design team
	Union supports flexible work assignments for hourly workers involved new product development
	Increasing informal autonomous activity by employees in work operations
	Corporate Leadership Through Quality efforts modified to complement union-management efforts
1986	Contract extends no-layoff guarantee; modifies restrictive absenteeism program; establishes classification for hourly group leaders; and contemplates pilot study of new forms of rewards and recognition—all with a mixture of hard bargaining and problem-solving
	Leadership Through Quality training completed for all managers and nearly all hourly employees
	Autonomous work groups increasingly established, prompted by early retirements of supervisors

Work Innovations in the United States

Richard E. Walton

Americans tend to do things by trial and error, and in dealing with changes in the way they work, they are no different. Whereas changes in European workplaces tend to be guided by government intervention and ideological rationalizations and involve an explicit transfer of authority, innovations in American workplaces are voluntary and pragmatic and involve no such transfer.[1] Despite its random nature, however, much change that has been planned has occurred in American workplaces during the past ten years.

Observers differ about whether work improvement is a fad or a long-term transformation in the nature of work organizations. Scientists differ in their theoretical explanations of why it works or when the conditions are right for it. Managers invariably wonder whether it has application in their organizations, and some union officials are concerned about its implications for the union as an institution. These concerns imply varying conceptions

of work innovation and hence indicate the amount of confusion that exists about what work improvement is.

In this article, I want to look at what has actually changed in workplaces, find out what we can learn from these work improvement activities, and derive some principles from what it reflected in the most successful ones. First, though, let us clarify what "work improvement" means and how I will be using it in the remainder of this article.

WHAT WORK IMPROVEMENT IS

The planned changes called "work improvements" have appeared in workplaces in many guises—as "quality of work life," "humanization of work," "work reform," "work restructuring," "work design," and "sociotechnical systems."

Although some of these terms have special connotations for the professionals who employ them, in method and goals the actual activities pursued under the various labels are not very different. I find it useful to distinguish three separate aspects of a work improvement effort.

1. Design Techniques

The element of work improvement activities that is most apparent is the specific changes in the way work is organized

[1] See Ted Mills, "Europe's Industrial Democracy: An American Response," HBR November–December 1978, p. 143.

Author's note: I wish to express my special thanks to Leonard Schlesinger, who has reviewed this manuscript at different stages of its development and made helpful suggestions for improving it.

and managed. For instance, the content of tasks changes when jobs are enriched, work teams affect the way tasks are organized and how they relate to each other, and consultative management gives workers the opportunity to influence decisions that affect them. The techniques may also affect the information provided workers as well as their compensation, security, physical environment, and access to due process.

The techniques employed and their possible combinations are many. For example, in changing assembly methods, auto plants have assigned related tasks to work teams, allowed them to decide how to allocate the work among themselves (provided they meet quality and quantity requirements) and created buffer inventories between adjacent work teams to increase latitude in the rhythm of their work. Also, management and unions in competitive manufacturing situations have designed plantwide schemes to share productivity increases and have structured mechanisms to ensure that workers' ideas for improvement are considered.

2. Intended Results

Another aspect of work improvement is the results it is intended to produce. They can be either economic (for the benefit of the organization) or human (for the benefit of employees). The business benefits can take many forms—quality, delivery, materials usage, machine capacity utilization, and labor efficiency. The human benefits can take form as real income, security, challenge, variety, advancement opportunity, dignity, equity, and sense of community. The relative importance of these depends on the needs and aspirations of the employees in question.

Most of the work improvement labels focus narrowly on either techniques or results. For example, "job enrichment" di-

rects attention to the techniques level and only to one technique. The connotation of "job design" is only slightly broader. "Quality of work life" has the same limitations. It refers directly to an objective that can be served in innumerable ways. Moreover, as labels, "quality of work life" and its first cousin, "humanization of work," have serious drawbacks; they refer only to human gains, which in today's business environment need to be closely coupled with improved competitive performance.

In my experience, I have found that organizations can improve business results in a humane way and improve the quality of the human experience in a businesslike manner by identifying the work cultures that promote both improvements simultaneously. Such work cultures are the links between technique and results in my three-level conception of work improvements.

3. Work Culture: The Intermediate Effects

The combination of attitudes, relationships, developed capabilities, habits, and other behavioral patterns that characterize the dynamics of an organization is a work culture.

Some changes in the culture, such as high cost consciousness, responsiveness to authority, and high activity norms, may promote performance but do little or nothing for people. Conversely, under some circumstances, high sensitivity to feelings and concern for the personal growth of the individual are cultural attributes that may be appreciated by the people affected but may not by themselves contribute to business performance.

In the most successful work improvement efforts, the culture simultaneously enhances business performance and the quality of human experience. In one food plant, for instance, management sought to promote employee identification with goals. Such positive identification increases not only workers' motivation to work but also their sense of belonging in the workplace and their pride in the plant's achievement. Similarly, a behavior pattern that influences both employee self-esteem and the soundness of business decisions is another desirable cultural attribute.

Identification and mutual influence are ideals common to many work improvement projects, but no single culture is ideal for all businesses or all people. What particular set of attitudes, capabilities, and relationships a company should emphasize will depend on its industry's strategic performance indexes and its employee's work life values. Whatever the work culture sought, it cannot be mandated by anyone. It can only be shaped over time by a combination of things— including the techniques by which work is organized and managed.

Let us review how these three aspects of work improvement activities relate to each other.

Techniques are the elements of the work organization that people can alter directly; intended results are the fundamental business and human criteria by which to judge effectiveness; and the work culture mediates the impact of the former on the latter. The techniques create the culture, which strongly influences business performance and the human experience at work.

According to this conception, one's choice of techniques is guided by continuously referring to the type of work culture that they promote, and in turn to projected business and human outcomes. For example, in a paper manufacturing plant, the business ends required that the manpower be flexible, and employees wanted the opportunity to acquire new skills. The plant adopted a design in which teams are responsible for a cluster of tasks and members are rewarded for acquiring the skills to perform all the team tasks. Such a design promotes both flexibility and opportunity. (The three-level conception of work improvement is shown in the Exhibit below; the arrows indicate influence.)

Three-level conception of work improvement

| Level 1
Design techniques ⟶ | Level II
Work culture ideals ⟶ | Level III
Intended results |
|---|---|---|
| Job design | High skill levels and flexibility in using them | *For business:* |
| Pay | Identification with product, process, and total business viewpoint | Low cost |
| Supervisor's role | Problem solving instead of finger pointing | Quick delivery |
| Training | Influence by information and expertise instead of by position | High-quality products |
| Performance feedback | Mutual influence | Low turnover |
| Goal setting | Openness | Low absenteeism |
| Communication | Responsiveness | Equipment utilization |
| Employment stability policies | Trust | *For quality of work life:*
Self-esteem |
| Status symbols | Egalitarian climate | Economic well-being |
| Leadership patterns | Equity | Security |

Note: The design techniques, cultural ideals, and intended results listed above are presented as illustrative, not as comprehensive or even universally applicable. Also, the items in the three columns are not horizontally lined up to relate to each other. The arrows indicate influence.

The exhibit illustrates how important it is to specify the proper business and work life outcomes for a particular company.

Applying this concept, one is also guided in the quality of choice one should make at each level. As one moves backward in the exhibit from intended results through work culture to design techniques, one's stance should become increasingly pragmatic. If the desired outcomes are clear and one's commitment to both business and human values is firm, then one can evaluate cultural attributes and in turn design techniques in terms of their efficacy in achieving the desired results.

The ruled insert (below) outlines some principles that arise out of the three-level conception of work innovation.

INTEREST IN WORK INNOVATION

Over the past decade, media attention has gradually shifted from focusing on the symptoms of disaffection with work to possible solutions. The amount of work improvement activity in plants and offices throughout the United States has grown steadily, appearing to be on the path of a classical S growth curve, in which growth climbs slowly at first, accelerates, and then slows again. Today, the rate of growth in these experiments continues to increase annually, suggesting that we are approaching the steeper portion of the curve.

Extrapolating from available information, I estimate that an important minority of the *Fortune "500"* companies are attempting some significant work improvement projects. And, not surprisingly, the companies that have greater commitment to and experience with such projects are among the leaders in their respective industries: General Motors, Procter & Gamble, Exxon, General Foods, TRW, and Cummins Engine. Less prominent but

---

PRINCIPLES REFLECTED IN THE THREE-LEVEL CONCEPTION OF WORK INNOVATION

Most effective work improvement efforts have reflected the following principles. I have induced them largely from experience rather than deduced them from social science theory.

1. In designing work structures, it is imperative to be absolutely committed to the results one chooses (shown on the far right of the Exhibit). One should become pragmatic in the choice of techniques to achieve these ends (shown on the far left of the Exhibit).

2. Recognize that no universally applicable set of human preferences and priorities regarding quality of work life exists. Hypotheses about what would enhance human experience at work may be useful, provided that they are tested with the people in question and are revised or discarded and replaced on the basis of that experience. The same points apply to the determination of the business results that the work culture should promote.

3. Accept that most techniques affect business and human results indirectly, altering first the culture of the organization. Even if in their designs planners ignore cultural considerations, the latter will nevertheless surface as the most important elements of the operation. Participants and visiting observers are quick to appreciate the motivation, cooperation, problem solving, openness, and candor that often mark a successful effort in practice.

4. Imagine the attitudes, relationships, and capabilities that would promote both business achievement and quality of work life in a particular setting, and then use these cultural attributes as proximate criteria for guiding the design of work structure. In many cases, duality of goals is absent, or the step of idealizing a work culture is omitted, or both. An elaborate methodology is not required, but a certain type of thinking is advantageous.

5. Be sure that at the technique level the many different elements of design and management practice—reward scheme, division of labor, performance reporting scheme, status symbols, and leadership style—are consistent with each other, each reinforcing or complementing the other. When these elements of the work structure send common or compatible signals, the culture will be internally consistent; if they send "mixed signals," people will feel ambivalent. Also, the more comprehensive the planned work structure and the more the design elements are aligned with each other, the more powerful the structure will be in shaping a distinctive work culture.

similarly well-managed manufacturing companies such as Butler Manufacturing and Mars, Inc., have also become increasingly active in this area. Citibank is one company with major work improvement efforts in the office environment.[2] Prudential Insurance is another

All of the manufacturing companies I have listed have regarded new plant start-ups as opportunities to introduce major new work structures. In recent years, major projects have begun in organizations of various sizes (from 100 to over 3,000), with varying technologies (from simple hand assembly to sophisticated continuous flow processes) and in different geographical locations (from upstate New York to the deep South and the West). As these companies extend their innovative work systems to other new plant sites, managers learn from the experience of the pioneers, and the systems cease to be regarded as experimental. Although the diffusion generally occurs slowly, the principles that underlie these new designs usually spread to companies' established plants as well. Let us look at some of these work innovations in detail.

Individual Projects

HBR readers have been exposed to a number of accounts of individual efforts (e.g., the Topeka Pet Food Plant) and to the distinctive approaches of several U.S. companies (e.g., Donnelly Mirrors and Eaton Corporation).[3] Although not fully representative of the diverse practices that one can observe, these experiments do illustrate the growing work improvement activity in the United States.

To my knowledge, the activity of General Motors is the most extensive of any company in the United States and may be more extensive than that of Volvo, whose pioneering efforts have been well publicized internationally. GM's dozens of projects take a variety of forms. One long-term effort at GM began in the early 1970s in an assembly plant in Tarrytown, New York. What began as a "What-have-we-got-to lose?" experiment in which workers and the union were involved in redesigning the hard- and soft-trim departments' facilities has blossomed into a plantwide quality of work life program involving over 3,500 people.

A different type of project at GM began in 1974 at a new battery plant in Fitzgerald, Georgia, where the pay system was set up to reward knowledge and skills acquisition. After four years, almost all workers there have become familiar with a wide range of jobs and have detailed knowledge of the production process. Initially, inspectors evaluated the workers' performance, but eventually the production teams themselves acquired the responsibility to ensure high-quality performance. Since 1977, work teams have prepared their own departmental budgets for materials and supplies. Managers provide workers with information such as cost data, which is traditionally not shown to them. The sparse and functional offices reveal the prevailing attitude about status symbols.

The pay system, self-supervision, and other design techniques have been combined at the Fitzgerald plant to create a work culture characterized by flexibility, mutual trust, informality, equality, and commitment. Reportedly, the Fitzgerald plant's performance has been very favorable, compared both with other plants and with its own plan. Those familiar with the

---

[2] See Richard J. Matteis, "The New Back Office Focuses on Customer Service," HBR March–April 1979, p. 146.

[3] See my article, "How to Counter Alienation in the Plant," HBR November–December 1972, p. 70; "Participative Management at Work," An Interview with John F. Donnelly, HBR January–February 1977, p. 117; and Donald N. Scobel, "Doing Away with the Factory Blues," HBR November–December 1975, p. 132.

plant attribute much of its superior performance to the work structure and to the fact that workers take pride in establishing new levels of output and quality.

Another innovator in this field is as much a leader in nondurable consumer goods as GM is in durable goods but shuns publicity of any of its work improvements. It regards the knowledge it has developed about implementing innovative work systems as proprietary, similar to other types of know-how that give it a competitive edge.

In the late 1960s in one plant of a major division, this company introduced a new work system designed around the idea that workers would be paid according to their skill levels. Under this system, the company does not impose quotas to limit the number who could advance to higher levels. The work system promotes the development of relatively self-supervising work teams. The basic features of this system have been adapted to the six new plants built subsequently as well as to departments in the preexisting, unionized plants of the division.

Because successful work improvement approaches have not always spread to other plants within the same company, it is worth noting why transfer did occur in this case. The acceptance of change in the existing plants has been fueled by their need to remain competitive with the newer plants, which employ more productive work structures. The change has been facilitated by transferring managers with experience from the innovative plants to the established ones. Also, whenever a new technology or project has been launched or major physical renovations planned, work innovations have been introduced in the old plants.

I have observed many of the plants in this company. Without a doubt, their innovative work systems have contributed significantly to the impressive performance of these plants and to the fact that by a wide margin the plants are usually regarded as the best places to work in their respective communities.

Although GM and the manufacturer of nondurable goods are leaders in the field of work improvements, they are not typical. Most companies, such as Butler Manufacturing, have only a few projects. In 1976, Butler introduced innovative work structures similar to the one at GM's Fitzgerald plant in two new plants. In one plant, the program is working exceptionally well; participants are enthusiastic about the work system and think it contributes strongly to their performance. According to pertinent internal criteria, this plant is 20% more productive and 35% more profitable than comparable plants in the same company.

The other new plant has experienced difficulties, and it is less clear that it has benefited from the work innovations.

The experience of a large paper company is also typical. With encouragement and support from the company's chairman, management launched two major facilitywide projects at the time of the plants' start-ups. When I last heard, the paper mill project was regarded as successful, but the other, in a converting plant, was not. Extenuating circumstances in the marketplace have contributed to the lack of profitability of the converting plant. Also, misjudgments in design reportedly have not been remedied, and optimism is declining.

Most companies experience both success and failure. One large company with four major plantwide projects has experienced almost the full spectrum. A plant that started up with a bold and imaginative work structure three and a half years ago has been very disappointing in terms of economic performance and the work system itself. Local management and union officials judge a second plant to be only somewhat more effective than it would have been without the innovations. A third is solidly effective, and a fourth is a big success according to both human and economic criteria.

The examples I have discussed so far are plant projects, but comparably conceived work improvement efforts have been occurring in office settings as well. In 1972, the clerical work in the Group Policyholders' Service Department of the Guardian Life Insurance Company was fragmented. To process a case file required several steps, each performed by a different person at a different desk in assembly line fashion. Files were hard to find, and responses to client inquiries were delayed. No one person performed or had responsibility for a whole job. Consequently, there was little basis for meaningful recognition of achievement, and morale was low.

The work improvement effort created natural units of work by combining policyholder services and accounting functions for a particular geographic area. The new "account analyst" became identified with a limited and stable set of clients with whom he or she maintained contact and for whom he or she provided a number of services previously assigned to different desks. Control over individual aspects of the work was removed, and individual accountability for overall results was increased.

Although the new work system at Guardian required people to go through complex training, with the result that 6 out of 120 employees could not meet the demands of the redesigned jobs, management reports that the system was effective in producing cumulative increases in productivity of about 33% in four years.

Top Management Interest

Part of the evidence supporting my projection of a continued acceleration of the growth rate of new projects goes beyond concrete activities; it is found in the trend toward increased top management attention to work innovation. Whereas five years ago it was plant or division level managers who invariably sought educational or consultative assistance for potential projects, today it is equally likely that inquiries will come from top corporate managers who are interested in advancing their own understanding of the field, formulating appropriate policies, and promoting constructive corporate activity.

Also, whereas before managers would invite professors to meet with them and report on developments in the field, today it is equally likely that managers with direct experience in promoting work innovations will address these management groups. For example, the chairman of the board of a major packaging company recently assembled his top corporate and divisional executives to learn about the work innovations of a major automobile company by a firsthand report of the auto company's vice chairman.

A particularly striking example of the trend toward top management interest in work innovations and toward more manager-to-manager consultation on the subject is provided by a November 1977 conference sponsored by the American Center for the Quality of Working Life. Convened for the purpose of exchanging experiences and examining from the "practical viewpoint of operating executives the principles underlying quality of work life efforts and their efficacy in society," the conference was attended by 40 senior executives from Xerox, General Motors, Nabisco, and Weyerhaeuser.

The "blue collar blues" may promote the adoption and diffusion of innovative work designs in a wide range of industries, from blue collar manufacturing work to white collar and service work and in both the private and the public sector, but a major reason companies are trying work improvement projects is competition. Another is the changing expectations of workers, whose consciousness of quality of work life issues continues to rise. Another is the implicit threat of legislation that might set new, more embracing quality of work environment standards or that might require workers to participate in the governance of private industry.

ASKING THE RIGHT QUESTIONS

Despite the many good reasons for attempting work improvement systems, their future depends on how managers approach some fundamental issues and whether they reject the myths surrounding these efforts. Some misconceptions yield easily to more valid assumptions; others appear to need more direct challenge.

Have Work Improvements Been Effective?

There has been a tendency for people to assume that work innovation projects are either spectacular successes or abject failures. At the expense of some widely held myths, however, people active in the field have become increasingly realistic, recognizing that, in fact, projects can and do fall at every point along a broad spectrum of effectiveness.

I have been deeply involved in 4 major projects and am familiar with aspects of another 30 or so. In terms of their effectiveness in achieving excellence in business and quality of work life outcomes, my impression is that these three dozen projects represent roughly a normal distribution around the mean, just as the effectiveness of more conventionally organized plants would be expected to form a normal distribution.

I believe that the average effectiveness of these innovative work systems is higher than the average of more conventionally organized but otherwise comparable plants. Certainly, however, the poorly managed innovative plants are less effective than the better managed conventional ones. I cannot offer proof that these assumptions are valid, but the mixed experiences of the companies I have discussed illustrate my observations.

Despite the evidence, the myths persist. I have visited a few innovative plants that were advertised as significantly successful, only to discover that they were at best marginally more effective than they would have been without the work innovations. And I have read reports of the "failures" of previously publicized projects, which, on investigation, I found were faulty. People had blown some difficulties encountered in the design or implementation of the projects way out of proportion.

Why these exaggerations? First, people view such efforts with emotion—some being deeply committed to work improvement activities, others being basically hostile to them. Second, where they are involved, the media deem dramatic successes and failures to be newsworthy. Third, because their expectations are high, people readily see any shortfall as a failure.

Even assuming that work innovations have merit, managers and researchers need to have the realistic expectation that their effectiveness will conform to some normal distribution.

What Are the Sponsors' Motives?

Myths have surrounded the motives of those promoting or undertaking work improvement activities. People see sponsors as narrowly interested in either productivity or the human condition, each at the expense of the other. During the early

1970s, when much interest in work improvement was stimulated by one of the two objectives, these beliefs had some basis in reality, but the situation has gradually changed.

In the successful innovations, managers behave as if both economic and human values count. I am familiar with several major innovative work systems that have taken a long time to become effective (and in one plant remain not very effective today) because management's choices were too heavily influenced by quality of work life considerations in the beginning.

In one case, for example, while stability of assignments and mastery of jobs was necessary to get the plant's new technology under control, employees were permitted to move among jobs and learn multiple skills that would advance their pay. Management later recognized that it had erred in not continuously keeping economic as well as human considerations in mind.

Conversely, I am aware of some abortive job redesign efforts in which management strictly viewed worker satisfaction either as a means to improve productivity or as an incidental by-product. Not surprisingly, management's orientation affected not only what changes were made but also workers' attitudes toward the changes. Many union officials believe it unwise to be publicly committed to productivity as well as to quality of work life goals lest the former be identified with speedups and other activities that achieve productivity at the workers' expense. Nevertheless, union officials often implicitly acknowledge the legitimacy of improved business results.

A commitment to dual outcomes is congruent with the values increasingly held by knowledgeable people, but also it has proved to be the most practical approach to making significant advances toward either end. Consider the point negatively.

When changes in the work structure do not improve the work environment from a human perspective, they will not increase employees' contribution to the business; likewise, changes in work structure that require managers to relate differently to workers but do not also benefit the business are not as likely to be sustained by those managers over time.

One should not confuse a dedication to achieving both results with the assumption that meeting one will guarantee the other; morale and productivity are not necessarily linked. Morale can be enhanced in any number of ways. Rather, a commitment to dual objectives sets in motion a search for the limited set of changes that will promote both human and economic ends.

Some issues will inevitably not yield to dual orientation. Planners and managers will have to make trade-off decisions in areas where achieving human goals can occur only at the expense of the business, and vice versa. Nevertheless, it is more important for those involved in work improvement to recognize that in most work structures there is an abundance of opportunities to make changes that will advance both objectives.

What Do Workers Really Want from Work?

Individuals and groups will always express broad differences in the types of work structure they prefer. Therefore, as the multiple-level framework indicates, the ideal culture and the design features of the work structure need to be responsive to the employee population at a given location. Even though researchers and managers are learning which questions about employees' needs and preferences will provide good guidelines to practice, they continue to ask a few either-or questions, which are more confusing than helpful.

Observers often ask variations of the following question: "Are people motivated more by intrinsic factors, such as tasks that use and develop their skills, or by extrinsic factors, such as variable pay for performance and the prospect of advancement?" Both kinds of factor are important, albeit one may be more important to any one group at any one time. The most significant question is how to integrate both extrinsic and intrinsic factors in a practical way.

My observation is that workers in innovative systems have not had to choose between more interesting work and more pay; and that where intrinsic satisfaction has increased, the pay has been improved, reflecting the workers' greater contribution. As Irving Bluestone of the UAW has said of the American worker, "While his rate of pay may dominate his relationship to his job, he can be responsive to the opportunity for playing an innovative, creative, and imaginative role in the production process."[4]

A related question people often ask is: "Are people more interested in finding meaning in the workplace or in minimizing the time spent there?" While the answer to this question may add to our understanding of the sociology of work today, it is not a productive question for improving current practice. It is better to assume that the work force as a whole would like both in some measure.

But, even if some workers care more about time off than a meaningful work life, it may still pay to heed the lower priority issue because improving the meaning of the workplace may be much more feasible than reducing the workweek. Speculating about workers' desires also leads to the related myths about regional differences and the need for selective hir-

[4] See Irving Bluestone, "The Next Step Toward Industrial Democracy" (Detroit: UAW Paper 1972), p. 4.

ing. Each myth is built on the assumption that a relatively small subset of the work force has attitudes and talents compatible with work restructuring. I have heard managers assert, "It may work in a plant located in a small town in the Midwest, but workers in the South (or the Northeast, California, big cities, and so on) are different."

If an innovative plant is located in an abundant labor market where supervisors screen, say, six times as many applicants as they actually hire, then their myth may be: "Only one in six is a high achiever who will be receptive to the new work structure. It is okay to redesign work if you can be selective but not if you are in a tight labor market."

Fortunately, since projects are launched in all regions of the country, in both rural and urban areas, in both tight and abundant labor markets, and appear to have a degree of effectiveness not determined by these factors, belief in these myths is weakening.

What Economic Benefits Can One Expect?

Managers frequently ask: "How much productivity gain can one expect from work redesign?" Unfortunately, some advocates answer: "One should be able to achieve 15% to 20% improvement in productivity." The question itself is emphatically misdirected, and the response just cited is meaningless without knowing what index of productivity the questioner has in mind and whether it is appropriate. For example, the number of output units per man-hour may not be an important index when labor is a low fraction of total costs. Moreover, prior to analysis of the operations in question, one cannot assume a basis for the estimates.

An inquiry and response should focus on methods by which managers can answer the question for themselves. The form of potential gains will vary significantly according to the technology used. The magnitude of possible gains will depend on how well the units is already performing and on whether the aspects of performance that can be improved are strongly influenced by employees' attitudes and skills. Finally, whether potential gains ever materialize depends on the quality of redesign ideas and their implementation.

The following examples illustrate how productivity indexes can take different forms:

- A facility that warehouses and supplies engine parts to dealers and dealer chains could gain new accounts by speeding up its delivery response; it could add very profitable business if it could promise certain large national chains 48 hours versus 72 hours for delivery.
- In a capital-intensive plant that machines casted parts, management determined that it was technically feasible to increase by 15% the maximum throughput of a $10 million segment of the technology manned by 10 employees. This rate has, however, been achieved only for brief periods of time because of the limitations of operating personnel. Running speeds and machine downtime play a similarly important role in other parts of this plant and strongly affect its competitiveness.
- In a relatively high labor-intensive business, management was experiencing a high rate of turnover. The particular tasks, mostly assembly line jobs, did not require great skill, but learning the idiosyncracies of the company's many different products took a lot of time. While the new employees were learning to deal with these peculiarities, their higher scrap rates and lower labor efficiency significantly affected unit costs. As a result, the turnover costs were significant.

To assess the potential of work improvements in the foregoing operations, one

should ask: "How much difference would it make if workers cared more and knew more about this work?" Let us examine the first example in light of this question to show how one can begin to analyze the situation.

First, one needs some facts: the replacement engine parts center employs about 100 hourly workers; the pay is good for this type of work in the area; turnover is relatively low; and labor relations are amicable. While workers do not especially identify with management and many are known to goof off whenever possible, they are not antagonistic.

After a preliminary analysis of the various ways in which performance is sensitive to employee motivation and knowledge, the management of the center estimated that:

1. Employees could reasonably handle a 10% additional volume, even allowing for increased time to be devoted to training and regular meetings. But the 10% savings would not create a net economic benefit because the wage increases reflecting greater job scope and skills would offset them.
2. The cost of errors (orders lost, wrong parts pulled, overages, underages, or damages in shipment due to carelessness) could be reduced by $100,000 per year.
3. The work system could reliably handle up to 25% of the facility's volume within a 48-hour response time, enabling the management to win over some additional accounts and increase the margins on some existing ones and thereby to add an estimated $200,000 more profit per year.
4. The potential benefits of $300,000 assumes a work force that cares more and knows more and that is amenable to flexibility in work assignments based on the needs of the business, the latter point being especially critical to reducing the center's response time.

The foregoing analysis illustrates good practice.

First, management identified particular points in the system where poor labor utilization, errors, and limitations in response time occurred. It did not rely on global hunches.

Second, by converting potential gains to annual dollar amounts, management could see the relative importance of error reduction and improved response time. Moreover, management could relate the benefits to other factors; for example, $300,000 would be a saving equals to 25% of the annual payroll.

Third, management understood these were potential benefits and not certain gains that would automatically flow from the adoption of some set of design techniques. Its ability to achieve any of these benefits depended on its ingenuity and skill. It always ran the risk that it would not be able to modify the work culture as intended.

Fourth, management knew that for any changes to be effective from a business standpoint, it would also have to improve the work from the workers' point of view.

Managers in the machining operation and assembly unit followed procedures similar to the one just outlined. However, their estimate of benefits took a different form. Because they could spread the large fixed interest and depreciated expenses, managers in the capital-intensive machining operation figured that increasing the output rate of finished parts by 15% would result in lower unit costs. The estimated annual savings represented 150% of the $140,000 payroll for the unit—that is, $210,000.

In the assembly line unit, the managers concluded that it was not feasible to reduce turnover significantly, that only modest improvements in scrap and labor efficiency were possible, and that costs associated with any changes contemplated would largely offset the estimated gains.

In cases such as those just described, management's analyses are limited by the same difficulties encountered in estimating the costs and benefits of untried technologies or management systems—that is, the estimates can prove to be incomplete, too optimistic, too conservative, and so on. Nevertheless, the analytic approach presented here illustrates the systematic and realistic efforts managers should make to assess the potential performance gains.

Which procedures a manager actually uses and the level of detail of the analysis is not the point. The important point is that planners have some systematic approach for assessing potential benefits that might accrue if the cultural ideas are actually realized. The methodology need not be elaborate.

SOME LESSONS FROM EXPERIENCE

For those who consider undertaking new initiatives and promoting the spread of successful innovations to other units in the organization, I offer the following guidelines. Though not comprehensive, they are nonetheless derived from observations of the contrasts between relatively effective work improvement efforts and less effective ones.

1. *Attempt work improvement because of its intrinsic positive values, not because it might be a way to avoid unionization.* Apart from the fact that I believe in the institution of collective bargaining, trying to avoid unionization has several drawbacks. One is that unions are more likely to join in efforts to adapt innovations to existing facilities if work patterns are not being used as an antiunion device in the new plants. Another is that, although most projects in the United States have been in nonunionized offices and plants, the amount of joint union-management cooperation is increasing. Such projects as Harman Industries, Weyerhaeuser, Tennessee Valley Authority, the Rushton Coal Miners, and Rockwell International attest to the benefit of cooperation.

As I stated earlier, GM and UAW have a very active program of work improvement. The approach contractually agreed on by the parties is oriented to quality of work life, but as the Tarrytown experience illustrates, management, union officials, and workers are all genuinely interested in the business results. Irving Bluestone, international vice president of the UAW, describes the joint GM-UAW program as follows:

> The objective of our quality of work life program is to create a more participative and satisfying work environment. If, as a result of increased participation, unit costs are improved because turnover rates go down and product quality goes up, that is fine.
>
> But if a plant manager is thinking of a quality of work life project as a means for increasing productivity, we don't proceed. There are certain other constraints—people must not be compelled to work harder, changes must not result in workers getting laid off, and the local and national agreements remain inviolate. The projects must be from the ground up and participation voluntary on the part of workers. The first phase of all projects is to improve the climate of mutual respect between union and management; if this doesn't succeed, there is no basis to proceed on. Plant management and the local union must both be committed.[5]

During the past half dozen years, as work improvement activities have been growing in number, diversity, and visibility, both labor and management have encountered doubt within their own ranks. UAW officials have not found it easy to

[5] Irving Bluestone, in personal conversation with the author.

convince union members that the program is not a management gimmick to increase productivity and perhaps weaken the union.

At GM, managers at certain levels express concern that the program will result in a loss of authority and prestige. These fears are diminishing gradually but can flare up at any event that seems to support them. Still, the commitment at the top of both organizations has been extraordinary and is bolstered by a growing constituency of local managers and union officials who have had positive experiences.

According to Bluestone, very few projects have actually failed, but more time must pass before the majority of projects currently under way can be declared successes.

2. *Recognize the basic difference between opportunities in new facilities and opportunities in existing ones.* Once, most people assumed that the major innovations introduced in new plant start-ups could serve as inspirational and instructive examples for managements and union officials of established plants. I have concluded that providing examples of what was done in a new organization is not helpful in enabling managers of established units to visualize alternative futures for their units and is not an effective stimulus for developing a program for transforming them.

The reasons are severalfold and go beyond the fact that a particular work structure that is successful in a new plant may be inappropriate in an old one. More fundamentally, the processes of innovation (diagnosing, planning, inventing, and implementing) are significantly different for new and existing units. In established facilities, the level of aspiration for change and the time frame allotted for achieving it must be much more modest than in new facilities.

In selecting aspects of work structure that can be changed, planners, need to be opportunistic—doing what they can when they can. Also, the main job of planners in old facilities is defrosting the old work culture and creating a sense of the potential for change. To do this, they need to give careful attention to the participative processes for deciding the direction and method of the change.

Fortunately, the literature is providing us with a growing number of instructive examples of productive change in established organizations. The Tarrytown plant is one such example.

3. *Avoid either-or conceptions of work organization.* An example of this faulty thinking relates to the sources and types of controls: "Traditional systems rely on hierarchical controls. The innovative system is the opposite; therefore, it must rely on individual or team self-management." Another example of this thinking is: "If we need to rely on self-discipline and peer group pressure to minimize counterproductive behavior, then there is no place for management-administered discipline."

Indeed, as managers in these work systems have sooner or later discovered, a selective emphasis and sensible mixture of management techniques are called for. A number of organizations have had to go through a period of permissiveness before management discovered the need to set and enforce certain boundaries on the behavior of members of the company.

Managers make a related mistake when they assume that an organization at start-up can be at an idealized, advanced state of development. Some plans for new plant organization neglect the important distinction between conceiving of the steady state design and designing the initial organization. These plants start up with workers and supervisors having roles and responsibilities that reflect the planners' idealized view of the mature organization. Workers lack the technical and human skills as well as the problem-solving capacities to perform effectively. Supervisors cannot merely "facilitate"—they must provide directive supervision.

Delegation is the cornerstone of new plant development. Such delegation must be rooted in careful diagnosis of the existing base of skills and capabilities in the work force and a realistic view of their ability to develop over time.

4. *Do not advocate one answer; spread a way of looking for answers.* Managers and planners need to inculcate their people with a way of thinking about the diagnosis and designing of innovative work structures, not the work structures themselves. This is a major implication of my three-level conception of work improvement activity. It is less appropriate (and sometimes counterproductive) to promote the spread of particular techniques—for example, enriched jobs, team concepts, productivity gain sharing—than it is to promote the diffusion of a diagnostic and innovative planning process.

VII

THE ROLE OF
FEEDBACK MECHANISMS,
COMMUNICATIONS
PROGRAMS, AND TRAINING
AND DEVELOPMENT

Many companies, especially large ones, have devised a variety of personnel programs and policies that serve both as upward and downward communications devices. A number of these approaches can also be viewed as top management feedback mechanisms. They also frequently identify training needs of both employees and managers. Before describing the purposes of these various policies and programs, let us list some of the communications programs that are in use today: attitude surveys; either on-premise or off-site employee counseling programs for personal and/or job related problems; employee meetings, sensing sessions, or forums conducted either by the supervisor, a personnel manager, or a higher-level member of management; speak-out programs; ombudsperson programs; employee newspapers and bulletin boards; question boxes; suggestion systems; and either the open door policy or another for-

mal complaint or grievance procedure. Although many of these programs are prevalent in large, nonunion companies or in the nonunion parts of large, unionized companies, many also may be found in unionized companies. In organized companies, the union of course establishes a network of communication channels as well as a formal grievance procedure, including arbitration.

OBJECTIVES

Formal communications programs and feedback mechanisms, which both supplement and check the employee-supervisor relationship, can serve one or more of five basic purposes. First, they can be a device to learn of and respond constructively to real or perceived general or individual employee problems. An employee's supervisor may not know the answers to some employee questions. At other times the employee's supervisor may be part of the problem. Consequently, a question box or a speak-out program can fulfill a real need. Moreover, there are times when an employee may not feel comfortable in discussing a problem with the supervisor. Such problems may be either job related or personal in nature. Speak-out programs are found by various names in many large companies. Citibank's program is called Citi-Line; Polaroid's program is called Confidential Interact.

Second, some upward communications programs represent a way for top management to help create and maintain a climate of openness and trust. They not only signal to employees that top management and/or the personnel department cares about and is interested in them as individuals, but they also provide a safety valve for employees to let off steam and frustrations. If, for instance, top-level managers have to sign the prepared responses to speak-out letters or meet regularly with hourly employees, they necessarily become more involved with employee concerns and problems. Their involvement, in turn, will help keep supervisors more in tune with employee relations issues. Moreover, in today's work environment, with agencies such as the Equal Employment Opportunity Commission and the Occupational Safety and Health Administration ready and willing to hear employee complaints about discrimination in employment or safety and health problems in the workplace, many managements would prefer an internal mechanism for employees to use. Without such programs, employees are forced to use the available external procedures. For the internal procedures to be effective, however, employees must have trust and confidence in top management.

Third, upward communications programs are a device for top management to learn first hand about employee concerns, suggestions, and grievances. Such programs educate top management not only about employee problems and views, but about working conditions and supervisory behavior as well. These out-of-the-regular-hierarchy devices, such as attitude surveys or employee meetings, avoid the filter problem of lower management telling top management only what it is believed top management wants to hear—namely, good news. They help top management keep its "finger on the pulse." Attitude surveys are a way to measure the morale of an organization. A "percent favorable" index can be calculated and used for comparison purposes. What is also important, of course, is the way in which opinion surveys are used, especially with respect to survey feedback meetings with employees. Employees asked to participate each year in an attitude survey, which in their view produces no results, will come to question the motives of management. Managers, therefore, must be trained to give feedback, and employees must see improvement and gain greater understanding of why things are as they are. Managers need to be given tools by which they can develop follow-up corrective action. It is therefore essential to break down survey results for the different operating units or functions within a company.

Fourth, some of these mechanisms give top management an opportunity to communicate downward facts and information of general concern as well as to respond to individual questions and problems. Whether in group or individual meetings or in written responses to general interest questions, management can talk about the state of the business as well as the problems facing the company. For real communication and education, there is, of course, no substitute for two-way face-to-face communication.

Finally, many of these approaches serve as an additional incentive for supervisors to perform the employee relations aspect of their jobs well. For instance, the supervisor who is sensitive to employee concerns and problems will minimize either the speak-out letters or open door complaints being filed by his or her employees; poor attitude survey results will also be minimized.

Because a supervisor does not want to risk being "chewed out" by bosses, the existence of formal programs can stimulate supervisors to engage in informal, problem-solving discussions with employees. If employees have the opportunity to complain to top management, the effective supervisor will give them as little as possible to complain about, especially with regard to items which might reflect unfavorably on him or her. While the supervisor who handles employees well has nothing to fear, many supervisors, especially weak ones, may be particularly resistant to the introduction and use of formal upward communications devices. They may see such programs as "supervisory by-pass" programs. Many of the approaches, it should be noted, make it easier to evaluate how effectively the supervisor carries out the human relations or people-management aspects of the job. But good supervisors will recognize both the need for and the purpose of such upward communication programs if they are administered well.

ORIENTATION AND TRAINING

Effective communication is particularly important because a significant number of people in the work force are cynical.[1] Cynicism, studies show, varies considerably by age, sex, race, and years of formal education. The younger, less educated members of the work force are the most cynical. With an "us against them" attitude, they are suspicious of other people's motives and do not trust others. Furthermore, they spurn innovation and create unrest. Their first loyalty is to themselves, not the company. With the knowledge that a number of the receivers of the formal messages will not believe them, management must think not only of the content of its message, but also of the sources of important information. Some information sources and communication techniques have more credibility than others. For example, Professors Kanter and Mirvis, the researchers who conducted the study cited above, recommend six approaches to corporate communication that they believe may be useful in lowering the cynics' barriers to communication and reducing their generally negative word-of-mouth influence. The six approaches suggested are:

1. A two-sided approach to presenting information, exposing both sides of issues so that cynics cannot say there was a coverup;
2. Management communication phrased in such a way that it allows people to make up their own minds rather than being a direct transmission of policy;
3. Do not unduly raise the expectations of workers, for later discrepancy between management's stated intentions and the final outcome will tend to disparage the sincerity of the original intentions;
4. Management presentations should be low-key, factual, and cool with the idea that management is offering information and not propaganda;
5. Spokespeople from senior management rather than from lower-level management because cynics are as interested in the source of information as they are in the substance; and finally,

[1] Donald L. Kanter and Philip H. Mirvis, "Managing Jaundiced Workers," *New Management*, Vol. 3, No. 4, Spring 1986, pp. 50–54.

6. The communication of important messages should be followed by informal, small-group meetings.[2]

Upward communication programs also help management and the human resources department develop appropriate orientation and training programs for employees and supervisors. For example, at Norway's Norske Shell, two questions, in the form of statements, are asked about pay.

1. My salary development is satisfactory.
2. My salary gives a fair impression of my work for the company.

Answers to the questions are given under one of the following six categories: disagree entirely; tend to disagree; disagree more than agree; agree more than disagree; tend to agree; and agree entirely. Under a six-part grading scale, if an employee marks disagree more than agree, the answer rates three points. If he marks disagree entirely, the answer gets one point. If he marks agree entirely, it gets six points. If the scores for the compensation questions are at unsatisfactory levels, management knows that some action needs to be taken. The action could be pay improvements. It could also be a training program for the supervisors on the pay plan, its administration, and the performance appraisal plan. It also might include a section explaining a government wage control program.

Illustrating the usefulness of department breakdowns, at Norske Shell one district showed an unusually low score on both of these salary questions for successive surveys. The problem, however, was isolated to a small group of employees in the unit who for a long time had sought to have their jobs reclassified and their salaries raised in line with other similar skills. In this particular case, because of the survey results, a team from company headquarters visited the site and successfully negotiated a solution that in turn led to subsequent improvement in the scores of the salary questions.

Training is not only for individual development but to enhance future productivity and organizational effectiveness. Some, in fact, think that future productivity advances may come more from improvements in the effectiveness and productivity of management than from technological advances. Although real development is self-development and most people learn on the job by doing the work itself and from effective coaching, formal training and management development programs can be important supplements.

To help the manager orient new employees, Hewlett-Packard, not unlike a number of other companies, developed an orientation checklist (see Figure VII–1). It is important that the new employee get off to a good start. The training required, of course, depends on the job. The initial training for some jobs is one or two hours; for other jobs the training required is several months. It may be several months, for example, before a college graduate hired to sell computers sees his or her first customer. This is also true for trainees for lending positions in banks.

According to a study by the American Society for Training and Development, private and public employers spend more than $30 billion a year for employee training and development. This is approximately half the cost of all higher education in the United States. In 1974 Xerox opened a $75 million training and management development center in Leesburg, Virginia, where it trains thousands of employees each year. In 1986 Motorola dedicated a $10 million center for continuing education near its corporate headquarters in

[2] Ibid., pp. 51–52.

Schaumburg, Illinois. Robert Galvin, Motorola's chairman and chief executive officer, in remarks prepared for the dedication ceremony, said the following:

> Training and education are part of Motorola's strategic response to maintaining a leading position in an increasingly competitive marketplace for advanced electronics. This is a place for all Motorola employees to learn new skills that will make them more productive and efficient.

At Motorola's Training and Education Center (called MoTEC by employees) a broad spectrum of courses is offered, from advanced computer sciences courses for engineers to word-processing skills for clerical employees. The courses a typical large company may sponsor will range from English as a second language, or welding, to manufacturing management, and human relations. Some courses aim to add knowledge; others are to develop and sharpen skills. Still others, such as modules on EEO, seek attitude and/or behavior change. In the late eighties, for example, a number of companies were hiring trainers and consultants to conduct "gender-awareness" workshops for company employees. These workshops focus on sex-role stereotypes in relations between men and women at work. Through role-playing exercises and discussions led by an outside expert, participants are encouraged to consider what behavior they expect of the opposite sex in a variety of common business settings.

Although there are important differences in the knowledge and skills managers need in different operating units and in different functional areas, there are also significant similarities. Increasingly, accordingly, large companies are designing and offering common courses for new first-level managers, for experienced first-level managers, for new managers of man-

agers as well as their staff equivalents, for experienced managers of managers, and for new and experienced executives. Some companies also offer courses to help participants decide if they want a management career.

MANAGEMENT DEVELOPMENT

A Bureau of National Affairs Study found that three-quarters of the companies it surveyed had in-house supervision training programs. More than half of the companies also provided training through outside seminars, professional or trade association meetings, and self-training courses. Formal courses are geared to the needs of the participants and the nature of the company. On the one hand, the new manager needs to know both the basic responsibilities of a manager and the company's basic policies and practices. He or she also needs some opportunities to practice the basic skills of managing people. These skills include coaching, counseling, and appraising and rewarding performance. Experienced managers, on the other hand, need learning opportunities that are broadening with respect to strategic planning, the global economy, societal values and expectations, and business-government relationships.

The organization chart for the management development function at one large, multinational company appears in Figure VII–2. Illustrating the importance this company attaches to management development, the 1987 salary and bonus for this company's director of management development exceeded $200,000. Larger companies tend to have more formal management development programs than smaller companies. Their thrust tends to be effective replacement planning—integrating at high levels manpower planning, based on business needs, with career plan-

FIGURE VII-1 Hewlett-Packard orientation checklist

MAKE THE NEW EMPLOYEE FEEL AT HOME

- Greet employee properly and welcome to HP.
- Introduce to co-workers.
- Explain working hours, breaks, lunch, and sick leave procedure.
- Give a brief tour of the work area, locate restrooms, etc.
- Explain the use of the phone for emergency and personal calls.
- See that employee has someone to eat lunch with.
- Explain how we get paid; time cards.
- Answer questions.

LET EMPLOYEE KNOW WHAT IS EXPECTED

- Explain all rules (smoking, visitors, parking, etc.).
- Cover importance of good housekeeping.
- Cover importance of good attendance.
- How to report absence or lateness.
- Reporting changes in address, telephone, marital status and dependents.
- High level of enthusiasm and interest.
- Look for better ways to do the job.

INSTRUCT EMPLOYEE IN THE PREVENTION OF ACCIDENTS

- Stress the importance of safety and explain safety regulations.
- Show the location of first aid supplies, safety glasses, etc.
- Teach employee to work safely, using the four training steps:
  1. Tell how to do it safely.
  2. Show the safe way to do it.
  3. Have employee show you how to do it safely.
  4. Follow-up to answer questions and check understanding.
- Stress the policy of reporting accidents promptly.

BEGIN JOB TRAINING

- Give a preview of your training plans.
- Explain where and how to obtain supplies, tools, etc.
- Discuss quantity and quality standards, department objectives.
- Do a job breakdown, listing important steps and key points, *before* training.
- Have the work area: in order, supplied, and arranged as it should be kept.
- Train in small portions, using these steps:
  1. Put at ease; find out what is already known; interest employee.
  2. Tell how to do the job, step by step, stressing key points. Show. Show and tell together. Show, letting employee tell how.
  3. Let person do the job, then do it again, explaining key points to you.
  4. Put employee on own but follow up frequently, tapering off gradually.
- Let employee know how much skill you expect and by what date.

FOLLOW-UP ON FIRST WEEK'S PROGRESS

- Check to see how employee is progressing.
- Check for questions.
- Take immediate action if, after understanding safety rules, person is not observing them.
- Continue job training, using the four-step method.
- Give feedback on punctuality and attendance—including positive comments. *(Be sure your absence and lateness records are accurate and meaningful—include type, reason given, action taken. NEVER neglect the first absence. Absenteeism and lateness are closely related, and the costliest corrective problems you have. Some causes: transportation, domestic worries, illnesses, personal problems, job dissatisfaction, poor attitude and morale.)*

EXPLAIN FIRST PAYCHECK

- Go over pay deductions, explaining how they are computed, if necessary.
- Remind that additional deductions are made as you become eligible for various benefits.
- Answer any questions about pay, vacation, sick leave, etc.

REVIEW WORK PERFORMANCE

- Review the quality of work. *If it is lower than it should be, check the following for causes:*
  1. Lack of understanding of the correct way to perform the job;
  2. Lack of understanding of required standards;
  3. Lack of ability to meet the standards;
  4. Defective equipment;
  5. Defective materials;
  6. Carelessness.

  (The presence of any of these conditions requires action from you.)
- Discuss your recommendations for improvement. Get employee's ideas and feelings about these areas; reach mutual agreement.
- Let employee know the date of first formal review.

13TH (OR 26TH) WEEK AND 52ND WEEK

CONDUCT A FORMAL PERFORMANCE REVIEW

- Ask first what employee thinks was done well and what should be done better. Listen. Find out how you can help. If you disagree, discuss your point of view, but make it clear you consider employee's judgment and feelings as well as your own.
- Discuss the performance expectations or goals which were set earlier and how well they have been met. Discuss the job, not the person.
- Ask what goals should be set for the next review period—add any of your own which are not covered. Agree on specifics and on a very general plan—document these agreed-upon goals, making sure that each of you have a copy. (May require additional sessions.)
- Discuss personal goals and objectives.
- 52nd week—Annual Performance Review.

Source: Company material. By permission of Hewlett-Packard.

ning, based on individual needs and objectives.

The best training approach depends on the desired objectives. In a survey to rate the effectiveness of nine standard training methods for achieving various objectives, Dr. John Newstrom of the University of Minnesota concluded that for almost every training objective there was a different "best" method. His findings are as follows:

Training Objective	Most Effective Method	Least Effective Method
Knowledge acquisition	Conference (discussion) method	TV lecture
Changing attitudes	Sensitivity training	TV lecture
Teaching problem-solving skills	Case studies	Films
Teaching interpersonal skills	Role playing	TV lecture
Acceptance by participants	Case studies	Programmed instruction
Knowledge retention	Programmed instruction	Sensitivity training

From "Evaluating the Effectiveness of Training Methods." Reprinted from the January 1980 issue of *Personnel Administrator*, copyright 1980, The American Society for Personnel Administration, Alexandria, VA.

Increasingly, management games, including those involving interactive video, are becoming part of both company and university management development programs. Video disk training, utilizing the personal computer, is becoming popular. Because of its high cost, its use seems to be primarily limited to large companies in which the number of trainees makes the economics of video disk training practical. *Business Week* reported that IAV (interactive video) systems train salespeople, train clerks to analyze insurance applications, and help service technicians learn to do a faster, better job of fixing defective equipment, among other applications.[3] Large companies are, in addition, establishing

[3] "Videos Are Starring in More and More Training Programs," *Business Week*, September 7, 1987, p. 108.

interoffice television through private television networks. They are investing in studios, satellite transmitters, and receiving dishes for regular broadcasts to convey information and to engage in two-way communications.

Dr. Newstrom advises training directors to improve their training programs by analyzing the use of different methods and the degree to which they achieve the objectives. It is important to have training objectives and to attempt to measure the effectiveness and the efficiency of training programs. This is easier to do for some kinds of training than for others.

IBM has an impressive record of developing managers. Through formal classes at its schools, the company devotes substantial resources so that its managers will have opportunities to develop themselves. Serious efforts are made, through stimulative kinds of training, to keep managers up to date on the latest management techniques and developments.

The Chase Manhattan Corporation, too, has an impressive array of development programs. For an overview of the work of the Chase Development Institute, see Figure VII–3.

When Alan F. Lafley, Executive Vice President in charge of corporate human resources for Chase, was asked in 1980 in an interview about the "people challenges" facing the bank and what the bank was doing in the area of staff development, he replied as follows:

Over the past three years, we've made significant investment in staff development in terms of people and dollars. We've initiated a wide spectrum of activities—from an advanced management program, that has now been attended by about 300 key officers, to a refinement of Chase's highly regarded credit training programs. We are now providing individually focused development programs on a worldwide basis, including marketing and sales training, management skills train-

FIGURE VII–2

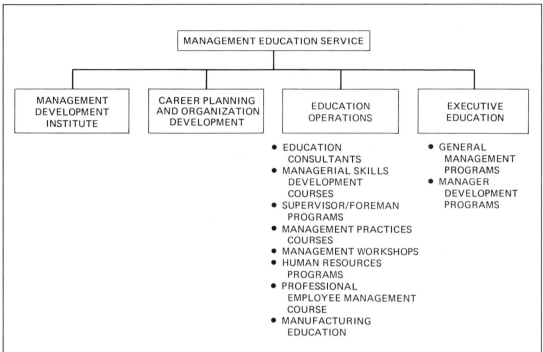

ing, supervisory training, and operations training. Additionally, we are focusing, with Chase's various business units, on tailored development plans to meet their particular needs. This incorporates informal on-the-job activities in addition to formal programs.[4]

As is the case at Motorola, training and development increasingly is being viewed in strategic terms as a key tool to meet today's competitive realities. It is being used as a critical device to implement new strategies, to reshape company culture, and as a lever for change. As Akio Morita of Sony put it: "Those companies that are most successful in Japan are those that have managed to create a shared sense of fate among all employees." Effective train-

[4]"An Interview with Alan F. Lafley," *The Chase Quarterly,* Third Quarter Ended September 30, 1980.

ing opportunities can help employers develop a "shared sense of fate" or common vision of the company and its future. Budgets for such training in many companies are being increased. In 1987 executive education was the fastest growing segment of higher education.

Stating that the pace of change in executive education is much faster than ever imagined, executive development consultant James F. Bolt has noted that several major corporations, including Federated Department Stores, Motorola, General Foods, and Xerox, have developed major management training and development programs aimed at assisting them to implement new corporate strategies. Shared characteristics of these successful programs are the following: (1) The programs are tailored and directly linked to the

FIGURE VII–3   Overview of Chase Development Institute programs

THE CHASE DEVELOPMENT INSTITUTE

The Chase Development Institute is a carefully planned set of experiences designed to develop and support excellence in managerial and professional performance. The Institute covers courses, seminars, workshops and other formal development activities Chase offers its employees.

The Chase Development Institute recognizes the following facts:

1. Chase is operating in a dynamic business environment and wants to maximize its ability to respond to opportunities in that environment.
2. Chase departments are interdependent and, therefore, have a high need for a consistent and integrated approach to management.
3. Chase is committed to the development of its people.
4. Chase's business needs must be the overriding consideration in any development decision.

Individual development can occur in many ways. Mastering one's current job, going into a new and different job, entering a temporary assignment, working on a task force, and assuming different responsibilities are a few of the forms that on-the-job development can take.

There are times, however, when formal development activities are appropriate. The Chase Development Institute includes a range of development activities that meet high priority needs:

Management

- Chase Advanced Management Course
- Chase Management Skills Program
- Chase Supervisory Skills Program
- Performance Management Project

Marketing

- Chase Marketing and Sales Management Program
- Selling Skills Programs (e.g. Xerox, Tratec, Hull)

Professional

- Commercial Banking Orientation Project

Development

- Managing Personal Growth Workshop
- Individual Development Seminar
- Affirmative Action Training Programs for women and minorities: officers, supervisors/professionals and advanced clericals.

The Managerial and Professional Development unit of Corporate Human Resources supports managers in the application of program content through development consulting services. Staff members can also be called upon to consult on developmental activities and the use of outside programs, vendors and consultants.

Source: From "The Chase Development Institute," introduction to descriptive brochure. By permission of The Chase Manhattan Bank, N.A.

unique strategies and goals of each company; (2) all were bottom-line-oriented in that they were designed to effect tangible improvements in financial performance; and (3) the senior executives of each company played key roles in both the design and implementation of each program.[5]

As an example of a management training program that is being used as a key ingredient of a company's effort to become more competitive on a global basis, Bolt

[5] James F. Bolt, "The Future Is Already Here" *New Management*, Vol. 4, No. 3, Winter 1987, pp. 27–29.

cites the case of Motorola. There, he reports, a six-day senior executive program called Focus on Asia was developed for three purposes: to identify and meet the competition, to understand the key factors in Asia that may affect the company's business, and to provide a perspective that would be helpful in the development and improvement of strategic plans.[6]

Illustrative of current developments are the changes that have taken place at General Electric's Management Institute in Crotonville, New York. According to Noel M. Tichy, professor of organizational behavior and industrial relations at the University of Michigan and, from 1985 to 1987, manager of GE's Management Education Operation, GE chairman Jack Welch and other GE leaders decided to make GE's Management Development Institute a "leadership development institute." Its mission is to enhance GE's global competitiveness by providing company professionals and managers with a broad array of experiences while also serving as an instrument for cultural change within the company. GE professionals and managers are required to participate in development experiences at critical transitional points in their careers.[7]

Five key career transitional points have been identified. The sequence begins with new hires and ends with corporate officers. At the first stage and within six months of joining GE, new hires attend Corporate Entry Leadership Conference I, a dialogue centering on global competition, GE's strategy for winning, values, and career and life goals. More than 1,200 new hires participated in this program in 1987. While in their third year, GE professionals attend Corporate Entry Leadership Conference II, in which the emphasis is on "competitive forces, customer orientation, collaboration needed to win in the market place, and what each individual can do to help a business win."

The second stage of corporate development is for all newly appointed GE managers, over 1,000 a year. These managers attend the New Manager Development Program, which concentrates on key skills and knowledge, effective teams, leadership behavior, and value clarification. The managers also learn how they are perceived by their peers through written feedback.

The third stage of development is designed for professionals who have attained top positions in their function, whether it be marketing, finance, information systems, or human resource management. Those participants attend senior-level programs designed to develop both functional depth and multifunctional problem-solving abilities.

The fourth stage is targeted for high-potential leaders moving toward executive management. They participate in three four-week programs to take courses that both broaden and stretch them.

The final stage, frequently neglected in many companies, is for corporate officers. They take part in workshops specifically designed to help them wrestle with the issues relating to their roles in the company. CEO Jack Welch participates, and action plans are completed that are "to leverage change in the company."[8]

Particularly impressive with respect to the GE program is the fact that so many senior line and staff executives teach in the programs. Over 80% of GE's officers teach in these programs. The chairman, vice chairman, and senior line and staff executives not only teach, but are excellent role models for the participants in the program. While a professional trainer can

---

[6] Ibid., p. 29.

[7] Noel M. Tichy, "Training as a Lever for Change," *New Management*, Vol. 4, No. 3, Winter 1987, pp. 39–41.

[8] Ibid., p. 41.

teach performance planning, counseling, and evaluation, the subject has more credibility if it is taught by a senior line manager who participates in the process regularly.

It should also be emphasized, however, that training need not be formal and of the off-site classroom variety to be effective. One of the authors, when he was a training director, held monthly meetings for about six years with mixed groups of ten or so foremen, superintendents, and middle management staff (finance and accounting, purchasing, production scheduling, design and styling, and so forth). It became clear over the years that one could do four different types of things in such meetings: (1) give out and discuss information, (2) discuss policies, (3) solve problems, and (4) give "training" in human relations skills. Of these four types of activity, by far the most frustrating and the least satisfactory was human relations skill training.

Looking upon these meetings as training never seemed appropriate because they were an integral part of running the business. For example, "giving out information" had enormous scope. It exposed foremen to officials and experts they would not otherwise feel they knew. It gave operating people a much better understanding of staff functions. It allowed discussion of many types of trends and developments. For example, once union demands were received, a quickly scheduled round of meetings on them was held. At these meetings we learned the relative importance of demands as foremen "read" employee attitudes. We also learned the positions foremen felt the company should take on issues. After negotiations were over, the results, including changes in the labor agreement, would be reviewed with foremen.

There is a vast difference between giving out information (a financial statement, for example) and discussing it. Even a simple change in procedure frequently warrants considerable discussion. A major problem is the relation of status to what you know. The whole question of top management support of an "open climate" is obviously very important. Saying that something is "confidential" can boomerang. But letting supervisors know what top management is thinking, and asking for their opinions, can be invaluable.

Discussion of policies was always significant. Not all policies nor policy changes are relevant. Any type of policy change directly affecting employees obviously requires discussion as to the whys, wherefores, and consequences. Even policy changes which are rather remote may be worth discussion simply to keep the group informed.

Problem-solving is somewhat complex. In the first place, various types of problems can be *identified* largely as an incidental consequence of meeting with supervisors. In the second place, supervisors' views as to the type of resolution can be elicited. Finally, task forces may be created to recommend solutions to specific problems. For example, all supervisors in one department were asked to work out a production schedule. They did work out a practical schedule. Participatory solutions obviously will be more readily accepted than answers from on high.

Teaching human relations or interpersonal skills involves attempts to change behavior. Supervisors who show little aptitude for handling grievances are not apt to be much changed by an intellectual discussion of the topics. It doesn't do much good to say "get the facts" if the individual has little perception of what facts are needed. On-the-job coaching by a good boss can be more effective, but this approach too has its limitations. Many companies do not have a broad enough perspective of the purposes of supervisory meetings. Moreover, they sometimes get the appropriate priorities confused.

The cases in this section of the book allow the student to examine many aspects of communication programs, attitude surveys, and management development programs. The Harvard University Staff Survey case shows a comprehensive approach to attitude surveys. An attitude survey can be an important tool to help management achieve some of its employee relations objectives. To be successful, however, effective follow-up is a necessity. The Harvard University Staff Survey case is a rich one because it permits the student to examine the attitude survey from several perspectives. The student must not only diagnose the sources of problems, but must also recommend a plan of action to deal with them.

The Apple Computer (Europe) case allows the student to wrestle with broad issues of communications, training, and corporate culture in a rapidly expanding high-technology company. Company culture can be a key vehicle for bringing together large numbers of people in a short period of time.

The United Parcel Service (A) and (B) cases are extremely comprehensive ones that go beyond the issues of training, education, and communications. An extremely successful domestic company must resolve several human resources issues in order to achieve a global strategy. The human resources imperatives of the revised strategy must be resolved if the company is to continue to grow and prosper.

The cases in this section also permit the student to focus on the role of the human resources department with respect to the development and administration of programs. These programs can be viewed as organizational audits by the department, as well as top management feedback devices. It is natural, therefore, to expect supervisory resistance to such programs. Students must not only try to understand the reasons for this resistance, but also to think how either top management or the human resources department should deal with it. Students should be able not only to develop ways to diagnose an organization's training and management development needs, but also to recommend methods by which those needs can be met. The cases also allow students to reflect on the role of the human resources department in the management of change. If top management and the leadership of the human resources function share a strategic vision for the company, the human resources organization is in a unique position, through symbols, words, and actions to partner with management in the attainment of the company's strategic goals through the planned management of change.

BIBLIOGRAPHY:
THE ROLE OF FEEDBACK MECHANISMS, COMMUNICATIONS PROGRAMS, AND TRAINING AND DEVELOPMENT

BAIRD, LLOYD, C. SCHNEIDER, AND D. LAIRD (eds.). *The Training and Development Sourcebook.* Amherst, MA: Human Resource Development Press, 1985.

BECKHARD, RICHARD. *Organization Development: Strategies and Models.* Reading, MA: Addison-Wesley, 1969.

BENNIS, WARREN G. *Organization Development: Its Nature, Origins, and Prospects.* Reading, MA: Addison-Wesley, 1969.

BERENBEIM, RONALD. *Nonunion Complaint Systems: A Corporate Appraisal* (Report No. 770). New York: Conference Board, 1980.

BURKE, W. WARNER. *Current Issues and Strategies in Organization Development.* New York: Human Sciences Press, 1977.

EWING, DAVID W. *Freedom Inside the Organiza-*

tion: Bringing Civil Liberties to the Workplace. New York: McGraw-Hill, 1977.

FOLLMAN, JOSEPH F., JR. *Alcoholics and Business: Problems, Costs, Solutions.* New York: American Management Association, 1975.

GARDNER, JAMES E. *Helping Employees Develop Job Skill: A Casebook of Training Approaches.* Chicago: Rand McNally, 1970.

KRAM, KATHY. *Mentoring at Work.* Glenview, IL: Scott, Foreman, 1984.

LAWLER, EDWARD E., III. *High Involvement Manager.* San Francisco: Jossey-Bass, 1986.

MCLEAN, ALAN A. *Mental Health and Work Organizations.* Chicago: Rand McNally, 1970.

MYERS, M. SCOTT. *Managing Without Unions.* Reading, MA: Addison-Wesley, 1976.

NADLER, LEONARD, AND GARLAND WIGGS. *Managing Human Resource Development.* San Francisco: Jossey-Bass, 1986.

ROBSON, R. THAYNE. *Employment and Training R&D: Lessons Learned and Future Directions.* Kalamazoo, MI: Upjohn Institute, 1984.

ROSOW, JEROME M., AND ROBERT ZAGER. *Cost Effective Design and Delivery of Training Programs.* Scarsdale, NY: Work in America Institute, 1986.

WARREN, MALCOLM W. *Training for Results: A Systems Approach to the Development of Human Resources in Industry,* 2nd ed. Reading, MA: Addison-Wesley, 1979.

WESTIN, ALAN F., (ed.). *Whistle Blowing.* New York: McGraw-Hill, 1980.

————, AND S. SALISBURY (eds.). *Individual Rights in the Corporation: A Reader on Employee Rights.* New York: Pantheon Books, 1980.

WIKSTROM, WALTER S. *Supervisory Training* (Report No. 612). New York: The Conference Board, 1973.

YODER, DALE, AND HERBERT G. HENEMAN, JR. (eds.). *Training and Development.* Washington, DC: Bureau of National Affairs, Inc., 1977.

YUILL, BRUCE, AND DANIEL STEINHOFF. *Developing Managers in Organizations.* New York: Wiley, 1975.

Harvard University Staff Survey

INTRODUCTION

Daniel D. Cantor was in his ninth year as Director of Personnel for Harvard University. Cantor had joined the university in 1976 after many years of personnel work in industry and in the Peace Corps.

Cantor viewed the decade of his tenure as an eventful and productive one for the personnel function. Of the programs enacted under his leadership, he thought the recently conducted 1985 attitude survey was one of his significant accomplishments. Although attitude surveys were common tools of the personnel trade in corporations, among universities only Stanford was known to have conducted a staff survey when Cantor had introduced the idea in 1984. In addition, Harvard had been experiencing a unionization drive, which subjected any move on the administration's part to scrutiny. As Cantor faced the difficult administrative task of collecting, assimilating and acting on the results of the attitude survey in an organization that was highly decentralized, he, nevertheless, was optimistic about the work that needed to be done in the weeks and months ahead.

This case was written by Hillery Ballantyne, under the direction of Professor Fred K. Foulkes, as a basis for discussion rather than to illustrate either the effective or ineffective handling of an administrative situation.

© Human Resources Policy Institute. School of Management, Boston University, 1988.

STRUCTURE OF HARVARD UNIVERSITY

Founded sixteen years after the arrival of the Pilgrims at Plymouth, Harvard University had grown from twelve students with a single master to an enrollment of some 16,000 degree candidates. This included students in the undergraduate college, in ten graduate and professional schools, and in an extension school, taught by a faculty of over 3,000.

The university had two governing boards. The Harvard Corporation, consisting of the president and Fellows of Harvard College, was the university's executive board. This seven-member board was responsible for the day-to-day management of the university's finances and business affairs. Significant matters of educational and institutional policy were also brought before the president and Fellows.

The Board of Overseers consisted of thirty members who were elected at large by graduates of Harvard. Through standing and visiting committees, the overseers learned about educational and administrative policies and practices of the university, provided advice to the corporation, and approved important actions of that body. Both the corporation and overseers had to approve major teaching and administrative appointments.

The expression "every tub on its own bottom" was often used to describe the decentralized organization and financial arrangement of the ten faculties overseeing Harvard's separate schools and colleges. Each faculty was headed by a dean, appointed by the president, and approved by the board of overseers and Harvard Corporation. Each was directly responsible for its own academic programs, finances and organization. President Derek Bok directly controlled approximately 10% of the university's $700 million annual budget. (Exhibit 1 shows Harvard's organizational structure.) As is shown in Exhibit 1, reporting to President Bok were five vice presidents (Administration, Finance, General Counsel, Development, and Government, Public and Community Affairs) and ten Deans.

Harvard's endowment and other funds were valued at more than $2.8 billion in 1985. Strong alumni support, through the recently completed Harvard Campaign, enabled the Faculty of Arts and Sciences, which is responsible for the education of more than half of Harvard's students, to renovate classroom buildings and the residential houses, strengthen the excellence of its faculty, and maintain its commitment to provide adequate financial aid for qualified students.

The number of exempt and non-exempt employees attached to each of these schools and the central administration was as follows:

	Exempt	Non-Exempt
Arts and Sciences	1,351	1,220
Business	230	264
Dental	22	60
Design	46	43
Divinity	38	32
Education	73	93
Government	93	114
Law	119	204
Public Health	235	212
Medical	467	490
Central Administration	993	832

These numbers included approximately 700 part-time employees, about half of whom were exempt personnel.

The university encompassed over 400 buildings spread across a radius of several miles. While most of Harvard was located in Cambridge, both the medically-oriented schools and the business school were located in Boston. The business school was just across the Charles River from Harvard College, the undergraduate houses, and the Kennedy School of Government and the other schools and administrative offices. The schools of medicine, public health and dental medicine, however, were in Boston, approximately three miles from the main campus.

THE HARVARD STAFF

In 1985, Harvard employed nearly 12,000 people, 9,000 of whom held staff positions. The fifth largest employer in the Commonwealth of Massachusetts, Harvard employed 10% of the people working in the city of Cambridge, Massachusetts. The staff was occupied in a wide variety of jobs, from grounds maintenance to skilled laboratory work to clerical, library and administrative positions.

Fourteen hundred of Harvard's staff belonged to seven unions. The unionized employees had jobs in food and custodial services, skilled trades, security, the print shop and the cogeneration plant. Of the 7,500 non-union staff employees, about one quarter were occupied in unskilled or semi-skilled work. Another quarter made up the bulk of the technical, secretarial and clerical workforce that supported the teaching, research, professional and administrative functions at the university. Approximately 82% of these non-exempt employees were women. Roughly 3,500 exempt professional and administrative positions made up the rest of Harvard's staff. The exempt staff included all supervisors and managers who were not faculty members.

THE PERSONNEL FUNCTION

Harvard's central personnel function in 1985 consisted of six department heads and eighty staff, half of whom were professionals (see Exhibit 2 for an organization chart). Each of the schools at Harvard had its own personnel officer who reported to the administrative dean with "dotted line" responsibility to the central organization.

The relationships between central personnel and the school's personnel offices varied, according to Dan Cantor, from "close and comfortable to we-don't-need-you!" Benefits were administered entirely by central personnel, from distribution of information to medical form processing. Central personnel issued wage guidelines by job grade to the schools. Posting for all open positions at the university was also done centrally, although actual recruitment was done both centrally and by the schools themselves.

UNION ORGANIZATION CAMPAIGN

In 1984 Dan Cantor had been aware of the potential results to be gleaned from employee surveys, and for years had felt that such a project would be beneficial for Harvard. But two major obstacles existed: the union organizing campaign and the decentralized structure of the university. Cantor described these dilemmas:

> The idea of doing an attitude survey was long thought of. We were so spread out in terms of how we govern that there was no coordinated way of getting feedback from staff. The union organizing efforts impacted the project both positively and negatively. It increased concern about how people feel but also hindered a survey project that might have been construed as an unfair labor practice.

Organizing efforts among technical and clerical workers had been going on since the mid-seventies, focused on the three schools in the medical area. But staff members there had voted against bargaining units twice in the past eight years. In 1984 the National Labor Relations Board handed down a decision requiring the union to treat the entire Harvard technical and clerical force as a single potential bargaining unit, forcing the organizing to go campus-wide.

BACKGROUND OF HARVARD'S STAFF MEMBER SURVEY

Dan Cantor felt that the 1984 NLRB decision enlarging the bargaining unit to the entire university created an opportunity for conducting an attitude survey among staff. He introduced the idea at that time to the Personnel Policy Council, a group that consisted of nine administrative deans and three of Harvard's vice presidents. Although Stanford was the only university known to have surveyed its people, the council favored the idea. Cantor had suggested a 100% sample of one-third of the schools every three years. To take the project forward, during the summer of 1984, the council appointed a committee headed by Robert Scott, Vice President of Administration. Scott was seen as best suited to chair the committee because of his extensive administrative responsibilities and his knowledge of computers and data analysis.

The committee was composed of administrators and personnel officers representing a cross-section of the university. They met more than a half dozen times over five months beginning in the fall. Dan Cantor also consulted with faculty experts from the School of Education and the Business School about how best to proceed.

The committee received proposals for

developing the survey from three consulting firms. The criteria used to make the selection were:

- The consultants' willingness and ability to understand the unique nature of Harvard's project
- The availability of a large database and the ability to use it
- Price
- Competence in developing and using data

The committee ultimately chose Opinion Research Corporation (ORC), a division of Arthur D. Little, to conduct the survey, although ORC's bid was not the lowest.

The allocation of the survey's cost was an issue because of Harvard's decentralized organization. The committee decided that the cost of the survey would be charged to each of the "tubs" on a per capita basis. The charge was higher for the units of the central organization than for the schools, but averaged under $10 per staff member. The decision was also made to survey the entire university rather than one-third at a time.

ORC developed a 24-page survey of over 100 items that varied in the number and type of possible responses. The main subjects of inquiry were compensation, performance evaluation, working conditions, career development and training, communications, and productivity. The survey was intended for the approximately 7,000 Harvard staff members, which excluded the faculty and members of bargaining units. Some of the questions asked may be found in Exhibit 3.

After the committee and other concerned individuals and groups had reviewed and approved the survey, it was mailed to employees at their homes in April 1985, seven weeks after the arrival of a letter to each employee from President Bok advising them of the survey and asking for their cooperation. (See Exhibit 4 for a copy of the letter sent to employees by President Bok.)

The questionnaire was sent to employees, with the covering letter signed by a vice president of ORC. All questionnaires were to be returned by April 19. So that ORC could analyze the results of the survey by various groupings of employees, respondents were asked to check off the Harvard unit where they worked; whether they were in academic/research, administration, or the library; the number of years they had worked for the university; the number of positions they had held at Harvard; their age, sex, and race; whether their immediate supervisor was a faculty member or a non-faculty member; their level of education; and whether their employment status was full or part time. Respondents were asked not to sign their names and they were assured that ". . . there are always enough people in any [employee] grouping so that no individual can be identified" and that if there were not 10 people in a group, the results of that group would not be released but instead would be combined with another group of employees.

Fifty-nine percent of the administrative/professional staff and 46% of the support staff completed the survey, which represented an overall response rate of 55% of Harvard staff members. During May and June ORC prepared a report that contained the principal results of the survey. ORC also prepared reports for each of Harvard's principal units. ORC delivered the results of the survey during the early part of the summer. Only President Bok and Messrs. Steiner and Cantor would see the complete results, including a comparison of responses by school. (See Exhibit 5 for a summary of the university-wide results prepared by ORC.)

With both President Bok and Mr. Steiner

on vacation, Dan Cantor studied the results carefully. He was scheduled to go on vacation in a week, and the beginning of the fall term was just six weeks away. Cantor knew, however, that a well thought out action plan was needed by the end of August or, at the latest, immediately after the Labor Day weekend. Cantor also recalled that in President Bok's February 21 letter to each Harvard staff member, he had pledged that "... you will receive results from the survey, and an opportunity to discuss the results."

HARVARD UNIVERSITY STAFF SURVEY STUDY QUESTIONS:

1. What is your evaluation of the first attitude survey conducted at Harvard?
2. What should Dan Cantor recommend at the end of the case?

HARVARD UNIVERSITY STAFF SURVEY
Exhibit 1

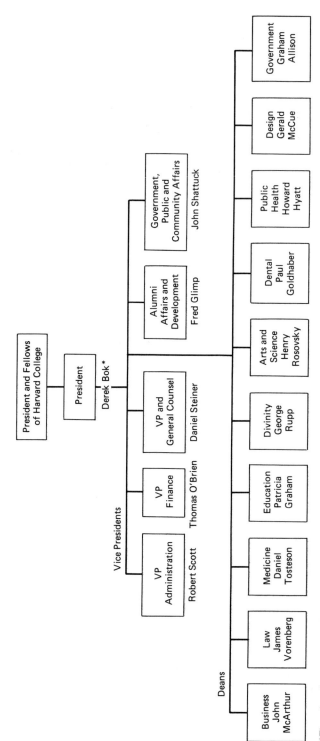

*The other direct reports to President Bok included the heads of University Health Services, the library system, and the minister of Memorial Church.

Exhibit 2 Personnel Department, table of organization, April 1985*

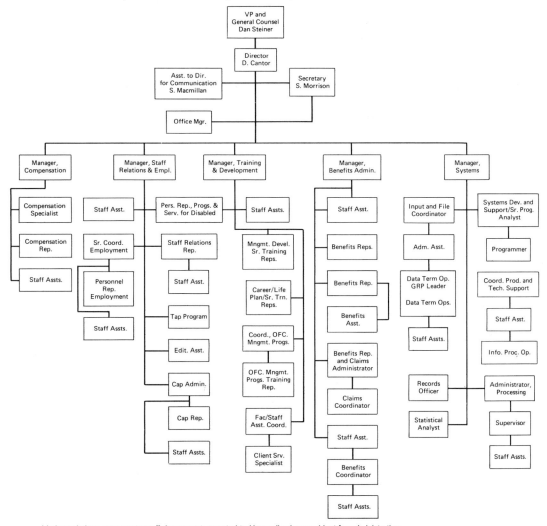

* Labor relations, a separate staff department, reported to Harvard's vice president for administration.

Exhibit 3 Sample questions from the 1985 opinion survey among staff members of Harvard University

---

1. How would you rate Harvard University as a place to work compared with other organizations you know or have heard about?

Circle
<u>one</u>
Number

1 One of the best
2 Above average
3 Average
4 Below average
5 One of the worst

. . .

4. Considering your experience here, as well as what you may know of other organizations, how would you rate Harvard University on each of the following?

Circle one number for each item	Very Good	Good	Average	Poor	Very Poor
Providing job security	1	2	3	4	5
Your pay	1	2	3	4	5
Applying policies and rules the same way to all staff members	1	2	3	4	5
Ability of <u>top administration</u>	1	2	3	4	5
Treating you with respect and consideration	1	2	3	4	5

. . .

8. How strongly do you agree or disagree with the following statements about your work at Harvard University?

Circle one number for each statement	Strongly Agree	Tend to Agree	Hard to Decide	Tend to Disagree	Strongly Disagree
I am committed to this university's success	1	2	3	4	5
My <u>unit administration</u> is in touch with its individual staff members	1	2	3	4	5
Decisions are often made at a high level that could be better made at a lower level	1	2	3	4	5

. . .

15. What do you think your chances are of achieving your personal career objectives by continuing to work for Harvard University?

Circle
<u>one</u>
number

1 Very good
2 Good
3 Average
4 Poor
5 Very poor
6 I have not yet clearly defined my career objectives
7 I have reached my career objectives

. . .

23. Indicate the 4 areas or programs listed below in which you would most like to see improvement at Harvard.

1 Parking facilities
2 Career development programs
3 Programs for learning about and applying for available positions within the University
4 Equal opportunity for minorities

Circle
<u>four</u>
numbers

5 Equal opportunity for women
6 Child care
7 Increased frequency of paycheck delivery
8 An independent "Ombudsperson" to listen to staff member complaints and help resolve them when justified
9 Short term disability
10 Salaries
11 Other (Specify): _____

HARVARD UNIVERSITY

OFFICE OF THE PRESIDENT

MASSACHUSETTS, HALL
CAMBRIDGE, MASSACHUSETTS 02138

February 21, 1985

To Each Harvard Staff Member:

I write to ask you help in an important University-wide effort that will soon begin. Harvard has retained Opinion Research Corporation (ORC) of Princeton, New Jersey, to conduct for us an opinion survey among all our administrative, professional, and supporting staff members. The purpose of the survey is to obtain information about a wide variety of work- and workplace-related subjects. We have chosen an outside organization to do the survey in order to obtain the expert help that will make the inquiry as useful and objective as possible.

Prior to the survey, during the week beginning February 25, a cross section of administrative, professional, and supporting staff members will be asked to participate on a voluntary basis in exploratory interview sessions with ORC representatives. These sessions, conducted on a totally confidential basis, will enable ORC to design a comprehensive questionnaire for Harvard. In the middle of April, all staff members will be invited to complete the actual survey questionnaire.

As you know, a survey of this kind is helpful only when staff members participate fully and candidly. You have my assurance and ORC's pledge that you will not be identified in anything you say in response to the questionnaire. The only reports Harvard will receive from ORC will be those showing patterns of opinion among major groups; Harvard has no access to any individual answers. In turn, you will receive results from the survey, and an opportunity to discuss the results.

In the past decade, we have conducted various surveys of staff members on specialized subjects such as benefits, salary systems, and security. Now, with your active involvement, a comprehensive survey can assist us further. I hope that you will join your colleagues in taking the opportunity to express your candid views.

Sincerely,

Derek Bok

Exhibit 5   1985 opinion survey results among staff members of Harvard University

This report contains the principal results of the survey conducted at the end of the last academic year for Harvard by Opinion Research Corporation (ORC). ORC began the survey by conducting a series of group and individual interviews of a representative cross-section of administrative, professional and support staff from all over the University. With the assistance of this group, ORC designed a questionnaire which was then sent to all administrative, professional and support staff by mail.

3,715 respondents, representing 55% of Harvard staff members, completed and returned the questionnaires. With a response rate of over 50% ORC views the overall results with confidence as being representative of Harvard staff members' attitudes.

The answers to the questions and the many comments received reveal that the people who filled out the questionnaire did so with much thought and care. As is the case in other surveys that ORC has conducted, there are some key questions to which staff members responded very positively and others to which the response is unfavorable. Overall, the results indicate considerable strengths in the relationship between Harvard and its staff, but also room for improvement.

Some of the survey deals with issues specific to individual schools or administrative departments. ORC understands that there will be opportunities to review and discuss these local issues later on. In this report, we concentrate on the major issues which emerge from the survey data for the University as a whole.

ORC
Opinion Research Corporation

North Harrison Street, Box 183, Princeton, NJ 08542-0183

413

Jobs: Respondents say they like their jobs, and a substantial number feel that their work provides them with both challenge and a chance to use their skills and abilities. 73% of responding staff members say they like their jobs "very much" or "a good deal." 56% say they would "definitely" or "probably" choose Harvard as a place to work, "if you could begin working over again, in the same occupation as you're in now." 52% of respondents feel their jobs provide challenging and interesting work. 60% believe Harvard provides "very good" or "good" job security.

Pay: Many respondents have concerns about pay. 22% rate Harvard as "very good" or "good" with respect to pay; 37% feel it is "average"; and, 40% think pay is below average. Similarly, two in five express concern about whether their pay is set fairly in relation to others at Harvard. Salary administration also raises questions because of a perceived lack of relationship between pay and performance; 27% say they "strongly agree" or "agree" that they are part of a system in which good performance leads to pay increases; 20% feel that is is "hard to decide," while 51% tend to or strongly disagree.

Supervision: Respondents give favorable ratings of the quality of their immediate supervisors. 65% answer "very good" or "good" to the question "How would you rate Harvard University on providing you with a supervisor you respect?" The majority of staff similarly rate their supervisors favorably on knowing their own jobs (79%), being friendly (77%), backing them when they are right (67%), and dealing fairly with everyone (61%).

Departmental Cooperation and Co-workers: Respondents generally rate cooperation within their own work units favorably, and give positive ratings to questions concerning co-workers. 65% rate the cooperation among people working in their unit as being "very good" or "good"; and 66% of staff give the same ratings when asked whether they feel Harvard provides them with a chance to work with people they like.

Benefits: A majority of respondents rate their overall benefits favorably, although there are variations in the ratings they give individual programs. More than six in ten rate vacations (77%), holidays (72%), cultural facilities (70%), the credit union (69%), and sick leave (64%) as being "very good" or "good." 67% rated dental insurance "poor" or "very poor" (the survey occurred before Harvard announced the new dental plans), while 23% feel retirement/pension plans and career planning assistance are below average.

Working Conditions: Almost half (47%) of the respondents give favorable ratings to their physical working conditions, although a number of specific local problems are identified. In the areas of ventilation, temperature, and parking, about half of the respondents give favorable or average rating while about half rate these working conditions below average.

Training: 44% of responding staff members answer "very good" or "good" when asked how Harvard does in "providing training so that you can handle your present job properly." 33% feel the training they get to help them qualify for a better job is "good" or "very good" while an equal percentage rate it "poor" or "very poor." Opportunities for training and development receive positive responses from 38% of the staff.

Career Advancement Opportunities: Respondents are generally critical of the lack of career development opportunities, of the difficulty of securing grade changes even when changes in their jobs warrant them, and of their ability to achieve their personal career objectives by continuing to work at Harvard. Almost one-half (46%) rate advancement opportunities below average. 21% give favorable responses to the question "When reasonable job-related criteria are met, job reclassification procedures function effectively." 28% feel they can achieve their personal career objectives by continuing to work at Harvard.

Performance Evaluation: Respondents who have had an evaluation of their performance generally regard the process favorably. 64% of the 2000 who say they had a performance review in the past year feel this review was "very effective" or "somewhat effective." About four in ten (44%) feel their unit has a fair system for evaluating performance. 69% give favorable responses to the question "I have a clear idea of what is required to achieve successful performance."

Communications: Respondents vary in their views of different facets of communications within the University. Six in ten feel they can always or usually believe information given out by Harvard's top administrators. 52% rate favorably the willingness of their unit administrators to listen to staff member problems. 42% feel the University is doing a "very good" or "good" job in letting staff know what is going on generally.

View of the University: Responding staff members generally feel positive about being part of the University community. Over half or 56% respond favorably to the question "How would you rate Harvard University as a place to work compared with other organizations you know or have heard about?" 71% "strongly agree" or "tend to agree" that they are committed to the University's success, and 70% give the same support to the statement that they are proud to be part of the University.

Apple Computer (Europe)

Over the five years since its creation in late 1980, Apple Europe had grown into a successful arm of Apple Computer, the parent company based in Cupertino, California. European sales had grown to $250 million by 1985, with a workforce of 580 employees, coordinated by a central European office in Paris.

Since the outset, human resource management had been as important in this growth as distribution or financial management—some would say the most important factor. Stefan Winsnes, architect of Apple Europe's human resource policies, had tried to free up initiative and build flexibility into the growing organization. An original approach had developed, differing significantly from that in other companies, just as Apple itself differed sharply from its competitors.

Following a worldwide reorganization in late 1985, Winsnes had moved to Cupertinto as director of international human resources. Now in February 1986, responsibility for human resources in Europe had been handed on to Michel Perez, formerly its training manager. Until this point, if Stefan had been the architect of human resource thinking, Michel had been its engineer.

Perez was deeply aware that although much had been achieved, difficult challenges still lay ahead. Systems still needed to be more fully implemented. Most of the local human resource managers in the European countries had only recently been appointed, and qualified HR managers still had to be found for Germany and Italy. New problems had developed, particularly in the areas of career development and communications. Above all, there was a danger that increasing size and a disquietingly different breed of recruits would dampen the creative spirit of the original pioneers. As the guardian of the culture that had led to Apple's success, how could these challenges be met while reinforcing, not stifling, a culture that would more than ever be needed in the future?

CORPORATE HISTORY

In 1975, Apple Computer started life humbly in a California garage when twenty-one-year old Steve Jobs and his friend Steve Wozniak designed a makeshift computer and dubbed it the Apple I. Seeing the market potential, the friends refined

Copyright © 1986 by INSEAD and CEDEP (the European Centre for Continuing Education). This case was developed by Alison Been-Farquhar, Research Associate, and Professor Paul Evans (Chairman of the Raoul de Vitry d'Avaucourt Chair Program in International Human Resource Management).

the product into the world's first personal computer. The Apple II was born.

With the financial backing and business expertise of a retired businessman, they formed their own Silicon Valley company in Cupertino. In their first year, 1977, sales from the garage reached a staggering $200,000 and the meteoric rise had begun. Elated as they may have been with their early success, Jobs and Wozniak surely did not foresee that sales would follow a compound growth rate of 150% through 1983, nor predict that their company would bring in nearly $2 billion in fiscal year 1985 with some 5400 employees (see Appendix 1). Wozniak retired from the venture in 1979 to pursue other interests but Jobs remained, strongly commited to running the company.

That growth was not without its ups and downs. Until 1981, the Apple II was still the company's only product and competition had never posed a significant problem. But the launch of a new product, the Apple III, was marred by design flaws. IBM also made its first move into the personal computer market, which would bring a radical change in competitive climate.

The widely predicted industry shake-out came in 1983, earlier than expected. After only two years, IBM had displaced Apple as leading supplier and the lure of high profits had by now attracted more than 100 companies to the PC market. Apple was competing in the higher price bracket, the business and education sectors, selling through independent dealers. Heavy expenses in advertising and R&D had to be compensated for by high volume, low cost manufacturing. To this end, a state-of-the-art production plant at Fremont, California, was built which would allow the automated assembly and quality control of the as yet unannounced Macintosh PC.

The major event of 1983 was the hiring from Pepsico of John Sculley, appointed as President and Chief Executive Officer of Apple Computer with the objective of introducing managerial discipline and long term strategic thinking to the company. The organization had to come to terms with the need for cost and overhead control.

Two new products were launched that year—the Apple IIe, a modified form of the original Apple II, and the Lisa, a PC with one million bytes of memory and a rolling box known as a mouse to simplify commands. The Lisa was aimed at the corporate market where Apple needed to expand, but it failed to meet expectations. However, it contained the Macintosh technology on which Apple intended to build its product line during the coming decade.

In January 1984, the MAC was launched. The Apple philosophy that PCs should not only be simple but fun to use was embodied in a product which was unlike any other on the market. At the same time the Lisa 2 was also brought out, followed soon by the stylish and portable Apple IIc.

Meanwhile, John Sculley was making his mark on the organization, pushing it towards a market orientation and curbing its tendency to technological arrogance. As Sculley put it: "The objective is to build Apple into a great consumer marketing company that makes money rather than having to break through in technology every year." Sculley also pointed out the folly of not respecting IBM and of trying to beat it at its own game. What was needed was to differentiate Apple as an innovative organization.

However, 1985 was the most turbulent year in the company's short history. Sales in the US reached only 40% of the target, stocks doubled at the dealers and the Lisa was abandoned. Although sales for the year reached an all time high of

$1.9 billion, Apple reported its first loss in the third quarter of the year and IBM continued to win market share at their expense.

For good or for bad, the computer industry slump of 1985 snatched away the luxury of gradual change. Some 180 firms had been attracted by the microcomputer industry over the years; many had since left it, and only some 30 were expected to survive. If Apple wanted to survive, it had both to lower its fixed costs and better serve its customers, dealers, third-party software developers, and production subcontractors. The company's organizational structure (see Appendix 2) which had been good in a period of explosive growth now contained too many redundancies. In a reorganization (see Appendix 3) costing $40 million, the Macintosh Division was absorbed into a Product Operations Group, the aim being to streamline and better organize the company around the three major markets of education, consumers, and business. Three factories in Ireland, Texas, and California were closed. The International headquarters, previously located in Paris, was regrouped in Cupertino, and four senior European executives moved there—recognition that international markets were now vital to Apple's future.

The final trauma of 1985 was the departure in September of Steve Jobs, Chairman and co-founder of the company. Relations between him and John Sculley had become strained by important differences in view on product development strategy, and the loss of Mac autonomy was a final blow. The departure was further embittered by legal wrangles over Jobs' announcement that he was intending to start another company and would be taking some Apple employees with him.

THE APPLE CULTURE

Since its creation, people have been attracted to Apple as a "different" company to work for, both in the United States and in Europe. The belief that the company can only survive by differentiating itself from its competitors has been reinforced over the years. For example, Apple has preferred to maintain its own unique computer standards despite the cry from customers for compatibility. Some forecast that this will change in the future, but an observer with the leading computer market research firm Dataquest says, "I think they'll make refrigerators first."

The average employee age on both sides of the Atlantic is only 30. The work atmosphere is striking in its informality and yet is highly dynamic. The Apple credo is that having fun is an integral part of work. Formality is minimal, dress is relaxed, and office areas are typically open. Hierarchical distinctions are kept to a minimum. The European headquarters in Paris is known as "The European Office in Paris" or EOP since there is a dislike of the connotations of headquarters. In the Paris office, a mirror stating "YOU make the difference" hangs in the entrance hall, and a basket of Granny Smiths is always on hand for the pleasure of visitors and employees alike.

The notions of creativity, innovation and fun embedded in the company's culture, are every bit a product of the Californian ethos in which they originated.

The Origin of the Apple Values

This ethos is encoded in nine Apple Values, the result of an attempt to maintain some cultural roots in the face of rapid growth.

Until 1981, Apple was run from a large warehouse-like building in Cupertino, with no separating walls. All employees worked in the same physical space regardless of rank or function, and the hubbub atmosphere was simply a part of Apple. As the company grew, force of numbers meant that certain functions would have to move into separate buildings. Some people worried that physical fragmentation of the company might lead to fragmentation of the culture they liked so much. A committee was set up, representing all levels and functions of Apple, to try to capture on paper how they felt about the company and what they valued most about it. Such a written set of values, they felt, would help the company retain its soul however it might be split up or moved around. The resulting nine values encapsulate the company's philosophy both on the *outside environment* (covering society, customers and dealers) and on *internal operations* (covering the individual, the team and attitudes towards work in general) (see Appendix 6 and later discussion).

Organizational Productivity

Beyond these values are basic management principles of maintaining high productivity and a lean organization. One Cupertino Vice President boasted that Apple today has the highest productivity ratio of any major firm in the Western world—including Japan.

These principles are the result of unhappy corporate memories of past lay-offs, reinforced by the concern not to follow the route of Victor, Atari and similar firms. The failure of the Apple III launch in 1981 had been followed by recriminatory sackings, and in 1983–4, there had been a general weeding out of sub-standard performers ("rotten apples"). More recently, the 1985 crisis reconfirmed the need for minimal slack in the company and a low breakeven point.

There are only four hierarchical levels between top and bottom of the organization, reflecting the company philosophy of maximum delegation and the belief that responsibility brings out hidden creative energy. Job descriptions have little place in a structure where job content is recognized to depend largely on the position holder.

Concern for the uncertain future is also reflected in the company financial policies which are highly conservative. Apple's auditors sometimes have difficulty with the speed at which capital investments are written off. For example, the state-of-the-art Fremont plant had two-thirds of its value written off in the first year. High productivity and this conservatism may well have been Apple's saving grace in times of difficulty since the resultant financial cushion prevented cash problems. In 1985, for example, the company had a "cash pot" of $400 million to fall back on.

John Sculley summarized his philosophy in a 1984 video address to some European managers by saying:

> Our goal isn't to become a large company, but rather to be a leader. But that probably means that we'll become big. Our challenge is how to keep the entrepreneurial spirit of values alive. We have to find ways of keeping it young. We cannot be a leader by being like all the others.
>
> This means that we must place a higher priority on leadership than on management. We don't want structure in this firm, we don't want hierarchy. We have to keep the business simple, invest a lot in training, keep good communications, maintain the accessibility of top management.
>
> The priority in 1983 and 1984 has been the United States. It was a survival issue. Today, Europe counts for 12% of worldwide sales. This will increase a lot in the future and we'll be giving much more emphasis to Europe as from 1985.

APPLE EUROPE

Apple Europe, based in Paris, was set up in late 1980 by Tom Lawrence, an American who had been managing director of Europe of Intel. Its function was to establish decentralized country distribution operations, provide the necessary support, and act as a liaison with headquarters in Cupertino.

Business was built up by acquiring or establishing distributors in the different countries—these companies then sell through a network of independent dealers who may or may not stock competing PCs. As in the USA, Apple Europe expanded at a rapid rate. By 1984, operations had been consolidated in nine different countries, and sales had reached $200 million with some 500 employees (see Appendix 4).

The Early Days

Needless to say, the company's growth in Europe has not been smooth. The European workforce increased to 80 employees in 1981, the first full year of operations. Stefan Winsnes was recruit #11 as director of human resources, and recruitment was the key challenge in these first two years. People brought in at the higher levels were mainly old business contacts of those already recruited, and there was little time for screening at the lower levels. The time lapse between initial contact and recruitment was also short. Mike Morren, hired to take responsibility for facilities, described the process:

> Stefan Winsnes and I had both been at ICL. The day after he joined Apple, I got a phone call asking me to come to his office. I remember it was Jean-Louis Gassée's birthday [Gassée became the general manager for the successful French company], and when I got there, everyone was sitting around on orange boxes. There wasn't a

stick of furniture! Anyway, I had an interview, if you could call it that, and was asked when I could start. My suggestion of ten days time didn't seem to appeal so I asked what would suit them. "Why don't you pull up a box," was the reply, and I've been with them ever since!"

Recruitment proceeded furiously into 1982, based on optimistic predictions of growth as new subsidiaries opened in France, Germany and Britain. The predictions, however, were exaggerated as Winsnes remembers:

> The realisation came that the planned growth couldn't be achieved, that 300 people had been recruited and that not one of them really knew what Apple was about. As a result, the operations more or less collapsed from a business point of view. Only 50% growth was realized against predictions of doubling or tripling sales.

An inevitable shedding of low performers ensued in 1983 and 1984. Rationalization was a painful step and Apple Europe, like the Cupertino headquarters, now operates on a lean headcount—further reinforced by the 1985 Cupertino-led drive to reduce fixed costs and increase profitability. The consequence is that the company tends to be more conservative in predicting market trends and operates its staff at full stretch.

The Shaping of the Organisation

The 1982 troubles led to the firing of Tom Lawrence. Mike Spindler, a German from Digital who had joined Apple earlier as European Marketing Director, was appointed as European General Manager in July 1983. Spindler's goals were clear:

> My first decision was that the front line was the country manager. We had to move more

technical and managerial power to these people—my own role is as a conduit with the USA and between these country GMs. In France, it is Jean-Louis Gassée [at that time the general manager for Apple France] who is on the front page of the newspapers, not me. That's a big difference from other firms like Olivetti, where de Benedetti is everywhere.

But in order to decentralise, you need strong country general managers and strong managerial teams. Building those teams has been my priority in recent years, even though it means some shake outs.

The organisation of today began to take shape (see Appendix 5). The staff functions reporting to the General European Manager are finance, operations, marketing, management information systems, human resources, and legal. Some 40 people today work at the Paris office, though operational responsibility lies entirely with the countries. For example, advertising is at the expense of the national distributor, although Apple Europe will occasionally subsidize a price cut or a special promotion. They also offer help on marketing strategy and promotional materials which the distributors may or may not choose to use. The countries themselves are France, Germany, the UK and the "General European Area" comprising Belgium, Holland, Italy, the Nordic area and Spain. Like Mike Spindler, most of the general managers had a background in marketing. All European production is carried out in Cork, Ireland.

Strategy comes from Cupertino, where the executive staff work on a five year time horizon. Paris looks one year ahead in its business plan, while subsidiaries deal only with the operational present.

From the outset, Cupertino seemed little interested in affairs outside the United States, except that Apple Europe was expected to implement their strategy and deliver the profits. Crises in the US would lead to headcount and cost restrictions in Europe. This has led to a European sentiment of "Them and Us." Until 1985, Apple International, responsible for all other regions aside from the USA and Europe, was also based in Paris, leading to divisive tensions.

Future Growth

The neglect by Cupertino of the international market is beginning to change, particularly at the insistance of Mike Spindler and his European colleagues. International sales accounted for 22% of total revenues in 1985 (15% from Europe), and Spindler predicts that they will account for 35% in two years time. U.S. domestic sales continue their long slump; Dataquest, the computer market research firm, forecasts that there will be up to 50% annual growth overseas against only 18% in the USA.

An important corporate reorganization in late 1985 recognized this. Responsibility for all international operations was regrouped at Cupertino (rather than Paris); Mike Spindler was appointed as vice president for international operations. Stefan Winsnes moved there as director for international human resources, while the international marketing function was also relocated from Paris. The fact that European managers were gaining recognition in Cupertino was further confirmed by the appointment as corporate manager for new product development of Jean-Louis Gassée, who had built the French company into Europe's most successful subsidiary.

Meanwhile in Paris, Roger Kermisch, previously European director of operations, took over as European general manager; Michel Perez was appointed as manager of human resources for Europe.

HUMAN RESOURCE MANAGEMENT IN EUROPE

From the very beginning of European operations, human resources has constituted one of the most important aspects of management, and its director has been the right hand of the general manager. "We're in a war, and in a war you need strong people," Mike Spindler affirms. "We can't afford any weak links." Stefan Winsnes, a Swede in his early forties and the architect of HR policy in Europe, adds:

> If you are going to grow at the rate that we in Europe have seen and that we intend to see internationally, then you need good people, good leadership and good management. And if you are going to keep the headcount low, and stay ahead of the competition, then you have to invest in those people.

Stefan Winsnes himself was attracted to Apple by the alternative image it offered:

> The people who created Apple Europe were part of the uproar generation who went to university in the late sixties. Students-for-a-Democratic-Society and all that. We had big ideals for Apple, we wanted to do something different. In the beginning, we saw ourselves as being on a yacht. The wind blew pretty rough at times, but we had control. Today, it's different. There's a new generation of people who are joining Apple. They have different values and they see themselves as joining a liner, not a yacht. Our approach to human resource management is having to adjust accordingly.

Certainly, the central preoccupations of the department have evolved considerably since 1981.

The Changing Focus of HRM

In 1981–82, the initial focus of HR activity was on *recruitment*. The Cupertino salary and benefits system was adopted, but there was little time to turn to other HR issues of importance. Only after the over-ambitious nature of this expansion became apparent was there time to look a little further into the future. Too many "doers" as opposed to "planners" had been recruited, and many of the over-zealously hired had to be shown the door.

The need for basic *induction training* was apparent, and Michel Perez was hired from Texas Instruments in 1983 to assume this responsibility, assisted by Mike Morren who moved over from facilities. This team began to turn to longer term issues.

In 1983–84, *Apple Values* were introduced into Europe in a series of campaigns, initially abortive, and gradually more successful. If their intention in the United States was to ensure the continuity of a culture, in Europe they were introduced to create a culture, to provide some "soul" to the 300 employees, whose varied nationalities and past experiences with the DECs and IBMs, ICLs and Bulls gave them little common ground. The Values were communicated through an induction course designed by Perez and Morren. This initiative was the first instance of what was to become a standard Apple practice—namely using the training function as a way of introducing new human resource concepts and techniques.

Further skill and managerial training were added to the induction training in 1984. Meanwhile, the Values needed to be concretised so as to develop policies and systems. Winsnes and Perez developed a set of *Principles*, expressing in popular metaphors the basic assumptions behind the human resource systems they wanted to build. The Amoeba, Spaceship and Garbage principles expressed the importance of flexibility, leadership and entrepreneurship, and they would form the foundation for the Apple's *performance management system* (the final accolade lay in its ultimate adoption by Cupertino—business strategy may come from the United States, but in terms of training and human resource management, Apple Europe has often taken the lead).

By late 1984, these human resources systems were beginning to take shape. However, the profit squeeze in the US meant that the strategic emphasis in the 1985–86 period was on reducing the breakeven point, with severe limits on headcount and costs. The target was to double turnover annually, but with only a 40% increase in headcount. The human resource department became heavily involved in replacing less effective management teams in Britain, Germany and Italy.

In theory, the human resource policies developed at the Paris office were to be administered by local human resource managers. Training programs initiated and tested by Paris were thereafter to be run locally. However, the work involved in reorganization, headcount restrictions, and turnover among local HR managers meant that there frequently was no local HR manager. Paris was obliged either to firefight in each country or to live with a vacuum.

New problems were also surfacing. *Communications* grew to be a major complaint. People found out about changes affecting their jobs belatedly and indirectly. Wild rumors circulated ("Paris office is being slashed and moved to Monte Carlo!"). Many individuals complained of being overstretched, though this varied from office to office. An emerging question among the new generation of Apple managers was also, "What are my *career prospects*?" At the same time, the older generation of pioneers asked whether the Apple spirit would not be destroyed in the drive to professionalise the company—the discontinued Saturday picnics of the Paris office became a symbol of loss of soul at Apple.

The Role of the Human Resource Department

When Michel Perez took over as manager of human resources for Europe in late 1985, Mike Morren assumed full responsibility for training, aided by an assistant. Backed by local human resource managers (all but one newly appointed, and two positions still remaining to be filled), this constituted Europe's team of human resource professionals (if "professionals" is not too misleading a word since none, bar Winsnes himself, had had much prior experience in personnel management).

However, the HR Department at Apple has never been intended to fulfill a classic personnel role, as Winsnes noted:

We view it as a business function rather than as a personnel department. About 60% of my time has been spent on organizational development, and troubleshooting in the local companies and on strategy formulation.

For example, we had two alternatives in Italy in 1983, either to set up our own company or buy the distributor. The European general manager left the decision up to me, and we decided to acquire the distributor. Then I became the project leader for the subsequent integration. Similarly, when a company gets into deep water, I'll spend some time figuring out the strengths and weaknesses, and after agreeing on what has to be done with Mike Spindler, we jointly implement the reorganization.

The rest of my time is spent with Michel, Mike and the others developing concepts, policies and practices that are right for Apple. Our focus here is on changing the attitudes of managers and providing certain services such as training.

Personnel management, the implementation of practices and issues such as career development are up to the local general and human resource managers. In all countries, the local HR guy has to work closely with the general manager, be involved in strategy formulation, and take the lead in creatively adapting policies and training.

His successor, Michel Perez, has a similar conception, also spending much of his time reorganising and troubleshooting. In addition, he sees the HR manager as guardian of the distinctive Apple culture. In an interview with *Le Monde* newspaper, he put it as follows:

> I don't believe Apple has lost its soul during its development. The role of the Human Resource Manager, the "priest" in whose hands the company's "Ten Commandments" lie, is to ensure the survival of this soul. Far from merely providing a functional service determing salary rises and fringe benefits, the human resource management function forms the very heart of a company, and its manager exists to confirm the company's particular values and try to apply them in practice.

Inside the firm no-one questions the vital importance of the Human Resource function although it is an inevitably controversial domain:

> Human Resources is the most difficult function at Apple. It has lost some credibility by

virtue of constantly changing track, by saying one thing and then another. The quality of their training is excellent, though there has been uneven access to the training. Those who need it most are those who often don't have the time. Winsnes himself is a powerful figure at Apple, though he is something of a theoretical politician.

> It's a very important area. The problem is that the people there are so busy that they are never available. They like to stay with the big picture, the big ideals, and they often ignore the vital little issues, the necessary administration and the follow through.

Views as to human resources vary considerably from country to country. They were particularly reserved in Germany. A weak and disorganised general manager was appointed in 1984, leading to political in-fighting. The local HR manager allied himself to the GM, and there were no performance reviews for an eighteen month period. The human resource function lost its credibility. "Everybody was concerned with protecting their own jobs so that no-one dared let Paris know of the problems," said one manager. "Winsnes and Perez were in their ivory towers, and it took a year and a half before they realized something was wrong, and stepped in."

HUMAN RESOURCE CONCEPTS, PRACTICES AND PROCESSES

Apple Europe's human resource management system, developed during these five years, can be seen as having four elements which are outlined in the subsequent part of the case:

- The *Apple Values* which constitute the guiding credo
- A system for *performance management*, with various sub-elements:
  - three basic conceptual principles
  - a system for objective setting and performance review

- the top management review board
- an original activity review system
- a system for compensation
- *Development systems*, mainly training, recruitment and induction, and career development, currently at varying stages of refinement
- Various actions and programs to improve *internal communications*.

THE APPLE VALUES

The nine Apple Values are supposedly the underpinning for these different systems and programmes. These values are as follows:

> Empathy for our Customers/Users; Positive Social Contribution; Innovation/Vision; Quality/Excellence; Achievement/Aggressiveness; Individual Performance; Individual Growth/Reward; Team Spirit; Good Management

Each value headlines something more specific (see Appendix 6 for details). For example, *Achievement & Aggressiveness* implies that Apple employees "will continue to set high goals and high standards of performance, because we realise that through meeting such challenges we will advance as a company and as individuals."

In the United States, these Values were an attempt to preserve the culture of the firm as it grew, whereas their introduction into Europe stemmed from the desire to mould a culture, as Stefan Winsnes recalls:

> In the middle of 1981, the average seniority here was about three weeks. Each person brought his own culture with him—there were Intel, ICL and IBM guys. They were developing the Apple Values in the U.S. and it made sense.
>
> So we invited Ann Bower [the person who developed the Values in the U.S.] over to make a presentation. But the people here just laughed at the ideas: "How can you talk of Values when I don't even have a chair to sit on?" They saw it all as Californian hype.

Winsnes concluded that Europe would have to work out what these Values meant in its own context. A poster campaign was organised, and then Michel Perez began to communicate the ideas behind the Values to the large numbers of recruits in the induction training. Slowly but surely, they started to become part of the firm:

In 1983, we had an open seminar for forty people to find out what they were most proud of at Apple. Innovation, Quality and Friendliness were the three themes that clearly emerged. And thus by 1984, we began to feel that the Values were taking root, that Apple was acquiring its soul.

In 1983 to 1984, a second poster campaign was devised, later exported to the United States which had never taken the Values much beyond their original creation. Their adoption was further encouraged by basing part of general managers' bonuses on Apple Value criteria.

Acceptance varies widely from country to country and from person to person, although it is fair to say that even those who claim not to like an explicit management philosophy seem to apply the Values naturally in their daily dealings. This seeming paradox is frequently seen. For example, one manager interviewed who purports not to believe in the Values at the same time states that those people who have been unsuccessful in Apple and have had to leave did so because they didn't have the Values within them. Stefan Winsnes relates the story of Germany, which seemed to resist the Values but nonetheless applied them in an exemplary way when the moment demanded:

> Look what happened there in 1984! In November 1983, the general manager suddenly quit and everyone was alone. We couldn't appoint a new GM until the following April. In a traditional organization, the group would have fallen apart or been split by jealousies over who should do what. But that didn't happen. They still made 92% of their business targets for the year! I don't think that could have happened in any other organization. That is Apple! Teamwork! Achievement! Innovation! Good Management! Whatever the Germans say, that is Apple Values in reality!

Apple people generally accept the theory of the Values, though the same cannot always be said for their practice. Work pressures in particular are felt to lead to inevitable compromises in terms of quality and excellence, however worthy these may be as ideals: "If someone finishes work everyday at 8:30 P.M., he can't be expected to think of them." Top management are as guilty as lower levels, for how can the ideal of "team spirit" not be viewed with cynicism when the company's chairman [Jobs] is squabbling over "his Mac Division" being reintegrated into the company structure?

There is a strong need for regular reiteration of the Values. As one employee puts it: "Working hard everyday, we forget the Values if we're not told about them in a special way, out of context from time to time." This is particularly the case for employees who have been in the company for over one year. The induction course is a distant memory and "these guys need a shot in the arm!"

For Stefan Winsnes, the Values have a broader role:

> In my view, the Apple Values are a catalyst in order to provoke discussion on what is "OUR way of doing things." I'm not worried that there is discussion about whether they are a dream or whether they are reality—as long as there is discussion! There probably are too many of them, and maybe one day we'll reduce the nine Values to three. But what is important now is that they continue to catalyze discussion.
>
> Hewlett Packard and IBM didn't write their values at the outset. They institutionalized them down the road. We have to find our own way, the way we feel good about. The deep value is that we are not like the others, we must find a different way of doing things, our own way.

PERFORMANCE MANAGEMENT

The Principles

In the Autumn of 1983, Stefan Winsnes decided that something had to be done to translate the Apple Values into something more concrete. Together with Perez and Morren, he gathered groups of people, including outsiders from other companies and consultants, in order to brainstorm the issue. The process was prolonged and intense and often went round in circles.

> We sat together and talked till we were hoarse. Sure, we generated hundreds of pages of ideas but we always ended up with procedures and structures when what we really wanted was to focus on the individual. Also, we were using traditional language to try to describe something far more subtle, something unique.
>
> Eventually, I said, "Let's ignore the bullshit, what is the picture which underlies all these words, how does this all relate to the individual in Apple?" And we came up with some basic HR principles on how to motivate and manage performance which have guided all our thinking since.

There is a fundamental concept behind the principles, known as the *Time Principle:* any job inevitably changes over time. Apple's environment is seen as so uncertain and its human resources so limited that flexibility is vital. Consequently, the company has tried to build an entrepreneurial organization on its people, not on "boxes." Boxes have fixed edges, and although their shape may be ideal at the time of the design, they become inappropriate when the environment changes. In contrast people evolve, they can adapt to changed surroundings. Consequently, as is clear in the first of the three Principles, traditional job descriptions are scorned as constraining the development of an organization, and little store is set by titles.

The Amoeba Principle When a person takes over a job, that job becomes something live, like an amoeba—the moment someone is assigned to it, the job as originally conceived changes. There are always facets of the job which the employee will leave aside, and there are others which he or she will add.

Admittedly, there is a *core* to every post, but that will be developed as the person feels appropriate and in line with their own particular aptitudes. There is a potential problem of overlapping responsibilities or neglecting essential parts of the work, but this is dealt with through a management process of negotiation called the "activity review."

The Spaceship Principle The second concept starts from the observation that while organizations inevitably formulate strategy at the top, this is typically implemented through top-down plans with minimal input from the people concerned. The traditional process is one-sided.

In Apple, on the other hand, there should be an interplay between management and their team which allows individual aptitudes and initiatives to be taken into account. A spaceship is used as an analogy. The pilot, or management, decides upon the destination and explains the vision of the enterprise to the crew. Formally speaking, this takes place at six-monthly performance reviews and objective setting discussions, when the manager discusses with his or her subordinates the challenges to be attacked, the desired destination. It is then up to each person to help in reaching that destination. In this way, the particular strengths of every individual are brought into play, and the spaceship moves along at a faster pace.

Winsnes and Perez are careful to emphasize the active role of the "crew."

> If you treat people as adults, if you let them understand how important they are, if you tell them where the opportunities lie, they'll aim that way. They will be motivated. What matters is that they are not sitting passively inside that spaceship. They have to be outside, pushing it along. Only that way can

they get an impression of the speed and the direction.

The Garbage Principle The third concept is abbreviated from the statement, "The garbage of my boss can be a challenge for me." This refers to the idea that certain tasks that a manager may no longer wish or have the time to carry out may represent stimulating opportunities for a subordinate, opportunities for increased learning and responsibility. The manager can and should release these tasks and focus his or her attention on new responsibilities which add further value to the firm, and which are fun. Subordinates are at the same time encouraged to seek new responsibilities and develop their jobs, part of their evaluation being based on these criteria. Thus in a rapidly growing organization, the Garbage Principle encourages managers to grow in their jobs and push responsibility downwards.

These Principles are reflected in the design of the performance management system, the management Review Board, as well as in the Activity Review system.

Objective Setting and Performance Review

Overall organizational goals can be seen as the destination of the famous spaceship, and they represent both quantitative objectives (the Apple business plan) and the qualitative objectives (the Apple Values). These objectives are communicated throughout the company, broken into work group and then individual objectives. During performance reviews, each employee defines goals with the boss, both quantitative and qualitative, for the next six months. At the end of this period, performance is measured and further objectives are set (see Appendix 7).

The system attempts to push people by distinguishing between standards and objectives. Standards reflect minimum, core job requirements, like attending necessary meetings, while objectives are performance targets, either to correct or maintain past performance or more particularly to develop something new requiring initiative and development ("propose a distribution cost reduction program for product Z within three months, reducing current costs by 20% and maintaining market share at present levels"). Once achieved, these *growth objectives* will often in turn become minimum standards.

The six-monthly performance review meeting with the boss is prepared by both individuals separately. It begins with an appraisal discussion—the comparison of actual performance with the original objectives, and a discussion of results and contributions. This leads to a joint agreement on overall rating on a 5-point scale (superior performer, exceeding requirements, meeting requirements, not fully meeting requirements or unsatisfactory performer). Following a discussion of individual development plans, the formal outcome is a summary review memo, sent to the Human Resource Department. This leads then to the negotiation of future task objectives, and the cycle repeats itself.

The Review Board

A recent development is the Review Board. This title reflects a currently informal top management process for the identification and development of leadership potential, also ensuring that appropriate action is taken in problem cases.

The review ratings are one input into the identification of "stars," individuals whose careers top management will more closely seek to develop. The conceptual guide is a *performance/potential matrix* (see Appendix 8). Potential implies more than high performance; it means consistent and continuous performance on growth objec-

tives, stretching the job and the individual.

High performance/high potential individuals are known as "Stars," while the low performance/low potential persons are called "Sleepy Dormice." Those who perform well but who have little potential are known as "Busy Bees," while those whose performance is below par but are thought nonetheless to have potential are labeled as "Sleeping Beauties." This has become a jargon for the discussion of career planning and job assignments. Senior management is concerned with providing horizontal moves to both Stars and Sleeping Beauties (in the latter case to find out whether they are simply in the wrong job, or in fact one of those Sleepy Dormice).

In a non-hierarchical company, the Human Resource Department is much concerned with identifying those people who really drive the company, as Stefan Winsnes points out:

> This company looks very nice and sweet on the surface, but it's remarkably clear what the true pecking order is underneath—and this has nothing to do with grades or rank. Those people who influence the organization are those who are creative, who grow and develop things. What's more, you can smell it in a room of Apple people. Within five minutes you can tell just which of them are the drivers of the organization. We have to try to ensure that the true drivers reach the company driving seats, that the formal organization reflects the informal one. That's what the performance review is designed in part to achieve. I think it works in Europe, but it's less of a success in the U.S. where they have had fewer reorganizations and have got a bit territorial.

The Activity Review

Change is built into the management philosophy of Apple Europe. Individuals are encouraged to grow their jobs, there are periodic formal reorganizations, and Apple wishes to encourage constant informal reorganization and improvement. The Activity Review was designed to facilitate change and to guide the negotiation of inevitable conflicts and overlaps that occur when people grow their jobs. The review process is in some ways Apple's answer to the role that static job descriptions play in more traditional organizations.

These 1–2 hour reviews by boss and subordinate have no set frequency, though they are intended to occur in a six to eighteen month cycle. The review can be invoked by the boss in order to undertake a departmental audit or to negotiate the implementation of business plan changes; or it may be requested by the subordinate to clarify responsibilities. The discussion should lead to an exchange on the core job content and wider professional activities of the person, ensuring that both manager and subordinate share a similar perception of job and future needs.

The *process* itself is relatively straightforward. By way of preparation, review forms are filled in separately by the individual and the supervisor. The discussion leads to a joint version, which is then referred to the supervisor's direct boss for comment and, if necessary, further discussion. Finally, completed forms are given to the human resource department which uses them both to keep in touch with changes and as an input into career development decisions.

The *review form* itself covers several areas. Aside from a section on personal data of the subordinate in order to update the human resource records, the first part reviews the *present job*. What is the boss's and reviewee's perception of its purpose? More specifically, "What would not be done at Apple if this job did not exist?" Then the two parties are asked to break down the job into its major duties, the essential training and skills that would be

required if a new person were to take over the job, the major recent accomplishments of the reviewee, and the new dimensions that the reviewee has brought to the job. This information may also be used by the Human Resource Department to revise the basic salary for the job, as is outlined later.

The next section looks to the *future* and asks first for proposals to improve functional effectiveness (elimination of overlaps or addition of new territories). Then quantitative and qualitative objectives for the next six months should be stated, leading to a renegotiation of these. The final part of the review concerns career development. Three suggestions are requested as to jobs the reviewee could fill over the next two years, two within the same job family and one in an area requiring the acquisition of entirely new skills. [There are four job families at Apple, namely (1) Manufacturing; (2) Sales-Marketing-Distribution-Education & Software; (3) Finance; and (4) Human Resources.] This latter part of the review is intended to provide further inputs into the Review Board process mentioned earlier, a guide to manpower planning.

In practice, activity reviews are undertaken less frequently than the human resource department sees as needed. A major reason is that the procedure is perhaps more cumbersome than is necessary. Moreover, the latter questions on career development often create problems in the review process. Some people find the idea of specifying desired jobs to be inconsistent with the philosophy that jobs change with the appointment of a person and over time. Others find the two-year time frame unrealistic: "No-one can say exactly what they want to be doing in two years' time. I don't know what I want to be doing then, though I do have an idea of where I'd like to be in ten years from now. Perhaps it's better to make people think in broader terms and further ahead." Indeed, career planning and development is one of the more problematic aspects of human resource management at Apple.

The Performance Management System in Practice

This system, together with the Principles and desired underlying attitudes, has been implemented through workshops and via supervisors. It is presented and discussed at *Human Resource Workshops* offered annually by the Paris training department. These workshops also emphasize the skills and attitudes that accompany an effective review (e.g., the evaluation of performance rather than personality, the importance of employee responsibility for achieving objectives, minimising demotivating criticism).

In theory, those who do not attend the workshops should learn through their superiors at actual performance and activity reviews. In fact, the consistency of reviews varies from manager to manager. Michel Perez, despite believing in decentralization to the countries, had no hesitation recently in threatening Germany with a salary strike when he discovered they were not carrying out performance reviews. This concentrated their minds with remarkable speed, and now reviews are dutifully undertaken.

The performance reviews are in general seen as a strength of the company, and for many the Principles contribute to making Apple different from other companies. If managers grumble good-naturedly about the time that the review process takes, they are indignant if their bosses do not hold regular reviews with themselves.

The Garbage Principle is the most controversial, and there are a few people who dismiss the Principles themselves, as does this member of management:

The Principles are simplistic. The amoeba and time principles are just verbalisations of what happened anyway because of the market we happen to be in. I don't find them particularly helpful. As for the garbage principle, there are plenty of pieces of my job which I could do without, which would free me to do more useful things, but subordinates are already so stretched that I can't dump my garbage even if it would be of interest to them, which isn't certain.

Most employees however saw the system as demanding a lot of individual initiative and responsibility:

You've got to be a very competent person here—I don't think anybody's going to lead you by the hand and suggest that you do this or that. The evaluation system makes it pretty clear—to be ranked merely as an "adequate performer," that is meeting requirements and no more, you have to add at least one new dimension to your job. And you can be sure no-one's going to tell you how to do it! Your supervisor should give support, but the initiative has to come from you.

Indeed "delegation" is a word that one rarely hears at Apple; people are expected to achieve their negotiated objectives and take initiatives rather than being told what to do.

As for the Activity Review, the process of questioning the contribution of each and every activity in an organization certainly helps Apple avoid complacency. The concept of redefinable jobs appears to have assisted in creating attitudes that are remarkably open to change. Six months rarely go by without some form of reorganization, to the extent that a certain uneasiness comes over people when time goes by without change! Winsnes notes a different attitude, however, among new employees:

The veterans have gone through so many restructurings that they know there's life beyond and can enjoy the excitement. For the new people, though, it's an incredible strain. They panic sometimes. I've watched them, and it takes a good two years before they can relax. What's interesting, then, is that they start actively looking for change. They develop a sense of urgency and I can assure you they don't let problems hang around for long. It's not like in some other companies where problems get swept under the carpet—at Apple, people almost fight to get at them!

Remuneration

The remuneration system can be seen as the last element of the performance management system, since it has a strong performance orientation.

A new recruit will not find much difference from most other firms who have adopted modern personnel systems. There are job grades according to level of responsibility, with corresponding salaries. Apple keeps track of salaries in other European high technology companies to ensure that theirs are competitive. And the core duties of jobs with Apple are compared and adjusted to ensure equity regardless of the person holding them. But here the similarities end.

All of this is only an entry ticket, a starting point. Over time, remuneration and job grade may diverge considerably. A salary increase typically does not reflect a promotion but rather the fact that the person has developed his or her job beyond its original scope; in a rapidly growing organization such as Apple, promotions will often simply be the confirmation of an already existing situation.

Salaries and Merits Increases An Apple employee will be paid at, above or below the base level for his or her grade according to performance. Those performing at a fully competent level receive between 95% and 105% of the specified core

salary. Those who are not yet proficient receive a salary in the sub 95% or learning range; those who are particularly effective contributors, expanding their job responsibilities, are paid over 105% of core salary. What is untraditional is that there is no upper limit on the salary which can be paid at any grade, so that a champion performer may be earning 200% of his core wage.

There is a salary review on each six-monthly anniversary of joining Apple, linked to the preceding performance review. Merit increases in addition to cost of living are determined by supervisors, with the local HR manager, on the basis of the performance evaluation (a merit increase of more than 7% does however require the approval of the European HR manager). Unsatisfactory performers may receive "negative merit increases" up to the same percentage as the cost of living increases, effectively reducing purchasing power.

Bonuses A bonus for an exceptional initiative may be awarded to an employee following an activity review, and supervisors can and regularly do award non-cash bonuses at their discretion—a trip for the family, an expensive dinner.

Managers above a certain grade are part of a *formal bonus system*. Half of the bonus is based on country revenue and profits (total European revenue and profits in the case of Paris managers). The other half is based on an assessment of individuals on six quality criteria: expense control, forecasting, general quality, development of staff, respect and implementation of Apple Values, and "other objectives." Zero to three stars are attributed on each criteria. In the case of development of staff, for example, one star would be attributed to a manager who took some actions in the field. Two stars would be given if the manager consistently gave his or her subordinates chances and pushed training. Three stars would be awarded if development of staff was clearly treated as a priority.

Profit Sharing   This is a basic Apple philosophy and is paid quarterly in proportion to salary unless the bonus amounts to a larger sum. There is a profit level threshold, however, and employees did not receive these benefits for almost two years until September 1985. Employees may also purchase stock at 80% of the lowest market value over a certain period, and Cupertino may on an ad hoc basis award stock options to managers.

DEVELOPMENT SYSTEMS

Although a broad menu of training programs is provided and the discussion of training needs and career development aspirations is part of the performance reviews, there is little obligatory training and the idea of career planning is rejected by the firm. Apple's policy is that training and career development are above all the responsibility of the individual. Apple could be said to help those who help themselves.

Training

Training is an important activity, for as company policy states, "The implementation of Apple's Human Resources management philosophy requires a set of strong, well structured and supportive training policies, the success of which will rely on a high degree of commitment by all parties involved." The quality and availability of training is highly regarded within the company. One often hears comments like: "The training is excellent. It's there for the taking if you want it" or "If I want to go on a course, I don't think I've ever been turned down. That's an opportunity I didn't have elsewhere." If there are complaints, it is that work pressures prevent people from taking advantage of the courses.

Its Evolution   Prior to the Spring of 1983, only a few courses were offered on presentation skills and team building. Michel Perez was brought in from Texas Instruments as Training and Development Manager and given a more or less free hand in developing the function, passing responsibilities later on to Mike Morren.

The early modules covered Apple culture and basic supervisory skills. Functional courses were added (e.g. marketing and distribution), as well as induction courses for recruits, and modules aimed at fostering the people's practice of Apple Values (enhancing "people's capacities for positive contribution," capabilities in "creative job design," time management). More advanced management courses came later, aimed at heightening the degree of professionalization, and recently there has been a move towards specific organizational development projects (e.g. implementing a sales information system to create a common language in Europe for sales management and raise the level of professionalism).

Although the Training Department is involved in design and monitoring, the majority of these courses are subcontracted, taught by outside consultants, with a balance between in-house and outside programs. The *Apple Management Institute* is an example of an outside program, a two-by-two-week advanced management program established in 1984 by Mike Morren with INSEAD and taught by both INSEAD faculty and Apple executives at Fontainebleau. In 1986, the Institute was opened up to high potential Apple managers from across the world. However, one area of training that is necessarily in-house is of course induction training.

The Training "Menu"   Aside from programs like the Institute and induction courses, what is offered is essentially a menu that employees can choose from according to their needs. The Paris department asks the different operating units to specify their specific training needs for the coming year. On this basis a training brochure is compiled. Employees then choose appropriate courses from this catalogue, applying to Paris for inscription. A secretary interested in marketing, for example, may sign up as long as the course does not coincide with other commitments, as well as a manager considering a functional shift to this field.

In practice, such an optional philosophy has its advantages and disadvantages. On the one hand, those participating are likely to be highly motivated. On the other hand, given Apple's lean headcount, a frequent comment is "I just don't have time!" As an employee from Apple Germany put it: "From the very top down there has to be a business calendar, forecasting meetings in advance so that you can plan for the year. Otherwise people say you can't go on the training because we need you." As mentioned earlier, this results in an uneven knowledge of Apple's values and philosophy, as well as difficulties in the implementation of human resource and other management procedures. Moreover, some employees feel out of depth confronted with choice:

> It's help yourself time. It's self help taken to the ultimate. So unless someone tells me that I'm going to be a good marketeer or sales guy or finance man by going on this or that course, I don't know which ones to go on. God knows, I might be the best salesman the company's ever known.

Apple would probably maintain that this employee should work it out for himself or leave.

Decentralization of Training? One of the thorny current issues has to do with the decentralization of training. Apple Europe's philosophy is to decentralize management to the countries, and the Paris Human Resource Department has always preferred merely to play an initiating role. As soon as a program had been developed and tested in Paris, it should in principle be passed on to the geographical units. Programs designed for a mix of nationalities and markets tend to be vague and of less specific local relevance.

Where there was no local HR manager, it was Paris' job to hold the fort. Now in February 1986 there is talk of total devolution of training, with initial design pushed out to local level where it can be better adapted to local circumstances. But the issue is hotly contested. In fact only one local HR manager has any training background, and training frequently comes low in subsidiary priorities even though a part of the bonus of country managers is based on development of staff. The countries themselves have little desire to take over training, and Winsnes himself now opposes earlier plans to move training out to the countries:

> Training is one of those things people turn to when there's nothing else to do, but this function is far too important for the future to be put in careless hands. Roger Kermisch agrees that we must say NO to decentralization of training. We will keep training optional but we are really going to have to drive it; we're prepared to kick people if they don't show the right attitude, if they don't attend or if they cancel at the last moment. One senior manager was already threatened with $8000 off his bonus if he didn't buck up staff development—that concentrated his mind wonderfully!

Career Development

Career development remains an area where Apple still has to formulate clear policies, although management has certain principles emanating from its Values and philosophy. There is no lack of ideas, but there is a definite need to weave them into a coherent set of processes.

The basic belief is that each individual should largely determine his or her own path. Stefan Winsnes is particularly insistent on this point:

> Let me give you an ideal example of career development. A distribution guy comes along to my office and says that he wants to become a general manager one day. Together we map out some modules, some developmental jobs that he would need—marketing, sales, experience in Britain and the U.S. This actually happened—six months later I heard that there was a sales job in the United States, and the guy in question got it.
>
> Other people come passively into my office and say, "What are my career development prospects?" My reaction is, "What do you want me to do? I don't even know you," and they leave in frustration, saying that those people in HR are so inefficient, there is no career development in Apple.

Apple also wants to avoid the trap of focusing only on the careers of so-called high fliers. All employees have the same rights and duties to grow in their jobs, though by their nature so-called Stars are likely to advance faster and choose career paths with more frequent diagonal moves; particular attention is paid to them in Review Board discussions.

Horizontal moves need to be managed, and the job of human resource management is to make sure that the right doors are open. But vertical promotions in a small and rapidly growing organization typically come only as recognition of an already existing situation. Horizontally or vertically, growth must be triggered by individual initiative.

The Flexible Career   In fact, the ability to follow a flexible career path within Apple accounts substantially for employee loyalty. There is little incentive to look outside for other jobs when one knows one can mould one's own. A senior manager in Apple Europe explains how this has affected him:

> I was attracted to Apple in the first place because of the opportunities it offered. After the constraining atmosphere of a large company, I felt a need to be involved. I wanted to know that my creativity would leave its mark, would be visible. I also wanted to know that I was not destined to stay in finance all my life. Not many companies can promise you that, especially when they've hired you as a specialist. Anyway, I spent four years with Apple in the kind of positions I was trained for—first finance, and then control—before deciding I was tired of the area. I made this quite clear to Michel Perez, expressed what I'd like to do. And here I am in a good sales and marketing position. The individual really does have a voice here.

This concept of career development is currently incorporated into the Activity Review, where the reviewee is asked to express three possible career moves, one outside his or her present job family.

Where possible, access to different functional areas may be facilitated by a mid-way post, a job which includes aspects of both disciplines. Other possibilities for diagonal growth accepted by the company are the creation of ad hoc posts and specially designed management projects. Job posting is becoming more widespread. On the other hand, geographic mobility is infrequent and treated on a case by case basis.

In any event, in order to encourage adventurous diagonal steps, Apple's policy is to minimise the penalties of failure. Failure in a vertical move would be serious, though in a diagonal move it should be looked upon as a lesson learned—the individual can always return to a vertical career in his or her original field.

The Problems What handicaps further elaboration of the career development system is that the theory of these developmental concepts is not always perceived in practice. Comments are heard such as: "All the major moves I've made have been at crisis point, rather than me saying what I want to do, and working towards that end."

Lean headcount contributes to the problems. Back-ups and deputies don't exist. Time constraints and difficulty in finding replacements are a barrier to training attendance and also hinder progression itself, for an individual cannot move on to another area without knowing that his or her post is filled. Although they may grow within their own jobs, opportunities for promotion are limited. One manager comments on the situation in Apple UK: "There is not only a flat hierarchy but also limited numbers. Therefore, there isn't room for advancement. I managed to have one or two good people sent to the States, but later, when Apple becomes more stable, I foresee a problem for progression in the lower ranks." On the other hand, few Apple employees until now view career development solely in terms of climbing a hierarchic ladder.

Another problem is that of guidance, which particularly concerns the more junior ranks. Lack of experience and confidence sometimes mean that Apple's policy of self-determination is far from desirable, interpreted as a sign that Apple doesn't care. When questioned on Apple's career strategy, their comments range from "I feel very stuck, and nobody seems to notice or care" to "The bigger we get, the less confident I feel. I just wonder if my boss has enough interest in me."

A clear split in attitude can be seen between senior and junior members of the company. Both are unclear as to what they will be doing five years down the line, but senior people tend to take the view, "I don't know and I don't care as long as I enjoy what I'm doing." More junior people tend to say, "I don't know where I'm going and I don't feel at ease with that."

Despite these problems, voluntary turnover at Apple is so low that it can hardly be measured. Enforced turnover runs at roughly 10% and is accounted for mainly by people who can't cope with the constant change. In Stefan Winsnes' words:

Most people get used to the instability, they see the light at the end of the tunnel when everything is in upheaval. Others don't, they panic. They will never be happy with Apple, so for their sakes and ours, we ask them to go. However, we spend a lot of time and energy on making these separations amicable, partly for those who are leaving but mainly as a reassurance to those who stay on.

The Changing Profile of Recruits

Another recent and troubling developmental problem is that newcomers to Apple clearly don't feel the same way about the company as the initial pioneers. When a candidate applied to Apple in the past, his or her candidature was itself proof of an adventurous, risk-taking nature. Now that the company is more well-known with a solid performance record, a job application proves nothing and attitudes to risk must be estimated by other judgmental means. There are indications that would-be recruits are coming to look on Apple as just another company, with no more or less to offer than others in the market. Careful recruitment, induction and integration become more vital than ever to bring on board enthusiastic, Apple orientated people.

Michel Perez is deeply concerned by what may become a serious problem:

More consistency in recruitment and integration of new hires would do much to remedy some of the difficulties we have in career development. Recruitment is very weak and new people don't always get an induction course at the local level. How can we expect them to take full control of their careers when they don't really know the rules of the game, and perhaps aren't even Apple types?

Perez is also sensitive to the risk of personnel problems plaguing other enterprises. Until now, unionization has been a non-concern, though today one sees some pressures to form works councils under local national legislation for the airing of grievances, especially for lower level staff.

While some managers bemoan the lack of recruitment procedures, poor training attendance is once more to blame. Guidelines for recruitment do exist, a manual of procedures and methods has been written on the subject including a guide to identifying what kind of people are "Apple material." However, those who have not attended the Human Resource Workshops continue to recruit poorly while complaining about the lack of company support. The problem is not helped by the fact that other managers wrongly believe that they have the requisite skills anyway. The HR Department sees no simple solution if Apple's "no compulsory training" philosophy is to be respected. It has been suggested that all new recruits should spend a week with the local training department before taking up their posts so as to allow better screening and induction.

Communications

Apple has hitherto prided itself on its open communications, its atmosphere of friendly exchange, its open door policy where each person has immediate access to bosses to talk freely about professional or personal matters. There is, however, a growing feeling now that people are communicating less. In part, this deterioration is blamed on Apple's growth, and Stefan Winsnes agrees to some extent: "When I was with ICL before, you could have a one day meeting to discuss something and inform everyone before reaching an important decision. But they were growing at 4% per annum—we're growing at 60%."

A 1985 survey showed that while there were few problems at the department level, interdepartmental information flows were poor and intercountry even worse. "Sometimes I have no idea of what's going on," was a not infrequent comment. There was a low awareness of what was happening in Cupertino. An extreme case occurred in 1985, when employees at the Irish manufacturing plant, including the paper manager, learnt about its closure through the newspaper before notification reached them from Cupertino.

Vertical communications were, however, the most serious problem. People were not informed about the reasons for changes affecting their jobs, or were finding out about these changes indirectly. Middle management was found to be the weak link in the top to bottom chain. A gap had come into being between top management and the lower ranks, creating an "us and them" sentiment that was totally out of keeping with company philosophy. The conclusion was that second line management needed to be more involved, particularly in the process of pushing information down through the organization, though how to achieve this was another matter.

Jon Bruce, the manager who had initiated the survey, felt that "the most Apple way to have an effective communications network is to pass back the responsibility for communication to Apple people themselves by forming informal communication circles." One existing model was the early morning meetings at the French subsidiary, nicknamed "Coffee-Croissants-Conversation," at which the different departments met to exchange news and views. Such circles have been formed in most countries, but their success has been varied—limited at best to those who attended them.

Perez feels that techniques and "gadgets" like an occasional special event do not constitute effective communication. This is above all a question of more basic management attitudes.

MANAGEMENT CONCERNS UNDERLYING HR

Behind the human resource system at Apple lie a number of concerns that are shared by senior executives in Europe and the United States. Three, in particular, can be singled out—a concept of organization and management that emphasizes leadership; a desire to remain lean and productive, and a concern, sometimes verging on an obsession, not to become a "traditional company." What links these management concerns is the conviction that survival in the maturing, though unpredictable, computer industry depends on leadership.

THE CONCEPT OF ORGANIZATION AND MANAGEMENT

The Apple concept of an organization is that of a network of strong, visionary leaders responsible for operations and countries, sharing a common sense of direction. These leaders each have a wide span of control over their managers. It is a flat, decentralised organization where there is no room for weak individuals who do not pull their weight. "Some people just won't fit into such an organization and we ask them to leave," says Mike Spindler.

Words like "manager" leave Apple executives uneasy, as do some of the connotations of "professionalism." Although there aren't better terms in the vocabulary, the notion of "manager" lacks the entrepreneurial qualities sought after at Apple, and executives are far happier with the notion of "leadership." Indeed, the Apple Value of "Good Management" is seen by some as inappropriately worded—it should read "Great Leadership!" In a similar way, the word "motivation" is not part of Apple jargon: "We don't want motivated people here, we want INSPIRED people!"

One of the side consequences of this wide span of control is that a number of employees complain of an *absence of recognition* for what they do. The communication survey had revealed that whereas all employees considered personal recognition to be important, a significant percentage thought it was neglected. To complicate the issue, opinions varied as to what constitutes recognition; some said that recognition was as important as money, others were equally adamant that "good recognition *is* money and not awards—It shows that the company is willing to make a sacrifice for someone." Many saw the firm in this respect as fickle:

> It depends on what phase the moon is in regarding Apple Values. If they're high, then we have the Apple Hero Award. But when Apple Values are low, the Hero Award disappears.

Others were more condemning still: "We used to give more in the old days. All we seem to be recognised for now is when we leave."

A LEAN AND PRODUCTIVE ORGANIZATION

A second management concern is to keep a lean organization, reinforced in recent years by the concerted profit drive and cost squeeze. In 1985 the goal was to increase turnover by 60% with a maximum 20% increase in headcount. Aside from the corporate concern with financial survival, another important reason is flexibility, as Mike Spindler, a former DEC manager, explains:

> People lock you in, and Digital is a good example. With a $4 billion turnover, they have too wide a product line—too much to focus on and strategize around. Their weakness is that there is no focus of attention. They've known this for some time, but why don't they do anything about it? Why? Because they have 45,000 people and they wouldn't know what to do with them otherwise.

However, this emphasis on a lean and productive organization has its price. One of the most common complaints is along the following lines: "The toughest problem now is that we don't have the resources. People are working day and night and at the weekends to handle everything." Some argue that this type of commitment is inconsistent with Apple's expressed value of "fostering the best environment for individual initiative" and of having fun in one's work. Resentment in some cases is vehement:

> I don't believe in strategies where you hire people, you take everything out of them, and then you kick them out and replace them. I've no private life. You can ask too much of people. You can't keep it up. They tend to soothe their consciences by saying the situation is only temporary and that next year we will be freer to devote time to home and family. The more realistic amongst them will admit that they said the same words last year and the year before that.

The pressures are also symbolised in what some call the consequent problem of "other halves"—problems in marriage, family and private life. When based in Paris, Stefan Winsnes was concerned about these sacrifices. He would make a point of walking through his department at six in the evening telling everyone to go home to their families. His intentions were appreciated, but everyone knew that the work normally done between six and eight o'clock or later would still be there the next morning along with another day's work.

Tight headcount, previously accepted as necessary for economic survival, is no longer considered indispensable. Instead of the positive feeling that they are helping the company through difficult times, some employees now have the impression that Apple is squeezing them for their last drop of blood. For the moment, Apple people seem still prepared to give, though this may not always be the case:

> It's alright demanding a lot of people when the culture is young and strong and the values are seen to be alive and well. But when it seems the company no longer cares as much and is expecting people to give without doing anything in return, then you have a recipe for trouble.

AVOIDING BECOMING A TRADITIONAL COMPANY

Senior management share a sense that in the same way as Apple's now legendary success story was founded on being different, so its future leadership position in the industry depends on maintaining that uniqueness. If Apple were to become a "traditional" firm, then its chance of competing with the IBMs and DECs, the Olivettis and the NECs are doomed.

Apple in Europe is growing, becoming

more established. Here, as in the United States, one acknowledges that a different generation of managers and professionals are coming on board, people who have no sense of the early pioneering days. One acknowledges also that competing with IBM requires more "professionalism." But how can one meet these realities and challenges without sacrificing the cultural basis for Apple's industry leadership? This remains a constant preoccupation.

THE CHALLENGES FOR THE FUTURE

Apple's approach to human resource management is widely regarded outside the firm as innovative. Winsnes and Perez are in much demand to lecture at universities and professional associations. Winsnes sometimes feels that there is excessive interest in Apple techniques rather than in the way that these were developed:

> We tried to come to grips with the realities of Apple's business development rather than applying traditional methods or the latest fad, and so we invented everything ourselves. That's the Apple way. But if others try to imitate our techniques, it'll take them ten years to put them in place—and by that time we'll be doing something different because the Apple reality will have changed.

Winsnes and Michel Perez are acutely conscious of the fact that if Apple's approach to human resource management is something of an innovative model outside the firm, there still remains much to be done inside the firm. Winsnes says this lack of complacency is typical:

> Apple people don't look back to the past and feel satisfied with the achievements that outsiders see as remarkable. They tend, instead, to look to the future and feel de-

pressed about how much is still there waiting for improvement.

A changed business emphasis in the coming years will intensify certain challenges. The focus on profits in recent years will swing more to a goal of recapturing and building market share, and sales growth of 30–40% is predicted for 1987. Inevitably many new people will have to be hired, and the company's ability to learn from past mistakes will be put to the test. These recruits will simply have to understand what Apple is, otherwise their sheer force of numbers could change the company's culture.

However busy they might be and however limited their resources, managers must make room for development activities, says Winsnes:

> Managers don't spend enough time on people management, they are becoming too much like individual contributors. They HAVE to use the garbage concept more often and more constructively. Everyone will have to sort out the wheat from the chaff, to get rid of everything which isn't necessary.

As for the exact direction which human resource management should take in Apple Europe, this is the major decision which he and Michel Perez have to reach.

APPLE COMPUTER (EUROPE) STUDY QUESTIONS:

1. Identify and evaluate the business strategy of Apple Computer.
2. Assess the strengths and weaknesses of Apple's approach to human resources management. In what ways, if any, has HRM contributed to the survival, growth, and business success of the company?
3. There are several challenges confronting Michel Perez. In developing his plan for 1986–87, what should be his top priorities? Why? In these priority areas, what do you suggest he do? Why?

APPLE COMPUTER (EUROPE)

Appendix 1 Apple Computer, Inc. sales ($000,000s), net income ($00,000s) and headcount, 1980–1985

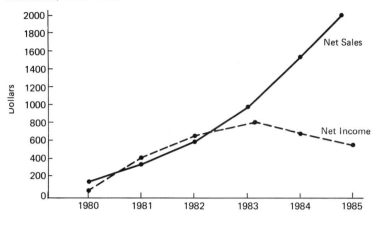

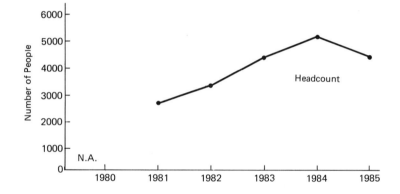

APPLE COMPUTER (EUROPE)
Appendix 2 Apple organisation chart (prior to 1985 reorganisation)

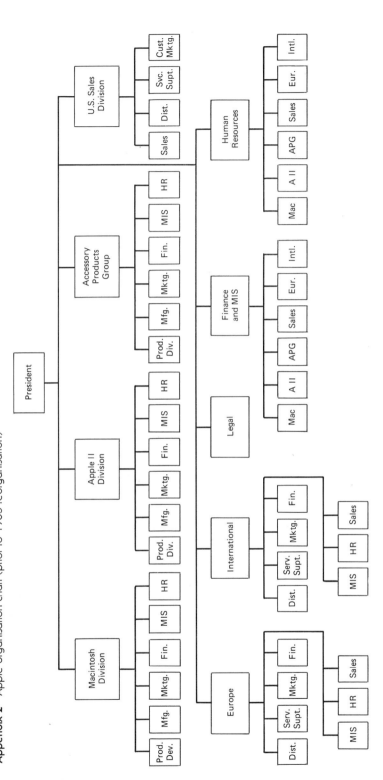

APPLE COMPUTER (EUROPE)

Appendix 3 Apple organisation chart (post 1985 reorganisation)

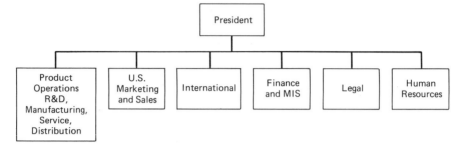

APPLE COMPUTER (EUROPE)

Appendix 4 Apple Europe 1980–1985: sales, new operations and headcount

Year	Sales	New Operations	Headcount
1980	$25m	Independent distributors	0
1981	$60m	Paris office (European HQ)	80
1982	$90m	France UK Germany	280
1983	$130m	Holland Ireland	400
1984	$200m	Italy Austria Sweden Belgium	500
1985	$250m	Spain	580

APPLE COMPUTER (EUROPE)

Appendix 5 Organization chart for Apple Europe

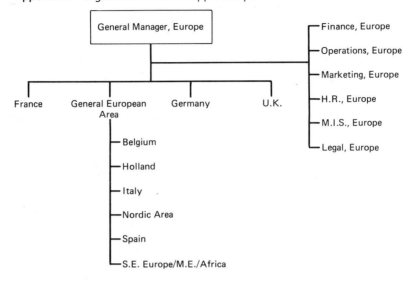

Empathy For Our Customers/Users

We provide our dealers and users with reliable products of lasting value and dependable service.
We expect our products to respond to the user's needs, and to be seen as friendly, natural tools that can extend each person's analytical and imagining abilities.

Positive Social Contribution

Apple contributes to society by providing the power and usefulness of the computer to individual people.
With this tool, people are improving the way they work, think, learn, communicate, and spend their leisure hours.

Innovation/Vision

Apple was founded on the conviction that the computer could be and should be a personal tool.
Innovation, aggressiveness, and responsible risk taking, combined with a vision of the future in which the personal computer will serve us all, will continue to motivate us.

Quality/Excellence

We take pride in our integrity and the quality of our products. We strive for absolute fairness in our dealings with customers, vendors, and competitors as well as among ourselves.

Achievement/Aggressiveness

We will continue to set high goals and high standards of performance, because we realise that through meeting such challenges we will advance as a company and as individuals.
We regard taking calculated risks as part of the adventure and the challenge of accomplishing something significant.

Individual Performance

The individual worth of each person is highly valued.
We recognise that each member of Apple is important and that each can contribute directly to customer satisfaction.

Individual Growth/Reward

We strive to support our people in achieving their personal objectives in line with their contribution at Apple.
We encourage the growth of each individual.
Sharing the tangible rewards of Apple's success is part of our management philosophy.

Team Spirit

We strive for a cooperative, friendly work environment that supports individual contribution as well as team effort.
We are all working together for a common goal.
We want to keep our organisation simple and flexible so that ideas and information can pass freely among those who need it.

Good Management

We want to foster the best environment for individual initiative while maintaining the highest standards in business ethics, personal and professional integrity, and achievement.

apple values

- achievement/aggressiveness
- individual performance
- team spirit
- empathy for our customers/users
- quality/excellence
- positive social contribution
- innovation/vision
- good management
- individual growth/reward

empathy for our customers/users

One person, one computer.

We provide our dealers and users with reliable products of lasting value and dependable service. We expect our products to respond to the user's needs. To be seen as friendly, natural tools that can extend each person's analytical and imagining abilities. Most of all, we want our customers to feel that they receive more benefit from Apple than they paid for.

achievement/aggressiveness

We are going for it and we will set aggressive goals. We are all on an adventure together.

We will continue to set high goals and high standards of performance because we realize that through meeting such challenges we will advance as a company and as individuals. We do not value risk taking for its own sake. Rather, we regard taking calculated risks as part of the adventure and the challenge of accomplishing something significant.

positive social contribution

We build products we believe in. We are here to make a positive difference in society, as well as make a profit.

Apple contributes to society by providing the power and usefulness of the computer to individual people. With this tool, people are improving the way they work, think, learn, communicate and spend their leisure hours. As a corporate citizen of this world, we will respect our social and ethical obligations. Our profits are the result and an important measure of how well we succeed in making the contribution.

individual performance

Each person is important, each has the opportunity and the obligation to make a difference.

The individual worth of each employee as a person is highly valued. We recognize that each member of Apple is important, that each can contribute directly to customer satisfaction. Our results come through the creativity, craftsmanship, initiative and good work of each person as a part of a team.

team spirit

We are all in it together, win or lose. We are enthusiastic!

We strive for a cooperative, friendly work environment that supports individual contribution as well as team effort. As a company, we know that we are all working together for a common goal. Accordingly, we want to keep our organization simple and flexible so that ideas and information can pass freely among those who need it. Indeed, our work environment serves to reflect and support all of our values.

innovation/vision

We are creative; we set the pace.

Apple was founded on the conviction that the computer could be, and should be a personal tool. From simple beginnings, the company has accomplished in a short time what many others thought impossible. Innovation, aggressiveness, and responsible risk taking, combined with a vision of the future in which the personal computer will serve us all, will continue to motivate us.

individual growth/reward

We want everyone to enjoy the adventure we are on together.

We are committed to providing a work environment based on mutual respect and will strive to support our employees in achieving their personal objectives in line with their contribution at Apple. We encourage the growth of each individual. Sharing the tangible rewards of Apple's success as well as the challenges and satisfactions that come with it is part of our management philosophy.

quality/excellence

We care about what we do.

We take pride in our integrity and the quality of our products. We strive for absolute fairness in our dealings with customers, vendors and competitors as well as among ourselves. In cases of dispute, we are willing to go the extra mile. The quality of our work stems directly from the care we express in all we do. It is an attitude that unites us.

good management

We want to create an environment in which Apple values flourish.

We want to foster the best environment for individual initiative while maintaining the highest standards in business ethics, personal and professional integrity, and achievement.

european operations

7, Rue de Chartres 92200 Neuilly. Tél. 624.21.13

apple computer

APPLE COMPUTER (EUROPE)
Appendix 7 Apple performance review environment

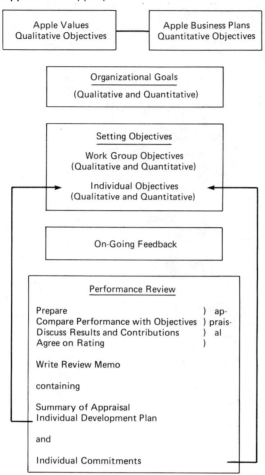

Apple Values
Qualitative Objectives

Apple Business Plans
Quantitative Objectives

Organizational Goals

(Qualitative and Quantitative)

Setting Objectives

Work Group Objectives
(Qualitative and Quantitative)

Individual Objectives
(Qualitative and Quantitative)

On-Going Feedback

Performance Review

Prepare   ) ap-
Compare Performance with Objectives) prais-
Discuss Results and Contributions   ) al
Agree on Rating   )

Write Review Memo

containing

Summary of Appraisal
Individual Development Plan

and

Individual Commitments

Salary Review

APPLE COMPUTER (EUROPE)

Appendix 8 The performance/potential matrix

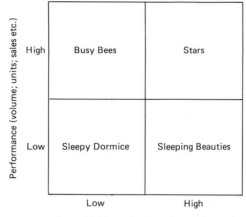

United Parcel Service (A)

The management committee at United Parcel Service (UPS) wrestled with the last item on the agenda. The head of the Information Services department had been invited to make a presentation.

"So you're convinced that we can't locate this talent internally or develop it in the smart computer-trained kids working in our districts?" inquired chief executive Jack Rogers.

"Oh, I think we can groom some from the inside, but we also have to get a large number of the senior programmers and middle managers from the outside. The field has gotten very specialized," replied Frank Erbrick, the head of the Information Services.

Erbrick was interrupted by Operations Vice President Frank Middendorf, "Look Frank, we don't need people to make the computers, just run them."

Erbrick turned to Middendorf, "Come on Frank, these people aren't Martians, but there's been a revolution in technology. We can hardly keep up with the language they speak. You'd do the same damned thing if you had my job."

Middendorf put one heel up on the ad-jacent chair and looked back at the others and growled, "'Yeah, but thank God I don't have your job. Someone has to make the money you're spending."

A playful banter of heated debate came to an end. As with most management decisions at UPS, consensus would be reached after an open airing of differences and the debate would be over. Critics would join the enthusiasts in support of whatever was decided concerning the staffing of Information Services. In considering the issue, Jack Rogers had asked for some discussion about the larger significance of the assimilation of new hires into the UPS culture.

A new plan for hiring outside talent for Information Services could represent a challenge to the company's long-established practice of equal pay across departments. Furthermore, management salaries were low and determined by hierarchical level. Senior managers, such as Rogers, earned at least one-third less in wages than their counterparts in comparable positions. Instead of short-term wages, the company relied upon a long-term bonus plan based upon annual stock grants from the company to all of its 15,000 full-time managers. With only six levels of management, the pay differences were slight, but substantial wealth was accumulated by UPS managers through their stock appreciation and dividends

This case was written by Associate Professor Jeffrey Sonnenfeld and Research Assistant Meredith Lazo as the basis for class discussion rather than to illustrate either effective or ineffective handling of an administrative situation. Reprinted by permission of the Harvard Business School.

over their long careers. The hiring of new specialized talent for assignments in key programming, financial, marketing, legal, engineering, and aviation positions at higher wages would challenge the strength of their long, successful career system.

Rogers commented on this: "What do you guys think we need to anticipate about the impact of these kinds of moves? As you know, our business is changing more in our eightieth anniversary than it has in any previous year."

John Alden, the head of business development, commented: "With the onslaught of new competitors chipping away at all parts of the business, we have to meet marketing and technological challenges, and that means recruiting more specialized talent."

Vern Cormie, another operations vice president, asked, "But how much can this system take? Can these people be routed out of their specialties into the districts?"

Joe Moderow, the corporate counsel, responded: "Well, specialists can still drive package cars." Moderow had joined UPS as a part-time clerk while earning a college economics degree. He managed Industrial Engineering and operating departments during his graduate schooling and after earning his J.D. He continued, "Engineers, analysts, programmers, and even attorneys can be broadened. I want my guys to have solid management skills, not just legal expertise."

Oz Nelson, the executive vice president, countered this by stating, "Well, as much as Joe has enjoyed getting away from other attorneys to work with managers, and who can blame him, many of the specialists we're bringing in do not want to be generalists. They have trained for years to become experts in their specialties and frankly, that's why we want them. Perhaps we can keep them more distinct from our operating culture."

Rogers responded, "Oz, I'm not certain that we can keep all such types hidden from the business. Some new acquisitions, for example, may hit us in the core. When outsiders are not in operations driving the business, I'm not as concerned."

The vice president of personnel, Don Layden, who was formerly a senior general manager, commented, "This is not the first time this company has attacked this sort of problem. We have moved into new nations, new industries, and new parts of the country. Each time we have had to face the challenge of introducing new people to the UPS system, orienting them, training them, matching their expectations, and helping them grow. The challenge is to be aware of whatever psychological contract is implicitly set up with each set of new hires, whether they are young college kids or mid-career avionics engineers."

Rogers responded, "Don, I think you're right. We made some mistakes in our national expansions to some regions but we did it right in our roll-outs in other regions. We knew that internal expansions could not be built with anything less than highly skilled managers. Perhaps there are other such lessons here."

Ed Jacoby, the new chief financial officer, added: "Our consultants, bankers, and auditors tell us we need to hire new talent and shouldn't worry about them fitting. We have this need to make everyone a member of the family with substantial stock and decades of service. After 30 years, I myself question this. Maybe we'd be better served by a cadre of fresh technical support that comes and goes and keeps us current."

Layden again recalled UPS's past experience, saying, "I think that even if we look at Germany . . ."

Rogers interrupted at this point, "That's right, Don. You led the operations team that corrected the crisis in Germany. Maybe you see what hidden patterns are emerging here. Why not throw out some observations for the committee meeting next week. We need to focus on how we bring outsiders to UPS as well as the extent to which we should do it."

COMPANY BACKGROUND

Jim Casey, with help from his brother George, founded the United Parcel Service (UPS) in 1907 under the name American Messenger Company. At that time messengers responded to telephone calls received at their headquarters; ran errands, carried notes, handbaggage, trays of food from restaurants, and delivered packages by either foot, streetcar, or bicycle.

As more advanced methods of communication became available to the public, the company placed a greater emphasis on services requiring package transportation. Only companies with a similar ground infrastructure could compete. And with the introduction of the motorcycle, they now could offer a faster and better delivery service.

In 1913, the new company acquired its first delivery car, a Model T Ford, establishing its identity as offering a state-of-the-art package delivery service. Two years later, its management adopted its trademark, the pullman brown color which continued to identify it through the years.

In 1919, Jim Casey, realizing that labor unions were unavoidable in the near future, invited the International Brotherhood of Teamsters to represent the UPS drivers and part-time hourly employees. He explained to his co-workers, "I think it's possible to be a good UPS member and union member at the same time." Because of this early relationship, UPS was able to forge a flexible union-management partnership with such noteworthy features as variable start time, working as directed with minimum work rules, working across job classifications, combinations of inside and outside labor, part-time employment for half the work force, and mandatory overtime as needed. Through the years, the relationship between the company and the union had been reasonably good, although there had been occasional work stoppages.

In 1922, UPS took a major strategic step when it began an experimental intercity "common carrier" service in Southern California. By becoming a common carrier, it was legally required to serve any shipper who was willing to pay, no matter how small the shipment or how remote the location within the service territory. Its common carrier service pioneered the automatic daily pick-up call, acceptance of checks made out to the shipper in payment of COD's, additional delivery attempts, automatic return of undeliverables, and streamlined documentation with weekly billing. This experiment was so successful that it grew to dictate the company policy and operating principles for service in future years.

Company operating features such as uniformed drivers; painted, well-maintained vehicles; an emphasis on courtesy; and an insistence on meeting service commitments were established at this time. Shortly thereafter, in 1929, *The Policy Book* was created to standardize these traits and other corporate ideals throughout all branches of the business. Although revised every few years by a special management committee, the book continued to serve as a template from which all new policy was made. Excerpts from *The Policy Book* are presented in Exhibit 1.

In spite of stringent regulatory restrictions on motor-carrier rates and routes in the U.S., by participating in repeated legal battles to obtain certificates of "public convenience and necessity," UPS had expanded its service to all or part of 50 states in the U.S. by 1980. With the passage of the Motor Carrier Act of 1980, deregulating the entire trucking industry, geographical restrictions were lifted and UPS was able to provide service to any point throughout all 48 contiguous states. As regulatory barriers vanished, other natural barriers like economies of scale, infrastructure, service recognition, and specialized skills took their place.

By this time, UPS had embarked as well on a strategy of diversification. As competition intensified with deregulation, it allocated large amounts of capital to modernize an antiquated data processing department. Beginning in 1976, it planned an aggressive international expansion. In 1982 it introduced Next Day Air Service in the U.S. By 1987 it owned 89 aircraft, leased 140, and had thirteen 757 Boeing jets, the most cost-efficient package freighters on the market, under construction. By 1987 UPS offered service to Canada, 16 European countries, and Japan. Foreign freight carriers, initially used for transporting packages from the planes to final destination points in foreign countries, became "service partners" or jointly run companies set up to participate in a full package delivery service in 1986.

By 1987 UPS was the largest transportation company and the largest air freight carrier in the world. Jim Casey, who continued to come to the office regularly until just before his death in 1981, lived to see this ambitious dream come true.

THE INDUSTRY

For years, UPS's major competitor had been the U.S. Parcel Service's (USPS) fourth-class parcel post. On a number of occasions over the years, UPS executives had argued that income from the USPS's large ($20 billion in 1986) first-class (letter) service was used to subsidize the price of parcel post service below true costs. Nevertheless, careful attention to service and cost-reducing ideas had enabled UPS slowly to overtake the USPS's parcel post in volume early in the 1970s. By 1986, USPS reported an average daily volume in its parcel post service of about 2.3 million packages per day compared with UPS's 8.3 million packages per day.

The USPS also competed in the air with its Express Mail service. From a volume of 7.7 million pieces in 1978, this service had grown to 40 million pieces in 1986. Most of these consisted of documents or very small items that could fit into an envelope.

In recent years the USPS had implemented many changes in its marketing and operating strategy that threatened UPS's leadership in surface small package shipments. In 1986, Preston Tisch took over as Postmaster. With a strong background in marketing, he aspired to change the USPS image by emphasizing customer service. The USPS also was making a concentrated effort to compete in the delivery of low-weight packages traveling short distances by offering reduced rates and expedited service. This service was also the fastest growing segment of UPS's business.

Deregulation   Deregulation, the competition it spawned, and the rapid growth of the overnight package delivery service by air were important characteristics of the package freight and document transportation business in recent years. The deregulation of the airline industry in 1978 had a significant impact on three major groups in the package delivery business: common carriers specializing in small package delivery on the ground, air freight forwarders, and existing air express carriers. Prior to deregulation, long-distance common carriers like UPS were unable to own or operate private aircraft without subjecting themselves to profit and pricing controls by the Civil Aeronautics Board (CAB). Instead they used passenger and freighter aircraft (operated by carriers such as United Airlines and Flying Tigers) to satisfy their air transportation needs. The second group, air freight forwarders (such as Airborne Freight), were companies that assumed responsibility for the local freight pick-up and delivery of freight to be transported on either commercial or freighter aircraft owned by others. After deregulation, many common carriers and forwarders purchased their own fleets and became integrated air carriers, offering a complete solution to a customer's express delivery needs. Owning their aircraft allowed the companies better control over service and costs associated with air delivery, something the Federal Express Corporation had been doing for several years as the nation's only major air express carrier. Deregulation of freight transport by air brought about by legislation, sometimes referred to as the "Federal Express Bill," assisted Federal Express by enabling it to increase substantially its package volume and revenues. To avoid CAB controls on all aircraft with total weight of over 7,500 pounds, Federal had transported all of its freight on small inefficient Dassault Falcons (converted executive jets) with cargo space of only 6,200 pounds. By 1976, the company was sending as many as six Falcons a night to one city and spending $25,000 a day more than it would with larger planes. With deregulation, it immediately purchased ten second-hand Boeing 727s and increased service to 300 cities. Accordingly, its daily package volume immediately increased by 34%.

Deregulation allowed UPS to service parcels up to 100 pounds. However, the company continued to restrict itself to a 70-pound limit. Because UPS had been run as an efficient operation during regulatory days, it was not underpriced by the influx of new entrants penetrating the market with lower operating costs and nonunion labor. However, with the threat of competition more apparent than in previous years, UPS began to fine-tune its operations, decreasing its costs and increasing its productivity. Management appropriated substantial funds for the information services department to develop new technologies that would enhance its customer service and keep the company in step with increased competition. Residential and business customers demanded that carriers have fast and reliable service, low rates, effective package tracking capabilities, and computerized documentation and billing of letters and parcels. UPS, although deficient in some of these capabilities, remained the leading carrier on the ground with the U.S. Postal Service posing the only major threat.

Federal Express

Incorporated in 1971 by Frederick Smith, Jr., as an air freight business specializing in the overnight delivery of small packages, Federal Express nearly went bankrupt before making its first profit of $3.6 million in 1976. Emulating the UPS hub concept by creating one hub in Memphis to serve the entire U.S., Fred Smith emphasized technology as an important element in his company's strategy. As a reflection of his interests, he was a member of the Advisory Committee to the National Academy of Engineering on technology in the service industries. In 1979, he created an Advanced Technology Center in Colorado Springs, Colorado, and by 1986 employed 95 information technology professionals in his organization.

This group had developed the COSMOS, ZODIAC, and DADS hardware and software systems for scheduling, tracking, and sorting packages and documents rapidly and accurately. The COSMOS system was used in receiving and scheduling pick-up requests at regional offices where technology and staffing combined to produce adherence to standards such as answering customer calls on the first ring. Packages and documents were bar-coded for identification and tracking purposes. Individual Federal Express couriers were assigned trucks with DADS terminals. A driver, using a hand-held Supertracker optical reader, recorded pick-up times and package numbers. The reader, when plugged into the DADS unit in the truck, communicated package status to a regional customer service facility. This information, combined with the ZODIAC system used in the hub for sorting by labels and positioning for reshipment to destination, provided comprehensive package tracking and control from the scheduling of a pick-up to delivery. It was described by one senior manager in the company as "the absolute bedrock of this company's success." The company had not been consistently successful with new technology, taking a reported $190 million after-tax write-off late in 1986 with the discontinuance of its electronic ZAPMAIL service. However, in 1986, Federal Express was handling about 537,000 packages and documents per day, realizing revenues for the fiscal year of more than $2.6 billion. Net income was $132 million, a 74% increase from the previous year.

Other Competitors

Airborne Freight, Inc., a traditional freight forwarder, had made a total commitment to the domestic and international package express market. It owned 33 aircraft and leased 43. In 1986, its express service handled 105,000 pieces per day, had revenues of $542 million, earned a net income of $13 million, and was the fourth largest express service. Its future plans included targeting the high-volume corporate user, expanding its sales force by 10–12%, and increasing the number of locations served with morning deliveries.

Emery Air Freight at one time had been the leading air freight forwarder in the U.S. The company began its express service in 1978 with later pick-up times and lower rates than Federal Express. However, by 1986, Emery lagged far behind Federal, UPS, Airborne and Express Mail services. Its volume reached only 42,000 pieces per day.

Purolator's specialty was in ground package delivery. Purolator's volume of next-day letters and packages in 1986 of 68,000 pieces per day was slightly larger than Emery's. However, Purolator realized less revenue and a larger loss than Emery in 1986. In 1987 the two firms merged, gaining 12% of the total one-day air express market.

In March 1985, Roadway Package Systems (RPS) began operations in 18 Midwest and Northeast states, with terminals in 33 cities and hubs in three other locations. A subsidiary of Roadway Services, Inc. (RSI), which included one of the largest over-the-road trucking businesses in the U.S., RPS had become a potential threat to UPS with a goal of capturing 10% of the small package market through business-to-business delivery service of small packages up to 100 pounds. Its parent company had a presence in 31 states, operating 83 terminals and 9 hubs. In 1986, RSI's revenues were $1.7 billion and net income was $16 million. It was anticipated that by the end of 1987 RPS could have a volume of 257,000 packages per day.

One particularly attractive feature about RPS was its sophisticated billing and package tracking system. A shipper could call a toll-free number at any time to find out the location of a package. UPS did not offer this service yet. The immensity of its ground network and the vast amount of computer memory needed to track the 2.3 billion packages it delivered in 1986 were given as reasons. Industry sources suggested that, despite its technological innovation, RPS's operations were marked by relatively high rates of damage, lost packages, and less efficient sorting. In 1986, however, UPS estimated that it lost several thousand packages per day to RPS. In 1987, industry sources predicted that RPS's daily volume would increase from about 3 percent of that of UPS to more than 7 percent by 1991.

Although UPS was clearly a giant on the ground in the early 1980s, it was a mere fledgling in the air. It began its overnight service four years after most of the competition. This delay set UPS far behind in service and image, forcing its management into a catch-up game for the first few years of its express operations. Although UPS had developed a two-day air service, Blue Label, in 1952, with the exception of ground pickup and delivery, UPS had subcontracted the service to various air carriers. For many years, UPS did not consider overnight air service to be within its mission. However, with the annual growth rates for the air express package market averaging 15 to 20% in the late 1970s and the leader of small package air freight transportation, Federal Express, doubling its profits and nearly tripling its revenues in the few years after deregulation, UPS management realized that air express was no longer a minor market niche.

To accommodate next-day service, UPS had developed a large hub in Louisville which, by 1983, could accommodate not only the Next Day Air operation but the Second Day Air service as well. By 1985, UPS air service included next-day air letters and packages, second-day packages and international shipments. Total air volume for 1986 amounted to 84 million packages.

Financial and employment data for major competitors in surface and air package delivery services in 1986 are shown in Exhibit 2.

UPS OPERATIONS

Over the years, UPS had pioneered the concept of daily pick-up and delivery service to retail and commercial accounts with delivery to all locations, including homes. Because of its relatively low rates and dependable service, retailers and manufacturers alike had come to rely on it for small shipments.

One analysis of the company's operations offered the following conclusions:

> [Among] the main reasons for UPS's strength is its emphasis on building route density [number of packages per stop and customers per route mile], standardizing the job of the route driver to allow for comparison and control, and designing its sorting facilities and transport equipment to handle packages of no more than 108 inches in combined length, width, and height and 70 pounds in weight. This single-minded approach to a service concept allows UPS to realize substantial profits while often charging its customers as little as half that of its competition.[1]

The core of the UPS service was provided by the package car, package center, feeder truck, and hub. The familiar chocolate brown package car and its driver represented the entire UPS operation to the public. Over the years, the standard car had been designed by the company and manufactured to its specifications.

---

[1] James L. Heskett, *Managing in the Service Economy* (Boston: Harvard Business School Press, 1986), p. 71.

Package Car

Most drivers treasured the customer contact. A 45-year-old former marine commented on his feelings about driving a package car:

> I thought this job would be a perfect transition to civilian life but it's been so much fun and the money is so good—I've stayed on. My wife is vice president of an insurance company, but I've got more job security and interesting work than she does. She works with papers and pens and I work with packages and people. A lot of guys with seniority go for feeder driver jobs. It pays a little better and is less physical. But I just love the customers on my route. I would hate to let them go. They count on me and I know all about them. Plus, the physical activity gives me such a good workout, I don't have to join a gym. Those feeder guys gain 50 pounds in just a few months!

Drivers generally worked more autonomously than employees inside the hub. The daily challenge was both physical and mental. The average driver had to deliver or pick up 360 packages per day regardless of any unanticipated problems. Drivers were held strictly accountable for every package in their car. They were given a complete instruction booklet on "Package Delivery and Pick-up Methods" and five days of one-on-one training to help train them. The booklet contained 31 detailed instructions on how to best perform the job from start to finish. It included turning on the delivery car's engine at the start of the day, ways to greet the customers during the day, and the final check-in procedure at the end of the day. Drivers had to determine for themselves how to handle abnormalities such as late starts due to delayed package center operations, adverse weather conditions, flat tires, or accidents.

UPS maintained a precise and comprehensive system of measuring performance by route. For this reason, little personal supervision of car drivers was required once the initial training was completed.

Package Center

A package center was the basic unit of UPS operations. Through package centers and a deliberate process of decentralization, UPS was able to maintain personal contact with every individual residing at an address anywhere across the U.S. and in many foreign countries.

At the 1200 package centers, packages were shifted from cars to feeder trucks for line-haul transport to one or more of UPS's 120 hubs at U.S. and foreign locations.

Although centers varied in size according to the district in which they were located, their operations were the same. At each center, packages received from hubs in feeders were unloaded and loaded onto package cars at night, ready for delivery the following morning. When package cars returned from their routes to the centers in the evening, part-time hourly employees unloaded the packages, placed them on sort belts, and reloaded them onto feeders that transported them back to hubs and on to their final destination points.

Because of limited car driver openings, only 10% to 15% of part-timers hired into the package center were eventually promoted into driving positions. To uphold its agreement with the Teamsters, for every three full-time driving positions, UPS filled two slots with people promoted from the hub and one with someone from outside the firm.

One could become a center manager usually only after he or she had driven a package car and held a full-time supervisor position. Two full-time supervisors reported to a center manager and three or four center managers reported to a division manager. In addition, delivery supervisors were employed at each center to perform "service checks" by accompanying drivers when they were delivering, observing and reinforcing safety guidelines, emphasizing techniques outlined by the prescribed job methods, and providing on-the-job training for all new drivers.

Full-time supervisors were considered first-level "partners" in the company, eligible for the management incentive stock plan. By 1986, there were 15,600 such partners throughout the company supervising another 152,600 employees.

Hub

The hub operation, although based on a simple concept of central unload, sort, and load, required complex and sophisticated coordination. Depending on the size of the hub, it had either two or three sort shifts which took place at noon (12 noon to 3 P.M.), twilight (5 to 8 P.M.) and midnight (11 P.M. to 2 A.M.). The completion of each task during a sort and adherence to service standards depended on the successful completion of the prior sort. The hub facility embodied a fantastic maze of incoming and outgoing belts and chutes that directed packages which were brought to the hub by large tractor-trailer trucks (feeders). Packages were manually unloaded from feeders and placed on various belts that led to outbound stations. The packages at each station were going to the same geographic area and were again loaded onto outbound feeders. The pace of work at a hub was furious during a sort. Employment and the volume of packages handled through each of three hubs on the UPS system are shown in Exhibit 3.

New hires were interviewed and selected by the personnel department on criteria such as independence, flexibility, physical fitness, and reliability. Ninety-five percent were students, recruited from local colleges. The department tried to employ the same percentage of white males, females, and minorities that lived in the community. Most new hires started as part timers inside the hub or as drivers. They were generally drawn to UPS for the supplementary income. Later, after recognizing the extensive opportunity to move into management or specialized areas like engineering or data programming, many decided to make UPS their career. Lengths of service for UPS employees are shown in Exhibit 4.

New hub operations were brought up-to-speed with the help of a team of visiting training managers and supervisors from various districts around the country. They typically stayed for eight to twelve weeks to help the new hub and its management in its initial development. The program they provided offered both formal training and an informal process of role modeling in which the old (and most successful) demonstrated to the new the attitudes and standards that represented a common thread throughout the organization.

POLICIES AND ORGANIZATION

Policies concerning employee ownership, decentralization, communication, managerial development, the unpretentiousness of its facilities, and its emphasis on customer service were particularly representative of the UPS culture. They were set forth in *The Policy Book*, examples from which are presented in Exhibit 1.

Employee Ownership

UPS was a private company, offering no stock to the public. A unique profit sharing and stock ownership plan caused many people to consider their UPS employment as a life-long commitment. The plan was designed so that in profitable years, all UPS employees shared in the company's profits, earning far more than they would from a normal salary. Jim Casey said in 1922 when 50 UPSers joined him in ownership:

> There is no bigger incentive than for someone to work for himself . . . the basic principle which I believe has contributed to the building of our business as it exists today is the ownership of our company by the people employed in it.

Although people in the full-time supervisory level and in upper management were considered partners or owners of the company, everyone was entitled to participate in at least one of the employment benefit plans. There were three main profit-sharing plans at UPS: a Thrift Plan for all regular employees who had completed at least one year of service; the UPS Management Incentive Plan, only for full-time managers; and the Stock Option Plans for the roughly 1200 employees holding positions equal to or above the division manager level.

UPS also offered a package of benefits designed to provide long-term financial security and immediate health care services for all employees. Both the retirement and health care plans were noncontributory for all employees who met minimum age and service requirements. The plans were designed to reflect the changes in the economy due to inflation. All employees, part and full-time, were provided with health and retirement benefits. Dale Orred, the National Benefits manager, commented about the UPS commitment to give its part-time employees the same medical benefits as full-timers:

> We can't think of a better way to spend our money. We don't look upon it as an excess nor should they [part-timers] see it as an entitlement. It is part of our management philosophy.

In a 1985 opinion survey given to a sample of 16,039 district employees, the majority of workers selected "good pay and benefits" as the most important job attribute at UPS. The president of Teamsters Local 804 in Long Island City, New York, recently had been quoted as saying that "if UPS announced it had 1,000 openings for drivers tomorrow, there would be 100,000 applicants."[2]

Decentralization

UPS emphasized decentralization. The operating organization was divided into regions, districts, divisions, and operating areas.

The district was considered the basic unit of the delivery operation. A district could be part or all of a metropolitan area, state, or several states. The district manager and staff formed a complete operating group with full responsibility for service and cost within the district. In 1986, UPS operations were divided into 70 districts in the U.S.

Regional management and staff provided services to all districts in their respective regions and arranged for an exchange of information among districts. Headquarters management performed a coordinating function on operational matters and provided certain services such as finance and real estate not available in the regions and districts themselves.

A chart of the UPS organization is shown in Exhibit 5.

Communication

In line with the partnership philosophy was an emphasis on corporate-wide communication. Believing that every department was entitled to know the activity of

[2] "Behind the UPS Mystique: Puritanism and Productivity," *Business Week*, June 6, 1983, p. 68.

the others, UPS's management designed tools to help build a network that would facilitate communication. A publication called "The Big Idea" was produced and distributed within every district to inform employees about national and local UPS news. Weekly Monday meetings were held at the company's headquarters in Greenwich, Connecticut, where representatives from each department gathered to meet with the top management committee. Each representative reported on his or her department's previous week's accomplishments and the following week's objectives. Issues like safety, employee recognition, new programs and policies, technology, customer priority, assignment changes, and training programs were reviewed. Minutes were taken during the meeting and then disseminated to the 15,600 managers at UPS. Each spring, a conference involving the top 200 managers in the company was held. Discussion about future strategic plans and present organizational accomplishments occurred during this annual conference. Managers from various regions and districts exchanged information, forged common objectives, and communicated best and worst performances and technological innovations. Upon returning to their districts and departments, the district managers presented a summary of the issues at the conference to a more immediate group of managers in a modified, day-long presentation that usually included a lunch or dinner for all local management.

In addition to the interaction between departments and districts, there was significant emphasis placed on communication within areas. Standard methods such as performance appraisals and opinion surveys were used to communicate opinions and performance levels in specified task areas. For verbal communication, districts held Prework Communication Meetings (PCMs). A PCM was a three-minute meeting held prior to the start of every work day in the hub or package center to discuss either specific questions about work tasks or larger issues involving competition and strategic direction. Either the immediate supervisor or a representative from a staff function such as customer service or safety would attend a driver or sort PCM and speak about a related issue concerning that operation. Customer service representatives alone gave over 50,000 PCMs a year. For more personal, one-on-one communication, a managerial tool called the "Talk, Listen, Act" (TLA) program was used to encourage closer coordination and interaction between managers, supervisors, package handlers, and drivers. A TLA was a scheduled meeting that gave employees protected time to express concerns, make suggestions, or simply establish more informal relationships with their managers. TLAs were required and monitored by the company for each employee and his or her immediate manager.

Internal Development of Employees

Through the dedication to its promotion-from-within policy, effective training schools, on-the-job training, and role modeling, the company had succeeded in preparing some of its most junior workers for top-level positions. However, because it had many more part-time employees than available full-time positions, it could promote only a small percentage of its part-time supervisors into full-time delivery jobs, which was the next step in the career track. Out of the total of 54,350 driving positions in 1986, 25% to 30% of them were filled by part-time promotions. Drivers then had the opportunity to move into full-time supervision and become eligible for ownership in the company. From the full-time supervisory level, an employee usually was transferred laterally for exposure to support roles and other functions of the company before moving up the vertical path. Paul Oberkotter, the former chief executive officer, commented on the benefits of internal development:

It's an intangible sort of thing. Everything we do to develop managers is in support of it. Individuals learn to get along and manage through personal influence and credibility of experience rather than through title and coercion. For example, we tracked Jack Rogers through 50 different types of permanent assignments and short-term projects. We saw his strengths grow and the areas where he needed work. Over time he became known throughout the organization. No one was frightened when he was named chief executive officer. He could make substantial changes in this business without worrying people about their security or continuation of the culture. He was not an untried personality. He had broad knowledge, experience, and UPS commitment.

Although UPS had always been a "people-oriented" company, the forceful management practices once common in many industries had often surfaced in first line supervision. Recently, top management had explicitly worked to close any lingering gaps between the long-held management philosophy of cooperation and actual supervisory practice. One training manager who had been with UPS 17 years commented:

The management style of UPS has changed. The mystique of the organization has not. The mystique is the belief that everyone who makes it at UPS must give 100% effort. The management style and method for motivating employees is different now. We use people policies, based on integrity and fairness, not force. At times we used to inject brown blood with a two-by-four. Now we do it through osmosis. I personally try to understand every individual I supervise and know what makes that person tick.

As UPS reached out to a new generation of workers with different needs and multiple employment opportunities, this new approach became more important. Instilling the "people policies" became a challenge for the 1980s. Structure and accountability were emphasized but now were sweetened with recognition, reward, and daily encouragement for a job well done.

Humility

Certain other aspects about UPS, however, had not changed. Over the last 80 years, the organization had retained a humility that was perhaps best reflected in the physical appearance of its facilities and by the attitude of top executives. The buildings were stark, contemporary, and simple. UPSers scrupulously emphasized cleanliness but also discouraged elaborate decor. Chairs and tables were functional. Walls, if not barren, displayed folksy, Norman Rockwell-type images of UPS package cars serving small communities. Carpets, where they existed, were thin and laid for the convenience of cleaning, not comfort. Offices were comparably sized. Parking spaces were available on strictly "first-come, first-served" basis. The parking lot was filled with conservative, mid-sized cars. People who drove flashy sport cars were subject to peer teasing. No one at UPS had his or her own secretary, including the CEO. All executives answered their own telephones. Executives did their own photocopying, travel arrangements, and scheduling. Even the board of directors shared the same conference room used for any meetings of managers or supervisors. There was no executive dining room in the national, regional, or district headquarters. Instead,

UPS provided a cheerful cafeteria where anyone from a clerk to a programmer to a senior manager could enjoy a morning or midday meal.

Customer Service

An entire section of *The Policy Book* was devoted to the company's service. It stressed such things as quality; low and uniform prices for all shippers, large and small alike; uniformity of service over wide geographical areas; and assistance to customers in improving their procedures.

Stories told at management gatherings often highlighted customer service. The following is typical:

> A few days before Christmas, a railroad officer called the Chicago office of United Parcel Service and confessed that a flatcar carrying two UPS trailers had unaccountably been left on a siding in the middle of Illinois. UPS is no Santa Claus, but it tries its best to deliver Christmas packages on time. So the regional manager paid for a high-speed diesel that whipped the flatcar into Chicago ahead of an Amtrak passenger train, and he ordered two of UPS's fleet of 25 Boeing 727s diverted to Chicago to get the contents of the trailers to their destinations in Florida and Louisiana in time for Christmas. In spite of the extraordinary expense, the manager neither asked permission nor even informed UPS headquarters in Greenwich, Connecticut until weeks later.
>
> "We applauded it when we heard about it," said Oz Nelson, then UPS vice president for customer service. "We give these guys complete authority to run their operations and do their jobs. We push decision-making down to the lowest possible levels."[3]

INFORMATION SERVICES

The information services department, called data processing until 1985, was cre-

---

[3] "Behind the UPS Mystique: Puritanism and Productivity," *Business Week*, June 6, 1983, p. 66.

ated in 1971 and operated out of the UPS facility on 43rd Street in Manhattan for five years. It was comprised of a small group of UPS mavericks. For many years, however, the high-spirited group was unable to exert influence over any function within the company other than accounting. With neither financial nor moral support from the national headquarters in Greenwich, Connecticut, the department suffered from what Jay Walsh, one of the original engineers in the group, called "a classic case of corporate neglect." The rest of UPS considered their data processing jobs "cushy," not understanding exactly what they entailed, but concluding that if it didn't require any physical exertion, it couldn't be that difficult. One driver in the Meadowlands commented, "No one has a cake job at UPS, except perhaps the people sitting behind those computers, pushing the keys or . . . doing whatever they do."

Data processing was operating with poor equipment and providing poor service and was rapidly falling behind the competition in technological and data programming capabilities. The department remained quite small and reclusive until 1981, when the threat of technologically more advanced competition suddenly brought it into the spotlight.

With the onslaught of Federal Express and RPS, most UPSers realized that to remain the dominant carrier in the package delivery service they would have to join their competitors in the age of computer technology. Although UPS had the most extensive ground network, it had fallen behind in certain technological innovations such as package scanning, radio dispatched pickups, package tracking, and data acquisition devices.

UPS could either go outside the company to fulfill its technological needs or it could develop a system internally. In keeping with the belief that if "given the proper tools, our people could do anything," it chose the latter. For the data processing department, it was like winning a lottery.

Funds were not the only thing that the group was given. The department was given organizational respect and the task of developing and implementing systems that would significantly affect the operations of every department within the company. Its collective mission was "To provide management with the information they need to meet the company's goals in a responsive manner and at a reasonable cost." The department's name was changed to information services.

In 1976, the department had moved into a larger building in Paramus, New Jersey. From 1976 to 1986, the I.S. capital expenditures grew ten fold. In 1987 its mainframe processed about 450,000 transactions per day, and served almost every department. It had concentrated on designing operations-oriented systems, but plans were to begin work on more service-oriented projects in 1988. Some of the major projects completed by mid-1987 included a trailer and package tracking system, an automated customer service telephone center, a plant engineering maintenance system, electronic call tag, and on-line billing and invoicing.

Since 1985, the department had experienced particularly rapid growth. The number of on-line terminals directly connected to the central computer had grown from 685 to an expected 3,000 by the end of 1987, with 15,000 projected by the end of 1991. In 1985, UPS had 700 personal computers in operation. That number jumped to 4,000 in 1986. In 1986, the department completed 269 projects for specific district needs.

To immediately staff the entire operation with people who had grown up with UPS and understood its needs and priorities but who were also specialists in computer science was impossible. These people

did not exist. The training that workers received in the hubs did not give them the technical skills necessary to "get the job done" in Paramus. Therefore, management had to make a choice. It could either hire people from within UPS, send them to school to acquire the necessary skills and delay service for a few years until these people were qualified, or it could hire people from outside organizations and try to mold them into UPSers.

Rino Bergonzi, the Systems and Operations Manager who holds one of the most senior positions ever given to an outside hire in the company's history, commented on the necessity of addressing this change:

I.S. inside of UPS has been weak. Skills are lower than we need and there is a tremendous need for recruiting. There has not been much specialization. We'd like our people to learn many different skills. Some are now overwhelmed. They didn't possess great technical expertise nor did they have strong contacts even within UPS. We are going to continue a lot of recruiting, building, and training. . . . Turnover may go up as we grow.

Department managers within I.S. sent out notices to the districts, informing them of their staffing needs and asking them to have interested workers take an aptitude test in engineering. If these people did well, they would go to Paramus for an interview and would usually be hired. All transfers, starting in Paramus in an entry level position, were immediately sent outside to the Chubb School in New Jersey for a ten-week training session. However, this process was slow and costly. Even after they graduated from the school, they were only qualified for the most junior positions, still requiring substantial guidance.

Although the need to hire people from the outside was recognized as a necessity by most employees at UPS, it was not completely accepted. People in the district felt that because these "outsiders" had not been exposed to operations (hub and package centers) they could not understand or appreciate the UPS service. In fact, they viewed the entire Paramus facility as a "different" and certainly less desirable environment in which to work. One 35-year-old Customer Service area manager commented:

> I was over in Paramus on special assignment last year. It was very different. It's not like the districts at all. I don't think we are doing a very good job of making them a part of the rest of UPS. UPS is one of the most efficiently run companies around. Why should I.S. want to be any different?

Employees at Paramus received mixed signals about what would be expected of them, how "outsiders" fit in, and what to expect in the way of career development. A 24-year-old systems programmer who was promoted from the district said:

> I am motivated by an opportunity to excel, to move into a higher level of management or a senior engineering position. Yet, no one is quite sure in I.S. what steps you must take to obtain those positions.

Another programmer about the same age, coming from the South Ohio district, where he was a part-time preloader while going to college, commented about the different cultures in Paramus and in the district:

> The managers in Paramus don't define the tasks as clearly. They often set deadlines for projects that are unrealistic. It's frustrating because they often don't realize how much time the job requires.

The I.S. department had done some experimental hiring of people from outside directly into UPS. It had set up a curriculum of entry and development programs to aid the assimilation process of an I.S. employee. The agenda encompassed the recruitment, interviewing, and selection processes and included an orientation, a training program, and a special two-week "district experience" for those who had not worked in a hub or package center. For recruiting purposes the personnel department drew up a profile of a "most desirable candidate." Gary Lee, a manager for the personnel department, described that candidate: technically qualified, career minded, mature, professional, hands-on, results-oriented, and adaptable to the culture.

Jim Segrue, another personnal manager for Paramus, explained how he selected people from outside UPS:

> First, I take them on a short walk to see if they can "maintain driver pace." Then, when we begin talking, I note whether this person can hold eye contact. Is he or she healthy, intelligent, emotionally stable, and accustomed to working hard?

If the person was technically qualified and the first interview went well, the person was invited to return for a second interview. Over the course of both interviews, the person was informed about the standards, expectations, and benefits of working for UPS. Segrue further explained:

> I tell them that we can offer life-time employment and that we like to promote from within. Yet, I also inform them about our long hours, no-beard policy, and other standards we uphold as a company.

Some were scared off by the stringent policies such as no coffee at desks, two 15-minute breaks during the working day, and no beards or long mustaches. Many also expressed concern about the necessity of working long hours and on Saturdays.

One systems manager, recently hired from Western Union, commented about the coffee and break policy:

> They shouldn't try to run an IS environment like a hub. . . . We should absolutely be allowed to have coffee at our desks. Instead, every day at 3:30 PM this place looks like a factory on break! Everyone jumps up from their chairs and goes to the cafeteria to socialize and drink coffee.

Other employees, after hearing in their interview and reading in the policy book that promotion-from-within was one of the most honored UPS policies, were confused and disappointed when they saw outside hires being placed in positions they thought they were being trained for. Some felt they had been misled. One entry level programmer commented:

> It's frustrating that management is not following the promotion-from-within policy. I understand that people with greater expertise are needed, but I wish they would have told us the real policy during orientation.

Many new hires from the outside were pleased with the culture. One of the first, who was hired in October, 1985, commented:

> I came to UPS because I liked its values and the work ethic. When the people who interviewed me told me about the low turnover, I knew the company was doing something right. My impressions were right. There is an incredible amount of trust and cooperation among people. That's what I was looking for after the bad experience I had with my last job.

The orientation program for these outside hires had been different than the one for internal recruits. The new hire from the district usually attended a special school beforehand for ten weeks of technical training. The outsider was usually hired with the expertise necessary to begin working right away. In place of technical training, the outside hire had a three-day orientation program and spent two weeks in a district with a driver. One programmer who had come from the outside who had not yet participated in the district experience said:

> I can't wait to see the guts and gore of this operation and finally understand what all of these old guys are really talking about. Yet, I would think you could only unload a truck for so long before you lose your mind!

Valerie Monte, an employment manager at the Meadowlands hub, reflected upon her experience as an on-car supervisor and hostess for the visitors from Paramus:

> At first we didn't like the idea of this district experience. We didn't feel like babysitting the technical part of the company during our peak season. But, much to our surprise, those people really dug in and helped us out. We gained a lot of respect for them and I know they respected us too. Later that month, we invited them all back and gave them awards for outstanding participation.

THE BIGGER QUESTION

Jack Rogers and other members of the top management group at UPS knew the issue of outside hires was not confined to information services. A rapidly growing air business confronted the company with a similar issue, although much of the growth had been accomplished to date by contracting air services from suppliers. If UPS were to acquire another firm, it would have to confront the issue of outsiders head-on. For several members of the group, the issue was not whether but how to approach the assimilation process.

. . .When the words, "we," "us" and "our" are used in this book, we should keep in mind that they are intended to include all the people in the company, as well as the company itself. This is true for the reasons that the policies apply to all. . .

. . .Please note that neither the policy's summary statement nor its explanation spells out <u>how</u> a policy is to be carried out. This Policy Book is not a "how-to-do-it" manual. . .

<u>Our Objectives Are</u>:

* To fulfill a useful economic purpose—satisfying the need for prompt, dependable delivery of small packages, serving all shippers and receivers wherever they may be located within our service areas—with the best possible service at the lowest possible cost to the public.

* To maintain a strong, forward-looking, efficient, and cooperative organization which will be ever mindful of the well-being of our people and enable them to develop their individual capabilities.

* To keep the ownership and control of our company in the hands of its managers and supervisors—to build an organization of people who think and act as partners rather than as "hired hands."

* To maintain a financially strong company earning a reasonable profit—which is the only way we can provide security for the members of our organization, continue to provide quality service for our customers, and reward our share with dividends and increases in value of owners the shares in which their money is invested.

* To develop additional profitable businesses which complement our efforts to maintain a financially strong company.

* To be alert to changing conditions and ready at all times to adjust our viewpoints and operations to meet them.

* To earn and preserve a reputation as a company whose well-being is in the public interest and whose people are respected for their performance, character, and integrity.

* To establish and maintain a high standard of excellence in everything we do.

Policy Group I

Our Company and Organization[a]

We Function as Partners. Although we are organized in corporate form, we function as partners in our working relationships with each other and we make our management decisions as partners.

Consolidated Parcel Delivery is Our Main Business. Our long experience in this specialized field helps us provide better service and greater economy for our customers and fill a need that could not be satisfied in any other way.

We use our management and technical skills to help us develop other businesses. The aim of these diversification activities is to complement our efforts to maintain a financially strong company. Our entry into other businesses does not lessen our concentration on consolidated parcel delivery.

Policy Group II

Our People[b]

We Promote From Within. Whenever possible, we fill managerial positions from our ranks. In doing so we take care to include for consideration and not overlook qualified people whose present job may make them less noticeable than other employees. We fill a vacancy from the outside only when we cannot locate one of our own people who has the capacity or the professional or technical skills which may be required by a particular assignment.

We Strive to Be Considerate and Understanding of Our People. In supervision we try to lead, not drive; request, not command.

We believe that when this attitude prevails it helps us gain the cooperation of everyone to work more efficiently and attain higher standards in everything we do.

Policy Group III

Our Service[c]

We Provide a Uniform Service. This service is provided in each area for all our customers, large and small alike. We maintain service standards of high quality and dependability and provide the features of service our experience shows shippers and receivers need and want.

---

[a]Two of 25 policies in this policy group.
[b]Two of 31 policies in this policy group.
[c]Two of 22 policies in this policy group.

<u>We Maintain a Dependable Delivery Service.</u> We make deliveries every delivery day in the entire service area, whether in a large city, small community, or rural area. Severe storms, floods, and other emergencies may occasionally make this impossible, but volume peaks or other operating problems do not excuse service failures.

The dependability of our delivery service is important to our customers and their customers. To assure on-schedule deliveries, we establish controls, conduct audits and otherwise measure performance in all districts. We regard each service failure as a serious matter.

Policy Group IV

Our Character and Reputation[d]

<u>We Insist Upon Integrity in Our People.</u> We present our company honestly to employees and in turn expect them to be honest with us.

<u>We Maintain Our Vehicles to Look Like New.</u> We paint and service our vehicles frequently, wash or clean them daily, and repair dents and scratches promptly to prevent them from becoming unsightly.

All vehicles should leave our buildings in a clean condition.

Policy Group V

Our Economic Stability[e]

<u>We Reinvest Earnings to Finance Our Growth.</u> Earnings retained in the business, year after year, have provided the major part of the capital required to finance our continued growth and development.

---

[d]Two of 31 policies in this policy group.
[e]One of 14 policies in this policy group.

UNITED PARCEL SERVICE (A)

Exhibit 2 1985–1986 comparative data, U.S. transportation companies[a]

Rank[b] 1986	1985	Company	Operating Revenues $Thousands	Assets $Thousands	Rank[c]	Net Income $Thousands	Rank	Stockholders' Equity $Thousands	Rank	Employees Number	Rank	Net Income as Percent of: Sales Percent	Rank	Stockholders' Equity Percent	Rank	Earnings Per Share 1986/$	1985/$	1976/$
1	5	UAL (Elk Grove, IL)	9,196,233	8,716,517	6	11,600	26	2,292,610	8	87,000	2	0.1	35	0.5	34	0.25	(2.09)	0.75
2	2	United Parcel Service of America (Greenwich, Conn.)[c]	8,619,703	4,801,133	9	668,966	1	2,469,798	7	168,200	1	7.8	6	27.1	2	3.96	3.36	M.A.
3	1	Burlington Northern (Seattle)	6,941,413	10,650,956	4	(860,485)	50	3,534,314	4	44,200	7					(12.07)	8.03	1.42
4	*	Union Pacific (New York)	6,688,000	10,863,000	3	(460,000)	48	3,408,000	5	32,700	12					(4.56)	4.18	2.09
5	3	CSX (Richmond)	6,345,000	12,661,000	1	418,000	3	4,873,000	3	48,000	6	6.6	7	8.3	25	2.73	(0.78)	1.44
6	6	AMR (Fort Worth)	6,018,175	7,527,969	8	279,132	4	2,484,896	6	54,300	4	4.6	11	11.0	15	4.63	5.94	1.97
7	4	Santa Fe Southern Pacific (Chicago)	5,801,600	11,610,800	2	(137,900)	45	5,040,300	2	53,423	5					(0.84)	2.67	1.27
8	8	Delat Air Lines (Atlanta)	4,460,062	3,785,462	11	47,286	16	1,301,946	9	38,901	8	1.1	29	3.6	30	1.18	6.50	1.76
9	14	Texas Air (Houston)	4,406,897	8,194,611	7	72,703	11	803,869	13	68,000	3	1.7	25	9.0	24	1.75	5.03	0.66
10	9	Norfolk Southern (Norfolk, Va.)	4,076,407	9,752,445	5	518,688	2	5,070,751	1	38,297	9	12.7	2	10.2	18	2.74	2.65	1.40
11	12	NWA (Eagan, Pa.)	3,589,174	4,322,854	10	76,941	9	1,105,916	10	33,427	11	2.1	23	7.0	26	3.26	3.18	2.39
12	10	Trans World Airlines (New York)	3,145,429	3,369,869	12	(106,328)	44	241,362	28	27,442	13					(3.87)	(6.10)	N.A.
13	11	Pan Am (New York)*	3,038,995	2,107,539	15	(462,814)	49	8,763	48	21,500	17					(3.42)	0.45	2.24
14	13	Federal Express (Memphis)	2,606,210	2,276,362	13	131,839	5	1,091,714	11	33,988	10	5.1	10	12.1	12	2.64	1.61	N.A.

UNITED PARCEL SERVICE (A)
Exhibit 2 (continued)

Rank 1986	1985	Company	Operating Revenues $Thousands	Assets $Thousands	Rank[c]	Net Income $Thousands	Rank	Stockholders' Equity $Thousands	Rank	Employees Number	Rank	Net Income as Percent of: Sales Percent	Rank	Stock-holders' Equity Percent	Rank	Earnings Per Share 1986/$	1985/$	1976/$
15	15	Consolidated Freightways (Palo Alto, Calif.)	2,124,467	1,275,440	20	89,109	8	655,048	16	24,600	14	4.2	14	13.6	10	2.31	3.10	1.56
16	21	Piedmont Aviation (Winston-Salem, N.C.)	1,865,473	1,717,650	16	72,363	12	783,888	14	20,798	18	3.9	16	9.2	23	3.48	3.89	1.22
17	16	US Air Group (Arlington, Va.)	1,835,199	2,147,081	14	98,352	6	1,057,953	12	14,976	21	5.4	9	9.3	22	3.34	4.05	2.19
18	20	Yellow Freight System (Overland Park, Kans.)	1,731,731	862,359	30	69,719	13	376,370	22	23,500	16	4.0	15	18.5	4	2.44	1.95	1.19
19	19	Roadway Services (Akron)	1,717,491	1,070,659	25	76,466	10	654,235	17	23,500	15	4.5	13	11.7	14	1.91	1.90	1.05
20	22	Leaseway Transportation (Beachwood, Ohio)	1,484,669	916,394	28	50,791	14	269,890	26	20,000	19	3.4	19	18.8	3	2.55	5.29	2.31
21	26	American President Cos. (Oakland)	1,466,714	1,343,304	19	17,956	22	640,562	18	3,970	38	1.2	28	2.8	32	0.71	1.86	2.61
22	27	Tiger International (Los Angeles)	1,110,948	883,457	29	45,063	42	(43,160)	50	6,200	27					(1.45)	(2.69)	1.61
23	32	CMW (Chicago)	959,490	1,691	50	43,040	17	397,275	21	9,500	24	4.5	12	10.8	16	2.31	(1.71)	0.62
24	25	McLean Industries (New York)	896,995	1,569,384	17	(248,773)	47	23,945	46	N.A.						N.A.	(1.89)	N.A.
25	35	PS Group (San Diego)	895,423	1,114,006	22	(13,930)	39	212,282	29	5,590	32					(2.25)	3.88	0.86
26	33	Emery Air Freight (Wilton, Conn.)	887,523	449,305	33	(5,440)	37	170,797	31	7,100	26					(0.28)	0.85	1.00
27	34	Purolator Courier (Basking Ridge, N.J.)	841,434	389,773	36	(57,643)	43	121,031	32	19,500	20					(7.54)	(3.86)	1.77
28	36	Southwest Airlines (Dallas)	768,790	1,078,190	24	50,035	15	511,850	20	5,819	31	6.5	8	9.8	21	1.55	1.54	0.37
29	28	Illinois Central Gulf Railroad (Chicago)	715,462	1,546,344	18	(171,674)	46	339,265	24	5,870	30					N.A.	N.A.	N.A.
30	38	Mayflower Group (Carmel, Ind.)	705,796	441,517	34	3,527	31	29,331	45	2,200	44	0.5	34	12.0	13	N.A.	N.A.	N.A.

* Not on last year's list.

[a] Source: "The Service 500," *Fortune*, June 8, 1987, pp. 212–213.

[b] All rankings shown in this exhibit are rankings among the largest 50 transportation firms.

[c] The firms with the largest operating revenues were UAL Inc. in 1986 and Burlington Northern in 1985. Both however, owned, non-transport businesses.

UNITED PARCEL SERVICE (A)

Exhibit 3 Comparative data from three UPS hubs, 1987

	Whites Creek (Nashville, TE) Hub	Meadowlands (NJ) Hub	Chelmsford (MA) Hub[a]
Capacity (packages per day)	360,000	700,000	800,000
Average daily volume	274,000	500,000	90,000
Number of management and hourly people[b]	643	1,700	350
Pre-seniority turnover[c]	32%	43%	9%
Seniority turnover[d]	22%	45%	13%

[a] The Chelmsford hub had been in operation only a few months.

[b] Full-time and part-time.

[c] Proportion of new hires who do not complete the 30-day trial period.

[d] Proportion of people (annualized) leaving the company after completing 30-day trial period.

UNITED PARCEL SERVICE (A)

Exhibit 4 Selected employment information, February 1987

Analysis of Work Force by Job

Job	Employees	Percent of Total
Service Workers	4,072	2.4%
Inside Clerical	8,749	5.1%
Inside Manual	62,611	36.3%
Package Drivers	48,129	27.9%
Driver Helpers	256	0.0%
Feeder Drivers	9,861	5.7%
Maintenance/Mechanics	3,793	2.2%
Clerical	11,199	6.5%
Supervisors	18,660	10.8%
Mid Managers	3,715	2.2%
Staff	1,401	0.8%
Total	172,446	100.0%

Analysis of Total Full-Time Hourly and Management

Years of Service	Number	Percentage of Total
Up to 5	28,574	35.8%
5–9	20,431	25 %
10–14	13,787	17 %
15–19	12,434	15 %
20–24	4,200	5 %
25–29	1,300	1.6%
30 and over	446	.6%
	81,172	100.0%

UNITED PARCEL SERVICE (A)

Exhibit 5 UPS corporate organization chart

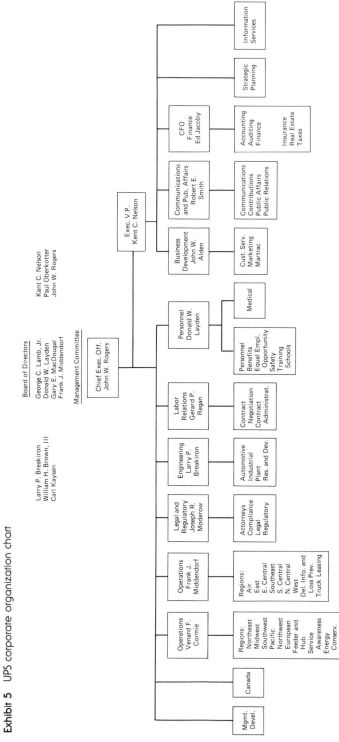

Board of Directors

George C. Lamb, Jr.
Donald W. Layden
Gary E. MacDougal
Frank J. Middendorf

Kent C. Nelson
Paul Oberkotter
John W. Rogers

Larry P. Breakiron
William H. Brown, III
Carl Kaysen

Management Committee

Chief Exec. Off.
John W. Rogers

Exec. V.P.
Kent C. Nelson

Operations
Venard F. Cormie

Regions:
Northeast
Midwest
Southwest
Pacific
Northwest
European
Feeder and
Hub
Service
Awareness
Energy
Conserv.

Operations
Frank J. Middendorf

Regions:
Air
East
E. Central
Southeast
S. Central
N. Central
West
Del. Info. and
Loss Prev.
Truck Leasing

Legal and Regulatory
Joseph R. Moderow

Attorneys
Compliance
Legal
Regulatory

Engineering
Larry P. Breakiron

Automotive
Industrial
Plant
Res. and Dev.

Labor Relations
Gerard P. Regan

Contract
Negotiation
Contract
Administrat.

Personnel
Donald W. Layden

Personnel
Benefits
Equal Empl.
Opportunity
Safety
Training
Schools

Medical

Canada

Mgmt. Devel.

Business Development
John W. Alden

Cust. Serv.
Marketing
Martrac

Communications and Pub. Affairs
Robert E. Smith

Communications
Contributions
Public Affairs
Public Relations

CFO Finance
Ed Jacoby

Accounting
Auditing
Finance

Insurance
Real Estate
Taxes

Strategic Planning

Information Services

470

UNITED PARCEL SERVICE (A)
Exhibit 6 UPS operations organization chart

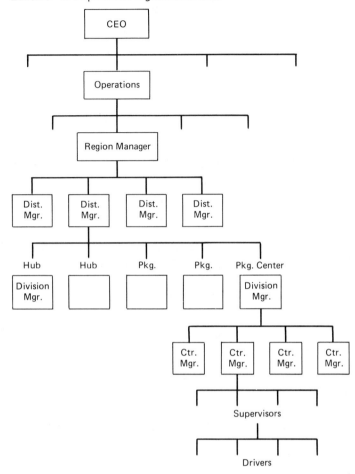

United Parcel Service (B)

EXPANSION

Opportunities in new geographic areas, new service functions, and new forms of technology had led UPS to embark on several programs of expansion in the late 1970s and 1980. The company soon found itself involved in foreign countries, air transport, and high-tech acquisitions. In the new areas of business, even more than in the modernization of existing operations, the need for employees with specialized skills presented a challenge to UPS' HRM policies and culture.

GERMANY

UPS first embarked on its mission to "unite the world with service" in Dusseldorf, West Germany, in 1976. It was the first step of an international plan, aborted due to cultural collisions with the traditional approach. Twenty UPSers were chosen from districts in the United States to begin a ground package delivery service in Germany like the one existing in the

This case was written by Associate Professor Jeffrey Sonnenfeld and Research Assistant Meredith Lazo as the basis for class discussion rather than to illustrate either effective or ineffective handling of an administrative situation. Reprinted by permission of the Harvard Business School.

Copyright © 1987 by the President and Fellows of Harvard College

United States but on a miniature scale. They were chosen on the basis of their competence as managers in the United States, ability to communicate, adaptability, and were preferable if they had at least a few years of academic instruction in German. Without an appreciation of German needs and attitudes, however, an operation evolved that was unsuited to the German community and not well understood by its American parent. According to UPS standards, it was an embarrassment. Four years later, in 1980, after a $59 million loss in 1979, an emergency team of 10 senior managers was sent over to rescue the failing operation.

By 1981 the German district had almost completely recovered, making a 20 million mark profit, and serving as an important link for further European expansion. Although UPS had badly stubbed its toes in the process, the experience provided them with invaluable lessons that would serve them in future years when they faced even greater barriers than culture and language.

The problems in Germany began almost immediately after the first twenty arrived in Dusseldorf. It became obvious that the majority of them didn't understand either the language or the culture. John Christensen, one of the original twenty in 1976 and the regional personnel manager from 1978 to 1984, recalled:

Most of the early American managers we brought over did not understand or recognize the immense cultural differences. It was like fighting World War II all over again. Americans adopted a "holier and better than thou" attitude while the Germans secretly sabotaged the American manager. Even some of the best managers in America were like fish out of water in Germany.

Recognizing that they had a problem, UPS managers sought the advice of a leading consulting company. From this point, the problems multiplied. Even the smallest step became a hurdle. All problems, ranging from staffing difficulties and specific German legislative complications to the major cultural differences in work ethic, added to the complexity of assimilating a foreign operation with one at home of rigid structure and policy.

The group arrived in Germany almost six months before they were scheduled to begin operation. Almost immediately, they began interviewing prospective drivers, hub operators, and staff support. However, without any buildings, trucks, or material written about the company in German, they could not offer prospective employees tangible evidence of their existence. Consequently, people were hesitant to wait four or five months for a job that they were not sure even existed. The personnel department also had difficulty selecting its future employees. Without fluency in the language or an understanding of the German business world, interviewing was ineffective as were their efforts in judging the quality of a person's previous experience. In short, they were lacking a profile of the ideal "German UPSer." Eventually, they staffed the personnel department with native Germans.

Other employment problems still remained. For instance, they did not realize that the wage for which they were asking the drivers and operators to work, 7 marks/hour in 1976, was not high enough to attract or maintain the committed, motivated workers typical of UPS. Theft among both hourly employees and managers was five or six times greater than in any hub of equivalent size in the United States. Almost half of the work force hired in 1976 was comprised of "guest workers," semiskilled migrant workers. This lack of parity with the native community gave UPS a negative stereotype and it was consequently not seen as a desirable place to work.

When they had completed the first round of hiring and were almost ready to begin operations, they encountered another problem. In order for their service to extend beyond a 50-mile radius of the constructed facility, they would have to obtain a new operating license for that surplus area and for every additional 50 miles of German territory they covered beyond that. Although problems like these caused a number of initial setbacks, the more serious long-range problems were realized when they began service. First, they could not draw as heavily from the student population as they did in the United States. Employment apprenticeships for students who did not go on to the university began when they were 15 years old. A teenager could not begin driving for UPS until age 18 when he or she could receive a driver's license. By that time, most applicable teenagers had secured a full-time apprenticeship in a different occupation.

Students going on to the university can only work 20 hours a week while they are in school or else they were heavily taxed. Until wages were raised and conditions such as the lack of sunlight and fresh air filtering through the hub were improved, manual labor inside the hub would not be attractive to the student. Students were subsidized by the state and therefore did not need an income to get an education. Perhaps more significantly, a driver's job in Germany was viewed as a highly unskilled and undesirable position. Thus, offering a negative social status and low pay, UPS had great difficulty attracting the quality individuals they were seeking. Among the workers they hired, there was an extremely high turnover rate of nearly 15–20% per month, excessive amounts of theft, and a fundamentally different work attitude than that to which the American management was accustomed.

It did not take the group long to realize that they were not attracting the right type of workers. In 1978, the group composed a comprehensive status report reviewing their operations. They attributed their labor problems to the low wage they offered their package handlers and drivers and sent the report to U.S. headquarters, requesting permission to raise their wages. Headquarters did not accede until 1980.

Thus, life was not easy for the American trying to set up the operation. They were told upon selection for the project that it was a "special assignment" and would therefore be a temporary relocation. Although at first most of them were eager, before long they felt abused and abandoned. When they arrived in Germany, appropriate housing had not been arranged and salaries were not adjusted to allow for cost-of-living differences and unfavorable exchange rates. Moreover, the job was twice as challenging as the one in the United States. Not only did they have to start an operation from scratch, but they had to do it alone and without a favorable UPS image in the community to fall back upon. They were constantly surprised by unanticipated problems with the culture and the German people.

The group encountered many other cultural barriers when trying to apply their American methods and management style to a German work force. Their values and aspirations required management to employ different motivational strategies to obtain the same service they got from workers in the United States. For instance, the Germans place an extremely high value on their free time. Working overtime in Germany was far less common or desirable there than in the United States. Therefore, they were not inspired by the UPS philosophy of working as long as it takes "to get the job done." According to the Regional Personnel Manager, Gale Davis: "Many Germans feel that a better way to handle an excessive work load is to hire more people. They consider stress and pressure bad things."

It soon became apparent that the "American" manager could not serve as an effective role model for Germans. To draw out the best in Germans, supervisors and managers would need to reflect German values and aspirations, not American ones. For instance, one American training manager that was on special assignment in Germany had difficulty coping with Germans because he didn't understand that calling a German by his first name is extremely offensive unless you are close friend. Yet, because at UPS everyone is on a first name basis, whether they know each other or not, he perceived this German norm as arrogance and said, "Those damned Germans are so arrogant. They think everyone should call them Mr. or Sir!"

Davis commented about one of the biggest incentives in the United States that has little meaning in Germany, "Promotion from within is not as highly valued in Germany as it is in the United States—and neither is lifetime employment."

The team was therefore forced to sell German employees on other aspects of the operation. By modifying the hub facility and by translating a successful assimilation strategy that American hubs used into German, they were able to turn the situation around.

One of the first physical adjustments involved installing windows in the hub. There was a strong belief in the German society that working in a place devoid of natural light and fresh air was extremely detrimental to one's health. This change helped make UPS a more desirable setting for employees to work.

The strategy the German operation adopted was to create appropriate role models. In 1980, the new management team reviewed the backgrounds and qualifications of 400 German drivers. Then they set up new criteria for hiring people, and employed native Germans who fit those qualifications and who understood the American operation. These people served as role model managers for the German district. The results of the profile showed that the average driver at that time was about twenty years old, single, Turkish, and had about ten years of total education and no previous driving experience. Concerned, the team developed new criteria on which to base all future hiring of drivers. These criteria included: an average age of twenty-five to thirty, married, German, ten years of education and at least three years of previous driving experience. Eventually further criteria were made for workers inside the hub. This management team was finally able to get the wages increased for the package handlers and drivers.

The new strategy proved to be effective. Up to 1980, the German operation had lost millions of dollars. The loss was greatly reduced in 1981 and in subsequent years it became profitable. The new management team was now working on reducing the still problematic full-time seniority turnover rate of 32.3% and full-time absentee rate of 4.9%. To gauge the attitude of their workers, they conducted a people survey with 100% of the employees. They had an 85% combined "favorable and average" response from the people regarding: "UPS as a place to work" and an 86% positive response to the question dealing with job satisfaction. Eighty-five percent of the people also responded favorably to their new pay structure. The social benefits like vacation pay, Christmas pay, and time off, however, were negative. The results of the survey helped them to understand where they were or were not meeting changing German needs. Whereas seven or eight years ago the labor problems stemmed from the low wage, in 1986 and 1987 it appeared management needed to change the wage-and-benefit plan again, this time enhancing benefits instead of pay. Larry Long, the regional manager for the European Region concluded:

> We have a lot of training to do with our management group to help them better understand and explain our work measurements.

AIR OPERATIONS

Seventy years after the last run of the UPS messenger service, UPS was back in the business of transporting information. On September 20, 1982, a Next Day Air Service was welcomed into the UPS family of operations. Although the decision to enter the market was slow in coming, two months after its inception, the service was expanded and made available to more than 130 million people and 29,000 communities in all or parts of 39 states and the District of Columbia.

In 1953, UPS had started a two-day air service called Blue Label. This service yielded a relatively small rate of growth in comparison with the ground operation. Because of the regulatory barriers in the airline industry, UPS forwarded all of its packages to either freight carriers or passenger aircraft. With the initiation of Next Day Air, Blue Label was renamed 2nd Day

Air. In 1982, the Louisville hub handled only the Next Day Air service. In 1983, however, UPS purchased additional planes and ground support systems in Louisville to support both the Next Day and 2nd Day Air load.

Total air volume had increased at an explosive rate over the last few years, rising more than 150% between 1982 and 1986. About 40% of the volume was in Next Day Air packages and the rest was in 2nd Day air packages. In 1986, air volume was approximately 3% of UPS total national volume and air revenues were nearly one-tenth of the total. The growth rate of the Next Day Air service had been most significant. In 1986, the growth rate for the Next Day Air service was 55%.

Transporting this volume were UPS's 89 major aircraft and 200 contracted smaller jets. In addition to the Louisville facility, now handling all domestic air activity, equipment in airport gateways and district hubs were designed and installed to support the network. However, to operate and maintain their planes, UPS used four other small package carriers. Pilots and general mechanics working for these carriers were not official UPS employees although most flew or maintained only UPS aircraft.

Conceptually, air consolidation and delivery ran similarly to the ground operation. Packages were brought to a central location from surrounding areas, sorted and consolidated and then sent back out, either locally or to further destinations where a more fine-tuned sort and delivery was then completed. The main differences included the existence of one central hub location, a surrounding area that spanned the entire nation; and technologically more complex operating equipment.

There were four main operating areas in a UPS airport facility. The first was the aircraft feeder load and unload area. From here the containers were unloaded and sent to three other ramp operations. Packages destined for nearby buildings went to a local sort facility. Containers loaded with packages all going to one particular building were moved to a transfer area. Packages going to more distant locations were led to a different sort and loaded onto a smaller "mosquito fleet." In both 1985 and 1986, UPS spent more than $5 million on ground equipment. Substantially more capital spending, for both air and ground equipment, was anticipated in 1987.

Along with the drastic increase in capital equipment, there was an insatiable need for management and line operators to run the operation. In 1985, the air functions, previously part of the package operations in the Kentucky district, were consolidated into one "air region." At that time, the UPS national support systems were brought into this new region. The major departments included Industrial Engineering, Information Services, National Accounting, Safety, Maintenance, Repair, and General Management. In 1985 a region manager was assigned from ground operations to create a top quality region staff from existing UPS management. He drew in top performers from the major staff departments. This inside team was supplemented by 25 top level outside hires. In 1986 that number grew to 150 and in 1987 it was expected to increase substantially. The concern again surfaced about the effective assimilation of new hires in specialized areas of expertise into a generalist UPS system.

The Regional Personnel Manager for Air, Jim Heck, commented on the struggles in the standard orientation process:

> At UPS we train people and then we move them. We can't do that now. We've got to have some stability now. It's hard enough to just keep them in their jobs.

The orientation program for managers in 1982 lasted three months. The UPS management felt that it was essential for outside hires to get a well-balanced understanding of UPS. However, the length of this program was progressively shortened as volume and time pressures increased.

Rick Syne, a quality assurance manager in the Air region who had worked for UPS for five years and came from Pan Am Airlines, commented:

> We're in an explosive situation. We can hardly afford to let our people go for two days let alone two weeks, to go to any of these orientations and seminars. Yet, this is a very people-oriented culture. We continually evaluate the importance of these programs. Do we need them or are they overdone? These jobs require special skills. It's a new function with new jobs. The situation requires more leadership effort than is needed for normal business expansions.

His solution, however, was not to cut back on the orientation programs but instead to overhire. Commenting on the necessity of the outside hires' exposure to the other UPS operations, he said:

> A traditional UPSer has been through a variety of jobs: hub, driving, IE, personnel. He doesn't have a professional occupation. He works for UPS. Yet, if you take someone who is midcareer and is a pilot or a manager of pilots, they are more interested in staying in aviation. My orientation was three months and I loved it: one month hub training, one month automotive repair, and one month package car delivery. Now our new hires don't know the business. If someone in their neighborhood asked them why a package was left on the back porch, they wouldn't know about the proper driver techniques.

Before outside hires were exposed to other UPS operation and support functions, many were unable to understand the UPS policies and management style. UPS took working procedures from its ground fleet such as a centralized location for mechanical parts, an insistence on cleanliness, and uniformity of outfits and behavior and applied them to the air operation. Also the participative management style was frustrating to outsiders accustomed to autocratic control. They could not find fast solutions to the immediate problems they encountered. Some also had trouble accepting the deflation or absence of titles at UPS. For instance, there was no distinction in title for the different levels of maintenance managers. They were all called Maintenance Representatives. For internal use, the lack of titles was common and accepted. Yet when these people had to interact with outside vendors, they did not feel respected. Thus, without a more comprehensive understanding of the entire UPS operation and the coordination that commonality throughout operations provided, many policies could appear needless or irrelevant. Yet, when midcareer hires from outside carriers were given that exposure, many received the deemphasis on titles and other such cultural values quite well.

Vince Pagliano, a 55-year-old maintenance manager who previously worked in maintenance for American and Pan Am Airlines, commented about his experience with UPSers who had been transferred from the ground district to the air region:

> When I ask people at UPS what they do, they say, "my present assignment is. . . ." That is real different than other places where they say, "I am an avionics engineer" . . . or whatever.

Pagliano, talking about his own commitment to UPS, later said:

> I've always looked for a place like UPS. I like the philosophies and the work ethic. When I went on my one-month orientation, they took me and accepted me as a partner and

they didn't even know me! It's a secure job and I've never been bored here. Perhaps it's the stage of my life; perhaps it's because I'm involved in the air operation—but I love it and I won't leave until either I die or they fire me.

Thus, coming from an unstable industry where many airline employees must question their employment with each passing day, UPS offered an alluring long-term job security. However, at present, UPS maintained a more distant relationship with its operating pilots and mechanics, employing their service through contract and not membership. Only management, specialized talent in engineering or support functions, and the hub operators had been officially hired as UPS employees. Thus while UPS was learning how to assimilate outside expertise into its operation, integrating contracted carriers and labor into the system continued to be a problem. Jim Heck concluded:

As much as the air carriers are chafing under the amount of controls and measurement, they've educated their people to new management controls. However, we are still unhappy with costs, maintenance delays, turnover (50%), safety and reliability. For example, in April, 13 aircraft with 30,000 packages each were grounded by FAA inspectors due to poor recordkeeping. We had to scramble to "make service" on those packages.

ACQUISITIONS

Gene Hughes, an industrial engineer with 20 years of employment at UPS, had tried for four years to sponsor a department inside of UPS that would develop applications for computerized mapping, computer-assisted vehicle routing and scheduling, mobile communications, and "on board" communications. Instead, in February 1986 a Strategic Planning group was created with a broader focus of "meeting the challenges of a changing business world and increasingly aggressive competitors." The group's formal and primary objectives were to:

1. Concentrate on ways to utilize technology at UPS to reduce cost and improve service.
2. Help the UPS organization develop a long-range plan for the future.

Heading this new department, Hughes embarked on a different strategy for obtaining the technology. He sent his group out to meet with dozens of leading technological companies to learn about their services. By the year's end, these meetings had resulted in the acquisition of two of the companies: Roadnet Technologies and II Morrow, Inc.

Roadnet Technologies, although a leader in computerized mapping and computer-assisted vehicle routing and scheduling, was four days away from bankruptcy when Hughes and his group confronted them. Roadnet was founded by Bob Leatherwood, a classic entrepreneur, to sell, install, and support the computer systems it had developed for wholesale food and beverage distribution industries. Although Roadnet saw UPS as a potential customer, they had no marketable services developed for them at the time of acquisition. Roadnet could only offer UPS the employment of 24 skilled engineers, a technology that could possibly be applied to UPS operations in a few years, and a purchase price of all the company's assets for $1.5 million. The deal was quickly enacted.

On December 29, 1986, Hughes' group suggested that UPS make another purchase and acquire the publicly owned II Morrow, Inc. II Morrow manufactured vehicle tracking systems for the aviation and marine industries, along with vehicle tracking systems for land-based mobile equipment such as buses, police cars, and trucks. With three months to put the deal together, the group had more time to evaluate this plan. II Morrow employed 167 people and had the capability to design almost any type of electronic device with their computer-aided design equipment.

Although UPS contended that the addition of these two companies gave it a three-year jump in technological development, merging the small, entrepreneurial cultures into the UPS well-established one required a slow and delicate process. Hughes struggled with the decision of whether to fully integrate the two companies. Commenting on the situation at Roadnet, he said:

> If I took the Roadnet people and put them immediately in the UPS environment, they would die. They would not assimilate and they would not produce. Yet, if they did not accept the UPS policies and culture, they would never become an integral part of UPS. . . . Roadnet is now the in-house development arm of UPS.

Hughes explained to the Roadnet employees that they would be slowly integrated into the system. Two groups within Roadnet were formed: a Roadnet Products division and a UPS Products division. Although the groups worked on different projects, they remained in the same building in adjacent offices. Eight UPS industrial engineers were sent down to the Roadnet office in Hunt Valley, Maryland, for permanent employment and were put on "special assignment" there. Rich Foard, the UPS product division manager at Roadnet, commented on UPS assistance, "You know UPS . . . if one of their divisions need help, they send up the 747, open its doors, and parachute the people down to help!"

Hughes wanted the little company to retain its innovative orientation but without any resources or staff support, it was entirely dependent on UPS to support its creativity. To facilitate the necessary cross-fertilization of UPS and Roadnet, he advocated that Roadnet immediately adopt and abide by the UPS policy book.

Roadnet employees felt anxious and skeptical as they anticipated forthcoming military rules and uniformity. They were surprised when the policy book was thin, written in simple English diction, and had blank pages in the back for suggestions and/or additions. Foard reflected:

> At first it was hard to adjust to the idea of adopting the UPS culture, replacing our own. Much of what I saw as a threat or an intrusion one year ago, I see as beneficial now.

However, the founder, Bob Leatherwood, deciding that he could not operate under the jurisdiction of a big company, resigned one year after the acquisition. Yet, the enthusiasm of employees remained high. One outside hire engineer in the UPS Products Division, who was brought in after the acquisition, commented on his attraction to Roadnet:

> I really liked the idea of working for, as Rich put it, a start-up company with the stability of a multimillion-dollar company.

Interestingly, one year after the purchase, the Roadnet facility looked as much like a UPS office building as the ones in Greenwich, Connecticut. The floors and desks were immaculately clean. None of the men wore beards and all were conservative in their dress. Just as the policies had been gradually accepted, some employees expressed initial frustration but final respect for the participative management style at UPS. One Roadnet manager in his mid-40s commented:

> I found it extremely frustrating when I wanted to get an answer but couldn't figure out who was in charge. But then they told me something I had never heard before. They said that the more people you include in the decision-making process, the more people you will have to help you in times of need.

Hughes did not pursue the same strategy of integration with II Morrow. He chose to let it remain more separate in both its culture and its operation. II Morrow, a larger and more self-sufficient company, was run by its own management and the founder, Ray Morrow, retained his title as CEO. Hughes elaborated on the situation at II Morrow:

> The culture at II Morrow is very different. I think that by imposing our culture, we would destroy much of their creativity. I told them they would have to get rid of the wet bars in the offices and could no longer hire relatives of existing employees. But beyond observing these major policies, they have been given a free rein.

UNITED PARCEL SERVICE (A) AND (B) STUDY QUESTIONS:

1. Identify and evaluate the business strategy of UPS. Why has UPS been so successful in the past? What key success factors have now changed?
2. Identify and evaluate the human resources strategy of UPS. Will the past human resources strategy work in the future?
3. Who are the major stakeholder groups in this case? What are their key concerns?
4. Should UPS attempt to maintain its traditional culture in the new areas of service? If so, why? If not, how should it go about creating a different environment, and what steps should it take to ensure that the different parts of the company continue to function smoothly as a whole?
5. What are the trade-offs between selecting potential information service people from within and training them, versus hiring experienced people from outside the company?
6. What human resources factors, if any, should be taken into account in UPS acquisitions?
7. What human resources lessons should UPS learn from its experience in Germany?